The Private Correspondence of Henry Clay

The Private Correspondence of Henry Clay

Edited by

Calvin Colton, LL. D.

Ross & Perry, Inc.
Washington, D.C.

© Ross & Perry, Inc. 2002 on new material. All rights reserved.

Protected under the Berne Convention.

Printed in The United States of America

Ross & Perry, Inc. Publishers
216 G St., N.E.
Washington, D.C. 20002
Telephone (202) 675-8300
Facsimile (202) 675-8400
info@RossPerry.com

SAN 253-8555

Library of Congress Control Number: 2002106099
http://www.rossperry.com

ISBN 1-932080-25-2

Book Cover designed by Sapna. sapna@rossperry.com

⊚ The paper used in this publication meets the requirements for permanence established by the American National Standard for Information Sciences "Permanence of Paper for Printed Library Materials" (ANSI Z39.48-1984).

All rights reserved. No copyrighted part of this publication may be reproduced, stored in a retrieval system, or transmitted, in any form or by any means, electronic, photocopying, recording, or otherwise, without the prior written permission of the publisher.

CONTENTS.

CHAPTER I.
CORRESPONDENCE FROM 1801 TO 1815, ... PAGE 9

CHAPTER II.
CORRESPONDENCE FROM 1815 TO 1820, ... 49

CHAPTER III.
CORRESPONDENCE OF 1825 AND 1826, ... 109

CHAPTER IV.
CORRESPONDENCE OF 1827, ... 156

CHAPTER V.
CORRESPONDENCE OF 1828, ... 188

CHAPTER VI.
CORRESPONDENCE OF 1829, ... 217

CHAPTER VII.
CORRESPONDENCE OF 1830, ... 251

CONTENTS.

CHAPTER VIII.
CORRESPONDENCE OF 1831 AND 1832, ... 293

CHAPTER IX.
CORRESPONDENCE OF 1833, 1834, AND 1835, ... 347

CHAPTER X.
CORRESPONDENCE OF 1836, 1837, 1838, AND 1839, ... 403

CHAPTER XI.
CORRESPONDENCE OF 1840, 1841, 1842, AND 1843, ... 443

CHAPTER XII.
CORRESPONDENCE OF 1844, ... 483

CHAPTER XIII.
CORRESPONDENCE OF 1848 AND 1849, ... 553

CHAPTER XIV.
CORRESPONDENCE OF 1850, 1851, AND 1852, ... 598

TO THE READER.

Mr. Clay was not in the habit of keeping copies of his own letters. It may easily be imagined, therefore, that the time and trouble required to collect original and properly authenticated copies, so as to compose an epistolary history of his life, have not been inconsiderable. It is ten years since the editor of this volume commenced this task, with very important facilities afforded by Mr. Clay himself, as will appear from some of the correspondence. In addition to a very thorough examination of Mr. Clay's papers, under his own supervision, in the winter of 1844–45, the editor, by permission of his family, made a new examination of all the papers at Ashland, in 1853. From some three thousand documents, more or less, collected at Ashland and elsewhere, the editor has sifted and shaken out the correspondence contained in this volume. For the first fifteen years of the present century, down to the treaty of Ghent, embraced in the first chapter, very few of Mr. Clay's letters could be obtained. From that period they begin to appear more abundantly, as will be seen. It was thought proper to introduce letters of the correspondents of Mr. Clay to some extent, especially those of distinguished persons, and on occasions of especial interest. It was not possible generally to obtain the immediate counterparts of the correspondence.

After having completed the "Life and Times of Henry Clay," in two volumes, first published in 1846, and having added, in 1854, a chapter to the second volume of that work containing the last seven years of Mr. Clay's life, the plan of the editor of the present volume has been to present an epistolary history of the same period, and chiefly of the same things, as viewed by the parties in correspondence from their own closets, in their epistolary communications with each other, with no design on their part of furnishing materials for history. Most of these parties are since dead. It must be seen that such materials, from such hands, are of a very peculiar character, naturally attractive and interesting; and some of them very instructive. They can not but cast light on events, in some cases very important, which could not otherwise be fully understood. There is a truthfulness in the *abandon* of private correspondence which the cautiousness of politicians and statesmen rarely betrays in their ordinary and public acts; or if they sometimes betray it, they do not avow and confess it. Not a little of such materials will be found in this volume.

As the letters are generally presented in chronological order, with constantly recurring chasms of other parts of the correspondence, and without any regard to their relations to each other, it is for the reader to connect them with history, as it may be found in the first two volumes of this work, and in other public records. Indeed, many facts of history will be found in this volume which can be found nowhere else; and some of them very interesting and important. Besides the new facts of history disclosed, much of this correspondence, very little of which was ever before published, will probably be felt and acknowledged as affording new and interesting light on a great deal of history before known. It will serve, in some degree, as a key to unlock and open to view many intricate and obscure events of no small importance hitherto unexplained.

Some will perhaps think there are too many letters in this volume of trivial import, and that some of the brief notes and others might as well have been omitted. But the editor has desired to present the *entireness* of Mr. Clay's character, so far as correspondence would reveal it, more especially in those parts which, from the nature and character of his career, have been very little before the public. His character as a public man is public property. But Mr. Clay has made such a mark on his age and the history of his time, that the public will naturally be interested, and perhaps have some right, to know more of all his relations in life than his brilliant career as a public man has permitted them to observe. They will find in this correspondence that nothing in his private and domestic relations, and in the minor details touching the interests of his own family, escaped his care and attention. They will see that that fidelity and rigid conscientiousness which controlled all his conduct as a politician and statesman, were exemplified in a similar type, and in a degree as much more careful and anxious as the case required, in all his private and domestic relations. He not only had a large family of the first generation, most of whom left the world before him, but he had numerous grandchildren. It is touching to observe the action of his parental feelings toward them all, according to their characters and conditions of health and comfort, as disclosed in this correspondence. An invalid granddaughter, Lucy, so often mentioned in his letters, was always a tender object of his solicitude.

Mr. Clay was necessarily a politician, because he was forever in the whirl of politics. Mr. Clay, however, did not seek politics, but politics sought him, on account of his peculiar and eminent qualifications for public life. But this correspondence will show how often, and, doubtless sincerely, he desired repose from political agitations, and how much he was disgusted with unfair and dishonorable political strifes. Take him all in all, he was the most popular public man, so far as his personal qualities were concerned, that has ever appeared in the history of the country, and that from the beginning to the end of his career. It was the unavoidable destiny of such a man, that he should be abused by his political opponents, and carried on the shoulders of his political friends; and in the same proportion as the former feared, the latter loved him. We know not of how many it can be said, but we fear of few; yet it can be said of Mr. Clay, and all the world will believe it, that he was an honest, fair, and patriotic politician. He never made a trade of politics, as many of his cotemporaries did, and as is generally the case now with those engaged in politics. His country, and the good of his country, in his strife with his opponents, were ever the ruling passion of his mind in all public affairs. His patriotism, true as the needle to the pole, will be more and more apparent as the events which excited it recede in the distance. Again and again, as a candidate for the highest trust in the nation, he sacrificed himself on the altar of his country, and of the principles which he adopted. "He would rather be right," or what he thought was right, than be invested with the highest official honors. That he was actuated by a laudable ambition fairly to gain eminence in his career, was doubtless an ingredient of his lofty aspirations; but his principles would not bend for such an advantage. Who does not know that his talents, and the charm of his character on the public mind, would have borne him to any place in the gift of the nation, if he had thrown himself on the popular current, in almost any of the exigences leading that way which fell in his path? But he would never sacrifice a principle for his own personal advantage. If he had had less faith in public virtue, it would have made no difference; for he would never sacrifice self-respect for influence. He trusted, and was deceived; but he has acquired more fame in history by his course than could have been achieved in any other way. The most rigid scrutiny of his character leaves his name untarnished by a single act in all his political relations.

That mill-stone on the neck of Mr. Clay's political history, the alleged bargain between him and Mr. Adams, was indeed cut loose, though not in time to save the victim from its disadvantages. The attempt at bargain, as since proved, was on the other side, and failing in the proposed arrangement, the best way to rebut an accusation to which the other party was liable, was found to be in bringing one of the same kind against Mr. Clay. Mr. Clay never believed that such an attack could answer its purpose. But it did. Several times Mr. Clay received proposals of such a bargain, more than one of which is revealed for the first time in this volume; and the lofty manliness and indignation with which he treated them is also shown. When proposed to make him President by a wrong to Mr. Webster, on condition that Mr. Clay would use his influence for a certain appointment, though Mr. Clay and Mr. Webster were not at the time on the most friendly terms, Mr. Clay insisted that the proposal and its conditions should be made known to Mr. Webster, and, as will be seen, it was no fault of Mr. Clay that this was not done. A subsequent letter of Mr. Clay will indicate further the estimate made by him of that transaction. No attempt on Mr. Clay's honor, as a politician, ever succeeded. He lived and died an American patriot of the loftiest character.

Forever cherished and followed by a great national party, and forced into the field as a candidate for public services and public honors, it was reasonable to expect that his correspondence will partake of this character. Numerous as his friends were, with whom he communicated very frankly—for frankness was a part of his nature —yet every man, and Mr. Clay was no exception, must have his bosom friends. Judge Brooke,* of Virginia, was a correspondent and bosom friend of Mr. Clay for more than half a century, and there was no other man in the nation to whom Mr. Clay opened his heart and mind so fully and freely on public and private affairs. Hence the use of this correspondence so largely in this volume. It always presents Mr. Clay's mind and views at the dates of the respective

* Judge Brooke and Francis Brooke, in the correspondence, are the same person.

letters, and on the topics considered. It is a perfect *abandon* of private friendship and correspondence, and, on that account, is always interesting and instructive. The Hon. J. S. Johnston, United States Senator from Louisiana, was also an habitual correspondent and bosom friend of Mr. Clay, and much of their correspondence is given in this volume down to the time of Mr. Johnston's death, by the burning of a steamboat on the waters of the Mississippi. The field of correspondence, from which this volume is a selection, was immense. It has been the aim of the editor not to insert letters which had been before published, and there are but few exceptions to this rule. The plan of arranging them in chronological order—the best, probably, that could be adopted—almost necessarily places nearly all the letters each in an isolated position. They are not, of course, all historical in the higher sense of the term. Some are introduced for their eccentricity, and some, doubtless, will be of little interest to the public generally. It is believed, however, that they are a fair illustration in kind of Mr. Clay's relations to the wide public. There are, as will be seen, sundry historical disclosures of considerable interest and importance, which will probably excite some attention.

The editor must crave pardon of numerous persons who have kindly furnished him with letters of Mr. Clay, which could not be inserted for lack of room, and for other causes. Notwithstanding the rules which he was obliged to adopt, the volume has swollen to unexpected dimensions.

Where the editor has used the letters of persons now living, he has been very careful not to insert any to the use of which he would imagine they would have any objection. On the contrary, he has used only such as he supposed they would be very willing, if not gratified, to see in such a place. If there should be any exceptions to this rule, the imperative demands for the truth of history in matters on which the parties concerned could not fairly claim to be consulted, must be the apology.

There will, of course, be found many peculiarities of style in such a variety of letters as are to be found in this volume. For the most part, however, they are good epistolary compositions, and not a few of them of a high order. The editor has not felt at liberty to make alterations, except to correct grammatical errors, and even some of these will probably still be found. The letters of foreigners were, for the most part, addressed to Mr. Clay in English, Lafayette's always, and they are given as found. In no case are they translations of the editor. There are, of course, imperfections of style in letters of this class. Mr. Clay's letters are generally a model of epistolary writing. The *fac-simile* presented is a fair exhibition of his chirography—always elegant, and never careless.

C. COLTON.

NEW YORK, September 1, 1855.

Wash. 17th Mar. 1840

Dear Sir:

I received your letter transmitting a schedule of alterations which the opponents of the Copy right bill are desirous of effecting. I do not think that what is out of element the holding of the Copy right to American citizens is just or liberal. Without the restriction, that would however probably be the practical operation of the measure. And rather than do nothing, I would accede to these alterations.

With good respect
I am Your ob. serv.
H. Clay

Geo. Allard Esq.

PRIVATE CORRESPONDENCE

OF

HENRY CLAY.

CHAPTER I.

CORRESPONDENCE FROM 1801 TO 1815.

MR. CLAY TO JUDGE BROOKE.*

LEXINGTON, December 30, 1801.

DEAR SIR,—I have received as well your letter by Mr. H. Taylor, as the one written a few days after, by the post.

I must request the favor of you to execute a small commission for me. The Acts of the Virginia Legislature, passed prior to the separation of this State, are extremely difficult to be procured, even by collecting fugitive Acts, in this country; but few indeed of the public offices possess entire collections. Will you be so obliging as to obtain for me, if you can, the old revisal, which reaches, I believe, to the year 1766, the Chancellor revisal, and the Acts passed since that, in a regular series to the year 1792. The last is most desired, but I could wish to possess all. Your revisal of 1791 would not answer my purpose, because it contains laws not in force in this country, and, if my recollection serves me, omits to give the respective dates of the passages of each law, all-important in many cases. These books you will be pleased to forward to William Taylor, Esq., merchant, in Baltimore, from whom I can easily procure them; or to either of our representatives in Congress, Mr. Brown, Mr. Breckenridge,

---

* Mr. Clay and Judge Brooke, of Fredericksburg, Va., were correspondents for more than half a century.

Fowler, or Davis, who will contrive some mode for them to get to me. I suppose they may be obtained from the Council Chamber.

What has become of the son of my much regretted friend, your brother? I feel myself under obligations of gratitude to the father, which I should be happy of having an opportunity of discharging to the son. What is the progress he has made in his education? We have in this place an university in a very flourishing condition. Could you not spare him to me in this country for two or three years? I live at a short distance from the buildings, have a small family, and need not add, that from the cheapness of living in this country, his expense to me would be extremely inconsiderable. We have, too, a distant hope of getting Mr. Madison, from William and Mary, to take the management of our seminary. Be pleased to let me hear from you on this subject.

JAMES BROWN* TO MR. CLAY.

WASHINGTON, September 16, 1804.

DEAR SIR,—Your last letter was dated at the Springs, where you were reveling in the enjoyments of ease, mirth, and engaging society. Since that time you have probably experienced the bustle and solicitude attendant on an election, for I discover your name at the head of the list of successful candidates.

* * * * * * * *

Nancy [Mrs. Brown] was delighted at finding that Lucretia [Mrs. Clay, sister of Mrs. Brown] had overcome her repugnance to writing, and by the next post replied to her letter. She begs me to press upon you the task of urging her to write more frequently, and authorizes me to declare that although her correspondents are numerous, Lucretia's letters shall ever receive prompt answers.

I have written to so many of my friends to-day, that I have much against my inclination, defrauded you of your share. My affectionate wishes for the happiness of yourself and family wait upon you.

---

* James Brown, brother-in-law of Mr. Clay, afterward American minister at Paris.

JOHN ADAIR TO MR. CLAY.

LEXINGTON, August 15, 1805.

SIR,— * * * * * * *
I need make no further apology for calling your recollection to the handbill that was shown in Frankfort last November, implicating my political principles as inimical to Mr. Jefferson and republicanism. From an application to Mr. Taylor and others who were present, it appears that the conversation alluded to took place principally between you and myself, although in presence of several gentlemen. I wish you now to recollect, as far as you can, the nature of that conversation—in what manner I spoke of the amendment to the Federal Constitution, whether positively as bad, or whether I did not merely doubt its future operation as unfavorable to republicanism, stating, as my reason, that it had been urged by the Federalists under the former Administration, and opposed by the party who had now carried it in opposition to them. I wish you likewise to state in what manner and by whom General Pinckney's name was first introduced, whether I discovered the least displeasure with the administration, or talents, or personal character of Mr. Jefferson ; on the contrary, whether I did not say I would prefer him as President to any man in the Union ; but observed that the people of America ought not to think their liberty or happiness depended on the election of any individual, but on their steady adherence to a virtuous observance of their laws.

Your answer by post to Frankfort will be deemed a favor.

MR. CLAY TO JOHN ADAIR.

LEXINGTON, August 24, 1805.

SIR,—Yours of the 15th instant, addressed to me at the Olympian Springs, did not reach me until a few days ago at Paris, or it should have been earlier answered.

I recollect, during the session of the Assembly of 1803, having had one or more conversations with you relative to the amendment of the Federal Constitution, providing for a designation of the President and Vice-President in the votes to be given for those officers. But I regret that my memory does not enable me to detail the particulars of those conversations. I remember, however, that you expressed doubts as to the propriety of the proposed amendment, urged some arguments to prove that the existing provision was best, and suggested your fears that a change would produce mischievous consequences. Whether your opinion was matured or not I can not say, but I do not think you expressed one decisively. If the name of General Pinckney was mentioned, and how or by whom it was introduced, at the times of the conversations, or at any of them, it has escaped my memory. I have heard you speak of that gentleman, I think, more than once, in terms of high respect, and it may have been when the topic of conversation was the amendment; but I do not believe that you drew any parallel between Mr. Jefferson and him, or contended that he was equally well qualified to fill the presidential chair.

When I saw the handbill to which you allude, I was surprised at some of the sentiments there ascribed to you; and am inclined to think had they been avowed in my presence and hearing, that they would have made an impression which would be still fresh.

JAMES BROWN TO MR. CLAY.

NEW ORLEANS, March 12, 1805.

DEAR SIR,—I received, two mails ago, your very acceptable favor of the 28th of January, and should sooner have answered it but for the pressure of business arising from two courts in session at the same time. I rejoice at every assurance I receive of the health and happiness of a family to whom I feel every attachment which a consciousness of their worth and a recollection of their friendship can inspire. The hope of a rapturous meeting with you shortly, consoles me under an absence which, without this delightful expectation, would be insupportable. With the young portion of my relations I feel confident of an interview, but poor old Colonel Hart*—am I never to see him again? He has frightened me by the very circumstance which he mentions as flattering to his hope of long life. He informs me that his weight has increased twenty-three pounds since his return from the Springs. I consider this as an unfavorable omen, but will feel perfectly relieved from all apprehensions if he survives the month of March.

* * * * * * * *

* Father-in-law of Mr. Brown and Mr. Clay.

It gives me real pleasure to hear from every quarter that you stand in Kentucky at the head of your profession. May you soon grow rich, and be able to retire from a profession, the duties of which are too severe in that inclement climate for the most robust constitution. My retreat from your State saved my life. One winter more would have fixed upon me a confirmed consumption. Here I have renewed my youth.

Nancy has written to Lucretia. She enjoys good health, good spirits, and, as you may suppose, the esteem of all who know her.

Let me hear from you more frequently.

AARON BURR TO MR. CLAY.

LOUISVILLE, November 27, 1806.

DEAR SIR,—Information has this morning been given to me that Mr. Davies has recommenced his prosecution and inquiry. I must entreat your professional aid in this business. It would be disagreeable to me to form a new connection, and various considerations will, it is hoped, induce you, even at some personal inconvenience, to acquiesce in my request. I shall, however, insist on making a liberal pecuniary compensation. The delay of your journey to Washington for a few days can not be very material. No business is done in Congress till after New Years. I pray you to repair to Frankfort on receipt of this.

AARON BURR TO MR. CLAY.

FRANKFORT, December 1, 1806.

SIR,—I have no design, nor have I taken any measure to promote a dissolution of the Union, or a separation of any one or more States from the residue. I have neither published a line on this subject nor has any one, through my agency, or with my knowledge. I have no design to intermeddle with the Government or to disturb the tranquillity of the United States, or of its territories, or any part of them. I have neither issued, nor signed, nor promised a commission to any person for any purpose. I do not own a musket nor a bayonet, nor any single article of military stores, nor does any person for me, by my authority or with my knowledge.

My views have been fully explained to, and approved by, several of the principal officers of Government, and, I believe, are well understood by the administration and seen by it with complacency. They are such as every man of honor and every good citizen must approve.

Considering the high station you now fill in our national councils* I have thought these explanations proper, as well to counteract the chimerical tales which malevolent persons have so industriously circulated, as to satisfy you that you have not espoused the cause of a man in any way unfriendly to the laws, the government, or the interests of his country.

AARON BURR TO MR. CLAY.

LEWIS INN, half past 3.

SIR,—At nine this morning Mr. Jordan received your letter in reply to one which he wrote at my request.

I have just arrived wet, and something fatigued, and send to inquire whether my presence in court is *now* deemed necessary or expedient.

I pray you to consider yourself as my counsel in the business moved by Mr. D. A more *technical* application will be made when I shall have the pleasure to see you. An early interview, at this house, would very much gratify me.

MR. CLAY TO THOMAS M. PRENTISS.

CITY OF WASHINGTON, February 15, 1807.

DEAR SIR,—I received your agreeable favor, with its inclosure, for which accept my thanks. Your New Year's ode was well adapted to the object in view, and the perusal of it afforded me much pleasure.

Colonel Burr has supplied much fund of conversation. No doubt is now entertained here of his having engaged in schemes of the most daring and illegal kind. Having left Kentucky under a belief that he was innocent, it was with no little surprise upon my arrival here that I found I had been deceived. Entertaining the opinion I did, I ventured at Chillicothe to speak with some

* Mr. Clay was now Senator of the United States.

freedom upon measures proposed there of a harsh character, and unjustified, as it appeared to me, by public exigences. It is to this cause that the strictures upon my conduct, alluded to in yours, are owing. They give me no pain, as I am conscious of having participated in no illegal projects of Burr, and know that I will not be suspected of having done so by any who know me.

Alexander has been discharged for want of proof. Bollmar and Swartwout remain in custody. They applied to the Supreme Court of the United States, now in session, for a writ of *habeas corpus*. Some of the judges doubted their power to grant it, as it was not included within the enumerated powers conferred upon that tribunal in the Constitution. The question has been discussed, and three judges to two [Chase and Johnson] have determined in favor of the application. The prisoners are to be brought before the Court to-day.

The papers inform you of the great events passing upon the European theater. A measure has been lately taken by Bonaparte of a most gigantic nature, the declaration that the islands of Great Britain are in a state of blockade. It is said that our minister at Paris has written on to Government that our commerce is not to be affected by it; I apprehend, however, that it will subject it to much embarrassment.

The session of Congress has not been so interesting as I had anticipated. No questions in relation to our foreign intercourse, involving much discussion, have been agitated; every thing depends upon the result of pending negotiations, and this will not be known, it is probable, until the session expires.

I expect to be accompanied to Kentucky by two young gentlemen, one proposing the practice and the other the study of the law. The latter will continue with me. I am glad to find that you have been getting acquainted with Strange. He is a valuable reporter, but occupies a second station only in the grade of merit. I calculate upon finding you much improved in your law knowledge. Two words will make any man of sound intellect a lawyer, industry and application, and the same words with a third, economy, will enable him to make a fortune.

My respects to your fellow-students; and tell them they have been very inattentive to me in not writing.

Present me also to the very amiable and sensible man with whom you reside.

MR. BROWN TO MR. CLAY.

NEW ORLEANS, September 1, 1803.

MY DEAR SIR,—Before I had the pleasure of your last very agreeable letter, the news of the death of our venerable friend [Colonel Hart] had reached us. Although in some degree prepared for the melancholy event by the account given in your former letter of the state of his health, I yet felt the loss with a degree of sensibility which was heightened by the regret I experienced by being forever denied the long expected pleasure of giving him a gleam of happiness in his last days, by restoring him the society of his beloved daughter. I need not tell you that she has suffered. You know the sensibility of her heart, and the warmth of her gratitude and attachment to the best of fathers. Reflection, however, should teach us the duty of yielding to the decrees of heaven. Our friend was not prematurely snatched away from us. He has left no needy infant orphans. He lived long and he lived well. His character is set before his family as a model of public and private virtues, worthy of their imitation. While they cherish his memory may they never depart from the example he has left them.

* * * * * * *

I am sorry that you do not live in better times, for you have talents to adorn a public station, and to be useful to your country. But to me character is more dear than every other thing; and can any man hope long to preserve it in the present miserable state of things? You have carried your election. I am rejoiced at it. Your enemies will be wounded. But I pray you to quit public life, or muster up sufficient philosophy to bear up under all the hard names with which you will be christened in the papers. You are, it seems, a Burrite. If Wilkinson deserves to be believed, seven thousand men in your State deserved the same opprobrious title. What you may next be called is uncertain; but as long as you retain your brains and your independence you will be abused. Republicanism demands that a man of talents should be kept down by detraction. Too much genius, like too much wealth, destroys equality, the very soul of democracy. But I forbear. You will say I have become splenetic, or rather that I have always been subject to that infirmity. Nothing is further from the fact. Ever since my arrival in this merry dancing country my temper has remained unruffled, with the exception of Wilkinson's winter of horrors. In domestic life I have nothing to wish, and my practice has been more prosperous than I had any right to expect. It is with pleasure that I discover that your rage for electioneering has not diverted your mind from the *main point;* and that the people, while they rail at the profession of law, vie with each other in filling the coffers of its professors. Happy in the bosom of your family may you long enjoy the fruits of your labors, and transmit liberal educations and competent fortunes to your descendants! * * * * * *

Present my affectionate regards to Lucretia and the family.

MR. CLAY TO JUDGE BROOKE.

WASHINGTON, January 26, 1811.

MY DEAR SIR,—I received your favor inclosing a statement relative to Garland's debt, and bank notes amounting to $35, being $3 more than was the balance agreeably to the statement. I have since received a letter from Mr. Hoomes, in which he acknowledges that I have overpaid the proportion of the purchase of Buzzard coming from me. But as I have the collection, in Kentucky, of some money for his father's estate, there will be no difficulty in adjusting the excess. I am much indebted to the kindness of your brother and yourself for your attention to this matter, and I can not agree that he shall be without compensation for his trouble. I must, therefore, request that you will pay him $20, for which, as well as for the $3 above mentioned, you shall be credited in the taxes upon your land. I do not think the present a very favorable period for selling your land, which I have no doubt is gradually rising in value. If, however, you are desirous to effect a sale, your object would probably be facilitated by such a descriptive survey of it as you mention. I can hardly suppose a survey necessary to the perpetuation of the boundaries; surveys in that county having been generally made in connection, in such manner that they tend to prove each other, and the removal of the corner of one would derange the whole block. Instances have, indeed, occurred there of such fraudulent attempts; but I believe they are rare. Should you desire to possess such an account of the quality of your lands as will enable you to satisfy the inquiries of purchasers, I need not say that, on this, as well as any other matter interesting to you, I shall take pleasure in promoting your wishes.

MR. CLAY TO ——— ———.

LEXINGTON, July 9, 1811.

DEAR SIR,—In acknowledging the receipt of your favor of the 7th inst., covering $100 for the Lexington Library, I must say you have furnished, what was not wanted, an additional evidence of that devotion to literature, and that disinterested liberality, which you have invariably so eminently displayed. I fear that, in this instance, your munificence has exceeded the bounds of self-justice, by the appropriation of a sum not warranted by the proceeds of the orations, with which you have favored us. Under this impression, I was about to obey my first impulse of soliciting you to permit me to return your benevolent donation. But apprehensive that, in so doing, I might excite some unpleasant sensation, I determined to give it the direction which your goodness has prescribed, and invest it in such of the books contained in your list, as are not already in the Library, which will be not more appreciated for their enlightened contents than by a recollection of the distinguished source whence they have proceeded.

LANGDON CHEVES TO MR. CLAY.

WASHINGTON (Davis' Hotel), July 30, 1812.

DEAR SIR,—Yours of the 15th July, inst., I received yesterday, at Philadelphia, at the very moment I was getting into the stage on my way to Carolina.   *   *   *   *   *

You ask me, " What notice you ought to take of Randolph's reply ?" certainly none—none whatever. Were you to notice it he would reply again, and it would never terminate. *He* spoke with great truth in the beginning of the last session, when he said the " Speaker of the House of Representatives was the second man in the nation ;" and if this be true, as I think it is, it does not become the Speaker to enter into altercations with any member of the House, or even of the nation, in a public

* The address of this letter is not given.

justification of his conduct, any more than it does to the *first* man in the nation—the President. I, therefore, thought you originally wrong. But if any notice of Mr. R.'s first publication was right, it was taken by you exactly in the manner, temperate and dignified, in which it ought to have been noticed. I think, as the question stands, you have entirely the advantage of the *argument;* and I think you would egregiously err, as the Speaker of the House of Representatives (it would be entirely different were it a question between Mr. Clay and Mr. R.) to put it on any other footing than that of argument. I have not heard one sentence on the subject of his reply, of any kind, from any person, except one in my own family, which resulted from my having received a copy of it, through the Post-office, from himself—it was not one to your prejudice. On this subject, although about the latitude of debate we differ, I am entirely and decidedly of opinion you are right; and *that,* I think, is enough for you as Speaker. I am sure of this, whether you think me right or wrong, you will be certain that I give you *candid* advice.

I have not a doubt of your willingness to put the question personally on any footing whatever, that might be deemed proper. But any such notice of it on your part would be most *inexcusably wrong.* It is always to be remembered that it is the Speaker and Mr. R. who are engaged; and really I should be afraid myself of the freedom of speech, if the Chair were supported in that way. No; if you had any feelings leading you that way, it would be a sacred public duty to suppress them. I ought to have said, besides, that there is not even a plausible reason and occasion for any such notice were you viewed merely as any other individual of the community. Present my most respectful compliments to Mrs. Clay. I have only arrived here fifteen minutes, and go away on my journey in fifteen more. I am, therefore, in great haste.

JAMES MONROE TO MR. CLAY.

WASHINGTON, August 28, 1812.

MY DEAR SIR,—Yours of the 29th ultimo and 12th instant have been received. The former should have been answered sooner, had I not been absent in Virginia, where I had gone to to take my family for the advantage of our mountain air.

We have just heard with equal astonishment and concern, that General Hull has surrendered, by capitulation, the army under his command at Detroit, to the British force opposed to him. The circumstances attending this most mortifying and humiliating event are not known; but, so far as we are informed on the subject, there appears to be no justification of it. I can not suspect his integrity; I rather suppose that a panic had seized the whole force, and that he and they became victims of his want of energy, promptitude of decision, and those resources, the characteristics of great minds in difficult emergencies. We understand that, after passing the river, he suffered his communication to be cut off with the States of Ohio and Kentucky, and without making any active movement in front to strike terror into the enemy, he remained tranquil, thereby evincing a want of confidence in his own means, and giving time to collect his forces together. No intelligence justifies the belief that he gave battle in a single instance. It appears that he surrendered on a summons from Fort Sandwich, on the opposite side of the river, after the firing of some cannon or mortars, which did no great mischief.

Before this disastrous event was known, the force, now, I presume, on its march, was ordered from Kentucky, and the appointment of brigadier had been conferred on Governor Harrison. Your letters had produced all the effect on those subjects, which their solidity justly merited.

I most sincerely wish that the President could dispose of me, at this juncture, in the military line. If circumstances would permit, and it should be thought that I could render any service, I would, in a very few days, join our forces assembling beyond the Ohio, and endeavor to recover the ground which we have lost. He left this to-day for Virginia, as did Mr. Gallatin for New York, but expresses being sent for them, they will probably both return to-morrow.

WILLIAM HENRY HARRISON TO MR. CLAY.

CINCINNATI, August 29, 1812.

I write to you, my dear sir, amid a thousand interruptions, and I do it solely for the purpose of showing you that you are present to my recollection, under circumstances that would almost justify a suspension of every private feeling. The rumored disasters upon our north-western frontier, are now ascertained to be correct. The important point of Mackinac was surrendered without an effort; an army captured at Detroit, after receiving three shots from *a distant* battery of the enemy (and from the range of which it was easy to retire), a fort [Chicago], in the midst of hostile tribes of Indians, ordered to be evacuated, and the garrison slaughtered; the numerous north-western tribes of Indians (with the exception of two feeble ones), in arms against us, is the distressing picture which presents itself to view in this part of the country. To remedy all these misfortunes, I have an army competent in numbers, and in spirit equal to any that Greece or Rome ever boasted of, but destitute of artillery, of many necessary equipments, and absolutely ignorant of every military evolution, nor have I but a single individual capable of assisting me in training them. But I beg you to believe, my dear sir, that this retrospect of my situation, far from producing despondency, produces a contrary effect, and I feel confident of being able to surmount them all. The grounds of this confidence are a reliance on my own zeal and perseverance, and a perfect conviction that no such *materials* for forming an invincible army ever existed, as the volunteers which have marched from Kentucky on the present occasion.

Fort Wayne is in imminent danger. Governor Meiggs is collecting a body of mounted men at Urbanna, and I suppose will send them to relieve Fort Wayne, before I can get up with the infantry. I dispatched Garrard's troop this morning, with orders to join any corps (at Piqua) which may be destined for that object. The three regiments of infantry marched also this morning; I shall follow and overtake them to-morrow. Should the relief of Fort Wayne not have been attempted, or the attempt have failed, it will be my first object upon my arrival at Piqua. I have made every arrangement in my power to facilitate the march of the regiments which are expected from Kentucky, after they shall arrive here, but I fear that I shall be obliged to advance from Piqua without them. With the assistance of a number of mounted men, however, which Governor Meiggs can supply, I may do pretty well. With troops that are awkward, and who, of course, maneuver slowly, mounted men are absolutely indispensable to mask their evolutions.

I am so much interrupted, that I can only add that I am your friend, etc.

WILLIAM HENRY HARRISON TO MR. CLAY.

CINCINNATI, August 30, 1812.

MY DEAR SIR,—After having been absent from home for so many months you will no doubt think it unreasonable that you should be asked to take a considerable journey, and that on an occasion entirely foreign to your ordinary public duties. I know you, however, too well, not to believe that sacrifices of private convenience will be always made to render service to your country. Without further preamble then, I inform you that in my opinion, your presence on the frontier of this State would be productive of great advantages. I can assure you that your advice and assistance in determining the course of operations for the army (to the command of which I have been designated by your recommendation), will be highly useful. You are not only pledged in some manner for my conduct, but for the success of the war—for God's sake, then, come on to Piqua as quickly as possible, and let us endeavor to throw off from the administration that weight of reproach which the late disasters will heap upon them. If you come, bring on McKee with you, whom you will overtake upon the road. An extract from this letter will be authority for the commanding officer of his regiment to let him come.

JAMES MONROE TO MR. CLAY.

WASHINGTON, September 17, 1812.

MY DEAR SIR,—I have had the pleasure to receive several letters from you in relation to our affairs to the westward, and I hope that one which I wrote you on the receipt of the first, has long since reached its destination. Every effort has been made by the government to remedy the shameful and disastrous loss of the army and fort at Detroit, and I hope the best effects will result from them. In aid of the force which has so generously volunteered its service from Kentucky and Ohio, fifteen hundred are ordered from Pennsylvania, and a like number from Virginia, so that I think you will have on the borders of Lake Erie, early in the next month, eight thousand or ten thousand men, well equipped, prepared to march on to recover the ground lost, and resume the conquest of Upper Canada. I have the utmost confidence in the success of the expedition which is set on foot, because the spirit of the people appears to be roused to that state which is best adapted to manly and heroic achievements. I am willing to trust to their sense of honor and to their patriotism, to efface the stigma which has been fixed on our national character. I hope they will exhibit a noble contrast to that degenerate spirit which has of late, and continues to exhibit itself to the eastward, in the dominant party there. The command of this force is committed to Governor Harrison, who, it is believed, will justify the favorable expectation entertained of him by those who are best acquainted with his merit. You and our other friends in Kentucky will find that the utmost attention has been paid to your opinions and wishes on all these subjects.

A large park of heavy artillery is sent on to Pittsburg, to be forwarded thence toward Cleveland, for the use of the army, whose duty it will be to retake Detroit, and expel the British from Malden and Upper Canada. In short, every arrangement is made to give effect to our operations in that quarter that has appeared to be necessary.

On the intelligence of the surrender of Detroit, the President expressed a desire to avail himself of my services in that quarter, and had partly decided so to do. He proposed that I should go in the character of a volunteer, with the rank of major general, to take the command of the forces. I expressed my willingness to obey the summons, although it was sudden and unexpected, as indeed the event which suggested the idea was. On mature reflection, however, he concluded that it would not be proper for me to leave my present station at the present juncture. I had no opinion on the subject, but was prepared to act in any situation in which it might be thought I might be most useful.

From the northern army we have nothing which inspires a confident hope of any brilliant success. The disaffection in that quarter has paralyzed every effort of the government, and rendered inoperative every law of Congress; I speak comparatively with what might have been expected. On the public mind, however, a salutary effect is produced even there, by the events which have occurred. Misfortune and success have alike diminished the influence of foreign attachments and party animosities, and contributed to draw the people closer together. The surrender of our army excited a general grief, and the naval victory a general joy. Inveterate Toryism itself was compelled, in both instances, to disguise its character and hide its feelings, by appearing to sympathize with those of the nation. If Great Britain does not come forward soon and propose honorable conditions, I am convinced that the war will become a national one, and will terminate in the expulsion of her force and power from the continent.

Should you see my old and venerable friend, General Scott, I beg you to present my best regards to him.

MR. CLAY'S PASSPORT TO GOTTENBURG.

To all who shall see these presents, greeting:

The President of the United States of America having appointed the Honorable Henry Clay, late Speaker of the House of Representatives, a Minister Plenipotentiary and Extraordinary, in conjunction with John Quincy Adams, James A. Bayard, and Jonathan Russell, Esquires, to negotiate and sign a treaty of peace with Great Britain; and the said Henry Clay, who is the bearer hereof, being now on his way to Gottenburg, in the kingdom of Sweden, for the purpose of fulfilling the objects of his mission; These are to request all officers of the United States aforesaid, civil and military, the officers and subjects of powers in amity with the said United States, and all others whom it may concern, not to offer to the said Henry Clay any hinderance or molestation whatsoever; but, on the contrary, to afford to him and to his secretaries and attendants, with their baggage, all necessary aid, comfort, and protection.

In faith whereof, I, James Monroe, Secretary of State for the United States of America, have hereunto subscribed my name and affixed the seal of my office.

Given at Washington City, this 4th day of February, A. D. 1814, and in the thirty-eighth year of American Independence.

MRS. CLAY TO MR. CLAY.

WASHINGTON, March 10.

MY DEAR HUSBAND,—Mr. Barker called to-day to let me know that he has an opportunity of sending letters to Gottenburg, and offered to take charge of one for you. I heard the other day from Lexington that it is more sickly than it ever has been. Nelly Hart had twelve negroes sick; Theodore wrote me that all our family were well. The children that I have with me are all well, and Henry is always talking of you, he comes up and kisses me for his papa. I long very much to be at home with my family, for I am very dreary here as I do not pay visits; indeed I found I could not go out without you in the evening, but I do all in my power to keep me from being melancholy. Our suit in this court was tried the other day; I have not heard that it is decided. Mr. Wickliff started on Sunday last for Kentucky. Mrs. Brown has at last made up her mind to go home with me and spend the summer. Judge Todd and his lady have been very polite to me since you left this; the Judge called the other day to examine the light wagon we were to have got from Mr. L. but he found it so completely worn out that I determined not to take it; we shall I hope get on without it. Mr. Bibb paid me the $500 as soon as he got here. You need not make yourself the least uneasy on our account, for I believe we shall do very well. Mr. Granger has been turned out of office. A great many blame Mr. Madison. Susan and Ann send their love to you. May God spare you to us. Do take care of yourself for our sakes

---

MR. CRAWFORD TO MR. CLAY.

PARIS, April 8, 1814.

DEAR SIR,—The events which have within a few days passed in this city, and in its neighborhood, have changed every thing in France but the character of the Parisians, and perhaps of Frenchmen in general.

On the 30th ult. a battle was fought in the vicinity of Paris by the French troops under the Duke of Ragusa, amounting to between fifteen and twenty thousand men, and the grand allied army. The loss was considerable on both sides, but that of the Allies was more than double. It is estimated from eight to ten thousand men. The disparity in the loss was the result of the strong positions of the French troops, and the desire of the Allies to get possession of the capital before the arrival of the Emperor Napoleon, who was advancing by rapid marches upon their rear. This desire was so predominant that they made no attempt to turn these positions, but marched directly up to the intrenchments, where they were repulsed four or five times. The battle commenced about 4 o'clock A. M. and finished about the same time in the evening. The Duke of Ragusa entered into a convention by which he agreed to evacuate the city, taking with him all his baggage, ammunition and artillery.

The next day the Emperor of Russia and King of Prussia entered Paris at the head of about fifty thousand of the finest troops in the world. The remainder of their immense army either defiled on the north or south side of the city, or remained in their positions on the east, which was the field of battle. The Emperor of Russia, with his Minister of Foreign Relations, went directly to the house of the Prince of Benevento, who convened the Senate the same evening, and had himself and three of his friends, with one devoted Bourbonite, named to the provisional government. The Senate had deposed Napoleon Bonaparte, and directed the provisional government to form a Constitution, which has been accomplished, and accepted by the Senate and the small portion of the Legislative corps who are now in Paris. The *Moniteur* of this day contains this Constitution, which you will probably see before you receive this letter. The monarchy is declared to be hereditary in the house of Bourbon in the male line. The present Senators remaining Senators of the realm by the same tenure. The Senate to consist of one hundred and fifty at least, and not more than two hundred. The ancient and new nobility to remain. All Frenchmen to be capable of filling all the offices of the government. The members of the legislative corps to hold their offices for five years, and to be elected directly by the people.

The proceedings of the Senate and of the provisional government, have overturned the authority of the Emperor with his army, and especially with his ablest generals. He seems to have sunk without an effort, at least without an effort corresponding in any degree with his former fame. Such at least is the conclusion which I draw from the facts which are communicated to the public. It is possible that these facts may be misrepresented. I believe, however, that it is certain, that he has agreed to retire with his family to the Isle of Elba upon a pension of six millions of livres. From the moment that he saw that it was impossible for him to reign he ought to have died. The manner was in his election. A strange infatuation seems to have influenced his conduct during the last six months. Still relying upon his talents and his power he refused, at Prague, to secure at least the neutrality of Austria, by giving her every thing she required. After having retreated across the Rhine he reluctantly accepted the basis which the Allies proposed, and which there is some reason to believe they were sincerely disposed to adopt. Lord Castlereagh's mission, however, according to the best view of the subject which I have been able to take, was intended solely to prevent this accommodation. Time will prove the accuracy or inaccuracy of this opinion. There must have been great address employed in managing the Emperor of Austria, who had rejected all idea of overthrowing the reigning dynasty. The infatuation of the Emperor, and his arrogance to his father-in-law (if we are to credit reports apparently well founded), greatly contributed to the success of the arts employed by the British Secretary. That the Emperor of Austria has been duped is clearly established by the declaration of the Allies after the breaking up of the Congress at Chatillon, and by the conduct of Lord Wellington. This declaration states that up to the 15th of March they were ready to make peace with the Emperor Napoleon, whereas the address of Lord Wellington, on the 2d of February, declares Louis XVIII. and raises the Bourbon standard. The introduction of the ancient dynasty is not acceptable to the great body of the people of Paris. Even now, after the Senate and provisional government have declared for that dynasty, there is not one man in a hundred who puts on the white cockade. On the day of the entry of the allied sovereigns, all the persons devoted to their ancient kings endeavored to make themselves as conspicuous as possible, and to conceal the smallness of their numbers by continual change of place. Exertions were made to excite popular feeling and popular tumult, but without effect. But for the National Guard popular tumult would have been excited, perhaps, but not in favor of the Bourbons. If the mob of Paris had been put in motion it would have been in favor of a free government.

The men now in power would, as far as I have been able to judge, have preferred the succession of the King of Rome, with a regency provided by the Empress; but the Emperor Alexander, who, under the modest exterior of submitting every thing to the will of the French people, dictates to the Senate and provisional government, at least this article of their Constitution.

I did not anticipate precisely the manner in which this European peace was to be consummated. I most sincerely wish you complete success in your negotiations, although I apprehend that great difficulties will be presented. Under existing circumstances, if peace is made, I presume that the treaty will be very short, concluding nothing but peace and the restoration of what territory may be in the hands of either party by conquest, if there is any such.

P. S. I send this by the Secretary of the Danish Legation, who sets out immediately for Copenhagen, which gives me no opportunity for reflection or revision of this hasty scrawl, as I have just been informed of the fact of his setting out.

MR. BAYARD TO MR. CLAY.

LONDON, April 20, 1814.

DEAR SIR,—The mail of last evening brought the intelligence of your arrival at Gottenburg. I present you my congratulations upon your safe passage across the Atlantic. Mr. Gallatin and myself left St. Petersburg on the 25th of January, and arrived at Amsterdam on the 4th of March. In that city we received the first advice of the direct negotiation proposed to be held between the United States and Great Britain, at Gottenburg, and of the intention of our government to send additional commissioners from America. Knowing that some time would elapse before your arrival in Europe, and also before the appointment of commissioners on the part of this Government, we thought it likely that more good might result from spending the interval in this country rather than in Holland.

We came over on the 9th inst. at a moment not very propitious for the objects we had in view. The Allies had taken possession of Paris, and the next day brought the news of Bonaparte's formal abdication of the thrones of France and Italy. The intelligence completely turned the heads of all ranks who seem to have thought of nothing since, but the means of manifesting their joy on the occasion.

It is much to be apprehended that this great and unexpected event will have an unfavorable influence upon the state of affairs between the United States and Great Britain. There is reason to think that it has materially changed the views of the British

Ministry. In fact the sudden reduction of their naval and military establishments would create much embarrassment, and the American war furnishes too good a pretense to avoid it. And the great augmentation of their disposable force presents an additional temptation to prosecute the war. You must also know that the temper of the country is highly excited against us, and decidedly expressed in favor of the continuance of hostilities.

I do not pretend, however, to speak at present with any certainty of the intentions of the Government, for we have had no communication with any member of it.

I think they have avoided any intercourse with us, but this may be attributed to the absence of Lord Castlereagh and the indisposition of the other ministers to interfere with the affairs of his department.

We can not learn that any step has yet been taken toward the selection of characters to be charged with the negotiation on the part of this Government. It is stated, and upon such authority as to deserve credit, that no appointment will be made till the Government is officially notified of the appointment of the American commissioners and of their arrival at the place of rendezvous. Mr. G. and myself have thought it, therefore, of sufficient importance to dispatch a special messenger to apprise you of the fact, and to enable you by his return, without loss of time, to make the official communication.

If there be a discretion on the subject, we would thoroughly recommend that some town in Holland should be substituted in lieu of Gottenburg, as the seat of the negotiation. There can be no doubt that the change would facilitate and accelerate the result. You may rely upon the friendly dispositions of the Prince of Orange, of which we had distinguished proofs during a short residence at Amsterdam.

One of the first acts of the Government of the Prince, was to nominate a minister to the United States.

I shall remain in London till I have the pleasure of hearing from you, unless (which is not to be expected), in the mean time commissioners should be appointed on the part of this Government.

This letter will be delivered to you by Colonel Milligan, who accompanied me as private secretary to St. Petersburg. He is deserving of your confidence, and I beg leave to recommend him to your attentions.

ALBERT GALLATIN TO MR. CLAY.

LONDON, April 22, 1814.

DEAR SIR,—We have just heard of your arrival, but have received no letters, and I am yet ignorant whether I am one of the new commission to treat of peace. My arrangements must depend on that circumstance, and I wait with impatience for the official account which you must have brought. For that reason Mr. Bayard addresses you and Mr. Russel in his own name; but I coincide fully with him in the opinion that the negotiations should by all means be opened here, or at least, in Holland, if this is not rendered impracticable from the nature of the commission. If this has unfortunately been limited to treating of peace at Gottenburg, which seems highly improbable, there is no remedy. But if the commission admits of a change of place, I would feel no hesitation in removing them, at least, to any other neutral place, whatever may be the language of the instructions. For their spirit would be fully answered by treating in any other friendly country as well as if at Gottenburg. On that point I feel great anxiety, because on account of the late great changes in Europe, and of the increased difficulties thence arising in making any treaty, I do believe that it would be utterly impossible to succeed in that corner, removed from every interference in our favor on the part of the European powers, and compelled to act with men clothed with limited authorities, and who might at all times plead a want of instructions.

You are sufficiently aware of the total change in our affairs produced by the late revolution, and by the restoration of universal peace in the European world, from which we are alone excluded. A well organized and large army is at once liberated from any European employment, and ready, together with a superabundant naval force, to act immediately against us. How ill-prepared we are to meet it in a proper manner no one knows better than yourself; but, above all, our own divisions and the hostile attitude of the Eastern States give room to apprehend that a continuance of the war might prove vitally fatal to the United States.

I understand that the ministers, with whom we have not had any direct intercourse, still profess to be disposed to make an equitable peace. But the hope not of ultimate conquest, but of a dissolution of the union, the convenient pretense which the

American war will afford to preserve large military establishments, and above all the force of popular feeling may all unite in inducing the cabinet in throwing impediments in the way of peace. They will not, certainly, be disposed to make concessions, nor probably displeased at a failure of negotiations. That the war is popular, and that national pride, inflated by the last unexpected success, can not be satisfied without what they call the chastisement of America, can not be doubted. The mass of the people here know nothing of American politics but through the medium of federal speeches and newspapers faithfully transcribed in their own journals. They do not even suspect that we have any just cause of complaint, and consider us altogether as the aggressors, and as allies of Bonaparte. In these opinions it is understood that the ministers do not participate; but it will really require an effort on their part to act contrary to public opinion; and they must, even if perfectly sincere, use great caution and run some risk of popularity. A direct, or at least, a very near intercourse with them is therefore highly important, as I have no doubt that they would go further themselves than they would be willing to intrust any other person. To this must be added, that Lord Castlereagh is, according to the best information I have been able to collect, the best disposed man in the cabinet, and that coming from France and having had intercourse with the Emperor Alexander, it is not improbable that these dispositions may have been increased by the personal expression of the Emperor's wishes in favor of peace with America. Whatever advantage may be derived from that circumstance and from the Emperor's arrival here, would be altogether lost at Gottenburg.

I have confined my letter to this single point, and hoping soon to hear from you and from Mr. Russell to whom you will present my best compliments.

MR. RUSSELL TO MR. CLAY.

STOCKHOLM, April 26, 1814.

DEAR SIR,—I did not reach this place until yesterday, a little before noon. The roads were very fine, but the weather, after the first day, execrable. I have announced my arrival to the minister, and he has assigned one o'clock to-morrow for our first interview, when I shall probably learn when I may expect to be presented to the king. This place, as far as I have yet seen it, promises to be agreeable.

Mr. Speyer received this morning a letter from Mr. Adams, dated the 11th of this month, in which he says he purposes to leave St. Petersburg about the 20th of this month, and hopes to arrive *somewhere* in Sweden, by the 1st of May—probably at Stockholm. This *route*, he says, will depend upon the thermometer of the next ten days.

I shall endeavor to complete my preparatory errand here, in season, to join Mr. Adams in his progress toward Gottenburg, should he come this way.

If you hear any thing of our wandering colleagues, please communicate it to me, as well as every thing else of an interesting nature at your residence.

Please say to our worthy secretary, and to Captain Angus, that I think Stockholm will fully indemnify them for the fatigue and expense of a visit.

I shall occasionally report progress, and give you a sketch of the times here. Make my compliments to Mr. Carroll.

MR. RUSSELL TO MR. CLAY.

STOCKHOLM, May 8, 1814.

MY DEAR SIR,—I received, day before yesterday, your communication, by the Consul General of Portugal, but not in season to return an answer by the mail of that day.

With regard to our power to enter into the negotiation elsewhere than at Gottenburg, I think the view which you have taken is quite satisfactory. A restriction of this power having been omitted in the commission, by the *express direction* of the President, appears to explain sufficiently his intentions, and to leave us at liberty, notwithstanding the incidental insertion of "Gottenburg" in the instructions, to treat wherever we may have the most promising prospect of success.

The only point, therefore, which remains for consideration, is that of expediency, and the reasons urged by Mr. Gallatin, Mr. Bayard, and yourself, have great weight.

The apprehension of any *serious* evil from this quarter, occasioned by our change of position, is, I trust, without foundation.

I regret, however, that I had not known the opinions of Messrs. Gallatin and Bayard in season to have shaped my communications here accordingly. Something like a retrograde movement will now be necessary, and it may require some address to reconcile this Government to the new arrangement. I hope it may be in our power to throw the responsibility on the British Government, but am somewhat afraid the original proposition will appear to have come from our colleagues.

My personal convenience and inclination are, indeed, opposed to the change, but considerations of this kind must yield to those of public utility.

I am placed rather in an awkward predicament by your communication, as the uncertainty in which it leaves our ultimate location, disqualifies me from adapting my movements here with sufficient precision to either alternative. This is a situation truly *diplomatic*, but I pray you to relieve me from its embarrassments the first moment it is in your power to do so.

I had, on the 29th ultimo, my presentations successively to the King, the Queen, the Duke of Sudermania, and the Princess Sophia. The early day assigned for this ceremony may be considered as some proof of a friendly disposition toward us.

The Crown Prince was to leave Paris on the 23d ultimo, and will probably be here by the 20th of this month. I hope, therefore, to have an opportunity of seeing him before my departure from Stockholm.

I wrote you soon after my arrival here, but my letter does not appear to have been received at the date of yours. I hear nothing more of Mr. Adams, but as the navigation is now open from Abo, he will probably soon be in Sweden.

Please remember me kindly to Mr. Carroll, and Captain Angus and his officers.

MR. CRAWFORD TO MR. CLAY.

PARIS, June 10, 1814.

MY DEAR SIR,—Mr. Carroll arrived a few days ago, and brought me your letters of the 10th and 14th ultimo. The change in the place of the negotiation for peace will enable me to write to you frequently, and will afford me the pleasure of receiving from you the most interesting details upon the advances which you shall make from day to day in the work of peace.

My expectations of a happy result are not strong. The arrogance of the enemy was never greater than at the present moment. The infatuation of that nation excludes almost the possibility of peace. The ministry are represented as being very temperate and moderate. In my former communications I have stated the reasons which I have for doubting the sincerity of their professions of moderation. I may have been wrong in my inferences. I wish that the result may correct me of this error. Admitting the possibility that the British ministers will consent to make peace, without deciding any thing upon the question of impressment, will your instructions justify you in accepting it? So far as I am acquainted with the nature of those instructions, their letter will not. But these instructions were given at a time when the great changes which have intervened in Europe were not only unknown, but wholly unexpected. What will be the effect which these changes will produce upon the determinations of the Government? Will the Government, after they are informed of these changes, give directions to conclude peace, leaving the question of impressment open to further negotiation? Will it consent to a peace which shall make no mention of this question? I presume it will. If the negotiators shall be of this opinion, ought they to hesitate to accept, in the most prompt manner, of a peace which they are convinced the Government will instruct them to make, as soon as it is informed of the actual state of things? I should answer promptly, No. A peace which omits the question of impressment entirely, will leave the American Government at perfect liberty to apply the proper remedy, whenever the evil shall be felt. I do not believe that you will be placed in a situation to determine this question. I believe they will insist upon the unqualified admission of their right to impress on board American vessels at sea. This, I trust, will never be conceded. It would be better to return to our colonial relations with *our mother country*, than submit to this condition. If it must be conceded, a federal President must make the concession. As there is but a faint glimmering of hope that the negotiation will terminate in peace, the next important point to be obtained is, that it shall break off, upon principles which will convince the American people, of all parties, that peace can be obtained only by the most vigorous prosecution of the war. I have the most unlimited confidence in the skill and address of our negotiators. I am perfectly satisfied that the negotiation will be conducted with a view to affect this important point. I have seen and conversed with several Englishmen in Paris, upon the question of impressment, and find the most of them very ignorant and arrogant. Sir Thomas Baring is an exception to this remark. But his mode of adjusting this question is wholly inadmissible. He proposes that no impressment shall be made in vessels engaged in the coasting trade—that no impressment shall take place in vessels engaged in the foreign trade, in sight of the American coast. He thinks the ministry will hardly go so far. A merchant of the name of Wilson says that an arrangement of a different nature would be satisfactory to the nation. It is this, that when a British officer should visit an American vessel, and designate any one of the crew as a British subject, and he should admit the fact, that the master or captain of the American vessel should deliver him up. If the man should deny that he is an Englishman, and the captain should refuse to deliver him, that the visiting officer should endorse the ship's papers with the name of the sailor, and with his allegation. The question of nationality shall be inquired into, at the first port at which the vessel shall touch, where there is a British consul; if found against the sailor, the captain shall pay a fine, or the expenses of the investigation, and the sailor shall be delivered up. If for him, the British Consul, or if in England, the British Government should be subject to the same payment. He says, that in the case of an admitted British subject, if the American captain should declare that the loss of the man would endanger the vessel, that he should be kept on board until the vessel entered the port of destination, when the captain should be bound to deliver him over to the British Consul, or officer authorized to receive him. I see no objection to this plan, except that the captain should not be permitted to deliver any man who denies the charge, until it is established against him. This arrangement will give the enemy the absolute control over their own seamen, as far as the fact of nationality can be established. It at the same time secures American sailors from arbitrary impressment. If the vessel should be bound to the ports of a nation at war with England, it might be made the duty of the American Consul at such port to ship him on board of an American vessel bound to England, to the United States, or to a neutral port, where the fact should be promptly settled. I do not believe that this arrangement will be acceptable to the Government of England, because I do not believe they will be satisfied with any arrangement which will prevent their seizing upon the sailors of other nations. If I am correct in my conjecture, the proposition will embarrass them, and the rejection will prove, to the most prejudiced mind, that they are determined to make the American sailors fight the battles which are to rivet the chains of slavery, which they have been forging for all maritime states, and especially for the seafaring men of these states, for a century past. I have thought that this arrangement ought to be suggested to you, because it may not have occurred to any one of our ministers. I think it highly improbable that the English negotiators will make any proposition of this nature. If their pretensions shall be so moderate as to afford rational ground for discussion, this arrangement may be proposed with advantage.

If their views are so unreasonable as to exclude discussion, that of itself will have the happy effect of convincing all parties that the peace must be obtained by the sword alone. But even in this case, when the rejection of the arrangement will be certain, I am inclined to believe that the proposition, coming from the American ministers, will have a tendency to elucidate the extent of the concessions which they demand upon this point, more satisfactorily than any other mode which has been presented to my mind. Mr. Wilson is a true John Bull, but, I believe, a very honest man, and, I am sure, sincerely desirous of peace. The rejection of the arrangement will probably have some effect upon the English nation itself. If this principle will be satisfactory to Mr. Wilson, it is probable that it will be acceptable to many others—in fact, to all reasonable men—to all men who have not formed the foolish and extravagant idea of re-colonizing the United States.

I have felt that it was my duty to present this subject to you in its fullest extent. I have verbally communicated it to Mr. Bayard. It is probable that Mr. Wilson may have communicated this idea to Mr. Gallatin, as he made his acquaintance, and that of Mr. Bayard's also, in London. He had not suggested it to the latter.

I will obtain the necessary passports for you, and send them on to Ghent, as the *Moniteur* of yesterday has notified that it is necessary to have them to leave the kingdom. I suppose it is equally necessary to enter it. From the letters which I have written to you, you will perceive that some of my inferences have been proved, by subsequent events, to be incorrect. I reasoned from the facts as they were presented to my mind, and I feel no mortification at the result. If it was my duty to communicate every thing to you which I knew, or believed, at the moment of writing, I do not feel any mortification that some of my conjectures, some of my inferences, have proved to be incorrect.

I have authority to draw on the bankers of the United States for diplomatic intercourse, and for disbursements for distressed seamen. Under the first head, I can satisfy Mr. Carroll's expenses, and shall do it with great pleasure on his own account, as well as upon your request. I am well acquainted with his father, and entertain the highest esteem for him.

This letter will be delivered to you by Mr. Bayard, who, I am happy to inform you, coincides with me in every question relative to the peace. He believes with me, if the nation can be united in the prosecution of the war, that the interest of the United States will be promoted by the failure of the negotiation. He will heartily unite with you in bringing the discussions to a close that will secure this great object. I think, from the English papers, that no armistice has been agreed upon. I rejoice that it has failed. It might have done us much injury, but could not possibly do us any good. God bless you, my dear sir, and bless your labors, and make them useful to your country. Mine, I believe, are like water spilled on the ground, that can never be gathered. Adieu.

MR. RUSSELL TO MR. CLAY.

STOCKHOLM, July 2, 1814.

MY DEAR SIR,—I have had the pleasure to receive your letter of the 27th ult. My distress at the delay which our joint errand has encountered, had almost become intolerable, and the kind of comfort I have received from Mr. Adams, has afforded very little relief. His apprehensions are rather of a gloomy cast with regard to the result of our labors, in which, I hope, however, he will be disappointed. He will show you a letter to Lord Castlereagh, which I have signed. I have done this in the expectation that the letter will not be delivered without the signatures of the other gentlemen composing the mission, and solely in the case that the conferences be not transferred to Holland, on the terms which you proposed, that is, if Messrs. Gallatin and Bayard, not being able to obtain your condition, and declining a removal without it, should again recur to you at Gottenburg, with new propositions. I think indeed that the condition itself was not of importance, although you had certainly reason to believe it to be so. Things have, however, come to my knowledge since my arrival here, which have entirely altered my view of the disposition and policy of this cabinet. Although the condition be not important, yet I find Mr. Adams, who also believes it not to be important, has definitively made up his mind not to remove without it, and is even uncertain if he will go with it. His reasons are that our present instructions will not admit of a negotiation on the basis which will be proposed by the adverse party, and therefore, the sooner we meet, the sooner shall we know the result, and be able to act accordingly. He is decided, therefore, that Gottenburg is to be preferred, unless Holland should already be agreed on. I have signed the above note to prevent the delay of applying to me, or the necessity of acting without me, should the circumstances occur in which it can be properly used.

I sincerely wish with you that the twenty prizes of the Rattlesnake, in Norway, could be condemned, but to this procedure there are insuperable difficulties. I do not recollect a single instance of a sovereign having *freely* consented to the institution of a foreign court of admiralty within his dominions, and the peculiar situation of Norway at this moment, presents additional difficulties. Both the contending parties must consider the friendship of England to be indispensable to their success, and so far from consenting to an extraordinary measure for the condemnation of the property in question, I am not without alarm that either of them would be willing to conciliate that friendship, by a violation of the rights of the captor.

The prince will be here to-morrow, and I shall follow Mr. Adams, who will hand you this letter, as soon as I learn the definitive location of the mission. I regret very much to learn the serious indisposition of Captain Angus. Please present my respects to him, and assure him of my best wishes for a speedy and perfect recovery.

It seems that a mail from England has at length arrived at Gottenburg, but I have not yet learned if it brought you any thing of a decisive character. A letter from Mr. Beasley, of the 13th May, informs me that Admiral Lord Gambier, Mr. Adams, and Mr. Goulbourn, are the persons who are to meet us, and that the place of the conference would be ascertained the next day.

MR. CRAWFORD TO MR. CLAY.

PARIS, July 4, 1814.

MY DEAR SIR,—I have but little to add to the contents of my preceding letters. Mr. Gallatin, and the young gentlemen who accompany, or follow immediately after him, will give you the ephemeral news of this capital. There is but little doing here which can interest an American citizen.

I am not sanguine in my expectations of peace. If the failure of your exertions, to put an end to the war, shall succeed in producing unanimity at home, we shall have no cause to lament that failure. I am thoroughly convinced that the United States can never be called upon to treat, under circumstances less auspicious than those which exist at the present moment, unless our internal bickerings shall continue to weaken the efforts of the Government. I sincerely trust that this will not be the case. In your letter to Messrs. Gallatin and Bayard, you state that the elections in the East had terminated against the Government, but by smaller majorities than on the preceding elections. I have not yet received any other information upon the subject, than what is contained in that letter. There is a chasm in my newspapers, delivered by Mr. Carroll, from the 19th of March to the 5th of April. If you can supply this chasm, you will greatly oblige me.

From what I have lately discovered of the councils of this nation, and of the temper of the principal maritime states of Europe, I am inclined to believe that the time at which they may be disposed to oppose the maritime usurpations of our enemy, will be more distant than I had previously imagined. At all events, I am fearful that it will be more distant than we shall be disposed to prosecute the war, to avoid concessions which they will feel as severely as we shall.

In the prosecution of the war, the great difficulty we shall have to encounter, will be the raising of money. The war will give us soldiers, and point out the officers qualified to command, but it will neither coin money, or increase our credit. If we can get through this campaign without any signal defeat, and without the loss of any of our principal commercial cities, and can raise for the ensuing year the sums necessary for the prosecution of the war, we shall find ourselves in much more eligible circumstances at the close of the next campaign, than we are at present.

I do not look forward with dismay; I believe we shall rise superior to all the difficulties with which we are surrounded. I trust we shall live to enjoy many happy celebrations of this anniversary of our national existence.

Give my best respects to your colleagues, and accept for yourself the assurance of my warmest friendship.

P. S. I will send by Mr. Todd, the passport necessary to enable you to come to Paris, after you close your diplomatic functions. I repeat my request that you will make my house your home, during your residence here. If you wish to take a disciple of Pestalozzi with you to the United States, one can be obtained. Upon him you can impose the condition of teaching the Greek and Latin. You will have, however, to maintain him, until he learns English enough to teach. The economy of Switzerland makes this expense very inconsiderable. I have learned with great pleasure, from the enemies of the system, that it has overcome the prejudices even of the priesthood.

MR. CRAWFORD TO MR. CLAY.

Paris, July 9, 1814.

My dear Sir,—I acknowledge with much pleasure your very interesting letter of the 2d instant, by the hands of Mr. Connell.

It appears that we differ in opinion upon two points. You believe that the British Government will not hesitate to make peace, leaving the question of impressment wholly out of view. You appear also to believe that the events of the present campaign will have a favorable effect upon your negotiation. I sincerely wish you may be right, but I am strongly inclined to believe that the result will prove your opinions to be incorrect.

When I foresaw that peace would probably take place in Europe, in the early part of the year, I did not expect that the manner in which the war has terminated would so inflate the arrogance of the enemy as it manifestly has done. I thought, as you now think, that England would not hesitate to make peace by waiving the question of impressment. I am even now convinced that her interest requires that this course should be adopted. There are, however, occasions in which nations, like individuals, blinded by some momentary but predominant passion, turn a deaf ear to the voice of interest. This I presume to be the case with our enemy at the present moment. Various facts which have come to my knowledge have led me to believe that she will now decidedly reject any proposition which you can make, which does not admit the legality of her practice of impressment on board American vessels at sea.

At the moment, however, when I presented to the joint embassy the idea of making peace, by omitting this question, even if your instructions did not literally warrant it, I still believed that England would consent to this course. At that time I expected the negotiation to open at Gottenburg, about the 1st of May. I did not expect that instructions could be received from the Government, founded on the recent changes in Europe, before the month of August. At the date of my letter to you of the 10th ultimo, my opinion of the views of the British Government had in some degree changed, but even then, I expected the negotiation to open a month sooner than it probably will. I also expected that the change of the seat of negotiations would probably postpone the receipt of the instructions expected from the United States. These reasons, together with those which arise from the expectation of a different result from our military operations from that which you entertain, aided by the express wish of Mr. Bayard that I should present the question anew to you individually, must plead my apology for its intrusion upon your attention.

If there was any rational ground to expect that by a longer prosecution of the war we should ultimately succeed in compelling the enemy to relinquish, by treaty, the practice of impressment, I would not hesitate to continue the war. I believe there is no such reasonable ground of expectation, unless we are disposed to bequeath this war as a legacy to our sons.

* * * * * * *

The Russian officers now in Paris who have been in England, are highly disgusted with that nation. They speak of a war with Austria as certain. In this I think they are mistaken. If war breaks out on the continent, I presume England, in her present temper, must have a finger in it. In this question, however, as she has no resentments to gratify, she will be governed by her interest. She will, therefore, be against that power which is most commercial, and the destruction of whose commerce will tend most directly to her interest.

I must really apologize to you for the length of my letters.

Present me most respectfully to your colleagues, and accept yourself the assurance of my most sincere friendship.

P. S. Mr. Carroll leaves Paris sooner than I expected. I will send your passport by Mr. Todd.

Remember me to the young gentlemen of the mission.

MR. CRAWFORD TO MR. CLAY.

PARIS, July 19, 1814.

MY DEAR SIR,—The departure of Messrs. Blanchard and Elliot, for Ghent, enables me to send you the passport which I have obtained for you. They will be able to give you the ephemeral news of this capital.

I dined a few days ago in company with the Marquis of Buckinghamshire. We conversed long and freely upon the subject of the approaching negotiation. The result of our conversation was that there can be no peace. He insists absolutely that the question of impressment shall be settled in this treaty, and of course, that it shall be settled entirely in their favor. He attempted to derive their right to take (for he insisted upon dropping the word *impressment*, to which I assented) their seamen from our vessels, from the law of nations.

DIPLOMATIC NOTE PROPOSED BY MR. CLAY AT GHENT.

The undersigned, ministers, etc., have the honor of recalling to the attention of his B. M. P. the note of the undersigned of the 30th ult., and to so much of what has passed in the subsequent conferences as is deemed material to the present communication.

In that note they stated that they objected to one of the alterations proposed by the B. P. in the first article, and to the modification which they also proposed of the eighth article, of the project which the undersigned had submitted for consideration.

By the first article of this project, the undersigned had proposed that there should be a mutual restitution of all territories, places and possessions, taken by either party during the war, without exception. The alteration in question, proposed by the B. P., contemplates a restitution of what belongs to either party. The alteration would be free from objection, if there were no places in the occupation of either party, which are claimed by the other. In that case the execution of the treaty would depend upon the question of who was the possessor at the moment when war was declared. But there are certain islands in the Bay of Fundy the title to which is claimed by both parties, and other portions of territory from that bay to the Lake of the Woods, the whole line between which is more or less liable to dispute, and which may by each party be supposed to belong to him. For the settlement of the respective pretensions of the two parties to those islands, and for other purposes, a mode of decision, suggested by Great Britain, has been assented to by the undersigned.

They can not consent to the proposed alteration, first, because by constituting each party the sole judge of what belongs to him, it makes the restitution to depend upon his uncertain exercise of judgment, and not on the precise principle of status before the war, on which alone in this respect they have repeatedly stated they can treat, and which has been agreed to by Great Britain; and secondly because it is repugnant to the principle on which it has been agreed to waive, at this time, the determination of the claims of the parties to the disputed islands, and to submit it to an impartial tribunal erected for the purpose. These objections apply equally to the alteration as proposed in general terms, and to the qualification by which it would be limited in its operation to the territories in dispute, or to the islands in Passamaquoddy Bay. It may be added that it is further objectionable as sowing, in the very instrument of pacification, the seeds of an immediate misunderstanding, the moment it is carried into practical execution.

On the other remaining subject of difference, the undersigned must observe that the demand of Great Britain of the navigation of the Mississippi, brought forward in the form of a modification of the eighth article of the project of the undersigned, was wholly unexpected by them, after the explicit declaration made by the British Plenipotentiaries that their Government had no demands to make other than was contained in their notes of the ——, etc., of which this was not one. As to that modification, the undersigned have offered three alternatives, first to strike out the article altogether, or to strike out the clause which grants the navigation of the Mississippi, or lastly, retaining that clause, to place the exercise of the right under restrictions to prevent its abuse or perversion, in consideration of the recognition by Great Britain of that liberty in the fisheries which she considers abrogated by the war. To either of these alternatives the undersigned are yet willing to assent. And it was with some surprise that they have been made acquainted, by the British Plenipotentiaries, that their Government declines to accept either of them, and offers as a substitute for the second, a clause referring to a future negotiation the adjustment of the proper equivalent to be given by the United States for the enjoyment of the liberty to the fisheries referred to; and of the proper equivalent to be given by Great Britain for the navigation of the Mississippi.

The undersigned can not consent to this substitute because it is either useless in itself, in providing for a future negotiation which the two governments, without any such provision, will at all times, if it be necessary, have it in their power to take up; or because it supposes, what the undersigned have declared their Government does not admit, that the liberty in the fisheries alluded to has been lost by the war.

To a general stipulation, similar to the —— article of the treaty of 1794, the undersigned will not object.

All other points having been substantially arranged either by the correspondence, or in the conferences between the Plenipotentiaries of the two countries, it remains only to dispose of the two existing topics of difference to conclude, so far as depends on the undersigned, a treaty of peace. For this happy result it is quite unnecessary to dwell on the testimony which, in every stage of the negotiation, they have constantly given of their anxious desire.

[The above note is in Mr. Clay's hand-writing, endorsed by him as follows:]

Proposed by me in lieu of the note which we sent on the 14*th day of December*, 1814.   H. C.

SIR JAMES MACKINTOSH TO MR. CLAY.

15 GREAT GEORGE STREET, Monday Forenoon.

Sir James Mackintosh is so eager to have the honor of Mr. Clay's acquaintance that he ventures to request his company this evening, to a small party, when Lady Mackintosh will be most happy to receive him, at nine or ten o'clock, with any gentleman of his suite who may be so good as to honor them with coming.

MR. CLAY TO HIS WIFE.

LIVERPOOL, July 14, 1815.

MY DEAR WIFE,—I expect to embark to-morrow on board the Lorenzo, of this port, for New York, and hope to have the pleasure of seeing you before this letter reaches you. As it is possible, however, that I may not, to guard against any accidents which may attend me, I inclose you a copy of a power of Attorney (accompanied by a copy of the original certificate) to transfer to me $4,444 44, in the 6 per cent. stock of the United States. The original of these copies is in my possession.

Messrs. Baring, Brothers & Co., bankers London, have in their hands £201 0s. 9d. sterling of my money.

On the other side is a memorandum of charges against the United States, which are to be brought forward on settlement of my account, besides my outfit and salary.

Dr. the United States to H. Clay,

To the sum lost by me in the rent of a house from Mr. Pritz, of Gottenburg, for one quarter, and which I occupied only one month; there remaining two months; Mr. Pritz agreed to be satisfied with rent for one of them (see Mr. Carroll) at $200 per month	$200
To expenses of my journey from Gottenburg to Ghent in consequence of the removal of the seat of the negotiation	500
To newspapers for one quarter, at Gottenburg, (see Mr. Hall's account)	£5
To newspapers at London	£5
To stationary at Gottenburg and London	25

MR. ADAMS TO MESSRS. BAYARD, CLAY, RUSSELL AND GALLATIN.

GHENT, January 17, 1815.

GENTLEMEN,—A letter from Mr. Hughes of which I subjoin a copy, was received by me this morning. I presume you will have heard more directly, and before this will reach you, what were the interruptions or difficulties which delayed his departure so long beyond the time he had anticipated by his former letter, and occasioned the disappointment of which he complains. No intermediate letter from him has been received.

I contemplate leaving this city this day week, and hope to find a passport from Mr. Crawford at Bruxelles.

I am with great respect, gentlemen, your very humble and obedient servant, JOHN QUINCY ADAMS.

[COPY.] ON BOARD THE TRANSIT,
6th January, 1815—Friday, 2 P.M.

GENTLEMEN,—I am at last under way; we are now about four leagues from Bordeaux; I came on board last night, and am in hopes that there will be no further interruption or difficulty to delay my progress to the United States. I am afraid I shall be the second or third herald, in point of time; yet the news is so happy for the country, that in the pleasure of contemplating its fine effect at home I lose almost all the mortification of the disappointment I have suffered.

I have the honor to be be very respectfully your obedient servant, C. HUGHES, JR.

American Ministers at Ghent.

MR. CLAY TO ADAM BEATTY.*

WASHINGTON, April 23, 1810.

DR. BEATTY,—This day was fixed by resolution of the two Houses of Congress for its adjournment, but that resolution has been rescinded, and the session protracted one week longer. On the great subject of our foreign affairs, I believe we shall adjourn without adopting any efficient measure. A bill to augment the duties fifty per cent. has passed the House of Representatives, but I fear, like Macon's bill, it will not be concurred in by the Senate. One of its valuable effects, if it passes, will be the encouragement of our manufactures. As the increase is not contemplated, however, to be permanent, I should prefer a smaller augmentation, and that it should be durable.

Two committees of the House of Representatives are engaged

---

* The remaining letters of this chapter, from Mr. Clay to Judge Beatty, were not received in time for their proper place *as to date.*

in investigating Wilkinson's conduct (who has at length arrived), one into the Spanish conspiracy, and the other into the causes of the mortality of the army last summer. On this latter subject it is expected a report will be made this session; upon the other a report will hardly be made before the next.

Howard is appointed Governor of Louisiana.

MR. CLAY TO ADAM BEATTY.

FRANKFORT, May 31, 1810.

DR. BEATTY,—I received your favor, with the specimen inclosed of your merino's fleece, and compared it with one which I took from a full-blooded merino of General Mason's, and find very little difference between them. If you could send your wool, or the yarn, to a manufacturer in Danville, he would make you the best piece of cloth that you could obtain from it. I do not recollect his name, but he is an Englishman, accustomed to the business, and has undertaken, for Judge Todd, to make him a coat which he warrants shall not be inferior to the best imported cloth in the State. I propose sending mine to him. If, however, you prefer having it made in the neighborhood of Lexington, there will be no difficulty in getting it wove, fulled, etc.

I am glad to learn that your election to the Legislature is deemed certain. Your presence there will be extremely necessary. I am solicitous for it on various accounts. You will have heard that I am no longer a candidate for the Senate, and that my successor will consequently be appointed. May not the Federalists attempt to rally in support of one of their party? This should be looked to.

In offering for the House of Representatives, I was influenced by a partiality for the station, and by the wishes of some of my friends, as well here as to the East. I contemplate, however serving out the term for which I am already appointed in the Senate, not wishing to give the trouble of supplying my place for the ensuing session, and being desirous to prevent the possibility of the State being partially represented during a considerable portion of it.

MR. CLAY TO ADAM BEATTY.

LEXINGTON, July 27, 1810.

DR. BEATTY,—I received your favor of the 24th June. The nett yield of our merino (owing to the neglect or fraud of the shearer of him) was not sufficient to make me a coat. Mrs. Clay therefore determined to have it spun, and either applied to other uses, or retained until we could get an additional quantity. A Captain M'Call, in this neighborhood, has undertaken to weave and full, for Jordan, some yarn spun from the merino wool; and if you can not better dispose of yours, I have no doubt Mr. Jordan can procure him to weave and full yours also.

I learned with pleasure your decision in favor of again offering for the Legislature. Your success, I am told, is not doubted. The Republican interests will require, and, I am sure, will receive your best support. Whether the Federalists will or will not attempt a Senator of their own kind depends on the issue of the election. I believe Daviess will not be elected here; and even Humphrey* dreads the result of the Franklin election.

P. S. I requested a Mr. Fowke, of Baltimore, to call on you for professional aid, which I hope you will afford.

MR. CLAY TO ADAM BEATTY.

LIMESTONE, March 31, 1813.

Henry Clay presents his respectful compliments to Mr. Beatty. His solicitude to reach home prevents him from having the pleasure to see Mr. Beatty, whose favors he ought to have acknowledged at the city. With every disposition to serve Colonel C. B., he regrets his inability to have done so. Under the regular establishment of the military there were no vacancies worthy his notice. Under the act for raising twenty thousand infantry for the term of one year, when Henry Clay left Washington it was understood that but one regiment would be allotted to K., and the field officers of that regiment were determined upon prior to Mr. B.'s application, although not announced. Henry Clay could not interfere with the contemplated arrangement.

Henry Clay paid Mr. Beatty's last year's subscription to the "Intelligencer," and was reimbursed before he left K. What is due he forgot to pay, but will discharge on his return to the city He can add no news to the public prints.

* Marshall.

CHAPTER II.

CORRESPONDENCE FROM 1815 TO 1820.

JAMES MONROE TO MR. CLAY.

WASHINGTON, October 30, 1815.

MY DEAR SIR,—Since the overthrow of France, Russia has acquired the highest degree of political importance in relation to these States. As a great power, friendly to a liberal system of neutral rights, and with whose dominions our commerce had become considerable, she held, before that event, a distinguished rank; but by it her weight in the general scale has been much augmented. Russia forms, in effect, at this time, the principal check on the overgrown power of England, on which account, and many others, it is immensely the interest of these States to cultivate a good understanding with her sovereign. The President is desirous of confiding to you a mission to that power, and will be much gratified to hear that it will be acceptable to you. I write you now that you may be enabled to consider the proposition before you leave home, and make the necessary arrangements for your departure, in case you accept the trust; though you will not infer from this intimation that all due and friendly attention will not be paid to your convenience as to the time.

It would have been very agreeable to the President as well as to me, to have had an opportunity of seeing and conferring with you on your arrival, but our absence from this city and your anxiety to join your family after so long a separation from them, were obstacles not to be surmounted.

In the hope of seeing you soon, I shall reserve for that occasion comments on other subjects.

THOMAS VAUGHAN TO MR. CLAY.

NEAR CARDIFF, December 1, 1815.

MY GOOD AND WORTHY SIR,—Having seen an account in our newspapers of your safe arrival in America, gives me great pleasure, and I hope this will meet you in perfect health, and every other earthly comfort. And I now take the liberty of informing you that we have received an account from my son's wife, Mrs. Vaughan, of his death, so long back as the 5th of April, 1814. We have also an account of it from a relation of mine, living near to Upper Bluelick, but on whom (I am sorry to say) we can set no dependence at all; and therefore take the liberty of begging that you will be pleased to have the goodness to inquire into the state of his (my son's) affairs and property, and, if possible, to get for his daughter (now with me from an infant, and thirty-two years of age) whatever is right, and justly her due; as she is a good, honest, and industrious young woman, and deserving of every justice and encouragement that can be lawfully given her; and your influence will, no doubt, have great weight in settling it justly, and we desire no other; but, by Mrs. Vaughan's account, there seems to be but little for her; and we are at such a distance, it is next to impossible for us to see into it; but I know, from all my son's letters, it was his intention to make his daughter nearly equal to his son; and by a letter of his to me, as far back as the 20th May, 1807, he referred me to you in case of his death (which was the only knowledge I had of his acquaintance with you, and the reason I took the liberty of writing to you in London), in the following words: "I will request Henry Clay of Lexington, Esquire, to give you every information respecting my property, etc., etc. He is one of our Senators, in Congress, which is now sitting; he is very friendly to me, and, I am sure, will do me any reasonable request," etc., etc.

If you will have the goodness to take the trouble on you to get for her what is right and just, and, after deducting for your trouble and every expense, will be pleased to remit the remainder, directed as under, whenever it may be convenient, will greatly oblige me and my grand-daughter (who begs her respectful compliments to you), and am, with deference and respect (although unknown), your obedient servant.

P. S. I am sorry we had not the honor of seeing you in Wales, as we made provision for your reception, after we heard, by my nephew, of your longer stay in London, and particularly as we have the largest iron and tin works in this neighborhood, that are in Great Britain, and through all of which I could have conducted you, and would have been well worth your seeing. I have written by this packet to my daughter-in-law at Bluelick, telling her I have written to you on the above subject, and also to invite my grandson over to England, as I should be very glad to see him here, for one whole year at least, if I live so long.

Whenever convenient, I shall be very glad of a few lines from you, to hear how matters go, and to give me your proper address, as I am at a loss whether to address you as minister, or commissioner, or as a private gentleman. Your goodness will excuse any defects you may meet with in this scrawl, from my age of eighty-five years, and want of memory, etc., although I am as healthy and as heart-well as ever, blessed be God for that, and all his other goodness to me. We are in general very happy to be at peace with America in particular, and with the rest of the world; but our farmers and manufacturers complain heavily, the former because grain, cattle, horses, etc., sell very low, and the latter for want of orders for their wares, etc. Almost every thing is lowered very much since you left England, and the surrender of Napoleon; but we are in hopes of our taxes being lowered to ease the farmers and trades, and traffic revived with you, and with other countries, to relieve our manufacturers.

I pray God bless you with good health, long life, and every other comfort that this uncertain world can give you, are the sincere prayers of your unknown friend and humble servant.

HENRY GOULBURN TO MR. CLAY.

Downing Street, March 8, 1816.

My dear Sir,—I am really very much obliged to you for your letter of the 7th of January, which I received a short time since, both because it has enabled me to relieve the anxiety which a friend of mine in this country (Mr. Harris) felt for the fate of the relation to whom it particularly relates, and not less because it has assured me that, though situated in so distant a quarter of the world, I nevertheless bear a place in your recollection.

I had already learned the death of Mr. Bayard before your letter reached me, and although I could not but regret the event, I was glad that he had at least the satisfaction of seeing his family before his death.

I have to congratulate you on your resumption of the arduous and honorable situation which you left in order to meet us at Ghent. I trust that this is an evidence that our joint work is approved in America. I assure you it is so in England; and whatever may be said in the newspapers on either side of the Atlantic, I have little doubt that it will continue to be approved by all rational persons. You seem by your papers to be fighting the same battle in America that we are fighting here, namely, that of putting peace establishments on a footing not unbecoming the growth of the population and the empire in which they are to be maintained. It is impossible that either country should feel any jealousy of the other so long as the augmentation does not exceed the necessity of the case, and I have not heard an argument any where to prove that it does so exceed in either case. From all that I know, I am sure I can take upon me to relieve the apprehensions which you seem to entertain of hostile movements on the part of this country in any quarter of the globe. Newspapers will, on subjects of this kind, propagate any intelligence, however false, which is likely to excite an interest on the part of their readers, but I am sure you will agree with me in thinking it the duty of every man to avoid giving the authority of his belief to any of the rumors which they so convert for their own purposes into facts.

When you see Mr. Gallatin, may I beg you to present to him my best respects, and if at any time I can be of any service to you or to him in this country, I trust you will have no hesitation in commanding me, for I can assure you that nothing could give me greater pleasure.

JAMES MADISON TO MR. CLAY.

MONTPELIER, August 30, 1816.

DEAR SIR,—Mr. Dallas seems to have made up his mind to retire early in October from the department in his hands, and the event may draw after it a vacancy in the War Department. Will you permit me to avail our country of your services in the latter? It will be convenient to know your determination as soon as you have formed it, and it will be particularly gratifying if it assent to my request.

MR. CLAY TO MR. MADISON.

ASHLAND, September 14, 1816.

DEAR SIR,—The last mail brought me the letter which you did me the honor to write on the 30th ultimo, stating your expectation of a vacancy in the Department of War, and communicating your wish that I would take upon myself the discharge of the duties of that office. Several considerations appear to me to require that I should decline accepting the honor which your favorable opinion has tendered. I regret the necessity of this decision the less, as I hope that you will fill the place equally agreeably to yourself, and I am sure more advantageously to the public interest. I pray you, however, to believe that I shall always entertain the highest sense of this new proof of your confidence, and that, with the greatest respect and esteem, I am your obedient servant.

JAMES MONROE TO MR. CLAY.

WASHINGTON, March 4, 1817.

SIR,—I had the honor to receive your letter of yesterday last night, advising me that the chamber of the House of Representatives would be put, by the officers of the House, in a condition to receive me to-day, for the purpose of taking the oath prescribed by the Constitution for the President of the United States. I have hastened to transmit the communication to the Chairman of the Committee of the Senate, and I beg you to accept my acknowledgment for your polite attention.

LORD GAMBIER TO MR. CLAY.

IVER GROVE, January 20, 1818.

MY DEAR SIR,—I had much satisfaction in receiving your letter of the 6th November, by the hand of Mr. Burgess, from whom and from Mr. Mills, I had the pleasure of hearing of your health and welfare. I return you many thanks for the kind and obliging terms in which you are so good as to express yourself toward me, and can with great truth assure you it would afford me much gratification if the course of events should approximate us so that I could have the pleasure of your society, and avail myself of any opportunity that might offer by which I could evince my regard and esteem personally for you. I hope Messrs. Burgess and Mills received every necessary assistance and kindness from the several persons, Mr. Wilberforce and others, to whom they were introduced, toward the object of their benevolent undertaking. I regret their short visit to this country deprived me of the pleasure of performing any kind offices of hospitality and respect that their own characters give them claim to, and which would have been gratifying to me to show to any person in whose interest you take a part.

If Mr. Adams should be near you when this comes to your hand, I will beg of you to communicate my best regards to him.

With every cordial wish for your health and prosperity, I remain, my dear sir, in great respect, your faithful and most humble servant.

MR. CLAY TO FRANCIS BROOKE.

HOUSE OF REPRESENTATIVES, April 16, 1818.

MY DEAR SIR,—In great haste I have to acknowledge the receipt of your favor of the 13th March. Walker would undertake to explore your lands, and report to you particularly their situation, quality, and value. He would charge for the service, only his expenses, that is to say, about $2 per day, for twelve or fifteen days. He is a man of perfect integrity, and may be relied on for such an undertaking. When I spoke, in a former letter, of him, I did not mean to imply any question of his veracity, but merely to convey the idea, that he was a laughing, talking, good-natured sort of a fellow, who might express himself somewhat at random, unless he knew precision to be necessary.

He himself recommends Daniel Ashley at Madisonville as a person on whom you may rely to report the desired information. Major Walker's address is "David Walker, Russellville, Ky."

MR. CLAY TO ADAM BEATTY.

WASHINGTON, April 21, 1818.

DEAR SIR,—The contemplated changes in the judicial establishment of the United States, were not made during the session of Congress just terminated. The opinion that these changes are necessary acquires daily additional strength; and I think there is reason to believe that they will be effected at the next session.

I am glad to learn that there exists a prospect of doing something towards turnpiking in Kentucky. I shall be very happy to co-operate with you in an object so worthy of the utmost exertions.

MR. CLAY TO ADAM BEATTY.

ASHLAND, July 25, 1818.

DEAR SIR,—I received your favor of the 9th. You mention that you have thought of becoming a candidate for the Senate, and, justly viewing me as one of your friends, you have asked my opinion.

In the first place, I beg leave to state that I have always felt a most lively and sincere interest in your welfare, and that it would give me, personally, much satisfaction to see you in the situation suggested. With respect to your prospect of success I am not a very good judge, having been so much of late years out of the State, and therefore knowing but little of the weight and standing of different individuals. I hinted at the subject to Barry, who seemed to think that, living in one extreme of the State, however much esteemed there, you were probably hardly well enough known at the other to count with any certainty upon your success. I did not mention it to Breckenridge, because I am quite sure that he proposes to himself the career of politics, and I have heard, though not from him, nor from any one that as far as I know, was authorized by him, that he is looking himself to the situation. I should think the event would greatly depend upon the persons who might happen to be your competitors. Should Colonel Johnson offer, (he has been talked of, with what authority from himself I know not,) or perhaps Breckenridge, you would probably fail.

I will now give you, in the frankness which is due from the

friendship I feel for you, my opinion. I do not think you ought to accept the situation, if you had a moral certainty of getting it. Although comfortable in your pecuniary condition, you are not rich, and you have a growing family. Instead of making additions to your fortune, you would most probably make annual subtractions from it, during your service. For if your pay should cover your expenses, while absent from your family, affairs would go on less profitably at home than they do now. Such, at least, is my experience; and such I believe to be in the nature of things. Congress, too, has greater attractions at a distance than near. After the novelty wears off (which it commonly does in the course of two or three months), the interest which was at first felt is diminished, if not extinguished, with most of those, at least, who are not perfectly at their ease in their circumstances, or who are not in pursuit of place, and are willing to venture every thing on getting it, or, lastly, those few individuals whose great attainments give them a high degree of prominence in the body and in the nation.

With respect to yourself (I write, you see, with the frankness and freedom which you have invited,) your talents are of the most respectable kind; but they are better adapted to the career which you have been wisely pursuing than to that of politics. While you would never fail to speak sensibly, your elocution would not perhaps procure for you that high degree of eminence which I am sure you would be ambitious of reaching. Besides, you have great reason to expect promotion in the judiciary of either the State or the United States, when vacancies shall occur. While judicial appointment might also be acquired in the situation to which we refer, it is perhaps not so direct a road to it as by a faithful and enlightened discharge of the duties of your present office. There is, moreover, always some risk (and it is greater as we are more advanced in life) in quitting an occupation with which one is familiar, and entering upon another with which he is less conversant. The intimate alliance between law and politics, and the habit which is so common in our country of participating in the consideration of its political affairs, diminishes but does not entirely remove this objection.

I have given you my candid sentiments. Your own better judgment will, at last, guide you, as it ought; and that you may be successful and prosperous, however you may decide, is my sincere wish.

[In pursuance of the advice of Mr. Clay, I concluded to retain my judicial station, and therefore declined becoming a candidate for the Senate of the United States. A. B.]

LAFAYETTE TO MR. CLAY.

LAGRANGE, October 26, 1818.

MY DEAR SIR,—The letter of which Mr. Newcomb was the bearer, is the last communication I have had from you. Permit me to solicit a more frequent correspondence. In this exchange of information you may be a loser as I now am returned to a private, solitary life, and can hardly write any thing but what you will collect from European papers. Indeed the gazettes of France, shackled as they are, to such a reader as you, may tell, and even foretell a great deal.

The French, or rather the European revolution, had raised against us the passions and the exertions of Coblentz and Pilnitz. In subsequent excesses, although it had put a stop to proselytism, it did not so generally operate abroad as the ambitious despotism of Napoleon who estranged from France the speculative love of freedom, and roused against her the masses of the people, our natural allies. In that situation of universal oppression and enmity, Bonaparte did twice squander away the moral and military resources of this nation, first in Russia, afterward, at Dresden, and Leipsic, and brought in the hosts of the coalition, leaving on the Niemen, the Oder, and the Elbe, the material means of defense which he had taken from our stores and fortresses. He capitulated for himself, while a restoration ushered by the Allies, and not unpleasing to the nation, was generally considered as a tolerable transaction between old princes and modern institutions. A month had sufficed to prepare the people for a change. It was impossible for any combination, but the folly of the royal Government, to make Bonaparte welcome, which proved to be the case with many, although few could love and trust him. But these interior vicissitudes were of no effect upon foreign courts and foreign nations. The latter, having no time to explain, were hurried again against their own interest, with revengeful and desperate fury. The courts were the more eager to avail themselves of their error, as they saw that Napoleon, unable to reassume his arbitrary doctrines, had been forced to acknowledge the first principles of the Revolution.

Two modes of resistance were left for France, to launch out of the imperial circle of men and measures into a national insurrection: or to support the actual ruler who, although he was a check upon the exertions of a people whom he did no more trust than he could be trusted by them, was justly reckoned the ablest of generals, and enjoyed the confidence of a standing army amounting to two hundred thousand men. The active majority having prefered this method, it remained for those who would have proposed a bolder and more popular system, to slide in with the adopted plan of defense, which was done with candor and determination.

Two weeks after the opening of the session, Napoleon had lost the only army that bore a proportion with the opposed forces, and leaving it to its fate, he flew back to the national representation, not to consult, but to dissolve it, recurring to a wild and desperate arbitrariness which, while it countenanced the attack, could not but damp and dishearten the defense. He was checked in the attempt, and with the assent of his best friends, obliged to abdicate.

Time was short. An attempt to raise some sort of *pudeur* in the Allies, and construe their word of honor into a suspension of arms proved fruitless. In the mean while the troops being rallied under the walls of the capital, more divested of Bonapartism, more actuated by patriotism than they had been said to be, were all alive to national colors and national independence. On my return from the diplomatic errand which I could not refuse, I was much disappointed to hear of the capitulation. The provisory Government and peers dissolved themselves. The House of Representatives were dissolved by force, but not before they had, in their declaration of the 5th of July, expressed what I think to have been for five-and-twenty years the true sense of the nation.

Further resistance to foreign powers was impeded. The President of the popular Government was a minister of the King before he had entered Paris. The imperial system of administration having been, during thirteen years, calculated for absolute monarchy had precluded the means of exertion. A Royal Government being reinstalled in the capital, many trusted its influence with the Allies, those who did not were afraid the impending evils should be imputed to their obstinacy. And above all, the high powers, made a more Machiavelian use of the King's name and hand successively to undo all the means of French resistance, after which you know what treaty has been dictated by them.

Two administrations have been tried. That of Talleyrand and Fouché, although the former had solicited and signed the coalition of Vienna, and the second put his name to the proscription of many of his associates and friends, and to the suppression of the liberty of the press, was not thought a match for the royalism of the two new chambers. The present ministry, the head of which, although for twenty-five years a Russian officer, is a Frenchman by birth, the last of the illustrious family of Richelieu, and among whom our friend Barbi Marbois is seal-keeper, have gone great lengths toward the spirit of reaction. You have in the papers the bills proposed by them, and their speeches in both Houses, which, nevertheless, keep ahead of the Executive. Among the influencing powers you may distinguish a British and a Russian interest, to both of which I am, thank God, a perfect stranger.

Unfit as I shall ever be for such complicated politics, and having, in my doctrines of legitimacy, much to say for the rights of men and the sovereignty of nations, I am returned to my retirement of Lagrange, and my agricultural pursuits. Here my son, his wife, two daughters, and eleven grandchildren, are now with me. We expect in a few days the pleasure to receive General Scott and Major Mercer.

The happy tidings we receive of increasing prosperity in the United States, fill my heart with delight. I hope the work of liberty and independence in the other parts of America, is going on, and am I to be discouraged with respect to the final establishment of freedom in the European world? The liberal part of the Revolution shall not be lost.

You have been pleased, my dear sir, to promise your kind inquiries and good care with respect to my Orleans business. The Pointe Coupée lands have been purchased by Sir John Coghill, Mr. Seymour, and the parish. The two former gentlemen complain that M. Duplansier, by refusing to answer some questions relative to a land tax, has exposed their property to be sold. They were ignorant of the duty. I hastened to write to the President and explain their situation.

There remain five hundred and twenty acres to be located, or I rather think, located in the vicinity of the town. Under the pressure of my affairs I have parted with one half of those town lots to Sir John, whose large capital, being employed on his alternate lots, would soon bring my share to a value much superior to the actual totality. Should the location be at a distance of more than two miles, the space between the bayou and the town, it becomes a common tract and the whole would have been paid above its value. In the contrary case, one half is mine. It is true, Sir John might challenge me to take back this half for the given price and interest. But if the location was made on the spot, I would, I think, easily find a capitalist to take Sir John's bargain. Let me add that he is willing, in case there was not room for a location of five hundred and twenty acres, to enter into some arrangements with the claimants, to make it complete. Such is, my dear sir, as far as I know it, the present state of the affair. M. Duplansier, who has been very unfortunate in his own concerns, has not, for several years, written to me. M. Allen Michel had the powers of Sir John who has since, I believe, sent a relation of his. The President, to whose kind concern in my behalf, I am highly obliged, knows probably more of my affairs than myself.

This letter will be delivered by Mr. Lakanal, member of the French Institute of the Academy, and Rector General of the Medical System with a handsome treatment, all which he abandons for a settlement in the neighborhood of Lexington, State of Kentucky. The high rank he holds in the scientific world, and his having been a distinguished member of our former assemblies will recommend him to your notice. But I have presumed to engage in your name you would favor him with your good advice, and with letters of introduction to the country which he intends to inhabit. I know you will be so kind as to render him in that way, the services which I beg leave to solicit on account of his own merit and my earnest desire to oblige him. Permit me to depend upon you to ask the same favor from our friends, Mr. Monroe, and Crawford, and others who may recommend him to public and private characters in the State.

MR. CLAY TO ADAM BEATTY.

WASHINGTON, January 22, 1820.

DEAR SIR,—I received your obliging favor of the 10th inst., from Frankfort, and thank you for the friendly feelings toward me of which it furnishes the evidence. On the subject of the next Governor I had communicated my views, prior to the receipt of your letter, to several friends at Frankfort, from whom you must have learned them before you left that place. I have regretted exceedingly my inability to conform to the wishes of those whose kindness has made them look to me for that office.

I am glad to find that the course which it seems to me fitting for this country to pursue, in respect to Spanish affairs, meets with your concurrence. The extraordinary one recommended by the President excited much surprise in Congress, and has, I think, very few of that body disposed to adopt it. The general embarrassments throughout the country, the deficit in the Treasury, and other causes, have communicated their influence to Congress, and produced the effect of great repugnance to war and to any augmentation of the national expenditure. Add to which the various alternatives which the failure of Spain to ratify the treaty presents to our choice, and I should not be surprised if the result should be that Congress will do nothing on Spanish affairs, but leave them where it found them. I should regret this very much, because I think it would be precisely the result most gratifying to Spain.

At present Spanish affairs, manufactures, and every other matter of public concern, have given way to the Missouri question, which engrosses the whole thoughts of the members, and constitutes almost the only topic of conversation. It is a most unhappy question, awakening sectional feelings, and exasperating them to the highest degree. The words, civil war, and disunion, are uttered almost without emotion, and a Senator of the United States, in his place, as I understand, said the other day that he would rather have both than fail in the resolution. I witnessed yesterday a display of astonishing eloquence, in the Senate, on the part of Mr. Pinkney of Indiana against the restriction. In that body the majority is with us; in the House of Representatives it is doubtful.

I think nothing will be done by Congress respecting the currency.

LAFAYETTE TO MR. CLAY.

PARIS, June 9, 1821.

MY DEAR SIR,—Permit me to entreat your kind welcome and good advice in behalf of M. Pette and M. Menardi, who are going to settle in the State of Ohio. Their partner, M. La Barthe, is already fixed near New Athens, and there enjoys the freedom which old Athens now struggles to obtain. Our cause has been unfortunate in Italy, but can not fail ultimately to prevail. European liberty chiefly depends on the interior politics of France. I hope our American newspapers take their paragraphs from the "Constitutionnel," the "Courier," or at least the semi-official "Moniteur," in what relates to the debates of the Chamber of Deputies; all the other journals make it a point to disfigure them scandalously. Where M. Pette and M. Menardi will find you I do not know, but am sure you will have the goodness to give them all the advice and recommendation in your power.

PETER B. PORTER TO MR. CLAY.

ALBANY, January 29, 1822.

DEAR SIR,—I arrived two days ago at this place, where not only the members of our Legislature, but most of the active political talent and mischief of the State are now congregated. I have not, during this period, been inattentive to the great question that at present engages the speculations of the politicians throughout the Union, and I think I do not deceive you when I say that your prospects here are highly flattering. You are probably aware that some six or eight months ago there was a partial understanding and commitment among some of our most active politicians in favor of Mr. C———d, and it is to this class that my conversations and views have been principally directed. Many of them are now ready to change their ground, and even the most zealous are willing to lie still at present, and eventually to be governed by future and clearer indications of public sentiment on this subject.

You will see Mr. Van Buren in Washington, and I beg you to pay him some attention. I am decidedly of opinion that he will yet be for you. His best and strongest friends here are so, and

I know that his own views have been essentially changed since last spring. He will not, I presume, avow his preference of any candidate during the present session of Congress, and perhaps it is desirable that he should not. Be civil also to Rochester of our State, who is a very clever young man, and strongly your friend. A rumor is in circulation here that you and D. Clinton are playing in concert, and that you and he will run on the same ticket. I need not tell you that such a rumor, once believed, would prostrate all your hopes here. The recent, and all but unanimous, rejection of the Clintonian judges by our Senate, shows the temper of the State in regard to that class of politicians. Can you with propriety say something in a letter to me on the subject of this supposed coalition which I may show *confidentially* to two or three persons? It might be attended with good consequences. Noah, the Advocate man, is now here. I have had several conversations with him, and although his predelections are still for Mr. C———d, his zeal and confidence have greatly abated. He finds that the State is not disposed to go with him, and expresses a willingness to be quiet, until the sentiments of the old republican party shall be more fully developed.

JOSE M. DEL REAL TO MR. CLAY.

BORDEAUX, February 23, 1822.

SIR,—Both by honor of my country and duty of friendship, I think myself obliged to make over to posterity the image of Don Josef M. Garcia de Toledo, my particular friend, and the first defender of the rights of his country, and as I was favored with the honor of your acquaintance in London, and convinced as I am of a great deal of interest you lay hold of for the liberty and independence as well as for all that belongs to the glorious revolution of South America, I take the liberty of sending you six stamps of his portrait, which I entreat you to have the goodness of accepting as an acknowledgment of my duty to you.

After a few days I shall embark to Carthagena, where, if it is in my way to render you any service, I should be very glad to be honored with your commands.

R. M. JOHNSON TO MR. CLAY.

WASHINGTON, April 1, 1822.

DEAR SIR,—I have seen the President, who has again assured me that he would get Mr. Wirt to re-examine your claim, and he will bring the thing to a close. I see that Fickler has republished a piece from the " Franklin Gazette," in favor of Mr Calhoun, and some letters from our friends who dislike his course. I do not know his motive in doing this. I have not written a word to him on the subject of the next President. I saw a letter of his to Mr. Johnson, in which he says he is for you. It is very possible that some of your particular friends may think that as I am intimate with him, I may have some influence in this respect, and knowing the disposition with some, to place every thing to my account, I hope you will not only believe me incapable of promoting any thing unfavorable to you, but whenever a different sentiment is communicated or hinted to you, my feelings may be explained. I intend, in this business, to keep a straightforward course, and while I consider it my duty to be on terms of personal friendship with others, if I find it reciprocal, no person shall doubt my course where I can be of any service to you.

ITURBIDE TO MR. CLAY.

MEXICO, May 6, 1822.

MY DEAR SIR,—Through the means of the captain of the navy, Don Eugenio Cortes, I have been informed of the great services by which you have furthered the success of his commission, and contributed to the prosperous advantages that resulted from it; this generous course, the fruit of this enlightened age, excites my gratitude, and obliges me to give you my most sincere thanks, and offer you my friendship; for this philanthropic conduct that emanates from a liberal education, and whose end is the civilization of nations, though it relates to the whole Mexican Empire, if its success should be in proportion to its promise, I offer you the gratitude which is due to you by all, and my most particular thanks for the present of books, and for the value you set on my portrait. In exchange for it, I am waiting for yours, which is announced by our common friend Cortes, and without seeing it, it gives me a satisfaction, from that common effect which can not be explained, in which men reciprocally love without knowing each other, in which the mind forms favorable prepossessions, and gives to the person (for so it delights in), as many virtues as it pleases, takes for true what it conjectures, and goes so far as to give to the portrait expression and gestures. But our case is different from this—your works are distinguished, my correspondence is a debt of justice to their merit, and I promise myself the continuance of duties so praiseworthy, and protest to render you the same in like circumstances.

EUGENIO CORTES TO MR. CLAY.

PHILADELPHIA, June 19, 1822.

THE HONORABLE HENRY CLAY:

I have the honor to deliver to you the inclosed letter from the supreme chief of the Mexican Empire, who directed me to present it to you personally, as a testimony of the gratitude, esteem, and distinction, which the supreme chief of the Mexican nation entertains for the virtues, talents and services displayed by you in favor of the just cause sustained by all the States of South America, to gain their independence.

This occasion affords me the opportunity of offering to you my respects, and of assuring you that I am your most faithful obedient servant.

PETER B. PORTER TO MR. CLAY.

BLACK ROCK, July 8, 1822.

DEAR SIR,—It has been the misfortune of this State, that for a number of years past, its political concerns have been managed, or rather distracted, by a few ambitious men, whose views have extended only to their own personal aggrandizement, and on almost every great national question, our strength has been scattered and wasted by premature and unadvised commitments, made by these headlong and selfish politicians. As regards the interesting question which is the subject of your letter, a new and more circumspect course of proceeding has been adopted. A mutual understanding now exists among the principal republicans of the State, that it is yet too early to act on this question, and that, whatever may be the private sentiments and predilections of individuals, it would be imprudent at present to promulgate them. Whenever the proper time shall arrive (and perhaps the next winter session of our Legislature may be selected as such), a full and friendly consultation and interchange of sentiments will take place, and we are not without hopes of producing, by this course, a unanimity that will insure to this State (what it has never possessed), an influence proportioned to its reputation and wealth. Whoever may be the candidate fairly designated by the majority, I shall consider myself bound, as a republican, to give him my support. I have indeed been one of the advisers of this cautious and circumspect policy, because I have deemed it the wisest that this State, under present circumstances, could pursue. If we had a favorite candidate in one of our own citizens, it would afford a fair apology for our taking the field early, but we have none, and you are aware of the jealousy that exists, particularly at the South, against the growing power of the *great State of New York*, and if we were to manifest our solicitude, by making an early selection, that very circumstance might weaken the chance of our candidate, and perhaps throw him into a minority.

The Republicans of this State have been so often and shamefully deceived and abused by the professed friendship, as well as open hostility of the opposite party, that the first requisite in their candidate will be, that he be a *Republican of the old school*, and I know of no one who, in addition to so many other splendid qualifications, can better sustain the integrity of this character, than my friend from Kentucky.

I expect to see a number of my political friends at my house during the summer, and among them, Mr. Van Buren, of the Senate. The subject of the next Presidency will of course be canvassed, and I will, in a future letter, give you my impressions in regard to the prevailing views of the Republicans of this State.

Mrs. P. is in excellent health, and desires her best respects to you.

LANGDON CHEVES TO MR. CLAY.

PHILADELPHIA, July 27, 1822.

MY DEAR SIR,—Your favor of the 5th instant was duly received. I have put your brother in nomination, and his and your wish will be duly and respectfully considered. The appointments for the Orleans office will be made on the 27th November next, at which time I will be merely nominally an officer of the bank, as I have determined to leave it a few weeks after.

I perceive you are again a candidate for Congress, in which I suppose you are right. The *great question* seems to be but little agitated yet. You will perceive from the "Sentinel" of this city, which is one of the oracles of the democratic party in this part of the State—the "Franklin Gazette" is the other—that there is a schism among the active men. The "Sentinel" appears to incline to Crawford. New York appears to be completely undecided, and apparently asking for an offer; but I really know nothing about it, and hear little.

PATRICK HENRY TO MR. CLAY.

August 21, 1822.

DEAR SIR,—You must make Clinton President, which, with your force and talents, public and private, you can accomplish. He has pretensions in every respect—a man of business, is bold and honorable—an elegant scholar—deeply read—liberal altogether in his ideas. He would return the favor with fidelity. He has no sneaking, tricky vices. You would be the next President, from character, pretensions, experience, and, coming from the West, you would be expected and attended to by the nation. You would be Vice-President or Secretary of State. The former would keep you out of turmoil and responsibility, and perhaps be the safest place. You would be happy in it, honored and supported by every body.

Clinton has name, fame, talents, and useful and lasting honors to sustain him for any or in any station he may fill. It would be worthy of Clay and Kentucky to join New York and Clinton in so glorious a career in saving the Union.

LAFAYETTE TO MR. CLAY.

PARIS, November 5, 1822.

MY DEAR SIR,—I am too happy in an opportunity to keep our friendly acquaintance, and would be still happier to converse with you on the business of freedom, as it relates to both sides of the Atlantic. You have had the pleasure, in which I was long ago ready to sympathize, of the acknowledgment of Columbian independence by the United States. May every part of that continent be also free, independent, and universally acknowledged! It is to be expected the nonsense of an American emperor can not last long. But while I rejoice in the emancipation of what was called the Spanish dominion, while I lament the hesitation of the Cortes in the acknowledgment which policy and necessity point out to them, I would be very sorry to hear of a serious quarrel between Spain and the United States. The embers of European freedom are now to be cherished in the peninsula. Old Governments, England particularly, employ a great deal of cunning in fomenting divisions among the nations, and in every nation among the parties, nay, the individuals who enlist in the cause of mankind. Their friendship is almost as bad as their enmity. The British papers, Whig and Tory, seem to vie in recommending an intervention, under the form of protection, in the affairs of this very Greece against whom Great Britain and Austria have acted so cruel and dishonorable a part. How happy should I be to see an American squadron in those seas! The American flag should be the natural, disinterested protector for the Grecian confederacy. Should the Ottoman navy prove impertinent, it might be crushed at once. A Grecian citizen who has left Corinth with orders from the Federal Government, tells me that two millions of dollars, two ships of the line, or three or four large frigates, could they obtain that sum and naval means from mercantile enterprise, would suffice to insure the liberties of that classic country. It is to be feared the assistance will be either withheld or lent with interested views, if not under degrading conditions. The decisions of the Vienna Congress are every day expected. While a common antipathy to the rights of men and nations link them together, the old systems and potent views of each Cabinet interfere with the general plan of the Holy Alliance. The situation of France under its counter-revolutionary Government is better understood by a series of intelligences lately collected from the papers of both parties, than I could explain in a letter. An actual invasion of Spain by foreign troops may be postponed from the fear of uniting the whole people in the defense of the country; but every countenance and protection will more and more be afforded to the enemies of the Constitution; and if the patriots are driven to excesses, in consequence of their provoked irritation it will become a pretense against them, against the liberals of every country, and the cause itself, much depends on the spirited resistance of Spain in the present crisis.

I have been requested by my former aid-de-camp in the national guards, and constant friend, M. de la Rue, to mention to you a claim of his lady, Beaumarchais' daughter, now under the examination of Congress. Their wish is that the affair may be referred to a judicial, I suppose the Supreme Court. It does not belong to me to decide on the propriety of the measure, nor the circumstances of the claim, further than to say, I have been a witness to very active exertions of Beaumarchais in the first period of our American contest; but I owe it to those remembrances, and to my affection for M. de la Rue, to make to you the mention of this affair, very important to him and family. It appears that American claims upon France are on the point of being examined in this country. I much wish justice may be rendered on all sides.

I have often the pleasure to talk of you with two amiable friends of ours, Miller and Wright, who are now in France, and most of the time in our family colony of Lagrange.

B. W. LEIGH TO MR. CLAY.

RICHMOND, November 9, 1822.

MY DEAR SIR,—I had the happiness to receive your letter of the 29th October this morning, and I am heartily thankful to you for it. It was the more welcome, as it served to assure me of the re-establishment of your health. The newspapers represented you, some weeks ago, as very dangerously ill; and one of them killed you outright—which your distant friends regard as a very unpardonable abuse of the freedom of the press.

It was considerate and kind in you to send me your report of our arrangements to the Legislature of Kentucky—the more so since I must plead guilty to the charge of having broken my promise to write to you on my return home. The truth is, that when I got home, I had to write so many letters which I was obliged to write, that I soon came to a conclusion to write none but such as were absolutely indispensable. I trust to your own experience in like cases to estimate the worth of this apology.

As to yourself in particular, I shall take this occasion to say, that there was no part of your conduct in regard to the peculiar state of your local politics (and I was very observant of it all), which impressed me with such high respect, and excited so warm a sentiment of approbation, as the constant effort I saw you making to impress it upon all parties, that there was no desperation either in the distemper of the State, or in the remedies that had been applied, and that it behooved all men to treat them both with patience, temper, and moderation, as well as frankness and steadiness.

Tell my friends in Kentucky that I remember them as I ought. Have the goodness to present my best respects to Mrs. Clay.

MR. CLAY TO FRANCIS BROOKE.

COLUMBUS, OHIO, January 8, 1823.

MY DEAR SIR,—You will have seen a note which I addressed to the editors of the "Intelligencer," on the subject of the business of Ghent. I wish to say one word to you on it. To those who have attentively read the controversial papers between Messrs. Russell and Adams, and particularly the appendix to the book of the latter, it must be apparent that the honorable secretary has labored to draw me into the controversy, by the manner in which he has alluded to my name, and the inconsistency which, on one occasion, he imputes to me. I had but one alternative, either to acquiesce, by my silence, in all misrepresentations; or, by a sort of protest, to reserve to myself the right of correcting errors on some future fit occasion. I might, indeed, have rushed into the controversy between those two gentlemen, or commenced a new one; but I hope my friends will believe me incapable of committing such an indiscretion, as I conceive that would be, of doing at this time the one or the other. I chose the latter because of the alternative stated, and I hope you will approve of the step I have taken. My purpose is answered, my ground is taken, and those who know me will not want to be assured that I will adhere to both. I shall write no more until I think the period has arrived which I have indicated. The honorable secretary seems to deplore its possible distance. I shall remain unmoved by any regrets he may feel on account of the want of fresh aliment for new strife.

The newspapers will communicate to you the events which

have occurred here. As they chose to have a second caucus, I was glad it took place before I reached Columbus. Considering the great efforts made from without to prevent any legislative expression of public opinion, the proof which is afforded by the vote here is extremely strong. My friends believe that from eighty to ninety out of the one hundred and three members, who compose the General Assembly, are in my favor; and there is among the former the greatest zeal, animation, and confidence.

I am anxious to learn the names of your commissioners. Expecting to reach Washington by the 22d instant, I shall be glad to have the pleasure of hearing from you on my arrival there.

MR. CLAY TO FRANCIS BROOKE.

WASHINGTON, January 31, 1823.

MY DEAR SIR,—I have received your obliging favor of the 29th instant. The considerations were so many and so powerful, calling upon your State to ratify the convention with Kentucky, that I confess to you frankly I did not anticipate the event which you say will probably happen. In that event I shall deeply regret that Virginia ever again opened the negotiation, after respecting the professions which Mr. Bibb and I submitted to your Legislature last winter. Why did Virginia ask a reference of the claim of her State limit? Could she suppose that Kentucky would refer it and leave herself exposed, after the decision of the referees, to the claim, as if it had never been submitted to arbitration? Could she think that the mockery of creating a tribunal was to be presented to decide a controversy, respecting which the parties were to be as free and unbound after the decision as before the reference. If she had no power to refer; if she had no authority to bind her constituents, then she ought not to have moved in the business; and the first error was committed at Richmond, and not at Lexington. For my part I believe the State line *bound* by the decision, and that the guaranty is the mere expression of a fair implication from the whole transaction without it. And it was only to render the convention more explicit, and to preclude the necessity of resorting to any interpretations about which disputes might arise, that it appeared to me to be expedient to insert the clause of guaranty. Upon the whole I must say, that if you reject the convention,

I think the impartial world will look upon you as being clearly in the wrong.

I am extremely sorry to find that any of my friends believe that I was not called upon to address the note which was recently published in the Intelligencer, respecting certain questions arising at Ghent. Had Mr. Adams, either before or after his several publications, designed to consult me about the use which he has freely made in them of my name; had he said to me " Mr. Clay, I have imputed to you such and such opinions, and made statements about the part you acted at Ghent; if I am inaccurate in any of them I will take pleasure in correcting the error," I should have felt myself required to address Mr. Adams personally, and not the public. But he never communicated to me any one of his publications, and I never had an opportunity even of seeing his book until my arrival here. Having chosen, without my knowledge or consent, to usher my name into the public journals; having imputed to me, as he does in his appendix, inconsistencies, and by an innuendo insinuated that I was the author of an editorial article in Kentucky, which I never saw until I read it in the paper in which it was printed, I felt myself absolved from all obligation to make any direct appeal to Mr. Adams himself. In addressing the note which I did to the public, it was my intention merely to enter a *caveat* against the correctness of all his statements, and to exhibit a public reservation of a right on my part to rectify mistakes, when the proper occasion should arrive. Considering the relation in which both of us now stand to the public, I thought the present an unsuitable moment even to hazard any controversy with him; and if I could prostrate him in the dust I would not write at this time.

I thank you for your kind information respecting the state of the public mind in Virginia. * * * * *
I look upon this struggle with all the philosophy which I ought to do. On one resolution my friends may rest assured I will firmly rely, and that is, to participate in no intrigues, to enter into no arrangements, to make no promises or pledges; but that, whether I am elected or not, I will have nothing to reproach myself with. If elected I will go into the office with a pure conscience, to promote with my utmost exertions the common good of our country, and free to select the most able and faithful public servants. If not elected, acquiescing most cheerfully in the better selection which will thus have been made, I will at

least have the satisfaction of preserving my honor unsullied, and my heart uncorrupted.

I shall remain here during the greater part of the term of the Supreme Court, in which I have some professional business, particularly the cause between the bank and the State of Ohio.

I shall be glad that your leisure may allow you to give me the pleasure of again hearing from you.

P. S. What course does Virginia mean to take after refuting the guaranty? Does she intend again to open the negotiation? To propose that the Board of Commissioners shall now proceed without the clause of guaranty? Or to make a rupture of all negotiations and fly to arms? I mean *forensic* arms.

B. W. LEIGH TO MR. CLAY.

RICHMOND, Feb. 12, 1823.

MY DEAR SIR,—I have received your truly kind and friendly letter. Far from being surprised at the indignation which the conduct of the Virginia Legislature, in respect to the convention agreed on between us last summer, has excited in your breast, I unite in the sentiment; but my indignation is aggravated by the sense of personal mortification at such a defeat of my best efforts for the public service, and of burning shame for the ridicule and dishonor which Virginia has brought on herself. If *you* be thus indignant, what must be the feelings of your colleague, Mr. Rowan? I fancy I can see his resentment, disdain, and contempt. Yet, my dear sir, this deed must not be imputed to us, the people of Virginia, nor even to the body of her representatives—it must lie at the door of a bare majority of the Senate. I am not sure that Kentucky is bound to take the distinction, but I hope you will. I believe that the sentiment of the people of Virginia toward Kentucky, is the same with my own individually, and that, I am sure, is what it ought to be.

It is impossible to say what our assembly means to do in this business. Some answer must be given to Kentucky. What it will be, or how it can be agreed on, considering the difference of opinion between the two houses, I am wholly at a loss to conjecture. The majority in the Senate for the present, so far as I can learn, are perfectly careless about it. But it is impossible, I hope, that they can continue so regardless of self-respect, so unconcerned about the comity due to a sister State, as to leave matters in their present condition. Mr. Johnson desired me a day or two ago, to tell you that he did not think it absolutely hopeless, and that the Senate will yet consent to the ratification of the convention.

MR. CLAY TO FRANCIS BROOKE.

WASHINGTON, February 26, 1823.

MY DEAR SIR,—I duly received your friendly letter of the 19th inst., as I did the preceding one to which it refers. The course which the business between our respective States has taken, fills me with so much regret and concern, that I will not dwell upon it, especially as it has probably terminated finally, and had, therefore better be forgotten as soon as it can be. What is done can not be changed, and it is not conformable to my temper or habit, to indulge in unavailing regrets. I prefer always looking to the future. I observe what you state with respect to the condition of the public feeling in Virginia, in regard to the next Presidency. I ever thought that the line of conduct which the Virginia gentleman had marked out for that State, that is, to take no forward part in the ensuing election, but rather to leave the decision of it to the residue of the Union, was wise and discreet. It would have been thought that Virginia was dictatorial, if after ceasing to furnish a chief magistrate, she should have displayed any early and anxious solicitude about the successor of Mr. Monroe. But has Virginia acted in consonance with this avowed purpose? Has not that point, which heretofore has invariably indicated her pleasure, distinctly taken its ground? Has it not been confidently proclaimed, and been believed, every where out of Virginia, that her choice was fixed? May not the effect of all this be, to jeopardize, not only that preference, if it be actually made, but also the election of him who would be her second choice?

Virginia may possibly decide the election by bestowing her suffrage on the gentleman referred to, though I doubt it extremely. But she certainly *can* decide it by lending her support to him who is said to be her second choice. She will, of course, as she ought to, determine as she pleases in such contingences.   *   *

In saying that it is my firm conviction that Mr. Adams is at present the most formidable, I pray you to believe that I do not mean (far from it), to indicate any preference for him, nor am I moved, at Mr. Crawford's expense, by the desire of advancing my own interests.   *   *   *   *   *   *

Connect yourselves with the West, and are you not, whether the election is won or lost, on the vantage ground? You see, my dear sir, that I write you with all the freedom of an ancient friendship, which could alone excuse the presentation to you of views, which, I dare say, have often been taken by you.

I pray you to give my best respects to your associate, Judge Green, whose acquaintance I had the pleasure of making last winter, and for whose character I have a high regard.

MR. CLAY TO FRANCIS BROOKE.

WASHINGTON, March 9, 1823.

MY DEAR SIR,—You will have seen that the Supreme Court has decided against the validity of our occupying claimant laws. The dissatisfaction which will be felt by the people of Kentucky, with the decision, will be aggravated in no little degree, by the fact, that the decision is that of three judges to one, a minority, therefore, of the whole court; and this aggravation will be further increased by considerations which belong to either of these three judges.

At the moment of some vexation about this unhappy result of a cause, the effects and possible consequences of which, fill me with extreme concern, I wrote you my last letter, and I fear that I expressed myself in it, on some points, in a manner which I ought not to have done, even to one whom I have ever regarded as one of my best friends. I must pray you, therefore, to commit it to the flames, and its contents to oblivion.   *   *   *

I shall leave this place in a few days, for Kentucky, by the way of Philadelphia, and I shall be glad to have the pleasure of hearing from you, when I reach home.

M. DE MENOU TO MR. CLAY.

MARCH 17, 1823.

M. de Menou has the honor of presenting his respects to Mr. Clay, and while acknowledging his polite note of yesterday, begs leave to thank him for his attention to the affair of Apollon which he regrets was not tried this term. He hopes Mr. Clay will have the goodness to give it his continued support next year.

Should Mr. Clay have no further use, at present, for the different papers relating to that business, and think fit to send them to M. de Menou, he would keep them in readiness to be returned to Mr. Clay on his return to Washington.

REPUBLIC OF COLOMBIA TO MR. CLAY.

FAVORITA, December 31, 1822.

The Secretary of State for Foreign Affairs, begs leave to offer his best respects to Colonel Todd, and will have the greatest pleasure in presenting to the Executive of Colombia, the portrait of the Honorable Henry Clay, to whom the Continental States of the *ci-devant* Spanish America, are so much indebted for his perseverance and enlightened sagacity.

The Secretary of State for Foreign Relations, entertains no doubt but that the Executive will accept a present which will at every moment recall to his mind, an American politician and a sincere friend of humanity. He does not hesitate, by anticipation, to offer to Colonel Todd his best thanks for his goodness and the particular confidence with which he distinguishes him.

BOGOTA, April 23, 1823.

C. S. Todd offers his respects to the Honorable Speaker of the House of Representatives of the Republic of Colombia, and, as a testimony of his esteem for the first Constitutional Congress, has the honor to present an engraved portrait of his distinguished friend and connection, Henry Clay, the eloquent advocate of the liberty of both Americas.

LA FAVORITA, December 31, 1822.

C. S. Todd's respects to Dr. Gual, Secretary of State for Foreign Affairs, and begs leave to present, as a slight testimony of his esteem, an engraved portrait of his distinguished friend and connection, Henry Clay; to be disposed of in such manner as Dr. Gual may deem most complimentary to the Executive Department of Colombia.

REPUBLIC OF COLOMBIA.

HOUSE OF REPRESENTATIVES, IN BOGOTA,
April 25, 1823.

To MR. C. S. TODD, *Chargé d'Affaires*—

The House of Representatives has received with the most lively sense of gratitude the valuable present you have had the goodness to offer. It duly appreciates the generous sentiments manifested in the address with which you accompanied it; sentiments very worthy of the country of Washington and of Franklin.

The House will not fail to pay that profound tribute of respect which is due to the Honorable Henry Clay, the intrepid advocate of the cause of Colombia; and while it reserves to itself the occasion of manifesting in a more conspicuous manner, the high esteem of which he is worthy, you will condescend to communicate to him, the wishes which the House cherishes for the prosperity of the United States. God preserve you.

DOMINGO CAYCEDO, *President of the House.*

C. S. TODD TO MR. CLAY.

BOGOTA, May 8, 1823.

MY DEAR SIR,—I had the pleasure of addressing you a short note from Merida, in December last, and avail myself, now, of the return of the Swedish Consul-General to Philadelphia, to transmit a correspondence with the authorities here, produced by the presentation of some of Tyler's engravings of you, three copies of which I had procured for the purpose; the receipt of that presented to General Soublette, Intendant-General at Caracas, has not been acknowledged. The correspondence was originally in Spanish, and you will see in the translation that I have made some progress in a language, which, besides its pre-eminent beauties, may become emphatically that of America.

I hope you know me sufficiently to be aware that I have not received with indifference, the account of the indications in Kentucky, Ohio, and Missouri, and in the prints of other States, favorable to your pretensions to the next Presidency. Death and some Siberian Missions may lessen the number of your competitors, and whatever may be the feeling of the United

States singly on the subject, there can be no doubt but that the united voice of continental America would elevate you to a station full of unexampled responsibility and of unrequited solicitude. I am persuaded, however, that you are yourself too national in your feelings, to give all the point which the people and Governments in the New States of Spanish America would wish to convey by their unqualified approbation of your conduct in relation to their supposed interests; since it has been made the occasion and the pretext for indulging in cold and unworthy feelings toward our Government, and extending, in a much greater degree than we could wish, even to our people and institutions.

I might refer you to Colonel Duane for detailed information with respect to the state of affairs here; and his opinions would be entitled to great consideration, having devoted many years to the acquisition of an extensive knowledge of the country, and in support of the cause which the people supposed they were maintaining. Being myself in the diplomatic service and, moreover, under the immediate eye of a statesman, who is characteristically known never to express more than he means to say, I may be excused from giving an opinion on the condition of things; but Colonel Duane, if he were to meet with you, would undeceive you with respect to many matters about which, he says, he has been heretofore under misapprehensions. He would tell you that though the county is separated from Spanish dominion and misrule, yet that Spanish duplicity in the Governors, and Spanish superstition in the people are but too painfully prevalent; while the hopes of the public councils are directed to Europe, and especially Great Britain, in the vain delusion, that it is by those powers alone, their interests can be promoted.

I need not say, dear sir, that any communication you may find it convenient to make me, will be peculiarly acceptable.

MR. CLAY TO FRANCIS BROOKE.

LEXINGTON, August 28, 1823.

I received, my dear sir, your very obliging letter of the 14th instant, and I pray you to believe that I do not place less value on your friendship because you have nothing to communicate "more favorable to my prospects." On the subject to which you allude, I assure you most sincerely I look with great calmness, and with a most perfect determination to acquiesce cheerfully in whatever choice the nation may make. It would be a poor compliment to our institutions, to say that their solidity, or the public happiness, materially depended upon any election that shall take place. I really think, however, that Virginia can not justify herself to the Union for the apathy which you say prevails there on the question. Judging, as I have done at this distance, from the " Enquirer" and other Virginia prints, I had supposed that great interest was felt and generally taken in its decision, and that there was even danger of her overstepping the line of cautious circumspection, which her leading politicians were understood to have marked out for her.

This indifference, you say, arises from the absence of any pledge that the great interests of the people of Virginia will be taken care of by any of the competitors for the chief magistracy. If, indeed, no such pledge is to be found in the principles, integrity, and characters, as heretofore developed, of either of the candidates, it is, I should think, quite too late in the day now for any pledge to be given or received. But, my dear sir, what interests have Virginia and the South separate from the Union? You have mentioned a single subject only, that of the encroachments of the Federal judiciary on State rights; and, as connected with this, the " broad doctrine now inculcated, that Congress has the right to extend, not to regulate only, the jurisdiction of the Federal Courts." On that subject I am entirely at a loss to conceive any peculiar interest in the State of Virginia, and the Southern States. All are equally concerned in the jurisdiction of the State sovereignties. All would be equally affected by Federal usurpation. But I must confess that it is the first time that I ever heard asserted such a doctrine as you say is now inculcated. The limit of the Federal judiciary is to be found in the Constitution, and Congress can vest in it no power which is not there found. If such a doctrine as you state is really attempted to be inculcated, you will find Kentucky now, as in the epoch of 1799, in spite of all your unkindness toward her, ready to co-operate with you in opposing it, and no man in the Union will be more prompt than I shall be to second the opposition. I can not suppose you to refer to the power that is claimed for the general Government, to give effect to its laws through its own judiciary. For, without that power, without Federal means to effectuate the constitutional resolves of the Federal will, there is an end to the general Government—that is inevitable, if not instantaneous anarchy.

But, my dear sir, on this subject of the Federal judiciary and State rights, I mean to say a few words to you, in the spirit of Virginia independence, and in the frankness of sincere friendship. Has not Virginia exposed herself to the imputation of selfishness, by the course of her conduct, or of that of many of her politicians? When, in the case of Cohans and Virginia, her authority was alone concerned, she made the most strenuous efforts against the exercise of power by the Supreme Court. But when the thunders of that Court were directed against poor Kentucky, in vain did she invoke Virginian aid. The Supreme Court, it was imagined, would decide on the side of supposed interests of Virginia. It has so decided; and, in effect, cripples the sovereign power of the State of Kentucky more than any other measure ever affected the independence of any State in this Union, and not a Virginia voice is heard against the decision. The Supreme Court is viewed with complacency, and as a very different sort of tribunal from that Supreme Court which decided Cohans' case.

Again: of all the irregular bodies, none can be more so than a Congressional caucus at Washington. None have a more consolidating tendency. Indeed, it is espoused upon the principle of preventing the exercise of State or Federal rights through the medium of the House of Representatives. Yet the Virginia politicians (at least if we are to judge from the papers) warmly advocate the constitution of such a caucus. Will it not be said that they are influenced by the consideration, not of preserving unimpaired State rights, but of giving to the State power of Virginia the utmost effect of which it is capable? Or that of securing the election of the alleged favorite, who, without the instrumentality of such an assemblage, is in danger of losing the election? It is in vain to speak of the inconveniences of a warmly-contested election. They are incident to our system, and are happily provided for by it. And the transitions from a Congressional caucus to a pretorian cohort or hereditary monarchy, to escape from those vexations, are not so great as we might at first imagine.

I am aware that on two subjects I have the misfortune to differ with many of my Virginia friends—internal improvements and home manufactures. My opinion has been formed after much deliberation, and my best judgment yet tells me that I am right. I have not time, nor would it be fitting as regards your comfort, now to discuss the policy or the power of fostering these interests. I believe Virginia and the Southern States as much interested, directly or indirectly, as any other parts of the Union, in their encouragement. When the Government was first adopted we had no interior. Our population was inclosed between the sea and the mountains which run parallel to it. Since then the west part of your State, the western parts of New York and Pennsylvania, and all the Western States, have been settled. The wars of Europe consumed all the surplus produce on both sides of the mountains. Those wars have terminated, and emigration has ceased. We find ourselves annually in possession of an immense surplus. There is no market for it abroad; there is none at home. If there were a foreign market, before we, in the interior, could reach it, the intervening population would have supplied it. There can be no foreign market adequate to the consumption of the vast and growing surplus of the produce of our agriculture. We must, then, have a home market. Some of us must cultivate; some fabricate. And we must have reasonable protection against the machinations of foreign powers. On the sea-board you want a navy, fortifications, protection, foreign commerce. In the interior we want internal improvements, home manufactures. You have what you want, and object to our getting what we want. Should not the interests of both parties be provided for?

It has appeared to me, in the administration of the general Government, to be a just principle to inquire what great interests belong to each section of our country, and to promote those interests, as far as practicable, consistently with the Constitution, having always an eye to the welfare of the whole. Assuming this principle, does any one doubt that if New York, New Jersey, Pennsylvania, Delaware, Maryland, and the Western States constituted an independent nation, it would immediately protect the important interests in question? And is it not to be feared that, if protection is not to be found for vital interests, from the existing systems, in great parts of the confederacy, those parts will ultimately seek to establish a system that will afford the requisite protection? I would not, in the application of the principle indicated, give to the peculiar interests of great sections *all* the protection which they would probably receive if those sections constituted separate and independent States. I would, however, extend some protection, and measure it by balancing the countervailing interests, if there be such, in other quarters of the Union.

I concur entirely with you in thinking that the north and east, but particularly New England, have laid, in a great measure, the other parts of the Union under contribution. And of all the ill-advised measures, of all the wasteful expenditures of public money, the Revolutionary pension list pre-eminently takes the lead. Never was there more public money spent, with less practical benefit. But who proposed it? Your own Monroe. I thought of it then as I think of it now; but opposition would have been silly and vain.

You will oppose my election, I suppose, in Virginia. I have no right to complain. Silence and submission are my duty. You will oppose me because I think that the interests of all parts of the Union should be taken care of; in other words, that the interests of the interior, on the two subjects mentioned, as well as that of the maritime coast, ought to be provided for. You will give your suffrages to Mr. Crawford or Mr. Adams; and if Mr. Crawford or Mr. Adams be elected, I venture to predict that we shall find, either in his inaugural speech, or in the first message or speech (perhaps the latter mode of communication may be revived) to Congress, a recommendation of efficient encouragement to domestic manufactures and internal improvements.

I am afraid that you will think me in a very bad humor. Far from it. I repeat that I never enjoyed more perfect composure. My health, it is true, is extremely bad, and I am now confined at home by the endeavor to re-establish it. But it neither affects my tranquillity or gives me the spleen. In regard to the election, as to which I will make no professions of affecting an indifference, which I do not feel, my friends continue to be very confident; and my own opinion is that my prospects are not surpassed by those of either of the other gentlemen, still I am not unaware that all things are uncertain; and I therefore continue resolved to preserve my philosophy, my principles, and my conscience, be the event what it may.

Has not our friend Southard been rapidly advanced? He certainly has merit, and his friend, the Secretary of War, has discernment.

It would have given me great pleasure to see you, as it will to meet you any where again. Can you not run up to Washington next winter? To a close observer there will be a scene there exhibited worth surveying. Wherever you are, I pray you to be persuaded that my best wishes attend you.

P. S. I send you my effusions as they are poured out through a mercurial course, on which the doctors have put me; and wish no copy for others. I write for yourself alone.

LAFAYETTE TO MR. CLAY.

LAGRANGE, October 13, 1823.

MY DEAR SIR,—I have been applied to by the amiable Madame de la Rue for a letter of introduction to my friend Mr. Clay; she is daughter of the celebrated Beaumarchais, whose name has been connected with the five years of our American contest; she is the wife of one of my faithful and zealous aides-de-camp in the National Guard; two motives which make it a very agreeable duty for me to present her to you.

Madame de la Rue has a claim upon the public treasury, long debated in Congress, the documents of which have been laid before you. It does not belong to me to anticipate your opinion in a matter upon which you have more data than I could offer; but I find a pleasure in contributing to gratify Madame de la Rue's wishes to be introduced to your personal acquaintance.

PETER B. PORTER TO MR. CLAY.

BLACK ROCK, November 17, 1823.

DEAR SIR,—I received your favor of September some days ago.

The singular results in our late elections, with the speculations on them in our newspapers, will show you the uncertainty of the ultimate vote of this State on the presidential question. The zeal and pertinacity with which Van Buren and his friends have pushed Mr. Crawford (who has no substantial popularity here) without any other argument in his favor than the necessity of *party discipline*, have disgusted the Republicans of this State, and produced great dissatisfaction and division in our ranks.

The cleverest fellow in our delegation is Dudley Marvin, a new member from Ontario, to whom I have given a letter of introduction to you. He was from New England, and educated a Federalist, but is a Republican in principle and practice, and has for some time been in the confidence of our party. He possesses a heart as well as a head of the first order. I hope you will notice him in *public* as well as in private, and I am confident your attentions will be amply repaid in the pleasure you will derive from his acquaintance.

P. P. BARBOUR TO MR. CLAY.

WASHINGTON, December 4, 1823.

DEAR SIR,—In answer to your note of this evening, I beg leave to say, that I should regret exceedingly, as far as I am personally concerned, to give you the slightest difficulty in the arrangement of committees. My own individual wish would be decidedly to be on no committee; but as that might *possibly* give rise to some misconstruction, I now so far modify my wish as to desire to be put upon none whose labor is very great; and further, not to be chairman of whatsoever committee I may be placed on—above all, the Committee of Ways and Means I should most object to. Wheresoever your general arrangement may make it convenient to place me, I assure you in sincerity I shall be perfectly satisfied.

MR. CLAY TO FRANCIS BROOKE.

WASHINGTON, December 20, 1823.

MY DEAR SIR,—A friend informs me that, at Richmond, my arrangement of the committees of the House of Representatives has been the subject of some animadversion, in consequence of Mr. Barbour, late Speaker, not being at the head of any committee. The truth is, that it was my intention to have appointed him chairman of one of the most prominent committees of the House, but he entreated me not to put him at the head of any committee, nor on any committee, which might require much of his time, as he wished to employ it exclusively in study. I should certainly not offer, even to a friend, any explanation of my official conduct in such a matter, if it were not to prevent misconception of my motives in respect to a gentleman between whom and myself unfortunately some competition existed. I am sure if he were apprised (he is now absent from Washington) of the erroneous impression existing at Richmond, he would himself hasten to correct it. I have a full share of human frailties; but a want of consideration for a competitor, in relation to any object, does not, if I know myself, happen to be one of them.

Did you get a *lengthy* letter that I wrote you in August or September last?

W. B. ROCHESTER TO MR. CLAY.

BATH, STEUBEN COUNTY, N. Y., December 20, 1823.

MY DEAR SIR,—Your election as Speaker, considering the majority, and that you were opposed by a professed friend of Mr. Crawford, has had the effect of making the few friends of the last-named gentleman, whom I have since conversed with, admit that he is not so strong a man throughout the Union as they had previously supposed. You were right in taking it; had you declined, you would have been charged with chaffering; indeed, Rufus King's paper, in New York city, has already, in substance, charged you with having graduated some of the first of your official acts (*ex. qr.* appointments of committees), with a view to serve private views. That editor, Mr. ———, is a sad fellow, for it is only about a twelvemonth since he avowed to me his preference of you, and ever since he has been *tôtis viribus*, for Adams!

The hollow apology which he made to me, was your publication disavowing any co-operation with Mr. Russell in his affair with Mr. Adams.

In answer to the inquiry in your favor of the 6th instant, whether I correspond with Mr. Van Buren, I reply affirmatively, though I have not as yet heard directly from him since his arrival at Washington.

I have just finished a hasty letter to him, which lies before me, and shall be forwarded by the same mail which takes this.

I repeat to you that Mr. V. B.'s preference will be of vast importance to his favorites in this State, let the choice be made as it may.

I am told your health has been poor, and as your duties are

doubtless arduous, let me once more beg of you to believe that I do not write with a view of extracting answers. . I need hardly say that my letters to you are written for the indulgent eye of friendship only. I have not time to transcribe and to correct, but shall occasionally drop you a hasty scroll as the tide moves on.

MR. CLAY TO FRANCIS BROOKE.

WASHINGTON, January 22, 1824.

MY DEAR SIR,—I duly received your obliging letter of the 18th instant. I am glad to hear of the probability of the recovery of Colonel Taylor's health. With respect to his opinions on the subject to which you refer, whatever they may be, they can not diminish that habitual veneration for him which I have ever cherished.

On the point of a caucus, in a spirit of perfect desperation, a continual effort is making to get one up. It will be defeated, you may rely, either by being voted down, in a general attendance of the Republican members, or by a resolution of a large majority of them not to attend. If they make one, it will be a faction—a cabal. My friends say, that on the score of mere expediency, they have no objection to a caucus which shall be composed of the Republican members generally; that they have no fears of the result of such a caucus; but that they have no idea of consenting to make part of a caucus in which they should act the part of mere *figuranti*, which would be the case if the friends of other candidates, who, it is well known, would not attend, should be absent. *   *   *   *   *   *

With great regard, I am faithfully your friend.

MR. CLAY TO FRANCIS BROOKE.

WASHINGTON, February 23, 1824.

MY DEAR SIR,—It is some time since I had the pleasure of hearing from you. In the interval, several events of importance have occurred. The miserable attempt at a caucus, you will have seen accounts of. Mr. Crawford never could have been elected, but I venture to predict that the mere fact of seeking, by means of a caucus so got up, and so constituted, will destroy whatever prospects he ever had. Mr. Calhoun has withdrawn. This has been produced by events in Pennsylvania, evincing, beyond all doubt, the determination of that State to support General Jackson. The circle of competition is thus much circumscribed, and you may rely upon it, that you will have, as your next President, Adams, Jackson, or myself. You will have, in Virginia, to choose between these three evils. It is madness, it is perfect infatuation, to think, at this time, of any body else. Our intelligence from New York, continues to be favorable to the hopes of my friends. Still we shall have nothing absolutely decisive from that quarter, until time has elapsed to enable us to hear what the consequences there will be of the caucus. The present moment is one of great importance to me in Virginia. Now is the time to make a demonstration for me there, if ever. My friends accordingly, I understand, contemplate the formation of an electoral ticket for me, at Richmond, and think of putting you at the head of it, if you consent. Such a ticket, announced at this time, whatever may be its ultimate fate to Virginia, will have the very best effects out of Virginia.

As soon as I hear from New York, I will communicate to you. In the mean time, I should be glad to hear from you. Mr. Crawford's friends will make an effort as long as they adhere to him, to exclude me from the House of Representatives, in the hope that my Western friends will take him, if they can not get me. They utterly deceive themselves. If they accomplish that object, and bring him into the house with Adams and Jackson, to my exclusion, he *can not* be elected. As I have told you before, the north-western States will go for Mr. Adams, if they can not get me. They will vote for no man residing in a slave State but me, and they vote for me because of other and chiefly local considerations, outweighing the slave objections. On that you may depend. Mr. Adams, then, will have the six New England States, and three north-western States, with the chance (and the best chance), for New York (if I am out of the way), New Jersey, Maryland, to say nothing of Alabama, Mississippi, and Louisiana.

MR. CLAY TO FRANCIS BROOKE

WASHINGTON, February 26, 1824.

MY DEAR SIR,—During your sojourn at home, I did not write you any letter except one, which I addressed to you some days ago, at Fredericksburg, with a direction to the post-master at that place, to forward it to you at Richmond, if you had gone thither. I hope it has safely come to hand. I am glad that you have returned to the metropolis. Inclosed, I transmit to you two letters which I have received to-day from New York, which you may return or destroy, after perusing the contents. Other letters, to other persons, have, from Albany, corroborated their statements, and represent, first that Mr. Crawford can not possibly obtain the vote of New York; secondly, that great dissatisfaction prevails at Albany, with such a caucus as was held here, and especially with the person nominated as Vice-President; and thirdly, that there is no contest in New York, but between Mr. Adams and me. Pennsylvania has gone inevitably to Jackson.

MR. CLAY TO FRANCIS BROOKE.

WASHINGTON, March 6, 1824.

MY DEAR SIR,—I have received the three last letters which you have done me the favor to write to me. On the subject to which they relate, there appears to be an eddy at this moment. We shall soon see which way the currents will break out. Information from every quarter assures us that the caucus here has impaired, instead of advancing Mr. Crawford's prospects. The convention at Harrisburg, no doubt, the day before yesterday, recommended General Jackson; and they probably forebore to make any recommendation of a Vice-President; or, if they did make any, I think it was Mr. Calhoun. At Albany they are probably looking to Harrisburg, and waiting for events. It is now believed, that the Senate of New York will reject the Electoral Bill, the committee of that body having made a report against it. But, rest assured, that all inferences derived from that fact in favor of Mr. Crawford are utterly fallacious. He can not obtain the vote of that State.

I concur with you in thinking that my friends at Richmond

and in Virginia ought to avoid, if possible, all misunderstanding with those of Mr. Crawford; and a temperate and conciliatory character would therefore be best to be given to any appeal made to the people in my behalf.

I have just heard that De Witt Clinton has arrived here. I pray you not to think it necessary to answer every letter which I may address to you. I should be glad to hear from you occasionally, and when perfectly convenient.

MR. CLAY TO FRANCIS BROOKE.

WASHINGTON, March 16, 1824.

MY DEAR SIR,—I received your obliging favor of the 14th. The ticket formed by my friends at Richmond, appears to me, upon the whole, to be extremely judicious; and its good effect elsewhere, I think I am not deceived in. The Senate of New York, has by a vote of seventeen to fourteen, postponed the Electoral Bill. The first and most certain effect of that note is to prevent Mr. Clinton from being a candidate; and I have no doubt that that was the principal object with the majority. If there had been a popular election of electors, he would probably have come out, and very likely would have obtained the vote of that State.

The course of Mr. Randolph's friends about Richmond surprises me. My conscience acquits me entirely of all blame toward that gentleman. Throughout all our acquaintance he has ever been the assailant. I have ever been on the defensive. The House of Representatives has ever taken part with me, and against him, in every collision that I ever had with him.

JAMES MADISON TO MR. CLAY.

MONTPELIER, April 24, 1824.

DEAR SIR,—I have received a copy of your speech on "American Industry" for which I pray you to accept my thanks. I find in it a full measure of the ability and eloquence so often witnessed on preceding occasions. But while doing this justice to the task you have performed, which I do with pleasure as well as sincerity, candor obliges me to add that I can not concur in the extent to which the pending bill carries the tariff, nor in some of the reasoning by which it is advocated.

The bill, I think, loses sight too much of the general principle which leaves to the judgment of individuals the choice of profitable employments for their labor and capital; and the arguments in favor of it drawn from the aptitudes of our situation for manufacturing establishments, tend to show that these would take place without a Legislative interference. The law would not say to the cotton-planter, you overstock the market, and ought to plant tobacco; and to the planter of tobacco you would do better by substituting wheat. It presumes that profit being the object of each, as the profit of each is the wealth of the whole, each will make whatever change the state of the markets and prices may require. We see, in fact, changes of this sort frequently produced in agricultural pursuits by individual sagacity watching over individual interest. And why not trust to the same guidance in favor of manufacturing industry, whenever it promises more profit than any of the agricultural branches; or more than mercantile pursuits, from which we see capital readily transferred to manufacturing establishments likely to yield a greater income?

With views of the subject such as this, I am a friend to the general principle of "free industry" as the basis of a sound system of political economy. On the other hand, I am not less a friend to the legal patronage of domestic manufactures, as far as they come within particular reasons for exceptions to the general rule, not derogating from its generality. If the friends of the tariff, some of them at least, maintain opinions subversive of the rule, there are among its opponents views taken of the subject which would exclude the fair exceptions to it.

For examples of these exceptions I take, first, the case of articles necessary for national defense. Second, articles of a use too indispensable to be subjected to foreign contingences. Third, cases where there may be sufficient certainty that a *temporary* encouragement will introduce a particular manufacture, which, once introduced, would flourish without that encouragement. That there are such cases is proved by the cotton manufacture, introduced by the impulse of the war and the patronage of the law, without which it might not for a considerable time have effectually sprung up. It must not be forgotten, however, that the great success in this case was owing to the advantage enjoyed in the raw material, and to the extraordinary abridgment of manual labor by mechanical agency. Fourth, a very important exception results from the frequency of wars among the manufacturing nations, the effect of a state of war on the prices of their manufactures, and the improbability that domestic substitutes will be provided by establishments which could not outlast occasions of such uncertain duration. I have not noticed any particular reference to this consideration in the discussions which have been published, the greater cheapness of imported fabrics being assumed from their cost in times of peace. Yet it is clear that if a yard of imported cloth, which costs but six dollars in peace, costs eight dollars in war, and the two periods should be, as for the last two centuries taken together they have been, nearly equal, a tax of nearly one dollar a yard in time of peace could be afforded by the consumer, in order to escape the tax imposed by the event of war.

Without looking for other exceptions to the general principle restraining legislative interferences with the industrious pursuits of individuals, those specified give sufficient scope for a moderate tariff that would at once answer the purpose of revenue and foster domestic manufactures.

With respect to the operation of the projected tariff, I am led to believe that it will disappoint the calculations both of its friends and of its adversaries. The latter will probably find that the increase of duty on articles which will be but partially manufactured at home, with the annual increment of consumers, will balance at least the loss to the Treasury from the diminution of the tariffed imports; while the sanguine hopes of the former will be not less frustrated by the increase of smuggling, particularly through our east and north frontiers, and by the attraction of the laboring class to the vacant territory. This is the great obstacle to the spontaneous establishment of manufactures, and will be overcome with most difficulty wherever land is cheapest, and the ownership of it most attainable.

The tariff, I apprehend, will disappoint also those who expect it to put an end to unfavorable balances of trade. Our imports, as is justly observed, will not be short of our exports. They will probably exceed them. We are accustomed to buy not only as much as we can pay for, but as much more as can be obtained on credit. Until we change our habits, therefore, or manufacture the articles of luxury as well as the useful articles, we shall be apt to be in arrears, to a certain extent, in our foreign dealings, and have the exchange bearing against us. As long as our exports consist chiefly of food and raw materials, we shall have the advantage, in a contest of privations, over a nation supplying us with superfluities. But in the ordinary freedom of intercourse, the advantage will be on the other side; the wants on that being limited by the nature of them, and on ours as boundless as fancy and fashion.

Excuse a letter which I fear is much too long, and be assured of my great esteem and sincere regard.

P. S. Mrs. Madison desires me to offer the proper return for the kind wishes expressed in your note introducing Mr. Ten Eyck, who with his companion made the time very agreeable which they passed with us.

MR. CLAY TO FRANCIS BROOKE.

WASHINGTON, May 19, 1824.

MY DEAR SIR,—I duly received your favor of the 16th inst. I did not become acquainted with Colonel Gooch while he was here. An incident that occurred may serve to explain the charge to which you refer. It is the duty of the Speaker to admit stenographers. Mr. Stevenson said to me, "Colonel Gooch is here, and probably would like to take down the debates, etc., for the "Enquirer" during his stay, but I am not authorized to apply for his admission." I replied, if Colonel Gooch wants a seat within the hall, *bonâ fide* for that purpose, he shall be admitted; but that I could not consent to his admission merely to give him a comfortable place, without reference to the duties of a stenographer. Mr. Stevenson said he should advise him not to apply, etc. He did not make an application. I afterward understood that he complained; but I was also told that, after an explanation with Mr. Stevenson, he left here entirely satisfied with my conduct.

I inclose you the extract of a letter which has been sent me from New York, respecting a contemplated call of the Legislature. I have very little doubt that such a measure has been determined on, and will take place, unless the Governor changes his intention. If my efforts on the tariff have injured me in Virginia, they have benefited me in other quarters.

MR. CLAY TO FRANCIS BROOKE.

WASHINGTON, May 28, 1824.

MY DEAR SIR,—The state of Mr. Crawford's health is such as scarcely to leave a hope of his recovery. It is said that he has sustained a paralytic stroke. His friends begin to own that his death is now but too probable, and that in any event he can no longer be held up for the presidency.

I conjecture that a visit which Mr. Van Buren and Governor Dickinson, of New Jersey, are about to make to Virginia, is connected with this circumstance, and that they are about to take measures for a fresh campaign. I thought, prior to my departure to-morrow, I would put you in possession of these matters.

Be pleased to make my best respects to Mr. Call, and believe me ever faithfully your friend.

SIR JAMES MACKINTOSH TO MR. CLAY.

LONDON, June 3, 1824.

MY DEAR SIR,—This note will be presented to you by Mr. Stanley, a grandson of the Earl of Derby, a young gentleman who has already shown in Parliament talents equally brilliant and solid, and whom I can hardly be mistaken in considering as destined to perform a great part in the public affairs of this country. He is accompanied by three other gentlemen, one of whom (Mr. Wortley) I know and highly value, and the other two I know to be most respectable. I know that you will consider this first visit of such a body of English travelers to the United States as an event which ought to interest and gratify the friends of both countries. I hope that I may venture to ask your good offices in guiding the inquiry and aiding the observation of Mr. Stanley, and in procuring access for him and his friends to those individuals and societies which may afford them sufficient specimens of the great English commonwealth in which you perform so distinguished a part.

The enlightened curiosity of Mr. Stanley will direct his comprehensive understanding to your laws, and government, and manners; to the state of industry, wealth, and knowledge, and to the effect of all those on the virtue and happiness of the people

There is no one more able than yourself to aid him in so difficul a study. I intended to have taken the same liberty with Mr. Adams and Mr. Crawford. But I am so very much hurried (besides being indisposed) at this moment, that I am reduced to the necessity of requesting that you would introduce Mr. Stanley to them as holding the first place among those who are the hope of this country. After this sincere testimony to his extraordinary merit, it is, perhaps, presumptuous in me to add that I should consider their attention to him as a most pleasing mark that they have not forgotten the degree in which I have had the pleasure of enjoying their society.

MR. CLAY TO J. S. JOHNSTON.

ASHLAND, June 15, 1824.

DEAR SIR,—I transmit you the inclosed just as I have received it. The person who writes it (and whose acquaintance I would like you to make, if convenient) became known to me at Columbus, in Ohio, in January, 1823. He traveled with Judge Burnett and myself from that place to Wheeling, and interested us both by the variety and extent of his information, particularly in regard to characters now on the stage. He subsequently manifested a good deal of zeal in my behalf, and has frequently written me letters, to which I have sometimes replied, respectfully but cautiously. If the communication from Mr. ——— is to be considered in the nature of an overture, there can be but one answer given. I can make no promises of office, of any sort, to any one, upon any condition whatever. Whatever support shall be given to me, if any, must be spontaneous and unbought. I can not but believe that Mr. ———'s friend must have allowed his zeal to cary him further than was authorized.

We have nothing new in this quarter. All that we believed in respect to the favorable disposition toward me is well founded.

Be pleased to make my best respects to Mrs. Johnston.

N. B. The endorsement on the letter, supposed to be by Mr. Johnston, is—" Mr. ——— wanted a foreign embassy."

MR. CLAY TO J. S. JOHNSTON.

ASHLAND, June 21, 1824.

DEAR SIR,—I received your obliging favor of the 7th instant from Philadelphia, with the proclamation of the Governor of New York inclosed. I was of course prepared to expect that measure, the only effect of which will be, should the Legislature pass the proposed law, to place the vote of that State to some candidate other than Mr. Crawford.

We have nothing new at the West, where I find every thing to be as I expected. You will see candidates announced for election in this State for Mr. Adams, General Jackson, etc. This is the result of the absence of all sort of concert by means of caucuses, or other nominating appendages in Kentucky. Every body who chooses puts himself forward as a candidate. The State is divided into three districts, according to which it has given its electoral vote for many years past. No change was made in consequence of one of its own citizens being brought forward, because it was known that no change was necessary to insure him the entire vote of the State. Nor is there a county, parish, or a respectable neighborhood in the whole State, in which he would not obtain the majority over all competition. In Ohio, Indiana, and Illinois, as well as in Missouri, the result I believe to be equally certain. I shall go to Columbus to attend the Federal Court, which begins there on the second Monday in July. Should you write to me at any time after the receipt of this letter, and before the 20th of July, be pleased to address me at that place. I am anxious to see the indications, which will shortly be given at the South, of the dispositions of Mr. Crawford's friends, should he be withdrawn, of which I do not doubt, sooner or later. My interest, I think, will be benefited by his being continued to be held up for some time to come. The tariff fever will have then somewhat abated. My respectful compliments to Mrs. Johnston.

LORD GAMBIER TO MR. CLAY.

IVER GROVE, June 29, 1824.

MY DEAR SIR,—I had great pleasure in receiving your very friendly letter by the hand of the worthy Bishop Chase, and in hearing of your well being from him. I have found him, as you truly describe him, a learned, pious, and highly estimable clergyman; he passed a few days with me here, on his first arrival in this country, and I have had much agreeable communication with him since that time; he gains the esteem and affection of all persons with whom he has become acquainted, he is highly respected, and has been received with great kindness wherever he has gone, and I am happy to say he has been very successful in the important object of his visit in this country. I very much regret that he is under the necessity of returning so soon to his diocese; but he leaves an excellent Christian savour among the good and pious of our land. I hope we shall add more to the collection that has been made for the good and laudable work in which he is so piously and zealously engaged.

It is a cause of great satisfaction to me that so much success has attended the good Bishop's visit to this country, for I greatly rejoice on every occasion that in any way promotes mutual friendship and good will between the people of our two countries.

I feel very sensibly the kind and friendly expressions in your letter, toward me, and happy in every opportunity of assuring you of my high esteem and sincere regard.

BISHOP CHASE TO MR. CLAY.

WORTHINGTON, October 14, 1824.

MY DEAR SIR,—I have delayed, I fear, far beyond the proper period, forwarding to you the inclosed letter from Lord Gambier. My apology is the very sincere wish I have all along entertained of a personal interview, on the subject of which I presumed the letter treated, namely, his lordship's great regard for you, and the essential service, of which your letter to him, proved to me.

I wished also to see you (perhaps at the United States Court), that I might assign the reasons and obtain your pardon, for using your name as the umpire, in a certain deed of donation of my estate to the contemplated Theological Seminary, for the education of young men for the Christian ministry. As it is, I can only send you a copy of that instrument; and to it beg your favorable attention.

The meeting of our Convention takes place, in Chillicothe, on the 3d of November next. Nothing of the kind could give me more pleasure, than to see you there, if business or the great importance to posterity of our plans should so incline you.

Your very sincere friend, Charles Hammond, who has been of such essential service in the great work of founding this Seminary will be there, and, as I trust, assist us with his most valuable advice. Pray communicate with him on the subject any thing which you think will do us good.

I take the liberty of sending you a letter addressed to Lord Kenyon, on the subject of my errand to England. Presuming you have seen what has preceded this, no apology is deemed necessary.

MR. CLAY TO J. S. JOHNSTON.

COLUMBUS, Ohio, July 21, 1824.

DEAR SIR,—Your favor under date at Philadelphia on the 27th of June, has followed me from Lexington to this place. I thank you for it. The position which it portrays of the condition of things in New York, compared with other modes of ascertaining its correctness, I should suppose faithful. It certainly offers every motive to animated and persevering exertion. I concur with you in thinking, that the appearance in my favor of two papers you have mentioned, as being willing so to come out, would be advantageous. On their part, it is perfectly voluntary. They are unbought. No imputation of that kind could possibly be made. None can be made against me, either of Clintonian or Federal taint. Or if such imputations were made they would not be credited by the unbiased or impartial, who must compose a large portion of the American population.

Before I came to this State, popular meetings in various counties had been held. Some have occurred since I entered it. The evidence derivable from their expression of preference among the presidential candidates, places beyond all sort of doubt the final result here.

I shall leave this place to-morrow, for Lexington.

J. S. JOHNSTON TO MR. CLAY.

NEW YORK, August 19, 1824.

DEAR SIR,—There is little feeling in New England for Adams. The ultra Federalists hate him, the moderate feel indifference, the Republicans are not cordial. He is supported merely on sectional grounds. But strange—the ultras will join the radicals—the extremes meet.

General Lafayette has been received with distinguished honors, and departed this morning for Boston. His whole journey will be a procession. What a glorious reward! I shall leave here in a few days for Philadelphia, where I think it important to be.

MR. CLAY TO J. S. JOHNSTON.

ASHLAND, August 31, 1824.

DEAR SIR,—Your obliging favor of the 9th inst., dated at Saratoga, and those subsequently at New York, have all safely arrived. They reached Lexington during my absence on a short excursion to one of our watering-places, from which I am but just returned.

I concur with you in thinking that, considering all the combinations that may arise, and the contingences that may happen, my friends ought to persevere in their support of me. That, I believe, is the course which they have determined on generally. And I think the six States heretofore supposed to be disposed to support me, may still be relied on. You have no doubt heard from Louisiana. Your Governor elect passed through Lexington, and I presume you will have seen him. The information derived from him and other sources, assures us of the unaltered state of Louisiana, although in the city of New Orleans, the Jackson ticket prevailed in the greater part. Those opposed to me in that State, admit a plurality of the Legislature to be for me, while my friends confidently claim the majority. What is most to be apprehended, is, that my friends in the West, or at least in some of the more doubtful States, may become discouraged by the little prospect of my being supported to any extent in the East, and especially by the statements in the "National Intelligencer," and other papers, according to which it would seem that I have not a friend in the New York Legislature.

The anticipated coalition in New York, I should suppose was very probable, unless it should be prevented by the apprehension of the imputation of corruption, bargaining, etc. Perhaps there may be nerve enough to encounter all the odium of those imputations, considering the quarter from which they must emanate. If there be a majority of the Legislature who prefer either of two candidates to a third, there is surely reason in an equal division of its vote between those two. The effect of such a division would doubtless be to exclude the third from the House of Representatives, and it would lead to the election of one or the other of them most certainly. In the actual state of the circumstances of the election, New York would have two strings to her bow by dividing her suffrage, and more certainly secure influence in the new administration, than by risking her whole vote upon one of the candidates, since, if she were so to concentrate it, she could not be sure of effecting his election.

What about the Vice-President? Is New York desirous of electing Mr. Sanford? Has he any, and what interest there? In Ohio there is a strong disposition to elect a Vice-President from New York, and Mr. Sanford has been favorably brought forward there. Here, also, his name has been advantageously announced to the public, and there would not be the slightest difficulty in his obtaining the votes of both States, and probably of the other States inclined to give me their suffrages.

Be pleased to present my respects to Mrs. Johnston, and believe me faithfully and cordially your friend.

J. S. JOHNSTON TO MR. CLAY.

PHILADELPHIA, September 1, 1824.

DEAR SIR,—I now hand you the letter of General M'Clure which I promised you in my last, when I handed you the printed letter.

I purposely avoided seeing General M'Clure at Albany, satisfied it was better for Rochester to communicate with him than me, and that the objects and views of your friends are better accomplished by a corresponding committee. Besides, I was told your friends were as firm and stanch as was necessary; and, from the tone and tenor of this letter, I have no doubt. I will now write to all of them, and let them understand distinctly the views taken of the state of your interests in New York.

* * * * * * * *

MR. CLAY TO J. S. JOHNSTON.

ASHLAND, September 19, 1824.

MY DEAR SIR,—I received to-day your favor under date the 4th, with its inclosures, as I did your former letters, including General M'Clure's letter. I thank you for them. I have directed twenty copies of the circular prepared by the Kentucky Committee of Correspondence (which I have not seen), to be forwarded to you for distribution. Copies have also been ordered to most of our friends in Philadelphia and New York. Although I have not perused it, I presume, from the pen from which it issues, that it is well composed. An address from the same quarter has been written to Virginia, intended for that region, but so guarded as to do mischief nowhere, if it be published, which is to be anticipated. These papers will, I think, contribute to arouse and animate my friends. The remark which you make is but too true, that there has not been sufficient united exertion among them. Every thing is yet going well in the West. It is amazing to see the mistakes or misstatements made about it at the East. For example: Stratten was said to be elected in Missouri, and was claimed by the " Franklin Gazette" for General Jackson. No, says the " National Journal," although he is elected, we *know* he is for Mr. Adams. Now, it turns out that Scott is elected, and that Stratten declared himself for me.

MR. CLAY TO J. S. JOHNSTON.

ASHLAND, September 3, 1824.

DEAR SIR,—I duly received your obliging favor of the 19th ultimo, under date at New York, transmitting a letter from Mr. Ingalls, from whom I had previously received a duplicate. I did not, however, answer his letter. Eight months ago, I supposed there would be no difficulty in my election as Vice-President, if my friends had thought it advisable to press me for that office. It would now be extremely difficult, if not impracticable, to effect that object, if it were desirable. My friends in the West do not attach any very great, perhaps not sufficient, importance to that station ; and it would be, I apprehend, nearly impossible now to induce them to divert their support of me from the first to the second office. And if they could be prevailed on to do it, the electoral colleges would hardly be induced, by any possible exertion, to unite their individual suffrages on any other candidate for the Presidency. There could, therefore, be no support secured for me in the Atlantic States for the Vice-Presidency, if it depended on concert among my Western friends, in regard to the office of President. And consequently, if I received any, it must be spontaneous, without reference to the direction which my interest would take as to the Presidency. If my Eastern friends think proper to bring me forward for the office of Vice-President, I wish it distinctly understood, that it is their own movement, unprompted by me. If an idea were taken up that the office was sought by me, after all that has occurred, it could not fail to be injurious to me. It would be said to display a most inordinate desire for office, which I certainly am not conscious of feeling. It would not look well, in any respect, if it were supposed that I was instrumental in the attempt to elect me. It is certainly a high and dignified office, such as no American citizen could readily decline.

With respect to the movement in Massachusetts to which Mr. Ingalls refers, while I concur with you entirely in the state of public feeling in New England toward Mr. Adams, I do not believe that there is the smallest prospect of diverting the vote of Massachusetts from him. There may be some probability of such a diversion in other States of that section, but none whatever, I apprehend, in Massachusetts. Depend upon it, that local pride, if not attachment, will secure to each of the candidates the support of his own State, doubtless with more opposition in some instances than in others. It would, therefore, be an act of extreme indiscretion, justified by no motive whatever, for me, or for any of my friends out of Massachusetts, to say to Mr. Ingalls, and to those who are co-operating with him, that I am willing to give up all pretensions to the office of President, and to be contented with that of Vice-President.

By the by, it has been said here that a feeling is prevailing in some of the Atlantic cities to make the Marquis Lafayette Vice-President. Such a disposition of the office would be highly creditable to the national gratitude, if it could be made without any constitutional impediment.

I do not anticipate much from the Philadelphia meeting. It is a little remarkable, that my support of the tariff has excited against me, in the South, a degree of opposition which is by no means counterbalanced by any espousal of my cause in Pennsylvania and other quarters, where the tariff was so much desired. Is this owing to the greater activity which the losing party almost always displays than the gaining?

I expect every day that the Committee of Correspondence, appointed by the Legislature of the State, will prepare their general circular, as suggested in my last. A copy of it shall be forwarded to you. Do you correspond with General Peter B. Porter? His residence is Black Rock.

I can not close without expressing to you my thanks for the zeal and interest which you manifest in my favor; nor without adding, that you have fulfilled entirely all my expectations as to the discretion which you would manifest.

J. S. JOHNSTON TO MR. CLAY.

PHILADELPHIA, September 4, 1824.

DEAR SIR,—I attended a meeting of your friends, to wit, Mr. Carey and son, Mr. Hemphill, Mr. Tilman, Mr. Wharton, Dr. Chapman, Dr. Godman, Mr. Edward Ingersoll, etc., to consult about the meeting of your friends. It was called without their knowledge. They determined to postpone the meeting until this day week. Mr. Carey consents to be chairman. A committee of correspondence will be organized, and delegates appointed. I have no doubt the meeting will be numerous and respectable. This State might have been secured at a proper time, and this State would have *secured you*. Your affairs have been trusted to providence. I send you two letters from Boston. I hope you have received General M'Clure's.

The friends of Crawford are still very anxious to make you Vice-President. Mr. Elliot often speaks of it; it is much a subject of correspondence among them. They count confidently upon most of your votes in that event. They say Gallatin would not be in the way.

MR. CLAY TO J. S. JOHNSTON.

ASHLAND, September 10, 1824.

MY DEAR SIR,—In respect to the Vice-Presidency, I wrote you some days ago. When my name was brought forward seriously, I resolved neither to offer nor to accept any arrangement in regard to myself, or to office for others. I have adhered to that resolution hitherto, and shall continue to abide by it to the last. I considered that I was and ought to be in the hands of the public, to be disposed of as it pleased. Most undoubtedly the office of Vice-President is one of high respectability and great dignity, preferable, in my opinion, to any place in the cabinet. If the acceptance of it were offered to me (I mean by the public having the right to tender it), I could not decline it; but I can not seek it, much less make any sacrifices of honor or duty to obtain it.

J. S. JOHNSTON TO MR. CLAY.

PHILADELPHIA, September 26, 1824.

DEAR SIR,—I have read with pleasure and with attention your favor of the 10th September. We agree in every particular with regard to the Vice-Presidency. You can not change your position, and your friends are not disposed. You must abide the issue. I have uniformly given the same reply. It was a strange idea of Crawford's friends to count on the Western States by your withdrawal. I have often explained that to them; they now see and feel the truth. The object of Crawford's friends *now* will be to put down Adams, and, if possible, to prevent his being returned, under the idea that his being withdrawn, the New England States will vote for him.

We receive General Lafayette to-morrow. The concourse of people here is very great. The preparations are very expensive and very grand.

I presume he will be received by both Houses in the center building.

There is no idea of making him Vice-President.

MR. CLAY TO J. S. JOHNSTON.

ASHLAND, October 2, 1824.

MY DEAR SIR,—I duly received your favor of the 16th and 19th ult., with the Philadelphia address. I also received one or two preceding letters from you, which I have not before acknowledged the receipt of.   *   *   *   *   *

Mr. Holley, just returned from an Eastern trip, saw Mr. Crawford about a fortnight ago, at Fredericktown, on his return from the Springs. He says that his gait, articulation, and general appearance indicated most clearly the paralysis under which he has labored, and that he appeared to be much more infirm than Mr. Jefferson at the age of eighty-two, whom he also saw.

I thank you for your kind admonition about the uncertainty as to the pending election, and the utility of repressing a too great anxiety. I hope you will not, as you seem to anticipate, have any occasion for philosophical exertion on account of your own election.   *   *   *   *   .*   *

I have some thought of passing through Virginia, and visiting Mr. Jefferson, Mr. Madison, and Governor Barbour.

———— TO FRANCIS BROOKE.

ALBANY, November 17, 1824.

SIR,—I have taken the liberty to address you, as a known friend of Mr. Clay, for the purpose of stating to you, in a frank and unreserved manner, the course of conduct pursued by the friends of Mr. Clay toward those of Mr. Crawford, in the choice of presidential electors. I trust, for my apology, that the subject will excuse my addressing you, without the pleasure of a personal acquaintance.

You will probably have learned the result by the time this reaches you, and will also have learned that twenty-five Adams electors have been chosen by the co-operation of Mr. Clay's friends in the Legislature. It appears to me that a full eqplanation is due from the friends of Mr. Clay in New York, to the friends of Mr. Crawford in Virginia, for this course. It is true that the friends of Mr. Clay had a perfect right to choose between Mr. Crawford and Mr. Adams; but it is also true, that a majority of the friends of Mr. Clay were disposed to take up

Mr. Crawford as their second choice, if, from any unforeseen contingency, the former should be withdrawn from the contest. With this feeling they came to Albany, and the same feeling led them to go into caucus with the friends of Mr. Crawford, at the commencement of the session. They were resolved to support Mr. Clay, because they preferred him, and because they really knew that he was the choice of three fourths of the democratic party, among the people. This led them, in caucus, to assert his claims with great zeal and force. But numbers was the only reply they received. The friends of Mr. Crawford had a majority in caucus, and though neither party had the majority in the Legislature, they, the friends of Mr. Crawford, thought proper to insist that the friends of Mr. Clay should submit to their numbers, and meekly yield to them, instead of consulting their own judgment, and the voice of the State. This was resisted with becoming spirit, and the consequence was, that they were, in effect, expelled from the caucus. They were treated with the most insulting contumely, and threatened with the high displeasure of the set of individuals known here by the name and style of the "Albany Regency."

This unfortunate state of parties was, for some days, productive of no other result than an obstinate adherence, in the House, to the respective candidates. Neither party would yield, and the consequence would have been, that the vote of the State would have been lost. At length, symptoms of respect for public opinion began to be manifested in the ranks of the Crawford party, which alarmed the leaders so much that they determined to set their hopes upon the hazard of a die, and to drive the friends of Mr. Clay to the support of Mr. Crawford. The mode of appointing electors, by our laws, enabled them to make this desperate attempt.

Each House nominates thirty-six electors. They then meet to compare their lists. If they agree, the whole are, of course, chosen; if not, they proceed to choose, from the two lists only, by joint ballot. No name, not on one or the other list, can be voted for. Here, then, the leaders of the Crawford party rashly, and, according to my ideas of honor and rectitude, corruptly and wickedly, determined to vote for the Adams ticket in the lower house, so as to reduce the question to Crawford and Adams. A fouler and more dishonorable piece of management could not, in my estimation, be adopted. They did it, however, and the consequence is as might have been apprehended. The friends of Mr. Clay, indignant at this baseness, voted for the Adams ticket on joint ballot, with the exception of seven Clay men on the Crawford ticket, and by this operation have prostrated the Crawford ticket, in this State, forever. They were forced into this course. They could not, consistently with their respect for themselves and for public opinion, pursue any other. The consequences must rest upon the heads of those who reduced them to that necessity.

I have the honor to be, sir, your obedient servant.

[It is thought proper to suppress the signature over which the above letter was written.]

MR. CLAY TO FRANCIS BROOKE.

HARDIN'S, near CHARLOTTEVILLE, Virginia, November 26, 1824.

MY DEAR SIR,—I felt, in your prompt public contradiction of the letter of Mr. Dayton, stating that my name had been withdrawn as a candidate for the Presidency, a new proof of your friendship, which I have ever so highly valued, and at the same time a self-reproach for my not having written to you since the adjournment of Congress. The truth is, that in the first letter which I received from you, after I reached home, you stated your intention to visit the watering places, and I did not well know where to address you; and the last which you did me the favor to write, was received but a few days before I sat out on this journey. I concluded, therefore, to defer the pleasure of writing you until I passed the mountains.

Your prediction has been well nigh verified as to General Jackson's taking the Western vote from me. My friends have prevailed over him in Ohio by only about seven or eight hundred votes.

Events on this side of the mountains have surprised me, particularly in New York, and North Carolina; in the former State especially. I know not the secret springs which have produced such a strange result as has occurred in New York. I have moved none of them. I know nothing but what we see in the public prints. From those it is evident, that, if the friends of Mr. Crawford and myself had all amicably co-operated, the vote of that State might have been secured to one or the other, or been divided between us. I am uninformed of what prevented that contest.

I propose visiting Mr. Jefferson to-morrow, and afterward Mr. Madison. I shall remain a day or two with each of them, and expect to reach Fredericksburg on my way to the city of Washington, on the 2d or 3d of December.

MR. CLAY TO FRANCIS BROOKE.

WASHINGTON, December 5, 1824.

MY DEAR SIR,—Your favor of the 29th October, addressed to me at Lexington, not finding me there, has returned and been duly received by me here. Events subsequent to its date render it unnecessary for me to say any thing in regard to Mr. Ritchie's communication about the Vice-Presidency. I have also received your obliging letter of the first instant. I had before learned the issue of the electoral vote of Virginia. I was prepared to expect it by all that I had previously observed. Two weeks ago a course might have been taken which would probably have prevented that result of the Presidential election now most likely to happen; and that was to have prevailed upon Mr. Crawford to withdraw, which might have been done, I should suppose, without mortification to his friends, by placing it on the ground of the continued precarious state of his health. As it is, I shall yield a cheerful acquiescence in the public decision. I should indeed have been highly gratified if my native State had thought me worthy of even a second place in her confidence and affection. The obligations and respect which I owe her forbid my uttering one word of complaint on account of her having thought otherwise.

Mr. Calhoun deserves all that you say of him. He is a most captivating man.

MR. CLAY TO FRANCIS BROOKE.

WASHINGTON, December 22, 1824.

MY DEAR SIR,—I received your letter by your son, and had great pleasure in furnishing him with a letter of introduction to Commodore Rogers.

I have also received that of the 21st instant, and will examine the claim to which it refers, with all the prepossessions which arise from your opinion, and my high regard to you.

The result in Louisiana did not surprise or affect me. There was much misfortune attending it nevertheless.   *   *   * We must not despair of the Republic. Our institutions, if they have the value which we believe them to possess, and are worth preserving, will sustain themselves, and we shall yet do well.

A bill passed the House of Representatives to-day (166 to 26) giving to Lafayette $200,000 and a township of land.

CHAPTER III.

CORRESPONDENCE OF 1825 AND 1826.

MR. CLAY TO FRANCIS P. BLAIR.

WASHINGTON, January 8, 1825.

MY DEAR SIR,—My position in relation to the friends of the three returned candidates is singular enough, and often to me very amusing. In the first place they all believe that my friends have the power of deciding the question, and then that I have the power of controlling my friends. Acting upon this supposition, in the same hour, I am sometimes touched gently on the shoulder by a friend, for example, of General Jackson, who will thus address me, " My dear Sir, all my dependence is upon you, don't disappoint us, you know our partiality was for you next to the hero; and how much we want a Western President." Immediately after a friend of Mr. Crawford will accost me, " The hopes of the Republican party are concentrated on you, for God's sake preserve it. If you had been returned, instead of Mr. Crawford, every man of us would have supported you to the last hour. We consider him and you as the only genuine Republican candidates." Next a friend of Mr. Adams comes with tears in his eyes,* " Sir, Mr. Adams has always had the greatest respect for you, and admiration of your talents. There is no station to which you are not equal. Most undoubtedly you are the second choice of New England, and I pray you to consider seriously whether the public good and your own future interests do not point most distinctly to the choice which you ought to make." How can one withstand all this disinterested homage and kindness ? Really the friends of all three gentlemen

* A playful allusion to a notable fact. It is all playful, though true.

are so very courteous and affectionate that I sometimes almost wish that it was in my power to accommodate each of them, but that being impossible, we are beginning to think seriously of the choice which we must finally make. I will tell you then that I believe the contest will be limited to Mr. Adams and General Jackson. Mr. Crawford's personal condition precludes the choice of him if there were no other objection to his election. As the only alternative which is presented to us it is sufficiently painful, and I consider whatever choice we may make will be only a choice of evils. To both of those gentlemen there are strong personal objections. The principal difference between them is that in the election of Mr. Adams we shall not by the example inflict any wound upon the character of our institutions, but I should much fear hereafter, if not during the present generation, that the election of the General would give to the military spirit a stimulus and a confidence that might lead to the most pernicious results. I shall, therefore, with great regret on account of the dilemma in which the people have placed us, support Mr. Adams. My friends are generally so inclined. What has great weight with me is the decided preference which a majority of the delegation from Ohio has for him over General Jackson. If, therefore, Kentucky were to vote for the General it would probably only have the effect of dividing our friends, without defeating ultimately the election of Mr. Adams. Three of the four States favorable to Mr. Crawford are believed to prefer Mr. Adams to the General. Virginia is one of them. I am inclined to think that nearly three-fourths of our delegation have yielded to the influence of these views, and will vote for Mr. Adams. My friends entertain the belief that their kind wishes toward me will in the end be more likely to be accomplished by so bestowing their votes. I have, however, most earnestly entreated them to throw me out of their consideration in bringing their judgments to a final conclusion, and to look and be guided solely by the public good. If I know myself, that alone has determined me. Your Representative is inclined to concur with us in these sentiments and views, and if they should meet your approbation, as I know he has great respect for your opinions, I would be glad if you would by the return mail address a letter to him to strengthen him in his inclination. Be pleased to show this letter to Crittenden alone.

MR. CLAY TO FRANCIS BROOKE.

WASHINGTON, January 28, 1825.

MY DEAR SIR,—My position, in regard to the Presidential election, is highly critical, and such as to leave me no path on which I can move without censure. I have pursued, in regard to it, the rule which I always observe in the discharge of my public duty—I have interrogated my conscience as to what I ought to do, and that faithful guide tells me that I ought to vote for Mr. Adams. I shall fulfill its injunction. Mr. Crawford's state of health, and the circumstances under which he presents himself to the House, appear to me to be conclusive against him. As a friend of liberty, and to the permanence of our institutions, I can not consent, in this early stage of their existence, by contributing to the election of a military chieftain, to give the strongest guaranty that the Republic will march in the fatal road which has conducted every other republic to ruin. I owe to our friendship this frank exposition of my intentions. I am, and shall continue to be, assailed by all the abuse, which partisan zeal, malignity, and rivalry, can invent. I shall risk, without emotion, these effusions of malice, and remain unshaken in my purpose. What is a public man worth, if he will not expose himself, on fit occasions, for the good of his country?

As to the result of the election, I can not speak with absolute certainty; but there is every reason to believe that we shall avoid the dangerous precedent to which I allude.

Be pleased to give my respects to Mr. ———, and believe me always your cordial friend.

MR. CLAY TO FRANCIS P. BLAIR.

WASHINGTON, January 29, 1825.

MY DEAR BLAIR,—I received this morning your very agreeable favor of the 17th instant. A letter from you is always refreshing; and I wish that I could entitle myself to expect them more frequently, by more punctuality and diligence on my part in our correspondence. My last letter informed you of the unction that was unceasingly applied to me by all the returned candidates for the Presidency, or rather their friends. Since then I have avowed my intention to support Mr. Adams, under actual circumstances, and thereupon the oil has been instantly transformed into vinegar. The friends of ———— have turned upon me, and with the most amiable unanimity agree to vituperate me. I am a deserter from democracy; a giant at intrigue; have sold the West—sold myself—defeating General Jackson's election to leave open the Western pretensions that I may hereafter fill them myself—blasting all my fair prospects, etc., etc. To these are added a thousand other of the most gentle and kind, and agreeable epithets and things in the world.

————, who are themselves straining every nerve to elect Jackson that the claims of the West may be satisfied and I be thereby pretermitted, are accusing me of acting on their own principles. The knaves can not comprehend how a man can be honest. They can not conceive that I should have solemnly interrogated my conscience and asked it to tell me seriously what I ought to do. That it should have enjoined me not to establish the dangerous precedent of elevating, in this early stage of the Republic, a military chieftain, merely because he has won a great victory? That it should have told me that a public man is undeserving his station who will not, regardless of aspersions and calumnies, risk himself for his country? I am afraid that you will think me moved by these abuses. Be not deceived. I assure you that I never in my whole life felt more perfect composure, more entire confidence in the resolutions of my judgment, and a more unshakable determination to march up to my duty. And, my dear sir, is there an intelligent and unbiased man who must not, sooner or later, concur with me? Mr. Adams you know well I should never have selected, if at liberty to draw from the whole mass of our citizens for a President. But there is no danger in his elevation now, or in time to come. Not so of his competitor, of whom I can not believe that killing two thousand five hundred Englishmen at New Orleans, qualifies for the various, difficult, and complicated duties of the chief magistracy. I perceive that I am unconsciously writing a sort of defense, which you may possibly think implies guilt. What will be the result? you will ask with curiosity, if not anxiety. I think Mr. Adams must be elected, such is the prevailing opinion. Still I shall not consider the matter as certain until the election is over.

MR. CLAY TO FRANCIS BROOKE.

WASHINGTON, February 4, 1825.

MY DEAR SIR,—I received your obliging letter of the 1st inst. Although my letter, to which it is an answer, was not intended for publication, I would rather that it should be published, and speak for itself, than that its contents should appear through the medium of Mr. Ritchie's representation of them. With regard to its publication, you will be pleased to do as you may think proper. All that I feel anxious about is, that the public should not receive an impression that it was my intention that it should be published.

My condition at this moment is most peculiar. The batteries of some of the friends of every man who would now be President, or who, four or eight years hence, would be President, are directed against me, with only the exception of those of Mr. Adams. Some of the friends of General Jackson, Mr. Crawford, Mr. Calhoun, and Mr. Clinton, with very different ultimate ends, agree for the present to unite in assailing me. The object now is, on the part of Mr. Crawford and General Jackson, to drive me from the course which my deliberate judgment points out; and for the future, on the part of Mr. Clinton and Mr. Calhoun, to remove me as an obstacle to their elevation. They all have yet to learn my character if they suppose it possible to make me swerve from my duty, by any species of intimidation or denunciation. But I did not expect that my old friend Ritchie would join in the general cry. He ought to recollect that he is struggling for a man, I for the country—he to elevate an unfortunate gentleman worn down by disease, I to preserve our youthful institutions from the bane which has destroyed all the republics of the old world. I might have expected, from the patriotism of Thomas Ritchie, that he would have surrendered his personal predilections, and joined with me in the effort to save us from a precedent fraught with the most pernicious consequences. I am so far disappointed: I say it with mortification and regret. But all attempts to make me unite with him, to induce me to give up the defense of our institutions, that we may elect a sick gentleman, who has also been rejected by the great body of the nation, are vain and utterly fruitless. Mr. Ritchie ought to awake, should be himself again, and love Rome more than Cæsar.

I observe what you kindly tell me about the future cabinet. My dear sir, I want no office. When have I shown an avidity for office? In rejecting the mission to Russia, and the department of war under one administration? In rejecting the same department, the mission to England, or any other foreign mission, under the succeeding administration? If Mr. Adams is elected, I know not who will be his cabinet; I know not whether I shall be offered a place in it or not. If there should be an offer, I shall decide upon it, when it may be made according to my sense of duty. But do you not perceive that this denunciation of me, by anticipation, is a part of the common system between the discordant confederates which I have above described? Most certainly, if an office should be offered to me under the new administration, and I should be induced to think that I ought to accept it, I shall not be deterred from accepting it, either by the denunciations of open or secret enemies, or the hypocrisy of pretended friends.

MR. CLAY TO FRANCIS BROOKE.

WASHINGTON, February 10, 1825.

MY DEAR SIR,—I received your letters of the 6th and 8th inst. In the former was inclosed a ten dollar note, about which not one word was contained in your letters. Was it inclosed by mistake? or did you intend that I should apply it to some object for you? Be pleased to instruct me.

The "long agony" was terminated yesterday, and Mr. Adams was elected on the first ballot. Exertions to defeat, and even to defer the result, of the most strenuous kind, were made up to the last moment. Without referring to the issue of the election, the manner in which the whole scene was exhibited in the House of Representatives was creditable to our institutions and to our country.

I have not yet received the "Enquirer," in which my letter has been published. It did not arrive to-day.

MR. CLAY TO FRANCIS BROOKE.

WASHINGTON, February 18, 1825.

MY DEAR SIR,—When the subject of the offer of the Department of State to me was first opened to my congressional friends, there existed among them some diversity of opinion as to the propriety of my accepting it. On the one hand, it was said that, if I took it, that fact would be treated as conclusive evidence of the justice of the imputations which have been made against me; that the House of Representatives was my theater; that the administration would want me there, if it should prove itself worthy of support, more than in the cabinet; and that my own section would not like to see me translated from the legislative hall to the executive departments.

On the other hand, it was urged that, whether I accepted or declined the office, I should not escape severe animadversion; that, in the latter contingency, it would be said that the patriotic Mr. Kremer, by an exposure of the corrupt arrangement, had prevented its consummation; that the very object of propagating the calumny would be accomplished; that, conscious of my own purity of intentions, I ought not to give the weight of a feather to Mr. Kremer's affair; that there would be much difficulty in filling the administration without me; that either of the other candidates, if he had been elected, would have made me the same offer; that it would be said of me that, after having contributed to the election of a President, I thought so ill of him, that I would not take the first place under him; that he was now the constitutional head of the Government, and, as such, I ought to regard him, dismissing any personal objections which I might have heretofore had to him; that I had, perhaps, remained long enough in the House of Representatives; and that my own section could not be dissatisfied with seeing me placed where, if I should prove myself possessed of the requisite attainments, my services might have a more extended usefulness.

On mature consideration, those of my friends who were originally averse to my entering the office, changed their opinion, and I believe they were finally unanimous in thinking that I ought not to hesitate in taking upon myself its duties. Those of Mr. Adams, especially in New England, were alike unanimous, and indeed extremely urgent in their solicitations. Several of Mr. Crawford's friends (Mr. McLane, of Delaware, Mr. Forsythe, Mr. Mangum, etc., etc.), and also some of those of General Jackson, in Pennsylvania, have expressed to me their strong convictions that I ought to accept. The opposition to my acceptance is limited chiefly to the violence of Mr. Calhoun's friends, and to some of those of Mr. Crawford and General Jackson.

From the first, I determined to throw myself into the hands of my friends, and if they advised me to decline the office, not to accept it, but if they thought it was my duty, and for the public interest, to go into it, to do so. I have an unaffected repugnance to any executive employment, and my rejection of the offer, if it were in conformity to their deliberate judgment, would have been more compatible with my feelings, than its acceptance.

But as their advice to me is to accept, I have resolved accordingly, and I have just communicated my final determination to Mr. Adams. I am not yet at liberty to communicate the names of the persons who will fill the other vacant departments; but I will say to you, that they will be Republicans. I entertain a strong belief, and sanguine hopes, that the administration will be conducted upon principles which will entitle it to liberal and general support. An opposition is talked of here; but I regard that as the ebullition of the moment, the natural offspring of chagrin and disappointment. There are elements for faction; none for opposition. Opposition to what? To measures and principles which are yet to be developed! Opposition may follow, it can not precede the unknown measures of administration, without incurring the denomination of faction. Mr. Adams is on his trial. Hear him, and then decide. This is the natural sentiment of every candid and impartial mind. He would not have been my President, if I had been allowed to range at large among the great mass of our citizens, to select a President; but I was not so allowed, and circumscribed as I was, I thought that, under all circumstances, he was the best choice that I could practicably make.

I received your kind letter of the 16th instant, and I am happy to find that your better judgment points to the course which I am about to take. I hope that, on further reflection, my other Richmond friends will probably unite in sentiment with you.

This is not written for publication in whole, or in part, but I request you to show it to Mr. Call, Mr. Leigh, and Mr. Ritchie, who will have the goodness to regard it in the same confidential light.

J. J. CRITTENDEN TO MR. CLAY.

FRANKFORT, Feb. 15, 1825.

DEAR SIR,—We are all waiting with breathless impatience, to know the result of the Presidential election. It was rumored here a few days past, that a coalition had been formed between Jackson and Crawford; that New York, Virginia, etc., follow into its ranks; that it was bearing on irresistibly and triumphantly; and that you and Adams were its destined victims. The mail of last night, however, brought no confirmation of this terrible rising, and we are all settling down again into the opinion which has for some time prevailed here, that Adams is to be the President.

I have seen the abuse that has been heaped upon you in some of the newspapers, and your card in the "Intelligencer." I confess that I feel some apprehension for you. There are about you a thousand desperadoes, political and military, following at the heels of leaders, and living upon expectations, that would think it a most honorable service to fasten a quarrel upon Mr. Clay, and shoot him. And this card of yours, evincing such a spontaneous and uncalculating spirit of gallantry, will be a signal, I fear, for some of these fellows to gather about you, and to endeavor to provoke you to some extremity. For God's sake be upon your guard, at least, as it respects these subalterns. As for the abuse there has been heaped upon you, you may safely regard it as the idle wind that passes by. I expected to hear you vilified. You occupy too lofty and imposing a stand, to escape. You prefer Mr. Adams under existing circumstances, and for that you are calumniated. And so it would equally have been, had you announced your preference for either of the other competitors.

If, notwithstanding your support of Adams, Jackson should be elected, that circumstance would certainly embolden your comparatively few adversaries in this State, and enable them for a little while to excite some petty clamor against you. But no such thing can displace you from the hold you have on the pride and affections of Kentucky. If Adams is elected, and you will accept a station in his cabinet, all will be quieted in a moment. This is my view.

I think I can see the policy which dictates the charges which are now made against you of " going over to Mr. Adams," of having " made your bargain" with him, and of a thousand other horrible conspiracies, etc. It is intended to intimidate you, if possible, from the acceptance of the Department of State which they think Mr. Adams must tender to you, and where they tremble to see you. They wish to obstruct your passage to it by heaping up the way with all the falsehood and calumny they can create and invent. This is the real secret of the whole business, as I think. Whether I am right or wrong, I trust you will hold on your course unshaken and unaltered by all the calumny, falsehood, and scandal of your enemies. It will not be long before it will all recoil on themselves. I think it is due to yourself, to your friends here, and to the expectation and wishes of the State, that you should accept the office of Secretary of State, if it should be offered to you. Some few of your friends think your present station the more elevated and commanding one, and of course that you should retain it. Whatever may be its nominal elevation, its practical importance and power is not to be compared with that of the Department of State. The Chair of the House of Representatives is undoubtedly a very high and lofty station, but all its honors and advantages are of the abstract, fruitless kind, and I am now convinced that no man will live to see the incumbent of that Chair transferred at once to the Presidency. You best know, however, what course to pursue. That it may be a prosperous and happy one, is my earnest wish.

W. CREIGHTON TO MR. CLAY.

CHILLICOTHE, February 19, 1825.

MY DEAR SIR,—I was gratified to learn by the mail of this morning that the long agony is over, and particularly that the contest was terminated on the first ballot. A protracted ballot could not have failed to produce great excitement, both within and without. Here there is entire acquiescence. The inflammable materials artificially excited in Pennsylvania and New York, will soon spend themselves. Thinking it probable, in the event of Mr. Adams' election, you might be invited to the administration, the question propounded in your letter of the 7th instant, is one on which I have thought a great deal this winter, and have endeavored, with the feeble lights I possess, to view it in all its ulterior bearings. Necessarily ignorant of many circumstances that may exist at Washington that may have a bearing, *pro* or *con*, my opinion is, if the offer is made, you ought to accept. This opinion is formed, regardless of the scurrility and abuse that the election has given rise to. If a man could suffer himself to be driven from his purpose by means like these, he would always be at the mercy of the profligate and unprincipled. In the expression of this opinion, it is taken for granted that Mr. Adams will pursue a liberal policy, and embrace within its scope the great leading policy that you have been advocating. By uniting with such an Administration, you could not be charged, by the most fastidious, with a dereliction of principle for place.

I could not, within the compass of a letter, detail my reasons for the opinion expressed, and therefore shall not attempt it. Should the invitation be given, your friends in Ohio will acquiesce in whatever decision you make.

Will our friend Cheves be invited to the Treasury?

MR. CLAY TO FRANCIS BROOKE.

WASHINGTON, March 4, 1825.

MY DEAR SIR,—I have the gratification to tell you that all my information from the West bespeaks a satisfied state of the public mind, in relation to the result of the late election. In Ohio the approbation of it is enthusiastic. In Kentucky, too, the expression of public opinion evinces general acquiescence.

I transmit to you, inclosed, two letters, which are from Crittenden and Creighton, two of the most discreet men in Ohio and Kentucky. Be pleased to show them to Mr. Pleasants.

JOHN TYLER TO MR. CLAY

CHARLES CITY, March 27, 1825.

DEAR SIR,—In the midst of the numerous accusations which have of late been urged against you from different quarters, and from none with more acrimony than from the seat of Government of this State, I have deemed it proper, and in some measure called for, to make known to you that one of the million at least, still regarded you as I am satisfied you deserve to be regarded. Instead of seeing in your course on the late presidential question aught morally or politically wrong, I am on the contrary fully impressed with the belief that the United States owes you a deep debt of gratitude for that course, resulting as it did in the speedy settlement of that distracting subject. Believing Mr. Crawford's chance of success to have been utterly desperate, you have not only met my wishes (which would be to you of little concern), but I do believe, the wishes and feelings of a large majority of the people of this your native State. I do not believe that the sober and reflecting people of Virginia would have been so far dazzled by military renown as to have conferred their suffrages upon a mere soldier—one acknowledged on all hands to be of little value as a civilian. I will not withhold from you also the expression of my approval of your acceptance of your present honorable and exalted station. To have refused it would have been to have furnished your enemies with fresh ground of objection. Against an insiduous and malicious attack you courted an investigation not only before the Representatives of the people, but by accepting the office, before the Senate, and gave just evidence of your purity by your readiness to encounter your accusers, supported as they were by the virulence and intemperance of party feeling on the part of some of your very judges. For a time the tide may run against you, but when the ferment, excited by the feelings of the day, shall have subsided, and men shall regard things with unprejudiced eyes, your motives and your acts will be justly appreciated and the plaudits of your country will await you. This is not the language of flattery to one lifted high in authority. As an American citizen I claim to be your equal. It is the voluntary offering of truth at the shrine of patriotism, and is called for by the circumstance of our having been, in times past, fellow laborers in the same vineyard of our common country, although I was at the time an unprofitable servant. When one, however, is assailed by unjust reproaches, the expression of confidence from a quarter even the most humble and the most retired can not but be acceptable. It is under the influence of this feeling and of this belief that I have thus ventured to address you.

I pray you to accept assurances of my sincere regard and unshaken confidence.

CHIEF JUSTICE MARSHALL TO MR. CLAY.

RICHMOND, April 4, 1825.

DEAR SIR,—I have received your address to your former constituents; and, as it was franked by you, I presume I am indebted to you for it. I have read it with great pleasure as well as attention, and am gratified at the full and complete view you have given of some matters which the busy world has been employing itself upon. I required no evidence respecting the charge made by Mr. Kremer, nor should I have required any had I been unacquainted with you or with the transaction, because I have long since ceased to credit charges destitute of proof, and to consider them as mere aspersions. The minuteness of detail, however, will enable your friends to encounter any insinuations on that subject which may be thrown out in their hearing. More of this may be looked for than any hostility to you would produce. There is unquestionably a party determined to oppose Mr. Adams at the next election, and this party will attack him through you. It is an old, and has been a successful stratagem. No part of your letter was more necessary than that which respects your former relations with that gentleman.

MR. CLAY TO FRANCIS BROOKE.

WASHINGTON, April 6, 1825.

MY DEAR SIR,—From your letter of the 5th instant, which I this day received, I perceive you are at home, and not at Richmond, to which I had transmitted to you one of my addresses to my constituents. The favorable opinion entertained of it by such early and valuable friends as yourself and Nicholas, is highly gratifying. Among other similar testimonies from Richmond, I have received, from the Chief Justice, a very satisfactory letter. Prior to the publication of my address, Mr. Tyler wrote me a letter, approving of my course (since he believed Mr. Crawford to have been out of the question), and declaring, in strong terms, his unabated confidence in me. From all quarters, in short, information is constantly pouring in upon me, in every form, evincing general and hearty approbation of my late public course. My triumph will be, as it ought, complete and entire over the base confederacy against me. As to Forsythe, he certainly advised me, in unqualified terms, to accept the Department of State. I myself attached no particular importance to his opinion, though I supposed others might. He was with me on the 30th or 29th of last month, had a long conversation, in the course of which he praised my address, and, *entre nous*, gave in his adhesion. I have no curiosity to see his letter. I understand him thoroughly. He did not mention one word about his letter to you, or his correspondence with you. What could he say to me?

I share with you in your grief for the death of Mrs. Randolph. I have known her from my earliest youth. She deserved all that you have so well said in behalf of her memory.

I find my office no bed of roses. With spirits never more buoyant, twelve hours work per day are almost too much for my physical frame. An entire harmony as to public measures exists between Mr. Adams and me.

I return you Nicholas' letter.

P. S. Was ever any thing so silly as for Eaton to publish his correspondence with me? I am greatly deceived if he has not come out worse than he stood before.

DANIEL WEBSTER TO MR. CLAY.

BOSTON, April 7, 1825.

MY DEAR SIR,—I am obliged to you for a copy of your address to your constituents. It has been widely circulated here, is universally read, and highly commended. I have heard but one opinion as to its general merits. Some think that part which relates to Mr. Kremer's letter, and the incidents connected with it, was an unnecessary labor, at least so far as regards the state of public opinion this way. That transaction seems to have made no impression here. The part of your address which sets forth your reasons for preferring another candidate to General Jackson is composed, in my opinion, with great skill and ability, and I have no doubt it will produce a very strong effect. It is a very good case, very ably managed.

We are very quiet in this quarter. There is very little dissatisfaction, and no disposition, that I discover, to opposition.

With almost all there prevails a very good spirit; and the exceptions are not important, from weight of character or influence.

I have heard nothing, since I left Washington, respecting the English mission. If any thing has occurred, not improper for me to know, I should be glad to learn it from you at your leisure; and I shall be gratified also to hear from you on other subjects and occasions.

JUDGE STORY TO MR. CLAY.

SALEM, April 8, 1825.

DEAR SIR,—I am much obliged to you for the copy of your address to your late constituents, which you have been pleased to send me. I read it with great interest and satisfaction. As a vindication of your character and conduct, it was to me wholly unnecessary, for I have never entertained the slightest doubt of the perfect correctness of the motives of your vote in the recent presidential election. I have considered it as a new proof of your integrity, independence, and firmness. Pardon me if I add, that if your vote had been other than it was, I would have found it somewhat difficult to have reconciled it with your known public opinions on subjects intimately connected with executive duties.

I have no doubt that the address will meet with general approbation, I do not say among warm partisans of other candidates, but among reflecting, considerate men of all parties. In this part of the Union it has received unqualified praise, and has given a new luster to your public fame.

I hope you may long live to enjoy the confidence of the nation, and to remain a blessing to the country; and I beg you will do me the favor of numbering me among those who cherish with the sincerest pleasure every expression of public regard toward you.

LEWIS CASS TO MR. CLAY.

DETROIT, April 14, 1825.

DEAR SIR,—I have just finished the perusal of your masterly address to your late constituents, and I can not refrain from expressing to you the high satisfaction it has afforded me. It is a triumphant refutation of the vile slanders which have been propagated respecting the motives of your conduct in the peculiar circumstances in which you were recently placed. You may safely commit your character to the judgment of your countrymen, and of posterity. They will not fail to award you full justice.

I must ask your indulgence for this almost involuntary tribute to your claims and services. So strong is the impression which your appeal has made upon me, that I could not restrain this expression of my feelings.

PRESIDENT HOLLEY TO MR. CLAY.

TRANSYLVANIA UNIVERSITY, April 18, 1825.

DEAR SIR,—I am much obliged to you for a copy of your address to your late constituents. It appears to me to be able, frank, and satisfactory. Your immediate friends did not need such a communication to keep them from yielding to the calumnies which were heaped upon you for the independent and magnanimous course that you pursued in regard to the election of the President. The publication, however, will, I am convinced, do great good, or rather has done it already. There is but one sentiment upon the subject in this vicinity, so far as comments have reached my ears. All are satisfied with the facts and the reasonings. I have no doubt that there are some among us, who would be better pleased, if you had not defended yourself, or if you had made your statement with less calmness, judgment, and ability. This number can not be great.

I have just read the correspondence between yourself and Mr. Eaton. I am blinded, or it was weakness in him to publish it. He has left the community to believe that he was concerned in Kremer's conspiracy, even to a greater extent than might otherwise have been supposed. He appears to begin with a demand for explanation, which is given only in reference to the first letter, and ends the correspondence without obtaining any satisfaction upon some of the most material points, and with new evidence fastened upon him of connivance, and indeed of active exertions in the base affair. I at first regretted to see Mr. Eaton's name in your address, but he has now shown himself worthy of reprobation from the community.

MR. CLAY TO GENERAL GAINES.*

WASHINGTON, April 29, 1825.

SIR,—Having met with General Brown to-day, and fearing that I might not have the pleasure to see you, I requested him to make a communication to you respecting an incident which occurred in the President's house a few days ago. Upon calling at your lodgings this morning I was unfortunate in not finding you at them. The incident to which I allude is this: Upon leaving the President, with whom I had been engaged in official consultation, I unexpectedly met, on coming out of his receiving-room, at the door of it, in the adjoining room, General Brown, yourself, and a young gentleman, Mr. ——, to whom, as your aid, I was introduced by General Brown. Both the meeting and the introduction were entirely unexpected by me. Upon being presented to Mr. —— I walked up to him and offered him my hand in my usual manner, which he declined receiving. I remarked nothing offensive in his countenance, but he distinctly evinced an unwillingness to reciprocate that mode of salutation. Attaching no particular virtue to the touch of his hand, I turned off and left the room. Upon reflection on the occurrence, it appeared to me that if the young gentleman designed an affront to a total stranger, he could not have possibly selected an apartment of the President's house, at the very door of his receiving-room, and within the hearing, if not in the view, of the Chief Magistrate, to give the affront. I had a right, therefore, to conclude that he had some cutaneous disease with which he was unwilling to infect me, or that, as he kept his hand inclosed in his coat or waistcoat, that some newly-established etiquette forbade the ancient and unfashionable mode of salutation. But on my return from the office to my lodgings yesterday afternoon, I perceived your visiting-card, unaccompanied by that of any other person; from which I have supposed that I may have misconceived the intentions of Mr. —— and that he really meditated offering me an insult. Upon that supposition this note is addressed to you, with the sole object that you may impress upon the member of your family, to whom I refer, the utility of the

---

* This letter was sent to General Gaines, at his lodgings in the city of Washington, on the day of its date, but he had left it, and the letter was never transmitted to him.   H. C.

observance of urbanity as a necessary part of that discipline for which the American army, generally, is so eminently distinguished.

MR. CLAY TO FRANCIS BROOKE.

WASHINGTON, April 29, 1825.

MY DEAR SIR,—I have just received your favor of the 27th. I did not know that the extract published by Mr. Pleasants was from a letter written by you. The same thing has been told to me by several, and, among others, by Mr. Wilson Allen, of the Bowling Green, and Colonel H. Mercer. I think you ought to take no notice of the contradiction of Mr. Ritchie. Your name is not before the public as the writer of the letter. If it were, you might be considered as pledged to sustain the assertion. Mr. Allen told me that Mr. Crawford's warmest friends in Fredericksburg, after seeing him, admitted his incompetency for the office. I think I would let it stand where it does. We ought to make great allowances for chagrin and disappointment. I wish Mr. Crawford could have been seen at Richmond. Mr. Van Buren told me that they had committed a great error in not withdrawing him in May last, on account of his want of health.

From all quarters, the testimony which I get, public and private, of the public approbation of my late conduct, is full, complete, and triumphant. They are preparing in Kentucky to give me an enthusiastic reception. But you see they will not let me alone. Ingham has just made his appearance, and I wish he would write by the league instead of the yard. The next shot will be from McDuffie, or from Nashville, or from both.

JAMES BROWN TO MR. CLAY.

PARIS, May 10, 1825.

DEAR SIR,—I received your letter of the 29th March, inclosing one directed to Mr. Schaffer, acknowledging, on the part of the House of Representatives, the receipt of his excellent portrait of our good friend, General Lafayette, presented to that body. This letter I delivered to Mr. Schaffer on the 5th instant, and at the same time intimated to him, in such terms as could in no way compromise the House, that you had been restrained only by the advice of General Lafayette and his son, from making a movement toward a more suitable return for that valuable present. Mr. Schaffer expressed his entire approbation of the course which had been recommended by his friends, and assured me that the acknowledgment had been made in the manner most agreeable to his feelings and wishes.

MR. CLAY TO FRANCIS BROOKE.

WASHINGTON, September 2, 1825.

MY DEAR SIR,—I received your kind letter of the 29th ultimo, and thank you for the friendly expression of sympathy which it contains. Our late affliction* was rendered still more severe by the circumstances under which it occurred. I did not yield to the urgent calls of duty here, until I had the strongest assurances from the attending physician that there was no danger. And, after leaving Lebanon, the first information I received of the sad event which occurred there, reached me, when I was within about twenty miles of this place, through the "Intelligencer."

I received, perused, and now retain Judge Duval's letter. His wishes in behalf of his son will be considered; but the fact that he has one son a governor under the general Government and another holding a captain's commission (this latter now applying for another appointment), will operate somewhat against his success.

You must feel gratified that our old friend Troop has finally concluded to abstain from surveying the Creek lands, and of course that all danger is dissipated of disturbing the public peace.

PRESIDENT KIRKLAND TO MR. CLAY.

HARVARD UNIVERSITY, CAMBRIDGE, September 22, 1825.

DEAR SIR,—I have the honor of informing you, that the government of Harvard University did, at the last Commencement, in expression of their sense of your professional and general attainments, and your distinguished character and standing, confer on you the honorary degree of Doctor of Laws.

* Death of a daughter.

The diploma will be made out and sent to you. In the hope of your favorable consideration of this token of our respect, I have the honor to be, etc.

DANIEL WEBSTER TO MR. CLAY.

Boston, September 28, 1825.

Dear Sir,—Under another cover I send you what has occurred to me on the subject of our trade with England. The object of this is, to express my sympathy for your domestic calamity, and to offer my congratulations on the welcome so ardent and so universal, which seems to have greeted you among your fellow-citizens of the West. The same kindness of feeling which has been expressed in that quarter, exists, I believe, in other places. I have been through New York in the course of the summer, and I found almost every where, a hearty approbation, and every where else, at least, an entire and not uneasy acquiescence, in regard to the events of last winter, and to your own agency in producing those events. In New England, with here and there a little expression of spleen from the disappointed, the great majority of the people have the best disposition toward the Government, in all its parts. Our ability in Congress is not so great as it might have been, and as it ought to have been. But that evil admits of no immediate cure.

You must allow me to admonish you to take care of your health. Knowing the ardor and the intensity with which you may probably apply yourself to the duties of your place, I fear very much you may overwork yourself. Somebody (was it not an Austrian minister?) on being asked how he could get through so much business, replied that he did it by repudiating two false maxims, which had obtained currency among men; that, for his part, he never did any thing to-day, which he could put off till to-morrow; nor any thing himself, which he could get another to do for him. Without following his example strictly and literally, I still think you ought to be a good deal governed by the same rules, especially the last.

MR. ADAMS TO MR. CLAY.

Boston, October 12, 1825.

Dear Sir,—I have received two letters from you, and several packets from the Department of State, concerning the contents of which I have thought it advisable to wait until I could have the pleasure of conferring personally with you. There is in my mind but one objection to the appointment which you suggest, and that is perhaps removed at least by the authority of respectable precedent. Although detained here longer than I had intended, I still purpose to be with you, at the latest, by the 25th instant.

I inclose, addressed to you, thirty and ten blank patents signed by me, received yesterday from Dr. Thornton, for my signature.

I pray you to present my kind respects to Governor Barbour, Mr. Rush, and Mr. Southard, from each of whom I have received letters, which perpetual motion has prevented me from answering.

JAMES BROWN TO MR. CLAY.

Paris, October 13, 1825.

Sir,—I had the pleasure of receiving your letter sent by the Brandywine, and most sincerely sympathize with you and Mrs. Clay in the sad calamity you have suffered in the loss of your dear little daughter. She had attained that age at which children are particularly interesting, and in the absence of her sisters, would have been for many years an agreeable companion to her mother. These, however, are misfortunes which it pleases Providence to inflict, and for which time and resignation are the only remedies. It has, perhaps, been fortunate that this melancholy event has been succeeded immediately by the variety of traveling, and the occupation attendant on forming a new establishment. These serve in some degree to divert the mind from its afflictions, and to blunt the edge of misfortune.

General Lafayette has arrived in good health at Lagrange, and I sincerely hope he will wisely avoid any interference in public affairs, and content with the honors he has received in the United States, will pass the remainder of his days in tranquillity.

LAFAYETTE TO MR. CLAY.

Lagrange, October 28, 1825.

My dear Sir,—I am the more anxiously waiting for the packet of the 1st instant, as an account of your having been sick, since my departure, has appeared in the French papers. Yet there are evident inaccuracies in the report. Now I must hasten these lines to the Cadmus, which sails on the 1st November. I have written to the President, sending him an article of the *Journal des Debats*, which may interest him and you. I also tell him a few words of what I have heard respecting the affairs of Greece, upon which I have seen nothing to alter my opinion. I came directly from Havre to Lagrange, and have been very friendly received by the people on the road, and here, on my arrival. Ministerial and court people have either kept aloof, or acted foolishly to their own damage. I have been only four days in Paris, to see several friends, and do not intend returning to town before the first days of January. The mass of the nation is quiet and industrious, though dissatisfied with the measures of the Government, and the incroachments of nobles and priests. I found Mr. Brown much better than I expected, indeed, almost quite well. Mr. Sheldon is better, also, and has wisely, I think, determined to nurse his health in Paris, rather than go to *ennuyer* himself in the South, while his time here is usefully employed. Mr. Somerville has been very sick; I hope he will be soon on his travels. Present my affectionate respects to Mrs. Clay and family. Receive those of my children and Le Valleur.

THEODORE WYTHE CLAY* TO HIS FATHER.

Lexington, November 11, 1825.

My dear Father,—I received yours with great concern for the deep distress in which our great loss [death of Eliza and Mrs. Duralde] must have thrown both yourself and my mother. I have not the power of deriving any consolation to myself, and have not, therefore, the means of offering you any. I would gladly render you happy by any sacrifice in my power.

---

* Theodore Wythe Clay, the oldest son, has now (1855) been in the Lunatic Asylum, at Lexington, over twenty years.

As I advance in years I feel the value of a relation more and more, because they must and should be the best friends. I hope, however, that you may not suffer your spirits to be too much depressed, for it is an inevitable effect that the health is thereby impaired; and that of yourself and my dear mother, by these repeated shocks, is more and more necessary to our happiness.

ALBERT GALLATIN TO MR. CLAY.

BALTIMORE, November 14, 1825.

DEAR SIR,—No one can be more sensible than I am, both of the importance of laying the foundation of a permanent friendship between the United States and our sister Republics, and of the distinguished honor conferred on the persons selected to be the representatives of our glorious and happy country at the first Congress of the Independent Powers of this hemisphere; but, without affecting any false modesty, I can not perceive that I am peculiarly fitted for that mission, either by knowledge of the language, things, or men, of South America, or by being known to them. My personal objection has already been stated. I had none, whatever, to a sea voyage, or to embarking from an Atlantic port. On the receipt of your friendly letter of the 11th, I had further private inquiries made from one thoroughly acquainted with the country, as if the object had been a commercial establishment, and without my name being mentioned. The result of these, and the decided opposition I would have to encounter in my family, compel me, though with great reluctance, to persist in declining the appointment. I will preserve a grateful sense of your's and the President's favorable disposition in my favor; and I beg you to accept my thanks for your friendly conduct toward me on this occasion.

LAFAYETTE TO MR. CLAY.

LAGRANGE, November 25, 1825.

MY DEAR FRIEND,—This letter will find you in the full occupation of Congressional business, and although your duties as Speaker are over, there will be enough for the Secretary of State to do. I am ever anxiously waiting for news from the United

States, and particularly from Washington. My American habits have been so happily renewed in the blessed thirteen months I have passed on your side of the Atlantic, that I can not easily submit to an interruption in these communications. Let me hear from you as often as you can.

You have but too melancholy motives to sympathize with the cruel anxiety I have had lately to experience; one of my granddaughters, the third daughter of George, has been on the eve of death. She is now out of danger. How often and how feelingly I have thought of you and Mrs. Clay you will easily conceive. I was gone to town, and expected to see Mr. Brown the next morning when a courier, announcing the dear girl's situation, recalled me suddenly to Lagrange. I suppose he has more than me to write about European politics. Indeed the politics of the Republican hemisphere, until this is greatly mended, appear to me the principal business of mankind.

I much wish to know what answer you have had to your South American and Mexican communications respecting the Congress of Panama, and who has been sent as minister from the United States to that momentous meeting where his good and honest advice will, no doubt, prove highly useful. They say the Empire of Brazil has been invited also to send a minister to Panama. I wish it might be to give Don Pedro a passport to Europe; for I apprehend this Brazilian spot will be a focus of European intrigues until it has adopted the Republican form of Government.

While British publications speak of their half recognition of American independence, as if no such feat of liberalism had ever existed elsewhere, the French Government are wavering between a sense of public discontent at their backwardness and their ridiculous notions of legitimacy; and when lately they thought of grasping at something like a *mezzo termine* on the part of Spain, they have been momentarily discomfited by a change in the Spanish ministry. Such is the diplomacy of Europe, and the fitness to have an American era of foreign as well as interior policy. However, an invisible current must soon wash away those difficulties.

Notwithstanding the quarreling spirit of the Grecian chiefs, and abuses attending a long interruption of national Government, there is an admirable heroism in the resistance of that people and a moral obligation to every liberal man, or body of men, to give them encouragement and the assistance which special situations can allow. The British Government is, as usual, under a conflict of interests opposed to each other, and wants to obtain, as cheap as possible, the first place in the poor career of European liberalism. While French committees are sincere and eager in their concern for the cause of Greece, the Tuileries holds a connection, most unpopular in France, with the Egyptian despot. The rumor of very peculiar acts of benevolence from the American squadron and Commodore Rogers in behalf of the Greeks, which has produced no party complaint that I know of, has in the enlightened and liberal part of the world added to the popularity and dignity of the American name. What has really passed I do not know, but very much lament the illness of Mr. Somerville which possibly keeps him in Paris. I have pressed him to come to Lagrange to refit himself, and from there pursue his journey; but when he will be able to support this short ride to our country residence I can not yet say. He is, however, a little better, as he himself writes to me, and you will no doubt get from him a later and more positive account. Present my affectionate respects to Mrs. Clay, to the President, to your colleagues, and all other friends in Washington as well as to their families. George and Le Valleur beg to be respectfully remembered. Be so kind as to forward the inclosed letters; and remember me to your own family, present and absent, and believe me forever your sincere friend.

I have received, before I left the United States, communications from my old comrades of the Connecticut and Massachusetts lines, intimating the purpose to present Congress, during this session, with a petition relative to the manner in which old accounts have been settled in their very interesting claims on their country's bounty, and also respecting the interpretation given in 1820, to the pension law of 1798. At all times I would have taken the most lively interest in their behalf, but now loaded as I am with the munificent bounty of Congress, I am more than ever anxious to hear they have had cause to be satisfied. There are few survivors; any thing done for them would, I hope, be gratifying to the people, and you know it would have an excellent effect abroad.

Mr. Connel returns to England by way of Liverpool. He will talk with you of several claims upon Europe, namely, that of Antwerp which he had been commissioned to pursue. I have seen M. and Mme. De la Rue. They know you are of opinion that Congress might with all propriety, and without hurting any person, instead of taking it for granted that the President is enlisted to introduce this French claim in the negotiation, express a positive vote upon it, and indeed I don't see any objection to express what every one considers as being already understood.

Here is a bundle of letters which, with proper confidence in your goodness, I beg you to forward.

MR. CLAY TO FRANCIS BROOKE.*

WASHINGTON, November 30, 1825.

If Virginia is to designate a Senator upon the principle of opposition to the administration, let that Senator be Mr. B. Giles. He would be a real friend, though a nominal enemy. I mean that his indiscretions, always great, and now greater than ever, would benefit more than his hostility would injure. But I should hope that no such principle would govern the choice. I should be delighted to see Governor Pleasants here, or General Tucker, or Mr. C. Johnson. Of the latter I know personally but little; but the accounts I have always had of him are highly favorable. It is of no great consequence, in respect to the success or movement of the Administration, who may be sent. The judgment which the public will form of it, depends upon its measures. And one Senator out of forty-eight can not, in that view of the matter, be very essential. You will hear with pleasure, that our harmony, in the cabinet, continues without the slightest interruption, and that we have daily testimonies of increased strength and confidence.

The President has acceded to the wishes of several of the new American Republics, that the United States should be represented at Panama. Our friends need have no fears of our contracting there unnecessary or onerous engagements, or menacing the peace or neutrality of the country.

There is a treaty now going on in this city with the Creeks, with prospects of a successful issue.

---

* We observe that Judge Brooke generally signs his name Francis Brooke —sometimes Francis T. Brooke. Mr. Clay also writes it both ways. Having begun as Francis Brooke, we shall continue it.

LAFAYETTE TO MR. CLAY.

PARIS, December 10, 1825.

Although no direct information from you, my dear friend, has confirmed the fatal report communicated to me for the first time by Mr. Brown and your sister, I but too well know I have again to sympathize with you in a most heavy calamity. I have also to mourn for myself. It was impossible to have formed an acquaintance with the most valuable daughter you have lately lost, to have been favored with her friendly welcome and affectionate attentions, without feeling a deep and lively personal regret. I condole most tenderly and mournfully with you, my dear friend, with Mrs. Clay, and the whole family so cruelly visited of late, and want words to express what I feel on the lamentable occasion.

A similar kind of misfortune has been very near attending me. My granddaughter, Clementine, the youngest daughter of George, has passed several days in a hopeless state ; she is now recovering. I was then thinking of a former, although a late loss. Far was I from suspecting what new blow had fallen upon you.

I have no heart to talk with you of other matters. The President will receive a letter from me. My son and Le Valleur share in my sad feelings, and beg to be remembered most affectionately.

I have written to the President that Mr. Somerville expected to proceed slowly toward his destination. Mr. Brown, whom I have just now seen, gives me a much more sad account than what I had received from poor Somerville himself.

LAFAYETTE TO MR. CLAY.

LAGRANGE, January 22, 1826.

MY DEAR SIR,—No letter from you, since your last most lamentable loss, and you can not write to a more sympathizing friend, has yet reached me ; but I have heard of you and Mrs. Clay by your sister and Mr. Brown. We have been here on the edge of a similar affliction, and I am sure you will feel with me at the not-expected recovery of my granddaughter. Poor Somerville, after a long and painful lingering, has breathed his last at Auxerre, on his way to Italy ; he hoped, while the physicians had no hope of him. Mr. Brown will inform you of the measures taken to secure his papers. He has expressed the affectionate wish to be buried at Lagrange, which was received with our best gratitude and respect, and, after consulting the public officers of the United States in Paris, executed in the properest manner we could, ignorant as we were of Somerville's religious persuasion. It was thought the parish cemetery, where two of my grandchildren are interred, was the proper spot, and I am taking measures, by an exchange, to annex it to the grounds of the farm. You easily will guess what title I would like to mention in the inscription. But it can not properly be done until you find no inconvenience in it. I have every day lamented an unavoidable delay. Every circumstance confirms me in that opinion.

Although the interior politics of Russia have been kept in the dark, two points seem to be ascertained: that Nicholas is the definitive Emperor, and that a plan to obtain constitutional guaranties had a great share in the late commotion at Petersburg. The Holy Alliance has received a blow. It is said another disappointment awaits them from the bad health of Emperor Francis, whose son, more of a fool than his father, which amounts to complete idiotism, is pretended to hate Metternich, the great counter-revolutionary intriguer. I believe the bad situation of the Greeks has been exaggerated, even by well-meaning persons. There is in the revolutionary spirit of freedom an elasticity which is seldom well appreciated. On no European power they can confide. But posterity, and it will begin immediately after their success as it would begin immediately after their fall, can not fail to give full credit to every honest measure taken in their behalf. I am very anxious to hear the name, or names, of the mission to Panama, and have with much pleasure heard of a Republican success over the imperial troops of Brazil. I more and more am confirmed in my eagerness to see the monarch of Brazil removed from his American throne.

Adieu, my dear friend. My best respects wait on Mrs. Clay and family.

MR. CLAY TO FRANCIS BROOKE.

WASHINGTON, February 20, 1826.

MY DEAR SIR,—In answer to your friendly inquiries, contained in your letter of 18th instant, respecting my health, I have the satisfaction to say it is improving. From the commencement until about four weeks ago it was very good. I was then attacked with influenza, which, after one recovery, has been renewed, and I have been a good deal reduced, especially in the relapse. I think I have no organic defect in my structure, and I therefore indulge the hope of a speedy return to health.

As to the Panama mission, it has encountered much delay and a good deal of opposition in the Senate, owing principally to the actual composition of that body at present. There are some fifteen or sixteen Senators determined to oppose the administration at all events, and that measure especially. There are eight or ten others whose private feelings are inimical, but who are restrained by the state of things at their respective homes. When these eight or ten unite (and they are disposed to lend to the regulars of opposition all the collateral countenance they can, without committing themselves), with the others, together they form a majority. The delay which has occurred in the Panama affair has been produced by a majority thus compounded; and the expedients to which it has resorted, to procrastinate the decision, will surprise the country, if it is ever allowed to know them. Nevertheless, it is confidently believed that a majority of the Senate will finally oppose the mission. It is understood they are to act on it to-day, and they may probably get through it this week, though that is by no means certain. In the House, and with the country, the administration need not desire to be stronger than it is. As to the peculiar condition, at this time, of the Senate, you can well imagine the cause.

LAFAYETTE TO MR. CLAY.

PARIS, February 28, 1826.

MY DEAR SIR,—Your letter of the 13th December is the last I have received from you. I know your avocations, but whenever you have time to drop a few lines, they will be received with the grateful feelings of patriotic interest and personal friendship.

My hopes of Greece have not been disappointed. They still fight, and often conquer, abandoned as they have been by all, and attacked or betrayed by many of the Christian powers. It seems now that England regrets not to have been more generous before an unforeseen and extensive conspiracy in Russia may make it a matter of necessity for Emperor Nicholas to wage war against the Turks. The Western powers would like to patch up some arrangement favorable to the independence of Greece, that they may not be dependent on the Russian empire. I wrote to you some private exertions were taking place, from only one part of the French Greek Committee, in favor of Duke d'Orleans' second son. Now the Duke himself does not deny it, but I doubt his obtaining a sincere support from the Court of· the Tuileries. Under those circumstances I did more lament the misfortune that has deprived poor Somerville of the pursuit of his mission, and I wish a respectable American squadron may appear again in those seas. My notions of the moral influence of the people of the United States are lofty and extensive, I confess; but at least I would sadly regret if it were not fully exercised at the Congress of Panama, and in every concern of South America, it would be, in my opinion, leaving the field to the intrigues of European monarchy and aristocracy. Nor can I be easy until the throne of Brazil is no more.

Present my affectionate respects to Mrs. Clay and family, to the President and family, to your colleagues in the cabinet, to all friends. Receive those of my son and Le Valleur, and believe me forever your affectionate sympathizing friend.

Will you please to forward the inclosed to our young Tennesseean friends.

LORD BEXLEY TO MR. CLAY.

GREAT GEORGE STREET, LONDON, March 9, 1826.

SIR,—Having some time ago been informed, by Bishop Chase, that you would permit small parcels of the periodical publications of some of our religious and charitable societies, for his use, to be occasionally addressed to you, I have taken the liberty, by the favor of Mr. King, to consign two small packages, containing a few Mohawk Prayer Books and some Reports, to your address for the Bishop.

I can not forbear taking this opportunity of expressing my sincere pleasure that a statesman in your eminent situation should be the friend of that excellent man; and I can not conceive a purer or stronger bond of union between our countries than that which is afforded by the co-operation now so happily established between them in religious and benevolent pursuits. I am sure you will find the patronage you afforded them not only an honor to your Government, but a source of sincere and increasing satisfaction to yourself amid the cares and labors of an official life; and which you will hereafter reflect upon as not among the least important of the services which your talents and character have enabled you to render to your country. I have the honor to be, Sir, with every sentiment of consideration, yours, etc.

LAFAYETTE TO MR. CLAY.

PARIS, March 27, 1826.

MY DEAR SIR,—As I am writing to you by the packet I shall only in these lines introduce to your acquaintance General Narvaez, a member of the Colombian Senate and of Bolivar's military family, who after having brought over the treaty with Great Britain, and paid a visit to Paris, is returning home through the United States. There he will witness the superiority of Republican Institutions over the half civilization, at best, of the European countries. May he also, and his fellow inhabitants of the south be convinced that from American diplomacy alone they can expect honest advice and sincere sympathies.

MR. CLAY TO FRANCIS BROOKE.

WASHINGTON, April 19, 1826.

MY DEAR SIR,—I duly received your kind letter of the 12th instant. Prior to my going out on the affair to which it refers, the only letter I wrote about it was addressed to you, and put into the hands of General Harrison, to be forwarded on a contingency which did not happen. In that letter, which he still retains, I briefly assigned the reasons which determined me on the course I took. The circumstances which most embarrassed me was the opinion which is entertained by some, as to the state of Mr. Randolph's mind. But I thought I ought not to be governed by that opinion which was opposed by the recent act of my native State electing him to the Senate. As for the future, it must be left to itself. Most certainly I should reluctantly engage in any similar affair.

Will you not come and see us this session? I should be glad if you would come up and pass some days at my house. On Wednesday next I expect some company to dine with me, as I generally do on that day of every week. Suppose you be of the party, and take your lodgings with me? My family is very small, and we have several spare bed-rooms.

LAFAYETTE TO MR. CLAY

PARIS, March 29, 1826.

MY DEAR SIR,—We are anxiously waiting for the arrival of two New York packets. I hope they will bring me some lines from you. At all events I will know what is going on at Washington and other parts of the United States, a food to my mind, a consolation of my heart, which has become more than ever necessary to me. I am happy to think the Panama mission is now on its way. I believe it of high moment for the welfare of South America and Mexico, for the prospects of mankind, and for the dignity of the people of the United States, that they preserve and exert the moral influence to which they are so justly entitled.

This letter accompanies an offer presented to you of the collection of General Foy's speeches, which have the additional merit of being a compliment of the national subscription in behalf of his children. The conduct of the people in that circumstance has been marked with feeling and propriety. The editors are men of remarkable talents.

The European newspapers, your correspondence with the American ministers, leave me but little to say on political topics. I am by this same opportunity writing to the President, and think it needless to repeat my observations. Present my best respects to Mrs. Clay and family, remember me to our friends, and receive the sincere wishes, in which my companions heartily join, of your affectionate friend.*

* It should have been mentioned before, that all Lafayette's letters to Mr. Clay are in English, which will account for the modes of expression found in them.

LAFAYETTE TO MR. CLAY.

PARIS, April 28, 1826.

MY DEAR SIR,—I have not by the last packet heard from you, or the President, or any of the public men at Washington, which I readily explain on account of your pressing avocations in these Congressional times. Mr. Brown writes, no doubt, to you. Mr. Dodge, consul at Marseilles, contemplates going from New York to the seat of Government, which is a very good channel of late information. I shall therefore confine myself to expressing my satisfaction at the result of a debate which has given me much anxiety, as you know nobody sets a greater value than I do on the moral influence of the United States, for their own sakes, for the sake of the new American Republics, for the sake of mankind, the general cause of which, the Government model, whenever they allow themselves to act, is called to further. I wish the commissioners may not have been too long detained.

My anticipations relative to the heroic resistance of the Greeks, have not been disappointed, but unless European policy, I mean that of their Governments, finds a selfish interest in rescuing them from the efforts of the barbarians, nothing is to be expected from the feelings of the Holy Alliance, Great Britain included. In the meanwhile, we have the joyful account of a complete repulse of Ibrahim Pasha, from the shattered walls of Missolonghi.

Present my most affectionate respects to Mrs. Clay, to the President, and both families, to your colleagues, to all friends at Washington. I have had a visit of the gout, which had very properly refrained from interrupting my enjoyments on the sacred beloved ground of the United States, but am now much better.

LAFAYETTE TO MR. CLAY.

LAGRANGE, May 28, 1826.

MY DEAR SIR,—My affection and regard for you are sure, and, I hope, anticipated pledges of the interest I take in every thing where you are concerned, and it were superfluous to expand on my feelings, which, I know, are not to you a matter of doubt.

Your official correspondent and good brother gives you regular accounts of political matters on this side of the Atlantic. I have already communicated my private observations on the strange and portentful contrast that exists between the liberal sentiments, the improving good sense of the people on this continent, more particularly in France, and the bold, but, I expect, imprudent encroachments of power and priesthood on the actual state of civilization. This anomaly is very striking in the dispositions relative to Greece. It appears that Great Britain and their continental partners have succeeded in tampering with the co-religionary movement of the Russians. The British commander of the Ionian Islands has boldly invited the heroic population of Missolonghi to surrender to the Turks, which amounts to the massacre of every man, the rape of every woman, and the conversion to Mohammedanism, if not the death, of every child, prisoners of war in their hands, while a scanty supply to the starving garrison, or at least the starving women and children, was so very easy a matter. On the other hand, renegade officers, protected by the French Government, have assisted in reducing that unfortunate population who have resolved to blow up, along with their enemies, such part of themselves as could not fight, and devote the other to destruction, among the havoc they made in the barbarian ranks of the Austrians. I shall only say that nothing can exceed or equal the infamy of their conduct. In the meanwhile, the popular feeling in favor of the Grecian cause has never been so warm and so general. Their adversaries are branded with the most poignant reproaches. Collections are going on, supplies are sent. The people of France, the ladies of Paris, and successively of every town, are acting a conspicuous and useful part in their behalf. I see in an English paper that some stipulations have been made at Petersburg in favor of Greece. But although public opinion is much excited, I question even this dilatory interference. I need not tell you, my dear friend, that I have been anxiously waiting for the arrival of the two private New York frigates, and persisting in the opinion that the presence of an American squadron on those seas would afford honorable opportunities, consisting with the rules of neutrality, to render essential services. And, indeed, such I have found the popular feeling in the United States. Such is now the general feeling in Europe, that every service rendered to those people would be looked upon with very favorable constructions.

I see in the papers that a Penitentiary is to be erected in the District of Columbia, under the control of the President; and I remember with pleasure the conformity of our ideas respecting the deviations from the late system of reformation, and namely the prevalence of solitary confinement that was contemplated at Philadelphia. Not that I object to solitary cells, not only as a transitory punishment, but also as a great improvement to separate the prisoners at night, a time when they spoil each other. I only think that in day-time they ought to be together in a certain number, which is susceptible of very useful modifications. I intrude upon this matter because I believe this is a good opportunity for the United States to give one more example, among so many, to the rest of mankind.

Permit me to put under your cover a letter to Mr. Skinner, inclosing one to Mr. Cormick and the Report of the Agricultural Society of Paris, with their very advantageous opinion about a new plow which I had been desired to present to their examination. Here is also a letter to my Memphis friends.

Present my best respects to Mrs. Clay and family, to the President and family, to your colleagues and other friends in Washington. I have been long suffering from the gout, and depend on the country air and country occupations to make me quite well. Part of my family are still in town, namely my daughter-in-law, who is one of the female collectors for the Greeks.

DANIEL WEBSTER TO MR. CLAY.

BOSTON, June 8, 1826.

MY DEAR SIR,—We are glad to learn, through the papers, that you have been able to leave the city for a little visit into Maryland, as it gives us reason to hope that you have recovered from your recent indisposition.

You will have noticed Mr. Lloyd's resignation. I did not expect it at this moment, although I was apprised of his wish to leave the Senate as soon as he could. It was with difficulty he was persuaded to attend the last session. The Legislature being now in session, his place will be immediately filled. I incline to think that the appointment will fall on Mr. Silsby. It has been intimated to me, indeed, that a different arrangement *might*, perhaps, be made, if I should approve it ; but my impression at present is against it, and I believe for very good reasons.

Mr. Silsby you know. He is entirely well disposed, and is a well-informed merchant and a respectable man. It is not likely he would take much part in the discussions of the Senate ; but would bring a good deal of useful knowledge into the body, and might be entirely relied on to support all just and proper measures. According to general usage here, a senator would now be appointed for six years, commencing next March, at the end of Mr. Mills' present term of office ; but I think it probable enough, that having to fill the vacancy, occasioned by the resignation of Mr. Lloyd, now, the Legislature may choose to postpone the other election to the winter. If the choice should come on now, I understand Mr. Mills will be re-elected. If postponed, it may be a little uncertain, it is said, as some suppose our Governor has an inclination for the place. There are here, in the Legislature and out, a few very busy persons, who are hostile to the administration. They have no system, but act, in every case, *pro re nata*, and content themselves with the general principle, applied in all cases, and indiscriminately, of opposing. They will probably support Mr. Lincoln against Mr. Mills, from an idea that Mr. Mills' appointment would gratify the friends of the President, or is a thing arranged by his friends, although Mr. Lincoln is known to be equally friendly. Some embarrassment may happen from this source, very possibly ; but I trust it can be overcome.

I have great pleasure in assuring you that nothing can be more correct or more decisive than public opinion in this part of the country, in regard to the various transactions of the last session.

The sentiment of the people is exactly what you would expect and wish it to be.

In New Hampshire the Legislature meets next week. The two senators will doubtless be present on that occasion, and we are looking with some interest to see whether Mr. Woodbury and the editor of the " Patriot" (publisher of the laws !) will be able to bring the Legislature and people of that State to their way of thinking.

GENERAL JESUP TO MR. CLAY.

WASHINGTON, April 1, 1826.

SIR,—Agreeably to your request, I called this morning on Mr. Randolph, for the purpose of delivering your note. Previous to presenting it, however, I thought it proper to ascertain from him whether the information you had received, that he considered himself personally accountable for any attack upon you, was correct. I accordingly informed him that I was the bearer of a message from you, in consequence of an attack which, you had been informed, he had made on your private as well as public character, in the Senate; that I was aware of the fact that he could not be made accountable elsewhere for any thing said in debate, unless he chose himself to waive his privilege as a member of that body. Mr. Randolph replied, that the Constitution did protect him, but he would never shield himself under such a subterfuge as the pleading of his privilege as a Senator from Virginia; that he did hold himself accountable " to Mr. Clay," but considered that he (Mr. Clay) had first two pledges to redeem. One that he was bound to fight any member of the House of Representatives who had acknowledged himself the author of a certain publication in a Philadelphia paper; the other, that he stood pledged to establish certain facts in regard to "a great man," whom he would not name. He added, however, that he would receive no message from Mr. Clay which was not in writing. I replied that the only message I had was in writing; that I had not been authorized by you to enter into or receive any verbal explanations, but that I had done so on my own responsibility, because I thought it proper to do so. I then presented him the note. He read it, and informed me that he would send, by a friend, a written answer to it, or he would send the answer by me, if I would take it. I observed that it would be better to send it by a friend, to which he assented.

GENERAL JESUP TO MR. CLAY.

WASHINGTON, June 24, 1826.

DEAR SIR,—I inclose a copy of the paper which I read to you to-day; it was drawn up with a view of being presented to you, within half an hour after your note had been presented to Mr. Randolph. It contains the substance of my interview with that gentleman.

GENERAL JESUP TO JAMES B. CLAY.*

WASHINGTON, January 19, 1853.

MY DEAR SIR,—I have received your letter of the 4th instant. You owe me no apology for writing to me on any subject; certainly not when the matter relates to your late father.

I have never seen Garland's book, but the statement which you understood him to have made, that Mr. Randolph, in the duel with your father, did not fire at him, is entirely incorrect. In that affair, when the parties came upon the ground, Colonel Tatnal, the friend of Mr. Randolph, having won the choice of positions, placed his principal in that which he preferred, and I placed your father opposite to him, distant ten paces. The other party, having the choice of positions, gave me the word. Mr. Randolph desired to know how I would give it when the parties should be ready. I repeated it. He desired to hear it again. While I was repeating it the second time, his pistol was discharged, whether by accident or not I was then in doubt, but I was soon satisfied that the discharge was accidental. Your father called to me—" It was an accident—I saw it." The parties resumed their stations, and exchanged shots, Mr. Randolph's ball striking a small stump in the rear of, and nearly in line with your father, and his ball cutting Mr. Randolph's pantaloons near the knee, and passing through his coat. The parties again took their stations, and the word was given by Colonel Tatnal— your father fired at Randolph, his bullet passing again through Mr. Randolph's clothes; the latter raised his pistol and fired in the air, exclaiming at the moment, " Mr. Clay, I came upon this ground determined not to fire at you, but the unfortunate discharge of my pistol, after I had taken my position" (and I think he added, " with the circumstances attending it"), " for a moment changed my mind." They sprang forward as if by a common impulse, and grasped each other by the hand, each expressing the pleasure he felt that the other was unhurt.

A statement, prepared at the time and signed by the friends of the parties, was published, giving an account of the whole

---

* It is thought proper to put this letter in this place, though of a later date.

matter. I have duplicates of all the correspondence, carefully packed among my private papers. I will open them, and have them copied for you, as soon as I shall find time to examine them. The other set of the papers, I have understood, was placed by Colonel Tatnal in the hands of Mr. Randolph's half brother, the late Judge Henry St. George Tucker, of Virginia, and was soon after destroyed by fire when his house was burned.

I will examine Garland's book, and take such public notice of the part to which you refer as truth and justice may seem to require. With respect and regard, I am, etc.

MR. CLAY TO J. S. JOHNSTON.

LEXINGTON, August 2, 1826.

MY DEAR SIR,—My visit home has been altogether highly gratifying. Far from any abatement, there is an increase in the number and ardor of my friends, who have given me the strongest testimonies of their attachment. From Missouri I learn that Scott's prospect of re-election is promising. Cook's is unattended with any doubt. Senator Reed writes me from Mississippi in great confidence of his re-election, upon the distinct ground of supporting the Administration. In Ohio and Indiana things could not look better. I think we may assume, first, that the Western States, whose delegation voted for Mr. Adams, will continue to support him; and secondly, that Mississippi will probably be added to the number. You will have heard of Gurley's re-election, and rumor says that Brent has also succeeded.

I shall set out on the 11th for Washington viâ Kanawba. I go that route to take advantage of the Virginia Springs, to improve my health, which just begins to feel the benefit of absence from my office. Mrs. Clay will probably go through Ohio to see James, and we shall meet at Washington, where we are very anxious again to join our friends. I may halt a few days at the White Sulphur Springs, and therefore shall not probably reach Washington till early in September.

You will have seen the tragical end of Beauchamp and his unfortunate wife. We live in an age of romance. Ask Mrs. Johnston if the story might not be wrought up into a fine popular tragedy, one similar to George Barnwell?

Mrs. Clay joins me in the communication of cordial regards to Mrs. Johnston; and I add assurances of my sincere friendship to yourself, etc.

MR. CLAY TO J. S. JOHNSTON.

WHITE SULPHUR SPRINGS, Va., August 24, 1826.

MY DEAR SIR,—I arrived without accident the day before yesterday, and after remaining about a week at it, for the use of the mineral waters, I propose resuming my journey about the 1st of September, and hope to reach the city the 10th or 12th. My health has improved on the journey, although I have not been able to secure all the tranquillity and abstraction from crowds which is necessary to its re-establishment; for they have invited me to a public dinner at Lewisburg, and not being able to assign any sufficient reason for declining it, I have accepted it. The administration has many friends in this quarter of Virginia.

There is much company at this place, but it shifts as frequently as the dramatis personæ of a theater. It is chiefly from the Southern States.

I am driving a gig-horse, which, though not so fine or showy as your finest carriage-horse, I am inclined to think might answer as a tolerable match for him.

With my best regards to Mrs. Johnston, and the hope of seeing you both very soon, I am truly your friend.

P. S. Mrs. Clay was to leave Lexington on the 22d inst., to proceed to the city, by the Ohio route, and I expect will reach you about the time that I shall.

MR. CLAY TO FRANCIS BROOKE.

WHITE SULPHUR SPRINGS, August 28, 1826.

MY DEAR SIR,—I was disappointed, on my arrival here, in not having the pleasure of meeting you; but I received your obliging letter, accounting for your absence. I have made a short halt for the use of the waters, which I have already found of some benefit. I shall resume my journey on the 1st of next month, and will, perhaps, reach Orange, by the way of Charlottesville, on the 8th or 9th. I purpose remaining a day or two there, with Governor Barbour, if at home, and Mr. Madison. I should be delighted to avail myself of your kind invitation, but that must depend upon information which I may hereafter receive, as to the necessity of my presence at my post. It will be very gratifying to me if I can render any service, which I will not fail to endeavor, to your friend, Mr. Carter.

MR. ADAMS TO MR. CLAY.

QUINCY, September 12, 1826.

DEAR SIR,—I duly received your kind letters of the 25th and 30th of July, and of the 12th ultimo, all from Lexington, which I have hitherto deferred answering, from an uncertainty where a letter would meet you. But supposing you would, about this time, reach Washington, I, two days since, inclosed to you a letter from the Governor of New York, with other papers, on a subject requiring at once mature deliberation and prompt decision.

I learn, with much concern, that your health did not derive, from your visit home, so much benefit as you had anticipated. I hope the tour to the Springs will have more favorable results. Your apprehensions with regard to Mr. Anderson were but too well founded. The public have lost in him an able and useful officer. The Panama Congress, it seems, have adjourned to meet in the neighborhood of the city of Mexico.

Your letter of instructions to Mr. Gallatin has been forwarded by me to the Collector of the Customs at New York, to be forthwith transmitted. Mr. Poinsett's treaty with Mexico has all the articles stipulating the delivery of criminals and fugitive slaves, which Mr. Gallatin thinks may be objected to. We shall have an opportunity, by the reference of the Mexican Treaty to the Senate, of ascertaining their views in relation to these subjects, and, probably, in season to give further instructions to Mr. Gallatin, before the termination of his negotiation.

I think that, unless some unforeseen emergency should indispensably require my return to Washington earlier, I shall be there between the 15th and 20th of next month, about ten days later than I have, until recently, expected.

LORD GAMBIER TO MR. CLAY.

Iver Grove, September 20, 1826.

My dear Sir,—Mr. Edward Thomson, the son of an esteemed and intimate friend of mine, being about to proceed to the State of South Carolina, will pass a little time at Washington, on his way from New York. I beg your permission to introduce him to your countenance and protection. You will find him, should he have the honor of presenting himself to you, to be an intelligent, well-informed young man, of most respectable character, and worthy of your notice. Any friendly office that you may please to honor him with, will be very gratifying and obliging to me.

I was happy to hear, from my nephew, Mr. Charles Gambier, who visited Washington the beginning of the present year, of your health and well-being. Most cordially do I wish you a continuance of the same, with the addition of every other blessing that may conduce to your present and everlasting happiness; being, my dear sir, with unfeigned esteem and regard, your faithful friend.

DANIEL WEBSTER TO MR. CLAY.

Boston, October 13, 1826.

My dear Sir,—The subject of the recent British order is exciting some little attention, as you will have observed, in the commercial cities, and there are those, doubtless, who would embrace this, as they would any opportunity, to find fault.

Mr. Lloyd has probably written you in regard to it. He feels more than a common share of interest on the occasion, as he recommended negotiation in preference to meeting the English proposition by an act of Congress. It may be well, perhaps, that some little statement, made at Washington, would appear, for the satisfaction of the public. I would not intimate that there is, in this part of the country at least, any dissatisfaction; but I see attempts are making, in New York and other places, to produce an impression that the national interests have, in this instance, been overlooked.

As to the general course of political affairs, we have nothing of much interest in this quarter. Our elections take place next month. In some districts there may be personal changes, but nobody will be proposed on the ground of opposition, nor any body chosen who is suspected, on good grounds, of being inclined to join the opposition. Some few, perhaps, may be chosen, who profess friendship, and who will yet fly off on the first, and on every close question, according to the example of last winter. But, on the whole, the great majority from this quarter will be well inclined, and steady in their course. The Jackson paper in this city (for we have also a Jackson paper), seems to occupy itself at present very much with Mr. Everett. Mr. Everett, however, is likely to be re-elected with great unanimity. I think, my dear sir, without intending a compliment, that your speech at Lewisburg has done real service. It was happy and excellent, even for you, both in matter and manner. We all rejoice here —I mean all who do not fear that you were born to prevent General J. from being President—in the improvement of your health; and you must allow me to express my most anxious and earnest hope that you will not overwork yourself the ensuing session and winter. What can not be done without the sacrifice of your health must be left undone, at whatever expense or hazard. I have often thought of suggesting to you one practice, if you have not already adopted it, which I have found very useful myself, when my own little affairs have occasionally pressed me; that is, the constant employment of an amanuensis. The difference between writing at the table and dictating to another, is very great. The first is tedious, exhausting, debilitating labor; the last may be done while you are pacing a large room, and enjoying in that way the benefit of an erect posture, and a healthy exercise. If I were you I would not touch a pen, except to write my frank. Make the clerks do all that clerks can do, and for the rest dictate to an amanuensis. I venture to say, that if you once get accustomed to this, you will find your labor greatly lightened.

I have had the pleasure of hearing from several Kentucky and Ohio friends during the summer; and have had much gratification in learning the favorable state of opinion in those important states. The only incident to be regretted much, in the West, is the loss of Cook's election. His friends must remember him, and sustain him, in some public service, according to his merits.

LAFAYETTE TO MR. CLAY.

LAGRANGE, October 28, 1826.

MY DEAR SIR,—Mr. Brown who is in the city, Mr. Gallatin, whom I had the pleasure to see for two days, give you French and English news, with the reports from other parts of Europe. I have therefore very little to say, and what should I say but that the British and the Continental Cabinets are patching up every gap from which liberty and equality might pop out on this side of the Atlantic. Nevertheless, the public mind is making slow progress, and at the end of a chapter, too long I fear, things will definitely come to rights.

I have given the President an account of my conversation, sought on their part with the last commissioners, from Hayti to this Government, the main point of which was to tell me that one of the American objections to the acknowledgment of their independence, might easily be removed, as they might even now assure you that the privileges complained of as a kind of vassalage, were not, at any rate, to last more than the time fixed for the payment of the stipulated money.

Permit me to inclose a letter to the President, containing the application of a lady, a packet for Mr. Graham, relating to my landed concerns, and one to my dear friends Fanny and Camilla Wright, the elder of whom had but lately recovered from a very alarming fever. I would much like to have your opinion of their philanthropic experiment.

I beg you to present my best respects to Mrs. Clay and family, to remember me to our friends, particularly Governor Barbour, to whom I will have the pleasure to write by the next packet. Here is the copy of a letter I have received from General Bolivar. It has been published in France, as well as my letter from Washington, at the request of M. Madrid, the Colombian agent to this Government.

MR. CLAY TO FRANCIS BROOKE.

WASHINGTON, December 11, 1826.

MY DEAR SIR,—I have occasion for all possible indulgence from my friends, on account of my irregularity in acknowledging and answering their esteemed favors. They will do me great wrong, if, in any case, they attribute my silence to insensibility to the value of their letters. I perceive from yours of the 7th inst., that you feel that I had neglected answering some of your prior letters. I must plead guilty, and ask for mercy. I am glad to learn that the message takes well at Richmond, or rather, that it is only objected to because it is without fault. Political prospects are good every where, to the North, East and West, and I think less gloomy in the South. In Kentucky, an Adams representative has been sent from one of the two Jackson districts, vacated by the death of their members, and my confidence in the support of that State to the administration, and in the re-election of Mr. Adams is entire. In Pennsylvania, the Governor comes out in his message in support of the administration, and sanctioning the late election of President. In New York, the great body of both parties is with us, and I verily believe that if the electoral law should even remain unaltered, Mr. Adams will obtain every vote.

I invite your attention to the documents (of which I will forward a copy by the mail), concerning the colonial question. I think we have put Great Britain unquestionably in the wrong.

MR. CLAY TO FRANCIS BROOKE.

WASHINGTON, December 23, 1826.

MY DEAR SIR,—I have yielded to the wish that I should write in behalf of Mr. Taylor, but a great deal too much weight is attributed to my recommendation, and I fear that the bank will hardly be prevailed on to deviate from their practice of sending out a cashier educated under their own eye.

From all recent indications at Richmond, we are to conclude that Mr. Ritchie has succeeded in putting a majority of the General Assembly in the honor of a permanent opposition to the general administration. I regret it extremely, not more on our account here, than on that of Virginia herself. It is consoling that every where else, things are going well, and the final issue is perfectly certain. Mr. McKinley, the new Senator lately elected in Alabama, is believed to have brought with him good dispositions toward the Administration. In that branch of Congress where it was weakest, it is now entirely safe.

LAFAYETTE TO MR. CLAY.

Lagrange, December 29, 1826.

My dear Sir,—After having passed a very pleasing summer in this rural abode, we have been lately afflicted with a sad calamity, the death of Louis Lasteyrie (husband to my daughter Virginia, and father to four children), whom we have lost after a cruel illness of two months. You are but too well acquainted with the feelings of family mournings, and will sympathize in our regrets. The so very strange murder of Doctor Brown has given me much pain, not only from motives of friendship to his brother and other relations, but on account of my personal acquaintance with him and his amiable family.

You are now in the midst of Congressional debates. I much wish they may relax of the unusual bitterness that has marked the last session. The choice of Mr. Poinsett to the Congress of Panama has afforded me great pleasure, as he well knows the concerns of South America and Mexico, including those of Guatimala, and will be a good adviser of the Republican measures, as well as a guardian against European influence. How do you find Mr. Canning's assertion in the British Parliament that he, Mr. Canning, has called to existence the new Republics of the American hemisphere? when it is known by what example, what declaration, and what feelings of jealousy the British Government has been dragged into a slow, gradual, and conditional recognition of that independence.

Gallant Greece is still struggling against the Ottomans and Egyptians; whatever has been the revolutionary tone of the British prime-minister, and in spite of the counter-revolutionary ultraism in France and Spain, it is well understood between all Governments in Europe, that a general commotion might carry them on a ground not very favorable to the interests of aristocracy and despotism; so that as long as they can keep the nations within the bounds of ancient institutions, or at best, of old and new octroyed charters, they will ever ultimately find means to patch up every political question that may annoy European slumbers.

Among the several publications relative to Lagrange and its inhabitants, which I have found in the papers of the United States, there is one that I am prompted to notice, as you will have, at Washington, frequent opportunities to contradict it.

The writer, with a kind intention, I don't doubt, but under a complete mistake, asserts that I am assailed by Americans in Europe, with demands for money. Happy I would be, to be sure, of an opportunity to oblige friends in distress. But those opportunities have not been offered.

Be pleased, my dear friend, to present me very affectionately to Mrs. Clay, your family, the President, Mrs. Adams and family, your colleagues in the cabinet, General Brown, Commodore Morris, General Bernard, Mr. Graham, and all other friends at Washington. Be pleased also to take care of the inclosed letter, and believe me forever your affectionate friend.

LAFAYETTE TO MR. CLAY.*

On Board the Steamboat, near York Town, October 18, 1824.

My dear Friend,—Your kind congratulations and affectionate letter are new testimonies of those sentiments which I am proud and happy to have obtained from you, and which are most cordially reciprocated. I am now on my way to the anniversary meeting at York Town, and shall from there proceed to Norfolk, Richmond, Monticello, Montpelier, and again to Washington, where I intend to await the meeting of Congress. It is my fond determination to visit the Southern and Western States, and I anticipate the pleasure to find myself under your friendly roof at Ashland. But it can not now be before I have met you at Washington, where every motive of propriety, respect, and gratitude demand my early visit to the members of both Houses, whose unanimous invitation has called me to the most honorable and gratifying enjoyments in which the human heart can delight. I am happy to think that the time is not far removed when I shall have the pleasure to present you in person the expression of my high regard and most sincere affection. My son desires his sincere acknowledgments and respects to you.

---

* This letter, from Lafayette, was mislaid, and is out of its proper place as to date.

CHAPTER IV.

CORRESPONDENCE OF 1827.

DANIEL WEBSTER TO MR. CLAY.

JANUARY 1, 1827.

MY DEAR SIR,—After company went out last night, and I had packed up my trunk, I sat down and read your letter through. Probably, I should have voted against any further publication; but I am now fully satisfied this will do good. The statement is clear, and the evidence irresistible. I am satisfied, upon my conscience, that the whole business originated with General J. himself; whether through mistake, or from intention, I do not say.

MR. CLAY TO FRANCIS BROOKE.

WASHINGTON, January 26, 1827.

MY DEAR SIR,—I duly received your favor of the 24th instant. You will have since seen the late Convention with England, which has been communicated to Congress, and published. A great and somewhat general mistake has prevailed in respect to the extent of the claim which existed on Great Britain, on account of slaves, and other property, taken away or destroyed. The claim, on the part of American citizens, arises out of the first article of the Treaty of Ghent, which stipulates, "All territory, places, and possessions, whatsoever, taken by either party from the other, during the war, or which may be taken after signing this treaty, excepting only the islands hereinafter mentioned, shall be restored without delay, and without causing any destruction, or carrying away any of the artillery, or other public property, originally captured in the said forts or places, and which shall remain therein upon the exchange of the ratifications of this treaty, or any slaves, or other private property." The parties differed about the meaning of this clause, and referred their dispute to the Emperor Alexander. He decided it in favor of the United States, and a Tripartite Convention was concluded at St. Petersburg, to give effect to this decision. The mixed commission (composed of Messrs. Jackson and Cheves), was created to execute that commission ; but they could not agree, and the late Convention, by which the United States agree to accept, in behalf of the claimants, a gross sum, was substituted to the commission.

Now it is evident, from this narrative, that the new Convention could only provide for that class of complainants who were comprehended in the first article of the Treaty of Ghent. Government, in fact, was only an agent or trustee for that class. If you go back beyond the Treaty of Ghent, perhaps one class of persons who had their property taken away or destroyed, during the late war, has as much equity as another. But the treaty did not provide for any but one class. To that limited extent, Great Britain has always been dissatisfied with the stipulation and the interpretation put upon it. Government, now, can do no more than see that the class provided for shall have the benefit of a most fortunate provision made for them in the treaty. It can not undertake to divide a fund, intended exclusively for that class, among those who are, unfortunately, not comprehended in the Treaty of Ghent. If it were to go out of the treaty, where would be the stopping-place ?

A board will probably be created by Congress, during the present session, but its duty will be restricted to a fair execution of the Treaty of Ghent, the Imperial decision, and the late Convention. The average value fixed by the mixed commission, and the definitive list sent to it from the Department of State, in pursuance of the Convention at St. Petersburg, will govern the new Board ; and it will belong to that to decide, under the limitations stated, upon all cases thus presented to it, and upon the sufficiency of the evidence by which they are made out.

Should there be a surplus in the fund, Congress alone possesses the power to dispose of it.

MR. CLAY TO FRANCIS BROOKE.

WASHINGTON, February 8, 1827.

MY DEAR SIR,—I send by this mail the copies of the British Acts of Parliament desired.

It is a subject of deep regret with me (and I beg you to say so to Governor Tyler) that his friendly letter to me, on the occasion of my vote in the House of Representatives, on the late Presidential election, should have been used to assail or annoy him. In any casual allusion which I ever made to that letter, it was far from my intention that it should have been made instrumental to his prejudice. The truth is, that it is one of a hundred similar letters which I received, about the period of its date, from all quarters of the Union, and from some of the most distinguished men in it. I have heard that the letter was inadvertently (and certainly with no unfriendly purpose toward the Governor) spoken of by a Mr. Clarke, a lawyer of Winchester, who had been, a few days before, with me, and to whom I expressed, what I certainly felt, much gratification with his election, and stated that I had the satisfaction to believe that Governor Tyler did justice to the motives which had influenced me on the above memorable occasion, as he had addressed to me, at the time, a letter couched in the most friendly terms. I understand that Mr. Clarke incidentally spoke of this conversation, not recollecting that a printer was by, who felt himself at liberty to make the matter a topic in his next paper.

Whether it was in this way or not that it got out, I can not tell. It may have been in some other manner; for there is an espionage prevailing which spares no privacy, and which, unless checked, must destroy all confidence.

Tell the Governor that he must not take the matter much at heart; to recollect how much I have borne, and with what philosophy and fortitude. Tell him, moreover, that we shall certainly prevail, and that I do not even despair of our native State. When he comes here, no one entertains the idea that he will renounce any of the great principles of his public action, and least of all, that by which he judges of men and things as they are, and not as passion, party, or prejudice may represent them.

MR. CLAY TO FRANCIS BROOKE.

WASHINGTON, February 16, 1827.

MY DEAR SIR,—The volume of the British Acts of Parliament, containing those which General Taylor desires, is in possession of the clerk of the House of Representatives. We have not been able to get it back, and I fear may not in time for the use of the General. But if I can regain it, I will send it by mail for his use.

I do not wish you to write to Governor Tyler. It will do to speak to him when you see him. I should regret very much if he feels hurt about the letter. I can only repeat, that any allusion which I made to it in conversation was far from any design to prejudice him, or any expectation that it should get into the public prints. I hope, on the other hand, that he has not permitted himself to attribute to me the violation of any confidential correspondence. His letter had nothing confidential in it. It was public in its nature, public topics were treated of, and it was addressed to a public man. It was spontaneous, and therefore more prized by me. We have no news.

PORTER CLAY* TO MR. CLAY.

FRANKFORT, February 22, 1827.

DEAR BROTHER,—Your favor of the 3d instant came to hand in due time, and I heartily thank you for the valuable inclosures, particularly your speech before the Colonization Society. Your views upon that subject have my most hearty concurrence, and I pray Almighty God may bless the institution with his approbation, and make it the means of extending the light of his glorious Gospel into that benighted land; that Ethiopia may stretch out her hands to God, and the isles of the sea be made to rejoice in the fullness of his free salvation. You are right when you say that "God may convert that which has been our great sin into an extensive blessing to that people"—not that we should be encouraged to do evil that grace may abound; God forbid: for how then should God judge the world? But that we through his all-wise providence should get to himself a revenue of glory by that which in us was originally wicked.

* Mr. Clay's brother, a Baptist minister, since dead.

JAMES MADISON TO MR. CLAY.

MONTPELIER, March 24, 1827.

DEAR SIR,—After your kind offer, I make no apology for inclosing another letter, which I wish to have the advantage of a conveyance from the Department of State. Its object is to obtain from Mr. Gallatin a small service for our university, and that with as little delay as may be.

While I was charged with the Department of State, the British doctrine against a neutral trade with belligerent ports, shut in peace and open in war, was examined at some length, and the examination published in a stout pamphlet. I have been applied to by several friends for a copy, which I could not furnish, nor do I know that they are attainable, unless obsolete copies should remain in the Department. If this be the case, I should be thankful for the means of complying with the application.

Mrs. Madison joins in offering to Mrs. Clay and yourself assurances of cordial regards and best wishes.

HENRY CLAY JR. TO HIS FATHER.

WEST POINT, March 27, 1827.

DEAR FATHER,—Since I last heard from you, Mr. and Mrs. Smith, with Margaret Ross, have been here. They remained but a day or two, and seemed delighted with the place. From them I learned that you were well, and that Theodore is going as a bearer of dispatches to the Congress of Panama, likewise, that it is your intention to visit Kentucky some time in May, but they do not inform me whether my mother goes with you or not. Should you come to the determination of leaving Washington, I should be extremely happy to see you here. The lakes will then be open, and will afford you a speedy and pleasant route. Worthington will be very little out of your way, and by calling, you will gratify James. *   *   *

MR. CLAY TO J. S. JOHNSTON.

WASHINGTON, April 2, 1827.

DEAR SIR,—I am glad to learn from your letter, dated at Wheeling, that you had safely advanced so far on your journey. I will attend to your wish about the note to your speech, so far as it is practicable. Since you left us, the city has been very quiet. From Albany, our friends write in a tone of confidence, as to ultimate success, about which, I think, they can hardly be mistaken. The developments of the "Intelligencer" have produced great effect in that quarter, and from other parts of Pennsylvania than those which you visited, our information still runs in a favorable current. They tell this anecdote of Buchanan. At a tavern in Harrisburg, where he was electioneering, he remarked that he "had heard much of changes from Jackson to Adams, but could see nobody that had changed." A member of the Legislature, from Meadsville, who was present, replied, "Yes, sir, here are eleven members of the Legislature, all of whom were the friends of General Jackson, and now are the friends of Mr. Adams. And I will tell you why—because the administration is right, and the opposition have been defeating the best measures."

ALBERT GALLATIN TO MR. CLAY.

LONDON, May 3, 1827.

SIR,—Mr. Colquhoun, the agent of the Hanse Towns in London, called on me yesterday, and informed me that the city of Frankfort having given her consent to that measure, the Hanse Towns had appointed Mr. Rumph their Chargé d'Affaires at Paris, special minister to the United States, with power to negotiate a treaty of commerce, that he had accepted, and intended to sail from Havre for America, in the middle of August.

Mr. Colquhoun also said that he was charged by the city of Hamburg, to obtain from me a communication of the answer I might receive from my Government, to the note of Mr. Sieveking, which I had transmitted at his request. I said that, having informed that gentleman that I had no authority or instructions on that subject, he had sent me this note in question, as an unofficial paper, that I had transmitted it as such, and that, under these circumstances, I did not think it probable that an answer would be made by my Government to that communication. The Government of the Hanse Towns is very economical; the sending a minister abroad, is for them an extraordinary measure, and as three months will elapse before Mr. Rumph's intended departure, I suppose they would wish to know whether there is a reasonable prospect of his succeeding.

It appeared to me, from the general tenor of the conversation, that not only are the Hanse Towns anxious of concluding a treaty of commerce with the United States, on account of its immediate advantages, but that they believe that it will have a tendency to increase the consideration in which they are held, and to strengthen the tenure on which they hold their situation of independent Republics. I said, of course, nothing that could commit my Government, but adverted in general to the liberal commercial policy adopted by the United States, and to their friendly disposition and feelings toward the free commercial cities of Germany. It is not probable that you will have any difficulty with them, as relates to either commerce or navigation, as generally understood. But you are undoubtedly aware that they are very narrow and selfish, as regards merchants residing within their own precincts, and that they may be unwilling to grant to citizens of the United States, who might be desirous of forming commercial establishments in any of those cities, the same privileges which foreign merchants indiscriminately enjoy, in common with our own citizens in the ports of the United States where they reside.

MR. CLAY TO FRANCIS BROOKE.

WASHINGTON, May 25, 1827.

MY DEAR SIR,—I took the liberty of sending you a few days ago, a copy of some speeches, etc., of mine, which have been recently published in Philadelphia, and which I hope you will have safely received.

Have you read the accounts about the execution of the six militia-men at Mobile, early in 1814? I think the Nashville Committee are entitled to the public thanks for bringing that matter to light. I had a vague impression about it, but I had really put it in the large class of doubtful reports. The Committee have undeceived me; and I think if they favor the public with many more similar disclosures, they will serve most effectually the cause they have espoused. What has become of the eloquent pen of Algernon Sidney? I think the case of these poor deluded militia-men furnishes a theme on which it might be employed with as much instruction and benefit as when it was formerly exercised with such powerful influence.

MR. CLAY TO COLONEL RUTGERS.

WASHINGTON, June 4, 1827.

DEAR SIR,—Long accustomed to regard you as one of the fathers of the Republican church, to which we both belong, I hope I shall be excused from that circumstance, if I am not authorized by our acquaintance, in taking the liberty of addressing this letter to you.

You have felt too deep an interest and had too much agency in the public affairs of our country to admit of your beholding with indifference what is now passing, or to allow you to forbear from giving, while you are spared among us, the benefit of your matured counsels. And I am greatly mistaken in the estimate I have made of your judgment and character, if you can approve the conduct of the opposition to the General Administration, or the object, or the means which they are employing to accomplish that object, of supplanting Mr. Adams and electing General Jackson.

During the administration of the father of our present Chief Magistrate, I was too young and too poor to take any part in the public councils ; but I, nevertheless, had very decided opinions, to which I gave all the effect I could in private circles, against some of the prominent measures of that administration, and what I believed to be its tendency, if not the ultimate aim of some of its principal supporters. But I could not allow myself to transfer my dislike of the Administration of the father to the person and public character of the son, who, I firmly believe, after an acquaintance with him of more than twenty years, to be sincerly attached to our free institutions, and to the general cause of liberty. When, therefore, the only alternative presented, on a late occasion, to my choice in the House of Representatives, was between him and General Jackson, who appeared to me to possess no other than military pretensions, I could not doubt the side on which duty and safety lay. Far from regretting the choice which I then made, I should make it again, under similar circumstances, and I must ever think that the election of General Jackson at that or any other time, would be a most unfortunate event for this country. I accepted a place in the Administration from a full conviction that it was a duty I owed myself, after the flagitious attacks made upon me, one object of which was to intimidate me, and under the unanimous advice of all my Congressional friends.

If there be one characteristic which, more than any other, distinguishes the Republican party, and of which, more than any other, they may be justly proud, it is their devotion to liberty and to the guarantees for its preservation which experience and reason demonstrate to be necessary. Does not the history of all nations and of all times prove, that the greatest danger to freedom is from mere military men? With this light before them, can the Republican party, if they are faithful to their own principles, and desirous to perpetuate to their posterity that liberty which they themselves enjoy, lend themselves to the election of a chief magistrate, who possesses no other qualification than that of being a successful military commander? I thought they could not, and yet believe that they can not.

It would be a great satisfaction to me to find that the opinions which I have now expressed receive your approbation. But whether I am so fortunate or not, I hope you will do justice to my motives in communicating them, and in addressing you at the present period, and at the same time be fully pursuaded that I have the greatest respect and veneration for your character.

MR. CLAY TO FRANCIS BROOKE.

WASHINGTON, June 4, 1827.

MY DEAR SIR,—I received your favor of the 2d instant. You ask me if I am going to Kentucky soon, and if I can be spared. I am compelled by my private business, and particularly by that of the estate of my deceased friend, Colonel Morrison, of which I am the only acting executor, to go to Kentucky, and I shall leave this city for that purpose on the 10th instant. It is my intention to return by the 1st of August. I shall leave the business of the Department in such condition, that I do not believe that any prejudice to the public will arise from my absence.

RICHARD RUSH TO MR. CLAY.

WASHINGTON, June 23, 1827.

MY DEAR SIR,—I have just read Lord Grey's speech, and can not resist the desire I have to send it to you. You will recognize in it sentiments I have expressed as regards Mr. Canning and the new States. If Earl Grey had been better informed, he would have said that it was you who did most to call them into being. I say this in no idle spirit of praise, having always, abroad and at home, expressed the opinion that, next to their own exertions, the South Americans owe to you more than to any other man in either hemisphere, their independence, you having led the way to our acknowledgment of it. This is truth; this is history. Without our acknowledgment, England would not have taken the step to this day. This is my belief. I give Mr. Canning no credit for the part he acted. It was forced upon him by our lead, which he never had the magnanimity to avow, but strove to claim all the merit for England, or rather for himself. He esteems civil and political liberty no more than Lord Londonderry did, though circumstances have made him appear to be somewhat more their champion. That our public should be inclined to rejoice at Mr. Canning's present triumph, is, I think, the effect of his character not being understood among us. Certainly, as regards the United States, he has been, of all British statesmen, the least disposed to do us justice; yes, truly, the least of any that ever we have had to deal with, without a single exception. Forgetting, if we can, all that he has said of us, let us take his acts; for was it not he who disavowed Erskine's arrangement, which, had it been sanctioned in England, might have prevented a war? Was it not he who in 1823 infused the unfriendly tone into that long negotiation at London, almost refusing to listen to nine out of ten of our claims, obviously just as most of them were? And was it not he, who, in 1826, most abruptly closed the West India trade against us, upon pretexts the most unexpected and flimsy? I could make the list longer, but that I should make too long a letter of it, having intended to do nothing more than send you Lord Grey's speech. I know how high you rate his speeches. Mr. Canning never liked the United States or their institutions, and never will, his Liverpool speech, and the conclusion of his late dispatch, notwithstanding. He will watch all our steps with a sharper and more active jealousy than perhaps any other English statesman living. Of all their public men, we have the least to expect from him.

HENRY CLAY JR. TO HIS FATHER.

WEST POINT, June 24, 1827.

DEAR FATHER,—I arrived here last Thursday, the 21st, and have already been examined, and, I am glad to add, have been admitted. Yesterday we came into camp, and I am now in my tent, sitting on my knapsack and writing on my chair. I am better pleased than ever with the Academy. I was well received by the officers on my return, and now start with the prospect of success hereafter—am delighted with the hardships accompanying a military life, but still give the civil the preference. My duties will prevent my writing more, although I had intended to have written a long letter concerning the discipline and course of study in use here. Give my respects to all my relations and friends. Tell Cousin Nannette that I am daily expecting an answer to my letter which was written before I left Washington.

BARON DE MAREUIL TO MR. CLAY.

NEW YORK, June 30, 1827.

SIR,—At the moment when I am about to depart, permit me to add to my official communications of this day, some more particular expression of the sentiments which I bear away with me, and the better part of which is assured to you. I have often regretted that conversation was not more easy between us, being persuaded of the interest and pleasure which you would have been able to throw over it, and eager as I would have been to make myself understood in those things of which the pen can not treat, but in which the heart and spirit may find satisfaction. I hope, however, that I may not have been misunderstood by you, and that I have made an impression upon you akin to that which you have left on me.

The extensive and beautiful tour which I have just finished, has much increased my admiration of North America. I have regretted that I was not at Black Rock, and that I was unable to deliver, in person, to General and Mrs. Porter, the recommendations with which you honored me. Madame Mareuil begs that Mrs. Clay will be pleased to accept her adieus and compliments. I venture to add my homage, and to beg, Sir, that you will accept, at the same time, with my thanks for the welcome treatment which I received from you during my residence in Washington, the assurance of the invariable sentiments of high consideration which I have professed for you.

DANIEL WEBSTER TO MR. CLAY.

BOSTON, July 24, 1827.

MY DEAR SIR,—Your reply to General Jackson's letter is admirable, and has been most favorably received every where, at least on this side the Alleghany. It places the General in a position where he can not remain. He must move, in some direction; and, whatever movement he makes, will either embarrass his friends, or still more embarrass himself. I have a suspicion that the respectable member of Congress is Mr. Buchanan. If this should turn out so, it will place him in an awkward situation, since, it seems, he did recommend a bargain with your friends, on the suspicion that such a bargain had been proposed to them on the part of the friends of Mr. Adams. I am curious to see how this matter will develop itself.

FRANKLIN LITCHFIELD TO MR. CLAY.

PUERTO CABELLO, COLOMBIA, July 30, 1827.

SIR,—I do myself the pleasure to transmit to you a case, containing the bust of President Bolivar, which is a most perfect likeness of this great South American statesman. This is the first copy ever taken of him in this style, and was lately executed by an Italian, at the city of Caracas, and I beg of you to accept the same in my name, as a token of respect for your disinterested and patriotic eloquence, displayed on the floor of Congress, in defense of the rights and independence of the native country of this distinguished liberator. Mr. Royal Phelps, Jr., is charged with the delivery of said bust, in person, and if you have no objections, I have requested him to have a portrait painting taken from it, *in oleo*, by one of our first artists. I have also requested Mr. Phelps to make several inquiries of you relating to my consular duties, and beg of you the favor to communicate to him your views frankly.

SAMUEL L. SOUTHARD TO MR. CLAY.

Waynesborough, August 8, 1827.

My dear Sir,—You have set the whole world in commotion —never did one speech produce such an effect. It meets almost universal approbation, and with the wise and good there is no exception. I think they praise it too much, good as it is—a little envy, you know, is sometimes pardonable. I am informed that General J. has given an answer to your letter—shall see it in the morning at Staunton. It is said to be mild, and to give up B. as the man.

I am satisfied that a rapid change is taking place in this State, and my hopes that even Virginia will be with us have been confirmed; they grow stronger every day. I find many men with us whom I looked upon as aliens. You may depend that I shall endeavor to encourage the process which is going on. Can not you give me some good news at the White Sulphur?

LAFAYETTE TO MR. CLAY.

Paris, August 12, 1827.

These few lines, my dear friend, are intrusted to Mrs. Shaw, a daughter of General Greene, and Mrs. Greene, her niece and cousin, who have passed with us most of the time of their sojourn in Europe, and who have inspired my family and myself with the sentiments of highest respect, warm affection, and every wish for their welfare. Mrs. Shaw will go to Washington, in pursuit of a claim on British compensation, and I beg you to favor her with your kind advice; both ladies, as our intimate friends, will tell you more about Lagrange and its inhabitants than I could do in a long letter. I have written to the President about my family and election concerns; Mr. Brown gives you an account of public affairs. I shall therefore content myself with requesting my respects to Mrs. Clay, remembrance of me to your family, colleagues, and other friends, being most truly and affectionately, etc.

MR. CLAY TO FRANCIS BROOKE.

WASHINGTON, August 14, 1827.

MY DEAR SIR,—I received your obliging favor from Waynesborough. I should be very glad if I could participate with you and Mr. Southard in the pleasure and benefit of the Springs. My health is, however, not bad.

I hope you are not mistaken in the good effect of my Lexington speech. Mr. Buchanan has presented his communication to the public; and although he evidently labors throughout the whole of it to spare and cover General Jackson, he fails in every essential particular to sustain the General. Indeed, I could not desire a stronger statement from Mr. Buchanan. The tables are completely turned upon the General. Instead of any intrigues on my part and that of my friends, they were altogether on the side of General Jackson and his friends. But I will leave the statement to your own reflections. I directed a copy to be inclosed yesterday to Mr. Southard. It must confirm any good impression produced by my speech.

Tell Mr. Southard that his children are much better, and that he need not entertain any fear about them.

With my best wishes that you may both realize much benefit from the mineral waters.

MR. CLAY TO J. S. JOHNSTON.

WASHINGTON, August 19, 1827.

MY DEAR SIR,—We have only imperfect accounts from some of the Congressional districts in Kentucky. These authorize the belief that Metcalf, Trimble, and Clarke are re-elected. And so far as I learn, the Administration tickets have generally prevailed in their districts. Captain Byers appears to have declined, and Beatty and Morris were elected without any great struggle. The inclosed letter from Mr. Robertson, late

Speaker of the House of Representatives, on his return home from Harrisburg, would justify the hope that Mr. Crittenden is elected, and Mr. Walton defeated by the Administration candidate in his district; but I do not think we ought yet to count upon these auspicious results.

The city has been extremely hot since you left us; but, for the last two days, the heat has been tempered by misty weather. I think you have made a lucky escape. I should find it very lonesome, if the occupations of business did not constantly engage me.

My best respects to Mrs. Johnston; and I pray you also to communicate them to Mr. and Mrs. Madison, and to Mrs. Cutts.

DANIEL WEBSTER TO MR. CLAY.

BOSTON, August 22, 1827.

MY DEAR SIR,—My letter to Colonel Johnson was not important, and the delay in its transmission is of no moment.

You speak very modestly of recent events, in which you have borne so distinguished and so successful a part. I can not think General Jackson will ever recover from the blow which he has received. Your speech at Lexington, in point of merit, as a clear and well stated argument, is certainly at the head of all your efforts; and its effects on public opinion have not been exceeded by those of any political paper, I may almost say, within my recollection. Buchanan is treated too gently. Many persons think his letter candid. I deem otherwise. It seems to me he has labored very hard to protect the General, as far as he could without injury to himself. Although the General's friends this way, however, affect to consider Buchanan's letter as supporting the charge, it is possible the General himself, and the Nashville Committee may think otherwise, and complain of Buchanan. I should expect this, with some confidence, if they received the letter a little earlier than they may have seen the turn which the Atlantic editors have attempted to give it. As these last have pretty generally agreed to say that the letter does support the General, the Nashville commentators, if they see the example in season, may be disposed to follow it. I do not yet learn what answer comes from that quarter to your speech.

R. P. LETCHER TO MR. CLAY.

LANCASTER, August 27, 1827.

MY DEAR SIR,—Yours of the 9th instant came to hand last night. The one by Mr. A., I received a few days since by private hand, from the county of Harlan. With your letter of the 9th, Mr. Buchanan's response to the hero was received. This answer is well put together. As they say, in Connecticut, "there is a great deal of good reading" in Buck's reply. It is modest and genteel, yet strong and conclusive. I am truly delighted with the manner in which B. has acquitted himself. I really feared and believed he was placed in such a dilemma, by the General, that he could not extricate himself with any sort of credit. But he has come forth victoriously. I am greatly gratified with the result, and must believe it will have a happy effect upon the Presidential election. It is impossible it should turn out otherwise. Virginia, after this, will not—can not support the General. I never had the least hope of Virginia until now.

I presume Buck's reply supersedes the necessity of any reference to the conversation in my room. I am glad of it.

MR. CLAY TO MR. ADAMS.

WASHINGTON, August 30, 1827.

DEAR SIR,—I received yesterday your letter of the 23d instant. After its date you must have received other dispatches from the Department of State, transmitted by Mr. Gallatin. From them you will perceive that he did not take the two points, proposed by the British plenipotentiaries, for reference to his Government, but for his own consideration (see his dispatch No. 87), and that he afterward decided to reject them, and gave to the British plenipotentiaries two written arguments, one relating to the point respecting the Commercial Convention, and the other to that respecting the North-western Boundary (see his dispatch No. 88). In this state of the case the matter stands. It does not appear that the British plenipotentiaries had, in consequence of that determination of Mr. Gallatin, refused to renew the Convention of 1818; but that, on the contrary, they had again taken the subject of the North-western Boundary into consideration. So the affair, I understand, was left on the 14th of July, 1827, when

Mr. Huskisson was compelled, by indisposition, to withdraw from the negotiation. It was expected that Mr. Grant would be substituted for him (see Mr. Gallatin's dispatch No. 96).

Under these circumstances, shall I instruct Mr. Gallatin to accede to the British demands on the two points referred to? I shall await your further directions, founded on the dispatches which must have been received by you subsequent to the date of your letter. Shall I confer with the other members of the Administration who may be here?

I am inclined to think that the British Government may waive both points. I should be sorry that the negotiation should break off on these points, but there will be still another year to go upon. As to the discrimination between rolled and hammered iron, I am inclined to think the weight of the argument is with the British; but Congress has at least twice decided otherwise. You will recollect Mr. Baldwin's argument, which, however, I think, was refuted by that of Mr. S. Canning.

On the other point, we should, by consenting to the restraint which the British Government wishes to impose against our military occupation of any part of the territory on the north-west coast, come into direct collision with the House of Representatives. What shall we lose if that part of the Convention is not renewed? What danger shall we encounter? None, unless from our own acts. What shall we gain by the renewal with the British modification? What danger avoid? None. We shall only have tied those hands by a treaty, which we may keep still without it. And it will be the Executive who will have co-operated in fastening the hands of Congress.

I do not think that we ought to be hastening any settlements beyond the Rocky Mountains. We ought to do nothing more, in my opinion, there than may be necessary to preserve our rights for posterity.

MR. BARBOUR TO MR. CLAY.

BARBOURSVILLE, August 30, 1827.

DEAR SIR,—The inclosed paper was delivered me yesterday by a servant, who immediately disappeared on its delivery; so that I know not from whom it comes.* Yet the information it

* Mr. Clay endorses the envelope thus: "Supposed to be from T. J. R." The result will be found on pages 174, 175.

contains, and the anxiety manifested by the writer, induce me to transmit it by the earliest opportunity afforded by the mail.

Mad as R—— is, I can scarcely believe he will move in the subject. But surely you can have no difficulty in deciding, should he do so, to treat his call with contempt.

If you have any thing new, let me hear from you.

STRICTLY CONFIDENTIAL.

Wednesday Morning, August 28.

DEAR SIR,—I should be wanting in common gratitude toward Mr. Clay, for the interest evinced by him in Mrs. Randolph, if I did not make every endeavor to apprise him in time of a piece of news which came to my ears yesterday afternoon.

I happened to go to Charlottesville, and there heard of the piece in the "National Journal," and that Colonel Randolph had left there, intending to take the Richmond stage of yesterday afternoon, on his way to Washington, determined that he would make Mr. Clay fight him. He was exceedingly exasperated, and, as you know, is capable of any violence.

The northern stage had already been gone several hours, when this news was communicated to me, and my first impression was that Colonel Randolph had gone in that. After a good deal of painful perplexity in endeavoring to fix on a course which would reconcile my duty, as a member of this family, to Mr. Clay, with necessary secrecy (for were it ever to come to his ears, or even suspicion, that I had taken this step, the consequence would be an immediate explosion against me), I determined on riding down to Barboursville in the night. Having ascertained that you were probably there, and supposing that you could possibly send off a messenger by the same stage, to Mr. Clay.

Having ascertained that he was to go to Washington viâ Richmond, I changed my plan. I inquired at the Post-office how far the northern stage went that night. Came home, wrote a hasty letter to Mr. Clay, inclosed it in one to Mr. Wirt (to avoid having it known in the neighborhood that any letter had been written under such suspicious circumstances to Mr. Clay), on the back of which I desired any one of Mr. Wirt's family to open the letter—sent it off by a confidential servant. This morning he brings me back the letter, with the disheartening intelligence that the stage, instead of stopping for the night at the house where I was informed at the Post-office that it put up, had left there an hour or two before sunset.

I should myself ride to Barboursville this morning, but for the certainty of this visit becoming known in the neighborhood, and thus bringing on consequences which would, in the present state of the family be deplorable to them, independently of any anxiety which I may, or may not entertain to avoid his ire on my own account.

Were you, sir, in Washington, I should desire you to be on your guard, for you are an object of deadly aversion.

This is written for no eyes or ears but yours and Mr. Clay's. Burn it, if you please, as soon as read.

In great haste, yours with grateful respect,

On second thoughts, I obliterate my name, that you may answer to any inquiries, the letter is anonymous, and also without any date as to place.

THOMAS M. RANDOLPH TO MR. CLAY.

WASHINGTON, September 1, 1827.

SIR,—Upon what I think sufficient ground, I believe that you have, several times since the month of December, 1824, made use of expressions, insulting in their purport, and injurious in their consequences with regard to me.

I believe that by such expressions, and by unjust representations, you occasioned that conduct toward me from the Department of War, which defeated the object of my mission to Florida, last winter.

Lastly, I believe that you are the author of the piece in the "National Journal" of last Saturday, August 25th, in which such abusive language is used toward me.

With respectful feelings I call upon you to declare whether my belief be well-founded, or not, in each of the cases stated.

MR. CLAY TO THOMAS M. RANDOLPH.

WASHINGTON September 1st, 1827.

SIR,—Mr. Wheaton having delivered to me this day a letter from you, in which you have called upon me to declare whether your belief be well-founded or not, in each of the cases therein stated, I take much pleasure in saying, First, that I have no recollection of having before or since the month of December, 1824, made use of any expressions insulting in their purport, and injurious in their consequences with regard to you; Secondly, that I am fully persuaded you labor under an entire mistake in supposing that, by any expressions or representations of mine, the Department of War was induced to adopt a line of conduct in respect to you which defeated the object of your mission to Florida last winter. I had no agency in your appointment, nor had I any thing to do with the relations which subsequently arose between the Department of War and yourself. I remember to have heard with satisfaction of the appointment about the time it was made, and I assure you that I could not possibly have entertained any other wish in regard to your mission, but that it should have been attended with full success; and, Thirdly, so far from being the author of the piece to which I understand you to refer, in the "National Journal," of the 25th ult. (the piece under the editorial head), I had not even read it, until since I have received your note. The paper is generally left at my house before breakfast, and I do generally throw my eye over it, but the number containing the article in question, was either not left as usual, or was not seen by me.

MR. CLAY TO GENERAL HARRISON.

WASHINGTON CITY, September 6, 1827.

DEAR SIR,—A speech of Mr. Senator Branch, of North Carolina (of which I transmit you a copy herewith), has been recently published as having been delivered by that gentleman on the occasion of the Senate's confirmation of my nomination to the office which I now hold. It is brought forward to impugn a statement contained in a speech which I delivered in July last, at Noble's, near Lexington. In the course of an argument, which I urged against the improbability of any such overtures having been made, as General Jackson stated himself to have received from my friends, I contended that if they had been received, General Jackson was bound, when, as a Senator of the United States, he was required to act upon the nomination, to have disclosed them to the Senate, and to have moved the appointment of a Committee of Inquiry; and that it was especially incumbent on him to have adopted that course, as it did not then appear that any other Senator knew of the alleged overtures. I observed that I had requested a Senator of the United States, when my nomination should be taken up, to ask of the Senate the appointment of such a committee, unless it should appear to him to be altogether unnecessary; and I added that I was afterward informed, "that when it was acted upon, General Jackson, and every other Senator present, were silent as to the imputations now made; no one presuming to question my honor or integrity."

Although it can not be regarded as material to the validity of the argument, as urged against General Jackson, whether Mr. Branch did or did not make a speech in opposition to my appointment, I am desirous that in the statement of any matter of fact made by me, even on a collateral or unimportant point, there should be perfect accuracy; or that, if a mistake has been committed, it should be rectified. You will, I think, recollect, that I desired you, as my friend, with much earnestness, to ask from the Senate the appointment of a Committee of Investigation into Mr. Kremer's charge, if, from the course the nomination should take in the Senate, it should appear to you to be at all necessary; that you afterward informed me that nothing had occurred to render the appointment of such a committee necessary, and that you had, therefore, forbore to ask it. The Senate acted, as usual, with closed doors, and, consequently, no one was present but the members and the officers of the body. The injunction of secrecy was removed after the decision upon the nomination.

After the publication of my speech at Noble's, upon seeing a statement in some of the public prints that Mr. Branch had addressed some observations to the Senate, in opposition to my nomination, an indistinct recollection occurred to me that you did inform me that no Senator but Mr. Branch had said any thing on the subject of my appointment; that he made a few remarks, which were but little attended to, and which appeared to produce no impression. I think you did not state, particularly, what they were, for, I am quite sure, if you had mentioned that Mr. Branch had assigned the reasons which he now puts forward, a more distinct and durable impression would have been made on my mind. It would, however, have been too late, at that time, for me to have applied to the Senate for the appointment of a committee, if I had even thought it to be necessary, as the Senate had finally acted upon the nomination.

My object in addressing this letter to you being to obtain from you a statement, according to your recollection, of the above transactions, so far as you had an agency in them, I shall be very much obliged to you to furnish me with a reply as soon as may be convenient.

FROM MR. CLAY'S MOTHER, ELIZABETH WATKINS.

WOODFORD, KENTUCKY, September 13, 1827.

MY DEAR SON,—Your kind favor of the 14th of August last, by mail, came safe to hand a few days ago. I feel glad that you have got again to the bosom of your family, and found them all well. Rest assured, my son, I have been a great deal worse since you last saw me than I was when I had the pleasure of seeing you. I am still very low. I can make out to walk across the house with the help of a cane, or some one to help me. I feel to-day somewhat better, having had a good night's rest. My cough is not as bad as it has been. Your aunt Moss is very poorly, and has been for two or three weeks; also, her son Philip is very low; at present, there is very little hope of their recovery. Mr. Blackburn has been very poorly, but is getting better, so that he is able to attend to his business. Your sister is well. As to your brother John, I have not seen him for two weeks; I expect him in a few days; he was quite well when he left me. Mr. Watkins still enjoys his usual health, but much worn out by attending on me, both night and day. Mr. Watkins joins me in love to you and Lucretia, and the rest of the family. Pray, my son, write me when convenient: and that God may bless you all, is the sincere prayer of your mother.

MR. CLAY TO J. S. JOHNSTON.

WASHINGTON, September 14, 1827.

DEAR SIR,—I have received your favor of yesterday, and thank you for the agreeable intelligence which it communicates. If we can succeed in the coming Maryland elections, in the Delaware election, and in that in the city of Philadelphia, our cause will again be put in good heart. From Kentucky my late information is more encouraging. The partial defeat in the Congressional elections has aroused our friends, and they think it will ultimately have a good effect. Letcher says he is more confident than ever of our cause prevailing. I think the exultation on the one side, and the depression on the other, will be found to be without any sufficient ground, and that it will be temporary.

I am glad that you conversed with Markley. It may be necessary for him to come out in the end with his statement, though I think that not necessary till we hear from the Hermitage. At the last date I saw from Nashville, Buchanan's statement had just reached there.

MR. CLAY TO FRANCIS BROOKE.

WASHINGTON, September 24, 1827.

MY DEAR SIR,—I received your obliging favor of the 21st instant, with its inclosure. Mr. Southard on his return from the Springs, brought home with him high spirits and good health, and communicated to me all interesting occurrences on his journey. The result of the Kentucky elections, though in some respects to be regretted, ought not to be regarded in the discouraging light in which it is. It should be recollected that they took place before Mr. Buchanan's statement reached the State, and before the extensive circulation of the speech which you and Mr. S. too highly extolled. Many local and other causes had also an inauspicious effect, which it is believed will not operate in future. Notwithstanding all circumstances the Legislature, in both of its branches, is decidedly friendly to the Administration, and of those who actually voted for members of Congress, there is a considerable majority for Mr. Adams. This happened by the Jackson members being elected, in several instances by small majorities, and the Adams, either without competition, or by large majorities. My letters speak with good confidence on the final vote of the State. Mr. Letcher writes that his confidence is greater now than ever.

As to Mr. Ritchie's boastful statement, that is all a *ruse de guerre*. My belief is that Mr. Adams will be re-elected and with ease. I speak of course with all the diffidence which one ought to feel when expressing himself on such a subject. It is a part of the system of the friends of General Jackson to make demonstrations—speak boldly—claim every body and every State, and carry the election by storm. The circumstance most to be deprecated is that this system has too much success in dispiriting our friends. You ask my opinion as to the project of a convention in Virginia to nominate, in January next, electors for Mr. Adams. It appears to me to be an excellent project, and one that can not fail to have good effect, even if it should not succeed. It will take by its novelty, and it will command respect by its fairness.

There is a great portion (I believe a majority) of the population of Virginia opposed to the domination of the Richmond party. That majority is kept down by the principle of representation, according to territorial division, instead of population. The election of electors is the only election in Virginia in which that principle does not prevail, and in which the decision is according to numbers, without regard to counties. There is reason to believe that the greatest strength of the Administration in Virginia is where there are the greatest numbers, and consequently it will be manifested in the vote for electors. This is, or will be known, and the desire of pulling down the Richmond influence will stimulate many to the greatest exertion, and may operate, in numerous instances, to induce men to discard their preference for General Jackson, in order to defeat the party of the metropolis. In every view of the matter I think it of the first importance to push the plan. You are to have the first meeting, I understand, at Fredericksburg. There should be great exertion to make it respectable. So matters strike me. I thank you for the opportunity of perusing my letter of 4th February, 1825. I think its publication would have good effect. Perhaps it had better be deferred a little while. You could take it with you to Richmond; show it to Pleasants, and he could, at a proper time, publish it by your permission. When published, it ought to be accompanied with the explanation of the first paragraph; that my letter to you of the 28th January, 1825 (the letter referred to in that paragraph) had found its way into the "Enquirer" where it was not correctly represented, owing, no doubt, to the erroneous information of its contents received by the editor; that you wrote to me expressing regret that it had been the subject of newspaper animadversion, and hence my letter of the 4th February. I return the letter, having retained a copy. Are you coming here, as Southard (now absent) told me was possible? or are you going shortly from home? If you come, pray come at once to my house, where there is always a bed for you. I have been a little indisposed; and I have some thoughts of an excursion of a week or ten days, to get out of the dust of the office and the smoke of the city. I know not whether I shall be able to get off; but if I do, I have a thought of a little tour, first to Harper's Ferry, and then round by Mr. Monroe's, and probably to your house. I beg you not to mention my visit in this respect—first, because I do not know that I can execute it; and second, if I should, I desire to go as much *incog.* as possible.

LAFAYETTE TO MR. CLAY.

LAGRANGE, October 10, 1827.

MY DEAR SIR,—Having accidentally missed the last opportunity to answer your most valued favor, August 10th, I avail myself of the next packet to offer my affectionate thanks, and request, as much as the pressure of business allows it, the very high gratification of your correspondence.

Your diplomatic accounts from Europe have little to say, and although a member of that House, by courtesy, called Representative, I am not the wiser, nor shall I be the more useful for it. A dissolution of the House is much spoken of. The ministry are recording the new electoral lists, in consequence of a late bill mingling the vote of election with the duties of juror, to which, however, some additions have been made. As the public mind is progressing, and several willful errors have been forcibly rectified, a liberal opposition can not fail to be more numerous. The question with Government is, whether they will this year meet a larger minority, with a seven years' new lease, or hereafter risk to have a majority against them, or at least a stronger opposition than that to which, in case of dissolution, they must now submit.

The account of the funeral of Manuel having been indicted before an inferior tribunal, and our speeches on his tomb making a part of the impeachment of the publishers, it became the duty of Messrs. Lafitte, Dechiness, and myself, to claim our share in the trial, which we could not obtain. But a judgment of the court, very properly and liberally worded, has acquitted the selected objects of the accusation. An appeal from that decision to the Superior Court, has, it is said, taken place.

The intervention of three great powers in the affairs of Greece seems to promise a respite, although it has not prevented the arrival of an Egyptian fleet, and a body of soldiers. There is, however, some good in the notifications made by the French and English admirals, impeding further progress. The mediation has been accepted by the Greeks. The Ottoman Porte hitherto refuses it. So far they oblige the mediators to commit themselves a little more, and, if they are sincere, the Porte must yield at last. It is obvious to every looker-on that those powers are jealous of liberty, of complete emancipation, and jealous of each other. If any body can play the difficult game, it must be Capodistria, who is now on his third station, that of Paris, before he proceeds to the Presidential chair. He unites in his person an exclusive coincidence of happy circumstances. After he has managed those discordant elements, there will be other discordances to be managed at home, for which he also seems to be the proper and exclusive man. Upon the whole, the existence of Greece is rather more secure than it has been of late.

I have received a letter from our friend Poinsett, and can not but observe with him the general and especial attempts that have been lately directed against the peace, harmony, and institutions of the Republican States of South America and Mexico. It is very natural to see the Republican minister of North America a butt to those monarchical and aristocratical factions. That the impression is given from Europe is not, I think, to be questioned. But I have received with deep regret the part of your letter alluding to a man whose glory, great talents, and hitherto experienced patriotism I have delighted to cherish. Several painful informations had reached me, which, all together, and many more beside, could not weigh so much with me as your own sense of the matter. I beg you to continue to write on the subject, and on every matter relative to public concerns, to my friends, and particularly to yourself, who know my old, grateful, and sincere affection.

Blessed as I have lately been with the welcome, and conscious, as it is my happy lot to be, of the affection and confidence of all parties, and all men in every party within the United States, feelings which I most cordially reciprocate, I ever have thought myself bound to avoid taking any part in local or personal divisions. Indeed, if I thought that, in these matters, my influence could be of any avail, it should be solely exerted to deprecate, not, by far, the free, Republican, and full discussion of principles and candidates; but those invidious slanders which, although they are happily repelled by the good sense, the candor, and, in domestic instances, by the delicacy of the American people, tend to give abroad incorrect and disparaging impressions. Yet that line of conduct, from which I must not deviate, except in imminent cases now out of the question, does not imply a forgetfulness of facts, nor a refusal to state them occasionally. My remembrance concurs with your own on this point, that in the latter end of December, either before or after my visit to Annapolis, you being out of the Presidential candidature, and, after having expressed my above-mentioned motives of forbearance, I, by way of a confidential exception, allowed myself to put a simple unqualified question respecting your electioneering guests, and your intended vote. Your answer was, that in your opinion, the actual state of the health of Mr. Crawford had limited the contest to a choice between Mr. Adams and General Jackson, that a claim founded on military achievements did not meet your preference, and that you had concluded to vote for Mr. Adams. Such was, if not the literal wording, at least the precise sense of a conversation which it would have been inconsistent for me to carry further and not to keep a secret, while a recollection of it, to assist your memory, I should not now deny, either to you, as my friend, or to any man in a similar situation.

Present my affectionate respects to Mrs. Clay. Remember me to all your family, and to our friends in Washington. I will write by the same packet to the President.

———

────── TO MR. CLAY.

[The following proposal to Mr. Clay, from the State of New York, dated October 22, 1827, over a signature which we think proper to suppress, is indorsed in Mr. Clay's hand as follows: "I was shocked by the proposal in this letter, and need not say, that it was impossible to comply with it."]

What I would now beg leave to suggest for your consideration is, the propriety of addressing me a letter on that subject, of the date of November, 1824, about the time we met to choose electors, and after your return to Washington. It might be so worded as to be in answer to my inquiries on that head, which, with your liberty, I would publish. It would be a knock-down argument against your bitter enemies. It is at you the fatal blow is aimed, and not Mr. Adams; if they succeed against you, they well know that Adams will inevitably fall with you. He would become an easy prey, and could not stand a moment.

I trust you will not be offended at my suggestion, whether you approve or disapprove of it, when I assure you that I am actuated through motives of friendship—a friendship, sir, that can not easily be shaken. Should you think proper to make the communication, it shall be sacred.

MR. CLAY TO FRANCIS BROOKE.

WASHINGTON, November 24, 1827.

MY DEAR SIR,—I duly received your favor of the 20th inst., and most truly do I participate in the wish which it expresses, that it was practicable for us to have a personal interview.

On the affair of the V. P., it was understood at the last session, that at the one now near at hand the friends of the Administration should bring together and compare the public opinion prevailing in the respective quarters of the country, as to the proper individual to be selected, and that measures should then be adopted to give effect to it. As for myself, I have no wish one way or the other about it, so far as I am personally concerned.

On the subject touched in your letter—the propriety of an address from the Convention about to assemble at Richmond—I concur with you entirely as to its expediency. The occasion calls for it. It will be expected from the enlightened men there assembled. And the public will be disappointed if it be not able, patriotic, and striking. There are so many members of the Convention more competent than I am to suggest what should be its character and its contents, that I will only barely take the liberty of hinting, that it should make a peaceful appeal to the uniform devotion of Virginia to the cause of human liberty, and to the providing of all possible guarantees of its preservation.

Then I should think you might awaken the magnanimity of Virginia. She has had four Presidents; the North but two.

Is it not her true interest to evince that she is not actuated by selfish ambition?

The influence of Virginia can only be preserved in this Union by numbers or by moral power. The first she has not. The last she has; and what augmentation of it would she not produce, by making the present generation feel, and posterity own, that she had thrown herself into the military crevasse which is letting in a fatal current, threatening to sweep all before it? Should the election of Mr. Adams be secured by the aid of Virginia, to her weight distinctly would it be attributed. She would then be the primary power.

These hints are respectfully suggested. They might be much extended; but I have neither time to enlarge them, or to throw them into the form of a regular composition. I am acquainted with Mr. Semple. He is ardent in the cause, but thinks that he can aid more effectually by indirect than direct exertion.

MR. CLAY TO J. S. JOHNSTON.

WASHINGTON, November 26, 1827.

DEAR SIR,—Shortly after my arrival in this city in the fall of 1824, to attend Congress, and before the commencement of the session, I conversed with you freely on the subject of the Presidential election more than once. I think one of these conversations was after I had seen Mr. Crawford, on whom I called the next day after that on which I reached the city. In the course of these conversations I fully expressed to you my views and opinions as to Mr. Adams, Mr. Crawford, and General Jackson, and stated for which of them I should vote, if I was called upon to decide between them. I shall be greatly obliged if you would state, in writing, the purport of these conversations, or of any other which I had with you in November or December, 1824, in reference to the Presidential election. It is proper to apprise you that I may make a public use of the statement.*

* The answer to this note not being found, was probably published as intimated it might be.

MR. CLAY TO FRANCIS BROOKE.

WASHINGTON, November 29, 1827.

MY DEAR SIR,—I have to thank you for Mr. Giles' book, and him for writing it. I care not how widely he diffuses my Tariff speech. I believe its principles will stand the test of the severest scrutiny. I hope, however, that General Taylor will now publish his speech. I understood from him that he had come under some promise to do so.

The two parties are beginning to assemble in great numbers, and we shall, doubtless, have a full house on the election of a Speaker. The contest will be close, and if luck did not seem to be running somewhat against us at this particular period, I should say Mr. Taylor will be chosen.

The rumor of the day is that Chilton is elected in Kentucky by twenty-seven votes.

MR. CLAY TO FRANCIS BROOKE.

WASHINGTON, December 6, 1827.

MY DEAR SIR,—I received your favor of the 2d instant. Mr. Sergeant informed me that he would, in answer to a letter from Mr. Call, put your Committee in correspondence with the contemplated convention at Harrisburg, etc. General P. B. Porter, who, as a member of the Legislature, will be at Albany from the first of next month to some time in April, and will be a very suitable person to correspond with. I will obtain some other names hereafter.

We were beaten in the Speaker's election. The truth is, that Mr. Taylor was heavy to carry, and the burden could not be well thrown off. Had some person been run on our side free from the objections applicable to him, the difference would not have been greater than two or three votes, but would still, perhaps, have been against us. Now that the Opposition have obtained the Speaker, I suspect that both he and they are greatly embarrassed as to the use which ought to be made of their triumph. If an opposition complexion is given to the committees, they assume all the responsibility of public measures. If another character is stamped upon them, it will be a virtual admission that no change of measures is desirable.

If any allusion is made in the public prints to Mr. Johnston's favorable opinion of the Panama mission, I hope the fact will be put on incontestible ground.

MR. RUSH TO MR. CLAY.

DECEMBER 18, 1827.

MY DEAR MR. CLAY,—Your invitation and Mrs. Clay's to your winter evenings, got to my hands this morning, and I have passed it to my wife's. She will be most happy to be with you, as often as in her power. For myself, I am a slave, a very slave, the charter of whose present existence cuts him off from all and every such indulgence, even though tendered by " Your Excellency," as Kit Hughes would say. In truth, I am so galled, so whipped up, so ground down, morning, noon, and night, and night, noon, and morning, by being head overseer, and journeyman too, of the octogenarian department, that I was forced to make a vow and covenant on the first day of the session, not to break bread out of my own house (and miserable brown stuff it is that I break there just now), by day or by night till the session is over, if it lasts till doomsday, and we know that it is to last almost as long. This is a hard fate to undergo, and for one who likes good cheer, and has always been accustomed to it, moderately at least; yet it is to be my fate without mitigation, unless perchance I should ever break its bonds by darkening the threshhold, once in awhile, of " our worthy little master" over the way. As to our most potent sovereign lords and masters upon the hill, they would scourge me to death, you know, or flay me alive, if I do not mind their business; so the only way in which I, or mortal man like me, can compass that, and mind all the other treasury business to boot, big and little, which never stops (including a daily quantum of the most horrible parts which I never should have had to mind if our said lords and masters had deigned to grant me the humble boon I once asked of a little more clerical aid at the desks of my superannuated beureaus), is by digging and fagging by night as well as by day. This is the long and short of the story. By leading this anti-social life—hard penance as it is—I shall hope to flounder through the session without being impeached; and if God spares me till it is over, as good Christians should say, I will resume good fellowship with you and others once more I trust. But, till then, farewell to evening parties all, farewell to dinners; farewell to such dinners, even, as yours, to which, when bidden, I have never heretofore said nay—to all, farewell. Othello's occupation's gone!

I have forced an answer upon you, and a long-winded one—though the requisition is scratched out from your kind billet.

CHAPTER V.

CORRESPONDENCE OF 1828.

CHIEF JUSTICE MARSHALL TO MR. CLAY.

RICHMOND, January 5, 1828.

DEAR SIR,—I thank you for the copy of your address on the charges made against you respecting the election of President, which I have read with the more pleasure because it combines a body of testimony much stronger than I had supposed possible, which must I think silence even those who wish the charge to be believed.

With sincere wishes for the improvement of your health, and with real esteem I am, dear sir, yours, etc.

JAMES MADISON TO MR. CLAY.

MOTPELIER, January 6, 1828.

DEAR SIR,—I have duly received the copy of your address politely forwarded to me. Although I have taken no part in the depending contests, and have been led to place myself publicly on that ground, I could not peruse the appeal you have made without being sensible of the weight of testimony it exhibits, and of the eloquence by which it is distinguished.

Having occasion to write to Mr. Brougham [since Lord Brougham] on a subject which interests our University, I take the liberty of asking your friendly attention to the letter which I inclose. I hope it may find an early conveyance from the Department of State, with dispatches about to be destined for London. Should this not be the case Mr. Brent will save you the trouble of giving the intimation, that a duplicate may seek some other channel. It is desirable that the letter should reach Mr. Brougham with as little delay as may be.

MR. CLAY TO FRANCIS BROOKE.

WASHINGTON, January 15, 1828.

MY DEAR SIR,—I am sorry to learn that you are indisposed and suffering much pain from a swelled knee; but I hope you will soon get over it.

I congratulate you on the proceedings of your Convention. I was particularly gratified that you were made its President. I hear the most flattering accounts of the address to the people which the Convention has adopted. Although I am eager to see it, I have not yet had an opportunity of perusing it. But I am prepared, in advance, to make my grateful acknowledgments for the friendly notice which is taken of me. I am rendered quite happy by the kind feelings which have been cotemporaneously expressed toward me by my native and adopted State.

The address of the Convention in the latter, I send you herewith, and after you have done with it I will thank you to hand it over to Pleasants, who may possibly think proper to publish it, or parts of it, in "The Whig." All, I hope and believe, will yet go well. The new year has been characterized by many cheering incidents.

MR. CLAY TO FRANCIS BROOKE.

WASHINGTON, January 18, 1828.

MY DEAR SIR,—I have duly received your favor of the 14th instant, prior to which I addressed a short letter to you at Richmond.

The proceedings of your Convention have been seen here with the greatest satisfaction. They are all marked by wisdom and discretion. The address is admired by every body, and fully realizes the high expectation which we formed when it was understood who was to compose it.

The duty assigned you as to the communication to Messrs. Madison and Monroe, is very delicate; but it appears to me that, by giving them beforehand sufficient notice of your intention hereafter to make an official communication to them, you have adopted the most prudent course. I am apprehensive that they will decline, which I should very much regret. If they do, it will be very desirable that it should not be done in such manner as to injure our cause.

Our news from the West is very cheering. Ohio is beyond all doubt safe. So is Indiana, and I think Illinois. Our friends in Kentucky are very confident of success, as is exhibited by a proposition in the Legislature, proceeding from them, for a general ticket. It was not decided when I last heard from Frankfort.

Southard has just returned from Annapolis. I have not yet seen him.

MR. VAUGHAN TO MR. CLAY.

WASHINGTON, January 19, 1828.

MY DEAR SIR,—I thank you for your loan of the message of the Governor of Maine, and as I am still disappointed of being able to procure a copy of it through the newspapers, I take the liberty of asking your permission to keep your copy. If you can not conveniently allow me to do so, I will return it immediately.

JAMES BARBOUR TO MR. CLAY.

WASHINGTON, January 27, 1828.

DEAR SIR,—I regret much as an apparent evidence of neglect the non-arrival of my letter to you and Colonel Mercer, in time. I intentionally delayed writing till the last moment, under a high hope of giving you some determinate information of the person best to present for the Vice-Presidency; but it was still in time for the period proposed by Colonel Mercer for his departure. Your own just views made the accident of no consequence. Here and every where your proceedings have been most favorably received. You did nobly. If Virginia is not mad beyond cure, she will yet be saved. We are in high expectations of Pennsylvania. Sergeant speaks with great confidence. In fine our prospects are evidently brightening. We are looking with intense curiosity as to Madison's course. The Opposition are in difficulty with their resolution of inquiry as to abuses—the friends of the Administration challenge them to proceed. If they recede they will be obliged to admit that the slanders of profligacy are groundless. If they proceed they will find the most economical Administration of the public affairs since the establishment of the Government. ―――― is a man just from the woods, and his resolution was for mere home consumption. One of his political associates warned the house, that young doctors always killed their patients. That the parties were too equal to admit of experiments—and he should not be surprised if by this tampering ―――― killed them. Let me hear from you occasionally.

MR. CLAY TO FRANCIS BROOKE.

WASHINGTON, February 2, 1828.

MY DEAR SIR,—I am sorry to learn by your letter of the 31st ultimo, that you have continued to be afflicted with the complaint in your knee, but as you proposed going to Richmond (where I address you), I hope you have by this time recovered from it.

Our late information from Albany is highly encouraging. The partisans of Clinton and V. B. are beginning already to display their suspicion and jealousy of each other; and my correspondents assure me that there is very little prospect of a union between them to nominate a P. and V. P. In the mean time, it is stated that a powerful reaction has taken place throughout tne State.

I shall be glad to have the earliest information of the decision of Messrs. Madison and Monroe, as to their names continuing on the electoral ticket.

Should you be able to execute your intention of visiting this city, I pray you to come at once to my house, where we have plenty of room for such accommodations as we shall take pleasure in affording you. It would add to Mrs. Clay's gratification and my own, if you would bring Mrs. Brooke with you.

MR. CRAWFORD TO MR. CLAY.

WOOD LAWN, February 4, 1828.

MY DEAR SIR,—Inclosed is a letter for Mr. Poinsett, our minister in Mexico, which I will thank you to forward to Mr. Poinsett, with as little delay as is consistent with your convenience. The object of the letter is to obtain from him some of the productions of Mexico, which will probably succeed in the

Southern and Western States. Perhaps an intimation from the Secretary of State on this subject may be productive of good effects.

I hope you know me too well to suppose that I have countenanced the charge of corruption which has been reiterated against you. The truth is, I approved of your vote for Mr. Adams, when it was given; and should have voted as you did, between Jackson and Adams. But candor compels me to say, that I disapproved of your accepting an office from him. You ought, I think, to have foreseen that his administration could hardly fail to be unpopular. Those who knew his temper, disposition, and political opinions, entertained no doubt upon the subject. By accepting the office of Secretary of State from him, you have indisputably connected your fortunes with his. And it appears to me that he is destined to fall as his father did, and you must fall with him. This State could not have been driven under the banners of Jackson by any other course of measures than that pursued by the Administration toward it. Mr. Adams' general measures, although very exceptionable, would not have ranged the State under Jackson's standard. Mr. Adams has professed to consider the Federal Government limited by the enumerated powers. Yet he has recommended to Congress to erect light-houses to the skies—a recommendation utterly inconsistent with the idea of the Government being limited by the enumerated powers. This recommendation, it appears to me, can be supported by no other construction than that Congress can do any thing which is not expressly forbidden by the Constitution. The whole of his first message to Congress is replete with doctrines which I hold to be unconstitutional.

Present my respects to Mrs. Clay, and accept the same yourself.

MR. CLAY TO MR. CRAWFORD.

WASHINGTON, February 18, 1828.

MY DEAR SIR,—I received your letter of the 4th instant, and I will take pleasure in having forwarded the letter which it inclosed, to Mr. Poinsett, with the first public dispatches. I should not hesitate to intimate to him my wish that he would comply with your request for the Mexican seeds, etc., if I were not persuaded that it would be altogether unnecessary for me to second any expression of your desire to him. Our country needs much the multiplication of the products of the earth, as well as of industry otherwise applied, and he deserves well of it, who will introduce a new, or more successfully cultivate an old article of agriculture.

I do, my dear sir, know you too well to suppose that you ever countenanced the charge of corruption against me. No man of sense and candor—at least none that know me—ever could, or did countenance it. Your frank admission that you would have voted as I did, between Mr. Adams and General Jackson, accords with the estimate I have always made of your intelligence, your independence, and your patriotism. Nor am I at all surprised or dissatisfied with the expression of your opinion that I erred in accepting the place which I now hold. When two courses present themselves in human affairs, and one only is pursued, experience develops the errors of the selection which has been made. Those which would have attended the adoption of the opposite course, can only be matter of speculation. Thus it is in the case referred to. We see, or think we see, distinctly, the errors of the alternative which I embraced. But are we sure that, if I had chosen the other, I should not have been liable to greater hazard, or more animadversion? The truth is (as I have often said), my condition was one full of embarrassments, whatever way I might act. My own judgment was rather opposed to my acceptance of the Department of State, but my friends, and let me add, two of your best friends (Mr. McLane, of Delaware, and Mr. Forsyth), urged me strongly not to decline it. It was represented by my friends that I would get no credit for the forbearance, but that, on the contrary, it would be said that that very forbearance was evidence of my having made a bargain, though unwilling to execute it. The office, they thought, was an office of the nation, not of the actual Presidential incumbent, and I was bound to look to the good of the country, and not to regard any personal objections which I had to him. Can you, who have contributed, said they, to the election of Mr. Adams, decline the Department of State? Will you not be charged if you do, with having co-operated in the election of a man, of whom you think so ill, that you will not serve in one of the highest places in the public councils with him? Even if he should be wanting in any of the requisite qualifications for the station to which he has been elevated, you are the more bound for that very reason to accept, in order to endeavor to guard the country against any danger from his mal-administration. Your enemies have sought by previous denunciation to frighten you. They do not believe that you have acted otherwise than from motives of the purest patriotism; but they wish to alarm you, and prevent you from entering the Department of State.

These, and other similar arguments were pressed on me, and after a week's deliberation, I yielded to their force. It is quite possible that I may have erred, and you may be right in predicting, as a consequence of my decision, that, being identified with Mr. Adams' administration, if he falls, I also shall fall. Should such be my fate, I shall submit to it, I hope, with the fortitude of a philosopher, if not with the resignation of a Christian. I shall at least have no cause of self-reproach, for I will undertake to affirm (and I appeal with confidence to Him who knows best the human heart, for the truth of the affirmation) that, throughout my public life, in the many trying situations in which I have been placed, I have been guided exclusively by the consideration of the good of my country. You say that I ought to have foreseen that Mr. Adams' administration could hardly fail to be unpopular. I certainly did not foresee that the tree would be judged of, otherwise than by its fruits. But the popularity of a particular course or proceeding (although I will not pretend that I have been altogether regardless of it), has not been the deciding motive with me of my public conduct. Is the measure right? Will it conduce to the general happiness, and the elevation of the national character? These have been always my first and most anxious inquiries.

I had fears of Mr. Adams' temper and disposition, but I must say that they have not been realized, and I have found in him, since I have been associated with him in the Executive Government, as little to censure or condemn as I could have expected in any man. Truth compels me to say that I have heartily approved of the leading measures of his administration, not excepting those which relate to Georgia. I have not time, if I had ability, and it were necessary, to vindicate them. But, my dear sir, I must invoke your frankness and justice to reconsider the only exceptionable measure which you have specified, that of his recommendation of light-houses to the skies. It is not the metaphor, I presume, but the thing (an observatory), which has provoked your censure. And can you justly censure Mr. Adams for a recommendation which almost every previous President had made? If there be no power in the general Government to authorize the erection of an observatory within the limits of a State, is there none to sanction its location in this District? The message, I believe, was silent as to the place where it should be built. But I will dwell no longer on public affairs. I should not have touched the topic but for your friendly allusion to it. I turn from it with pleasure to the recollection of our amicable relations. Whatever you may have thought, or may have been sought to be infused into your mind, my friendly feelings toward you have never ceased; and, although our correspondence has been interrupted four or five years, I have always entertained a lively solicitude for your welfare, and availed myself of every opportunity to inquire particularly about your health and situation. I have heard with unaffected pleasure of the improvement of your health. That it may be perfectly reestablished, and that you may be long spared for the benefit of your family, and the good of your country, is the sincere wish of your faithful friend and obedient servant.

MR. CLAY TO FRANCIS BROOKE.

WASHINGTON, February 22, 1828.

MY DEAR SIR,—Your favor of yesterday is received. General Porter had been ill and absent from Albany. He had returned, however, and I have a late letter from him. All accounts concur that the political effect of Mr. Clinton's death will be favorable to the Administration; and intelligence generally from that State, especially from the western portion of it, is very cheering.

I really do not know (and who does?) what Mr. R. means by his allusion to my letter addressed to you. I do not think there is any necessity for you or myself saying any thing on that subject. As to a statement of a conversation which he represents himself to have held with me, he has been so contradictory in the House about it, that, although my first impression, when I heard of it, was to have authorized a counter-statement, my friends think it is not worthy of such a notice. If I take any of it, I shall do it in some other way, and at a future day.

I have a curious but friendly letter from Mr. Crawford, in

which he says he never countenanced the calumny against me; that he would have voted, as I did, between Jackson and Adams, etc. I have answered it in the most friendly terms, combatting, however, some of his opinions.

The inquiry in the Senate of Kentucky has terminated with the adoption of resolutions friendly to the Administration and myself. My friends there claim a decided and triumphant victory.

MR. CLAY TO FRANCIS BROOKE.

WASHINGTON, February 27, 1828.

MY DEAR SIR,—Your favor of the 25th instant is received. The House of Representatives of Kentucky having been limited to an adjournment on a fixed day, when the resolution came to it from the Senate, there was not time to act on them, and it adjourned without taking them up. My friends there think we have gained a great victory. It will possibly lead to some further publications that may render it more decisive. The general ticket has passed, so that the entire vote of Kentucky may, I think, be now anticipated.

Mr. Crawford's letter to me has been seen by several of my friends, and has been spoken of, I understand, generally in this city. I should regret that the subject should get into the newspapers, but with that exception I do not know that I ought to object to its being mentioned. It is not confidential; and, in my opinion, does Mr. Crawford as much credit as it does me.

FRANCIS BROOKE TO MR. CLAY.

RICHMOND, February 28, 1828.

MY DEAR SIR,—I have received answers to my circular from Mr. Madison and Mr. Monroe, which you will see in "The Whig" next week. They decline to accept the appointment, as was apprehended, though with the expression of sentiments, if not perverted, rather flattering to the friends of the Administration. The fact is, that they have used an expression susceptible of construction more favorable to General Jackson than was intended. They speak of the high estimation in which they hold both of the candidates, which may be interpreted now, and not then, as was intended.

MR. CLAY TO FRANCIS BROOKE.

WASHINGTON, March 1, 1828.

MY DEAR SIR,—I was prepared to anticipate the declension, communicated in your letter of the 28th ultimo, of Messrs. Madison and Monroe, to stand on your electoral ticket I regret that there should be any thing ambiguous in the terms which they have employed to express their refusal, though in that, also, I am not much disappointed. It will, for the moment, produce a bad effect, but I am persuaded that it will soon pass off. Our prospects are better, at this time, than they have been for many months.

You will have seen the allusion made in Kentucky to a correspondence between Mr. Blair and myself,* and the defiance that has been thrown out as to my allowing the publication of it. I have a copy of the letter, on which reliance is placed. It is written in a style of playfulness, and friendly familiarity, which constitutes the only objection I could possibly have to its publication. I shall let them go on making confident assertions in regard to its contents, and perhaps I may hereafter cause it to be published. With honorable men, it will do me good rather than harm. By the by, this is not a bad time to have the letter published which you did me the favor to submit to my inspection, last fall.

At present, we have no messenger to send abroad. We rarely employ one to go to France or England, on account of the great regularity of the packets. I will bear in mind your wish concerning your nephew, should an occasion arise to dispatch a messenger.

MR. CLAY TO FRANCIS BROOKE.

WASHINGTON, March 10, 1828.

MY DEAR SIR,—I have received your favor of the 8th instant. If you do not, I do, feel the attacks on you, because I fear that they are the effect of our long-standing friendship. Their effect is less, it is true, considering the quarter from which they proceed. Pleasants, of "The Whig," has not the merit of first evincing a thorough knowledge of that being, Mr. ———. Mr. Jefferson long ago understood him, when he made an allusion to

* For this correspondence see pp. 109, 111.

the same physical defect. We ought to be ashamed of ourselves, in reflecting that such a *thing* should be capable of inflicting any pain.

I wish my letter to you of February 4, 1825, could be drawn out; but how is that to be done? I have a copy of mine to Blair, mentioned by you, and although there is a playfulness, not to say levity, about it, which renders it, perhaps, unfit for the public eye, I do believe that good, rather than evil, would attend its publication. The difficulty, and the only difficulty, with me, is, whether I ought to lend my sanction to such a violation of private intercourse, and whether, after yielding to it, there would not be other and further efforts and insinuations to deceive public credulity? If I authorize its publication, I do not think the time has yet arrived when that ought to be done. I will, if I do not forget it, send you hereafter a copy of the letter.

Since the publication of my address, I have received a large mass of additional evidence, to the same tenor. Some of it is as strong as, if not stronger than, any which is now before the public. Ought I to publish it? I am afraid, on the one hand, of teasing the public, and on the other, of omitting any thing that is due to the occasion.

You are assailed for the first time seriously. May I take the liberty of suggesting that you should not allow this wanton attack to affect you, in the smallest degree? Above all, you should not permit yourself to use one expression, or to perform any act hastily. An unsullied character of more than threescore years duration, can surely successfully withstand the imbecile assaults of a miserable creature.

I will send you a copy of the report of the committee respecting the six militia men.

I am sorry for Leigh, quite as much on his as on public account. The gratification of private antipathy will never be allowed, before God or man, as a sufficient motive for the neglect of patriotic duty. Unless he fears R—— more even than he hates Mr. ———, the world and his own conscience will both condemn him.

Our accounts are truly encouraging. From New York the current of favorable intelligence is steady, unchecked, and such as to justify a confident anticipation of our success The Kentucky prospects, too, are good; and if, as I believe, we shall succeed there, we shall owe our good fortune, in no small degree, to our Virginia friends.

MR. CLAY TO FRANCIS BROOKE.

WASHINGTON, March 24, 1828.

MY DEAR SIR,—I received your favor of the 20th instant. I had previously seen in the Whig my letter to you of the 4th of February, 1825. It is believed here that its publication will do good.

I am glad that you do not allow yourself to be affected by the calumnies of Mr. ———. Here, I assure you, they do you no prejudice, and create no other than a feeling of detestation toward the author. "The Whig" has found out his sensitive part, and if man ever forfeited all claim to commisseration, on account of a physical misfortune, and justified the allusion to it by the wanton and unprovoked attacks which he makes upon others, Mr. ——— is that man.

I hope you will not fail to visit us in April. I think you would pass a week or two here very agreeably, and you are so near home that half a day will at any time take you there. Southard and Taliaferro are my next door neighbors, so that at my house you would be in the midst of your friends.

The general aspect of our political news continues good, especially from Kentucky and New York.

REV. ISAAC BARD TO MR. CLAY.

GREENVILLE, Kentucky, March 27, 1828.

DEAR SIR,—I know you will not think it strange if an unknown friend should address a letter to you. Have you not given yourself to your beloved country, devoted yourself to her cause, and may not the citizen claim you as his property and inheritance? If so, why should an humble citizen be shy and stand aloof from him whom he has long loved and admired?

Will you be so kind as to indulge me in some desultory remarks? When I was pursuing my education in Lexington, I first heard you deliver an oration at the laying of the corner-stone of the Hospital. As a student and a boy I was much pleased. Once on Poplar Row, on the pavement, I met you and there were none else on the whole street, and you spoke to me so politely and friendly, it, though a little thing, made no small impression. The next time I saw you was when I was on at

College and the Divinity School, you passed through Princeton, sitting by the driver on an outside seat of the stage, spoke to Mr. Wm. Warfield, who was with me coming up street. To say the least, the way you spoke to him (an acquaintance) impressed me that you, in no ordinary degree, were a man of friendly feeling, of openness and urbanity of manners.

But it is not merely the pleasing qualifications and attractions of private character, your eloquence and ratiocination, the boon of God, but your political course, and those important national principles of internal improvement, smiling on rising Republics, that enhance you in the approbation and give you such a scope in the affections of your fellow citizens. You have already established an imperishable reputation. A wreath of evergreens encircles your brow, and will entwine around your name while time shall last. Your reputation, the storms of persecution have tried to carry away; but it is built on a basis that moldering ages can not waste. Ethiopia will remember your colonization efforts. South America and Greece will couple your name with liberty and independence. Your Tariff speech of 1824 has opened the eyes of the American people, and they will not forget you. Roads, and canals, and manufactures, in fine, the American system, will hail you as their founder and father. Sir, if I understand flattery it is stating what is false; but I believe I am telling the truth. Truth that is already written in American history—written in the hearts and affections of the American people, more indelible than letters engraven on adamant.

For many years I have read with pleasure your speeches and observed your public course. I have witnessed with heart-burning and disgust the vituperation and slander of ambitious, wicked men. In private conversation I have often pleaded your cause, and that of the President, and of your policy. I approve heartily of your course. When my friend told me that Mr. Adams was President, and you had voted for him, a sudden exultation of joy flashed through my bosom.

We (of Greenville) had a large number of your defenses printed at Russelville, and I have spread them from my store far and wide (for I am a merchant and Presbyterian preacher). Be assured they are operating powerfully. It is the best antidote against lying and slander that has ever been used. Many of the Jackson men of this county (Muhlenberg) have turned completely around. We are decidedly Administration here, by a very large majority. I hope you and Mr. Adams will not be discouraged, but keep up good spirits.

In writing you this letter I mean no more than an expression of my friendship for you, my country, the prosperity of the nation, and the welfare of civil and religious liberty. I am in the habit of praying for you in secret and in public. If I have any interest at the court of Heaven, I have tried to make it for you. Think; they did n't say, at Hopkinsville, they knew I was an Administration man from my prayer, as I prayed for the President, etc. But it is not a cause I am ashamed or afraid of; for if even "Old Hickory" should be elected, we will not give up you. You must come next. You are consecrated to your country and you are ours.

Permit me to say, I have named my first-born son Henry Clay Bard. I did it for two reasons: 1. As a mark of affection and friendship for you; 2. That your character might stimulate him to worthy deeds.

Will you be so good as to give my respects to Mrs. Clay. Will you be so good as to give my respects to the President, Mr. Adams. Tell him I pray for him and his Cabinet. May God bless Mr. Clay. May God bless the President. May God guide and direct him and his counselors. May you all fear God, pray to him, keep his "commandments that it may be well with you."

MR. CLAY TO FRANCIS BROOKE.

WASHINGTON, April 29, 1828.

MY DEAR SIR,—I was much disappointed in not having the pleasure of seeing you. Having understood from Mr. Maury that you would certainly be here on a particular day, I even made arrangements to get some friends to meet you at dinner.

I transmitted to Mr. Call copies of my letter to Mr. Blair, which have formed the subject of newspaper animadversions, and requested him to send them to some friends in Richmond. I will thank you, also, to look at them.

I send herewith copies of Mr. Crawford's last letter to me, and my answer, which, after having perused them yourself, you will be pleased to exhibit confidentially to such of the gentlemen who saw Mr. Blair's letters as you may think proper.

Our news from Kentucky is very good.

MR. CLAY TO FRANCIS BROOKE.

WASHINGTON, May 18, 1828.

MY DEAR SIR,—Your two favors of the 4th and 6th instant, reached this place during my absence on a trip to Philadelphia for the purpose of obtaining medical advice, which I am happy to inform you was favorable.

I can not object to Mr. Tresslitt's speaking of the contents of the letter which you showed him, though I do not desire at present that they should be published.

I will endeavor to procure and forward the documents you request.

I regretted much that the considerations to which the President felt himself bound to yield, did not seem to him to admit of the appointment of our friend T———. New York has not, in the person of any citizen of that State, a single representative at this place, in any one of the high executive offices. Judge Savage is a man of undoubted qualifications, and standing high in the esteem of the people in that State. Under these views, the President thought he ought to be appointed, and his appointment has given very great satisfaction.

MR. CLAY TO FRANCIS BROOKE.

WASHINGTON, May 28, 1828.

MY DEAR SIR,—I sent the documents to you by mail requested in your favor of the 20th instant. My intention is to leave this place in about a fortnight on my contemplated journey, which I propose taking through the valley of Virginia, by the White Sulphur Springs, and thence by the Crab Orchard to Kentucky. I shall not return to the city until late in July, or early in August. If I do not then find myself entirely re-established, I will go to some of the sea baths.

The last appointments of the President have given general satisfaction, as far as I have heard. I do not think that a better arrangement could have been made. We shall lose no strength in the Cabinet by the introduction of Porter.

Our information from Kentucky continues to be very encouraging. We must be greatly deceived if Metcalfe should not be elected by a respectable majority.

I hope you were pleased with the address of our friends in Congress to the people, on the prospects of the election.

MR. CLAY TO FRANCIS BROOKE.

WASHINGTON, June 5, 1828.

MY DEAR SIR,—I received your favor of 2d instant. My health remains pretty much in *statu quo*. I do not anticipate any considerable improvement of it until I commence my journey, which I propose doing about the 15th instant. I shall go through Virginia, but by what route I have not yet positively decided. I think I shall go to the mountains by the shortest.

I have prepared a letter to the Central Administration Committee of Kentucky, in answer to one received from it on the subject of Amos Kendall, and his correspondence with me. I think some letters from him which I have authorized to be published, will fully establish his infamy.

I am not preparing, nor shall I prepare, any answer to the address of the Jackson Central Committee of this place. My opinion is, that it is unworthy of notice from me. But I shall probably publish, by way of supplement to my former address, a mass of testimony which has since accumulated on my hands, and I may publish it without comment. I have also addressed a letter to Kentucky to a friend (which he is authorized to publish), respecting my private affairs, which will relieve my friends from any anxiety on that account.

Judge Savage declined the office of Treasurer, and it has been given to General Clarke, late Treasurer of Pennsylvania, who was turned out by the Jackson party last winter, because he is a friend to the Administration. There is some reason to hope that circumstances will hereafter admit of something being done for your friend.

I regret that I have no copies of Mr. Burgess' two speeches, which I have never seen.

DANIEL WEBSTER TO MR. CLAY.

BOSTON, June 8, 1828.

MY DEAR SIR,—You will have seen some proofs of the prevailing sentiments, on public subjects, in this quarter. The best possible feeling was indicated at the meeting on the 5th. I do not mean in regard to myself, but on general subjects, and in respect to others. The toast in which you were named was received with the most enthusiastic applause. I do not think I have ever seen, in Boston, a meeting comprising so much character, talent, influence, and respectability. I hope it may do good.

One objection, my dear sir, which I have to writing to you, is, that your courtesy and kindness lead you always to answer me, and I feel that it is wrong, in the present state of your health and of your engagements, to impose any new duty, though it be a trifling one, upon you. I will really take it as a greater proof of friendship and confidence, if, how often soever I may write, you will forbear all reply, unless when there is something which you wish to say.

MR. CLAY TO J. S. JOHNSTON.

NEWMARKET, June 25, 1828.

DEAR SIR—At the moment of my departure from Washington, I received two letters (one from Duralde and one from Dupuy) recommending Mr. Gibson, editor of "The Argus," as Surveyor of the port of New Orleans. I had not time to consult with you and Mr. Bouligny, and directed the letters to be laid before the President. I have no wish on the subject but that a competent person should be appointed—one who is not tainted with Jacksonism, and who may be agreeable to friends. Will you confer with Mr. Bouligny on the matter?

We are now about one hundred and twenty miles from the city. My horses stand the journey better than I do. The heat is excessive. I shall stop a few days at the White Sulphur Springs, in Green Brier, where a letter, put into the post-office the day you receive this, or the next, would overtake me.

My best respects to Mrs. Johnston.

DANIEL WEBSTER TO MR. CLAY.

BOSTON, July 7, 1828.

MY DEAR SIR,—I am in hopes this will find you in Kentucky, in good spirits and renewed health. If you are as well as we wish you, this way, you need be no better. A strong manifestation of kindly feeling toward you, personally, has very generally appeared in all the numerous celebrations of the 4th instant, in this quarter of the country, which have fallen under my observation. As far as I can judge, the general aspect of things is favorable.

P. B. PORTER TO MR. CLAY.

WASHINGTON, July 15, 1828.

DEAR SIR,—Notwithstanding I have been overwhelmed with business in the office, ever since you left here, I would have written you sooner, but that, from the accounts which Mrs. Clay has given me, at different times, of your progress, I calculate that you will not reach Lexington sooner than this letter.

For the first ten days of my official labor, or, rather, *reconnoissance*, I found myself located in a field so entirely new and strange, that I could not move a single step without encountering some serious obstacle. I have now become familiarized to a small extent of ground, over which I move with tolerable ease, but my horizon is yet extremely circumscribed. I hope, however, to be able, by great assiduity, gradually to extend it.

I call, almost daily, on the President, who treats me with great kindness. His health and spirits have, I think, both improved since you left us.

RICHARD RUSH TO MR. CLAY.

WASHINGTON, August 3, 1828.

DEAR MR. CLAY,—Although I have had little or nothing to say, I should, at least, have dropped you a line since you went away, if only to tell you that we are all alive here; but you have been whirled about so from post to pillar, that I have not known where to aim a letter at you. You have been bargaining all over the land, no doubt. No sooner have I heard of your being at one place, but the next mail has fixed you at another, and the third somewhere else again ; but now that you are in Lexington, I may hope that you will remain at moorings awhile.

First and foremost, I am glad to learn that your health is better. Next, I congratulate you on the issue of the Louisiana election, hoping that you will follow suit in old Kentuck.

The President sets out for the North to-morrow. He expects to be gone a couple of months. I am highly pleased with our new colleague, General Porter. If I do not mistake, there is a fine mixture of suavity and energy in him. The former is very apparent and attractive ; you would come at the latter, I suspect, as soon as you get below the surface.

Adieu. Be sure you bring good tidings from Kentucky, or we will give you no welcome on your return.

P. S. August 4.—Hearing to-day that you are expected to leave Lexington on the 10th, and not being sure that this will reach you there, I will just fold it up to wait your arrival.

MR. CLAY TO DR. R. PINDELL.

WASHINGTON, October 15, 1828.

MY DEAR DOCTOR,—I observe that some of the Jackson party in Kentucky, for the purpose of withdrawing public attention from the alleged connection between General Jackson and Colonel Burr, have gotten up a charge against me of participation in the schemes of the latter. I have not myself thought it necessary to notice this new and groundless accusation ; but, prompted by the opinions of some of my friends, and actuated also by the desire to vindicate the memory of an inestimable but departed friend, who fell in the military service of his country, I communicate the following statement, which you are at liberty to publish.

Public prosecutions were commenced in the Federal Court of Kentucky, against Colonel Burr, in the fall of 1806. He applied to me, and I engaged as his counsel, in conjunction with the late Colonel John Allen, to defend him. The prosecutions were conducted by the late Colonel Joseph Hamilton Daviess, a man of genius, but of strong prejudices, who was such an admirer of Colonel Hamilton, that, after he had attained full age, he (Colonel

D.), adopted a part of his name as his own. Both Colonel Allen and myself believed that there was no ground for the prosecutions, and that Colonel Daviess was chiefly moved to institute them by his admiration of Colonel Hamilton, and his hatred of Colonel Burr. Such was our conviction of the innocence of the accused, that, when he sent us a considerable fee, we resolved to decline accepting it, and accordingly returned it. We said to each other, Colonel Burr has been an eminent member of the profession, has been Attorney-General of the State of New York, is prosecuted without cause in a distant State, and we ought not to regard him in the light of an ordinary culprit. The first prosecution entirely failed. A second was shortly afterward instituted. Between the two I was appointed a Senator of the United States. In consequence of that relation to the General Government, Colonel Burr, who still wished me to appear for him, addressed the note to me, of which a copy is herewith transmitted. I accordingly again appeared for him, with Colonel Allen; and when the grand jury returned the bill of indictment not true, a scene was presented in the Court-room which I had never before witnessed in Kentucky. There were shouts of applause from an audience, not one of whom, I am persuaded, would have hesitated to level a rifle against Colonel Burr, if he believed that he aimed to dismember the Union, or sought to violate its peace, or overturn its Constitution.

It is not true that the professional services of either Colonel Allen or myself were volunteered, although they were gratuitous. Neither of us were acquainted with any illegal designs whatever of Colonel Burr. Both of us were fully convinced of his innocence. A better or braver man, or a more ardent and sincere patriot than Colonel John Allen never lived. The disastrous field of Raisin, on which he fell, attests his devotion to his country.

The affidavit of a Mr. John Downing has been procured and published, to prove that I advised him to enlist with Colonel Burr, and that I told him I was going with him myself. There is not one word of truth in it, so far as it relates to me. The ridiculous tale will be credited by no one who knows both of us. The certificate of some highly respectable men has been procured as to his character. His affidavit bears date on the third, and the certificate, on a detached paper, on the fourth instant. I have no doubt that it was obtained on false pretences, and with an entire concealment of its object. I was at the period of the last prosecution preparing to attend the Senate of the United States at the seat of Government, many hundred miles in an opposite direction from that in which it afterward appeared Colonel Burr was bound. So far from my having sent any message to Mr. Downing, when I was last in Lexington, I did not then ever dream that the malignity of party spirit could fabricate such a charge as has been since put forth against me.

It is not true that I was at the ball given to Colonel Burr in Frankfort. I was at the time in Lexington. It is not true that he ever partook of the hospitality of my house. It was at that time a matter of regret with me that my professional engagements, and those connected with my departure for Washington, did not allow me to extend to him the hospitality with which it was always my wont to treat strangers. He never was in my house, according to my recollection, but once, and that was the night before I started to this city, when, being myself a stranger in this place, he delivered me some letters of introduction, which I never presented.

On my arrival here, in December, 1806, I became satisfied, from the letter in cypher of Colonel Burr to General Wilkinson, and from other information communicated to me by Mr. Jefferson, that Colonel Burr had entertained illegal designs. At the request of Mr. Jefferson, I delivered to him the original note from Colonel Burr to me, of which a copy is now forwarded, and I presume it is yet among Mr. Jefferson's papers. I was furnished with a copy of it, in the handwriting of Colonel Coles, his private secretary, which is with my papers in Kentucky.

This, my dear doctor, is a true and faithful account of my connection with Colonel Burr.

LAFAYETTE TO MR. CLAY.

LAGRANGE, October 28, 1828.

My DEAR SIR,—The critical time of Presidential election is now come; the busy time of the session is coming on; yet I know you ever have a thought to spare for your affectionate friend on this side of the Atlantic. Mr. Brown, whose excellent lady, to our inexpressible gratification, is now in much better health, keeps you informed of European political news. The Russians have met with more difficulties than was expected. It is said that mistrusts relative to the suppressed conspiracy have somewhat added to them. Mahmond is a spirited sultan. Yet at the long run the power of Russia is considered to have the better chance, unless the influence of England and Austria succeed in patching up a peace during the winter. Amid these broils and intrigues, France is acting a noble part quite the reverse of the Spanish Expedition, a contrast which has been observed by Ibrahim Pacha himself in his conversation with the French Generals. The session will not open until the 20th of January. Some particular points we wish to obtain have been stated in a public dinner at Meaux, an account of which I inclose. There are some others that will be mentioned; but while the present ministry are less advanced in their own liberalism than we wish them to be, they find at court a heavy drawback in their endeavors to move on the popular road. Some progress, however, is made.

Mr. Cooper is now on his travels; his late publication will give to European readers more correct notions of the United States than are found in most books on that matter, and yet I hear it is criticised in America as being too complimentary to his own countrymen. I don't find it is so, and while foolish slander is propagated in almost every British publication, don't think that feeling, or rather profession of humility, to be seasonable.

I understand Mr. Cooper has resigned his Consulship of Lyons. The emoluments of the station do not allow a special mission from the United States. I am told applications have been made in favor of my friend Mr. Bradford, a New Yorker, nephew to Mr. Philip Hone, late mayor of that city, and I hope I don't break upon my determination, not to solicit preferments, when I tell you that Mr. Bradford, whose intimacy with us has given me full scope to know him well, is one of the best, most sensible, and noble-minded young gentlemen I ever met in my life. He is universally beloved.

Be pleased, my dear sir, to remember me very respectfully and affectionately to Mrs. Clay and family.

MR. CLAY TO FRANCIS BROOKE.

WASHINGTON, November 9, 1828.

MY DEAR SIR,—I received your favor of the 7th as I did the previous one, inclosing a letter from Mr. Spotswood. I need not say that it would have afforded me much satisfaction if I could have gratified this gentleman with the appointment to the vacant clerkship in the Department of State. But Mr. Trist came recommended to me by so many powerful considerations, of ample qualifications, a knowledge of foreign languages, etc., the necessity of his appointment to the personal comfort of Mr. R., that I could not decline appointing him. In his behalf, I declined appointing a brother-in-law of the President, who was urged on me.

I can give you no satisfactory news about the election. The most discouraging aspect of our cause is that it is necessary that we should succeed in five or six disputed States to insure Mr. Adam's election. It will be wonderful if we do not fail in some one of them. The same mail that carries this letter will take you some information from New York, which will enable you to make an approximation. My solicitude about Kentucky is extreme.

Have you read my Russell correspondence? I am deceived if the publication of it does not essentially benefit me. I wish, after the smart of the election is dissipated, that Pleasants would republish it.

MR. CLAY TO ADAM BEATTY.

WASHINGTON, November 13, 1828.

MY DEAR SIR,—I received your letter of the 6th instant. From the information which it communicates, and that which I derive from other channels, there is reason to apprehend that the vote of Kentucky has been given to General Jackson. Without that event, there is but too much probability of his election. To this decision of the people of the United States, patriotism and religion both unite in enjoining submission and resignation. For one, I shall endeavor to perform that duty. As a private citizen, and as a lover of liberty, I shall ever deeply deplore it. And the course of my own State, should it be what I have reason to apprehend it has been, will mortify and distress me. I hope, nevertheless, that I shall find myself able to sustain with composure the shock of this event, and every other trial to which I shall be destined.

You kindly promise me the suggestion of your ideas as to my future course. I shall await it with anxiety, and shall receive and deliberate upon it in the friendly spirit by which I know it will be dictated.

MR. CLAY TO FRANCIS BROOKE.

WASHINGTON, November 18, 1828.

MY DEAR SIR,—I received your favor of the 11th instant, from which I am very sorry to learn that a late political event has produced on you so serious an effect. It is certainly not very agreeable, and, though feared, was not expected by me. It is undoubtedly calculated to weaken our confidence in the stability of our free institutions. But we ought not to allow this, or any other of the ills of human life, to deprive us of hope and fortitude. For myself, I declare to you most sincerely, that I have enjoyed a degree of composure, and of health too, since the event was known, greater than any I experienced for many months before. I shall continue at my post, honestly and faithfully discharging my duty, until the 4th of March, when I shall surrender my trust to other hands, which I hope may serve the public with more success—with more patriotic zeal they can not. In my retirement to Ashland, I shall find tranquillity, and whatever my future situation may be, I shall continue to employ my best exertions for the preservation and perpetuation of those great principles of freedom and policy, to the establishment of which my public life has hitherto been sincerely dedicated. I believe the other members of the Administration, including its head, will, in their respective spheres, calmly exercise equal diligence, till the arrival of the same period.

A most wild and reprehensible suggestion has been made by some anonymous correspondent of the Editors of " The Intelligencer," whose letter is published in their paper of this day, to defeat the election of General Jackson, by the Electoral Colleges, or some of them, taking up a new candidate. Nothing could be more exceptionable than such an attempt at this time.

It would be a gross violation of the pledge which has been implied, if not expressed, in the choice of all the electors. Calamitous as I regard the election of General Jackson, I should consider the defeat of his election, at this time, by any such means, as a still greater calamity.

CHIEF JUSTICE MARSHALL TO MR. CLAY.

RICHMOND, November 28, 1828.

MY DEAR SIR,—In consequence of my inattention to the post-office, I did not receive your letter of the 23d till yesterday afternoon. I need not say how deeply I regret the loss of Judge Trimble. He was distinguished for sound sense, uprightness of intention, and legal knowledge. His superior can not be found. I wish we may find his equal. You are certainly correct in supposing that I feel a deep interest in the character of the person who may succeed him. His successor will, of course, be designated by Mr. Adams, because he will be required to perform the most important duties of his office, before a change of administration can take place.

Mr. Crittenden is not personally known to me, but I am well acquainted with his general character. It stands very high. Were I myself to designate the successor of Mr. Trimble, I do not know the man I could prefer to him. Report, in which those in whom I confide concur, declares him to be sensible, honorable, and a sound lawyer. I shall be happy to meet him at the Supreme Court as an associate. The objection I have to a direct communication of this opinion to the President arises from the delicacy of the case. I can not venture, unasked, to recommend an associate justice to the President, especially a gentleman who is not personally known to me. It has the appearance of assuming more than I am willing to assume. I must, then, notwithstanding my deep interest in the appointment, and my conviction of the fitness of Mr. Crittenden—a conviction as strong as I could well feel in favor of a gentleman of whom I judge only from general character—decline writing to the President on the subject.

P. GUAL TO MR. CLAY.

TACUBAYA, November 20, 1828.

ESTEEMED SIR,—I take the liberty to recommend Colonel Belford Wilson, a son of the illustrious friend of America, Sir Robert Wilson, to your attentions and civilities. This gentleman, after having conducted himself admirably well among us, returns now, with honor, to the bosom of his country and family. As he first thinks of visiting those States, I assure you that I will be very grateful for any demonstration of regard which you may have the goodness to bestow on him.

It is with particular pleasure I avail myself of this occasion to renew to you the assurances of the ancient esteem and respect for your person, with which I am ever your affectionate and obedient servant.

MR. CLAY TO H. NILES.

WASHINGTON, November 25, 1828.

MY DEAR SIR,—I received your favor of the 22d. The inauspicious issue of the election has shocked me less than I feared it would. My health and my spirits, too, have been better, since the event was known, than they were many weeks before. And yet all my opinions are unchanged and unchangeable, about the dangers of the precedent which we have established. The military principle has triumphed, and triumphed in the person of one devoid of all the graces, elegances, and magnanimity, of the accomplished men of the profession.

Our course is a plain one. We must peaceably submit to what we have been unable to avert, firmly resolved to adhere to our principles, and to watch over the Republic like faithful sentinels. We should especially avoid gratuitous propositions of support to the new Administration, or, on the other hand, a rash and precipitate opposition. Many of our friends have got under the hostile standard. We should endeavor to recall them to their duty by kindness. A blind and precipitate attack would produce union where now there is nothing but the elements of discord.

I thank you and Mrs. Niles for the high compliment you

have lately paid me. It is a better evidence of the fidelity of your friendship than of your discretion, at this time. With my best wishes for the mother and son, I remain your friend.

J. J. CRITTENDEN TO MR. CLAY.

FRANKFORT, December 3, 1828.

DEAR SIR,—Though recent occurrences have a good deal depressed my spirits, my principles forbid me to despair. I have yet a strong confidence "that truth is omnipotent, and public justice certain," and that you will live to hail the day of retribution and triumph. Your political enemies render involuntary homage to you, by their early and spontaneous apprehensions of your future elevation, and your friends find their consolation by looking upon the same prospect. The combination that has been formed against you will dissolve—its leaders have too many selfish views of personal aggrandizement to harmonize long; your friends will remain steadfast, bound to you more strongly by adversity; you will, of necessity, be looked to as the great head and hope of the great mass that constitutes the present Administration party. This is the spirit already visible here, and I am sanguine of its final result.

What an excellent philosophy it is which can thus extract good from evil—consolation from defeat! But enough of it.

You will, of course, go on with the Administration to the last moment, as though Mr. Adams had been re-elected, and with all the good temper and discretion possible. But what then? That you should return to your district, and represent it again in Congress, seems to be the general wish and expectation of your friends here. It is certainly mine.

HENRY CLAY, JR., TO HIS FATHER.

WEST POINT, December 16, 1828.

MY DEAR FATHER,—When last in Washington, I mentioned to my mother that it would be in my power to be absent from West Point during the two months of the next encampment; and intimated that it would be highly agreeable to me to visit

Kentucky. My feelings on this subject still remain the same, but I must confess that I am not very eager to go, all things being considered. For if I am to remain in the army, it will be of the last importance to me to enter as honorable a corps as possible, and this may, in some measure, be influenced by my going, for it is but reasonable to suppose that my mind will be somewhat estranged from study. You will perceive that I am beginning to lose all other ambition than that of being an honest man. A professorship of mathematics in some college, or, lastly, a post in the army, are all that I now aspire to. My talents, I am forced to coincide with you in what I have long supposed to be your opinion, are not above mediocrity. This presents to me an insurmountable obstacle to the profession of law; for in this profession there is no medium. A good lawyer and a great man, a poor lawyer and a contemptible man, are synonymous terms.

MR. CLAY TO FRANCIS BROOKE.

WASHINGTON, December 26, 1828.

MY DEAR SIR,—Having nothing to offer you from this place, I am anxious to learn from you what is passing at Richmond. Here we are in a political eddy, the currents from which will not break out and show themselves until about the Ides of March. There is nothing but vague speculation in regard to the intentions of the President-elect, with which it is not worth while to trouble you. Toward the bottom, indeed, there is some movement in the water already, but it does not show itself upon the surface. It is said that a good deal of jealousy is felt, and in private circles sometimes manifests itself, among the partisans of the Vice-President and the Governor-elect of New York.

I get a great many letters from all quarters, conveying strong sentiments of unabated confidence and ardent attachment. I am frequently, too, favored with the advice of friends of a directly opposite tenor. One tells me, for example, that I should retire from public life for two or three years; while another is equally positive that I should forthwith return to the House of Representatives. I have as yet decided upon no course for myself, and shall decide upon none until my return to Kentucky. In the meantime, I should be glad to be favored with your opinion, and that of other friends whom you may think proper to consult.

Mr. Madison's letters are sought after with great avidity. They have produced much effect, and I think are likely to produce much more. This is evidenced by the violence of some of those who are opposed to the Tariff. You will be shocked when I tell you that one of them, and one, too, from Mr. Madison's own State, I have been told, said that he ought to have died, or that he wished he had died, five years ago.

But to return to Richmond. What will be done with the Convention question? What is the tone of party spirit? Is it a proscription there, as in some other places?

CHAPTER VI.

CORRESPONDENCE OF 1829.

MR. CLAY TO FRANCIS BROOKE.

WASHINGTON, January 10, 1829.

MY DEAR SIR,—I perceive from your letter of the 5th instant, at St. Julien, that you had not then received one which I addressed to you at Richmond, where I presume it is now awaiting your return.

We are here absolutely without any thing new or interesting. Congress is in no disposition to do business. The present Administration is winding up their public affairs, originating no new measures, and endeavoring to turn their stewardship over to their successors in the best state possible. In respect to the purposes of the new Administration, or rather the intentions of the President-elect, nothing seems to be known here. We have vague speculations only in place of positive information. Washington, therefore, is not at present the source of news. We must look to other quarters for it. And accordingly we have been turning our attention toward Richmond. There appears in your Legislature to be so many projects in regard to the basis of the representation in your Convention, that we are at a loss to conjecture whether any thing or what will be done.

As far as I can learn (and on that subject a good deal of information reaches me), there is a good spirit prevailing among our friends every where. They seem to be generally impressed with the belief that our true policy, at present, is to do nothing but look on; that they ought to avoid alike hostility or professions of support toward the new Administration; that until it begins to act, there are no means of judging what its course will be; that in the mean time, holding fast to all our principles, and keeping constantly in view the danger to civil liberty of the predominance of the military spirit, we should preserve stout hearts, and be prepared to act, under contingences, according to the impulses of a generous patriotism.

Whether I ought to be brought out, and when, must be left exclusively to my friends. This latter point, supposing the first affirmatively settled, is one of great delicacy. Precipitancy and tardiness should be equally avoided. The public wants tranquillity after the late agitation. To present formally candidates for the succession, before the President-elect enters on the duties of his office, would be premature and offensive to the quiet, that is, the larger portion of the community. It would be otherwise if the candidates of the Jackson party were announced.

Where Jacksonism has prevailed, and secured majorities in the Legislatures of the different States, those majorities are more inimical to me, at this time, than majorities in those Legislatures ever will be hereafter. They have been elected under an excitement, and I have remarked always that the representatives of the people, when so elected, are ahead of the people themselves in reference to that particular excitement.

It will be time enough, upon my return to Kentucky after the 4th of March, to decide whether I shall remain in private, or again seek to enter public life. I should be glad to know your views, and those of other friends, on that point. I presume there will be no difficulty in my return to the House of Representatives, if I should permit myself to be a candidate.

The health of Mr. Southard has been bad throughout the session. He is now confined to his house, but I hear is better to-day. Without, perhaps, there being any cause of immediate apprehension, I think his situation is one full of anxiety to his friends and connections.

Do you not mean to visit us? I need not say that I should see you with great pleasure, and although this city presents less attractions than usual at this season to the ladies, we should be most happy to see Mrs. Brooke also with you at my house.

HENRY CLAY, JR., TO HIS FATHER.

WEST POINT, January 21, 1829.

MY DEAR FATHER,—I have received your letter of the 14th instant. By it all my fears are quieted; and I can now look forward to something honorable. You can hardly conceive of a more wretched state than that in which I was before this letter was received. I have always had an inclination for the law, which arose from an entire conviction that it was the path which led to distinction. When, therefore, it was first proposed to me to come to West Point, I thought that I saw all my hopes blasted forever, and, though I desired to acquire the education given here, yet I must confess to you that I looked upon my stay at this place with a kind of horror. But now that I see that your intentions have all along been in unison with my wishes, I feel sensibly how much I have erred in the supposition, too hastily formed, that you purposed that I should become a member of the army. Feeling as I now do, I can not but beseech you to forgive me for the uneasiness which my but half-suppressed discontent must have caused you.

RICHARD HENRY LEE TO MR. CLAY.

LEESBURG, January 23, 1829.

DEAR SIR,—When I last enjoyed the honor of your company, I took the liberty of asking the favor of you, to prepare for me a list of all the treaties negotiated by yourself and by our foreign ministers, during your occupancy of the State Department. You were kind enough to promise me the enumeration I desired. I am obliged to you for the call of my attention to the principle you mentioned, so favorable to our navigation interests, and for the history of its introduction into our later treaties.

Permit me to obtrude again on your attention, so far as to beg that, amid the various and important business constantly engaging your mind, you would not forget the memoranda I want. You will add to the favor, if you will attach a note to the name, etc., of any treaty, noticing any novel principle contained in it, and elucidating the history and the intention of its introduction, and its actual or probable effect upon our national interests and national relations.

In composing the history I took the liberty of telling you I intend to write, if I have the leisure and opportunity of writing, I shall devote no small portion of it to the first Department under the Executive, and to the labors and character of its head. I say this, my dear sir, without any purpose of flattery or courtier-like spirit (my Republican spirit is above this), but because its concerns and the character and labors of its officer, of the period I shall be writing of, belong to the history and glory of my country. When I again have the pleasure of seeing you, I will take the liberty of submitting it to you, whether it would be your wish that an historian, if thought adequate to his task, should take any notice of the false and malicious imputations cast upon you and Mr. Adams, of intrigue and corruption. For myself, I am inclined to think that to notice them would be beneath the dignity of history and of your characters.

MR. CLAY TO FRANCIS BROOKE.

WASHINGTON, January 30, 1829.

MY DEAR SIR,—Ten days confinement from a severe indisposition produced by cold, has delayed my answer to your favor of the 14th inst. I am now better, though I still feel much debility from the attack.

I should be extremely gratified to be able to accept for myself and Mrs. Clay your kind invitation to visit you and Mrs. Brooke, at St. Julien, but I regret that it will not be in our power to avail ourselves of it. At the season of the year when we shall return to Kentucky, that is, about the 10th of March, we have no alternative but to proceed to Wheeling or Pittsburg. The roads on every other route will be then almost impassable. From the present time, until the period of our departure, we shall be constantly occupied with winding up my official business; with packing up, sending off, and disposing of furniture; and with other arrangements for the journey.

I should be very much pleased to visit Richmond. It would afford me much satisfaction to see my friends, and I doubt not that there are many of them that would be happy to meet me. But I must own to you frankly, that I should not expect to derive any political benefit from such a visit. The contest has been too recent, passions have not yet sufficiently abated, prejudices are yet too high and strong, to make me an acceptable guest at Richmond, where a large majority of the Legislature is of an opposite faith from that which I profess. I should, undoubtedly, find among that majority much of the courtesy which characterizes our native State. I should even, now and then, find a friend, but the great mass would be animated by a spirit, positively, if not bitterly hostile. You must have remarked what I have often observed, that when a particular popular current prevails, the representatives of the people elected under its impulse, are in advance of the people themselves in violence. It is on this principle that I am inclined to think that the Jackson majorities in the Legislatures, this winter, are more adverse to me than they will probably be at any future time.

With respect to any movements in regard to the successor of General Jackson, I believe I have already said to you that I think it would be premature now to commence them. The next six months—the next six weeks—may develop important events, and shed brilliant light upon our path. At all events, I do not wish that our friends should disturb the public in the enjoyment of that tranquillity, of which, after the late violent agitation, it has so much need. As to the danger which some apprehend, of the separation and dispersion of our friends, I do not participate in their fears. The same principles which have guided them heretofore, will continue to unite them together. In every demonstration which has been made during the present winter (witness the Senatorial elections in Ohio, Delaware, Maine, etc.), they stand firm and unshaken.

Should any thing occur to me prior to my departure for Kentucky, as being expedient to be done, in relation to the Presidential succession, I will communicate it to you.

JAMES BROWN TO MR. CLAY.

PARIS, February 13, 1829.

MY DEAR SIR,—I am happy to find that you have borne your disappointment and loss of place with so much true philosophy. If you have lost your office, you will regain your health and improve your fortune, and therefore I think you may felicitate yourself on the result. I hope, as you love a little agitation, you will obtain a seat in the House of Representatives, where your weight of talents will be felt, and where, by resuming your cheerfulness and former popular manners, you will again fill a high place in the esteem of the nation. The outs have acted wisely in resolving not to set up opposition until the new Administration shall have done something which merits opposition.

MR. CLAY TO FRANCIS BROOKE.

WASHINGTON, February 21, 1829.

MY DEAR SIR,—I received the last letter which you did me the favor to write me, and I have since received the publication relating to the Tariff, to which it refers. From the course which that business is taking in your Legislature, I apprehend that a majority will oppose itself to the opinions of Mr. Madison.

After a great deal of speculation in relation to the new Cabinet, an arrangement of it is now spoken of with great confidence. If that be executed it will consist of Mr. Van Buren for the State Department, Ingham for the Treasury, Eaton for the War, Branch for the Navy, Berrian for Attorney-General, M'Lean to continue Post-master General, or to be put upon the bench of the Supreme Court; and, in the latter case, Colonel Johnson, of Kentucky, to be appointed Post-master General. Van Buren has, from the first, run upon all the tickets for the State Department, and I conclude, therefore, that he will be appointed. I was at first incredulous as to the other persons spoken of as Secretaries; but I have been compelled at last to believe that they are, at least at this time, designed for these respective places.

I should be glad to hear from you after the decision of the Tariff resolutions in your House of Delegates. Let me know if there is any diminution in the number of those who have heretofore opposed the power. From your silence in your last letter, I infer, as I had anticipated, that the tone of the Jackson portion of your Legislature, with two or three exceptions, is decidedly hostile to me.

FRANCIS BROOKE TO MR. CLAY.

RICHMOND, February 23, 1829.

MY DEAR SIR,—I hasten to answer your letter of to-day. The intelligence it gives of the proposed Cabinet had reached here on yesterday, and filled the Jackson party with consternation. Some affect not to believe it, and some few to palliate it; you will see the vote on the Tariff, the minority has increased from forty-nine to seventy-five, and would have been higher but for the absence of some members. You have not drawn the intended inference from any letter. There can be little doubt that a large portion of the Jackson party are favorable to you, at least, this is my information from every quarter. I think the people must say with Hamlet, "Look at this picture and look at that," and for this only has been the mighty strife. I confess I am myself disappointed. I thought General Jackson, if he could not get splendid talents and information, at least would have brought around him great moral worth, as those who have least of it are not insensible to its value. Feeling must have superseded this instinct. I think that now his future course will not be doubtful. He must put himself into the hands of the Secretary of State, who will be *de facto*, President, etc.

LAFAYETTE TO MR. CLAY.

PARIS, March 8, 1829.

MY DEAR SIR,—A precious book, beautifully bound, and containing several of your admirable speeches, has been lately presented to me, by your excellent brother, Mr. Brown, as a new token of your friendship. That it has been received with every sentiment of affection and gratitude I need not, I know, to assert, but I want to express, and so I want to add that while I am happy to acknowledge your personal kindness along with your public eloquence, there is one speech, strongly tinctured with both, which although not recorded in the book, as it relates to a more private object, shall ever be engraved in my heart.

Four days are now elapsed, my dear friend, since you have been restored to a life of repose; it will probably not last long, and I anticipate the approaching time when you will be returned to Congress, and probably to the Chair of the House. I hope the intervals will be consecrated to the restoration of your health, above which, and also above every thing that concerns yourself and family, I beg you to give me frequent and minute information. They become the more necessary to me as we are going to lose Mr. and Mrs. Brown, a loss that is deeply felt by every American on this side of the Atlantic, by none more than by me, and my family who are attached to them by every tie of gratitude, affection, and respect. Mrs. Brown's health is now better than when they took the resolution to return home. We have been much alarmed on her account; it is now over, as to danger, and a few days ago she looked quite well. But all the particulars relative to her health she, no doubt, gives to her sister, and these lines will go by the same opportunity. Packets now run three times in the month. Miss Brown, who lives with them, is a most amiable young lady.

Of the affairs of Europe you have, in your official capacity, heard a great deal, and much of them is to be found in the public papers. It appears the two great despots of the East will try the fortune of war. The conduct of the French Government has been liberal and disinterested. Not so with the rulers of England; they strive to contract the limits and independence of Greece. Their connections with Don Miguel, and late behavior at Terceira, have roused a general cry against them. The American stars have lately lighted on a dextrous and honorable private attempt, of which I feel very proud. Austria is as bad as ever. Italy deserves the leaden inquisitorial yoke. It is impossible for Spain and Portugal to go on as they are now governed. The downfall of the Villele administration, and a better choice of deputies which occasioned it, has set the interior affairs of France on a somewhat improved line of march. But very slow, timid steps indeed. Far even from what could be done within the so very limited circle of an *octroid charter*. Yet, I think it a duty to assist in the little progressive good that can be obtained.

On reading again your observations on our Colonization Society, of which to have been chosen a Vice-President is to me a great honor, and a most highly valued gratification, I have thought you will employ some of your time of leisure in promoting the most important object that it remains, in my opinion, for our part of America finally to obtain. The settlement of Liberia may in future times civilize Africa, and facilitate a gradual abolition of slavery. I have seen with much pleasure that measures of the kind were talked of for the District of Columbia. You know that while I feel, as much as any man, the cursed evil entailed upon America by Great Britain, I am not insensible of the immense difficulties, but think that if an incessant attention, in the Southern States, to that momentous object of self-interest as well as of humanity, is directed that way, means may be found out consistent with prudence and possession, to limit, lessen, and perhaps, in time to eradicate that only obstacle to Southern improvements, that only objection to the example proposed to the world in the superior state of American civilization.

I am told our friend Mr. Adams intends to remain with his family in the District of Columbia; if you see them, and your former colleagues in the Cabinet, remember me very affectionately to them all. Present my best respects to Mrs. Clay and family.

My son requests me to present his best respects. Le Valleur is now a partner in a bookselling firm under the name of Malker & Co., Faubourg, St. Germain, where he has settled his family and himself. You know that M. David, one of the first statuaries in the world, and the first in Paris, member of the Institute, etc., has presented Congress with a marble bust, made on purpose to be offered as a tribute to them. It has been much admired by the artists of Paris.

MR. CLAY TO FRANCIS BROOKE.

WASHINGTON, March 12, 1829.

MY DEAR SIR,—I have not written you very lately, because, having nothing to communicate which the papers did not contain, I did not wish to make you pay postage for the thousand rumors with which this city has been filled. Among the official corps here there is the greatest solicitude and apprehension. The members of it feel something like the inhabitants of Cairo when the plague breaks out; no one knows who is next to encounter the stroke of death; or which, with many of them is the same thing, to be dismissed from office. You have no conception of the moral tyranny which prevails here over those in employment. It is, however, believed that the work of expulsion will not begin till after the adjournment of the Senate.

It is said that Amos Kendall, of Kentucky, is to be appointed an auditor, and Tom Moore minister to Colombia!

I take my departure to-morrow. My inclination at present is not to return to the next Congress, but I shall reserve a final decision of the question, for a consideration of all circumstances, after my return home. The major part of my friends, whom I have consulted, think a seat in the next Congress inexpedient. Among them all the best spirit prevails, and high and confident hopes are cherished by them. Every movement of the President, though dictated by personal resentment toward me, conduces to my benefit, especially his Kentucky appointments.

Let me hear often from you, and believe me ever your devoted friend.

MR. CLAY TO J. S. JOHNSTON.

WHEELING, April 1, 1829.

MY DEAR FRIEND,—W. C. C. Claiborne having decided rather suddenly to throw himself on board a steamboat about departing for Louisville, I have only time to say that we reached this place the day before yesterday, nine days after you, in good health. I found here your letter, informing me of your journey, etc. The same snow that you left on the mountains remained, and smoothed our passage over them, although it rendered us somewhat uncomfortably cold.

My journey has been marked by every token of warm attachment and cordial demonstrations. I never experienced more testimonies of respect and confidence, nor more enthusiasm. Dinners, suppers, balls, etc. I have had literally a free passage. Taverns, stages, toll-gates have been generally thrown open to me, free from all charge. Monarchs might be proud of the reception with which I have been every where honored.

The work of proscription has commenced at Washington and elsewhere. Our poor friends, Cutts, Watkins, and Lee, are among the sufferers. Editor Hill has succeeded the first, Editor Kendall the second, and Major Lewis the last. So we go.

Let me hear from you, and often, I entreat of you, for no one feels more warmly actuated in the welfare of you both than your constant friend.

MR. ADAMS TO MR. CLAY.

MERIDIAN HILL, WASHINGTON, April 21, 1829.

MY DEAR SIR,—Your favor of the 12th instant, inclosing a letter to you from Mr. Child, with your answer, has come to hand. The letter to Mr. Child has been forwarded to him as you desired.

I have no design or wish that old party distinctions should be revived, and do not believe that they will or can be. A struggle by certain individuals of the old Federal party to recover the ascendency they had lost, may render a reaction of the Republicans necessary for their own defense; it can be necessary for no other purpose of which I am aware, and I have no wish to fortify myself by the support of any party whatever.

The objection there appears to me to be against applying the denomination of Federalists to the opposers of protection to manufactures and internal improvement is, that I believe the fact to be otherwise. The old Federalists were generally friendly to those interests. Washington was pre-eminently so. The remains of the Federal party now are divided upon those questions, as they are upon all others of present political interest. They have now no public principle peculiar to themselves.

The Federalists have generally supported the measures of the two last Administrations. Those Administrations have adopted and practiced upon many of their favorite opinions. Most of the New England manufacturers are Federalists, and would hardly be gratified by the application of their names to their opponents.

The composition of the new Administration indicates the intention to conciliate the South. Perhaps means will be found also of propitiating the West. New England will not be a favorite; nor, it would seem, will Virginia; but there is now no propensity to opposition in either.

You will have time, between this and next August, to fix your opinion, whether it will be advisable for you to come to the House or not. I have no doubt your presence here will be salutary. But whether, at the present Congress, a seat in the House would conduce to your health or comfort may admit of doubt.

Wherever you may be, you will have with you my respect and esteem.

RICHARD HENRY LEE TO MR. CLAY.

WASHINGTON, April 22, 1829.

DEAR SIR,—From a late paper, I learn that you and your family have arrived at home, without accident. Permit me to express to you the pleasure this intelligence has given me.

I was chagrined, that through misinformation of the time of your departure from this city, I did not enjoy the friendly privilege of presenting to you the parting assurances of my respect and remembrance. I felt this circumstance so much, that I determined to take the earliest opportunity of presenting them to you, which I do now, when they are as strongly entertained.

No one, my dear sir, of your friends and fellow-citizens, has traced the course and incidents of your return to Kentucky with more interest and gratification than myself. "I will not despair of the American Republic" while I observe the redeeming and purifying leaven which yet remains in her citizens. It is essentially diffusive, and will yet leaven the whole mass. It is not the frothy effervescence of sordid interest and ignorance, but the genuine risings of enlightened and fearless patriotism. To drop all figure, the gloom in which you left us here was dispelled by the events of your journey. I rejoiced in the testimonials of the confidence and gratitude of the country, so generously and enthusiastically offered you. They have cheered more than half a million of freemen, who, as you truly observed, are not surpassed by any body of men on earth, in civic virtues and intelligence. I was cheered with them, not only because they prove the sense of justice to be strong and fearless, but because they give us reason to hope that by concentrating all our efforts upon a statesman, we may yet be able to bring back the people to a just estimate of civil services, civil qualifications, and civil freedom.

Mr. Adams (whom I have lately seen, in fine health and spirits) has very much gratified his friends by his letter to the citizens of New Jersey. The irony of the last paragraph was keen, and just toward him, who, on such an occasion, had the indecorum to charge him with corruption and abuse of office, and to libel half a million of his fellow-citizens. The truth and faithfulness of the portraits Mr. Adams has so glowingly drawn, have struck the public with a force which has exceedingly annoyed the unwilling beholders, whose eyes could not be altogether turned away from the brilliant colors and the striking resemblances. That letter has blistered the tribes of error in all their gradations.

I can not but hope, my dear sir, that in considering your own plans and views, and the wishes of your friends and fellow-citizens, you may decide that your duty requires you to appear again in public in the House of Representatives. Aside from all public views, which you are best able to take and correctly to weigh, it would afford me great gratification to be able to renew the personal intercourse with which you honored me.

You have said, that "the country needed repose." However true this may be, *I know* that it is contemplated in Virginia, in less than two years, to accept your pledge to serve your country, which will be signified by public meetings, the number and character of which will be impressive to others, and imperative upon you. I expect to return to my native State in two years, and to mingle my efforts in giving impetus to these movements.

I once mentioned to you my design of writing a History of the Administration of Mr. Adams. My relation, Mr. Fendall, had anticipated me. He will execute this just and grateful task, while we will compare our views and unite our researches.

FRANCIS BROOKE TO MR. CLAY.

St. Julien, April 29, 1829.

My dear Sir,—I may now congratulate you on your safe arrival with your family at Lexington, and on your triumphal journey from Washington to your peaceful home. The unsolicited and unbought respect and affection of numerous bodies of your fellow-citizens, must much enhance the feelings with which a consciousness of having discharged faithfully your duties to your country inspires you, and give an example to others which will stimulate them to do the like, in despite of the slanders that may annoy them.

MR. ADAMS TO MR. CLAY.

Meridian Hill, Washington, May 2, 1829.

Dear Sir,—I have received your obliging letters of the 16th and 19th ultimo, the latter covering a copy of my correspondence with the New Jersey Committee, printed upon satin. I am happy that my letter was satisfactory to you, and I have learned that it has been generally gratifying to our friends. There was a testimony due from me to all the members of the late Administration, and in a special manner to you. No better opportunity could have been afforded me to give it than that presented me by the New Jersey Address, and I availed myself of it with pleasure.

The Catholic Question has assumed in England an aspect entirely new; and is presenting appearances quite unexpected. Brought forward in Parliament by the Duke of Wellington and Mr. Peel, carried in the House of Commons by a majority of more than two to one, it is almost doubtful whether it will yet overpower the cry of "No Popery" in the House of Peers, among the people, and with the king. Mr. Gallatin, who is here, and called upon me a few days since, thinks it will pass the House of Lords by a small majority.

May 11, 1829.

I was interrupted in the writing of this letter by information of a domestic calamity, of which you will have seen some account in the newspapers, and which has disqualified me for the time even for the performance of some of the duties of social life. The loss of my eldest son has been followed by an aggravation of the infirm health of his mother, and by an effect upon my own spirits, calling for more than the consolations of philosophy.

Mr. Southard, before he left this city, had met with an affliction similar in its nature, though not equally severe, in the loss of his youngest daughter. He has returned home, and, I have learned, is recovering his health. Mr. Rush has sailed for England.

I expect to leave this place toward the close of this month. I have no intercourse with any member of the Administration, and am a silent observer of passing events.

JOHN L. LAWRENCE TO MR. CLAY.

NEW YORK, May 2, 1829.

DEAR SIR,—Since our separation at Gottenburg, I have had but few opportunities of presenting myself to your remembrance, except in the way of recommending to your notice, personally or officially, some whom I deemed worthy of it. Let my motive excuse me for now obtruding on a subject, immediately relating to yourself, but interesting to the nation at large.

A report reached us on the 30th ult., that a duel had been

fought in which Mr. Pope was your antagonist, which terminated fatally to you. Although it came in so questionable a shape as to warrant disbelief, it filled the minds of our worthiest citizens with apprehensions of its truth. Idle as the arrival of successive mails has proved the rumor to be, it has forced the community to reflect, most seriously, on the consequences that would flow from the reality, and has created feelings, of which, I am sure, you will not be regardless.

In looking for relief from the evils, actual and prospective, to which an inconsiderate admiration of great military talent has exposed the country, the eyes of the largest portion of the intelligent and reflecting turn to you, as the instrument of our deliverance. From you, therefore, duties are manifestly owing of higher obligation than any purely personal. It is undoubtedly difficult to repress the sensibilities of an honorable mind smarting under wrongs, and goaded by their repetition ; but the effort is noble in itself, and is imperatively demanded by your present relations to your fellow-citizens. The sentiment, that in a crisis like this, all private considerations should yield to our regard for the national welfare, is one to which you are pledged by repeated declarations. I submit, whether you have not thus offered the guarantee of your personal reputation, that no matters merely affecting yourself shall tempt you to endanger the public cause ?

It is not my intention to enter into prosing remarks on duelling, or to say that it never ought to be resorted to. Your own affair at Washington was perhaps unavoidable, situated as you then were. But your position has materially changed with the times, and brings a corresponding change of obligation along with it. Public sentiment would now condemn what then it might excuse or even approve. The honest prejudices of the people exact from you a homage which need not before have been accorded. In a large section of the Union the practice is regarded with horror. In our own, where the pistol has been as fashionable and as fatal as elsewhere, appeals to it, as the arbiter, have become absolutely disreputable. Even in those States where duelling is yet countenanced, I apprehend that it is a necessary recourse only when one's character for personal courage might suffer by declining. This motive can not operate in your case. Were your worst enemy required to pronounce on that point he would probably censure you for being too chivalrous.

Besides the considerations above stated, there is another demanding much attention. The new Administration is essentially belligerent; and without a corps of sharp-shooters its arrangements would seem incomplete. It might, peradventure, be imagined by some self-constituted legion of honor, that your removal from "this world of woe" were a meritorious service! If it be understood that you are to take the field whenever an adversary gives occasion, you may make up your mind to successive hazards of your life, until the catastrophe shall be accomplished.

I have been thus plain, perhaps I ought to say abrupt, on this subject, because I have seen and felt how intimately it is connected with the best hopes of the country. A repetition of apology is needless to one of your own frank disposition. On that disposition I rely for permission to add my confidence, that if similar reports shall hereafter reach us, we may at once stamp them with discredit and denial.

MR. CLAY TO FRANCIS BROOKE.

ASHLAND, May 12, 1829.

MY DEAR SIR,—Your favor of the 29th ultimo is duly received. I must refer you to the public prints for the incidents of a journey which, though performed at an unpleasant season, and over bad roads, was full of gratification, on account of the testimonials of esteem, public and private, by which it was attended. On Saturday next I am to attend a public dinner, which promises to be the largest ever given in this State.

I have been much occupied, since my return, with repairs to my house, grounds, and farm. As far as I have yet been able to learn the state of public feeling and sentiment toward me, it is far from being unfavorable, except with a few of the most violent of the Jackson party. Many of them have come out openly for me, and several of the most prominent of them in this district have communicated their wishes that I would offer for Congress. I could not only be elected with the most perfect ease, but I have reason to believe that there would be no opposition from any quarter whatever. The public, nevertheless, confiding, perhaps, too much in my judgment as to what is best to be done, is entirely disposed to acquiesce in any resolution I may take. That which I have adopted, is, to offer for no office at present, and until I can see more distinctly than I do now how I can be useful, but to remain in private life, attending to the care of my private affairs, and the re-establishment of my health. I was consulted repeatedly to know if I would serve in the Legislature, but I thought it best to decline.

There is enough in passing events, God knows, to alarm, to arouse, and to urge to the most strenuous exertions; but, if I were to put myself forward, my motives and my actions would be questioned, and perhaps the reaction so desirable would be retarded, instead of being accelerated. Others, I think, had better take the lead, who stand in attitudes less likely to excite passion and prejudice. Above all, we must rely upon the reflections and convictions among the Jackson party themselves. Already they begin to repent, that is, many of the better portion of them. Pride restrains them from denouncing openly, with their mouths, an Administration which they detest from their hearts. As time elapses, and new events are developed, they will take courage, and finally concur in restoring the civil rule.

I have not determined to return to the practice of my old profession, and nothing but necessity will compel me to put on the harness again. That I hope to be able to avoid.

I must request that you will keep me informed of all that relates to your Convention, its composition, etc., etc.

HENRY CLAY, JR., TO HIS FATHER.

WEST POINT, May 19, 1829.

MY DEAR FATHER,—You caution me against remitting my efforts in my present pursuits, in my eagerness to enter upon the study of the law. I hope, and at present feel confident, that I shall preserve my rank in my class. The course of studies of his year is by no means so difficult as that of the last, or of the coming year. I now find time to attend to some studies which I believe will be useful to me when I commence the study of law. I am reading Montesquieu's Spirit of Laws. I take much interest in it. The subjects treated of are such as would present themselves continually to a man's mind in our country of laws and of free inquiry. The style of the work is very different from the general style of the French, for it is both concise and comprehensive.

I shall be with you by the 1st of July. Remember me to our friends.

P. S.—I would be glad if you would send me an application by you for a furlough for me. I believe I have not mentioned this to you before, although it ought to have been done, for by a regulation of the Academy, it is required that the application of the parent or guardian should be handed in, together with that of the cadets, on the 1st of June.

MR. CLAY TO ADAM BEATTY.

ASHLAND, June 2, 1829.

MY DEAR SIR,—I have lately purchased in Washington County, Pennsylvania, fifty full-blooded Merino ewes, the choice out of three hundred, part of one of the finest flocks in the country, which belonged to the late Mr. R. W. Meade, whose persecution and sufferings were so well known in Spain. The choice was made by a friend of mine, himself one of the largest sheep owners in Pennsylvania, and one of the best judges that I know of. There are about sixteen or eighteen lambs with them, and I suppose an equal portion of rams. I expect them all at Maysville in the course of eight or ten days, on their way to my residence.

It is my intention to let a few of my particular friends have about a dozen of them, at reasonable prices. If you wish any of them you may have your choice of an ewe with the ram lamb belonging to her, at $25 for both. Should you decide to take them, you may show this letter to Messrs. January & Co., as their authority for delivering them to you.

Is there not danger, my dear sir, of an adverse result to the Congressional election in your district? I fear it, and I hear perhaps some things that you do not. There is much dissatisfaction among our friends in Bourbon, as I regret to learn. They think that they are entitled to the member. Can you not devise some plan to collect and concentrate public opinion in behalf of one candidate of the party of our friends? There is no one in the district that I should be more happy to see elected than yourself; and I hope, if you continue to offer, that you may be. But if it be impracticable, from any cause, perseverance might display resolution without leading to any good issue. Perseverance indeed, without success, might lead to the worst consequences to yourself and to the district. It might give a permanently unfriendly character to the district. Such I have several times observed to be the effect of divisions elsewhere among our friends.

There is always danger, which I trust I need not guard you against, of the opposite party practicing deception in regard to the prospects of candidates among their opponents.

I pray you, my dear sir, to appreciate the friendly motives which have dictated these observations, to which you will give just so much weight as they deserve.

Under all circumstances and every contingency I pray you to believe me sincerely your friend.

MR. CLAY TO ADAM BEATTY.

ASHLAND, June 7, 1829.

MY DEAR SIR,—I have been mortified by the late movements in Bourbon, in bringing out Mr. Marshall for the House of Representatives, lest you might suppose that when I wrote to you a few days ago, I had some knowledge that they were in contemplation. Such a supposition would be very far from the fact. I had no more knowledge or information about them, when I wrote that letter, than the man in the moon. I had indeed understood from Mr. Marshall himself, that he would not be a candidate, and I was well pleased with that decision, because I believed it to be in conformity with the best interests of his family. And now I have no doubt, indeed I have heard that he had been brought out, most reluctantly on his part, in consequence of the state of things to which I alluded in my last, as existing in Bourbon.

I derived information of that state of things, principally from Mr. Rain, the sheriff of Bourbon, and Mr. Spiers, who were at my house the day after the dinner at Fowler's garden. They both represented the dissatisfaction in Bourbon, among our friends, to be very great, because a candidate was not selected from that county, and they both concurred in expressing the belief that they could not be prevailed upon to rally at the polls on any candidate out of Bourbon, Mr. Rain expressing that opinion with more, and Mr. Spiers with less, confidence. I urged them to support you. They said that they hoped some measure would be yet adopted to collect the sense, and unite the exertions of our friends throughout the district. I of course supposed that that measure would be some such as was adopted last year. I went to Madison on Tuesday last, and it was not until my return on Thursday, that I learned what had transpired in Bourbon.

I have thought these statements due to our long and warm friendship, and I hope they will be received in the spirit in which they are made.

I have not yet heard of my sheep having been started.

MR. CLAY TO J. S. JOHNSTON.

LOUISVILLE June 26, 1829.

MY DEAR SIR,—I quit this city with much regret, on account of my not seeing you. The trial of young Wickliffe, fixed for Tuesday next, and the preparations incident to it, oblige me to go. I have, during four days, been in constant expectation of your arrival. I am informed by rumor only, of your being on board the Hibernia.

I have not time to enter into details on public affairs. Unless my friends are greatly deceived, there is not a particle of doubt about the disposition of Kentucky to support me, and although it is too early to draw the line between those who are for, and those who are against me, we have reason to hope the friendship of the majority of the next Legislature.

I should be extremely delighted to see you at Ashland. Can you not visit us? If not, do let me hear from you.

MR. VAUGHAN TO MR. CLAY.

WASHINGTON, July 1, 1829.

MY DEAR SIR,—I return you my very best thanks for the promptitude with which you have executed my commission, and procured for me a genuine Kentucky rifle. I shall hope to receive it about the time of the meeting of Congress, if not before. I find the opportunities of sending any thing from Washington to Kentucky by private hands rarely occur. I have long had in my possession, the portrait of a spaniel dog, lithographed by a very young boy, the son of our friend Christopher Hughes. Among many copies which he sent to me to distribute among his friends at Washington, was one for Mrs. Clay. To send it by the post would be to risk spoiling it. Do suggest to me some means of forwarding it.

I have a letter from Christopher Hughes, dated the 10th of May, when he was waiting with anxiety to know his fate, whether he was to be *envoyé* or *renvoyé*. I am very sorry to know that by this time he must be aware that he is to be superseded by Mr. Preble, and I do not yet hear what other appointment he is likely to get.

Mr. Ouseley is to embark on the 8th, at New York, for England, with the first statement on the part of the United States, respecting the Boundary Question, referred to arbitration. I think the statement well done.

I am glad of an occasion of opening a communication with you. You will be glad to know that I am perfectly satisfied with the conduct and feelings of the present President, in all communications which I have had with his Government, as British minister.

I leave it to others better informed than myself, to tell you the news of Washington. I am glad to find that you justly appreciate the conduct of the Duke of Wellington, in carrying through the Catholic Relief Bill. The difficulties were insurmountable for any other man.

With kindest regards to Mrs. Clay and all your family, not forgetting Johnny, believe me ever yours, etc.

MR. CLAY TO ADAM BEATTY.

ASHLAND, July 9, 1829.

MY DEAR SIR,—I duly received and have attentively read your favor of the 26th ultimo, with the inclosure, the address to the voters of the Second Congressional district. I entertain no doubt that you have correctly represented the purport of your interviews with Major Allen, and that you have been unjustly dealt by on account of them.

I view with inexpressible regret the state of things in your district, and I should be most happy to learn that any mode had been adopted to concentrate on yourself, or any other friend, the votes of those who concur in their political principles. Can no such mode be fallen upon? Is it not yet practicable to convene persons together from all parts of the district? Of what avail to the present candidates, on the same side, can it be to persevere, with the certainty of defeat before them all? How will the honor of any one of them be vindicated by such a course? Defeat can neither gratify friends nor the candidate himself. It may display his resolution, but it can prove nothing else. Most certainly neither of the candidates can feel gratified by being the instrument (should such be the result) of the failure of his competitor on the same side.

The existing state of things can afford pleasure to none but our opponents. They alone will profit by it. And I fear that it may lead, in your district, to pernicious consequences permanently.

I have not seen nor heard directly from Mr. Marshall since he was announced. I believe him utterly incapable of deception; and I therefore feel confident that he has been brought out contrary to his wishes; for he told me in April that he had no desire whatever to be a candidate. I do not know him, if he would not concur in any honorable expedient by which a member can be returned favorable to those views of national policy which both he and you entertain.

But I must leave this painful subject, fearing, I confess, that owing to the unhappy divisions among friends, we are destined to add another to the long catalogue of defeats, from the same cause, which we have sustained within a few years.

I have been disappointed in not receiving the Merino sheep, which, I presume, have been kept to be sent when the weather is somewhat cooler. You shall be advised of their arrival.

MR. CLAY TO J. S. JOHNSTON.

ASHLAND, July 18, 1829.

MY DEAR SIR,—I received your obliging letter of the 8th instant, under date at Maysville, and I perused with great satisfaction the information and reflections it contains. Although I have an aversion to some long letters, it does not extend to that, and you would greatly oblige me by frequently writing me similar ones. I agree with you in most of the reflections which you have communicated. The elements undoubtedly exist for a serious, if not doubtful struggle, at the next presidential election. I believe with you, that, on certain contingences, General Jackson will be again brought forward. But whether he should be or not, if the party that elected him can be kept together, in any considerable extent, it will be formidable, whoever else may happen to be taken up. The next session of Congress will, I think, greatly add to the dissolvents of that party which are now operating. Whatever the President may say or recommend in his message to Congress, his friends in the body must divide on certain leading measures of policy. Each section of it will claim him as belonging to it, if he should be silent, and a quarrel between them is inevitable. On the contrary, if he speak out his sentiments (probably the safest course for him, whatever they may be), he must throw from him all of his party who are opposed to his sentiments, and those thus cast off, must, sooner or later, attach themselves to the party which has all along been adverse to the General. If, for example, he comes out for the Tariff, the South leaves him, and will try another change, if it can effect it, of the office of chief magistrate. If he comes out in opposition to the Tariff, there will be such an opposition to him in the Tariff States, as must prevent his re-election.

The worst course for those who were opposed to his election, and are now unwilling to see him re-elected, is that he should declare himself unequivocally for the Tariff. The best course for them is, that he should come out clearly against the Tariff. In the former case, it would be difficult to detach, in sufficient numbers, the friends of the system from him, and make them comprehend the expediency of supplanting the head of an Administration favorable to their views. This was done in the case of Mr. Adams, but that was an exception, from various causes. In the latter supposition it would not, I think, be at all difficult or impracticable to unite the friends of the Tariff, and place at the head of the Administration one who would promote their policy. In short, I think matters have come, or are rapidly tending, to such a state of things, that those who are in favor, or those who are against certain measures of policy, must govern. Masks must be cast off, and the real color and complexion of men and their opinions must be seen.

In respect to my future personal movements, I hope so to conduct myself as to satisfy my friends. I appeared for young Wickliffe with some reluctance. I would have avoided doing so, if I could have avoided it honorably. But the case had such a triumphant issue, that I have been greatly benefited by it, in this State, instead of being injuriously affected.

I will write you after the result of the August elections is certainly known. Prospects continue very good, but they are better for the State Legislature than for Congress. In Chambers' late district you saw what they were. Mr. Marshall has declined, but Beatty's election is still regarded uncertain.

MR. CLAY TO J. S. JOHNSTON.

ASHLAND, August 26, 1829.

MY DEAR SIR,—The result of our Congressional elections was not as favorable as might have been, owing to bad arrangements. Beatty was beaten by a majority of only twelve, owing to Bedinger's perseverance as a candidate, and his own want of tact. In Tom Moore's old district our triumph is complete.

In both branches of our General Assembly we have large majorities, bordering upon two thirds in each, of friends of the late Administration. The majorities friendly to me are still larger.

Ought our Legislature to do any thing, and what, at the ensuing session? Let me know your opinion, and that of our friends in your quarter.

It may adopt either of two courses: Make a direct nomination, or, avoiding that, limit itself to an expression of undiminished confidence and attachment, and a discrediting of calumnies, etc., etc. What is best? Or is it best to embrace neither course?

My health continues good. Mrs. Erwin remains at Ashland, but I shall accompany her to Russellville about the 10th of next month.

My affectionate regards to Mrs. J.

MR. CLAY TO ADAM BEATTY.

ASHLAND, September 5, 1829.

MY DEAR SIR,—My friend Mr. Ewing informs me that he sent my sheep on the 26th ultimo, from his residence, near Washington, in Pennsylvania, in the care of a man whose name he has omitted to mention. They were to proceed by land, and were expected to travel at the rate of about fifteen miles per day. If no accident has happened, they ought to be at Maysville about the time this letter reaches you. I will thank you to take measures to secure a knowledge of their arrival, so that you and Mr. Foreman may make choice of the ewe and ram lamb which I have reserved for each of you. Should you prefer not to take the dams of the particular lambs which you may choose, you are at liberty to take other ewes, without lambs, in lieu of them. As the weaning-time is at hand, I thought this option might be agreeable to you. This letter is an authority for the selection which you may make, as well as your friends.

I received your favor in regard to the unfortunate issue of the election. You have no friend who more sincerely regrets it than I do; but as that is now unavailing, I hope, with you, that it may lead to no lasting consequences of a nature to be deprecated.

ALEXIS DE SARCY* TO MR. CLAY.

SEPTEMBER 6, 1829.

SIR,—To address you directly through the mail is hazardous, and as I have information to communicate which I deem of importance as well to you personally as to the country, you may expect in a few days to hear from me, under cover to some friend in Lexington. In that dispatch you will learn the mode of communicating with me.

There is a Virginian at present residing in Franklin, in Louisiana, a Dr. John N. Field, he is an active zealous friend to you, and has influence which he uses freely; he receives "The Focus;" send him "The Reporter." The cause derives benefit from his efforts.

HENRY CLAY, JR., TO HIS FATHER.

WEST POINT, September 18, 1829.

MY DEAR FATHER,—I received your favor of the 3d instant. I am glad to be able to write, in answer to a portion of it, that I am not only satisfied about West Point, but, in fact, am so well persuaded that advantages closely connected with my fu-

---

* An assumed name.

ture welfare may result from the continuation of my academic course, that nothing would now induce me to leave this place. My dear father, your kindness and indulgence have convinced me that I have greatly erred, and that I can not too soon ask your forgiveness of my offense. When I wished to act in direct opposition to your decided advice, by not returning to West Point, my unwillingness to return did not arise from any obstinacy of opinion as to the utility of the course of this school, but merely from a sanguineness of success which so often leads young men to suppose that they are as competent to contend against the difficulties of the law, at eighteen years of age, as they will be at any future time. However, all this has passed by, and I am now completely submissive. You tell me that you wish me to receive your opinions, not as commands, but as advice. Yet I must consider them as commands, doubly binding, for they proceed from one so vastly my superior in all respects, and to whom I am under such great obligations, that the mere intimation of an opinion will be sufficient to govern my conduct.

MR. CLAY TO FRANCIS BROOKE.

ASHLAND, September 5, 1829.

MY DEAR SIR,—I received both your favors of the 11th July and 4th ultimo, to which I should have sooner replied, but for my absence from home, and that I did not suppose there was any urgency in my transmitting a reply.

On public affairs, I have but little to say in addition to what you will find in the public prints. The result of our election to the Legislature of Kentucky, gave a decided majority, beyond all doubt, to our friends, in both of its branches. The people of the State would, to-morrow, give a different decision from what they did in November last, upon the same state of the question on which they then acted; that is, a contest between the same parties. The manner in which the power of patronage has been exercised, has dissatisfied thousands who voted for Jackson. There is a large class of his supporters who now avow that their opposition was to Mr. Adams, and not to me. This same distinction is taken in other Western States. I have every reason to be satisfied with the state of things in Kentucky. Whether any measures, in relation to myself, will be adopted at the next session of our Legislature, and if any, what its character may be, will depend upon intervening events, and upon consultation among my friends after they assemble at the seat of Government.

I hardly know what to say about your land near Madisonville. It would afford me much pleasure to render you any assistance in my power, but I am afraid to assume any direction about it, lest I should not be able to do what might be necessary. The land is remote from me, and it would be as difficult for me to attend to the tenanting or processioning of it as it would be for you to perform the same operation on a tract of land in Franklin or Pittsylvania. I have great confidence in Triplett, and I think when you hear from him, he will account satisfactorily for his silence. My personal acquaintance in that quarter is very limited. I shall set out, in a few days, on a trip to Russellville, and perhaps I may meet with some one, during the performance of it, who may give me useful information in regard to your land, and I will bear the subject in mind, so as to make inquiries when opportunities shall occur. But I must advise that you would rely more particularly on some one residing nearer the land than I do. If it has no intruder upon it, you are in no danger. But if there be any person settled on it, claiming under an adverse title, it may be necessary for you to adopt measures, by bringing suit, or otherwise, to prevent the operation of the law of this State, commonly called the Seven Years' Limitation Law. According to that law, a peaceable and undisturbed possession, during seven years, under a title derived from the State, protects the occupant against any outstanding adverse claim. I need not tell you that the validity of the law is controverted; but it is wise not to be obliged to depend upon that plea exclusively. Pray remember me affectionately to Mrs. Brooke, and believe me ever cordially your friend.

MR. CLAY TO J. S. JOHNSTON.

ASHLAND, October 5, 1829.

MY DEAR SIR,—I received with great thankfulness your several interesting communications from Northampton, which shall be returned as you desire. I have also received your last favor, without date, from Washington. I have perused with great attention these several letters. The contents of some of them are highly curious.

I envy you your pleasure at Boston. How much should I have been delighted, if I could have shared them with yourself and Mrs. J.

I have just returned from my dreaded tour to the southern part of this State. I went as far as Hopkinsville. Mr. and Mrs. Erwin, and four or five ladies from Mississippi, accompanied me to Russellville. From that point they proceeded to Nashville. The tour was full of gratification. Every sort of enthusiastic demonstration of friendship and attachment, on the part of the people, was made toward me. Barbecues, dinners, balls, etc., etc., without number.

I have been really in danger of that gout with which I have been threatened by some of the Jackson party. And tell Mrs. J. that if I had a younger heart, that also would have been in danger amid the blaze of beauty in the State of Green River. I thought the men, and women too, would devour me. I devoured many of their good dishes at their numerous festivals.

In spite of all my prudence, which nobody, I am sure, will question, I was forced to speak often and long. At Russellville, and Hopkinsville, I spoke upward of three hours together, to at least three thousand persons at each place. My addresses were never better received by all parties, nor were they ever more satisfactory to myself.

Things could not be expected to be more favorable in Kentucky than they are at this time. I entertain not a particle of doubt of there being at this moment a decided majority for me against all and every person whatever.

From what I hear, the Legislature will do something at the next session, to testify its regard for me. What that will be may depend on subsequent events. But something will be done. Should things remain pretty much as they now are, it may not, and I think, ought not to be a nomination. We ought not to take upon ourselves the responsibility of a premature agitation of a certain question. Still, events at Washington may possibly occur early in the winter, to render necessary, and to justify that measure. I think our friends may place all reliance on Kentucky, and on the discretion of the next general assembly.

Present me affectionately to Mrs. J., whose leisure I hope will permit her often to write me during your abode at Washington.

MR. CLAY TO J. S. JOHNSTON.

ASHLAND, October 8, 1829.

MY DEAR SIR,—Will you think of the suggestion contained in the inclosed letter, from a very worthy and intelligent friend, formerly in Congress, and send it to Niles, or some other complacent person to act upon, if you do not disapprove it?

I have nothing to send you from this quarter. In Kentucky and I believe generally in the West, we have every reason for encouragement.

I shall go to the last (I must sincerely hope) of the public barbecues in this State next week. That is in Mercer, to which I am invited by a majority of Jackson men. You know Mercer is the center of our State and Tom Moore's headquarters. If my addresses should satisfy me as well as those did at Russellville and Hopkinsville, it will do good.

JAMES BROWN TO MR. CLAY.

NEW YORK, November 1, 1829.

MY DEAR SIR,—You will see by the papers our safe arrival announced in the unusually short passage of twenty-four days, during which time we enjoyed fine weather, excellent accommodations, and good society, in a splendid packet with an obliging captain. Mrs. Brown suffered throughout the voyage from seasickness, but I am happy in assuring you that her general health, if not materially improved, is certainly not impaired by the voyage. We have been received with the most flattering attentions by the respectable inhabitants of the city.

Be so good as to write to me in Philadelphia and let us know how you are, and what you are doing. They say here that many are anxious to make you President. Are you not tired of the troubled ocean of politics, or will you again launch into the busy strife? I hope my poor bark is once more safe in port, and it is not my intention again to meddle with politics unless driven to it by ill usage or persecution, which I do not now apprehend.

Be so good as to present our love to Mrs. Clay and all our dear relations. We are impatient to see them, but find Mrs. Brown's health too delicate to bear the journey.

D. MALLORY TO MR. CLAY.

NEW YORK, November 2, 1829.

DEAR SIR,—I had the pleasure of meeting your friend Mr. Johnson, the Senator of Louisiana, a short time since, and during our conversation, which related mostly to you, he advised my writing to you " fully and freely."

You have known me a great many years, and during this long period of time, I think I can boast of having possessed your confidence to a flattering extent, considering my humble pretensions to influence. You have often honored me with your approbation, and have at various times given to my views and opinions attention and respect. If I have not succeeded in all respects to the extent my vanity and zeal had projected for your interest, I have the approbation of numerous acquaintances that industry and attention have not been spared to accomplish these views.

I have but recently returned from a visit to several of the New England States, and my information is certainly cheering as it relates to you. In Boston, during a stay of nearly two weeks, I had various and highly interesting communications made to me on the state of public opinion. The result of these, and numerous others made at other times and in other States and places, is, that there is scarcely a doubt but that nearly all the States north and east of this will join heartily in your nomination. The excitement on this subject in these sections of the country is much greater than I had supposed. We can securely rely on Connecticut, Massachusetts, Rhode Island, and Vermont, and if by any casualty the " hero" is out of the question, no reasonable doubt can be entertained of the other two.

The wish is very general that you should visit them during the ensuing summer. I do not, however, consider a visit to them half so important or politic as a visit to New York. Some time previous to the late Presidential election, while I had the honor of a seat in the City Convention, I introduced a resolution expressive of a wish that a committee should be formed to invite you to the city. At that time, and since, but one opinion prevailed. It was unanimous among our party, and much good was anticipated by such an event. If it was deemed so important at that period, it surely is much more so now.

Mr. Johnson informed me that he believed it was your intention to visit General Porter next season; if so, I trust you will not refuse us the gratification of a visit. Indeed, it will do much good. Thousands of people are anxious to see you, and among them are many leading and influential men.

I wrote to Mr. Smith, the editor of "The Reporter," a few days since, on the subject of a likeness of yourself, which I am about publishing from the portrait by Wood: will you do me the favor to request him to answer as early as his convenience will admit of it. I shall feel greatly honored and obliged by an early reply from yourself.

MR. ADAMS TO MR. CLAY.

WASHINGTON, December 11, 1829.

MY DEAR SIR,—On my return here from the North a few days since, I received your letter of the 23d October, written at Frankfort, and inclosing the printed copy of Mr. Jefferson's letter to Mr. Breckenridge of 12th August, 1803. It corresponds in opinion with his letter to Mr. Dunbar of nearly the same date, which had been published before.

The sacrifice of principle, by Mr. Jefferson, in sanctioning the assumption by Congress of the power to do that which he thus acknowledges could rightfully be done only by an amendment to the Constitution, is destined to produce consequences from which I turn my eyes.

I have written a reply to the Confederate Appeal of Mr. Giles' auxiliaries; but have hitherto forborne to publish it. The friends to whom I have communicated it are not altogether agreed as to the expediency of its immediate publication, and I have cheerfully postponed it for the present. When published, I shall not fail of transmitting a copy of it to you.

I offer you my warm and sincere thanks as well for your condolence as for your congratulations. I have had the pleasure this day of seeing Mr. Clarke, and of hearing from him the entire re-establishment of your health. I saw Mr. Southard last Saturday at Philadelphia, and rejoiced at meeting him quite recovered both in health and spirits. Mr. Brown is also at Philadelphia; but my stay there was so short I did not see him. I heard that Mrs. Brown's health was much improved.

MR. VAUGHAN TO MR. CLAY.

WASHINGTON, December 18, 1829.

MY DEAR SIR,—Mr. Clark has delivered to me the rifle, and it seems to me to be, in workmanship, most perfect; and I am as well pleased with it as any child you ever saw with a new toy. Mr. Clark and Mr. Letcher have promised to teach me how to use it, and it will not be my fault if we have not a field-day very soon.

Gratified, as I feel, by your kindness in executing the commission which I took the liberty of giving you, to procure for me a genuine Kentucky rifle, which you have so admirably executed, it is very painful to me to be obliged to accompany my thanks with a severe scolding. Your friends tell me that they were specially instructed by you (in diplomatic phrase) not to allow me to reimburse you, through them, for the heavy expense which my commission has brought upon you. This is too bad, and makes me very restless. The only way in which you can soothe me is by telling me what article you want, or would covet, from England, as I shall have time to get it out before your friends return to Kentucky, after the session of Congress. If you will not make choice of something useful, I shall be obliged to send you some article which may prove very useless and very unacceptable. Exercise, therefore, your frankness, and pray put me in a way of executing a commission for you, in as acceptable a manner as you have just executed one for me. I shall ever be proud of the rifle as a memorial of your friendship.

I have not any public or private news to send you. I rejoice at the termination of the war in Turkey, and the opening of the commerce of the Black Sea has pleased all the world. As to politics at Washington, you will know better than I do what is the state of them. Congress has opened, it appears to me, in a perfect calm.

I have been lately out of spirits, on account of the death of a brother, who was younger than myself, and who was a clergyman of exemplary life and character, and who has left behind him a widow and thirteen children.

Mr. and Mrs. Johnston, Messrs. Letcher and Clark, and some others, your friends, are to dine with me on Christmas day, when we shall drink your health.

My kind regards to Mrs. Clay, and to Johnny.

MR. CLAY TO J. S. JOHNSTON.

ASHLAND, December 25, 1829.

MY DEAR SIR,—I received your obliging favor of the 12th instant. I shall leave here for New Orleans, from the 16th to the 20th of next month, and I purpose remaining there until early in March. There will be time for a letter to reach me after you receive this, if you write by the next mail. Tell me how I can serve you while there—who is to be soothed, who to be won, to secure your next election. Whatever I can do on that subject, with propriety, shall be done.

Will you do me the favor to place the endorsed letter for Hughes in a train for reaching him? Poor fellow! he has met with most unkind and most unjust treatment.

With the compliments of the season to yourself and Mrs. Johnston.

MR. CLAY TO J. S. JOHNSTON.

ASHLAND, December 31, 1829.

MY DEAR SIR,—Your favor of the 20th instant, under cover to Major Tilford, and franked by Judge Clarke, came safe to hand; and I thank you for the views and information which it communicates.

There is the best and most friendly disposition prevailing so far with our Legislature at Frankfort. They are disposed to do any thing right and politic; but, from what I learn, I presume nothing will be done but to present an argumentation-report in favor of the Tariff and Internal Improvements, in which will be embodied some friendly expressions concerning me. The Governor gets along without difficulty. Much good spirit exists in regard to the State's doing something for its own improvement; but the great obstacle is the want of means, and the want of union as to objects to be first undertaken.

I am busy in making preparation for my intended voyage to New Orleans. I purpose leaving home in less than a fortnight, about the 12th of next month. I regret to find that my expected visit there has already excited more expectation than I would have wished. I have heard nothing of General Van Rensselaer. I am afraid that the frightful state of our roads has deterred him from making his intended detour. I shall lament this the more, because I think we should have arranged it to descend the river together.

P. S. Should you address me, as I hope you may, while I am at New Orleans, your letters put under cover to Nicholas Bertrand, Esq., Shipping-port, Kentucky, would quickly reach me.

REV. JOHN S. BARGER TO MR. CLAY.

DEAR SIR,—I could not conscientiously drink to you a toast, but I indulge the hope that you will permit me to offer to Almighty God an humble prayer for the Hon. Henry Clay.

May God the Judge who "putteth down one and setteth up another" reward you with the confidence and highest honor of your happy country, for whose glory you have so arduously and faithfully toiled. May your labors for your country's glory be at least equaled by your competitor and surpassed by your efforts to secure your Maker's favor and to proclaim your Saviour's renown. And having faithfully served your country and your God, may you largely and forever share with his saints the honors and kingdom of our common Saviour. Amen.

CHAPTER VII.

CORRESPONDENCE OF 1830.

MR. CLAY TO J. S. JOHNSTON.

ASHLAND, January 12, 1830.

MY DEAR SIR,—Your Alma Mater is a petitioner to Congress. The affliction which has recently occurred, presents her in that posture. Transylvania University was the first temple of science erected in the wilds of the West. Do not these circumstances give some claim to the charity of a generous Government? If you think so, will you say one friendly word in behalf of the application?

REV. WM. HAWLEY TO MR. CLAY.

WASHINGTON, January 14, 1830.

MY DEAR SIR,—Permit me to return you my humble but sincere thanks for the very able, interesting, and I trust, useful speech in favor of the Colonization Society, which you have given to the public, a copy of which I received yesterday.

I had read it the day before in the "National Intelligencer" with a pleasure and satisfaction I will not attempt to describe. Not a word is out of place, nor is there a sentence too much or too little. The whole subject is presented in so clear a light and happy arrangement that he who runs may read and understand the object, the importance and the usefulness of the institution. The appropriate manner in which you have introduced the subject of Christianity and exhibited the powerful operation and extensive effects which would be produced by the successful accomplishment of the objects of the Society, in a religious point of view, will, I doubt not, command the united approbation of all denominations of Christians, and insure their cordial co-operation.

Our anniversary takes place next Monday and I hope to succeed in having this speech placed on the pages of our Report; for it ought to be in the hands of every man, woman and child, throughout the country.

In your retirement from the honorable, but arduous situation, which you recently occupied, I hope your health has improved, and that the subject of religion, which you so eloquently advocate, and which my feeble endeavors to impress on your mind may have failed to accomplish to the extent of my wishes, will now occupy that portion of your time to which it has so powerful and just a claim both as it regards this world and that which is to come. In this world true religion sweetens all our joys, mitigates all our sorrows and eventuates in preparing us for the death of the righteous, and for those mansions of bliss prepared by the Saviour of the world for all those who truly love and obey him.

You have my earnest prayer that your life may be long preserved to your family and to your country, and that you may yet receive her highest reward for the many useful services you have rendered the Republic, and finally obtain an unfading crown of glory at the right hand of God.

Mrs. Hawley unites with me in affectionate regards to Mrs. Clay and yourself, and I beg you to accept the assurance of my very high esteem and respectful consideration.

ALEXIS DE SARCY TO MR. CLAY.*

February 11, 1830.

It will not be in my power to meet you so soon as I expected, but you may rest satisfied that all goes well. Be true to yourself, be discreet, and there is nothing to apprehend. Say nothing about Mr. Adams, nothing in allusion to him; the reasons assigned in your speech, not long since, for accepting office under him, were injudicious. It will be impracticable for me to be in Kentucky earlier than May or June.

---

* This note, and the following extract from a long letter of bold advice, are written over an assumed name, Alexis de Sarcy, but the writer appears to have been well-known to Mr. Clay, and a sort of Mentor. How he was entertained in this capacity, is not known. See another note from same, page 241.

ALEXIS DE SARCY TO MR. CLAY.

Sir,—You are reputed to possess judgment, tact, a deep and correct knowledge of the human character, and a self-possession that never falters. I am not disposed to controvert the opinion, yet I think if you are to be judged by the events of the last five years, your claim to these qualities must be denied. During that period, you have committed errors so palpable and gross, that no man so distinguished could have been betrayed into. It might be ungracious, as well as unnecessary, to notice all the blunders of that time, but you will permit me to mention one, that remarkable one, your defense of yourself against the charge of "bargain, intrigue, and management." Had you avowed a bargain, instead of denying, explaining, and defending, I am grossly mistaken in the character of the American people, if you had not sustained your popularity at its highest flow. If, instead of your letter to your constituents, and all your other letters and speeches and sayings, and the sayings of all your friends, you had promptly declared that your vote for Mr. Adams was the result of a bargain, of a pledge on his part, to support the American system and internal improvements, while General Jackson's silence, reserve, and affectation of offended dignity at being approached, left you, the founder of the system, and all its other friends, in doubt as to the policy of his administration upon these subjects—that this consideration, added to your other objections to the General, had decided your course upon that question, and that you accepted the Department of State under the influence of the same motives, to aid in extending and supporting the system, with a determination to resign and oppose the Administration, if Mr. Adams played false—that it was the operation of such considerations which induced you to disregard the recommendation of the Kentucky Legislature, and offer yourself a victim on the altar of your country, as General Jackson had himself done in declaring martial law at New Orleans—had you done this, my life on it, the newspaper clamor would have been hushed, that prolific theme been removed, and your adversaries confounded. It is over! How shall we repair the loss and correct the evil?

MR. CLAY TO J. S. JOHNSTON.

NEW ORLEANS, February 27, 1830.

MY DEAR SIR,—Your several letters addressed to me in Kentucky, and at this place, have been received. Owing to the Ohio river being closed by ice, I did not receive the former as early as they would have reached me by land. That obstruction being now removed, and boats daily arriving from Louisville, I shall receive the letters of my friends with more regularity, during the ten or twelve days that I propose yet to continue in this city. Except the two short excursions to Mr. Goniot's and Mr. Millegan's, I have not been out of the city and its immediate neighborhood. I have been treated throughout with the greatest respect and attention. Some of the more prominent Jacksonians, especially those who are expecting offices, keep at a distance; but all others, embracing many of that party, have been extremely civil. I have been invited to public dinners at Memphis, Vicksburg, Fort Gibson, Natchez, and Baton Rouge, but I have declined all, except that proposed at Natchez.

I have been often with your friend, Judge Porter, who I think worthy of all the fine things you have said of him to me. I like him extremely, and hope that our acquaintance will leave impressed upon him toward me the same sentiments of esteem and friendship which I feel for him.

I shall expect eagerly Mr. Webster's second speech on Mr. Foote's resolution, of which your letters and those of other friends have communicated such flattering accounts. The triumph which he enjoyed was a noble one. I fear his resolution against Duff Green was premature, and dictated by a chafed and proud spirit, indignant at his vile misrepresentations. His ninth Thermidor has not, I fear, yet arrived.

I have been agreeably surprised to find the opinion in favor of the Tariff so general and so strong in this State. You must not be surprised to find yourself shortly instructed by the Legislature to support it. From what I learn, at least two thirds of the Legislature, if not more, are in favor of it; but they have great difficulty in collecting and keeping the members at Donaldsville.

Duralde has declined being a candidate for Governor, at a moment when, they tell me, his election would have been certain, if Roman had declined, and probably if he would not. He did not wish to produce divisions among friends, and really cared nothing about the office.

My best respects to Mrs. Johnston.

MR. CLAY TO J. S. JOHNSTON.

On Board the Caledonia, near Baton Rouge, March 11, 1830.

My dear Sir,—You will perceive, from the inclosed, that my anticipation has been realized. You will now be at liberty to pursue your own judgment in relation to the great measure referred to. On that subject two grounds will naturally suggest themselves to you, as forming a justification for your future course : 1st, the will of your constituents ; and, secondly, that you will not assist in disturbing an established policy.

I expect to reach Natchez to-morrow morning, and I shall remain there until Sunday the 14th, when I shall ascend in the George Washington.

All parties tell me that your re-election is safe. I think you were wise in declining being a candidate for the office of Governor. Roman, I believe, will be elected. I think it the interest of our friends to unite on him. There is a good prospect of our returning those friends to the House of Representatives ; and yet I am not without fears that we may lose the majority in your Legislature. The city of New Orleans is the pivot ; and it is extremely difficult there to animate our friends to proper exertion. It will be well for you to come here after the close of Congress. My cordial regards always to Mrs. Johnston.

MR. DURALDE* TO MR. CLAY.

New Orleans, March 18, 1830.

My dear Sir,—I received, by the return of William Claiborne, your letter of the 14th instant. I was glad to hear that Henry, so far, had been a good boy, and had given no trouble to those around him. I shall feel greatly relieved when I hear of your safe arrival at Louisville.

Your friends here feel grateful toward the people of Natchez

* Son-in-law to Mr. Clay.

for having treated you so kindly during your short stay among them.

The resolutions concerning the Tariff, which passed the Senate unanimously, have also passed the House of Representatives by a large majority, there having been but seven dissenting votes.

Unless a very great change should take place, I have no doubt but that A. B. Roman will be elected Governor of this State in July next.

Mr. Thomas Hart, who is the bearer of this, will give you the pocket-handkerchief you had left at Donaldsonville.

Present my best respects to Mrs. Clay, and to the rest of the family, and remember me to my dear, dear little Henry.

MR. CLAY TO FRANCIS BROOKE.

FRANKFORT, March 25, 1830.

MY DEAR SIR,—I reached this place this morning from Louisville. My passage from Natchez in the George Washington comprehended all the agreeable circumstances. Nothing could surpass the warmth of my reception in Mississippi. Both parties attended the dinner and ball at Natchez, and they vied with each other in their testimonies of respect. I had the satisfaction to make the acquaintance of Drs. Duncan and Mercer, with both of whom I was much pleased.

I believe that I have not heretofore said to you, that I found in Louisiana an unanimous and strong opposition to the acquisition of Texas. Your brother is disinclined to offer at the next election for the Legislature. I endeavored to overcome his repugnance. I think he ought to be there, where he might essentially serve you. He has an excellent standing in the House. General Thomas will beat Ripley with ease for Congress, if those two only offer.

MR. CLAY TO J. S. JOHNSTON.

ASHLAND, April 6, 1830.

MY DEAR SIR,—I received your favor of the 14th ultimo, transmitted through a friend. It discloses a state of public affairs at Washington, both curious and mortifying. Your accounts and conclusions are substantially concurred in by other friends who write me. If the incompetency of the President could be manifested to the public, I have no doubt, with you, that his re-election would be impracticable. But how is that to be done? How, especially, will that large portion of it which contributed to place him where he is, be made to believe his unfitness?—particularly when majorities in both Houses continue to support all, even his most exceptionable acts?

I say, continue to support them. For I infer, from what I have seen, that the principle of removal, in its most odious form, has been sanctioned by the majority. What does the Senate believe will be thought of its dignity and independence, in after time, when it will sanction (as in the case of the Treasurer of the United States) the removal, without cause, of a high public officer, whose appointment it only a few months before approved? Does it imagine that the miserable sophistry of that pliant tool, Felix Grundy, will justify it? According to him, the Senate can not look beyond the mere question of fitness of the person nominated; the President acts upon his responsibility, and there is no remedy but in impeachment! Does he not see that he strips the body of one of its most important constitutional functions—that of operating as a check upon the executive? Does he not see that the Senate, after making itself a particeps with the President in a dangerous and pernicious proceeding, will be a very unfit and unsafe tribunal to arraign him before for that identical proceeding?

The consequence, I fear, will be, of this approbation in both houses of the worst acts of the President, that the Jackson portion of the public will be lulled into security, and believe that all is right. In this point of view, I have thought it of much importance that, when any great principle was involved (such as the appointment of editors, or removals without cause), the Senate would show itself worthy of the esteem which it once enjoyed, by putting itself against the evils to be dreaded.

You perceive no effect, at a distance, from the state of things which you describe at Washington. Witness the result in New Hampshire.

If Mr. Calhoun really intends to set himself up in opposition to General Jackson, I should begin to think there was a prospect of some division that might lead to beneficial results.

Do not imagine from any thing that I have said that I at all despair of the Republic. I only fear that the day of soundness and sanity is more distant than you believe.

Mr. Chilton's last letter on the comparative expenditures of the two Administrations, like his first, will do good.

I shall not disappoint my friends in remaining still. I shall remain more than ever at Ashland, the occupations of which I relish more than ever.

Duralde writes me that the Tariff resolution, which I informed you had passed the Senate of Louisiana unanimously, has passed the House with only seven dissentients. I sent you a copy of the resolution, which I hope you received.

I heard nothing more, after I wrote you, of Waggerman's opposition to you. I hope it will not take place. Our friends were very confident of your success, but you should go home after the session. Duralde thinks Roman will be elected Governor.

I will thank you to remit me the amount you may receive from Mann, in a check of the office of Discount and Deposit, at Washington, on the Bank of the United States, at Philadelphia. My warmest regards to Mrs. Johnston.

WILLIAM HENRY HARRISON TO MR. CLAY.

STEAMBOAT TELEGRAPH, near MAYSVILLE, April 11, 1830.

DEAR SIR,—I would have written to you immediately upon my arrival in the United States if I had not heard that you had gone on a visit to New Orleans, to inform you that I had forwarded your letter to General Bolivar, from Bogota, and that I had received a note from him acknowledging its reception and adding that there "was no answer." Herewith I send a pamphlet which I have lately published, in which you will find a letter addressed by me to the same distinguished character, to which also he did not think proper to reply. I could have inserted many interesting circumstances which I omitted from the fear of injuring persons who still remain subject to the power of the Colombian Government.

Accept for yourself and family my best respects.

MR. CLAY TO REV. JAMES E. WELCH.

ASHLAND, April 17, 1830.

DEAR SIR,—I have to acknowledge the receipt of your very friendly letter of the 5th instant, and to thank you for the information which it contains, and for your kind endeavor to vindicate me from the aspersions to which I have been exposed on account of my public conduct. I have almost daily proofs of the general conviction which prevails of my having been wronged; and I have full confidence that my fellow citizens will ultimately render me perfect justice. These good feelings were strongly manifested toward me during a late visit I made to Louisiana. Every where I was received with warmth and cordiality, and, in some instances, with enthusiasm. When the passions lately so strongly excited, shall subside, and the people come to reflect on the past, and to reason upon the promises made by or for the successful Presidential candidate, and the shameful violation of all of them at Washington, they can not fail to come to right conclusions.

I met Colonel Drake to-day and delivered him your message, as I will endeavor to recollect to do to the other gentlemen mentioned by you.

Accept my best wishes for the success of the cause in which you are engaged, and for your individual prosperity.

DANIEL WEBSTER TO MR. CLAY.

WASHINGTON, April 18, 1830.

MY DEAR SIR,—We have heard with great pleasure of your safe arrival at your own home, after your interesting trip down the great river; and we all enjoyed, as sincerely as you could have done, the tokens of regard and affection which the good people manifested toward you at the various points of your tour. More than all, it was gratifying to hear from Mr. Poinsett such excellent accounts of your health.

* * * * * * *

The President means to be re-elected. He has meant so all along. Seeing this, Van Buren has been endeavoring to make a merit of persuading him to do so, on the ground of its being necessary to keep the party together. Calhoun is more than half reconciled to it from two considerations : first, he hardly feels as confident as he has done, of his own present strength ; second, he regards the chance of succession, in seven years, as pretty important. If any thing should prevent General Jackson from being a candidate for re-election, my hopes would now be exceeding strong of beating both Van Buren and Calhoun. How it will be expedient for us to act, in case the present incumbent should actually be candidate again, we can better determine hereafter. My own firm belief is, that if we were to let the Administration, this session and the next, have their own way, and follow out their own principles, they would be so unpopular as that the General could not possibly be re-elected. I do not mean by this, that we should let them disturb the Tariff, or injure any other existing interest ; still less that we should, in the slightest degree, vote or act against our own principles. All these being safe, and all existing interests preserved, I still think if we leave to them to decide on new measures of internal improvement, etc., according to their own will, they will soon find what the sense of the people is. But I forbear further talk.

MR. CLAY TO FRANCIS BROOKE.

ASHLAND, April 19, 1830.

MY DEAR SIR,—I received your favor of the 8th instant. I returned from Louisiana about three weeks ago. My visit to that State and to Mississippi, was full of gratification. Not a single painful incident occurred. Every where my reception was warm and cordial, and sometimes enthusiastic. The Legislature of Louisiana paid me a compliment, the more estimable because it was spontaneous, and without previous concert. When I unexpectedly attended it, the whole body (Speaker and all), without distinction of party, rose to receive me. While I was in that State, its Senate passed unanimously a resolution in favor of the Tariff, which has since been concurred in by the House of Representatives, with only seven dissentients. Nothing could have surpassed the cordiality of my reception and entertainment at Natchez. At one of the largest public dinners I ever attended, I found myself in the midst of about equal numbers of both parties. A Jackson man sat on my right, an Adams man on my left. From all that I learned, I should think that the vote of

Louisiana would certainly be given me against any one, and that of Mississippi against any one but Jackson. Against him also, if he continues, during the next two years, to lose his popularity there in proportion to his loss this last year.

As to the state of things at Washington, you are probably as well, if not better informed than I am. My friends, prior to the recent nomination in Pennsylvania, were sanguine, extremely sanguine, of success. They represent great animosity as existing between the partisans of Calhoun and Van Buren, insomuch that each party prefers me to the other; and that there are not thirty members of Congress who desire Jackson's re-election.

Events which may have already happened, or which may occur in the course of the residue of the present session of Congress, will throw great light on the future. If the three great States of Virginia, Pennsylvania, and New York, should unite on any particular candidate, opposition to that candidate will be unavailing, in all probability. If there should be no such union, Jackson himself or either of the two prominent members of his party, may be beaten. Of the prospect of the supposed union, you can form as correct a conjecture as I can.

Meantime I assure you, most sincerely, that I feel myself more and more weaned from public affairs. My attachment to rural occupation every day acquires more strength, and if it continues to increase another year as it has the last, I shall be fully prepared to renounce forever the strifes of public life. My farm is in fine order, and my preparations for the crop of the present year, are in advance of all my neighbors. I shall make a better farmer than statesman. And I find in the business of cultivation, gardening, grazing, and the rearing of the various descriptions of domestic animals, the most agreeable resources.

I presume your new Constitution will be adopted. It has incorporated in it some very exceptionable elements of aristocracy. I should, nevertheless, vote for it, if I had a vote, as being, with all its defects, preferable to the old Constitution. I am curious to learn those anecdotes occurring at Richmond, which you are afraid to intrust to the mail. I think a letter communicating them, put under cover to the Honorable R. P. Letcher, at Washington, would reach me in safety. I have never been able to comprehend Mr. Madison's course. At a distance, it appeared to me marked by some inconsistency, which I regretted.

Mrs. Clay unites with me in best regards to Mrs. Brooke.

MR. CLAY TO FRANCIS BROOKE.

ASHLAND, April 24, 1830.

MY DEAR SIR,—Upon my return home from New Orleans, I found here your two favors of the 28th December last, and 6th ult. Although I met a vast accumulation of correspondence and of business, I should have immediately answered your letters but, to tell the truth, for my desire to see the issue of the elections in your Legislature. My anxious looks were directed toward Richmond, on account of yourself especially, and other friends. The papers have at length brought the intelligence I desired, and I offer you my cordial congratulations on your election, which, under all circumstances, is as honorable as I hope it will prove satisfactory to you. You are not, I remark again, appointed President of the Court, but, considering every thing, I do not think you should be mortified or even regret that the choice and the responsibility have fallen on a younger man. It would have given me inexpressible pain if I could have believed that your friendship to me, which has been of such long duration, and such great value, had affected you injuriously.

Important events at home and abroad have happened since I last wrote you. These changes in Europe are so rapid that we have scarcely time to speculate on one before it is succeeded and supplanted by another. You will have heard probably by the time this letter reaches you, the decision of the question of a general war in Europe. I regret that such a war now seems to me almost inevitable. That regret will be diminished if we can remain at peace. But if there should be a general war, embracing England, she will make every endeavor to involve us in it. Such a purpose was openly avowed to me by men high in authority, when I was in England, on the contingency supposed.

Among the incidents at home, the correspondence between the President and Van Buren, is perhaps the most important occurrence during the late session of Congress. I think it lowers them both, although confining our consideration to the parties to the controversy, Mr. Calhoun must be allowed to have obtained the advantage.

What course he may take in respect to the next election I am uninformed. From the knowledge I possess of his character and disposition, I believe he will be regulated altogether by his estimate of the probability of successful opposition to Jackson. If he thinks he can be defeated by himself or another, he will oppose his re-election directly or collaterally, according to circumstances. If he believes he can be defeated by no one, he will support his re-election, make a merit of a magnanimous sacrifice of his sense of his wrongs, and endeavor to enlist the gratitude and sympathies of the Jackson party to elevate himself hereafter. In any event, we can not fail to profit by the controversy.

Mr. Crawford's conduct, in respect to myself, surprised me. That he should, at the very period of holding such language toward me as he did in his letters, have been addressing letters to others containing the most improper expressions, betrays great duplicity. But, after his letter to me of March, in the last year, ought we to be surprised at any thing he may do? I have never written to him since I received that letter, nor do I desire any correspondence with him again. I shall not, however, permit the publication of his letter of March. It could only be justified by some public good, and I see none that it would accomplish. The public feeling of Louisiana in regard to the President is all that we could desire. Not a doubt can be entertained of the vote of that State by any one acquainted with it. There have been numerous changes, and some of very influential individuals. In Kentucky, both parties are preparing for a vigorous campaign. Our friends are confident of carrying majorities both in the General Assembly and in the House of Representatives. I was so greatly mortified with the issue of our last August election, that I am unwilling either to indulge or inspire hopes. I can not, however, but believe that nothing but a corrupt and most extensive use of money can defeat us. Of that there is some reason to fear.

As to the issue of the contest generally, my opinion remains the same that it has been for the last eighteen months. If Jackson loses either New York, Pennsylvania, or Virginia, he will be defeated. If he unites the votes of all three of those States, he will succeed. And I have generally supposed that the degrees of probability of loss to him of those States were in the order in which I have placed them. If I am right, he is most certain of Virginia. Of course I am unable to estimate the effect upon her of recent transactions, especially the correspondence and votes of your Senators.

The movement in Philadelphia is strong and encouraging. It remains to be seen whether it will be seconded in other parts of the State. I am afraid it will be. In New York some progress has been made toward effecting an union of the various parties opposed to the present Administration, but the problem is yet to be solved whether such an union can be accomplished.

The whole case presents one encouraging view. Jackson has lost, is losing, and must continue to lose. If the ratio of his loss hereafter shall equal what it has been in the two last years, he will be defeated.

I am much pressed to visit the north this summer; and although my judgment is opposed to any journey having a political object, or which might be construed into such an object, I have been somewhat shaken in my resolution by the great anxiety manifested. But I believe I shall resist it, and remain in Kentucky, where (will you believe it?) I am likely to make an excellent farmer. I am almost tempted to believe that I have heretofore been altogether mistaken in my capacity, and that I have, though late, found out the vocation best suited to it.

I received from our friend Call a very kind letter, and I have to request that you will ask him to consider this equally intended for his eye and your own. It has been a long time since I heard from him, but I see nobody from Richmond of whom I do not inquire about him; and I learn from all that he retains generally his good spirits, and his attachments with great constancy; of mine to him and you I pray you both to be fully persuaded.

MR. CLAY TO J. S. JOHNSTON.

ASHLAND, April 30, 1830.

MY DEAR SIR,—I received your favor of the 13th instant, communicating the rejection of Hill, and your expectation that Kendall will follow the same fate. This latter anticipation, from what others tell me, I apprehend, has not been realized. I attach some consequence to the rejection of these men. Who is the uncertain Senator? Is he from Indiana? If he be, it is to be attributed to his approaching election. If my information from that State be correct, he need not fear the issue, unless he proves treacherous to our cause.

I observe that you regard the movements of Harrisburg and Albany as putting Jackson in nomination. They may bear that interpretation, but they are also susceptible of another. The terms in which the two caucuses express themselves do not necessarily import the presentation of Jackson as a candidate. May not the movements be regarded as a stratagem of Van Buren to gain time, to disconcert his rival, to concentrate the Jackson party upon himself, and to come out, at a suitable time, as a candidate?

Ask Mr. Webster to show you a letter which I wrote him a few days ago, stating a proposition which I received from Mr. Crawford, and be pleased to regard that matter as strictly confidential, resting between you two. Mr. Crawford, supposing him to be in the secrets of Van Buren and his faction, does not appear, on the 31st of March, to have suspected that Jackson would be a candidate.

You inform me that my friends contemplate taking some decisive measures in regard to me, before they separate. I shall acquiesce in whatever decision they may make. If Jackson should be a candidate, and can unite upon himself the three States of Virginia, Pennsylvania, and New York, opposition to him will be unavailing. If either of those States can be detached from his support, I think he can be beaten. Whether that be practicable or not, you have better means, and are otherwise more competent to judge, than I am. * * *

The disadvantage of delay, if we mean to act, is the uncertainty in which our friends among the great body of the people, are left. Already I have been frequently spoken to, and sometimes have been written to, to know if I am a candidate. Of course I give but one answer, which is, that I shall never present myself as a candidate.

G. W. FEATHERSTONHAUGH TO MR. CLAY.

PHILADELPHIA, May 4, 1830.

MY DEAR SIR,—The appearance of our friend, General Van Rensselaer here, within a few days, and some other incidents, have induced me to write you a few lines, before a contemplated voyage to Europe takes place. I was exceedingly pleased with the cheerful accounts General Van Rensselaer gave me of your health, spirits, and well-deserved popularity at the West and South. The value of my political attachment to you consists in its disinterestedness. Having no selfish views, I am not obliged to seek selfish connections. Independent of my ardent wishes for the prosperity of the whole human race, I have lived too long here, and been too nearly and dearly connected with the United States to see with indifference its best interests the sport of irresponsible men, who owe their distinction to the temporary delusion of popular favor, and who know not how to vindicate their claims to distinction, in the eyes of men of sense and honor. My intercourse with you has always been very frank. I may never see you again, though I hope I shall. Wherever I am, I shall be most happy to see the Government of this country in your hands. I have been long satisfied you are the man America wants. * * * * * * *

MR. CLAY TO ADAM BEATTY.

LEXINGTON, May 4, 1830.

DEAR SIR,—I received to-day your favor of the 29th ult. I had received from Mr. Yates a similar letter to that which he addressed to you, which I immediately answered, communicating all the information I could give him upon the subject to which it related. I therefore now return his letter to you, with the accompanying papers.

There is not the smallest ground for the intimation which you have received of Mr. Van Buren being disposed to decline in favor of Mr. Calhoun. On the contrary, there is the greatest animosity prevailing between these two rivals and their respective partisans. The late movements at Harrisburg and Albany, are well understood to have been prompted by Mr. Van Buren, to arrest the progress which Mr. Calhoun was making with the Jackson party, and I have no doubt that they are not to be taken as evidence that Jackson will ultimately be a candidate.

It is impossible that any reception could have been more warm and cordial than that which was given me below.

I am very busy farming, to which I am becoming every day more and more attached.

MR. CLAY TO J. S. JOHNSTON.

ASHLAND, May 9, 1830.

MY DEAR SIR,—I received your favors of the 28th and 29th ult. I do not think that the object of Colonel Benton and Colonel Hayne, in detaching the West from New England, has been at all promoted by their speeches on Foote's resolution. It has been well understood, and I think has entirely failed. However extensively their speeches have been circulated, they have not been so widely or so generally read as Mr. Webster's, and his triumph in that matter has been complete. Great aid has been afforded to him by the speeches of Mr. Sprague and Mr. Holmes. We are waiting anxiously, however, to see yours, and I hope you will not omit to send me the proof-sheets promised by you.

I am rejoiced at the passage in the House of Representatives, of the bill for the Maysville road. I sincerely hope you are correct in your anticipation of the concurrence of the Senate. The South will of course be opposed to it. If, as I hope, the New England Senators shall generally vote for it, there will be a fine commentary upon Colonel Benton's text. We shall then be able practically to know who are our real friends. Give my respects to our friends from New England, and tell them not to deprive us of the benefit of this weapon. The road, considered as a section of one extending from the Muskingum or Scioto, through Kentucky and Tennessee, to the Gulf of Mexico, is really of national importance. We observe that the New England delegation well entertained the measure in the House, and we trust that similar support will be given to it by her senators.

I have much information from both ends of the State of New York. It substantially corroborates the letters which you sent me. There seems to be perfect chaos in that State, and no one now can see what will come of it. If the friends of the late Administration, the workingmen party, and the anti-masons, should unite, they will compose a majority. Is it not probable that they will? The anti-masons will bring out Granger. I should think that the friends of the late Administration would support him against Troop or Foote; and even supposing those parties only were to co-operate, Granger would be elected.

By the time of the close of the Tariff debate, which Mr. McDuffie, I suppose, has precipitated, you will have a clearer view of the whole ground. Its effect can not fail to widen the breach between the sections of the Jackson party.

I have entire confidence in the discretion of my friends as to the course which they may mark out. If Mr. Calhoun should be announced as a candidate, it will be clear. If not, the question will be as to the consequences of delay, or immediate action. The first part of it (delay) involves a consideration of the discouragement or separation of our friends which might ensue, and the second the concentration of all the fragments of the Jackson party upon Jackson, which might be the result. I shall be glad to hear from you soon.

MR. CLAY TO J. S. JOHNSTON.

ASHLAND, May 10, 1830.

MY DEAR SIR,—I received to-day your favor of the 30th ult., with the first part of the proof-sheets of your speech, which I have perused with much satisfaction. The editor of "The Reporter" promises to publish it in his next week's paper. With the candid its views will be regarded as large and liberal, and its vindication complete.

I regret Hendrick's course. It was not necessary to secure, but may endanger his re-election. He was already distrusted in his State, but was forgiven, or rather there was a disposition to overlook his course, in consideration of the circumstances under which he was placed. But if he votes for the printers, I think it probable he will be abandoned.

I am very anxious, as you may well suppose, about the passage of the Maysville bill. I hope our New England friends will not desert us in that measure. Their support of it will be worth a thousand of Benton's speeches.

MR. VAUGHAN TO MR. CLAY.

WASHINGTON, May 13, 1830.

MY DEAR SIR,—I have procured for you from England a single-barrel gun, and with a percussion-lock, after having consulted with our friend Letcher, who was of opinion that you would prefer it to the common lock. You will find in the case containing the gun a plentiful supply of percussion caps. In consequence of Judge Clark informing me that an opportunity offered of sending the gun to you, I sent it yesterday to his lodgings, and I trust that it is already on its way to Kentucky. I only hope that you will be as well satisfied with it as I am with the excellent rifle which you have presented to me, and which 1 am proud to have, as a memorial of your friendship.

It is expected that this session of Congress will close on the 31st instant, and I shall take the opportunity of sending to Mrs. Clay the lithograph print of a dog, executed by the son of Christopher Hughes, by our friend Mr. Clark or Mr. Letcher, and which has been due to her for so long a time.

I am happy to infer from what I read in the newspapers about your movements, that your health is very much improved. It will give me great pleasure to meet you again, and, with kind regards to Mrs. Clay and Johnny, believe me, etc.

MRS. ERWIN (ANNE B.) TO HER FATHER, MR. CLAY.

SHELBYVILLE, May 15, 1830.

I HASTEN, my dear father, to answer your kind letter of the 1st, and to assure you that mamma and yourself can not desire that we should be with you more than we both wish it. Mr. Erwin always spoke of our joining you early in the summer, but his father being compelled to go to Georgia in a few days, he now feels himself obliged to remain here until he returns. We shall, however, be with you the last of July or early in August, and I hope we shall not then be separated for a great while, as we shall be guided pretty much by your movements.

I am happy to hear that you have been so good as to purchase us a pair of horses, as we are now without a good pair, intending to purchase when we should be in Lexington. As we shall not want them until then, you will please keep them for us. The pony you speak of has, I presume, been raised on the farm; it will, therefore, be doubly prized by me. Mr. Erwin wrote you, I believe, that he had sold your horses. I enjoyed a great many good rides from them, as we had just then purchased a servant who proved to be an excellent carriage-driver, besides being a very good boy in other respects.

Mr. Erwin and his friend, Mr. Denton, arrived on the 10th,

four or five days earlier than I expected them. They were not so fortunate as I was in getting up all the way by water, but they were detained at the mouth of the Cumberland, and then had a most tedious trip by land to Nashville.

I was a little surprised to see, by the last papers, uncle Porter Clay's marriage announced, although I presume it was a very suitable match, so far as age is concerned.

My little children have grown very much since you saw them. Henry now talks quite plain, and James runs about every where, and begins to say a few words. He has fattened so much since we have been here that he is becoming quite a beauty, at least, for his opportunities, not having any to inherit from either side of the house.

Father Erwin requested me to remember him affectionately to mamma and yourself. Mr. Erwin joins me in love to all the family both in town and at home. Believe me always, my dear father, your devoted daughter.

PETER B. PORTER TO MR. CLAY.

BLACK ROCK, May 23, 1830.

MY DEAR SIR,—I have noticed, with great satisfaction, the accounts of the numerous demonstrations of confidence and respect shown to you by the people of the South, during your late tour; and I feel equal pleasure in assuring you that the same sentiments that animate your Southern friends, are entertained, and I trust in a still higher degree, by the citizens generally in the Northern States; and that these kind and partial feelings have been, and still are, constantly increasing, as opportunity is afforded for comparing and contrasting the professions and acts of the present men in power, with those of their predecessors.

MR. CLAY TO FRANCIS BROOKE.

ASHLAND, May 23, 1830.

MY DEAR SIR,—Your favor of the 10th instant was safely conveyed to me through the friendly channel to which you committed it, and I have perused its contents with much interest. The project of Mr. Van Buren, and his partisans in Virginia, of attaching that State to his support upon the ground of an overthrow of the Bank of the United States, I should suppose was frustrated, for the present, by the events which have occurred at Washington, on that subject. The President's message, in referring to it, committed two radical errors: First, it was premature; and in the second place, he brought forward a rival institution, far worse than the Bank of the United States can be supposed to be by its most violent enemies. A comparison has been naturally made between the two institutions, and the result of it has been every where the same. The reports of the two committees of Congress have been widely circulated, and have confirmed the unfavorable impression which that part of the message produced, when it was first published. It is too soon yet to entertain, much less decide, on the question of the renewal of the charter. We have yet to acquire the experience of five years, which may bring about important developments. The national debt will, in the meantime, be paid, the duties reduced, etc., etc.

I have no intention of visiting the North, or any other place, this season, with any political object. I am urgently solicited to go to almost every quarter of the Union. If I were to yield to these entreaties, I should be perpetually traveling. My own judgment is decided, that I ought to go nowhere for any political purpose, but remain at home. Should I make any excursions this summer, they will relate entirely to business or to my health.

I have received a most singular letter from Mr. Crawford, of which I beg, however, you will speak to no one, as I can not but think, from the nature of the proposal which it contains, it indicates some want of self-possession. He says, that he perceives from the papers, that Mr. Calhoun, Van Buren, and myself, will be run for the next Presidency; that his friends also think of bringing him forward; that no one candidate would be elected; but that, if the contest be limited to the three first, Mr. Van Buren would be finally elected by the House of Representatives; that I should not get a vote in New England, which would support Mr. Van Buren; and that all the South would go for Mr. Calhoun. Therefore, he proposes that I should not be brought forward, but support him, whereby he would get the votes of all the Western States, which, with the aid of Virginia, North Carolina, Georgia, Delaware, New Jersey, and probably

Maryland, with some few other States, would secure his election. Then, he says, I would, of course, come again into the cabinet, and finally succeed him! He intimates that his friends may make a similar proposal to Mr. Van Buren, but he prefers that I should accede to it. He supposes that General Jackson will not be again a candidate. I have not answered this most extraordinary letter, which bears date the 31st day of March last. I shall not answer it. I could not answer it in terms consistent with the friendship which I once bore to Mr. Crawford.

I think Mr. Calhoun has sealed his fate by his recent vote for Kendall. He had previously boasted to some of my friends that he had constantly adhered to principle; that he would still pursue it, and that he disapproved the system of proscription, and the appointment of editors, etc. Now it so happens, that a finer opportunity could not have occurred to test the sincerity of these declarations. Kendall was a printer, and, besides, a man of unenviable character. Yet, Mr. Calhoun's casting vote saved him! I knew, weeks before the nomination was decided, that it depended upon Mr. Calhoun's vote; and, knowing him as well as I do, I stated to some of my friends what the issue would be. It is remarkable that, weeks before the event, Kendall wrote to some of his Frankfort correspondents, that, if the Senate was full, it would be equally divided, and that he would get Mr. Calhoun's vote. This fact ought to be generally known.

I perceive that your new Constitution is adopted. I noticed the provision in relation to the judiciary, both on account of the principle which it involves, and as it affected you. I most sincerely wish you may be re-appointed; and, considering the stability which has generally characterized your State, I presume you will be. If you submit the question to the consideration of those who best know you, they will be unanimous for your re-election. Twenty years hence it will be time enough to talk of old age, and its too frequent concomitants.

I have received several copies of the new edition of Algernon Sidney sent me by Mr. White. I wish that the principles which they so eloquently illustrate and establish, could be every where diffused. Bolivar appears to be reading us a lesson on the same subject, which ought not to be lost. I hope you approved of my letter to him, recently published.

As to the other publication to which you refer, I can not so well judge as you can, as to the most fit time of its appearance.

I should, however, think that it would not be too early after the adjournment of Congress.

I can not return this letter through the channel that you sent yours, for an obvious reason.

MR. CRAWFORD TO MR. CLAY.

WOOD LAWN, March 31, 1830.

MY DEAR SIR,—I perceive by the newspapers that your name, Mr. Van Buren's and Mr. Calhoun's names, are likely to be run for the next Presidency, in the event of General Jackson's not being a candidate. My friends are also solicitous that my name should be put in nomination. I do not profess to know much of public opinion, but I am very sure that if four names are run for the Presidency, no election will be made by the electoral colleges. If your name, Mr. Van Buren's, and Mr. Calhoun's name, should be held up for that office, I am under the impression that Mr. Van Buren would be elected; for, giving you all the Western and South-western votes, and Mr. Calhoun the votes of South Carolina, North Carolina, and Pennsylvania, which are all the votes that his most sanguine friends can claim for him, Mr. Van Buren would still have a majority of the colleges, unless you could divide the New England votes with him. This might happen for aught I know, but I do not expect it. In the first place, I think it probable that Mr. Adams' interest in New England would not be concentrated upon you. 1st. Because the men who would support Mr. Adams from principle, would probably be opposed to you. Mr. Adams and yourself are so different in manners, habits, sentiments, and principles, that it is not probable that you can be supported by the same men. Nothing but this discrepancy between you, could have given the vote of Ohio against Mr. Adams in the late election. 2d. In the election of 1824, almost every man of respectable standing in New England was against Mr. Adams, yet he got every vote in those States by a majority of five sixths. My impression, therefore, is, that you will not get a vote in New England. It is true Mr. Van Buren does not live in New England, but he lives near it, and you live a great way from it, and that circumstance will in all probability be decisive.

It has occurred to me that if you are desirous of filling the

Presidency, the most likely way of success will be to avoid the contest for the next Presidency. If you do this, and my name should be substituted for yours, and receive your support, I presume there would be no doubt of my receiving the vote of the Western and South-western States. To this vote might be safely added that of Georgia, North Carolina, Virginia and Delaware, and perhaps Maryland. The aggregate would fall little short of a majority, and the remainder could hardly fail to be received from the States north and east of those mentioned. In the event of success you would come again into the Cabinet, and could hardly fail of success when I retired. Your union with Mr. Adams has effectually destroyed your popularity in the Atlantic States south of the Chesapeake. I have even injured my own standing in this State, by defending you against the charge of corrupt bargaining. If such is your standing in this State, you can well imagine what it is in the other Southern Atlantic States. Do not suppose that I feel any solicitude upon the subject of this letter. I feel none, but supposing from what I have seen in the public papers, that you may feel some, it occurred to me that the most certain mode of gratifying that feeling, was to adopt the course which I have suggested. If you should be of a different opinion, let the matter rest where it is, and there will no harm have been done. On the contrary, should you concur in the suggestion I have made, I shall be happy to hear from you as soon as leisure will permit.

P. S. It is possible that my friends at Washington may make the same suggestion to Mr. Van Buren. Should it be accepted, it is probable the same result would be effected as to myself, but I should rather it should take place with you.

DANIEL WEBSTER TO MR. CLAY.

WASHINGTON, May 29, 1830.

MY DEAR SIR,—We are all with the foot in the stirrup, and are not leaving in a very composed state. The passage of the Indian bill, and the rejection of the Maysville Turnpike bill, have occasioned unusual excitement. The quarrel, yesterday, between Stansbury and others who voted for the bill, and Polk,

Bell, etc., was very warm. There is more ill blood raised, I should think, than would easily be quieted again.

We think all recent occurrences have been quite favorable, and that the present prospect is cheering. We have had no formal meeting. After much consideration, that idea was given up. We found it difficult to assemble a few friends without giving offense; or a great number without the danger of attracting too much notice. We have had, however, a very full and free interchange of opinions, for the last three weeks, and are all harmonious in purpose and design, and in good spirits. We incline to think no formal nominations at present advisable, though friends press us to such a measure from divers quarters of the country. It has seemed to us, on the whole, that a formal nomination would not be popular enough in its character and origin, to do good. It would be immediately proclaimed to be the act of your friends acting at your instance. It would excite jealousies on the one hand, which are now fast dying away, and on the other, check discontents and schisms among our opponents, from which much is now to be hoped. Such is our view.

I am much pressed to assent to a nomination of you by the Massachusetts Legislature now in session. But to this I steadily object, on the ground that every body knows we are perfectly safe and strong in Massachusetts, and a nomination there would only raise the cry of coalition revived. It has seemed to me the proper scene for the first formal action is Maryland. Her Legislature is elected in October. Our friends have the utmost confidence they will carry the State. Indeed there can be little doubt of it. In that event, the Maryland Legislature, next December, will occupy a position from which they can speak to advantage. Without detail, you will see, I think, at once, many advantages in a nomination from this quarter. None could be more favorable, unless it be New York, or Pennsylvania, neither of which, I fear, is as likely to be so soon ready for it.

I hope you will think that, under all circumstances, we have done wisely in doing nothing. If you run against General Jackson, there will be an election by the electors; and, as you justly state, General Jackson will be chosen, unless either Virginia, Pennsylvania, or New York can be detached from him. Of the three, I have, at present, most hope of New York, and least of Virginia. Late occurrences will strengthen General Jackson in

Virginia, and weaken him much in Pennsylvania, and perhaps also in New York. I am in hopes that "working men," "anti-mason," and "anti-auction men," etc., etc., will break down the regency. This we shall know in October. If it should turn out so, New York will then open a very fair field. For myself, I reckon on recent events as having insured us Maryland, Ohio, Kentucky and Indiana. This is one very good breadth. South of it I look for nothing but Louisiana, every thing north of it is worth a contest.

I hope your friends at the West keep a steady regard to Missouri. I am told there is a good chance, or some chance, of Mr. Barton's re-election. This is matter of very great importance. Nothing, indeed, is more momentous to the country than the approaching election of Senators to the next Congress.

On the whole, my dear sir, I think a crisis is arriving, or rather has arrived. I think you can not be kept back from the contest. The people will bring you out, *nolens volens*. Let them do it. I advise you, as you will be much watched, to stay at home; or, if you wish to travel, visit your old friends in Virginia. We should all be glad to see you at the North, but not now. You will hear from the North, every town and village in it, on the 4th of July. Parties must, now, necessarily, be started out anew; and the great ground of difference will be Tariff and Internal Improvements. You are necessarily at the head of one party, and General Jackson will be, if he is not already, identified with the other. The question will be put to the country. Let the country decide it.

I had intended to say a word about myself, but it would be to make a long letter still longer. When I came here it was my purpose to follow your example, and to vacate my seat at the end of this session. Events have suspended the execution of that purpose. How I shall think of it when I get home, I do not know.

I pray kind remembrance to Mrs. Clay, and beg to assure you of my unaltered regard and attachment.

MR. CLAY TO ADAM BEATTY.

ASHLAND, June 8, 1830.

MY DEAR SIR,—We are all shocked and mortified by the rejection of the Maysville road and other events occurring at the close of the late session. Meetings of the people are contemplated in several counties in this quarter, to give expression to public sentiment and feelings. At those meetings it has been suggested that the public sentiment may be expressed in terms of strong disapprobation of the act of the President. 2d. In favor of Internal Improvement. 3d. Disapproving Mr. Bibbs' conduct and recommending to the Legislature his recall. 4th. Approbation of Mr. Letcher, particularly, and of the other members who voted with him. 5th. Against the nullifying doctrines of the South. 6th. Against the re-election of Mr. Rowan, because he supports them, is opposed to Internal Improvements, and the Tariff, in opinion, and has supported the most obnoxious nominations. 7th. Proposing an amendment to the Constitution, substituting a majority of all the members elected to Congress, instead of two thirds, to pass a bill returned by the President. This is right I think, on principle. Your own reflections will suggest the immense advantages that we shall derive from supporting this amendment, while our opponents will oppose it. It is thought by my friends that these public meetings will furnish suitable occasions for making a nomination for the next Presidency, and recommending to the next Legislature to second and support it. They urge that this will be a popular measure, and not one of caucus agency. That the nomination connects itself naturally with the question of Internal Improvements. That the time has come. That Congress having adjourned, no counteracting measure can be adopted by members of Congress at Washington. That other States look to Kentucky for the first movement. That it will have good effect on the August elections. That it can do no harm, and may do much good, etc. I think there is much force in these suggestions. Will you have a meeting in Macon? If you do it will have beneficial consequences that there should be as many meetings as practicable in adjoining counties. Let me hear from you; and believe always that I am with constant and cordial regard yours, etc.

P. S. My opinion is that, with powerful, bold, and decided action, much may be made of the events of the moment.

MR. CLAY TO J. S. JOHNSTON.

LEXINGTON, June 14, 1830.

MY DEAR SIR,—Not knowing for some time past where to address you, I have omitted to write; but your letter from Washington of the 5th instant having informed me that you will be at Louisville, I commit this letter to the chance of reaching you. I regret that I could not have the pleasure of seeing you here.

I am perfectly contented with the course my friends took at Washington, and I think it was the wisest.

The decisions of the President in respect to Internal Improvement have produced great effect in this quarter of Kentucky. The larger number of all who supported Jackson, in the circle of my immediate acquaintance, have left him. Few but desperate leaders remain to him. Measures have been devised, and are now in a train of execution, to give expression to public sentiment. It is contemplated to disapprove of the exercise of the Veto, the Indian bill, etc, and to propose an amendment of the Constitution, requiring only a majority of both Houses of Congress (of all elected to each) to pass a bill returned by the President. I think such an amendment right, and I attach much importance to the discussion which it will provoke.

MR. CLAY TO FRANCIS BROOKE.

ASHLAND, June 16, 1830.

MY DEAR SIR,—I received both your late favors of the 4th and 6th instant. In regard to Mr. Crawford's strange letter, I could not answer it without violating the regard I once had for him and the respect due to myself, and therefore I did not answer it. I think his proposal was insulting and derogatory. I do not apprehend that the injury to me, which you fear from my silence, can accrue; 1st, because he says in his letter—"Do not suppose that I feel any solicitude upon the subject of the letter. I feel none. But supposing from what I have seen in the public press that you may feel some, it occurred to me that the most certain mode of gratifying that feeling was to adopt the course which I have suggested. If you should be of a different opinion, let the matter rest where it is, and there will have been no harm done. On the contrary, should you concur in the suggestion I have made, I will be happy to hear from you as soon as leisure will permit." This, you will agree, is a strong manifestation of *sang froid* and disinterestedness. But it also evinces that no answer was expected in the event of my disapproval of the proposal, which he seems to have anticipated as possible.

In the second place, I have communicated the contents of the letter, in confidence, to a sufficient number, to protect me against the presumption of any assent of mine, from my silence. Besides, there will be no sort of evidence, direct or collateral, of such assent. It seems to me, that when a base proposition is made, as I regard this, the most proper treatment of it is silent contempt.

As to publishing his letter, although I feel no objection of honor or of confidence which forbids it, I incline to think that under all circumstances it had better not now be done. Mr. Crawford is not, nor likely to be, formidable. His friends, though few of them were mine, are generally respectable. Their feelings would be affected. He has been high in public confidence. Ought that to be shown as having been misplaced, especially as he may not be in his right mind?

In regard to Blair's letter, I took some time ago public ground, from which I think I ought not to recede. I stated that I would not publish it, at the instance of Mr. Amos Kendall, but that it might be seen by any gentleman, and it was seen by many, and by him, though not of that number. The infamous story is now stale, and it can not be revived, even by Thomas Ritchie. I long since resolved to say nothing more to the public about it. I feared indeed that some portion of it [the public] may have considered me to have manifested too much sensitiveness concerning it. Such, I am sure, would be the judgment of many, if I were, in any form, again to present myself to the public respecting that matter.

Great sensation has been produced in this quarter about the President's course relative to Internal Improvements. Public meetings of the people, in various places, are about to be had, at which spirited resolves, etc., will be passed. They mean to attack the Veto, by proposing an amendment of the Constitution, requiring only a majority of all elected to each branch of Congress, instead of two thirds of a house, to pass a returned bill. Such an amendment I think right. If Congress pass a bill on their own reasons, and again pass the same bill, after a full consideration of the reasons of the President in opposition to it, the bill ought to be a law. The policy of proposing such an amendment, in the present condition of parties, is obvious. If our opponents agree to it, it will be adopted. If they oppose it, we shall get the weather guage of them. Will you mention this matter to Pleasants? As he and others of my friends in Virginia approve of the recent exercise of the Veto, there may be some objection in espousing an amendment of the Constitution, which has been suggested by what we deem an abuse. But if, on principle, you should agree with us that the amendment is proper, it might be supported by you without reference to the late exercise of power.

HENRY CLAY, JR., TO HIS FATHER.

CAMP EATON, July 4, 1830.

MY DEAR FATHER,—The anniversary of the Declaration of Independence was celebrated here on yesterday. From peculiar considerations I again appeared before an audience of between four and five hundred, and was once more eminently successful. At the dinner given by the corps, at which about one hundred invited guests were present, the wit and eloquence of the sons of Kentucky were toasted with applause. But the toast of Mr. Skinner, the editor of " The American Farmer and Turf Register," " The orator of the day, in the language of the turf, blood will show itself," drew forth enthusiastic cheers. Do not accuse me, my father, of too broad an exhibition of vanity. I confess that I, in common with all my fellow-men, am subjected to that besetting sin of the human race. But I have thought that, to you, a candid expression of my sentiments would be far more acceptable than any affected air of indifference that I might force from my self-love.

MR. CLAY TO ADAM BEATTY.

COLUMBUS, July 19, 1830.

MY DEAR SIR,—I received your obliging favor of the 13th instant, and, at the same time, the paper containing the proceedings of the meeting in Macon. I perused the preamble and resolutions with much satisfaction. They appear to me to be very appropriate and judicious. I find but one sentiment prevailing here in respect to the late popular movements in Kentucky, and that is, that they are very proper, must do good, and can do no harm. It was well enough, for a certain time, to leave the other party to its own divisions, but that time is now passed. The fact can not, and need not be concealed from that party, that an opposition will be made to the re-election of its chief. So far as that fact will prevent the creation of divisions in its ranks, that consequence will attend it whether we act or not; and by not acting, I apprehend, more loss among our friends than gain among those of the other side.

I have seen here many persons from New England and New York, as well as all parts of this State. Mr. Creighton has just got home, after having made the tour of the former, passing from the city of New York to Buffalo. Without troubling you with the details, the information derived from all these sources is highly encouraging. I shall leave this place in a few days to return home by the way of Cincinnati.

BARON DE KRUDENER TO MR. CLAY.

PHILADELPHIA, August 16, 1830.

SIR,—I can not depart from this country without taking leave from you, and offering once more to you my thanks for the uncommon kindness which I experienced from you during the first part of my residence in this country, and through which, this stage of my diplomatic career, in America, was made so pleasant, so easy, and so honorable to me. The Emperor has granted me a permission to leave my post. I should certainly not have availed myself of it with so much eagerness had circumstances not interrupted the relations in which I had the honor of standing with you. At the time when these circumstances occurred, they were considered by me as a very untoward event. But these disagreeable views of the past have been changed into future prospects of such brightness, that it remains only for me to praise the divine Providence, and to admire its splendid interference in the affairs of your nation.

Having notified my departure to Mr. Van Buren, and considering myself now as a mere traveler and spectator, I feel no remorse in expressing to you my decided partiality, and my hope of seeing the Presidential chair, and the Federal Government, restored by you to their former dignity. You know, my dear sir, enough of my independence of mind to be convinced that this language is dictated by no other feelings than those of conviction and sincerity.

Accept, sir, my best wishes for your personal and political prosperity, and the expression of my devotedness and great respect.

I beg to be remembered to our common friend, the excellent Mr. Letcher.

MR. CLAY TO FRANCIS BROOKE.

ASHLAND, August 17, 1830.

MY DEAR SIR,—I received your letter of the 20th of July. A letter, purporting to have been written by Mr. Jefferson to some manufacturer in Massachusetts, has been recently published in the "Literary Subaltern." It first caught my eye in the public prints, when I was recently on my way to Columbus, and I confess to you that I then had some doubts of its genuineness. They arose from two considerations, one of which was that it uses the terms American system, the first application of which, within my recollection, to the Tariff, was made by myself in my published speech on that subject in 1824, posterior to the date of the letter. The other was, that, although it bore a strong resemblance to the style of Mr. Jefferson, I thought it spoke with more explicitness in relation to the election to the Presidency of myself, than he would permit himself to do, in respect to any person. I communicated these doubts to General Vance at Columbus, and to one or two other friends, before I saw the authenticity of the letter questioned in the public prints. I had even thought of indicating my suspicion to the public in some form; but then I did not know but that the letter might be genuine; and if it should prove to be so, my calling it in question would seem very strange. I therefore remained silent. Subsequent occurrences have tended to strengthen instead of removing the doubts. And I now fear that Mr. Southworth (with whom I have no personal acquaintance, although I think it probable I may have seen him) has acted improperly. He had before given me several occasions to regret his intemperate zeal.

Under these circumstances, ought I to do any thing? Or to leave him to get out of the scrape as he can?

One thing has occurred to me, about which I wish to trouble you. The late Colonel T. M. Randolph, about three years ago attributed to Mr. Jefferson some very disparaging opinions of me, and published them. I knew they were inaccurate at the time. I know that Mr. Jefferson entertained friendly and favorable opinions of me, although I did not know the extent. And I know that Colonel Randolph greatly misrepresented the purport of a conversation between Mr. Jefferson and me, in his presence, and in the presence of Governor Metcalf, who, although I have never spoken to him about it, I am sure would contradict Colonel Randolph.

Shortly after the appearance of Colonel Randolph's statement, I received from his son, Thomas J. Randolph, a letter of which the inclosed is a copy, addressed to me spontaneously. I could make no use of it during the life of the father, for obvious reasons. After his death, I obtained from the son permission to use it as I pleased, although I have never availed myself of it. I observe that the statement of Colonel Randolph is again relied upon to obviate the effect of the Southworth letter. Now, it has occurred to me, that it may be useful to publish Mr. T. J. Randolph's letter; and if you think so, I would be glad that you would obtain his second permission to publish it. It might then be stated in "The Whig," or some other paper, that it had obtained a copy of the letter, with authority to publish it. I should prefer, if published, that it should not appear as my act, or to be done at my instance.

The publication of this letter will destroy the effect of Colonel Randolph's statement, and prove that Mr. Jefferson entertained friendly sentiments, although not the extent of them.

Our elections are just over, and have secured us a majority of not less, on joint ballot in the Legislature, than twelve, and perhaps eighteen. They show that there is about five thousand in the whole State against Jackson, which would have been swelled to from ten to fifteen thousand, if the direct question of the next Presidency had been before the people. Our majority in the Legislature would have been thirty, but for the operation of local causes, divisions, and the impossibility of making the Presidential question every where bear on the election. Mr. Rowan will be permitted to retire.

The results in Indiana, Illinois, Missouri, so far as we have yet heard from them, are still more favorable. Benton's re-election is considered certain.

P. S. Should you decide to publish the letter of Mr. T. J. R., perhaps, it will be better to make no allusion to the letter of Mr. Southworth.

PETER B. PORTER TO MR. CLAY.

BLACK ROCK, October 6, 1830.

DEAR SIR,—This cursed anti-masonry embarrasses every thing, and defeats all attempts at systematic operation against the common enemy. Of one thing, however, I can assure you, which is, that you personally, as well as the leading measures of policy which you have so powerfully and conspicuously advocated, are visibly and rapidly gaining ground in every part of our State; and I am now much inclined to believe that, if we had, two months ago, started a candidate for Governor under the banner of Clay and the American system, we should have succeeded.

MR. MADISON TO MR. CLAY.

MONTPELIER, October 9, 1830.

DEAR SIR,—I have just been favored with yours of the 22d ultimo, inclosing a copy of your address delivered at Cincinnati. Without concurring in every thing that is said, I feel what is due to the ability and eloquence of the whole. The rescue of the Resolutions of Kentucky, in '98 and '99, from the misconstruction of them, was very apropos; that authority being particularly relied on, as an ægis to the nullifying doctrine, which, notwithstanding its hideous aspect and fatal tendency, has captivated so many honest minds. In a late letter to one of my correspondents, I was led to the like task of vindicating the proceedings of Virginia in those years. I would gladly send you a copy if I had a suitable one. But as the letter is appended to the "North American Review" for this month, you will probably have an early opportunity of seeing it.

With my thanks for your obliging communication, I beg you

to accept assurances of my great and cordial esteem, in which Mrs. Madison joins me, as I do her in the best regards which she offers to Mrs Clay.

J. S. JOHNSTON TO MR. CLAY.

PHILADELPHIA, Tuesday, October 19, 1830.

MY DEAR SIR,—We have been greatly shocked to-day by the sudden and unexpected death of Mrs. Brown. She expired about eleven o'clock, without the slightest pain or suffering, and probably without any consciousness of the approaching event. The disease which has proved so instantaneously fatal was water in the chest, which had been gradually increasing and rendering her respiration more difficult. The collection of water burst and extinguished life in a moment. She drove out on Saturday as well as usual; saw several of her friends on Sunday evening, and did not retire until eleven. Monday she was not so well, and for the first time kept her room; she slept well Monday night, and until late in the morning; had her breakfast at nine; said she was much better, and would dress and go down stairs. Mr. Brown went to the reading-room as usual. Doctor La Roche was with her ten minutes before, and left her without apprehension. She expired so easily, that Miss Brown supposed she had fainted. Mr. Brown has been greatly distressed. They had just established themselves in their new house. Mrs. Brown supposed she had the asthma, and that she might live as her father had done for many years. On Saturday she selected a lot to build on. This event, painful as it is to Mr. Brown and his friends, is most happy for her in the manner of it. She has been spared all the anticipations of death, which she seemed to put far away from her.

All the arrangements are made for the funeral, which will be numerously attended. Mrs. Brown is a great loss to the city, and her death has made a great sensation. I returned last evening from Boston.

I have been with Mr. Brown this evening, and he is more composed. Miss Susan will write Mrs. Clay as soon as she can; in the mean time they both request me to write you, which I have done in great haste.

MR. CLAY TO J. S. JOHNSTON.

Ashland, November 1, 1830.

My dear Sir,—I have received several letters from you, which I should have acknowledged, had I known where to address you. The last, from Philadelphia, communicates the death of Mrs. Brown, an event which has filled us with affliction, although we were not altogether unprepared to expect it. To Mr. Brown it must have been irreparable. They had lived so long together, and entered so entirely into each other's pleasures, pursuits, and habits, that I fear he will hardly ever recover from the shock. He ought forthwith to leave Philadelphia and travel.

I have received a confidential communication that Senator Barnard has renounced Jacksonism, and, at a time when he may deem suitable, will exhibit evidence of his renunciation. I put you in possession of the fact that, if true, you may not be unapprised of it. Should it prove correct, the change may neutralize the loss of Marks, which, I suppose, is inevitable. We shall gain, I think, one Senator in Kentucky; and there being now two to elect in Illinois (Mr. M'Lean is dead), if we are in good luck, we shall gain at least one there. On the other hand, I fear, from all that has reached me, Barton may not be re-elected. Ohio will re-elect Burnet, or some other friend. Indiana will re-elect Hendricks, or some less equivocal friend. On these data you can estimate the probable state of the Senate.

Should the elections to the Legislature terminate favorably in New York (as some friends calculate), you may possibly get a friendly Senator there. Of that you will be able to judge by the time this letter reaches you.

Upon the whole (let the issue of the New York election be what it may), I think the campaign of this year has not closed discouragingly. Great faults have been committed, but they are not exclusively confined to our side. In this State, the proposed Convention will take effect, and one of its best results, I hope, will be to guard us against future *faux pas*.

My best regards to Mrs. Johnston.

NICHOLAS BIDDLE TO MR. CLAY.

PHILADELPHIA, November 3, 1830.

MY DEAR SIR,—I have purposely delayed answering your favor of the 11th of September, until I could speak with some degree of confidence as to the course which will be adopted in reference to the subject of it. In the mean time I have read repeatedly, and with renewed interest, all your remarks, proceeding, as I know they do, from one who, with ample materials of information and great sagacity in employing them, gives the result of his reflections with a sincere desire to serve the institution. For this, in any event, you will accept my grateful thanks.

After keeping the subject long under advisement, in order to observe the latest development of facts, I am now satisfied that it would be inexpedient to apply at present for the renewal of the Charter. My belief is, from all that I have seen, and read, and heard, that there is at this moment a majority of both Houses of Congress favorable to a renewal; and, moreover, that the President would not reject the bill. The temptation is therefore great to take advantage of a propitious state of feeling like this. But then the hazard is not to be disguised. A great mass of those who, if they were obliged to vote at all, would vote favorably, will prefer not voting if it can be avoided, and the dread of responsibility, the love of postponement, and the *vis inertiæ* inherent in all legislative bodies would combine to put off the question during the approaching short session. To pass both Houses and be rejected by the President—to be rejected in either House, to be postponed in either House, to be brought forward in any shape, and not be finally and favorably acted upon, are degrees of evil—but the mildest of them, a great evil, much to be deplored, and to be avoided, if possible. My impression, then, is, that nothing but a certainty of success should induce an application now. To this I am the more inclined, because time is operating in favor of the Bank by removing prejudices, and diffusing a general conviction of its utility.

Having made up my own mind on the subject, I am gratified that this, which is the first expression I have made of this opinion, should be communicated to you, whose views have so largely influenced my own. It will always afford me great pleasure to receive the benefit of your further suggestions on this or any other subject, being with great respect and regard yours, etc.

MR. CLAY TO J. S. JOHNSTON.

ASHLAND, November 14, 1830.

MY DEAR SIR,—The same information communicated to you, and which is contained in your letter of the 5th instant, respecting the rupture between two high officers, has come to me from Nashville, pretty directly. I think, therefore, it may be presumed true. I should not be surprised if Jackson should denounce the nullifiers in his next message, and mount that hobby to regain his popularity. But what will—what can the Vice-President do? South Carolina is rather too contracted a position for him to start from. Besides, he is not very secure in that. It appears to me that Van Buren has completely out-maneuvered him.

In regard to the attempt to turn out Duff, I can supply you with some facts which may throw light upon the object. Blair, of "The Kentucky Argus," is now on his way to Washington, with his family, to set up a new paper, and it is highly probable that the alternatives which the Jackson party mean to offer you, are Duff and Blair! Will not their division admit your friends appointing some respectable editor? If not, I think it will be most expedient for them to present such an editor, and adhere to him to the last, without mixing in the contest between the above two.

The divisions in New York have led, I perceive, to the issue that might have been anticipated: the triumph of the Jackson party in all the elections.

I believe I mentioned to you, in a former letter, that Poindexter dined with me, and that he talks like an independent man, who felt that he was denounced, and was resolved to cling to principle.

MR. CLAY TO JOHN BAILHACHE.

ASHLAND, November 24, 1830.

DEAR SIR,—I received your favor of the 18th inst., communicating a very full and satisfactory account of your late election, and of the causes which led to its results. Upon the whole, we have much reason to be satisfied with those results, although we may regret that our friends in the reserve did not bestir themselves more. On the subject of the operation of Anti-Masonry on the interests of our cause, respecting which you request my views, I will explain them very frankly.

The leaders of Anti-Masonry are in the pursuit of power; the great body of their party are endeavoring to remove what they honestly believe to be a great evil. The former would desire power, without regard to the means of acquiring it; the latter seek it only as an instrument of effecting their paramount object. To accomplish this object they believe, and their leaders industriously inculcate the belief, that a change of the administration of the actual Government (whether general or State) is necessary. Hence, in the Western reserve, and in Vermont, where our friends are in the majority, the Anti-Masons connected themselves with the Jacksonians to get hold of the Government, and to dispossess those who possessed it. For the same reason, in New York and Pennsylvania, when the Jackson party was in power, the Anti-Masons sought a coalition with our friends. If this coalition was not complete, and if the Anti-Masons did not succeed, it was not their fault.

I think it may be assumed that whenever Anti-Masonry is in the minority, it will seek a connection with any other party, which, in the same place, is also in the minority. This will account for the various and apparently conflicting directions which it takes. It is only an apparent inconsistency, for the object every where is the same, the acquisition of power.

In this respect, Anti-Masonry does not differ from any other party, for the natural tendency of all the divisions of a minority, is to cohesion. This will generally take place unless it is counteracted by some stronger feeling or sentiment than that of hatred to those in power, as was the case with a portion of our friends in the late New York election.

I do not know that it is to be regretted that the Anti-Masons did not succeed in Pennsylvania and New York. If they had been successful, they would probably have brought out an Anti-Masonic candidate for President. Still, if I had been in New York, with a right to vote, I should have given my suffrage to Granger. I will not now trouble you with the reasons.

I regret that the failure of Mr. Granger is so well ascertained to have been, because our friends about Albany, and in the river counties, would not concentrate on him. Unless this circumstance should produce an alienation between our friends and the

Anti-Masons, I should think we will ultimately obtain their support, for the following reasons:

1. It is in conformity with the general nature of minorities, already noticed, that they should vote with us, if they have no candidate of their own party.

2. They agree with us as to the American System.

3. They have been violently assailed in New York by the Regency.

4. They believe that, although I am a Mason, that I have no bigotry, and that I have no very great ardor for the institution.

5. General Jackson has, as they think, persecuted them, which they believe I should not do, as most certainly I should not.

I can hardly believe that they will now present a Presidential candidate, although they still talk about it. Immediately after the election in New York, Mr. Ward (the editor of the "Anti-Masonic Review") told a friend of mine that they could not support me, and would present a candidate of their own, etc. The next day he called on that same friend, and informed him that the Executive Committee of the Anti-Masons had resolved, 1st. That the late election in New York had shown that they could not directly support me: 2d. That it be recommended to the convention at Baltimore, to nominate an Anti-Masonic candidate; and 3d. That the papers of the party in New York, be advised to abstain from attacking me, and to conciliate my friends.

If there be an Anti-Masonic candidate, I am inclined to think that it would operate in Pennsylvania and New York, more against General Jackson than me, should we both be the candidates, while in your State, it would operate more against me than him. In that contingency, should our friends in New York and Pennsylvania unite with the Anti-Masonic party, Jackson would probably lose one or both of those States, in either of which cases I think he would be defeated.

What I think not unlikely, is, that this time two years hence, the Anti-Masonic party will present in New York a candidate for Governor, without any electors for President and Vice-President, and that our friends will offer these, without any candidate for Governor. Upon that supposition, if there be concert between the two parties, each would succeed in its object. I do not know that any such arrangement has ever been thought of. None such has ever been suggested to me, and I infer it only from the natural operation of causes.

I am inclined to think, upon the whole, that a conciliatory course on our part, toward the Anti-Masons, is wisest. There is no occasion for our friends to attack them. Let us leave that to the Jackson party.

We shall have some trouble about a Senator, though I yet think we shall succeed in the election of a friend. I have been pressed of late to offer. Mr. Adams' example is quoted. But both my feelings and judgment are strongly opposed to my return to Congress. Nothing but a contingency, which I sincerely hope may not arise, would overcome them.

MR. CLAY TO FRANCIS BROOKE.

ASHLAND, December 20, 1830.

MY DEAR SIR,—I believe I am in arrears to you, and that I omitted to answer your last, in which you requested me to say something on French affairs. Events followed in such rapid succession, that I had no time, except to put in a flying shot, which seemed to me hardly necessary. I sincerely hope that the work, so gloriously begun, will be happily consummated. They have two dangers: the first, in retaining a Bourbon on the throne, which they thought ought to be done to consiliate foreign powers; and the second, the humane desire to screen the former ministers from punishment. It would have been better to have suffered the law to proceed against them, and to have forborne the offer of the project of abolishing capital punishments until it had pronounced its sentence. It would have been better not to have mixed the two subjects together, or not to have given color to such an imputation. After their conviction, if convicted, I think it would have been easier to have commuted the punishment for banishment, or some other milder form. As to Belgium, the rock on which I feared the French Government would split, they appear to me to have acted discreetly. Belgium will ultimately go to France, unless a totally new way of thinking has taken place since I was there.

But I did not commence to write you now on French affairs. Perhaps, before my letter reaches you, some new and important turn may have taken place in them.

My object was to say to you, that I go in a day or two to New Orleans, to pass a portion of the winter there with Mrs. Clay, and to request you to let me hear from you at that city.

I am extremely anxious to know how your Legislature disposes of the Judiciary, or rather, Judges. In these late times of political trouble and strife, nothing has distressed me so much as the suffering of my friends, and I have feared that they would make a victim of you on my account. Do let me know what may be done.

The political events of the year, taken altogether, are not discouraging. Except in Maine and New York, they justify strong hopes of the future. And in New York, so far as the election of Governor was concerned, it is far from certain that the issue should be regretted.

In this State, the Legislature has not yet appointed a Senator. Our friends are in good spirits, and count upon success. But the vote will be a close one, owing to the fact that five or six members, opposed to the Administration, believe themselves pledged to vote for a Jackson Senator. It is not impossible that no election will be made this session.

HENRY CLAY, JR., TO HIS FATHER.

WEST POINT, December 20, 1830.

MY DEAR FATHER,—I have just learned with certainty by your letter, that you and my mother are going to New Orleans. You will find there such a reunion of friends and relations, that I am sure you can not fail to spend a very agreeable winter. Would that I formed one of your party, but next to enjoying your society myself, is the pleasure I feel in knowing that you are re-established in health and spirits, and surrounded by your friends.

In regard to study, an object has presented itself to my view, and I eagerly pursue it. My perseverance and assiduity in this pursuit, may perhaps be to my prejudice in others, but still I am willing to give up excellence in every other department of knowledge, to attain an honorable rank as a speaker. I am well aware that a general acquaintance with the whole circle of arts and sciences, and in fact with every branch of human knowledge, is indispensable to the accomplished orator, and this I shall endeavor to acquire, without weakening or confusing my mind by too abstracted an attention to minutiæ. I am glad that you are improving Ashland. I have a kind of filial affection for it, which seems to increase with my years, and distance from it.

CHAPTER VIII.

CORRESPONDENCE OF 1831 AND 1832.

MR. CLAY TO ———.

NEW ORLEANS, February 16, 1831.

DEAR SIR,—I found, on my arrival in this State, a general alarm pervading it in respect to the attack meditated on the Tariff, and which had been actually commenced in the House of Representatives. The people of Louisiana, an excellent race, and greatly attached to the Union, contemplate the success of that attack as involving their utter ruin. If, say they, we had remained a colony of France or Spain, our productions, and especially our great staple, would have been protected, in the parent country, against the rival productions of foreign colonies. And shall we, as an independent State, a member of this great Republic, fare worse than if we had continued a distant colony?

I must confess that they have made a convert of me, and have fully convinced me of two propositions: 1st. That the repeal or reduction of the present duty on foreign sugar would totally disable them from continuing the culture of the cane; and 2d. That all parts of the Union would partake of the distress which would be certainly inflicted on them.

Most erroneous impressions prevail, in other parts of the Union, as to the profits upon capital invested in sugar plantations. It happens to this business, as to all others, that now and then a planter, by the practice of the greatest economy, by a favorable season and the concurrence of fortunate circumstances, makes a large profit. These rare instances become the theme of general conversation, and hence it is rashly inferred that all the planters are growing rapidly rich. The conclusion is just as unwise as it would have been prior to the Tariff of 1824, to argue that the cotton manufacture was prosperous because that at Waltham was doing remarkably well. These cases of good fortune are neutralized by others of an opposite character. For example (and the instance is by no means singular), a planter, whose acquaintance I have formed, who is remarkable for his intelligence, and his accuracy and great attention to business, has, in partnership, an estate which cost upward of $220,000. His partner, a skillful and diligent manager, resides on the estate. Minute and regular accounts are kept of their receipts and expenditures. They sold last year their crop, and, after deducting all expenses, the nett sum of $800 remained to be divided between them!

But it is not on these extremes, on either side, that the statesman should be guided in adjusting his measures to the wants or necessities of a community. His conclusions should be drawn from the average profit deduced from a view of the entire branch of business, which his duties call upon him to consider. Proceeding upon this principle, I am persuaded, from all I have seen and heard here, that Mr. Senator Johnston, in his late excellent letter to the Secretary of the Treasury, in assuming as the average rate of profit upon capital employed in the culture of sugar cane, from five to six per cent. rather exceeds than falls short of the true standard. It is evident, then, that the Louisiana planter, if he were not protected by the existing duty, could not sustain a competition with the sugars of foreign colonies. They would compel him to abandon the business; and the repeal of that duty would be almost as fatal to him as if Congress were to order the dykes to be razed from Point Coupée to the Balize.

But if Congress, after having by its whole course of policy during a long series of years, inspired confidence in the inhabitants of this State as to the permanency of protection, and thereby invited them to invest their capital in their present pursuit, could overwhelm them in irretrievable ruin, their sufferings would not be confined to themselves, but would extend to every other part of the Union. If manufactures in any country deserve protection because of the home market which they create for the productions of the industry of other classes, the sugar planter of Louisiana is equally entitled, for the same reason, to protection. The seven or eight hundred sugar plantations in Louisiana are, in fact, but seven or eight hundred great manufactories. The raw material is, it is true, produced on their plantations by the cultivation of the earth, but it is only produced to be there manufactured also into sugar and molasses. As consumers of the objects of the industry of other classes, the Louisiana planters are even more important than manufacturers exclusively employed in fabrication ; for they neither make their food, nor their clothing, nor their implements of labor, all of which they purchase from other States. Nay more, their very laborers themselves, in consequence of the institution of slavery, are chiefly brought from other States. Manufacturers, strictly so called, on the contrary, either make their own clothes, or their implements of labor, or both.

I had no adequate conception, prior to my present visit to this State, of the extent of this dependence of the Louisiana planter upon other States for his necessary supplies. He draws from them his flour, bacon, pork, beef, the greater part of the Indian corn fed upon his plantation, his carts, axes, spades, plows, hoes, steam-engines for his sugar-house, stone-coal, boilers, horses, mules, cattle, the clothing of his slaves, whisky, and a great variety of small articles. These are obtained principally from Pennsylvania and the Western, Middle, and Northern States. His slaves, annually in great numbers, are brought from Virginia and Maryland.

Let us suppose the market for these various articles to be suddenly cut off, the inevitable consequence of the repeal of the duty upon sugar, and am I not correct in saying that every part of the Union, in this view of the subject, would be deeply and sensibly affected by the destruction of the business of the Louisiana planter ? Every article which I have enumerated would immediately fall in price, and no section of the Union would be altogether exempt from the consequences of a measure so disastrous.

Would they be compensated by any permanent reduction in the price of sugar, the illusive object sought by those who, in aiming to repeal the duty, would lay the ax at the root of the prosperity of this interesting State ? It is confidently believed not. The present low price of sugar is attributable to the competition which has been produced between the West Indian and Louisiana planter. The eighty or one hundred thousand hogsheads which the latter annually throws into the general consumption have diminished to that extent, the demand for the produce of the former, who has been consequently compelled to reduce the price. This has obliged the Louisiana planter also to reduce the price, and he has found himself sustained only by the possession of the home market, the principal part of which is given him by the existing duty. If that duty were repealed, and if Louisiana continued permanently to produce the quantity which she now annually yields, undoubtedly there would be a permanent reduction of price. But the effect of a repeal of the duty would compel the Louisiana planter to abandon cultivation of the sugar cane. Absolute ruin would attend him if he continued to prosecute it. Then what would happen? The eighty or one hundred thousand hogsheads now contributed by Louisiana would be withdrawn from the general consumption. A demand would ensue for eighty or one hundred thousand hogsheads more of the production of the West Indies. This demand would speedily augment the price, and the probability is, that it would rise to what it now is, or nearly so. It may be argued that when, after falling, the price should again rise to the present rate, the Louisiana planter would resume the cultivation. But this admits of several satisfactory answers. In the first place, if he was now out of the business, he probably would not embark in it, such are the discouragements produced by low prices and the dread of a change of public policy. He continues the business because he is in it, has built his houses, made his canals and ditches, established his manufactory, consisting of mills, steam-engines and boilers, and effected all his other arrangements with a view to his present pursuit. Supposing that abandoned; supposing all these arrangements overturned, and his plantation appropriated to the cultivation of cotton, rice, or any other article, it would not be so easy, under the temptation even of a high price of sugar, to return to the planting of cane. The establishment of a sugar plantation, with all its manufacturing and other apparatus, is not suddenly accomplished, but is a work of long, patient, and arduous industry. Finally, he could not fail to reflect that the encouraging price of sugar, for the moment, resulted from the absence of Louisiana competition, and that, whenever this returned, a depressed and ruinous state of the market would be inevitable.

Other views of this interesting question might be taken, but I will content myself with noticing only an additional one. If the cultivation of the sugar cane be abandoned, the labor now employed in it must be directed to some other object; and that object undoubtedly would be cotton. But this article is already produced in excessive quantity. Would it be wise in Congress, by curtailing the pursuits of the people of the United States, to compel a large portion of their industry to seek employment in a business already overdone? The effect would be most injuriously felt in Tennessee, the northern parts of Alabama and Mississippi, the upper parts of Georgia and South Carolina, and generally those districts of the cotton region which are the least adapted to the production of that staple.

I found the sensibility of the people of this State, on my arrival here, greatly excited on another subject. Shortly after the cession of Louisiana, an act of Congress required all the inhabitants to register their titles to lands granted to them by the previous governments, and denounced, as a penalty for a neglect to comply with this law, that the proprietors should not be allowed to use their unregistered titles in any court of justice. The object at which Congress aimed was a proper and legitimate object, it being to discriminate between the public domain and private property; but it may now be well doubted whether the means were not rigorously and disproportionately severe. Many, from no disrespect whatever to the Legislature, but from a perfect confidence in the security of their titles, resulting from ancient possession and complete grants, and strengthened by a positive stipulation in the treaty of cession guaranteeing their property, omitted to register their titles. Many, from ignorance of the law, promulgated in a language not their own, also omitted to register their titles. An opinion has prevailed among the bar, that in the case of perfect titles, the ceremony of registry was unnecessary.

Notwithstanding this state of conscious security, the lands of many of the ancient proprietors, who never dreamed of danger, have been thrown into the market. Sales have been actually made, in several instances, of plantations which have been in cultivation from fifty to one hundred years; and the first knowledge of them which the unfortunate planters acquired was a notice from the speculator, not to remove, at their peril, any thing whatever from the plantation. A church even, long dedicated to public worship, has been actually sold! The interposition of the Executive has, I understand, been in vain invoked. I do hope that that of Congress, to which the Legislature has appealed, will be afforded, and that some efficacious remedy will be provided.

What that remedy should be, Congress is most competent to

decide. The effect of the introduction to the proprietor of the use, in courts of justice, of his title paper, is a forfeiture of his land. But is not that punishment altogether too severe, and disproportionate to the offense, if offense it can be called, of non-registry? Especially when that was never contumacious, and in most, if not all, instances proceeded from ignorance of law or language, or forgetfulness. It seems to me that some mode might have been adopted to discriminate between the public and private lands other than that of obliging the inhabitants to register their titles, already recorded in the archives of preceding governments, under the pains and penalties of forfeiture of their estates. Had they committed the crime of high treason, under ancient law, the punishment, as to their estates, would not have been greater; but even the crime of high treason, in the mitigated spirit of modern institutions, does not draw after it a forfeiture of the culprit's estate. It may indeed be well questioned whether the act of Congress is not repugnant to that amendment of the Federal Constitution, which forbids a man's property to be taken from him without due process of law.

I do not know the extent of the evil which I have depicted. I have understood that perhaps one third of the plantations from Point Coupée down the Mississippi are in that condition. This, you know, comprises the best and longest settled, as well as the richest part of the State. And what aggravates the misfortune is, that the omission to register has been chiefly on the part of the Creole planters, affording a strong presumption that it has proceeded from ignorance of the American laws and language, the American planters having most generally taken the precaution to comply with the law.

Thus threatened with the loss both of their lands and their produce, it is astonishing how patiently this good people bear up under their afflictions. Complaints there are among individuals, but neither the Legislature nor any public assembly has, for a moment, forgot its loyalty to the Union, or its respect to the public authorities. We have no menaces of violence, no charges of the oppression and tyranny of the majority, no threats to execute the powers of nullification. They appear to abide in perfect confidence that, when their condition is fully understood, in the general family council, right and justice will be done them. That they may not be disappointed I sincerely pray.

RICHARD RUSH TO MR. CLAY.

York, Pennsylvania, April 14, 1831.

My dear Sir,—Is there no way in which, without doing violence to whatever opinions or feelings you may have as respects masonry, or without offending that institution, you could conciliate to a fair and reasonable extent the good will of Anti-Masons, between this and September? I am sure that, in this State, there are many, very many, of the latter, who notwithstanding what is said in the newspapers, ardently desire to give their support to you, for the sake of the great public objects and principles inseparably interwoven with your name, and which they fear the permanent prostration of, should General Jackson be reelected. I throw this out again, not to put you to the trouble of a reply, but only for you again to think of it, in conjunction with discreet friends in the West. You will do, I know, now as always, what duty, honor, and true patriotism require. With the direct aid of Anti-Masons, we should carry your banner to a glorious victory, even if we do not without.

MR. CLAY TO FRANCIS BROOKE.

Ashland, May 1, 1831.

My dear Sir,—Prior to the receipt of your favor of the 17th ultimo, I had written you a long letter, which I hope will safely reach you. I infer from your last a determination to accept your recent appointment. I think you ought to accept it, and I should regret that you did not. Under all circumstances, it was an honorable testimony. I share with Messrs. Johnson and Leigh in their disappointment in not getting Mr. Stanard on the bench; and I concur with them in the superiority which they assign to him over his successful competitor.

We live in an age of revolution. Who could have imagined such a cleansing of the Augean stable at Washington? a change, almost total, of the Cabinet. Did you ever read such a letter as Mr. Van Buren's? It is perfectly characteristic of the man—a labored effort to conceal the true motives, and to assign assumed ones, for his resignation, under the evident hope of profiting by the latter. The "delicate step," I apprehend, has been taken, because, foreseeing the gathering storm, he wished early to secure a safe refuge. Whether that will be on his farm, or at London, we shall see. Meantime, our cause can not fail to be benefited by the measure. It is a broad confession of the incompetency of the President's chosen advisers, no matter from what cause, to carry on the business of the Government. It is a full admission of that unfitness of those advisers for their respective stations, which the whole country felt when they were first selected. And if, as I presume, Ingham and Branch were dismissed, or compelled to resign, further dissentions must be sown in a party on the verge of dissolution.

Nor can the injury to his cause be repaired by any successors to the vacant places, whom the President may call around him—certainly not by those whom rumor designates. Edward Livingston to be Secretary of State—a recorded defaulter to an enormous amount—the reviler of Jefferson, whom he pursued in his retirement with a malicious and vexatious suit—a man notoriously destitute of all principle. Louis McLane to be Secretary of the Treasury—a man who glories in his federalism, to be appointed by the Republican party—one whose degrading supplications, at the Court of London, for a worthless privilege, must have disgusted every man who was not insensible to the honor and dignity of his country.

I expressed, in my former letter, my conjectures as to the course of Mr. Calhoun. Late events, tending to show the great probability of the defeat of Jackson, may now determine him to take bolder and firmer ground against the President. The occurrence at Washington is certainly not intended or calculated to subserve Mr. Calhoun. The rumored successors will all be adverse to him. I understand that Judge Smith was one of the advisers of the President in respect to the recent change, and he will advise nothing which can promote Mr. Calhoun's views. Thus situated, the Vice-President may declare, or cause himself to be declared, a candidate, or aid, without such declaration, any and every opposition to the President. Unless I am deceived as to his strength, he will not be a candidate himself, but will push forward, most probably, Judge McLean. I observe a hint of such a purpose, on the part of his friends, in "The Whig." I long since learned that there was (what shall I call it?—a bargain?) between the Judge and Mr. Calhoun, an understanding that he of the two was to be supported who could command the greatest probability of success.

I observe what you state, as to the impression, in regard to my constitutional principles, which Mr. Ritchie has made on the Virginia public ; but I can not concur with you as to the utility, at this time, of any publication about them, from myself, in any form. If I am not now understood by the public, nothing that I could say, during the pendancy of a warm canvass, would make me intelligible, and I must submit to any misconception of me which may, unfortunately, prevail. I need not say to you that my constitutional doctrines are those of the epoch of 1798. I am against all power not delegated, or not necessary and proper to execute what is delegated. I hold to the principles of Mr. Madison, as promulgated through the Virginia Legislature. I was with Mr. Madison then ; I am with him now. I am against all nullification, all new lights in politics, if not in religion. Applying the very principles of Mr. Madison's famous interpretation of the Constitution, in the Virginia address, I find in the Constitution the power to protect our industry, and to improve our country by objects of a national character. I have never altered my constitutional opinion which I ever entertained, and publicly expressed, but that in relation to the bank ; and the experience of the last war changed mine, and almost every other person's, who had been against the power of chartering it. Such are my views, but I will not consent to any publication of them, under existing circumstances, if I were even sure of achieving the conversion of my old friend Ritchie, who, by the by, knows them perfectly well.

I adhere to my opinion, that there is no sufficient public reason, at this time, for publishing Mr. Crawford's letter. I should be glad that that of Mr. T. J. Randolph could be published, without any direct agency of mine ; but if it can not be so published, I must acquiesce.

What am I to do with the perpetual importunities to visit the North, etc., etc.? My judgment is against all and every excursion for, or which might be fairly construed to have in view, mere political effect. But I should like to be fortified or corrected by the opinion of yourself and other Virginia friends.

MR. CLAY TO FRANCIS BROOKE.

ASHLAND, June 4, 1831.

MY DEAR SIR,—I received both of your favors of the 15th ult., from Richmond, and of the 26th from St. Julien. I should be very happy to meet you in August at the White Sulphur Springs and Lewisburg; but I believe I shall find it necessary to remain this summer in Kentucky. My private affairs require some portion of my time. I have several Executorships also to close, and I wish to avail myself of the leisure I can command this summer to settle them.

I regret that I have not a copy of the pamphlet of Mr. Livingston to which you refer. I will endeavor to procure one from New Orleans. Lately I have seen extracts from it, in which the author speaks very harshly of Mr. Jefferson.

I should be very glad if you could obtain the consent of Mr. T. J. R. to the publication of the letter, but I fear his apprehensions will lead him to withhold it.

Can you not, when at Lewisburg, extend your journey this far? I should be delighted to see you here, and beg you will come, if it be possible.

MR. CLAY TO ADAM BEATTY.

ASHLAND, June 4, 1831.

DEAR SIR,—I received your favor of the 31st ultimo, with the newspaper communicating the death of our friend Colonel Rochester. I offer you my sincere condolence on that afflicting event. To his family and numerous friends it is no small alleviation that he lived to a ripe old age, honored and beloved, and dies with the deep and general regret of all who knew him, as the "Rochester Gazette" truly testifies.

I congratulate you on the improvement in the price of wool, and the consequent encouragement to the cultivation of sheep. I received for my common wool, unwashed, 33 cents, and was offered 62 for my merino, washed on the back of the sheep.

A lame ram of mine was left the summer before the last with, I think, a Mr. Foreman, in your neighborhood, and I have never since heard of him. Will you be good enough to apply for the ram, if living, and use him this fall if you want him?

HENRY CLAY, JR., TO HIS FATHER.

WEST POINT, June 21, 1831.

DEAR FATHER,—I have favorable news to give you in regard to myself. I have finished my examination and have graduated second; and in the engineer corps. You know that it is the highest honor conferred upon graduates to be admitted into the engineers; and one not often conferred upon the heads of classes.

General Scott is President of the Board for this year; you know he is your warm friend, and consequently mine. I have received from him many manifestations of the kindest attention to my interests. He wishes me to be stationed in New York, should I remain in the army. If you should advise me so to do, I shall be employed on the fortifications of New York Bay and Harbor. In the mean time I deem it proper to say that my talents remain the same as before this honor, and I believe I may say my inclinations also.,

---

MR. CLAY TO FRANCIS BROOKE.

ASHLAND, June 23, 1831.

MY DEAR SIR,—I received your favor of the 12th instant. I believe I have answered all your previous favors, although my last, at the date of yours, had not, I suppose, reached you. In that I informed you that I could not visit Lewisburg. It would have afforded me very great satisfaction to have been able to visit it, on account of yourself and other friends whom I should have met there, or at the Springs; but it will not be in my power. Can you not come here, when you will, at Lewisburg, have penetrated so far to the West? I assure you that we would give you a warm and cordial reception, if you would visit us; and I hope you will be able and inclined to do so.

I am sorry to have troubled you with Mr. T. J. Randolph and his letter. Certainly their prudence is much to be admired. As it is but a small affair, I beg you to desist from the pursuit of it, if you encounter any further obstacle. I am not insensible to the value of the good opinion of his grandfather, as I desire indeed to deserve and possess that of all men. His father bore evidence, which was widely promulgated, of an unfavorable opinion entertained of me by his grandfather. He voluntarily contradicted it in a private letter to me. During his father's lifetime, from considerations of delicacy, I did not desire the publication of the contradiction. After his (father's) death, he expressly permitted it. If he now refuses the publication, and chooses to allow his father's erroneous testimony to stand unrefuted, I must, without repining, acquiesce in the decision.

Our flattering prospects in Kentucky daily increase, instead of declining. And letters which reach me from all quarters of the Union (the four Southern Atlantic States excepted) exhibit a tone of the greatest confidence. Anti-Masonry seems to be the only difficulty now in the way of certain success, both in Pennsylvania and New York. I have been urged, entreated, importuned, to make some declaration, short of renunciation of masonry, which would satisfy the Antis. But I have hitherto declined all interference on that subject. While I do not, and never did, care about Masonry, I shall abstain from making myself any party to that strife. I tell them that Masonry or Anti-Masonry has, legitimately, in my opinion, nothing to do with politics; that I never acted, in public or private life, under any Masonic influence; that I have long since ceased to be a member of any lodge; that I voted for Mr. Adams, no Mason, against General Jackson, a Mason, etc.

Mr. Rush, among others, has urged me to make some declaration. Notwithstanding his late impassioned address, he is firm in his devotion to our cause, and, I think, is worthy of all confidence. I do not believe that he would accept a nomination for the Presidency from the Antis, nor that he would allow of any use of his name prejudicial to me.

How Anti-Masonry will finally operate is an important question. They may, and probably will make a nomination at Baltimore, in September, of some person who is not a Mason. They can not nominate Calhoun, on account of his political principles. They will not nominate Van Buren. If they nominate Rush, I think he will not accept the nomination. It is said that Judge M'Lean will not. Granger they intend to run as Governor of New York. If they do make a nomination which shall be accepted, I think they will, before the next spring, discover how hopeless it is, and abandon it virtually, if not formally.

Upon the whole, I do not apprehend ultimately any serious mischief from it.

Mrs. Clay unites with me in respectful remembrances to Mrs. Brooke.

MR. CLAY TO ADAM BEATTY.

ASHLAND, June 25, 1831.

DEAR SIR,—The same anxiety displayed by our friend, Mr. Rochester, as evinced in the extract from his letter which you were good enough to send me, in regard to the pending Kentucky elections, pervades our friends throughout the Union. And I do believe that, if they should result, as we hope and believe they might be made to result, the Presidential contest would, in effect, be decided. My information as to our prospects in the State is highly flattering. Still no energy or exertion ought to be spared that can be thrown into the canvass. I concur with you fully in the efficiency of the plan suggested by you for bringing out the voters, and hope you will have it carried into effect in your quarter. Such a proceeding is contemplated here, and it will be also suggested to the Central Committee.

We can not tell, at this distance of time and theater, how the Anti-Masonic excitement will result. Should they make a nomination in September, their first difficulty will be to prevail on any prominent person to accept. I am quite sure, from the tenor of recent letters from Mr. Rush to me, that he will not. I have heard that Mr. M'Lean would not. They can not nominate Calhoun, without utter ruin to themselves. But if they should succeed in getting some prominent person to stand, I think, before one year, they would discover the hopelessness of the effort, and perceive that perseverance might be highly injurious. As between Jackson and me, I have every reason to count upon their preference.

MR. CLAY TO FRANCIS BROOKE.

ASHLAND, July 18, 1831.

MY DEAR SIR,—According to the wish expressed in your letter of the 2d instant, duly received, I transmit a copy of Mr. Randolph's letter to me. I have another from him, written subsequent to his father's death, on which, however, I have not been able to lay my hands, in which he expresses his consent to my publication of the letter now sent. Notwithstanding, if there be any objection now existing to its publication, on his part, I do not desire it to be done.

I have been much importuned to make some declaration in regard to Masonry (not a formal renunciation or denunciation), which would conciliate and satisfy the Anti-Masons. I have declined to do so, and shall not depart from this resolution. I think it best not to touch the subject. Principle and policy are both opposed to my meddling with it. At the same time I believe it would be politic to leave the Jackson party exclusively to abuse the Antis.

Information has reached me, in which I confide, that about one hundred of the most prominent Jacksonians in and about Philadelphia, have addressed the hero, and requested him not to run again. He had not answered them at my last dates.

GENERAL BERNARD TO MR. CLAY.

WASHINGTON CITY, July 19, 1831.

SIR,—I have the honor to inform you that it is with deep regret I am about to leave this hospitable land, and to return to Europe, whose political situation places me under the moral obligation to tender once more my humble services to France.

Before leaving this abode of liberty and peace, permit me to express to you, one of the great citizens of this noble Republic, how my heart is full of gratitude for the honorable and generous patronage you have bestowed upon me during the fifteen years that I have served this great people.

While I shall always remember with pride your kind regard toward me, my family will never forget how much we are indebted to Mrs. Clay for her polite attentions toward us during her stay at Washington.

Be so indulgent, sir, as to receive my most fervent wishes for your happiness, and the expression of my everlasting sentiments of gratitude.

MR. CLAY TO J. S. JOHNSTON.

HARRODSBURG, July 23, 1831.

MY DEAR SIR,—In passing through Lexington from my residence, yesterday, to this place, where I purpose spending a few days, I received your favor dated at the Balize, and sincerely hope that this letter may find you safe in port. I should have written you before, as at Louisville I intimated I would do, but you appeared to be in such constant motion in Louisiana, that I did not know how to take you on the wing.

Of the events at Washington which have occurred since I saw you, I need say but little. Every one, fond of his country, must have seen them with mortification and regret. The only consolation deducible from them is, that they may contribute to dispel the delusion which placed those in power who have occasioned them.

I think we are authorized, from all that is now before us, to anticipate confidently General Jackson's defeat. The question of who will be the successor, may be more doubtful. The probabilities are strongly with us. It seems to me that nothing can disappoint the hopes of our friends, but Anti-Masonry. If that party should nominate a candidate at Baltimore, and adhere to him, they may prevent any election by the colleges, and possibly may lead to the election of the present incumbent. I believe they will make a nomination of an Anti-Mason. The wish of many of them, I understand, has been to make such a nomination, and then, that the person designated should decline. Accordingly an application was made to Judge M'Lean, to sound him, and to the surprise of the party he has expressed, it is said, a willingness to accept the nomination! This has produced embarrassment. Whether they will now nominate the Judge, or some person not so accommodating, remains to be seen. Should they nominate Mr. Rush, I presume he will decline. This gentleman has written me several letters since the publication of his famous address, in all of which he has expressed the strongest sentiments of attachment and friendship to me. His main object in them was to prevail upon me to make some declaration against Masonry, which would satisfy and conciliate the Antis. I was opposed to it, both upon principle and policy. I was opposed, not exclusively upon Masonic, but also upon other grounds. I think we ought not to admit the right of mixing Masonry or Anti-Masonry, or any other society, whether literary, benevolent, or religious, with politics. I concluded, and so informed Mr. Rush, not to touch the subject, but to stand still. Reflection since has confirmed my resolution.

Should the Antis make a nomination, as supposed, in September, of an Anti-Mason for the Presidency, it will be an interesting question what course our friends ought to take in relation to it in New York and Pennsylvania. I submit some observations :

I think our friends in New York erred, last summer, in not hoisting their own colors. The consequence was, that, as a party, they acted with no concert, neither with the Antis nor with the Regency, exclusively, but with both. They got the gratitude of neither. What is more, the Antis were more embittered by the loss of some eighteen or twenty thousand of our friends, than they were gratified by their gain of upward of sixty thousand of them. And they obtained these sixty thousand as a clear addition to their own ranks, or, in fact, so many Antis. The further consequence was, to exhibit a great nominal increase of Anti-Masons since the election of the previous year. This apparent augmentation has had the effect of extending the Anti-Mason principle to other States, which had before been almost exempt from it. If, last fall, Anti-Masonry had, in New York, been restricted to its own legitimate numbers, it would now be less formidable there, or any where else, than it is.

We are taught by past errors what to do in future. That, I think, ought to be done this fall which was omitted the last. Our standard should be raised, whatever may be the number, small or great, flocking to it. There may then be in New York and Pennsylvania, three distinct tickets. Three consequences will ensue: First, that the Anti-Masons will be reduced to their proper numbers, and be taught by the reduction, moderation ; secondly, that the Jackson party may be the strongest of the three ; thirdly, by union, that the Jackson party may be defeated, whereas, by division between the Antis and the National Republicans, the Jackson party may succeed. And if the canvass should be conducted in a conciliatory manner by our friends toward the Antis (which policy evidently enjoins), this final consequence next fall may follow : that they (the Antis) will then come to our support.

The policy of the Antis is to force us into their support. Ours should be to win them to ours. Taking the Union at large, we are certainly the strongest party. Taking any single State in the Union (New York, Pennsylvania, and Vermont, for example), we are the strongest party. Upon the laws of gravitation, we ought to draw them to us, instead of being drawn to them. They and we agree as to every thing the general Government can or ought to do. We differ only about Masonry, respecting which the general Government has nothing to do. In what part of the Federal Constitution can they find any warrant or authority to put down Masonry? If they, by a pursuit of the delusive object which, as it respects federal politics, they are prosecuting, should endanger the safety, or occasion the loss of great political principles, they will incur a great responsibility, and an overwhelming odium.

I would not abuse them; I would not even attack them. I would leave that to the Jackson party.

Such are my general views on this perplexing question.

We are on the eve of our great Kentucky contest. I think we shall achieve a signal victory. As to the Legislature, we can not fail. But such is the arrangement of the Congressional Districts, and so nicely are many of them balanced, that we may be deceived as to some. Yet I believe we shall gain, at least, seven or eight out of the twelve. Prodigious efforts, seconded by a vast expenditure of money, are making from Washington; and if we fail, it will be because the power of corruption is superior to the power of truth. Be pleased to make my best regards to Mrs. Johnston.

MR. CLAY TO FRANCIS BROOKE.

OLYMPIAN SPRINGS, August 15, 1831.

MY DEAR SIR,—I avail myself of the conveyance afforded by a passing traveler to drop you a few lines in respect to our recent elections.

I have not seen all the returns, but the results of enough are ascertained to enable me to say, that we shall certainly have the majority in the Legislature, and consequently will elect the United States Senator. As to the members of the House of Representatives, we have heard of the election of five of our friends. There are opposite rumors as to the sixth. If he be elected, the parties will probably stand six to six. Two years ago they were ten to two.

The most extraordinary efforts have been made by the general Government to carry the election; and there is reason to believe that, in some instances, highly improper means have been employed. For example, in the county of Floyd, composing a part of the district from which I now write, where, in the contest between Daniel and Trimble, the vote was nearly equally divided, Daniel obtained a majority of upward of three hundred votes out of six or seven hundred. That county is in the mountains of Sandy, the most eastern county of the State. It is almost inaccessible. Yet an engineer of the United States arrived there in seven days from Philadelphia, on the 27th ultimo, just four days before the election, upon a service of reconnoissance, to effect objects of internal improvement. It is strongly suspected that he used some efficacious instruments. In every other county of the district, Daniel lost upon the vote between him and Trimble; other parties in the recent contest received respectively about the same support that was given on that occasion. But in Floyd, Daniel got the majority that has been stated. That extraordinary majority is believed to be the result of extraordinary causes.

Upon the whole, the issues of our late elections ought, perhaps, to be deemed satisfactory.

If the Berrian correspondence had reached Kentucky in time to be circulated throughout the State, prior to the election, there would not have been more than two or three Jackson members elected to Congress.

GENERAL DEARBORN TO MR. CLAY.

Brinley Place, Roxbury, September 3, 1831.

Much respected Sir,—From conversations with a number of your most influential friends in this State, I am induced to urge upon you the expediency of your going into the Senate of the United States. The next session will be of a very interesting and momentous character, and your talents, independence, and influence extremely desirable. Your presence will be a host. Not only the great interests of the country require your services, but your fellow-citizens, who claim you as their candidate, can not be so well subserved, as by your being in Washington. We hope that no motives of delicacy will restrain you. The times are portentous, and there is no man in the land who can do so much to restore confidence in the stability of the Republic.

There will be many Richmonds in the field, and each endeavoring to augment his forces by all means within his power. We want an abler and better man than any of them, to defeat their ambitious schemes of aggrandizement, and it is indispensable that you should be at the post of conflict.

I trust in your magnanimity to excuse this freedom, but I am but expressing the opinion of your best friends here.

MR. ADAMS TO MR. CLAY.

QUINCY, September 7, 1831.

MY DEAR SIR,—A very few days after transmitting to you a copy of an oration composed at the request of my neighbors at this place, I had the pleasure of receiving your friendly letter of the 26th July, which I have delayed answering till I could have the opportunity of forwarding with my answer a copy of another discourse prepared by invitation of the City Council of Boston in honor of our deceased friend and ex-President, Monroe.

I have availed myself of both these occasions to lay before our countrymen throughout the Union, the opinions which I have constantly entertained upon the doctrine of Nullification, and you will have seen that among the States which I have charged with directly asserting, or imprudently giving countenance to it, is your beloved State of Kentucky, as well as my own Massachusetts. I believe we are even indebted to Kentucky for the word, my remark upon which you will perhaps think savors of hypercriticism. A letter from Mr. Madison to Edward Everett, published last autumn in the "North American Review," disclaims explicitly all intention of resorting to force, by the interposition of the State Legislatures to arrest the operation of acts of Congress, deemed by such State Legislatures unconstitutional. Holding, as I do, that in our country all the powers of Government that can lawfully be exercised emanate from the people, it follows, as a necessary consequence, that neither the General Government, nor the State Governments can lawfully interfere with the appropriate functions of each other, nor exercise any authority or power not delegated to them by the people. The State is the creation of the people. Each of the thirteen original States passed by the will of its people, from the condition of a subject dependent colony, to that of an independent State, united with twelve others, and this operation was effected, not by the separate action of each colony, but by the joint operation of the people of the whole; and the Congress of 1776, assuming to speak in their name, and by their authority, fully sanctioned by their acquiescence, proclaimed this Union to the world in the Declaration of Independence.

The State then is the body corporate formed by the association of the people. The Constitution is the organic law or commission of Government. It is the delegation of power to be exercised by the public functionaries for the common good. Those functionaries can not lawfully travel out of the record in the exercise of power. Despotic or autocratic power is not only foreign to our institutions, but is expressly interdicted by the Declaration of Independence.

I assumed then that the people of no one State in the Union have ever delegated to their Government the right to interpose by legislation, to obstruct the operation of any act of Congress. That a State legislature may, as an assembly of individuals, remonstrate or petition I do not deny, and this was the only plausible ground upon which the Hartford Convention attempted to legalize their convocation and proceedings.

The Government of the Union, is, and necessarily must be, the judge of the extent of its own powers. So is the Government of each State. This is an essential attribute not only of sovereign but of independent power, and this is after all the refuge to which the school of despotic sovereignty must fly when pursued by the absurdities of their own argument. The Government of the Union, and the Governments of the States, are in their lawful action each independent of the other. But the Constitution of the United States expressly prohibits the States from the exercise of certain powers—high and transcendent powers—and this prohibition and its lawfulness is expressly recognized in the tenth emendatory article. Prohibits! who prohibits? If the States were the parties to the compact what right would either or all of them have to prohibit the exercise of any power by any one of them. They might stipulate the non-exercise of any given power; but to prohibit is the action of authority upon obedience—the relation of law to submission. The prohibiting power of the Constitution is—We the People of the United States. That "poor little thing" as Patrick Henry called it, "the expression, We the People, instead of the States of America." If, therefore, any one State, whether by an act of the Legislature or by a convention of its people, authorizes resistance or obstruction to the execution of any act of Congress, it exercises a power out of the pale of the Union; nullifies its own portion of the Constitution of the United States, violates the Declaration of Independence, and levies war against the United States.

This is and ever has been my opinion. Now the Virginia and Kentucky resolutions of 1798 and 1799; the opinion of Judge M'Kean and the Olmsted case in Pennsylvania; the Hartford Convention, and the proceedings of the Legislature of Massachusetts and Connecticut authorizing that assembly; the opinions of the Judges Parsons, Sewell, and Parker, of the Supreme Court of Massachusetts, given to the Legislature of the State; Spencer Roane's project of a bill in the "Richmond Enquirer," and the doctrines of Calhoun and his squad at this day, all assert or countenance a right of interposition by the States, against acts of Congress, which I find nowhere delegated to the States. Mr. Madison disclaims for the Virginia Resolutions all purpose of counteracting legislation; his southern disciples appeal from the commentary to the text, and Hamilton, the nullifier, charges him with desertion of his own principles.

The doctrine, in all its parts, is so adverse to my convictions that I can view it in no other light than organized civil war. That it has the sanction of high and venerable names makes it but the more portentous of evil to the Union. Mr. Calhoun is but a pupil of the Hartford Convention, though he takes special care not to include them in his citation of authorities. Parsons and Roane, and M'Kean, and Jefferson have all been nullifiers when in a passion. Mr. Madison alone has explained, when cool, what he said when warm, and it extracts from the doctrine its venom if not its sting.

The doctrine has never yet been carried into effect. In the Olmsted case the issue was made, but nullification, after lighting the match, flinched from her quarters. It is the odious nature of the question that it can be settled only at the cannon's mouth. The South Carolina nullifiers appear determined to come to that point, and I hear our sober friend Langdon Cheves has made up his mind that the Union must be dissolved for incompatability of interests between North and South. What shall we do with these heroes?

The papers in the "United States Gazette" upon the colonial trade arrangement, were written by Edward Ingersoll.

Mrs. Adams unites with me in offering our respectful regards to Mrs. Clay. We hope her health is entirely restored, and rejoice at the good account we have of yours, particularly from Mr. George Eustis, who lately saw you.

MR. CLAY TO FRANCIS BROOKE.

ASHLAND, October 4, 1831.

MY DEAR SIR,—I was rejoiced to learn, by your letter of the 4th ultimo, that both your health and spirits were good. I hope they have so continued, and may long remain.

I have received no letter from Mr. Randolph lately. I do not think it worth while longer to press him on a point which he evidently evades.

It appears to me to be right that I should put you in possession of at least a brief outline of the policy which I think adapted to the present state of the country. This I do, not for the purpose of publication, but that you may have the means of correcting any error that may fall in your way as to my real opinions. Such a correction might also, if necessary, be made in "The Whig;" not, however, to be done at my instance, nor upon my authority.

I agree with Mr. Calhoun, that the next session of Congress is a suitable time for such a modification of the Tariff as is called for by the near approach of the payment of the public debt. The modification may be prospective, to take effect on the happening of that event; or, if there be any particular article, the duty on which is burdensome, there might, as to that duty, be an immediate reduction, or abolition. There is a great advantage to merchants, as well as to consumers, to have adequate notice of a change in the existing Tariff. The Executive, too, might avail itself of the contemplated and distant alteration, to secure, in consideration of it, more favorable terms of commercial intercourse with foreign nations.

There ought, I think, to be a dispensation with duties to an amount, after the payment of the public debt, equal to the sinking fund of ten millions, which are annually appropriated to that object. This should be effected by an abolition or reduction of duties on articles not coming into competition with the produce of our agriculture, or the fabrics of our manufacturers. In other words, I think the principle of protection should be preserved unimpaired, in its application to our domestic industry; but, at the same time, that no more revenue should be collected than is necessary to an economical Administration. Laws ought to be passed to enforce strict execution of the Tariff, by detecting and punishing all evasions. An arrangement of the Tariff upon the principles stated, would be in conformity with what was always admitted by Southern statesmen, that is, that protection might be incidentally afforded in the collection of revenue.

I have no idea of the propriety of laying or continuing duties for the purpose of accumulating surpluses. And as to the doctrine of distributing any such surpluses among the several States, I think there is not the slightest authority for it in the Constitution. The general Government can no more devolve upon the States the duty of discharging any one of its own powers than the States can delegate to the general Government, without an annulment of the Constitution, the duty of local or municipal legislation.

In regard to internal improvements, I never have thought or contended, that a single cent of duty ought to be laid or continued for their promotion. I believe the power is possessed by the general Government. In any prudent adjustment of the Tariff to produce a revenue, say of twelve millions, sound policy requires that a deficit should be guarded against by laying duties enough. In some years, owing to the fluctuations of commerce, there may be a surplus, which might not be wanted. Such an occasional surplus, I would apply to the purpose of internal improvements.

But the great resource on which I think we should rely for that object, after the payment of the public debt, is the proceeds of the sales of the public lands. There is an obvious fitness in such an appropriation. And I think that a more liberal application to the Western States ought to be made, of this fund, than to the others, for two reasons; 1st. That the public domain is there situated, and improvements in that quarter have a tendency to enhance the value of the unsold residue; 2d. As a sort of counterbalance to the expenditures on a navy and fortifications, which are for the more immediate benefit of the maritime frontier. It is true, that each part of the Union is concerned in the safety and prosperity of every other part. But this interest is sometimes only indirect. The maritime States would have quite as much of this indirect interest in internal improvements made under the authority of the general Government, in the West, as the Western States would have in Eastern fortifications and a navy. But I would leave the consideration of what is due to the Western States, from the above views, to the enlightened sense of Congress.

I think the Charter of the Bank of the United States ought to be renewed upon equitable conditions. I am perfectly willing to abide by the reasons which I assigned for a change of my opinion (the only change of opinion I ever made on a great political question) relative to that institution, and which are to be found in my published speeches.

I have thus hastily sketched my views of the policy which is applicable to the present condition of our country. I repeat that they are not intended for publication, nor, for reasons which will readily occur to you, do I wish any copy of this letter given to any one, for any purpose.

The doings of the Anti-Masonic Convention at Baltimore, have not yet reached us. From all I have heard, I presume Mr. M'Lean, of Ohio, has been nominated. I do not believe that he has the moral courage to accept the nomination. But, to quote from your neighbor, *nous verrons*. If the alternative be between Andrew Jackson and an Anti-Masonic candidate, with his exclusive proscriptive principles, I should be embarrassed in the choice. I am not sure that the old tyranny is not better than a new one. That can endure, at the furthest, only four or five years more, while the latter might be of indefinite duration. The one is an exhausted volcano, the other would be the bursting of a new eruption, spreading no one can tell to what extent, nor how long it would last.

I believe, either that Mr. McLean will not accept, or, if he does, that he will be ultimately abandoned, from the impracticability of his election, in which case the great body of the Anti-Masons will support me, not because they love me, but because they hate Jackson more, and because there is greater coincidence between their political principles and mine.

You suggest the propriety of publishing an extract from a letter you addressed to me, disclaiming any wish for a federal appointment in any contingency. I have seen nothing which questions your disinterestedness; and, therefore, why make the publication? Might not such a publication be deemed a gratuitous and unnecessary display? I request your reconsideration.

I am glad that Virginia resolves to be represented in the Baltimore Convention. Whatever doubts might originally have existed about the policy of that movement, it has now proceeded too far to be abandoned. And it is therefore desirable that there should be a full and respectable assembly.

I am strongly urged to go to the Senate, and I am now considering whether I can subdue my repugnance to the service.

DANIEL WEBSTER TO MR. CLAY..

Boston, October 5, 1831.

MY DEAR SIR,—Mr. Everett was kind enough to show me your letter to him, stating the results of the Kentucky election.

It is doubtless true that some regret was felt in this quarter, that those results were not more strongly in our favor, but, upon the whole, a general satisfaction as to that matter now prevails, and all think that Kentucky has at least, by a certain, if not by a great majority, declared against the present Administration. For my own part, I can say, with great truth and sincerity, that I know no political men more deserving the thanks of the country, than our friends in Kentucky. I have some conception of the obstacles with which they have had to contend, not for once, but for many times, and their spirit, zeal, and perseverance in maintaining the cause of good government, place them, in my judgment, in the first class of really patriotic citizens. This opinion I often express, and it gives me always pleasure to express it. Whatever events may come upon us, I feel, for one, a debt of gaatitude to the good men of Kentucky, for the firmness with which they have breasted a storm, which has threatened, and I think still threatens, to overturn, not only the interests and institutions, but the Constitution of the country.

You must be aware, my dear sir, of the strong desire manifested in many parts of the country, that you should come into the Senate. There is, certainly, a strong feeling of that sort, all along the Atlantic coast. I learn its existence from private letters, as well as from the public newspapers. The wish is entertained here, as earnestly as any where. For myself, I hardly know what my own wishes are, because I suppose Mr. Crittenden will, of course, be thought of again. He has so much talent and fitness for the place, is, according to my apprehension of his character, so true and trustworthy, has done so much for the general good, and been so marked an object besides, for the opposition and reproach of the present dominant party at Washington, that I find myself incapable of desiring any thing incompatible with his wishes or expectations. But I know not what his wishes are. Independent of considerations of this kind, the force of which you can weigh infinitely better than I can, I should entirely concur with others in deeming it most expedient for you to come now into the Senate. We are to have an interesting and an arduous session. Every thing is to be attacked. An array is preparing much more formidable than has ever yet assaulted, what we think, the leading and important public interests. Not only the Tariff, but the Constitution itself, in its elementary and fundamental provisions, will be assailed with talent, vigor, and union. Every thing is to be debated, as if nothing had ever been settled. You perceive imposing proceedings, under high names, going on in Philadelphia. You see measures adopted to try the Constitution, further South. You see, every where, I think, omens of a contest of no ordinary character. At the same time, discouraging things are happening, such as the Baltimore nomination and its acceptance. I assure you, my dear sir, with the prospect of toil and labor which is before me, if honor and conscience were not in the way, I would give my place to another. But these dictate to me, or seem to, that, so far as depends on so humble an individual as myself, the crisis must be met. But it would be an infinite gratification to have your aid, or rather your lead. I speak in unaffected sincerity and truth, when I say that I should rejoice, personally, to meet you in the Senate. I am equally sincere in saying that the cause would, under present circumstances be materially benefited by your presence there. I know nothing so likely to be useful. Every thing valuable in the Government is to be fought for, and we need your arm in the fight. At the same time, my dear sir, I would not, even thus privately and confidentially to you, say any thing not consistent with delicacy and friendship for Mr. Crittenden, for whose character I have great regard, and toward whom you and others have taught me to entertain the feelings of a friend. Would to God we could have you both, at this crisis in the public councils.

I ought to thank you for your kindness to several friends of mine, who have visited you in the course of the season. They express themselves highly gratified by your hospitality and good offices.

I pray a most respectful remembrance to Mrs. Clay, and hope that at some time, on one or the other side of the mountains, Mrs. Webster may have the pleasure of making her acquaintance. Clark, Letcher, and Kincaird, I believe, are not at great distances from Lexington. If you see them, tender my regards to them. I hope you will let me hear from you.

TIMOTHY PICKERING TO MR. CLAY.

BOSTON, October 22, 1831.

DEAR SIR,—Will you permit an ardent political friend to address you upon a subject of the highest importance.

You are already aware that the Hon. William Wirt has been nominated by a very respectable Convention at Baltimore, for the high office of President of the United States.

You are aware that at the election of J. Q. Adams, you were accused of bargain and corruption. You may be aware, also, that no respectable man of good information does now believe it.

You recollect that you stated your conviction of General Jackson's inability, and notorious incompetency to fill that high station, and put your character and motives upon the issue.

You are aware that the present organization renders your election impossible.

You are aware that the sentiments of Mr. Wirt, upon the great and important points of our domestic policy are in unison with your own.

Now, sir, since your own election is impossible, would it not be the greatest blessing which you could possibly confer upon your country, to retire from the contest, and let all your forces be brought over to Mr. Wirt's side, and thus, by securing his election, you would be the means of delivering the country from the domination of the present weak and imbecile Administration.

Please to accept these remarks from a constant political friend.

MRS. ERWIN TO HER FATHER, MR. CLAY.

NEW ORLEANS, December 8, 1831.

MY DEAR FATHER,—I wrote mamma last from Cahaba. Not being certain whether she would go to Washington or not, I addressed my letter to Lexington, so that you will probably receive this one before that. We went on board of the boat a few hours after I wrote, and had a very pleasant passage of two days to Mobile, where we remained a week with our friends. We left there on the 4th, expecting to be here in twenty-four hours, but, owing to the steamboat being badly managed, we were two days and three nights in coming. We had a most comfortless time, and on arriving here found our friends very anxious about us, as there was a report that we were lost. I was delighted at finding Henry here. He has not been very well for a day or two past, but is in good spirits and appears to be very much pleased with the prospect of settling here. All of our friends have been very kind and attentive to him. Old Mr. Henderson gave him a dinner at which he invited some of the oldest gentlemen in the city to meet him. This was intended, of course, as a great compliment to his understanding. We found our rooms, that Mr. Erwin had engaged last spring, ready for us, and I think we shall be quite pleasantly situated. I am as yet the only lady in the house, but as we have a private table I shall prefer it, as I must necessarily be a greater belle, there being no competition in the case; and you know, my dear father, too well for me to disguise the fact, that all ladies like the attention of gentlemen. I have not as yet had time to see any of my friends except Aunt Clay. The weather for the last two weeks has been detestable. Judge Porter called this morning to see us. He appears to be in good health, but is of course very dejected. His daughter will remain in the city this winter with Mrs. Judge Matthews, and will spend next summer with me in Kentucky.

* * * * * * *

I hope, my dear father, you will not be so entirely absorbed in politics but that you will find time to write us frequently. Present me affectionately to all those persons who remember me in Washington, and give Mr. Erwin's love as well as mine to mamma.

MR. CLAY TO FRANCIS BROOKE.

WASHINGTON, December 9, 1831.

MY DEAR SIR,—I have received your favor of the 7th instant. That to which it refers was not received by me until after my return from Illinois, and after my election to the Senate. As this latter event brought me nearer to you, I concluded to postpone writing until I reached this city, and even now I have nothing material to communicate which the papers do not present. Parties have not yet exhibited their respective strength; nor, except the election of Speaker, has there been any occasion for its display. In that instance, there was evidently no concert between those opposed to the Administration ; and such a concert I apprehend to be extremely difficult, if not impossible. You will have seen from the message, and from the reports of the Secretary of the Treasury, and his colleagues, that the entire policy of the Government, in relation to every one of the great interests of the country, is proposed to be changed. Was there ever a wilder scheme than that respecting the public lands?

The impression here is, that the Baltimore Convention will make a nomination of me. I wish I could add that the impression was more favorable than it is of the success of such a nomination. Something, however, may turn up (and that must be our encouraging hope) to give a brighter aspect to our affairs.

I shall be glad to receive the long letter promised in your last.

HORTON HOWARD TO MR. CLAY.

COLUMBUS, December 19, 1831.

ESTEEMED FRIEND,—I had but one objection to thy going to Washington at present, and the good that I hoped would result from it overcame that objection. I nevertheless feel it my duty, as one of thy real friends, to caution thee to be at all times on thy guard. I have no doubt that attempts will be made, in many ways, to get thee out of the way.

Now, so long as thou bears in mind that thou art accountable to thy Creator for the talents he has committed to thee for the promotion of his glory, and that while on earth it must be promoted by rendering benefits to his creature man, so long his protecting Providence will preserve thee from harm. So long as the knowledge thou possesses that this nation claims thee as its property, and has a right to thy services in this eventful period, continues to be duly estimated, so long, I conceive, thou wilt so far disregard the machinations of the wicked as to contemn the foolish laws of honor, as they are falsely called. They have already been an injury to thee. Thy country knows thou possesses courage enough of this kind, as well as of a much higher and dignified kind. If insults or challenges should be again offered, it now expects thee to give the most unequivocal evidence that thou also possesses courage of a vastly more exalted and dignified character, and of course that with the stern independence and elevation of mind which has marked or distinguished thy political course, thou wilt with fearless intrepidity discountenance such false pretenses to honor, both by example and precept.

I do not fear its giving offense, and make no apology for this freedom of communication.

MR. CLAY TO FRANCIS BROOKE.

WASHINGTON, December 25, 1831.

MY DEAR SIR,—With the compliments of the season, I acknowledge the receipt of your favor of the 15th instant. Here we have nothing new. Opinions are in a progress of formation on the leading measures of the session. That of the Tariff will be the most difficult and agitating. I fear that there will be no agreement among parties, either as to the amount of the reduction of the revenue, or the objects on which it shall be effected. The ultras of South Carolina are very wrong-headed on the latter point. They appear to be bent on the destruction of the system of protection, or on their own destruction.

The Executive is playing a deep game to avoid, at this session, the responsibility of any decision on the Bank question. It is not yet ascertained whether the bank, by forbearing to apply for a renewal of their Charter, will or will not conform to the wishes of the President. I think they will act very unwisely if they do not apply.

You say the Calhoun party has almost disappeared at Richmond. Judging from the number of the members of the General Assembly who attended the late caucus, I should suppose all parties but that of Jackson had disappeared in Virginia. I see

" The Whig" has repeatedly admitted that the National Republican party is in the minority. I suppose it is so, but is it politic to make such an admission? Will such an admission secure additional strength, or any credit even for candor? Is it consistent with the purpose of making a struggle, if that be designed in Virginia?

MRS. ERWIN[*] TO HER FATHER, MR. CLAY.

NEW ORLEANS, January 7, 1832.

MY DEAR FATHER,—I to-day received your favor of the 25th of December, and read it with more than ordinary pleasure as we had not heard a word from you since your arrival at Washington, although we had been tantalized with a sight of your handwriting, as you had inclosed the Message both to Mr. Erwin and Henry. You have no doubt heard before this, that Claiborne has declined returning this winter; it is owing to his health, which is much better than it was when he left here; but he writes that his eyes are still so much affected that he thinks it prudent for him to remain at least another year. They have elected Mr. Dixon to fill his place; he is a warm partisan of yours, and was elected by one vote over Mr. Marigny, but the opposite party speak of contesting the election. It is not supposed, however, that they will succeed in turning Mr. Dixon out. So much for politics. You see it is impossible to be the daughter of a politician without, at least, knowing what is going on.

We have been suffering here with the same influenza which appears to be prevailing at the North. The Creoles have felt it more than the Americans. Indeed in some cases where the individuals were old, it has proved fatal. Mrs. Clay has been severely attacked. She was confined to her bed for several days, and has not left the house for more than two weeks. I am glad to be able to say that she is much better now. Mr. Duralde also has been quite sick with it; but I believe he is well enough now to go down to his saw-mill.

Henry has commenced the study of law under Judge Porter's

---

[*] Mrs. Erwin was a favorite child, and obtained the strongest hold on her father's heart. Mr. Erwin had a country seat at Lexington, adjoining Ashland, called the "Woodlands," a beautiful place, where the family resided in summer.

directions. He complains a little of the large folios he sends him, and thinks the Judge does not estimate his talents quite high enough when he supposes it will require two years of hard study to prepare him to commence the practice. The Judge's family appears to be completely broken up since the death of Miss Eliza. He has taken lodgings in town, and his daughter is passing the winter with Mrs. Mathews. I have invited her to spend the ensuing summer with me, and her father has promised that she should accompany us on our return to Kentucky. We have not heard a word from Lexington since the 29th of November. The river being frozen up, there is no communication at all between this and the Western country. The last letter I received was from James. I was very much gratified to find that he writes an uncommonly good letter for so young a boy.

I have been so fortunate as to find an infant-school established here upon the same plan as those at the North, where I send the boys. They did not like to go much at first, but by giving them a few sugar-plums every day I hired them for the first week, and they are now becoming interested in it. It is a very great relief to me to know that they are doing well and are out of mischief from nine until three every day. Little Lucretia grows every day. She is the most mischievous child of her age I ever saw. Aunt Lotty and she have at least a dozen quarrels a day. I can not thank my dear mother enough, for having spared Lotty to me. She is the best creature I ever saw, and appears to be quite as much attached to the children, as she ever was to yours.

Tell mamma I shall certainly execute her commission with a great deal of pleasure, and if she can think of any thing else she wishes, you will have quite time to let me know, as we we shall not leave this before the 1st of March. I have begun to make her the collection of baskets she wished me to get for her. The children all send a kiss to their dear grandparents, as well as their love to Henry Duralde. Mr. Erwin joins me in love both to mamma and yourself. If Uncle Brown is with you, you will remember us both affectionately to him. You will please say to him that Mr. Erwin will be happy to render him any service in this country in his power.

JOSEPH HOWARD TO MR. CLAY.

TIFFIN, Ohio, January 27, 1832.

MUCH ESTEEMED FRIEND,—Permit me to herewith inclose to thy acceptance the last Annual Report of our Canal Commissioners, by which it will be seen that one more link will shortly be completed in the great chain which, I hope, when completed, will add greatly to the strength and perpetuity of our Union. As it is at all times a source of gratitude to the parent to see his children as they advance in years advance toward perfection, so it must be a source of great satisfaction to the great parent and author of a system which but a few years ago existed only in theory, now to see it rapidly advancing toward the highest state of perfection that was anticipated by its author. Under this view of the subject it is then that I take the liberty of presenting the inclosed document to the universally-acknowledged author of a system which has, either directly or indirectly, contributed greatly to the projection and consummation of this stupendous work; a system which, if cherished, will be a rich legacy for future generations.

LESLIE COMBS TO MR. CLAY.

LEXINGTON, January 27, 1832.

MY DEAR SIR,—You have made a very sensible speech on your proposition to take off certain duties and reduce others. You occupied the true ground on every point you made, and did it with becoming temper. I regret that the Southrons are crazy, but let them fret; you must not quarrel with them. You occupy higher ground than any of them, and must look down upon them and sooth them, not yourself play the gladiator. That would do for me, if I were in Congress; as I am not, others must do it. Your course must be above all partisan warfare, and God will speed you. It must be for the Union, the whole Union, and nothing but the Union.

I am daily laboring to raise the caloric in our friends on this side the mountains. They are too cold, and selfish, and lethargic for me, but I never give up a good cause while there is a man in the field or a shot in the locker.

PATRICK HENRY TO MR. CLAY.

WASHINGTON, February 18, 1832.

SIR,—I have not yet had the honor of a personal acquaintance with you, but as we claim Virginia as our nativity (where I live and expect to die), and as my admiration for your character and principles admits of no comparison with the most distinguished living, I feel at liberty to make a suggestion, and, if it should meet with your views of liberal policy, for which you have been so much distinguished, I shall be very much gratified. It is that Henry Clay should forthwith introduce a resolution for the purchase of Mount Vernon; the improved grounds including the park, extending to the gate leading to Alexandria, with any other addition of land to the north and south of the mansion as may be thought desirable by Congress. If it should be the pleasure of Congress to make the purchase, the country would not only be in possession of the remains of the Father of the Republic, but would be enabled to preserve and use the property for some national purpose. It would be advisable (should this project meet with your approbation) first to ascertain through your friend, G. C. Washington, whether the proprietor of Mount Vernon would be willing to sell the property to the United States. Wishing you all the honors that can be conferred by your country, I am, sir, your most obedient servant.

MR. CLAY TO FRANCIS BROOKE.

WASHINGTON, February 21, 1832.

MY DEAR SIR,—I have been so constantly occupied, that I have not been able to write you as much or as often as I wished. That terrible long speech of mine in the Senate, which gave me less trouble in its delivery than it has since occasioned me, is now in the hands of the printer, and being disposed of, leaves me at leisure to say a few words.

Every thing is going on well. Van Buren, old Hickory, and the whole crew, will, I think, in due time, be gotten rid of. The attempt to excite public sympathy in behalf of the little Magician has totally failed; and I sincerely wish that he may be nominated as Vice-President. That is exactly the point to which I wish to see matters brought. Do urge our Jackson friends (if there be any that you can approach) to nominate him on the 28th. It will be so consistent that they should support him who is, or at least pretends to have been, for the Tariff, and oppose all others who are for it.

We have had various affairs here, and of which the papers will give you some account. The most bitter of the opposition is the Calhoun element. I heard to-day that a South Carolina Governor is in correspondence with a Virginia Lieutenant-Governor. Will our friend Lloyd on that occasion call out the posse, as he was supposed by some here to have intended to prevent the removal of the remains of Washington?

HENRY CLAY, JR., TO HIS FATHER.

NEW ORLEANS, February 28, 1832.

DEAR FATHER,—I am now living at Judge Porter's, on the coast. I found that in the city I was so much interrupted by the kindness of friends and acquaintance, that I could not devote that time to study which I desired. At the solicitation of the Judge, I therefore determined to spend in the country the few months that I shall be in Louisiana.

Judge Porter's residence, as you will recollect, is near the battle-ground, three or four miles from the city. He has an excellent library, and is himself a learned man in the law, animated with the best spirit of learning, that which applies useful maxims to the common wants of mankind.

The civil law begins to open before me. What I thought the study of a year, I perceive now would exhaust the energies of a lifetime. But I am determined, if ever I shall arrive at an independence of fortune, to carry what little talents and attainments I may possess to another tribunal than the bar of justice, the tribunal of public debate.

I am at present making all exertions to gain a knowledge of the law, and I have no reason, I think, to be dissatisfied with my progress. By the winter after next, I shall be able to come to the bar with a fair prospect of ultimate success.

JAMES BARBOUR TO MR. CLAY.

BARBOURSVILLE, March 7, 1832.

DEAR SIR,—You have obliged me much by furnishing me with your speech on the Tariff. It is the strongest view I have ever seen on the subject. If the facts are true to which you refer as the basis of your argument, your argument is unanswerable. I duly appreciate the necessity which induced you to introduce some remarks merely *ad captandum*. Contending as you are with an enemy using poisoned weapons, the right of defense extends to the employment of what otherwise might not be considered very legitimate means.

Your positions are judicious, and you have ably defended them. Great perspicuity is your leading characteristic.

HARRISON GREY OTIS TO MR. CLAY.

BOSTON, March 8, 1832.

DEAR SIR,—I had read your admirable speech with great delight, and pondered its contents, before I received the copy which you did me the honor to transmit. This, however, was not the less acceptable, as, in addition to the value of the attention, it gives me a right and an excuse for making my personal acknowledgment, without claiming or expecting a reply; knowing by long experience that no class of men are more in need of "protecting duties" from the uninvited consignments of correspondents, who expect remittances which interfere with time and convenience, than the members of Congress. And though the voice of one individual contributes little to swell the note of acclamation which you hear from all quarters, yet mine is entitled to something of more value than that of anybody, inasmuch as the only lance I ever broke with you was in defense of hemp and molasses, when you came forth as the champion of Mr. Baldwin's bill, which I dare say you have forgotten. But *tempora mutantur*, and I am among those who have been coerced by the policy of government *mutari cum illis*. Among the excellencies of your speech, that in my mind predominates which calls the agricultural, and especially the mechanical class, to look to the case as their own.

MR. MADISON TO MR. CLAY.

MONTPELIER, March 13, 1832.

J. Madison, with his best respects to Mr. Clay, thanks him for the copy of his speech "In defense of the American System," etc. It is a very able, a very eloquent, and a very interesting one. If it does not establish all its positions, in all their extent, it demolishes not a few of those relied on by the opponents. J. M. feels a pleasure in offering this tribute to its merits. But he must be pardoned for expressing a regret that an effusion of personal feeling was, in one instance, admitted into the discussion.

MR. CLAY TO FRANCIS BROOKE.

WASHINGTON, March 17, 1832.

MY DEAR SIR,—I received your favor of the 15th. I am sorry that I can give you no satisfactory information as to the course of Georgia in respect to the recent decision of the Supreme Court. It is rumored that the President has repeatedly said that he will not enforce it, and that he even went so far as to express his hope, to a Georgia member of Congress, that Georgia would support her rights.

The Committee of Investigation into the conduct of the Bank, leave here on Wednesday, for Philadelphia. The impression now is, that the Bank Charter will pass at this session. Mr. Adams, being appointed one of the Committee, took the occasion to ask to be excused from serving on the Committee of Manufactures, as its Chairman; whereupon the head was immediately knocked out of a barrel of oil, and the whole quantity poured on him by Southern gentlemen, and other anti-Tariffites. He was induced to postpone his motion.

I have requested Messrs. Gales & Seaton to send fifty of my speeches to Mr. White.

MR. MADISON TO MR. CLAY.

MONTPELIER, March 22, 1832.

DEAR SIR,—I have duly received yours of the 17th. Although you kindly release me from a reply, it may be proper to say, that some of the circumstances to which you refer were not before known to me.

On the great question before Congress, on which so much depends out of Congress, I ought the less to obtrude an opinion, as its merits essentially depend on details which I never investigated, and of which I am an incompetent judge. I know only that the Tariff, in its present amount and form, is a source of deep and extensive discontent; and I fear that, without alleviations, separating the more moderate from the more violent opponents, very serious effects are threatened. Of these, the most formidable, and not the least probable, would be a Southern Convention, the avowed object of some, and the unavowed object of others whose views are, perhaps, still more to be dreaded. The disastrous consequences of disunion, obvious to all, would no doubt be a powerful check on its partisans; but such a convention, characterized as it would be by selected talents, ardent zeal, and the confidence of those represented, would not be easily stopped in their course; especially, as many of the members, though not carrying with them particular aspirations for the honors, etc., presented to ambition on a new political theater, would find them germinating in such a hot-bed.

To these painful ideas I can only oppose hopes and wishes, that notwithstanding the wide space and warm feelings which divide the parties, some accommodating arrangements may be devised that will prove an immediate anodyne, and involve a lasting remedy to the Tariff discords.

Mrs. Madison charges me with her affectionate remembrances to Mrs. Clay, to whom I beg to be at the same time respectfully presented, with a re-assurance to yourself of my high esteem and cordial regards.

MR. CLAY TO FRANCIS BROOKE.

WASHINGTON, March 28, 1832.

MY DEAR SIR,—You will have seen the disposition made on Thursday last of my resolution respecting the Tariff. On that occasion some developments were made of a scheme which I have long since suspected—that certain portions of the South were disposed to purchase support to the anti-Tariff doctrines, by a total sacrifice of the public lands to States within which they are situated.

A more stupendous, and more flagitious project was never conceived. It will fail in its object, but it ought to be denounced. A majority of the Senate (composed of all the anti-Tariff Senators, and some of the Jackson Tariff Senators), referred a resolution concerning the public lands to the Committee of Manufactures! Can you conceive a more incongruous association of subjects? There were two objects. The first I have suggested; the second was to affect me personally, by placing me in a situation in which I must report unfavorably to the Western and South-Western States, which are desirous of possessing themselves of the public lands. I think I shall disappoint the design, by presenting such views of that great interest as will be sanctioned by the nation. Meantime, I should be glad if you would give some hints to our friend Pleasants, and let him sound the tocsin. In Illinois there are about forty millions of acres of public land, and about one hundred and fifty or one hundred and sixty thousand people. What think you of giving that large amount of land to that comparatively small number of people? If it were nominally sold to them, it would, in the end, amount to a mere donation.

We have nothing new about the course of Georgia, and the President's intention as to the decision of the Supreme Court. The current opinion is that he will not enforce it.

We shall report in part, in a day or two, a bill limited to a repeal of duties on the unprotected class of foreign imports, reserving for future report the other class, as to which, however, I do not anticipate that any thing can be done to satisfy South Carolina.

MR. CLAY TO FRANCIS BROOKE.

WASHINGTON, April 1, 1832.

MY DEAR SIR,—I received your favor of the 29th ultimo, communicating the tenor of a conversation with Governor Floyd. At the time that the Governor appeared as a witness before the public to testify against me, during the late Administration, I was surprised and hurt, and thought he took a course utterly inconsistent with the friendly relations which had previously existed between us, to say nothing of the opposite views which he and I took of the matter to which his testimony related. But, whatever feelings were excited in my mind at the time, they have been long since thrown aside, with a mass of analogous feelings awakened during an ardent and angry Presidential contest. My nature is such as to prompt me to forget these things, and I should be sorry if it were otherwise.

The clew to the motives which induced Governor Floyd voluntarily to make that explanation, I have discovered here since I received your letter. A design exists, on the part of Mr. Calhoun and his friends, to have his name presented as a candidate, provided they conceive that he will stand any chance of getting three or four Southern States; and provided, as the means of their accomplishing that object, our friends will co-operate in Virginia, and south of it, with his, to give him their votes. Mr. Calhoun had, at his instance, a conversation with a friend of mine, which was general, and understood by that friend to be preliminary to another which Duff Green subsequently sought with him. In the course of this latter, Duff explained fully the views and wishes of the Calhoun party. These are, that his name shall, in the course of the ensuing summer (say August), be presented as a candidate; that, if no ticket is run in Virginia by our friends, and if they will co-operate with his, he can obtain the vote of that State; that, with a fair prospect of receiving the vote of Virginia, he will obtain those also of North Carolina, Georgia, and South Carolina, and probably of Alabama and Mississippi; that the result would be to defeat the re-election of General Jackson, and to devolve the election on the House; that there they suppose I would be elected; and that they would be satisfied with my election. Such is the general outline of their project, the details of which were communicated by Duff after the previous general conversation with Mr. Calhoun. My friend presumed their intention was that he should communicate to me what passed, and he has accordingly communicated it. Duff stated that the success of the whole plan of the campaign, on their part, required that our friends should not present an electoral ticket; and, moreover, should support them in Virginia.

I have neither said nor done any thing in reply to all this, to commit my friends or myself. I could not, without dishonor, have ventured upon any sort of commitment of them. They are, in fact, free, and so I wish them to remain, to act according to their own sense of propriety.

As to the project itself, I have supposed that Mr. Calhoun has too little capital any where, out of South Carolina, to engraft upon ; that it would be impracticable, if it were desirable, to induce our friends in Virginia to abandon all purpose of supporting a ticket on our side, and of co-operating in the support of one for Mr. Calhoun; that if such a concocted movement were made, it would be very probably defeated by the imputations which would be brought against it; and that the whole idea has sprung out of the desperate condition of Mr. Calhoun's prospects. If there could be any movement at the South which would secure to Mr. Calhoun the vote of three or four Southern States, next to their being given to our cause, it would, undoubtedly, be the best thing that could happen for us. It would every where else stimulate our friends to the greatest exertions, by holding out the hope of certain success. It would break the power of Jacksonism, and discourage his friends in other States quite as much as it would animate ours.

Let me, my dear friend, hear from you on this matter, and particularly your views as to the strength of the party of Mr. Calhoun in Virginia. Has it not relapsed into Jacksonism? Could it be brought forth again, in its original force, to the support of Mr. Calhoun? Supposing Mr. Calhoun is not put forward as a candidate, what course, generally, will his friends in Virginia pursue? Could our friends be prevailed upon to unite on a ticket for Mr. Calhoun? Or, in the event of no ticket being put up for our cause, would they not divide between Jackson and Calhoun, the larger part probably going to Jackson? When do our friends contemplate bringing out the ticket which has been thought of for our side?

How long will you remain at St. Julien? that is, when will you return to your official duties at Richmond?

If I am to judge of what I see and hear, and know, there is a general persuasion in the public mind of the insecurity and danger in the existing state of the general Administration. That there is too much cause for that persuasion, I sincerely believe. The important inquiry is, what ought to be done—what can be done? As to myself, I am ready to consent to any disposition that would rid the country from impending perils, if any disposal of myself could contribute to that most desirable result. You are upon the judgment bench, and, perhaps, may there see more calmly than we can who are in the contending arena, what the good of our common country, in the present crisis, really demands from her true and devoted sons, among whom, whatever to the contrary others may profess to think or say, *I* know none to be more sincerely and zealously attached, than your faithful friend.

R. S. BROWNING TO MR. CLAY.

ROME, April 5, 1832.

SIR,—In visiting the relics of ancient Rome, my attention was naturally called to the tomb of Cicero. It stands on the spot where that immortal orator was assassinated by some base creatures of Mark Antony, near his villa, at Mola. I could not contemplate the monument, whose solidity had defied the ravages of nearly two thousand years, or tread the consecrated sod, without feelings of excitement. His unrivaled eloquence, that was ever raised for the rights of man—his fearless defense of the Roman Republic—his eminence as a lawyer—the ability with which he presided over the Roman people—all hurried upon my memory in rapid succession. Nor did I forget that the enemies of Cicero were numerous. But they were the enemies of the Republic, and sought to destroy Roman liberty by blasting the character of its most able defender. But Cicero was virtuous, and the Roman people were not yet dazzled by the success of a military chieftain, and rewarded his virtue by their highest gift. How could these reflections cross my mind without recalling you to my recollection? Your eloquence in defense of our Republic has been heard from the Mississippi to the Rhine. Your legal knowledge and abilities as a statesman, that give you the first rank in "the land of liberty," like Cicero's, have ever been directed to the good of the people. And you, too, have your enemies. May wisdom and virtue weaken their strength. May the Republicans of the United States prove to the world that they are not deluded by the success of a military chieftain, by rewarding your virtue and talents with the first gift of the nation. May they show themselves superior to the Romans by never deserting the cause of liberty, and by confiding only in wise and virtuous lovers of liberty.

With these reflections, I cut a bough of an abavita, that shaded the tomb, and have had a cane made of it, which I forward you by the bearer of this note, and beg your acceptance of it.

MR. CLAY TO FRANCIS BROOKE.

WASHINGTON, April 9, 1832.

MY DEAR SIR,—I received your favor of the 5th instant. I have some thoughts of running away from this place for a few days, wearied and exhausted as I am by public business, and I have an inclination to go to St. Julien, if you will give me an asylum, and receive me *incognito*. If I go, it would be on Thursday or Friday. Will you be at home for four or five days? Will you receive me, and promise, upon your sacred honor, not to invite to your house any company in consequence of my enjoying the advantage of your protection? Perhaps I may carry with me a friend. I shall be governed by your reply. Whatever that may be, I pray you always to consider me faithfully your friend.

MR. CLAY TO FRANCIS BROOKE.

WASHINGTON, April 17, 1832.

MY DEAR SIR,—I shall leave here on Thursday next, in the steamboat for Fredericksburg, and reach St. Julien, if I can, that evening. General Vance and Mr. Letcher will probably accompany me. Mrs. Clay thinks she had better remain here with our grandson, etc.

Mr. McDuffie of the Bank Committee, has returned from Philadelphia, and the rest of the Committee are expected this evening or to-morrow. It is understood that the Committee were not very harmonious, but it is not known what will be the character of their report.

FRANCIS BROOKE TO MR. CLAY.

ST. JULIEN, April 23, 1832.

MY DEAR SIR,—I was deeply affected by our last conversation on the subject of your health, and I conjure you to take care of it. I have some experience, and no little information from books, of the effect of diet, etc., upon the animal economy, and I am aware of the truth of the vulgar maxim, that "what is one man's meat, is another's poison," and therefore will not pretend to prescribe any specific course to you. It is perfectly true that if you will not permit your inclinations to control your judgment, you will better decide than the most experienced of the faculty, what diet is most conducive to your health; but there are some general principles that we can not be mistaken in, and one is, that after high excitement from any cause, there is invariably a consquent debility, which will always increase materially any predisposition to torpor, and even paralysis. High excitement, then, from any cause, ought to be avoided, and especially from causes that always precede great debility. I think I can not warn you too strongly, against the excessive use of tobacco, in any form. As Milo learned to carry the ox by carrying the calf every day, the quantity of tobacco may be diminished from day to day. This also may be said of wine; but there is another cause of high excitement which is more pernicious, and more difficult in your situation to be avoided, that which results from dwelling too much on the deplorable condition of our public affairs, and on the relation in which you are placed in regard to them. It is the more difficult for you to look on them in the calm lights of a mild philosophy, but yet you ought to be satisfied with performing your duty, and to leave the rest to others, and to that Providence which has heretofore watched over us. It is in vain to attempt to do more, and I shall be truly rejoiced when I find you less anxious, and, of course, less excited. There are times, when, as we have seen in history, patriotism made things that were bad, worse. I trust that we are not yet in that condition, but if that virtue is worth any thing, you ought to take care of your health; it is of great importance that you should. I hope I shall have a letter from you, giving me a better account of it than when you were here.

HENRY CLAY, JR., TO HIS FATHER.

ASHLAND, April 24, 1832.

I wish to communicate the joyful intelligence that you are grandfather by a new title. Heaven, as if jealous of our fondness for Anne, has attempted to divide it by a new object of affection, but it will only give rise to a new source of feeling. Yesterday, between 2 and 3 P. M., Anne gave life and light to a fine daughter.

We shall be happy to introduce you when you come, to the youthful stranger. Mary is to be her name, and her aunt, Miss Mary Erwin, her godmother.

I am now, for the first time for many years, enjoying the pleasures and scenes of a youthful spring in Kentucky. It is a charming country, and Ashland and the Woodlands have a thousand interests for me. I do not at all envy you your heated political atmosphere at Washington. I much prefer the serene happiness which the perusal of the elegant Thompson infuses, while surrounded with the beauties which the season of bloom opens to the view.

When may we expect you? My mother, I suppose, will not precede you. I hope to show her when she comes, that Ashland has not fallen into bad hands. A little severity, which I used in the fir t place, and a continued exertion of energy, have introduced a system and regularity into the concerns of the place, which were much wanting when I came.

MR. CLAY TO FRANCIS BROOKE.

WASHINGTON, April 26, 1832.

MY DEAR SIR,—I have received your affectionate letter of the 23d instant, and the interest which it manifests in my health and prosperity has affected me sensibly. Among the many circumstances to disgust me with life and my fellow man, the warmth, fidelity, and duration of your friendship have ever been a source of cheering satisfaction. You have described, I believe correctly, the true causes of my indisposition; and your advice is full of wisdom. Naturally ardent, perhaps too ardent, I can not avoid being too much excited and provoked by the scenes of tergiversation, hypocrisy, degeneracy, and corruption which are daily exhibited. I would fly from them, and renounce forever public life, if I were not restrained by a sentiment of duty, and of attachment to my friends. I shall endeavor to profit by your kindness, and to avoid as much as possible, in future, all causes of irritation. I have quit the use of tobacco, in one of the two forms to which I had been accustomed, and will gradually discontinue the other. I will also endeavor to moderate the interest excited by public affairs.

Since my return I have felt, with the exception of one day,

better. I wish I could have remained longer with you. Should I not feel my strength and health returning, I will make another excursion to Maryland or Philadelphia.

Nothing material has transpired here. Our friends are acquiring daily more confidence, and the Jackson party are greatly alarmed. It was remarked to me this morning that they have become panic struck.

A report is anticipated from a bare majority of the Bank Committee, recommending further investigation to be prosecuted in the recess. There will probably be a counter report.

Two reports may be expected from the Secretary of the Treasury, and the Committee of Manufactures, next week, on the Tariff, and presenting different plans of modification.

AMBROSE SPENCER TO MR. CLAY.

Near ALBANY, April 28, 1832.

DEAR SIR,—I thank you for the copy of your report on the public lands, which you kindly sent me, and I avail myself of the occasion to trouble you with a letter. I have considered myself unfortunate in never having had the pleasure of seeing you, or corresponding with you. When you were in power I had no favor to ask, although as far as my influence extended it was in favor of the last Administration. I admit that there were some passages in your public life which I disapproved; but I am happy also to be able to say that explanations given to me at Washington by honorable men, removed impressions of an unfavorable nature. The report you have sent me, and the general tenor of your public life, have indelibly impressed me that you are actuated, as a public man, by the purest principles and the sternest integrity.

You may think it strange that I should open a correspondence in this manner, but I consider it proper and necessary you should be informed by me of the undisguised state of my past and present feelings toward you. * * * *

Being myself thoroughly convinced that we are doomed to national degradation, and to the ruin of all our most valuable institutions, if General Jackson is re-elected, I will endeavor to do my duty in averting these calamities.

CHIEF JUSTICE MARSHALL TO MR. CLAY.

RICHMOND, May 7, 1832.

DEAR SIR,—On my return to this place, from a visit to my friends in our upper country, I had the pleasure of receiving your report on the public lands, which I have read with attention. The subject is of immense interest, and has long produced and is still producing great excitement.

My sentiments concur entirely with those contained in the report, which are so clearly and so well expressed that it must, I think, be approved by a great majority of Congress. Unanimity is not to be expected in any thing.

I thank you for this mark of attention, and am with great and respectful esteem your obedient servant.

MR. CLAY TO FRANCIS BROOKE.

WASHINGTON, June 2, 1832.

MY DEAR SIR,—I did not answer your last, because I had some hopes of seeing you here, and because I wished to be able to communicate to you something about the proceedings of the N. R. Convention at Harrisburg. The inclosed letter from Mr. Sergeant (which you can return after reading) will give you the latest information from that place. Other letters which I have received corroborate his views. The progress of the work of co-operation between the Anti-Masons and N. R.'s in New York continues, and every day adds to our confidence that it will be secured, and that its result will be to deprive Jackson of the support of that State. It is an affair, however, of much delicacy and of no little difficulty, from the fanaticism of some, and the perverseness of others, of the Anti-Masons. The letter which you procured Governor Barbour to write to Rose has had good effect, and if he could repeat the anodyne it would not be amiss. Stevens (the Anti-Masonic candidate for Lieutenant-Governor in New York) was here a few days ago, and assured me that he was fully persuaded that we should succeed in New York. Lieutenant-Governor Pilcher (now a member of the House of Representatives from that State, and elected as a Jackson man) said to me, last evening, that he had no doubt of our success there.

We are going on with the Bank in the Senate, and, I presume, will pass the bill on Monday or Tuesday. In the House of Representatives Mr. M'Duffie's Tariff bill had only about forty-four supporters. No time of adjournment yet spoken of. Mr. Hith, from Richmond, is here, and I am highly pleased with him.

MR. CLAY TO FRANCIS BROOKE.

WASHINGTON, June 29, 1832.

MY DEAR SIR,—Pennsylvania continues daily to exhibit signs of the most cheering character, and there is just reason to hope that she is lost to General Jackson.

A Tariff has passed the House of Representatives by a large majority. It will finally pass the Senate with or without modifications. It is a law which, with some alterations, will be a very good measure of protection.

The Bank bill will, I think, pass the Senate in a few days; and if Jackson is to be believed, he will veto it.

Congress will adjourn on the 9th or 16th, most probably on the latter day. Afterward I believe I shall go to the White Sulphur Springs, but it may not be until the 1st of August that I shall reach there. I hope I shall find you there.

A DAUGHTER OF MASSACHUSETTS TO MR. CLAY.

WASHINGTON, July 4, 1832.

SIR,—I beg leave, through this medium, to offer you my sincere acknowledgment for your recent noble and spirited avowal of your belief of the Christian religion, and of your reverence for its precepts; and I can assure you, sir, that a large majority of the daughters of the descendants of the Pilgrims unite with me in the same sentiment.

Our prayers will be offered to Almighty God, and our influence exerted with our friends, for your elevation to that office which is the first in the gift of the people of this Union; and should our prayers be answered, may you prove " a terror to evil doers, and a praise to those who do well."

MR. CLAY TO FRANCIS BROOKE.

WASHINGTON, July 20, 1832.

MY DEAR SIR,—I intend to take my departure from this city on Monday next (the 23d), and hope to reach St. Julien that evening. I design going from your house by Colonel William Bolling's, in Goochland, and thence viâ Charlottesville or Lynchburg to the White Sulphur Springs. I do not think we can remain longer with you than Tuesday, and I hope, on one account, my dear sir, you will not invite any company to St. Julien.

Nothing new, or at least nothing that will not keep new until I have the pleasure to meet you.

NICHOLAS BIDDLE TO MR. CLAY.

PHILADELPHIA, August 1, 1832.

MY DEAR SIR,—You ask what is the effect of the veto? My impression is, that it is working as well as the friends of the Bank and of the country could desire. I have always deplored making the Bank a party question, but since the President will have it so, he must pay the penalty of his own rashness. As to the veto message, I am delighted with it. It has all the fury of a chained panther, biting the bars of his cage. It is really a manifesto of anarchy, such as Marat or Robespierre might have issued to the mob of the Faubourg St. Antoine; and my hope is, that it will contribute to relieve the country from the dominion of these miserable people. You are destined to be the instrument of that deliverance, and at no period of your life has the country ever had a deeper stake in you. I wish you success, most cordially, because I believe the institutions of the Union are involved in it.

MR. CLAY TO FRANCIS BROOKE.

WHITE SULPHUR SPRINGS, August 5, 1832.

MY DEAR SIR,—We reached here safely on Thursday last, and find a very great crowd. Two of your sons are here, and we saw the third at Staunton. They are all well. I feel much better already, and hope the water will completely eradicate the disease under which I was suffering at St Julien.

I am informed, from Washington, that the President has resolved to suspend the execution of the parts of the law passed at the last session, relating to internal improvements, to which he objects. What think you of this high-handed measure? What of his daring violation of the Constitution, in re-appointing Gwinn? Is proud Virginia ready to bend her neck to these usurpations?

Speaking of your State, I do believe, with proper exertions, it might be carried against Jackson. The two parties exhibit, at this time, apathy and confidence on one side, and despondency on the other. If you would exchange for your despondency zeal and concert, I am half persuaded that you would triumph. Your strength is greater than you are aware of. The weakness of the other side is greater than is believed. Let our friends organize, throughout the State; let each county be divided into sections, and let one or more members of your Committees of Vigilance be designated in each to bring the voters to the polls, and I incline to think that you would win the day. All this should be put in motion by some central committee. What would serve to animate our friends, and to dispirit our opponents, is the high probability of success, whatever may happen to be the vote of Virginia.

We shall remain here until the 15th. Be pleased to make the respects of Mrs. Clay and myself to Mrs. Brooke and the young ladies, and believe me your affectionate friend.

JAMES BROWN TO MR. CLAY.

PHILADELPHIA, September 3, 1832.

MY DEAR SIR,—I have received, with feelings of the deepest sorrow, the intelligence of the decease of our lamented Mrs. Hart, conveyed by your letter. I had resided, for twelve months after my marriage, under her hospitable roof, during which time, and ever since, I received from her every proof of kindness and affection which could have been bestowed on me by my own mother. Alas! how much, in many essential particulars, she resembled my dear Nancy, and how soon she has followed her! I fondly trust that that beneficent Father of the Universe who has, during their lives, bestowed on them so many blessings, has graciously re-united them in the regions of everlasting bliss.

JAMES BROWN TO MR. CLAY.

PHILADELPHIA, November 5, 1832.

DEAR SIR,—I had the pleasure to receive, by the newspapers, the intelligence of Henry's marriage, and to learn by your last letter that his choice is every way agreeable to his family, and what is more important, such as to promise him future happiness. Be so kind as to accept my congratulations on the event, and to offer to the newly married pair my sincere wishes that they may enjoy a long life of union and prosperity.

The intelligence of your death was accompanied, perhaps preceded, by its contradiction. I sincerely hope that you may feel no serious consequences from your indisposition, and that you may resume your seat in the Senate with a disposition to be satisfied with a place which I would have preferred to any within the reach of American ambition. You know that I have never for a moment doubted that General Jackson would be reelected. He will have a large majority in this State, and I shall not be surprised should he be the choice of every State south of the Potomac, and west of the Alleghany. If I have proved more generally correct in my calculations than many of our active politicians, it may be accounted for by the fact that I derive my information almost exclusively from my knowledge of the American tendencies, my acquaintance with nearly all the prominent actors in the political theater, and the perusal of the journals, without entering into the busy scenes of active electioneering, by which my deliberate judgment might be warped, or conversing with eloquent and heated partisans, who might inflame my imagination.

HENRY CLAY, JR., TO HIS FATHER.

LOUISVILLE, November 27, 1832.

MY DEAR FATHER,—In regard to myself I am now perfectly happy. I am united to a lady who possesses my entire love and veneration, and who returns me, in over-measure, the affection to which I am entitled. We are not rich, but it will be a source of pleasurable occupation to become so. Like all young men of ambition and aspiring temperaments, the mere possibility of ill success keeps alive in me a thousand unnecessary and annoying fears. But I hope ere long to become settled in life, and then I shall begin in good earnest to mold my future destinies. In the meantime, I shall devote my principal energies to the law, and shall endeavor to compose my mind to a state of profitable study.

Whatever, my dear father, may have been my errors, I have always entertained for you the most unvarying filial attachment; and it shall always be my highest pleasure to endeavor to meet your wishes and commands.

Julia desires me to express her love to you all in the most tender and affectionate terms.

SAMUEL L. SOUTHARD TO MR. CLAY.

TRENTON, December 1, 1832.

MY DEAR SIR,—I should have written to you several days ago, but I feared that you would leave Lexington before my letter reached there.

I am in deep distress at the situation of our country. I fear that the Union and Government are gone. Nothing can save them but a wisdom and patriotism which I almost despair of finding, in the present day of madness. I should despair, if I did not feel, that a citizen can commit no crime short of treason, worse than to despair of the Republic.

The recent elections have greatly astonished me. Even in New Jersey, no one of any party, who was well informed, doubted a different result. We owe our defeat to two causes—The overconfidence of our friends, who feared no danger, and the course of the Anti-Masons. We were assured that they would support our ticket, in preference to General Jackson's, until the last moment; but the result shows that my early and constant fears respecting them were well founded. They tried me—painfully.

I am now myself in as unpleasant a condition as any man can well be. Forced into an annual office, to gratify my friends, and promote the success of the party—giving up a practice necessary for the comfort of myself and family, and destined, in all probabiliy, to be cast out in another year. But for myself I care little. I have never looked to popular favor for happiness, nor to office for support. I have always given more than I received when I have accepted public stations.

There are many who wish me to change my position to the Senate, in place of Dickenson, under the belief that I can, in the present melancholy times, do more good to the country there than where I now am. Whether this will be the wish of the joint meeting in January I know not. I took this office with no anticipations of good to myself. I felt it a sacrifice of myself to my country, and I am now content to remain in it; and while I do, let the period be short or long, to do my duty, and my whole duty, fearlessly and fully, and meet, without flinching, all consequences. What shall I do? Of the future I anticipate nothing of good to the country, unless trials and calamities may open blind eyes. What are we to do with South Carolina? Do tell me your plan—prophecy for me. I would write on that topic, I intended to do so when I began, but my time is out. Other duties call me. Let me hear from you, and fully.

MR. CLAY TO FRANCIS BROOKE.

WASHINGTON, December 12, 1832.

MY DEAR SIR,—On my arrival here, a few days ago, I found your favor of the 28th ultimo. Mrs. Clay did not accompany me, but remained at home, in consequence of the shortness of the session, and the apprehended bad state of the roads, both in coming and returning.

It is useless to dwell on the issue of the Presidential election, respecting which we were so greatly disappointed. From whatever causes it proceeded, it is now irrevocable.

You ask, what is to be done with nullification? I must refer you to the President's proclamation. One short week produced the message and the proclamation—the former ultra on the side of State rights, the latter ultra on the side of consolidation. How they can be reconciled, I must leave to our Virginia friends. As to the proclamation, although there are good things in it, especially what relates to the Judiciary, there are some entirely too ultra for me, and which I can not stomach. A proclamation ought to have been issued weeks ago, but I think it should have been a very different paper from the present, which, I apprehend, will irritate instead of allaying any excited feeling.

Congress has not yet been called upon, and I sincerely hope it may not be necessary to call upon it, in this unfortunate affair. How is the proclamation received at Richmond?

I shall leave here to-morrow, to accompany my fourth son as far as Philadelphia, on his way to New England. And, in great haste, I add assurances of my constant and cordial esteem.

MRS. ERWIN TO HER FATHER, MR. CLAY.

THE WOODLANDS, December 13, 1832.

MY DEAR FATHER,—I suppose, by the time this reaches you, that you will have arrived safely at Washington. We heard from you at Wheeling, but not since; you have been seeing new faces and new things every day, while we have been going on in the same quiet routine—I will not say dull—that you left us in. The only change in our society is the arrival of Henry and Julia from Louisiana; they came a week since, and are at Posttethwaites. They have been out frequently, and we all spent a very pleasant day yesterday with mamma, whom we found in good health and spirits. Theodore went home the day after you left, and although mamma is now fully convinced that he is deranged, he has so far conducted himself quietly, and she is much happier than if he were any where else.

Henry has recommenced the study of the law with increased energy. He is disgusted with the prospect of making a living at the bar in Kentucky, and as a last determination, which he does not intend to change, he is to go to New Orleans in February, and at last open an office this winter, preparatory to commencing business next year. This I think a wise course, and I hope he will persevere in it. His health and spirits are better than when he left us.

Nothing has occurred worth noticing in the family, except the very sudden death of Alfred Shelby, who fell in a fit of apoplexy, and died a few hours afterward. Mrs. M. Harrison gave birth to a fine son on Saturday, who, I hope, will not prove, like his father, a good Jackson man.

We are positively to leave on the 15th, that is, day after to-morrow, and we have every prospect of a quick and pleasant passage, as the weather is fine, and both rivers in fine order. I leave the boys with mamma. I expect they will occasion me to return very early in the spring.

Give my love to all those who may be so kind as to inquire for me, and particularly to James; do, my dear father, make him write me to New Orleans, if you can not find time to do so yourself. Mr. Denton begs to be respectfully remembered to you. Mr. Erwin and the children join me in love to you.

CHAPTER IX.

CORRESPONDENCE OF 1833, '34, AND '35.

MR. CLAY TO FRANCIS BROOKE.

WASHINGTON, January 17, 1833.

MY DEAR SIR,—I received your two last favors, and should have written to you before and oftener, but that I really have had nothing interesting to communicate. As to politics, we have no past, no future. After forty-four years of existence under the present Constitution, what single principle is fixed? The Bank? No. Internal Improvements? No. The Tariff? No. Who is to interpret the Constitution? We are as much afloat at sea as the day when the Constitution went into operation. There is nothing certain but that the will of Andrew Jackson is to govern; and that will fluctuates with the change of every pen which gives expression to it. As to the Tariff, now pending before the House, whether it will pass or no in that body depends upon his command.

I have been thinking of some settlement of that question, but I have not entirely matured any plan; and if I had, I am not satisfied that it would be expedient to offer it. Any plan that I might offer would be instantly opposed, because I offered it. Sometimes I have thought that, considering how I have been and still am treated by both parties (the Tariff and the Anti-Tariff), I would leave them to fight it out as well as they can. The lingering hopes for my country prevail over these feelings of a just resentment, and my judgment tells me, that disregarding them, I ought to the last to endeavor to do what I can to preserve its institutions and re-establish confidence and concord. I shall act in conformity with this judgment, but I am far from being sanguine that I have the power to effect any thing.

You will have seen the late Message. It is able and elaborate, freer from passion than the proclamation, but not more compatible with the doctrines which prevail at Richmond.

MR. CLAY TO FRANCIS BROOKE.

WASHINGTON, January 23, 1833.

MY DEAR SIR,—You mistake very much my feelings in supposing that the doubt which I sometimes entertained of making any effort to rescue the country from its present difficult situation, proceeded from any spirit similar to that which actuated Coriolanus. That doubt sprang from the facts, that there was an organized party ready to denounce any proposition that I would make, because I made it; and that the other party (the Anti-Tariff party) contained many individuals, in whose view the great interests and even the peace of the country, were subordinate to the success of the dominant party to which they belong, and to the success of the designated successor of the present chief magistrate. It is mortifying—inexpressibly disgusting—to find that considerations affecting an election now four years distant, influence the fate of great questions of immediate interest more than all the reasons and arguments which intimately appertain to those questions. If, for example, the Tariff now before the House should be lost, its defeat will be owing to two causes—1st, The apprehension of Mr. Van Buren's friends, that if it passes, Mr. Calhoun will rise again as the successful vindicator of Southern rights; and 2d, Its passage might prevent the President from exercising certain vengeful passions which he wishes to gratify in South Carolina. And if it passes, its passage may be attributed to the desire of those same friends of Mr. Van Buren to secure Southern votes. Whether it will pass or not, and if it does, what will be its fate in the Senate, remains altogether uncertain.

You ask me in your last letter if Tyler is not a nullifier? I understand him to be opposed both to nullification and the proceedings of South Carolina. Will he be re-elected? We feel here some solicitude on that point, being convinced, that under all circumstances, he would be far preferable to any person that could be sent. I hope, if you can say a proper word in his behalf, you will do so.

REVERDY JOHNSON TO MR. CLAY.

BALTIMORE, February 13, 1833.

MY DEAR SIR,—You will pardon me, I am sure, for trespassing a moment upon your time, in thanking you for the effort you are making to quiet the unhappy and alarming dissentions of the country. Like yourself, decidedly friendly to the protection of domestic industry, I am satisfied, and have been satisfied for some time, that nothing but a liberal spirit of compromise can save the system from almost immediate destruction. The incalculable mischief which, in a mere pecuniary point of view, this will bring upon us, is, of itself, alarming enough, but it is comparatively insignificant, when contrasted with the strong probability, that it may cause a struggle vital to the Union itself. The plan which you have proposed, will, I think, if any plan can accomplish it, save the manufacturers for the time, and in its consequences (gradually brought about) open the eyes of our Southern brethren to the manifold benefits of the system which they have so violently opposed. I can not but believe, that a few years of quiet and sober reflection will satisfy them that their present hostility to the prevailing policy, is the merest creation of prejudice that was ever known, and that their true interests, like that of their Northern countrymen, is in protecting the nation and its industry, against foreign restrictions. God grant that your efforts may prove successful, and that we may again see our country not only, as it is, prosperous in fact, but happy and free in the estimation of every citizen of the Government.

I repeat that I am satisfied you will take this communication in the spirit in which it is sent, and consider me as authorized to suppose that you will receive it in all kindness.

MR. CLAY TO FRANCIS BROOKE.

SENATE CHAMBER, February 14, 1833.

MY DEAR SIR,—I had forborne to communicate to you the plan of accommodation which I intended to submit, because, although I had long since settled in my mind the principle of the plan, I had not finally arranged the details. That work was only completed a few days ago. You will see in the papers that I have presented it to the Senate in the shape of a bill. I was fully aware of all the personal consequences, and personal risks to which I exposed myself; but "what is a public man worth that will not sacrifice himself, if necessary, for the good of his country?" The measure has been well secured. Still every contrivance will be resorted to by the Van Buren men, and by some of the Administration party, to prostrate or defeat the project. That, you know, I anticipated. What will be the final issue of the plan, I can not certainly say. I hope for success. We had a meeting this morning of the Committee—with the constitution of which I am satisfied—and things look as well there as I expected. Webster, and some other of the New England Senators, will oppose the plan.

JOHN M. CLAYTON TO MR. CLAY.

WASHINGTON, February 20, 1833.

MY DEAR FRIEND,—Prepare yourself fully for the debate tomorrow. We shall hear a labored speech from our opponents.

To-morrow will be the most eventful period of your eventful life. Your friends depend on your efforts, and I as one of them suggest to you this thought—consider whether it be not your best course to declare in your speech on the bill that you are no candidate for the honors of office—that you look only to the imperishable glory of preventing civil war and again uniting your distracted countrymen in the bonds of fraternal affection, while at the same time you insure the continuation, the perpetuity of that great system with which your fame is identified. I advise this course at present. We have a yawning gulf in our Rome, and it will never close till some patriot rides into it. This will stop the cry of coalition, save yourself and your friends from calumny, and your country from ruin.

MR. CLAY TO FRANCIS BROOKE.

SENATE CHAMBER, February 23, 1833.

MY DEAR FRIEND,—The compromise of the Tariff proposed by me is likely to be adopted with great eclat. It has passed the House, and will pass the Senate by a large majority. It will be popular everywhere, even in the East. The Eastern vote in the House has been given against it, rather from policy than from any dislike of the measure. Mr. Webster and I came in conflict, and I have the satisfaction to tell you that he gained nothing. My friends flatter me with my having completely triumphed. There is no permanent breach between us. I think he begins already to repent his course.

As to the publication of my letter, do as you please; but I think it hardly merits it.

I shall go to the North, or directly to the West, immediately after the close of the session. I regret that I can not have the pleasure of seeing you. Make my best respects to Mrs. Brooke.

NICHOLAS BIDDLE TO MR. CLAY.

PHILADELPHIA, February 28, 1833.

MY DEAR SIR,—I have a great deal to say, or rather to ask, about the manner in which you have been able to draw out the lightning from all the clouds which were lowering over the country; but I will not trouble you now, and I only hope that you will come up when the session is over, and talk into conviction all the doubters, even my friend Mr. Walsh himself. The fact is, that for forty-eight hours your friends held in their breath with anxiety, till they saw you fairly across the chasm, and are proportionally gratified at seeing you in such a firm and commanding position. Of all this hereafter, when you come to see us. What makes me write now is, that I think you may find an opportunity on Saturday or Sunday of saying a few words which may make a strong and favorable impression upon two large masses of the community whom I wish to see well disposed to you, especially at the present moment. I mean the friends of the Bank and the Western States generally.

MR. CLAY TO FRANCIS BROOKE.

WASHINGTON, March 11, 1833.

MY DEAR SIR,—At the date of your last you could not have received a letter which I had addressed to you at St. Julien. I shall leave here in a day or two, viâ Baltimore, Frederick, and Wheeling, for Kentucky. I have been detained by the Court. I regret that I could not have seen you.

You ask how amity was restored between Mr. Randolph and me? There was no explanation, no intervention. Observing him in the Senate one night, feeble, and looking as if he was not long for this world, and being myself engaged in a work of peace, with corresponding feelings, I shook hands with him. The salutation was cordial on both sides. I afterward left a card at his lodgings, where, I understand, he has been confined by sickness.

I heard to-day that Livingston is to go to France, Barry to Spain, and Stevenson to England; and that M'Lane will be made Secretary of State, Woodbury of the Treasury, Forsythe of the Navy, and Colonel William Wilkins Post-master General. Caring nothing about these arrangements, I vouch for nothing.

You may like to know that there is no breach between Webster and me. We had some friendly passes, and there the matter ended. Since, we have occasionally met on friendly terms. I think (of course I do not know) that if he had to go over again the work of the last few weeks, he would have been for the compromise, which commands the approbation of a great majority.

HENRY CLAY, JR., TO HIS FATHER.

NEW ORLEANS, March 11, 1833.

DEAR FATHER,—This morning I stood my examination in open court before the Judge of the Supreme Court, and I intend immediately to commence the practice. My visit to Mobile and my examination and license there were entirely unnecessary. I was admitted to an examination on the plea of residentship. I am full of hope and energy, and loving the civil law as I do, I indulge a subdued confidence of ultimate success. At all events, I shall continue the trial for two seasons after the present.

CHIEF JUSTICE MARSHALL TO MR. CLAY.

WASHINGTON, March 13, 1833.

DEAR SIR,—My nephew, Marshall Jones, purposes to remove to New Orleans with a view to the practice of the law, and is, I believe, now in that place. The circumstances under which he left Virginia increase my solicitude for his success. A personal rencounter with a young gentleman who had abused him wantonly and grossly, terminated very unfortunately in the death of his adversary. This compelled him to fly from Virginia and from very flattering professional prospects. After visiting Canada and Texas, he has at length, I am told, determined on trying his fortune in New Orleans. I am extremely desirous of promoting his object, but with the exception of Mr. Johnston, am not acquainted with a single individual in that place. May I ask the favor of you to mention him to some of your friends, not as a person known to yourself, but as my friend and relation whom I strongly recommend. I have the most entire confidence in his honor, integrity, and amiable qualities; and shall feel myself greatly obliged by your bestowing on him so much of your countenance as may favor his introduction into society, and his professional exertions. For the rest, he must depend upon himself.

With great respect and esteem I am, dear sir, your obedient servant.

MR. CLAY TO J. S. JOHNSTON.

WASHINGTON, March 15, 1833.

MY DEAR SIR,—You observe that your letter of the 13th found me here. I had, prior to its receipt, sent you a copy of my speech which is to be published by Gales & Seaton in the order of the debates. They have not published one word of the commendation of the bill, which has been put forth by other editors. To preserve an attitude of impartiality they, in effect, make themselves partisans of those who oppose the measure. Do you think it necessary that I should revise the speech which I made on the introduction of the bill? That which was published for me was done without my seeing it.

I am very sorry that Sergeant and Binney disapprove the measure, but I can not help it. I communicated it to them confidentially before I brought it forward, and they opposed no remonstrance. As for Walsh, he has but one god, and Mr. Webster is his prophet.

I hope you sent on my letter to Lawrence which I inclosed to you. That part of the subject ought to be well understood among our friends.

I have been detained here by the most violent cold I ever had; but I hope to be off on Sunday at furthest, for the West. I can not go now to Philadelphia. I gained my cause, Minor against Tillotson.

PELEG SPRAGUE TO MR. CLAY.

BOSTON, March 19, 1833.

DEAR SIR,—It affords me the highest gratification to be able to assure you that public sentiment here has wonderfully changed in favor of your great measure, since its introduction. It is now popular, and becoming more and more so as it becomes better understood, as the real condition of the country and of the views and opinions of the Administration are more known, and as the bill itself and your course previous to its being offered in the Senate are explained. In New York I scarcely found an individual who did not approve it. In Providence and in Boston there is yet some diversity of opinion among the politicians, but so far as I learn none among the actual business men, engaged in manufactures. I have seen several of the principal and most intelligent; they are only apprehensive that it will not be permanent, that it will be again put afloat. They say that they do not think fit to come out publicly in favor of the measure, because it might create uneasiness in the South, and generate a disposition to make further demands, and because it would carry a censure upon their delegation in Congress. I have seen and conversed with many of the principal men, and was at first surprised that there was so much of error and misapprehension in nearly all in relation to the bill. I yesterday spent nearly an hour in conversation upon this subject with the Governor, most of the members of his Council being present, and I also have conversed with the Lieutenant-Governor, the Speaker of the House of Representatives, several members of the Senate, and many members of the House, with Crowningshield and Dwight, formerly members of Congress, with both the Everett's, President Quincy, the Lawrences, and many other merchants and manufacturers, whose names are unknown to you; and I can not doubt from their representations that the bill is now considered a good one, and will be extremely popular when fully understood. Indeed I am entirely mistaken if, in six months, it be not considered in New England as the most wise, patriotic, beneficent and splendid act of legislation that any individual in this country has ever achieved. It ought not to be matter of surprise that some time is required to bring the public here to a correct understanding of the measure, for every member of their delegation, in whom they have justly so much confidence, voted against it, and some, in the early stages, united in a feeling of hostility to it. The debate has not yet been published, which is very unfortunate, and the impressions of the nature of the bill have been received from the objections which are understood to have been made to it in the Senate. I have found the impression almost universal that it relinquished the principle of protection after 1842, and not one have I seen here, as I recollect, who did not think that after that period the duties were to be equal on all articles, except such as the bill itself specified should be free. I have, ever since I arrived in New York, carried the bill in my pocket in order to convince them of this error, which has always been the first and prominent objection, and I have not met with one to whom I have had an opportunity to present the truth, who has not been satisfied, and wondered how they should have been so mistaken. I have made it a business, since my arrival here, to put the matter right, and also to correct another erroneous impression which has been the source of much prejudice from the beginning, and that is that your course was adopted without consultation with your Tariff friends, and operated as a surprise upon them all, and particularly upon Mr. W. I have taken the liberty, every where and upon all occasions, to state the truth upon this point, which I know. I thought myself not only at liberty, but bound, in justice to yourself, to make your course known, and have been delighted to find how relieved and rejoiced your friends here have invariably been to learn the truth. I have not hesitated to state the conferences which were had, formal and informal, the propositions and suggestions which you submitted, and the remarks of Mr. W. and others. Rely upon it the intelligent men here are getting to understand the subject; it requires but a few persons to explain it, and it will be highly satisfactory and almost universally popular. I regret deeply that the debate has not been published, while the public mind is awake and inquisitive in regard to it, especially as all the members from this State were opposed to it in their votes, and of course are stopped from saying much in its favor. I shall remain here several days longer, and shall see a great many more of their intelligent and leading men, and I have no doubt all will be satisfied except a particular, and I trust very limited class of politicians, who wished to carry matters to extremities with South Carolina, and to see her put down, prostrated by force of arms, and with whom this feeling was paramount to any regard for the Tariff.

Excuse me for writing so much, and so many repetitions, but the subject is one in which every hour's reflection and observation increases my interest, and I have the strongest solicitude that every body should view this splendid and glorious act as I do, and appreciate and do justice to the mover, which I have no doubt they will. Your promised visit here is looked forward to with great eagerness. Your reception will be all that you can wish. You must not disappoint them, nor us in Maine.

N. B. Since the passage of your bill there has been a material rise in the value and market price of almost all manufacturing stocks, and of wool, and woolen goods, which is extending now to cottons, and other articles. An infallible test of the real opinion of the interested.

NICHOLAS BIDDLE TO MR. CLAY.

PHILADELPHIA, March 25, 1833.

MY DEAR SIR,—I duly received your last favor from Washington, and did not fail to bear in mind its interesting contents. It confirmed an opinion previously formed, confirmed by subsequent reflection, and since repeatedly declared, that it was of great importance to the country not to permit the difference of sentiment on the Tariff to produce any alienation between those who had hitherto acted in concert on all the other great public measures; and that more especially no estrangement should be allowed to grow up between the two most prominent leaders who were opposed on that question. During the visit of our friend, I was in habits of constant and confidential intercourse with him. In regard to the measure itself, he retains all the opinions which he publicly expressed; but they are, I think, unaccompanied by any thing of an unkind or unfriendly feeling toward yourself, as you will perceive when the speech made on that occasion is published. There was a strong disposition among many of his friends, to give him a public dinner; but this I discouraged, because I feared that it might oblige him to say more on that subject than it is prudent to express at the present time, and because it would probably furnish an occasion for his less discreet friends to do and to say things excusable at a moment of excitement, but which might afterward be regretted. For such an exhibition, I substituted a large meeting of gentlemen at my own house, where his friends could have the pleasure of seeing him, without imposing upon him the necessity of making any exposition of his views on any subject. I stated to him without reserve, the share which I had taken in preventing a public dinner, and my reasons for it, in the propriety of which he entirely acquiesced. In short, he has left us two days ago, in a frame of mind entirely satisfactory, and your mutual friends seem to understand each other perfectly, that there ought not to be, and that there shall not be, any alienation between you, however you may have differed on one measure of policy. For myself, I entertain for him so sincere an attachment, that I should have been greatly pained at a different result. These good dispositions will, I doubt not, be strengthened during the visit which we meditate, to your country, in the course of the spring, since no one can be insensible to the attractions of personal intercourse with you. Few, I need not add, appreciate that pleasure more highly than yours, with great respect, etc.

ABBOTT LAWRENCE TO MR. CLAY.

BOSTON, March 26, 1833.

MY DEAR SIR,—I have great pleasure in acknowledging the receipt of your letter of the 13th inst., with your speech upon the Tariff Bill.

Your letter gave me individually, inexpressible pleasure, as it has placed in my power the means of satisfying the minds of many prominent citizens among us, who had supposed the whole scheme was brought forward without the knowledge of your friends. I have given the letter free circulation where it has been required, to remove any prejudices that might have existed, and I have a general response from all, that they are entirely satisfied with the purity of your motives, as well as your enlightened patriotism. The newspaper presses are now silent here upon the subject, and will remain so. I know the editors well, and have taken some pains to place the whole subject upon true ground. I had, as you know, strong objections to any concessions whatever; yet I am now well satisfied with the course the whole subject took in Congress; so are the people of this State, and of New England. Our interests have been greatly promoted by it, and it is hoped and believed that time will prove to us that it was the dictate of wisdom to have adopted the bill proposed by you, and carried by your influence. I do not think there is the least unkind feeling toward you, in New England, and I do not take, I think, too much upon myself, when I say you were never more popular than at the present moment. I look for a great change in public sentiment upon the American system, before the end of nine years, or even five years. If the system of internal improvements could go on for a few years, with vigor, there is not a doubt upon my mind, that this Union would be bound by ties stronger than all the constitutions that human wisdom could devise. A railroad from New England to Georgia, would do more to harmonize the feelings of the whole country, than any amendments that can be offered or adopted to the Constitution. It is intercourse we want, and what I desire. Your Land bill is a great favorite here, and receives the hearty support of all parties, with the exception of some few office-holders. I wrote you about the 10th inst., at Washington; when you write again, will you tell me whether it was received?

I have only to ask you now when we may expect to welcome you here. I am often asked the question, and should be glad to answer it. Our mutual friend, Mr. Sprague, remained here four days, and made the most of his time in explaining the principles of your bill, and the motives that influenced you in bringing it forward. I have a letter which he sent me from Mr. Senator Johnson, which is read in connection with yours of the 13th.

MR. MADISON TO MR. CLAY.

Montpelier, April 2, 1833.

Dear Sir,—Accept my acknowledgments for the copy of your speech on the bill modifying the Tariff. I need not repeat what is said by all on the ability and advantages with which the subject was handled. It has certainly had the effect of an anodyne on the feverish excitement under which the public mind was laboring; and a relapse may happily not ensue. There is no certainty, however, that a surplus revenue will not revive the difficulty of adjusting an impost to the claims of the manufacturing and the feelings of the agricultural States. The effect of a reduction, including the protected articles, on the manufacturers is manifest; and a discrimination in their favor will, besides the complaint of inequality, exhibit the protective principle, without disguise, to the protestors against its constitutionality. An alleviation of the difficulty may, perhaps, be found in such an apportionment of the tax on the protected articles most consumed in the South, and on the unprotected most consumed in the North, as will equalize the burden between them, and limit the advantage of the latter to the benefits flowing from a location of the manufacturing establishments.

May there not be a more important alleviation in embryo—an assimilation of the employment of labor in the South to its employment in the North? A difference, and even a contrast, in that respect, is at the bottom of the discords which have prevailed, and would so continue, until the manufacturers of the North could, without a bounty, take the place of the foreign in supplying the South; in which event, the source of discord would become a bond of interest, and the difference of pursuits more than equivalent to a similarity. In the mean time, an advance toward the latter must have an alleviating tendency. And does not this advance present itself in the certainty that, unless agriculture can find new markets for its products, or new products for its markets, the rapid increase of slave labor, and the still more rapid increase of its fruits, must divert a large portion of it from the plow and the hoe to the loom and the workshop? When we can no longer convert our flour, tobacco, cotton, and rice, into a supply of our habitual wants from abroad, labor must be withdrawn from those articles, and made to supply them at home.

It is painful to turn from anticipations of this sort to the prospect, opened by the torch of discord, bequeathed by the Convention of South Carolina to its country, by the insidious exhibitions of a permanent incompatibility, and even hostility, of interests between the South and the North, and by the contagious zeal in vindicating and varnishing the doctrines of nullification and secession; the tendency of all of which, whatever be the intention, is to create a disgust with the Union, and then to open the way out of it. We must oppose to this aspect of things confidence, that, as the gulf is approached, the deluded will recoil from its horrors, and that the deluders, if not themselves sufficiently startled, will be abandoned and overwhelmed by their followers.

As we were disappointed of the expected visit last fall, from yourself and Mrs. Clay, we hope the promise will not be forgotten when the next opportunity occurs. For the present, Mrs. Madison joins in cordial regards and all good wishes to you both.

JOHN SIBLEY TO MR. CLAY.

NATCHITOCHES, May 22, 1833.

DEAR SIR,—Illy fitted as my mind is to write a letter at this time, and painful as the task is, I must in grief tell you that J. S. Johnston, and his son William, were, last Sunday morning, on board the steam-boat Lioness, on their way to make me a visit, when, about thirty-five miles above Alexandria, in Red River, a large quantity of powder in the hold of the boat exploded, and blew the boat to atoms. Fifteen or sixteen passengers were lost; among them our friend Johnston.* William was blown off a distance, much hurt, but not killed; is, I hope, safe with his uncle, a few miles below where the disaster happened. His wife, my poor child, was left in bad health, in Philadelphia. I can now only commend her to a merciful God, and implore your condolence to her. I will write you more particularly when I can.

MR. CLAY TO FRANCIS BROOKE.

ASHLAND, May 30, 1833.

MY DEAR SIR,—I duly received your favor. I should have written to you before, but in this remote quarter we have rarely any thing interesting to communicate. Since my return from Washington, I have been principally occupied with the operations of my farm, which have more and more interest for me.

* The Hon. J. S. Johnston, United States Senator, and correspondent of Mr Clay.

There is a great difference, I think, between a farm employed in raising dead produce for market, and one which is applied, as mine is, to the rearing of all kinds of live stock. I have the Maltese ass, the Arabian horse, the merino and Saxe merino sheep, the English Hereford and Durham cattle, the goat, the mule, and the hog. The progress of these animals from their infancy to maturity, presents a constantly-varying subject of interest, and I never go out of my house, without meeting with some of them to engage agreeably my attention. Then, our fine green sward, our natural parks, our beautiful undulating country, every where exhibiting combinations of grass and trees, or luxuriant crops, all conspire to render home delightful. Notwithstanding, I shall leave it early in July, to make a journey which I have long desired to perform. I shall go through Ohio to Lake Erie, thence to Buffalo, Niagara, Montreal, Quebec, Saratoga, and toward September, to Boston, where I have a young son of sixteen. The papers have attributed to me an intention of visiting New England, as if it were the principal object of my excursion. It is the least important one, and I should not go there but for the sake of my son. I intend traveling with as much privacy as practicable, and absolutely to decline every species of public entertainment. I wished to have been accompanied by Mrs. Clay, and my son, and son-in-law, with their respective wives; but neither of the young ladies are in a traveling condition, and my wife hesitates about going without either of them.

You perceive that the journey I have sketched will not admit of my having the pleasure of meeting you at the White Sulphur Springs. I visit no place in the summer with more gratification than that finest of all, our mineral springs; but I have never seen the Falls of Niagara, and unless I avail myself of this summer to go there, I shall probably never have another opportunity.

I have not decided whether I shall return to the Senate or not. If the Land bill had passed, I certainly should not have gone there again; and the condition in which that measure has been left, creates the only doubt which I feel. But have I not done all that was incumbent on me? Twice have I pressed the bill in the Senate, where it has twice passed, and once in the House. I regret most deeply that the South, hitherto, has opposed that measure. They will regret it some day, if it fails; for the public lands will be lost to the country, without some such measure is adopted. They will be used as an instrument to advance the ambitious views of some Presidential aspirant, by offering motives to the new States to support him. Already they are attempted to be applied to that object; for how otherwise can you account for the opposition of Mr. Van Buren's friends, in New York, to the Land bill, and thus separating themselves from the rest of the North, and evidently arraying themselves against the interest of their own State?

You tell me that Messrs. Leigh, etc., speak of me as a candidate for the next Presidency, and even think of having my name forthwith announced. I am greatly obliged by their favorable opinion; but I really feel no disposition to enter again on an arduous and doubtful struggle for any office. I have seen no evidence of any favorable changes in respect to me, that are of an extent sufficient to justify the opinion, that a result of a new contest would take place different from former experiments. Nothing is so abhorrent to my feelings as to be placed in a position in which I should appear as a teasing suppliant for office. That of President is full of care and vexation. One borne to it by the willing suffrages of a large majority of his countrymen, may get along well enough in it; but if it is to be obtained in a hard contest, by a bare majority, or by a decision of the House of Representatives, between several candidates, no one having a majority, it has no charms, at least none for me. I doubt very much whether any successful opposition can be made against General Jackson's designated successor. The press, patronage, and party, will probably carry him triumphantly through. I have borne the taunts of the Jackson party and principles long enough. The country has not thought proper to sustain my exertions. Distinguished men, who could not possibly have viewed things differently from me, have stood by with a cold indifference, without lending any helping hand. What can one man do alone against a host?

If I am asked what I think of the present state of things, and of the future, upon the supposition of success on the part of the candidate referred to? I answer, Bad enough, bad enough, God knows. But what can I do? Have I heretofore ever ceased to warn the country against it? Worn out and exhausted in the service, why should I continue to sound the alarm, with no prospect of my being more heeded hereafter than heretofore?

I want repose. I have reached a time of life when all men want it. I shall not neglect the duties which belong to one who has aimed to be a good citizen, and a patriot, even in retirement; but the country had better try other sentinels, not more devoted or zealous, but who may be more successful than I have been.

Such, my dear sir, is the true state of my feelings. Your partiality and friendly wishes about me, may not—your unbiased judgment must—approve them.

Mrs. Clay unites with me in warm regards to Mrs. Brooke. For yourself, I need not repeat the assurance of my cordial esteem and friendship.

J. W. P. TO MR. CLAY.

PETERSBURG, May 31, 1833.

RESPECTED SIR,—The last speech which John Randolph, of Roanoke, ever delivered, was at the late Jockey Club dinner of our Newmarket races, to a party of about two hundred gentlemen. *Inter alios*, he alluded to yourself, somewhat thus : " I admire and respect such men (the old Federalists) far more than such Republicans as the Janus-faced editor of ' The Richmond Enquirer,' who has contrived to keep in with every Administration, save the short reign of John Adams the Second, and then he kept an anchor out to windward for Henry Clay, who, by the way, gentlemen, is a much better man than Ritchie. Clay is a brave man—he is a consistent man, which Ritchie is not; an independent man, and an honest man, which Ritchie is not."

These remarks were responded to by the company with rapturous applause, and I now communicate them to you (privately and *incognito*), because I like to impart pleasure to a generous mind, and it must be some gratification to you to hear that these were the last public declarations of one of your most envenomed and distinguished political enemies, and that they were uttered and applauded in a part of our country which has been, hitherto, most decided in its opposition to you.

MR. MADISON TO MR. CLAY.

MONTPELIER, June, 1833.

DEAR SIR,—Your letter of May 28th was duly received. In it you ask my opinion on the retention of the Land bill by the President.

It is obvious that the Constitution meant to allow the President an adequate time to consider the bills, etc., presented to him, and to make his objections to them ; and on the other hand, that Congress should have time to consider and overrule the objections. A disregard, on either side, of what it owes to the other, must be an abuse, for which it would be responsible under the forms of the Constitution. An abuse on the part of the President, with a view sufficiently manifest, in a case of sufficient magnitude to deprive Congress of the opportunity of overruling objections to their bills, might, doubtless, be a ground for impeachment. But nothing short of the signature of the President, or a lapse of ten days without a return of his objections, or an overruling of the objections by two thirds of each House of Congress, can give legal validity to a bill. In order to qualify (in the French sense of the term) the retention of the Land bill by the President, the first inquiry is, Whether a sufficient time was allowed him to decide on its merits? The next, Whether, with a sufficient time to prepare his objections, he unnecessarily put it out of the power of Congress to decide on them? How far an anticipated passage of the bill ought to enter into the sufficiency of the time for Executive deliberations, is another point for consideration. A minor one may be, whether a silent retention, or an assignment to Congress of the reasons for it, be the mode most suitable to such occasions.

I hope, with you, that the compromising Tariff will have a course and effect avoiding a renewal of the contest between the South and the North, and that a lapse of nine or ten years will enable the manufacturers to swim without the bladders which have supported them. Many considerations favor such a prospect. They will be saved, in future, much of the expense in fixtures, which they had to encounter, and, in many instances, unnecessarily incurred. They will be continually improving in the management of their business. They will not fail to improve, occasionally, on the machinery abroad. The reduction of duties on imported articles consumed by them will be equivalent to a direct bounty. There will probably be an increasing cheapness of food from the increasing redundancy of agricultural labor. There will, within the experimental period, be an addition of four or five millions to our population, no part, or little, of which will be needed for agricultural labor, and which will, consequently, be an extensive fund of manufacturing recruits. The current experience makes it probable, that not less than fifty or sixty thousand, or more, of emigrants, will annually each the United States, a large portion of whom will have been trained to manufactures, and be ready for that employment.

With respect to Virginia, it is quite probable, from the progress already made in the Western culture of tobacco, and the rapid exhaustion of her virgin soil, in which alone it can be cultivated with a chance of profit, that of the forty or fifty thousand laborers on tobacco the greater part will be released from the employment, and be applicable to that of manufactures. It is well known that the farming system requires much fewer hands than tobacco fields.

It is painful to observe the unceasing efforts to alarm the South by imputations against the North of unconstitutional designs on the subject of the slaves. You are right, I have do doubt, in believing that no such intermeddling disposition exists in the body of our northern brethren. Their good faith is sufficiently guaranteed by the interest they have, as merchants, as ship-owners, and as manufacturers, in preserving a union with the slaveholding States. On the other hand, what madness in the South to look for greater safety in disunion! It would be worse than jumping out of the frying-pan into the fire. It would be jumping into the fire from a fear of the frying-pan. The danger from the alarm is, that the pride and resentment excited by them may be an overmatch for the dictates of prudence, and favor the project of a Southern Convention insidiously revived, as promising by its counsels the best securities against grievances of every sort from the North.

The case of the Tariff and Land bills can not fail of an influence on the question of your return to the next session of Congress. They are both closely connected with the public repose.

DANIEL WEBSTER TO MR. CLAY.

COLUMBUS, June 10, 1833.

MY DEAR SIR,—I have at length reached this point, after having been greatly delayed by the state of the roads, produced by excessive rains. Such are the accounts here of the state of health, in the towns and near the rivers, and to the southward of it, that my future movements, and the extent to which I may prosecute my journey, have become uncertain. The season, too, seems now rapidly advancing into hot weather. I have thought it due to your kindness and proffered hospitality to make this suggestion, lest you should stay at Lexington, in expectation of my being there, after the time when it would be agreeable to you, under existing circumstances, to leave home. I pray you not to stay a day for me, since it is so uncertain whether I shall get to Lexington.

I have heard only to-day the dreadful account about poor Johnston. It is inexpressibly shocking.

DANIEL WEBSTER TO MR. CLAY.

CHILLICOTHE, June 22d, 1833.

MY DEAR SIR,—Your kind letter of the 17th was put into my hands at Cincinnati, on the morning of the 20th, just as I was getting into the carriage on my departure for this place. With whatever reluctance, and it was certainly very great, I found it unavoidable that I should give up the Kentucky portion of my journey; since, even though I felt no fear about personal safety, I should yet find those whom I wished to see either in alarm or in affliction. Now that the scourge has departed, as I hope, from your immediate neighborhood, and although Providence has kindly protected your own roof, yet I can well conceive that you must have lost valued friends, and that so terrible a visitation has left a shock which must continue to be felt for some time.

It is my purpose to proceed immediately to Pittsburg, and thence by the shortest route to New York and New England. I find Mr. Ewing here, as well as General M. Arthur and other friends. He expresses great pleasure at the escape of your family from the calamity. There is no sickness here, though a case of cholera is reported as having occurred at Portsmouth.

I sincerely hope you will not give up your intended visit to the North. All along the country there is a very general expectation of seeing you, and the disappointment will not be small, should you not come.

I beg you to make my best regards to Mrs. Clay, and say to her, that I will venture to give her my word that if she will visit the North, she will find her tour pleasant and agreeable, and her welcome every where hearty.

MR. CLAY TO FRANCIS BROOKE.

Ashland, August 2, 1833.

My dear Sir,—I duly received your favor of the 20th ultimo, and take great pleasure in transmitting an account of the remedy most successfully applied in the treatment of the cholera in Lexington. I send you herewith a number of the "Western Journal," which contains an article bringing into review almost all that has been written on the subject of the scourge. The description and treatment of the disease by Mr. J. Kennedy (the first work reviewed) resemble most the appearance of it here, and accord best with the most approved practice.

From all that I saw and heard about it here, I have drawn the conclusions:

1. That certain reliance can be placed upon no remedy after the disease has reached the state of collapse and cramps.

2. That, prior to that state, no sure reliance can be placed on any treatment which does not embrace the use of calomel in moderate doses.

3. That if the disease commences, as it generally does, by a complaint in the bowels, calomel in doses of from five to twenty-five grains, taken every hour, or two, until the discharge from the bowels is checked, may be relied upon with a high degree of certainty.

If there be considerable discharge from the bowels, opium, in the proportion of one grain to every two of calomel, or fifteen or twenty grains of laudanum, were advantageously given with calomel.

The use of emetics and bleeding was much controverted. I believe them both good, in certain cases, and they were both occasionally resorted to with benefit, though I think neither indispensable. In the early stages of the disease only, and when it has not assumed what Mr. Kennedy calls the rapid type, would it be advisable to employ the emetic? Ipecac., salt, and mustard, and warm salt and water, were all used. We had among our slaves a number of cases of violent pain in the abdomen, which we feared might terminate in cholera. In most of them we administered salt and mustard in equal proportions, about a tablespoonful of each forming a dose, which was, however, repeated until vomiting ensued, and, after the operation, twenty grains of calomel, combined with twenty grains of rhubarb. All of them were relieved. The same remedy, with the same success, was employed at Mr. Erwin's, and at a bagging factory in the city.

The attack made upon Mr. Dudley's practice was in consequence of his use of the emetic ; and, I think, was unfounded.

Some of our physicians employed enormous doses of calomel, but I believe with no advantage.

I send you a letter I received from Dr. M'Nairy, containing an account of his practice, which, as I understand, was very successful.

Most sincerely do I hope that you may not have occasion for any application whatever to this terrible disease. It still rages with great violence in some parts of our State.

You seem to think that I despond as to our public affairs. If you mean that I have less confidence than I formerly entertained in the virtue and intelligence of the people, and in the stability of our institutions, I regret to be obliged to own it. Are we not governed now, and have we not been for some time past, pretty much by the will of one man? And do not large masses of the people, perhaps a majority, seem disposed to follow him wherever he leads, through all his inconsistencies? He does not, it is true, always govern positively, by enforcing the measures which he prefers ; but he prevents those, although adopted by the representatives of the people, to which he is opposed ; and although manifestly for their good, they acquiesce in and applaud whatever he does, and take sides with him against the legislative authority. If that single man were an enlightened philosopher, and a true patriot, the popular sanction which is given to all his acts, however inconsistent or extravagant, might find some justification. But when we consider that he is ignorant, passionate, hypocritical, corrupt, and easily swayed by the base men who surround him, what can we think of the popular approbation which he receives?

One thing only was wanted to complete the public degradation, and that was, that he should name his successor. This he has done, and there is much reason to believe that the people will ratify the nomination. Although that successor may be now, in some places, unpopular, when we reflect that the whole patronage of the Government will be directed for three years to insure his success; and that a system of organization exists, in the largest State of the Union, wielding about one seventh of the whole electoral vote, the probability of his final success must be admitted to be great. To these chances we have to add others. In the South, it is now pretty evident that you are about to reenact the scenes of 1824, when, under a romantic notion of adhering to your candidate, you threw away your votes upon Mr. Crawford, a paralytic, although it was perfectly notorious that he stood no earthly chance of being elected. Now, under the erroneous idea that other parts of the Union contemplate an attack upon your slave property, and with the purpose of adhering to what are called your principles, Mr. Calhoun, or somebody else, will be brought out, and a great effort will be made to rally the South in his support. The contest will be between him and Mr. Van Buren. The latter, aided by the dominant party in Virginia, may secure that State. But it will so turn out that, whatever votes the Southern candidate may get, will serve Mr. Van Buren almost as effectually as if given directly for himself; because they will be so many abstracted from some other formidable competitor. Thus, by the operation of the instruments now in full employment to secure his election, and by the divisions of those opposed to him, he will obtain the majority, or enter the House of Representatives with a resistless popularity.

His election once secured, the corrupt means of preserving and perpetuating power, now in successful operation at Albany, will be transferred to Washington. And there we shall have a state of things which will prepare the public mind for a dissolution of the Union, to which, unfortunately, there is less aversion now than could be wished by those who love their country.

I hope I may be deceived in these predictions; but I fear that I will not. Believing in them, you can not be surprised that, at the age of fifty-six, and after the struggles which I have made to maintain the public liberty, and to avoid the evils which now menace us—struggles, I repeat, in which I have been too little sustained—I should think seriously of a final retirement from the theater of public life.

My daughter* was happy to find herself in your friendly recollection, and desires me to assure you of her cordially reciprocating your esteem. She is very happy, possessed of the affections of her husband, residing upon a beautiful place adjoining mine, and enjoying affluence and every blessing.

Mrs. Clay desires to be kindly remembered to Mrs. B. and yourself, and I remain always your sincere friend.

HARRISON GRAY OTIS TO MR. CLAY.

BOSTON, October 22, 1833.

MY DEAR SIR,—I had long indulged a most gratifying anticipation, that upon any visit you might make to this city, I should be among the foremost to receive you with a cordial welcome, and to promote among my fellow-citizens those public demonstrations of respect, to which your claims, to say the least, are, in my opinion, equal to those of any man in our country. My family also would have been too happy in uniting with me in every effort in our power to contribute toward making the stay of yours among us agreeable and convenient. The chagrin, therefore, which I should feel in a disappointment which forbids the accomplishment of these purposes, would be mortifying and deep, if arising from any human source. But we are under an affliction which comes from above, and precludes all emotions but those of anxiety and sorrow, and dispenses from all duties but those of resignation and obedience. My youngest son, the delight of our eyes and our lives, is suddenly arrested by disease, in the bloom and vigor of youth, and is, as his physicians fear, on his dying bed. This trouble is too serious to be mentioned as a ceremonious apology; but I could not, without a sense of self disparagement, permit you to remain a visitor in my native city, under an impression that any ordinary cause would prevent me from showing you, by all that depends on me, the sense which I think every man who loves his country should enter-

---

* Mrs. Erwin, the much-loved child, and most worthy of it. We have heard Mr. Clay speak of her, many years after her decease, with the most tender emotion. He delighted to dwell on her character with a sympathizing friend.

tertain of the claims of a patriot, who has always carried his principles in front, and is ignorant of all political disguise, except that which he has seen worn by others, and whose public services have been, and, I trust, yet will be, of inappreciable value to his country. If I can trust myself to behave with decent firmness and composure, for ten minutes, I shall steal them, to take you by the hand. If I do not, accept from a full heart the wish that God Almighty may secure you and yours in his holy keeping.

I pray you not to think of replying to this.

MR. CLAY TO FRANCIS BROOKE.

SENATE CHAMBER, December 11, 1833.

MY DEAR SIR,—I have delayed acknowledging the receipt of your favor, in consequence of an uncertainty whether my answer should be addressed you at St. Julien or at Richmond, and I am yet at a loss which direction to give it.

My journey was full of gratification. In spite of my constant protestations that it was undertaken with objects of a private nature exclusively, and my uniformly declining public dinners, the people every where, and at most places, without discrimination of parties, took possession of me, and gave enthusiastic demonstrations of respect, attachment and confidence. In looking back on the scenes through which I passed, they seem to me to have resembled those of enchantment more than of real life.

From indications which have been as yet given, it would seem that the session opens with a majority in the House for the Administration, and a majority in the Senate against it. We passed a pretty strong measure yesterday, resuming the appointment of committees by the Senate itself. On that vote, parties stand twenty-two to eighteen. We hope to reverse the majority in the House, and to strengthen it in the Senate, if we have no desertions.

Are you in habits of intimacy with Floyd? If you are, you may ask him to show you a long letter I have recently addressed to him, in answer to a long letter I had received from him on public affairs.

Mrs. Clay joins me in respects to Mrs. Brooke.

AMBROSE SPENCER TO MR. CLAY.

ALBANY, December 14, 1833.

DEAR SIR,—Knowing that your time is wholly taken up in the arduous duties before you, I have hesitated to divert your attention a moment by any thing I can suggest; but I am not willing that an acquaintance which gave me unspeakable pleasure, should be suffered to fade away. If you have not leisure to answer my letters I assure you that your silence will give me no offense. You can hardly conceive what favorable impressions your short visit among us created. Those who were prepared to love and admire you, were confirmed in all their anticipations, and they admire and love you with the more intensity; and even those who have been in the habit of thinking and speaking unkindly of you, were generally compelled to think better of you. I revert to the few happy hours I spent in your company with renewed delight. You may say this is flattery; but if you understood my character, this is a vice never imputed to me by friend or foe, but enough of this.

* * * * * * *

I am aware that it is quite premature to think or speak of the next Presidential candidate, but it seems that, *nolens volens*, the press will talk of it, and consequently the public will think of it. In my opinion the national Republicans ought to keep themselves wholly uncommitted, unless a great change should take place in the public mind, and the prejudices of party be greatly abated, the annunciation of any one of our distinguished friends would have the effect to unite the whole Jackson phalanx on some one of their leaders, and I think Mr. Van Buren would probably be that man. From present appearances the contest on the part of our adversaries will be between Van Buren, Judge M'Lean, and Mr. Cass. I had no opportunity to obtain your opinions of the two latter, but I confess I feel strong repugnance to both of them. The question is not whether they are as unprincipled as Jackson, for I console myself with the belief that we, under no circumstances, can elect a worse, or more incompetent man. If we are driven to a choice between the three, which of them will be the least mischievous? M'Lean's judicial course has been jesuitical and trimming, and it will be a strong objection to him that he enters the arena with the robes of office on. As to Cass, I once thought well of him; but did he not write an article in the "North American Review" expressly to propitiate the favor of Jackson, chiming in with his crude notions that Georgia had a right to abrogate the laws, etc., of the Cherokees and subject them to their jurisdiction? This was in July, 1830. Did he not write an essay for "The Globe" reviewing Judge Marshall's opinions in the case of the Missourians, to prepare the public mind for the President's refusal to obey and carry into effect the mandate of the court? Is he not the one of the Cabinet who gave an oral opinion against removing the deposits, but saying if they were removed he would stand by the President? If he has done all or any of these things, he is a fit instrument for a tyrant, and I despise him. Can you enlighten me on any of these matters at a leisure moment?

I feel as I did when I saw you, most desponding at the prospect before us, and yet were I called to act, I would, if possible, nerve myself for the contest and fight the battle on the last inch of ground left.

Excuse, I pray you, my want of method. I write on just as I feel. We are all well. Present my respects to Mrs. Clay and say to her, Mrs. Spencer presents her respects and will long remember her with affection.

P. S. Mrs. De Witt Clinton told me she regretted very much you did not call on her. She has not one remaining prejudice against you, and her husband's were conceived in error, and were, I doubt not, produced by misrepresentation.

HENRY CLAY, JR., TO HIS FATHER.

MAPLEWOOD, December 14, 1833.

MY DEAR FATHER,—I must now write you upon a very painful subject. Anne, Mr. Erwin, and the rest of the family, with the exception of myself, determined, from the great and apparent increase of Theodore's malady, and from the positive risk and danger of his going at large, that he ought to be again placed in the Hospital in this place. The Commissioners have taken him once more under their protection. They applied to me to know if I consented to it. I told them that I should have nothing to do in the matter, but that as one nearly related, but without any authority or desire to act, I had no objection. When he was placed in the Hospital I was applied to as his brother, the nearest relation present, to advance $50 for his board, and to give my bond for $500. I advanced the money promptly, and have expressed my willingness to give my bond. This is my part in the affair. I am not the mover in the business, nor, I may say, a participant, for Anne selected her course without consulting with me. She placed him where he is. But now let me say, my dear father, without I beseech your having my motives impugned, that Anne has done right. Theodore endangered the lives of all in the house with him. He was worse than he ever had been. But he is now doing better. To look at him was enough to melt the heart. His health wasting away, his face pale and emaciated. The day exhausted in forming suspicions of plots and conspiracies, the night in ceaseless and terrible alarms. Let me say, with a full knowledge of what I owe to you and to my mother, that we should allow the best physicians to operate with this most subtle and distressing disorder. When he was in the Hospital before, his health was reestablished and his mind certainly improved. Let us then curb our feelings and not destroy our brother and our child by mistimed affection. If the malady is a great affliction to us all, and the most awful calamity to which a human being is subject, then let the remedies be applied with proportionate care. Let the wisest men and the most skillful in cures take our patient under their charge. I have every hope, and others entertain hope also that Theodore will be eventually cured, if left in the Hospital. His disorder, from being confined to a few subjects has, I think, become more general, and I hope unsettled. At all events we ought never to resign hope; and the experience of mankind informs us that the living and discipline of a Hospital are the best remedies for the disease. Is the discipline, even when the worst, as painful as the amputation of a limb, and shall we do less to preserve our mind than our body? But you know the truth of what I write and my mother too will adopt it, I hope; for I think if she will reflect upon Theodore's case, she will recognize the exact coincidence with it of what I write. Theodore is now doing well, and I, at least, feel much better satisfied with what is going on for his good than when he was at large, a source of mortification and affliction to you and his friends, and in a progress to the gradual but complete destruction of his mind, his health, and happiness.

MR. CLAY TO FRANCIS BROOKE.

WASHINGTON, December 16, 1833.

MY DEAR SIR,—I addressed a letter to you at Richmond, but understand that you are at St. Julien, to which I direct this letter.

We were highly gratified to-day in the Senate. We carried the appointment of every chairman of the committees as we wished; and as far as we proceeded, every member of the several committees, with one unimportant exception. There is a fair prospect of our having in the Senate a majority of twenty-six or twenty-seven.

Whether it will be practicable to rescue the Government and public liberty from the impending dangers, which Jacksonism has created, depends, in my opinion, mainly upon the South; and the course of the South will be guided mainly by Virginia. Hence the very great importance of this State taking a patriotic direction. I understand that you are thought of for the Chief Magistrate. I know the sacrifices you must make, if you except that station; but can not you make them? "What is a public man worth who is not ready to sacrifice himself for his country?" Depend upon it, that every thing for which you fought, or which you and I hold valuable, in public concerns, is in imminent hazard. By means of the Veto, the power as exercised of removing from office, the possession of the public treasures, and the public patronage, the living existence of liberty and the Government is, in my judgment, in peril.

I mean myself to open and push a vigorous campaign. It is the campaign of 1777. I want aid—all the aid that can be given. I mean—which will surprise you—to be very prudent, but very resolute. Can you not assist us?

ERASTUS ROOT TO MR. CLAY.

DELHI, January 12, 1834.

DEAR SIR,—I have read your speeches on the removal of the Deposits with much pleasure and deep interest. I perceive in them that force of argument and that commanding eloquence which I was wont to witness in former days, in the efforts of Henry Clay, in the cause of liberty and the Constitution.

When, my dear sir, will the mad career of the "military

chieftain" be checked? or is it never to meet with a check? Will a thoughtless multitude, led on or encouraged by knavish politicians, always sing pæans of praise to the usurpations of a despot, if emblazoned with military renown? I fear the splendid and enormous bribe he has seized, and is now distributing, will insure the object of his wishes—the succession to his throne.

Under the Constitution, as now understood, is the Secretary of the Treasury an officer impeachable for high crimes and misdemeanors? Can the instrument be convicted of the crime it has perpetrated? He might be forfeited as a deodand.

In your speeches on this occasion, I discover the same ardent patriotism, the same devotion to public and personal liberty which I so much admired when associated with you in the House of Representatives; but from what you hinted to me last winter, I have some reason to fear that when the repeal of the Force bill shall come under consideration, in your House, you will cause me to regret a blot in your bright escutcheon. You were not present on the final passage of that odious bill, but I got the idea (I hope an erroneous one) that had you been present, you might have voted for it. With the sword and the purse, and that bill at his command, an American Cæsar might sink into comparative insignificance that puny whipster of a Cæsar whom you so eloquently described as swaying the final destinies of Rome. A part, and the most odious part, of the Force bill, I believe, will expire with the present session, but the Statute Book ought to be purged of that foul stain.

MR. CLAY TO FRANCIS BROOKE.

WASHINGTON, January 14, 1834.

MY DEAR SIR,—I received your favor of the 12th. That written by you early in December never came to hand, and I regret it. As to the repeal of the Force bill, there are parts of it which are permanent, and which, in my judgment, ought to remain, independent of and distinct from any excitement in South Carolina. The two sections (the first and fifth) contain some provisions, to which I objected on their passage. If the repeal of them were asked, not on the ground of the truth of the principles of nullification, but as expedient, since the necessity for them has passed by, to tranquillize the South, it might not be objectionable, although, even in that view, those parts of the act expiring with the present session, by express limitation, there is no great utility in the repeal. But it is not asked on any other ground than that nullification is right, and to that I can not assent. If I could forget myself and my principles so much as to adopt those of nullification, it would prove my utter ruin as a public man. Nullification is every where in the minority but in South Carolina. In Kentucky, it can not hold up its head. And I think Mr. Calhoun has been unfortunate in stirring this matter, which had better be left to sleep quietly.

What is doing in your Legislature about the deposits? We want all aid here on that subject which can be given us from Richmond. What has been done there has been of immense service to us. Virginia is herself again, and has once more the power to rally around her standard the friends of freedom. But bold, determined conduct on her part is necessary; and particularly on the subject of the public treasury. If she now falters or falls back, it would have been better that she should have never excited any hopes; for then we might have all sunk quietly into the abyss of despotism.

MR. CLAY TO FRANCIS BROOKE.

WASHINGTON, February 10, 1834.

MY DEAR SIR,—I should have written you oftener, but for the best reason in the world, that I had really nothing to write that was interesting.

The debate on the deposits continues. We are gaining both in public opinion and in number in the House of Representatives. We are probably still there in a minority, although the majority is not large, and will melt away if the current of public opinion continues to mix with us.

I transmit you a letter in answer to one I received. I wish you to read and deliver it, unless you think I had better not have it delivered. We are here so accustomed to vetos, that I voluntarily, you see, subject my letter to yours.

Our city is full of distress committees. The more the better.

MR. TAZEWELL TO MR. CLAY.

NORFOLK, February 19, 1834.

DEAR SIR,—An absence from this place for some weeks past has prevented me from receiving your favor of the 1st instant, until a short time since. I now hasten to reply to it, merely to give you some evidence of the consideration with which I regard any communication of yours. The opinion you asked of me upon the abstract question you proposed, even if entitled to more respect than my opinions ought ever to receive from you, can be of but little value now, when all the difficulties we encounter proceed from the practical operation of measures, which, whether they may be traced to usurpation or to the mere abuse of power, reach the same actual results. But as you have asked my opinion, I will give it to you freely.

Many years ago, soon after I became a member of the Senate, and before you last entered that body, I was under the necessity of discussing this question at large; and to that end I then examined it very carefully. The result of this examination was the conviction of my own mind, that all the executive power created by the Federal Constitution was confided thereby to the President, to be exercised by him at his discretion, and upon his high responsibility, except in the cases of appointments and of treaties, if indeed the latter may be considered as an executive power under this Constitution. In this opinion the majority of the Senate then concurred.

Under this view of the subject, it seemed to me of little use to inquire, in regard to the power of removal from office, whether this was a substantive power or one merely accessorial to the power of appointment. For, as it was clearly an executive power, if it was a substantive power, it would then be embraced in the general Grant of all executive power, which, by the Constitution, is given to the President; and if it was but an accessorial power, it must follow its principal, and appertain to the same functionary, to whom the principal power of appointment was granted by the Constitution in terms, although in the exercise of the power of appointment, he was required to consult his advisory council, the Senate.

This conclusion seemed to me the more apparent when I adverted to the other powers that are, obviously, merely accessorial to the power of appointment, such as the power of nominating to office, and of commissioning. No one could suppose that the Senate enjoyed either of these powers, although the Constitution required of the President to obtain their advice and consent, before he could exercise his power of appointment. The only reason for this is, that while the Constitution exacts of the President the duty of consulting the Senate in all cases of appointment, it imposes upon him no such obligation with regard to nominations or commissions. Then, as the exclusive right of the President to these new auxiliary powers must be conceded, I could discover no reason for denying to him the similar right to the other auxiliary power of removal, as to which also the Constitution was equally silent.

The treaty-making power, too, seemed to me to furnish a strong illustration of the correctness of my position. Whether, under the Federal Constitution, this ought to be considered as an executive or legislative power, in either case it must carry with it the accessorial powers of negotiation and ratification. Now although the consent of the Senate was required to give validity to every treaty, yet none could suppose that the advice of this body was requisite to justify the President in commencing a negotiation, or that he was bound to ratify a treaty because the Senate had consented that this might be done.

In the course of this debate, it was said by some Senator, that whatever might be the case elsewhere, under the Federal Constitution, the power of appointment was not an executive power, but belonged to an anomalous class, because it was confided to other depositaries than the executive; that being an anomalous power, all its incidents must partake of this character, and appertain to the same depositaries to whom the principal power was intrusted by the Constitution.

I could not admit the general character of the depositary to be the proper test by which to ascertain the nature of the power confided, especially as all our Constitutions furnished many examples of the grants of power admitted to be purely executive to mere legislative or judicial functionaries. It seemed to me more correct to say that the character of the depositary was changed *quo ad hoc*, than that of the power granted. I denied, therefore, that the power of appointment was an anomalous power, and contended that it was strictly executive. I could not admit either that this power of appointment was confided to the Senate, merely because the President was required to consult them before he exercised it effectually. As well might it be said, that the veto allowed to the President by the Constitution constituted him a part of the Legislature. In either case, the powers granted were negative, and not positive, and therefore could not be considered as active powers, which all legislative and executive powers must be. The Senate, in the case of appointments, were authorized to give or to withhold their consent when asked by the President; but they had no authority to proffer their advice unasked; nor was the President bound to follow it when properly given, although he could not act without it. Therefore, the power appertained to him and not to them. I could not discern how the character of the power granted, let this be ascertained how it might, could influence in any way the question of incidental authority. The accessory must follow its principal, whatever might be the name or nature of that principal. If they are once separated, and the powers confided to different hands, the accessory changes its character immediately, and becomes a new principal power, the matrix of other incidents. Otherwise, the greatest absurdities, and the most irreconcileable conflicts, would ensue.

But I will not fatigue you with any further repetition of the arguments then urged, except to say that it appeared to me manifestly absurd to regard the President as responsible for the acts of subordinate agents, and yet to deny to him the uncontrolled power of supervising them, and of removing them from office whenever they had lost his confidence.

While announcing these opinions, justice to myself requires of me to add, that in claiming for the President the exclusive right to all the executive power created by the Federal Constitution, I hold him accountable to Congress, to the people, and to the States, for every misuse of the discretionary power so granted to him. Believing that all the powers of all our Governments are derivative and not sovereign, I can not recognize any other than a mere verbal distinction between the abuse and the usurpation of any power. None can have the right to do wrong, although in cases where no tribunal exists to determine what is wrong, the mere possession of power must necessarily be regarded as the sole evidence of the right to use it at will. But in this country, where all political powers are granted, and therefore limited, there always exists a tribunal competent to decide upon the legitimate extent of powers. Here, then, the abuse of power granted is both in kind and in degree, an equal offense with the usurpation of power not granted, unless we could conceive the impossible case of power granted to be abused.

I have never heard any so wild as to claim for the President any other executive powers than such as are created by the Federal Constitution. Nor have I supposed that any could be so foolish as to regard what is called executive power in England, or in any other country, as the measure and standard of such power here. The absurdity of such a pretension is so monstrous, that I can not consider it as meriting any serious refutation. Once admit it to be true, and the Constitution would become a dead letter. We should then be sent abroad to learn the nature of our own Government, and might soon see the President proroguing, or even dissolving Congress at his pleasure, nay, creating a peerage, declaring war, and concluding treaties, without consulting any other department of the Government.

It will always give me pleasure to hear from you. Our principles may not, perhaps, be in exact accordance, nor shall we always agree in the application of those in which we do concur. But we have each seen so much of the world now as not to consider such diversities as either injurious to its interests, or as constituting any proper cause to disturb relations that, with us, have been of long standing.

MR. CLAY TO FRANCIS BROOKE.

WASHINGTON, March 10, 1834.

MY DEAR SIR,—I received your favor of the 6th inst., as I did that about the Compiler, with the subscription money which Mr. R. declined.

I should write you oftener, but that I have really nothing of interest to communicate. Almost daily, too, I express in the Senate what I have to say on public affairs.

The view taken by the writer in "The Whig," as to the effect of either House not concurring in the sufficiency of the reasons of the Secretary of the Treasury, had not escaped me. It would be conclusive, if the act of removing the public deposits was conditional, but it is a perfect and performed act, before the reasons are communicated to Congress. I have always believed that if both houses concurred in pronouncing the insufficiency of those reasons, it would, without any further or other legislative action, become the duty of the Secretary to restore them, and I have wished to be able to think that such would be his duty, if either House disagreed with him. But if one House agree, and the other disagree, is not the result a state of neutrality?

We shall look to the issue of your approaching election with very great anxiety.

MR. CLAY TO FRANCIS BROOKE.

WASHINGTON, April 17, 1834.

MY DEAR SIR,—I leave here to-day for the Virginia Springs, on account of Mrs. Clay's health, which continues feeble and precarious. I shall return as soon as I can leave her with propriety. My own situation requires also relaxation. I feel very much prostrated. I hope I shall be able soon to return to my post with re-invigorated health.

We are very thankful for the kind invitation contained in your letter of the 13th, but the condition of Mrs. Clay at present, is such, that she would only be a burden at St. Julien, without being able to enjoy its pleasures. I transmitted to you at Richmond some letters from New York, communicating the issue of the great three days' contest. It is felt by both parties here, as the precursor of the complete overthrow of Jacksonism.

We are still anxious about your elections, but feel confident of their being no variation from the last Legislature, in the aggregate result.

The nullifiers are doing us no good here. You will have seen a badly-reported speech of mine, in answer to Mr. Calhoun.

MR. CLAY TO FRANCIS BROOKE.

WASHINGTON, March 23, 1834.

MY DEAR SIR,—I received your favor, transmitting a copy of the address of the minority of your Legislature. It did not strike me as possessing much ability, but on some points was very weak and vulnerable. I am not aware that any answer to it from this place will be attempted.

I received also your subsequent favor.

Things remain in *statu quo* here. There is a small, but as yet inflexible majority, sustaining the Executive in the House. If the elections in Virginia and New York, should be adverse to the Administration, that majority probably will be changed, but in an opposite event, it may be increased. Mr. Van Buren yesterday offered to bet me a suit of clothes upon each of the elections in the city of New York and in your State. The Administration party is very confident, and our friends are not without fears as to the issue of matters with you. It is with politics as with the currency. In certain states of both, a slight circumstance produces much effect. We were not prepared here for the unfortunate result in Bouldin district. It depressed our side, and elevated the other, far beyond what such an event would have done at any other time.

What are your real prospects? I should confide much in your judgment. Would you like to take up Van's bet?

I told him yesterday, that if the people entertained the Administration in its late measures, I should begin to fear that our experiment of free Government had failed; that he would probably be elected the successor of Jackson; that he would introduce a system of intrigue and corruption, that would enable him to designate his successor; and that, after a few years of lingering and fretful existence, we should end in dissolution of the Union, or in despotism. He laughed, and remarked that I entertained morbid feelings. I replied, with good nature, that what I had said, I deliberately and sincerely believed.

ALEXANDER COFFIN TO MR. CLAY.

HUDSON, NEW YORK, May 12, 1834.

SIR,—Nearly a century has passed over my head; and, although I have witnessed, with much apprehension for the result, many hazardous scenes which my dear native country has struggled through in that time, not one has excited that trembling sense of alarm which the measures of the present Executive have done. I have remarked, in their whole course, an unbridled lust of power, that attacked the very foundation of our free institutions. And, notwithstanding, a temperament naturally sanguine leads me to contemplate things under a cheering aspect, when I beheld his bold claims to lawless power sustained by men in whom I had placed trust. I confess a very gloomy prospect of the future presented itself; my spirit sunk within me; and I began "to despair of the Republic." But, thanks be to God, who breathed into a phalanx of good men in the Senate of the United States, a spirit to breast the storm; and has enabled them, as I hope, to rescue the country from the danger that impended over it. Allow me to testify to you, sir, as a distinguished individual in that phalanx, my respect, together with my thanks, for the very important share you bore in that conflict; and also, to tender my most hearty congratulations upon the prospect we now enjoy of seeing the Constitution and laws, redeemed from the grasp of usurpation, restored to healthy action.

May I beg you to accept, from a man far advanced in his 94th year, the cane which will be handed you herewith, as a token of his gratitude for your eminent services rendered to our beloved country? It was made from the jawbone of a spermaceti whale, the head from a tooth of the same, by the mate of a ship belonging to one of my grandsons, upon her homeward passage from the Pacific.

JOHN NITCHIE TO MR. CLAY.

AMERICAN BIBLE SOCIETY, NEW YORK,
July 5, 1834.

SIR,—It affords me much pleasure to inclose to you a certificate of your membership for life in this society. The occasion of your being made a Life Member you will find from the extract of the letter of the individual making the needful contribution which is copied on the back of the certificate.

Permit me, respected sir, in the name of the benevolent, but anonymous donor, to ask your acceptancy of this compliment; and also, to assure you, of my earnest desire that you and yours may have an eternal interest in the promises of that blessed Book, which it is the design of this Society to spread abroad among the nations of this fallen world.

Extract of a letter to John Nitchie, General Agent and Assistant Treasurer of the American Bible Society, dated July 3, 1834.

DEAR FRIEND,—I send you the sum of thirty dollars, which I will thank you to present to the managers of the American Bible

Society, to be devoted by them to the circulation of the Holy Scriptures.

In consequence of this contribution, you will please enroll the name of the Honorable Henry Clay, of the United States Senate, among your Life Members.

The above is from a friend, which has arisen from the continued savings of a Missionary, by his laying aside portions of fees and presents at the time they were received; the entire amount of fees received on Sunday and Thursday of every week, also, free-will offerings under peculiar Providences: one tenth of his regular salary, and one tenth of the balance of his receipts during the year over his family expenses.

You will please forward to Mr. Clay, a certificate of his Life Membership; also, beg him to lay aside a portion of his income, and thus constitute in like manner, at least one of his friends, a Life Member of your important society, and in so doing, I would beg him to request that friend thus constituted, to constitute some other individual a Life Member. In this way passing the excitement round from friend to friend, an amount of good will accumulate, which the full glories of the Eternal World alone can unfold.

This is to certify, that Honorable HENRY CLAY, of the United States Senate, by virtue of a contribution of thirty dollars, made by a clergyman of the Protestant Episcopal Church, is a Member for Life of the AMERICAN BIBLE SOCIETY, New York, July 5th, 1834.

JOHN COTTON SMITH, *President.*
J. N. BRIGHAM, *Cor. Secretary.*

Attest—JOHN NITOHIE, *General Agent and Assistant Treasurer.*

FRANCIS LIEBER TO MR. CLAY.

PHILADELPHIA, November 8, 1834.

MY DEAR SIR,—I feel convinced that you will not ascribe my delay in answering your favor to any unsubstantial reason; on the contrary, I did not write immediately, because I was desirous of writing to you as definitely as possible. My wish is to see you in Lexington, and to become personally acquainted with the College, etc., as well as to give those, who might desire to engage me for the College, an opportunity of personal acquaintance. The salary, as you yourself intimate, is not large, and I should not be able to incur the expenses of removing thither, and furnishing there my house again, if I had not some hopes of being able to have some young gentlemen living in my house.

I should ere this have set out for Lexington, had I not actually been engaged in the publication of a work, which made my stay here indispensable.

I send you in the mean time a testimonial, such as you mention. If more are desired, I may send more from here, as Messrs. Joseph Ingersoll, Sergeant, N. Biddle, Richard Peters, or in fact any gentleman of note here or in Boston, might be applied to.

If you should make a trip to Philadelphia, in the course of this winter, I would beg you to send me word that you are in town (in case that you should be here only for a day or two); you would greatly favor me with a personal interview.

Politics seem, this moment, so sickening, that we avoid speaking of them, whenever possible. News, of the very worst kind, are here from New York. We are already in a revolution, as nations so often are long before they know it. "The Globe" plays very cheering preludes with regard to attacks upon the Supreme Court. My letters from Europe are of the worst kind, with reference to the moral influence of our general affairs on those of rational freedom, and the sway of law in that part of the world.

A letter from you, though it consist but in a few lines, is always a great delight to me; and you will much oblige me by informing me whether this letter has not perhaps missed you. Please present my best respects to Mrs. Clay, who, I trust, has continued to improve in health.

NICHOLAS BIDDLE TO MR. CLAY.

PHILADELPHIA, January 4, 1835.

MY DEAR SIR,—I have been thinking for some days past whether the time had not come when another interposition of yours is not needed to save the country from great trouble. In all this French negotiation, mismanaged as it has been from the beginning, nothing is so inexplicable as the manner in which the overture of France has been treated, and I have been looking for some movement from you for the production of all that will be told of that communication. You know, I presume, the contents of it—if you have not seen it all; at any rate, you are sufficiently aware of the dates and circumstances, which would enable you to make a distinct call. If I do not mistake, Mr. Pageot communicated it on the 11th of September, a few days before the orders went which will occasion Mr. Barton's return.

On the 2d of December he sent it with a letter to the Department, and although it was sent back, yet his letter might be called for.

It seems to me that this dispatch of the Duke de Broglie ought to have settled the matter in five minutes; and yet the country is to be cursed with a quarrel in which every disadvantage is on our side.

If there is any thing connected with it which you wish to know, I think I can obtain the information; and I forbear to add any thing, because I am under the impression that you are apprised of the whole. Had you been at the head of the Government, and the French ministry had said that they would deem that a happy day, when they would be able to surrender this sum deposited in their hands, you would certainly have thrown no unnecessary obstacle in their way.

CHANCELLOR KENT TO MR. CLAY.

NEW YORK, January 9, 1835.

MY DEAR SIR,—Let me remind you to send me, when printed, one of the twenty thousand copies of your Report. I rather guess I shall like it. Like it! why, God bless you, I sympathize with you in all your public feelings and doings since the beginning of the reign of the present dynasty. My prayer is, that length of days may be in your right hand, and in your left hand riches and honor.

ELEUTH COOKE TO MR. CLAY.

SANDUSKY CITY, January 22, 1835.

DEAR SIR,—I can not withhold from you the heartfelt expression of applause with which the Report of the Committee on

Foreign Relations, in reference to our affairs with France, has been received in this quarter. All see, and most acknowledge, in it the evidence of that enlightened patriotism and consummate statesmanship which have more than once elevated the character of our country, and rescued it from impending dangers. Whatever has been, and whatever may continue to be, the measure of injustice and ingratitude to its author, by that country, now thrice saved by his wisdom, posterity can not fail to assign him ample justice on her brightest page.

Excuse this frankness; you know it is not flattery. I speak from the midst of those who at all times, and through all changes, have been your fixed and steadfast friends, not from a sordid hope of favor, but from an admiration of your exalted talents, your lofty independence, and a love of your principles.

God knows what we are to do to preserve our country. Pressed as you must be with public duties, I dare not ask you (confidentially) what are the prospects?

MR. MADISON TO MR. CLAY.

Montpelier, January 31, 1835.

Dear Sir,—Perceiving that I am indebted to you for a copy of your Report on our Relations with France, I beg you to accept this return of my thanks for it. The document is as able in its execution as it is laudable in its object of avoiding war without incurring dishonor.

It must be the wish of all that the issue may correspond with the object. But may not a danger of rupture lurk under the conflicting grounds taken on the two sides? That taken by the Message, and by the Report also, in a softened tone, that the treaty is binding on France, and is in no event to be touched; and the ground taken, or likely to be taken by France, with feelings roused by the peremptory alternative of compliance or self-redress, that the treaty is not binding on her, appealing for the fact to the structure of her Government, which all nations treating with her are presumed and bound to understand.

It may be well for both parties if France should have yielded before the arrival of the Message, or not decided before that of the Report, or, at least, should not be inflexible in rejecting the terms of the treaty. A war between the two nations, which may cost them many millions, for a stake not exceeding a few, would be an occurrence peculiarly unpropitious to the cause of popular representation in the present crisis of the political world.

War is the more to be avoided, if it can be done without inadmissible sacrifices, as a maritime war, to which the United States should be a party, and Great Britain neutral, has no aspect which is not of an ominous cast. Enforce the belligerent rights of search and seizure against British ships, and it would be a miracle if serious collisions did not ensue. Allow them the rule of " free ships, free goods," and the flag covers the property of France and enables her to employ all her naval resources against us. The tendency of the new rules in favor of the neutral flag is to displace the mercantile marine of nations at war, by neutral substitutes, and to confine the war on water as on land to the regular force ; a revolution friendly to humanity as lessening the temptations to war and the severity of its operations, but giving an advantage to the nations which keep up large navies in time of peace over nations dispensing with them, or compelling the latter to follow the burdensome example. France has at present this advantage over us in the extent of public ships now, or that may immediately be brought into service, while the privilege of the neutral flag would deprive us of the cheap and efficient aid of privateers.

I do not relinquish the hope, however, that these views of the subject will be obviated by amicable and honorable adjustment.

Should the course of your movements at any time approach Montpelier, I need not express the pleasure which a call from you would give to Mrs. Madison and myself.

JOHN BROWN TO MR. CLAY.

FRANKFORT, April 20, 1835.

Mr. C. J. Ingersol has given me the melancholy intelligence of the death of my dear brother.* You may imagine, but it would be impossible for me to express how deeply, how painfully my feelings have been excited by this event. I understand that Charles Ingersol and my niece are absent on a jour-

* James Brown, brother-in-law of Mr. Clay, and his correspondent for thirty years.

ney for her health, and as I do not know that any person in Philadelphia has authority to take charge of my brother's effects, I have concluded that it was expedient that I should go on to attend to that business. It is certainly important that his papers shall be carefully preserved, and that his private correspondence shall not be exposed. I presume he has left a will, but know not who he has named executors. If you can give me any information on this subject, I pray you to drop me a line by mail, and advise me how to proceed and inform what you would wish to have done. I expect to set out on Wednesday, or Thursday at furthest.

STUDENTS OF WASHINGTON COLLEGE TO MR. CLAY.

WASHINGTON, Pennsylvania, May 16, 1835.

SIR,—We take great pleasure, as a Committee of the "Clay Institute of Washington College," in communicating your election as an honorary member of our Association.

We offer you this inadequate testimonial of our esteem, not, we hope, from a spirit of man-worship, but from an honest admiration of your virtues as a statesman, a philanthropist, and a man. We do not expect that by it we will confer honor upon you, but rather, as was said in the epitaph of a distinguished poet, " That you will confer honor upon us."

Permit us, sir, to request your acceptance of this humble tribute, and of our warmest wishes for your happiness through life.

HARRIET MARTINEAU TO MR. CLAY.

WHITE SULPHUR SPRINGS, June 30.

DEAR MR. CLAY,—Your frank, which overtook me at Cincinnati, was highly acceptable on its own account, as well as for the very delightful letters it inclosed from my mother and the Furnesses. My mother is in excellent health and spirits, and Mr. Furness writes me the happy news that his family will be in the neighborhood of Boston, and that he will preach there during the month of August, at least.

We enjoyed our ten days' visit at Cincinnati very much, and found your kind introductions of eminent service. We staid longer there than we had intended, from finding it impossible to travel at all in the interior of the State. A gentleman escaped out of the mud to his home, at last, after traveling at the rate of one mile an hour—a process which does not suit the taste or convenience of Miss Jeffery or myself. Our voyage and journey hither were quite prosperous, and the only disappointment we have met with is the non-arrival of Mr. and Mrs. Smith. As we see and hear nothing of them, and as the Lorings are obliged to go (by Mr. L.'s physician's advice) to the Hot Springs, where we do not want to go, we have accepted the offer of Mr. and Mrs. Sullivan of Boston, to travel together as far as Harper's Ferry. They have engaged an extra, which will afford us plenty of room, and have stipulated to be eight days on the road, seeing the Natural Bridge and Weir's Cave, by the way. As we are not in need of imbibing sulphur, and this pretty place is soon understood, we have no hesitation in embracing so very advantageous a plan of traveling, though it takes us away tomorrow. The Lorings flew to meet us on our arrival yesterday, and we find quite a throng of friends here from the Atlantic cities, and could make ourselves happy for a month, if we could stay so long. We shall leave our Philadelphia address in the post-office, in case of the arrival of any letters; but we expect no more from you. I almost hope there may be none, we have given you so much trouble already.

Mr. Calwell will be most happy to see you; and in the mean while, all has been done to fulfill your request about making us comfortable. We shall never forget how much we owe to yourself and very many of your friends to render our stay in this country happy. We shall always love Mr. and Mrs. Erwin like near and dear connections of our own. I hope Mrs. Clay and Mrs. Erwin are both better. Pray present our respects and love to all your circle, and believe me, dear sir, ever respectfully and gratefully your friend.

P. S. Mr. Prather has been here a few days, improving hourly in health. He requests me to mention the safe arrival of the party, and that they are anxiously looking for Mr. and Mrs. Smith. I have been introduced to Mr. P. since I wrote the first part of this letter.

I have also been weighed; and find my ponderosity to be one hundred and sixteen pounds;—within two of Mr. Erwin's guess;

and Louisa weighs one hundred and ten. So now you know another important circumstance about us. Poor Mrs. Loring weighs only eighty-five pounds. Mr. L's. eyes are no better. This P. S. is for Mr. Erwin, if you will be kind enough to show it to him.

MR. CLAY TO ———.*

ASHLAND, July 14, 1835.

DEAR SIR,—I received last night your favor of the 8th instant. Having experienced the constancy and fidelity of your friendly attachment to me, and entertaining a high opinion of your discretion and judgment, I shall answer it with all the frankness and freedom with which I would address any friend, on the interesting subject of the next Presidential election.

After the result of the election of 1832, I have felt no desire to have my name again presented as a candidate, unless I was satisfied that it was the wish of a probable majority of the people of the United States. Under the influence of this feeling, far from encouraging any movements in my favor, I have, in several instances, dissuaded them from being made, when I was consulted. I have indeed sometimes thought, since that period, that a state of things might arise which would induce a majority of the people to turn their attention toward me; but it has not occurred. It is possible that if the Whigs had manifested no inclination toward other candidates, and had thought proper to have adhered to me, such a state of things might have arisen. But the solicitude of other gentlemen, perhaps more entitled than I am to be chosen Chief Magistrate, and the discouragement of the use of my name, resulting from the issue of the last contest, have led respectable portions of the Whigs, in different States, to direct their views to other candidates than myself. The truth is that I was strongly disinclined to be presented as a candidate in 1832, fearing the issue which took place, but I was overruled by friends, some of whom have since thought it expedient, in consequence of that very event, that another name should be substituted for mine.

Without meaning to pass my opinion upon the measure adopted by the Whig members of your Legislature, at the last winter session, except in regard to its operation upon the prospects of

* The latter part of this letter, with its address, is lost.

my election, I must say that I think it was highly injurious to those prospects. Ohio had been considered as a State which (Jackson out of the way) would certainly bestow her suffrage on me, if I were a candidate. It was believed, and probably is yet believed, that no candidate would unite so much strength in opposition to Mr. Van Buren as I could. When, therefore, it was seen that Ohio, instead of manifesting a disposition to support me, was disposed, through her Legislature, to bring forward another gentleman, it exhibited a division in our party, and a distrust of the extent of my strength which had an unfavorable effect on my pretensions. There were many too who could not see the policy or propriety of selecting, as a candidate, a gentleman who was an original friend of Jackson, in preference to all who had been uniform in opposition to him. The principle, on which such a selection was founded, looked too much to support expected to be derived from the Jackson ranks, without sufficiently estimating the amount that might be lost in our own from positive aversion, or apathy and indifference.

I have never said that I would not consent, under any circumstances, to be a candidate. I have said that I did not wish to be a candidate, except on the condition before mentioned, that is, that I was desired by a probable majority of the country, or at least that there was strong reason to believe that I should not be again defeated. I could not have declared that my name should not be used, in any contingency, without violating a principle of public duty, which subjects the services of every citizen of the country to the call of the majority. But I have reserved to myself the right of controlling and arresting, as far as I could, any movement which might be attempted in my behalf that was likely to end in defeat.

I must now, in frankness, say that the condition on which I should be willing to be run has not heretofore existed, and does not seem to me now to exist. I have no reason to believe that I should be elected if I were brought forward; none to think that I am the wish of the majority of the people. And it is repugnant to my feelings and sense of propriety to be voluntarily placed in an attitude in which I would seem to be importuning the public for an office which it is not willing to confer. It is possible indeed, as many of my friends think, and so I am inclined to believe from the information I possess, that, if I were the only Whig candidate in opposition to Mr. Van Buren, I would receive a greater support than any other; but I apprehend it would fall short of securing my election.

I have appropriated too much of this letter to myself, the least important part of yours. But I will now give you my candid views as to the state of the country and the best policy, as it seems to me, for the Whigs to pursue.

I will not take up time in dwelling on the calamity of Mr. Van Buren's election. It is enough for me to express my conviction that it would lead to a system of general corruption, and end in a subversion of the Union.

I feel too with you the absolute necessity to secure his defeat, of union and concert among those who are opposed to him. Can that union and concert be produced on Judge White? I think not, for a reason already stated. He has been throughout a supporter of Jackson's administration, and holds no one principle (except in the matter of patronage) as to public measures in common with the Whigs. Although for other reasons he is to be preferred to Van Buren. I apprehend that it would be impossible, if we were to take him up as our candidate, to infuse among our friends the spirit and zeal necessary to insure success, especially in States where internal improvements and the American system have been popular. The Judge, however, seems to be the favorite of the South and South-west; and, from all the lights which we possess, it is probable that he will obtain their undivided support. At least it is so probable as to make it a justifiable basis of future calculation.

While Mr. Webster has attainments greatly superior to those of any other nominated candidate, it is to be regretted that a general persuasion seems to exist that he stands no chance. I believe that, if he stood a fair chance elsewhere, by great effort, the vote of this State might be given to him. In this opinion, however, I differ from many of my friends.

General Harrison could easier obtain the vote of Kentucky than any other candidate named. Judge McLean has not recently been much spoken of, was never generally popular here, but against Van Buren perhaps he might obtain the vote of Kentucky.

You will say this is not a very favorable account of the prospects of the several candidates opposed to Mr. Van Buren. It is not, and I regret it, but I believe it to be true.

What then is to be done? Nothing toward an union upon

either of them by public assemblies, in my opinion, until after the election in Pennsylvania. Great confidence exists that the Jackson candidate for Governor there will be defeated, and as great that, in that event, the State will not support Mr. Van Buren. Mr. Webster's friends, General Harrison's, and Judge M'Lean's, each persuade themselves that the vote of the State will be given to their favorite. Now, if we can have reasonable assurance that Pennsylvania will support either of them, I should think it would be our true policy to rally upon that one, and employ all our energies to give him as great an amount of support as possible.

There would then be three candidates: Mr. Van Buren, Mr. White, and the Pennsylvania favorite. And if White gets the South and South-west vote, or nearly all of it, and Pennsylvania and the Whig States North of the Potomac, and in the West, including Louisiana, unite on a candidate, he would enter the House with the largest vote, and Van Buren might have the smallest vote of the three.

I agree with you that whoever is returned to the House will be elected. If his plurality is considerable, after the experience which we have had, and upon general principles, it is desirable that he should be chosen.

On a late occasion of a public dinner, given to Governor Poindexter, I avowed publicly my opinion in opposition to Mr. Van Buren. This I should not have done, but for the report that I favored his pretensions in a contest with Judge White, which was industriously circulated. You will see what I said in the public papers. The truth is, that I think the election of either Mr. Van Buren or Judge White would be a great misfortune, although that of the Judge would be the least. I did not express my preference between the other candidates, which it appeared to me improper to do. But I have no hesitation in saying to you that either Mr. Webster, General Harrison, or Judge

* * * * * * *

LOUISA CAROLINE JEFFERY TO MR. CLAY.

NEW YORK, July 19, 1835.

MY DEAR SIR,—Will you allow "little insignificant me" (to parody Miss Kemble's words) to answer your last kind letter addressed to Miss Martineau? She has received safely the different letters and newspapers you kindly forwarded to her, including the parcel transmitted through Sir Charles Vaughan. Since we left the Virginia Springs, we have made a very pleasant journey through the valley to Harper's Ferry, with Mr. and Mrs. William Sullivan of Boston, visiting the Natural Bridge and Weir's Cave by the way, which objects are greatly inferior to the Falls of Niagara and the Mammoth Cave, in interest. We have been spending a few days here, visiting Long and Staten Islands, and on Tuesday morning we go up the North River to West Point, Catskill, and probably to Saratoga; thence to Stockbridge, and after visiting some of the pretty New England villages, we shall go to Boston about the 14th of August.

Miss M. received rather unfavorable accounts of the political state of England from her brother. He appears to think that the Tory influence (used in intimidating and bribing electors) will be too strong for the Whigs; that they will not carry large enough measures to satisfy the people, and there will follow that dangerous state of things, pressure from without; and to what is this Tory reaction to be attributed? To the imbecility of the Whigs, I suppose the Radicals will say. I should rather attribute it to the fears of the timid, arising from the constant complaints of the Radicals since the passage of the Reform Bill, and the confidence these disputes inspired the Tories with, that they might rise through the want of union among their opponents. Did you see that Lord Stanley asserts, on the authority of a friend at Washington (of course Mr. Murray), that Americans are all Conservative? If by Conservative he means Tory, I think he would find himself mistaken, and I can not think Mr. Murray could mean to make such an assertion. You, in the great kindness of your heart, will excuse my want of talent to condense all my matter into one page.

We feel very grateful for Judge Porter's kind regards and remembrances, and though passing through a very excellent channel, they might be still more welcome did they come more direct. When you write to him next, will you just mention that Miss M. and I sent him a joint packet, which we trust he received safely, though it was only directed, Attacapas, La. Give my very kind love to Mrs. Erwin; tell her I trust she will pardon me for my neglect in not writing to her ere this, but she shall certainly have my impressions of Yankee land.

I feel very grateful that my name is joined with my companion in the recollections of the kind and excellent inhabitants of Woodlands and Ashland. Some of my most pleasing associations are connected with my visit to Lexington. I am fully aware I have no claim on your very valuable time, but if, in the exceeding benevolence of your heart, you put pen to paper and honor me with a few lines, to tell us how our very good friends are and something of their thoughts and feelings, I shall feel more grateful than any lady in whose album you have written, inasmuch as a few words from Mr. Clay's heart are worth pages of his handwriting, though that has its value. I do not give you so difficult a subject to treat on as "the compatibility of the Roman Catholic religion with freedom."

We shall be much pleased to meet Mr. and Mrs. Smith. We are much grieved to hear of Mrs. Clay's continuous indisposition. Remember us most kindly to her, and our best love to the dear inhabitants of Woodlands; and, with our united kind regards and grateful recollections to yourself, believe me yours, etc.

JAMES BARBOUR TO MR. CLAY.

BARBOURSVILLE, August 2, 1835.

On the subject of politics, since our retrograde movement in April, in this State, I have desponded almost to despair. That our jugglers should succeed in seducing the people into a belief that it was premature to discuss the Presidential election, and that the issue should be Leigh, the bank, instruction, and all that kind of stuff, and the moment they had succeeded, turn right round, claim a Van Buren victory, send delegates to the Rump Convention, and immediately demand of their partisans implicit obedience—and all this juggling to be acted in broad daylight, without producing an immediate and violent reaction, seems to me to render our scheme of self-government highly doubtful. Not having left my house scarcely since, personally I know but little. If there have been any changes in the State, as yet, I fear they are few. The Whigs seem generally to have determined to support White. A small accession from the Jackson ranks might give us the majority in the State, but the leaders of the latter have told their creatures that the Whigs are playing false; they wish to divide the Jacksonians, so as to bring the election into the House (of which they express a holy horror), with a view to elect Webster, yourself, or some other Whig. It is this which constitutes the most formidable obstacle to our success in this State. The running of three candidates they seize upon in confirmation of their charge, and it is this that alone gives them hopes of success here. For being apart from this weapon, and the endorsement of Jackson, would not obtain five hundred votes in the State. But I am quite satisfied that no candidate can succeed against him here, notwithstanding his unpopularity, unless it be one maintaining the favorite doctrine of the State, especially one who has been opposed, and is now opposed to the Bank. For independent of the long cherished hostility to that institution, since Jackson's hostility has been avowed, and his party acquiring success by their incessant clamor on that head, all those in pursuit of office, whatever may be their real opinions, have joined in the denunciation. Opposition, therefore, to this institution, is now a fixed maxim in the political creed of this State, as much so, as the undivided Godhead with a Mohammedan. White happens in this respect to stand well, and therefore I think is the strongest man that can be presented to Virginia. In addition to this, the slave question begins, as I learn, to excite a strong sensation among some of our people. Locality associates Van with the fanatics of his State, and it is not improbable will have a greater influence in the South, than any other circumstance in the contest. Webster is out of the question here; McLean is not thought of; Harrison, next to White, stands foremost I should conclude. It seems to me, however, on the whole, that we have no prospect of excluding Van, but by the plan you suggest of selecting two candidates that will be strongest in their respective sections. White, I apprehend for the South, Webster, for the East, North, and West, or whomsoever Pennsylvania prefers—for in my view, she holds the election in her hands. By running two popular men, we have the prospect of retaining or acquiring the ascendency in the State Government, an object of great importance, and almost a compensation for the loss of our Presidential candidate. For example, even here, we hope, through White, of regaining our ascendency, where, with an inferior candidate, we should be in a decided minority. Fortunately in Pennsylvania, the division in the Jackson ranks promises success to the Whig candidate for Governor. If he succeed it will be sovereign in the contest for President. This election occurring in October will become a beacon to us in the difficulties with which we are surrounded. With its aid, the ensuing winter, you may decide upon the best course our affairs furnish. Hence, I threw cold water on Pleasant's proposed meeting in this State for this month, and it has been prudently abandoned. Personally dissatisfied with White, I will support him only because he is a lesser evil than Van. I shall wait patiently the development of events, and be prepared to follow any course esteemed best to exclude Van. I read, and was much pleased with your remarks touching this gentleman, made at the Poindexter fête.

MR. CLAY TO JOHN BAILHACHE.

ASHLAND, September 13, 1835.

MY DEAR SIR,—I received your favor this evening of the 9th instant, returning $15 collected of me at Cincinnati, for your paper published at Columbus. I own to you that there was something in the time and circumstances under which the demand was made that gave me momentary mortification. I believed then that it was without your instructions or sanction, and your letter confirms my belief. Had the application been made to me at home, and not in the presence of strangers; had it not been made as if I were a person of doubtful integrity, it would not have excited any feeling. Your friendly letter has perfectly relieved me. It has preserved you on the ground of honor and delicacy where I had always been accustomed to regard you. The only regret I now feel is that you did not retain the sum, while you made the explanation. Although your paper was sent to me, as stated by you, and as many others have been forwarded, I ought to pay the subscription, having received the value. And you must allow me to consider myself indebted to you the amount, to be paid at some time when I shall have the pleasure of seeing you, which I hope and sincerely desire may be soon.

I shall be glad at all times to hear from you on public affairs, or any other topic. I saw a good deal of General Harrison at Cincinnati. Very little passed between us on the subject of the Presidency. He was very respectful and cordial. He appeared to be in good spirits, and I thought seemed confident. I adhere to the opinion expressed in my former letter, that, if Pennsylvania will give satisfactory demonstrations of an intention to support him, it will be expedient, under all circumstances, to run him as the most available candidate against Mr. Van Buren. The issue of the Rhode Island election following that of Connecticut, proves, I fear, that it is in vain to look even to New England for the support of Mr. Webster.

HENRY CLAY, JR., TO HIS FATHER.

BORDEAUX, September 17, 1835.

DEAR FATHER,—I send to-day by the ship Tuskina, the Spanish ass Don Manuel. Mr. Haggerty in New York will have him put upon grass until he can hear from you. I have written to him to draw upon you for the expenses of transportation. The captain carries him for $50, I finding every thing. The captain's bill, and the charges in New York and on the way to Kentucky, will be all that are to be paid. May I beg that you will meet this bill, and that you will write to James Haggerty of New York, whom you know, such directions as will be proper. The ass has been rode and he is as gentle as a dog, so that a small boy might ride him. He is a very fine ass, about thirteen and a half hands and half an inch or one inch high. I am induced to send him because the Tuskina is a large packet and the only fine one in port. I shall go in a few days to the Hautes Pyrenées department where I hope to procure some good Spanish asses. There is a mistake about them in America. The few I have seen are very handsome.

MR. CLAY TO HIS WIFE.

MAYSVILLE, November 19, 1835.

MY DEAR WIFE,—I got to Governor Metcalfe's, last night, in good time, and reached here to-day, at two o'clock. The weather has been very fine, and my ride was a very good one. They tell me that a steamboat will be here this evening, in which, when it arrives, I shall embark. I have directed Aaron to go to Governor Metcalfe's to-morrow night, and the next day home.

I feel very uneasy about our dear daughter, Anne. I sincerely hope that she may get well, and that all my apprehensions may prove groundless.

I feel too, my dear wife, most sincerely and excessively alive respecting your lonely situation. I regret it extremely, and whatever you may think to the contrary, I should have preferred, greatly, your accompanying me. But I hope and believe that this is the last separation, upon earth, that will take place, for any length of time, between us. And I hope that you will make every effort in your power to be cheerful, contented, and happy.

MR. ERWIN TO MR. CLAY.—DEATH OF MRS. ERWIN.

THE WOODLANDS, December 15, 1835.

MY DEAR SIR,—I feel myself scarcely equal to the task which my duty imposes, that of writing you at this time, and speaking of the late dreadful calamity with which it has pleased God to afflict us—by which, at the same fatal blow, has been taken from you a daughter, unequaled in filial devotion and love, and from me a wife, the most devoted, kind, and virtuous, with which man was ever blessed.

Other friends have, I learn, given you the particulars of this sad event, which will spare me the pain of presenting to you the heart-rending scene which was so unexpectedly produced by the hand of Providence.

My home, lately the happiest, which I have shared for years with a beloved wife, who returned my affection with a devotion almost unknown, who, whether I was worthy or not, honored me with a love and confidence which I would not have exchanged for the whole world beside, that home is now to me insupportable. Every object that presents itself—each tree and flower, once so dear when objects of her care—now serve only to make known to me my loss and my misery. The beloved object who gave life and animation to all, has left me to lament over my wretched fate.

You, my dear sir, I am fully sensible, can and will extend to me more sympathy than any other human being—you who best knew her exalted worth, who have daily witnessed our happiness, not surpassed, I vainly believe, in the annals of wedded life—you who shared our pleasures and our joy, who bestowed upon me the choicest gift of heaven, can feel for me, but who,

I fear, will require for yourself all the sympathy of your friends, and all the philosophy with which you are endowed, to support you under this sad bereavement. Mrs. Clay, although in reality scarcely able to support herself under this severe trial, has suppressed, as far as she was able, her own feelings, intent only in rendering to me and my dear children every kindness which her judgment and affection could suggest. She has abandoned her own home and remained with us, exerting herself to preserve the babe, which has cost us all so dear.

My children, now ten-fold more dear to me than before, afford me much consolation, yet they are the objects of my greatest solicitude; for me to remain here is impossible, and to part from any of them, at this moment, will be equally trying. Mrs. Clay at once kindly proposed taking charge of all of them, and to have Miss Brulard remove to Ashland, for the present, and teach them as before. Miss B. wishes to return South, and the plan now is, to leave the three youngest at Ashland, the babe, with Lotty and a wet nurse, under Mrs. Clay's care, and for the two boys, Henry and James, to accompany me.

I expect to leave for New Orleans two days hence. My boys will be important to me, and I shall take care not to let any feeling prevent their having the best means for their improvement afforded them.

I shall hope to hear from you very soon after I reach New Orleans.

CHAPTER X.

CORRESPONDENCE OF 1836, '37, '38, AND '39.

GOVERNOR M'DUFFIE TO MR. CLAY.

ABBEVILLE, C. H., January 27, 1836.

MY DEAR SIR,—I am from home, and you must excuse the foolscap on which I write. Perceiving the message relative to the French indemnity referred to your Committee, I am irresistibly compelled to make a suggestion or two. You again have it in your power for the third or fourth time, to save the country from a great calamity. It is perfectly obvious that if the Annual Message of December last had been permitted to reach France before any additional cause of irritation was given by the President, the indemnity would have been promptly paid by the French Executive. The king and the ministry have all along been most anxious to adjust the difficulty and pay the claim. They have had to struggle with a refractory Chamber, who have co-operated with General Jackson's weakness and folly to produce war. Now it seems to me that the course for Congress to pursue, for the interest and true honor of the country, is perfectly plain; and that is, to be as courteous and civil as the President has been rude and insulting. State, what is evidently true, a confidence that there is a desire, on the part of the king and ministry, to adjust the matter without war, and a belief that they will pay the indemnity, when they read the annual Message, and that consequently no preparations for war are necessary. I have not a doubt that such a course would insure a peaceable and prompt adjustment of the existing differences.

If war ensues, Congress must now be responsible. It will proceed from their acts, and not those of the President. Even his last Message would be nothing to France, if Congress would again adopt the course you recommended last year. If it should fail, there will still be time to prepare during the session for non-intercourse, for I can not believe a war possible. A non-intercourse act on our part would not, I am sure, lead to a declaration of war by France. They could not make it a ground of war.

I beg you, my dear Sir, to excuse this liberty. The magnitude of the interests involved must be my apology. A war with France would be utterly ruinous to the Southern States, and God knows what would be its effect upon public liberty. It would be the most signal example of the folly of nations the world ever witnessed. We go to war for five millions, which is sponged out by the declaration, and with a certainty that we shall lose ten times as much, *and never can compel France to pay one cent.*

MR. CLAY TO LESLIE COMBS.

WASHINGTON, March 9, 1836.

DEAR SIR,—I received your favor of the 26th ultimo. My impression is that both the legacy was paid and the land assigned to Morrison Boswell, agreeably to the will of Colonel Morrison; but all the papers of the estate being at home, I can certainly affirm nothing and do nothing until my return.

We learn from Kentucky that Morehead has declined, leaving the field to Clarke. I hope no feelings unfavorable to his success will remain. Mr. C. A. Wickliffe is to be run as Lieutenant Governor with him, as we learn. Any arrangement as to individuals ought to be held subordinate to the great object of the prevalence of principles.

I have hopes, not unmixed with fears, about the Land bill. I do not know why your Pension case moves so slowly, or rather does not move at all, in the House. Crittenden and I spoke the other day of starting it in the Senate; and if it does not mend its pace in the House we may attempt that course.

MISS JEFFERY TO MR. CLAY.

BOSTON, March 10, 1836.

MY DEAR SIR,—I sail from New York on the 1st of April, in the packet ship Orpheus. Can I take any parcel or communication for you to your son or to Mrs. Henry Clay? And will you favor me with a letter of introduction to the latter? as I think she might be pleased to see in a foreign county, a person who had seen and known her own relations; and though I am afraid I can do but very little to increase her pleasure, yet I should wish to show, at least, how very grateful I feel for all the kindness I have received from you and yours, by adding my mite if I can. Will you remember me to Mrs. Clay and assure her of my lively recollections of her kindness. I am afraid there is nothing in the world I can do for you; but should you ever wish for any thing which I can procure in England, I shall be very much pleased to be employed. Remember me to Judge Porter.

GEORGE TUCKER TO MR. CLAY.

UNIVERSITY OF VIRGINIA, June 30, 1836.

MY DEAR SIR,—Before you receive this you will have learned the death of our venerated friend, James Madison. I take the liberty of asking you to have the inclosed resolutions published in "The Intelligencer," and I can not lose this opportunity of letting you know, or rather of giving you a further proof of the high place you held in his estimation. When I was last with him, a few days after the short interview I had with you in Washington, we were conversing on the affairs of the nation—and especially on the then agitating question of the efforts of the Abolitionists—when, with that absence of his habitual reserve on political topics, of which he had of late afforded me many flattering proofs, he said, "Clay has been so successful in his compromising other disputes, I wish he could fall upon some plan of compromising this, and then all parties (or enough of all parties, I forget which) might unite and make him President." Knowing his desire to be at peace with all, and to escape the coarse and reckless vituperation of the newspapers, I never ventured to mention this except to one or two discreet friends, nor would I now do it to any one who would make it public, as in the virulence of party feeling, it would operate with many prejudiced minds to abate the respect that the nation will be disposed to show to his memory, and by thus detracting somewhat from the weight and influence of his good opinion, deprive you of your just rights. I never, however, intended that such a remark should be buried, as that would have been a still greater injustice to you, and meant, and still mean in good time to make it known. You see I write frankly, but I trust not at the expense of delicacy

Would it be practicable, and if practicable, would it be safe and prudent to extend the franking privilege to Mrs. Madison? You can appreciate the real objections, if there be any, without being deterred from your views of right, by chimerical apprehensions. I pray you then to consider of it, if not too late, and act accordingly.

I forwarded to you last year two copies of my discourse before our Philosophical Society—one for yourself and the other for Miss Martineau. Did they reach you in time before she left you?

You must have a mixed feeling of triumph, contempt, and amusement, that the majority have been obliged, virtually, to pass your Land bill, under another form.

HARRIET MARTINEAU TO MR. CLAY.

NEW YORK, July 26, 1836.

DEAR SIR,—I am just about to sail for England, and I do not know where you are, but I can not help writing once more, to assure you of my respectful and affectionate remembrance; and of the earnestness with which I shall always watch for tidings of you and yours. If you should ever chance to visit England, you will give my mother and me the pleasure of seeing you at "17 Pludyer St., Westminster;" and if, in the mean time, I can be of any service to you whatever in furnishing information, or in any other way, pray write to me there; and it will delight me to be of use to you.

Pray remember me most kindly to Mrs. Clay and Mr. Erwin, and believe me ever yours faithfully and affectionately.

MRS. MADISON TO MR. CLAY.

MONTPELER, November 8, 1836.

The continued and very severe affection of my eyes, not permitting, but with much difficulty, even the signature of my name, has deferred, dear friend, the acknowledgments due for your very kind and acceptable letter of August 18th. I should sooner have resorted for this purpose to the pen of an amanuensis, but that the failure of my general health combining equal, and sometimes greater suffering, rendered dictation very painful, and hope still flattered me that I might yet use my own. So much time having elapsed with but little improvement in my situation, I can submit to no longer delay in offering this explanation of my silence, nor omit the expression of my deep sensibility to that pure and true sympathy which I am conscious I receive from such highly valued friends as Mrs. Clay and yourself.

The sources of consolation in my bereavement which you suggest, are those which my heart can most truly appreciate. The reflected rays of his virtues still linger around me, and my mind now dwells with calmer feelings on their mellowed tints. He left me, too, a charge, dear and sacred, and deeply impressed with its value to his fame, and its usefulness to his country. The important trust sustained me under the heavy pressure of recent loss, and formed an oasis to the desert it created in my feelings.

In fulfillment of his wishes I have, therefore, devoted myself to the object of having prepared for the press the productions of his own pen. It will form the surest evidence of his claim to the gratitude of his country and the world. With the aid of my brother, who had prepared copies of the debates in the Revolutionary Congress and in the Convention, under Mr. Madison's eye, triplicates have been completed for publication here and abroad. My son went, in July, as far as New York, and remained there for the purpose of negotiating with the most eminent publishers, and I have had communication with those in other cities, but no offer has been made by any entitled to confidence, which would free me from heavy and inconvenient pecuniary advances and the risk of impositions and eventual loss. Under these circumstances I have been advised by a friend to offer the work to the patronage of Congress, asking their aid so far as to relieve the work from the charges upon it, principally for literary and other benevolent purposes, and, after their use by Congress, to give me the stereotype plates. This would at once allow me to throw them into general circulation on a scale that would remunerate me more in accordance with the expectations entertained by their author, and would also allow the price to be so graduated as to insure their general diffusion.

As this plan was suggested by one favorable to the Administration, he advised also that the channel of his friends, as the majority of those who were to decide on the proposition, should be employed in making it, and pledged their support. This work being a record only of what passed preceding the existence of present parties, can not associate the name of Mr. Madison with either, and therefore its introduction and advocacy by the one can be no bar to the favor of the other. On your part, I am sure that, in my yielding to it this direction, you will perceive no deviation from the high respect and friendly regard I entertain toward yourself, but approving an adoption of this course as most conducive to success, you will, with your friends, insure it on the merits of the work alone, uninfluenced by adversary feeling toward the source from whence the measures originated.

It was my intention to have gone to Washington, principally with a view to obtain in personal conference the advice of my best friends, but my protracted ill health, and the approach of an inclement season I fear may prevent the journey.

In addition to three volumes of the Debates (near six hundred pages each) now ready for the press, matter enough for another volume is expected, and nearly four hundred pages copied, of writings and letters on Constitutional subjects, considerable selections have also been made from his early correspondence, which may form a volume on the legislative proceedings of Virginia, and historical letters of the period from 1780 up to the commencement of the new Government. His Congressional and Executive career may furnish two more. His writings already in print, as " Political Observations," a pamphlet in 1795, " Examinations of the British Doctrine," etc., it is thought should be embodied with his other works for more permanent preservation.

It is important that these manuscripts should be prepared and committed to the press as early as they can follow the Debates, and the success of the latter will much facilitate the publication of the former, even if Congress should decline a like patronage to them, a mode which would be much preferred.

The near approach of the time which will call you to your Senatorial duties rendering it uncertain whether this would reach you ere your departure from home, I deem it safest to address it to Washington, whence I hope, on your safe arrival, you will favor me with an acknowledgment of its receipt and any suggestions your friendship may offer.

Accept for Mrs. Clay and yourself my affectionate respects.

MR. CLAY TO FRANCIS BROOKE.

WASHINGTON, December 19, 1836.

MY DEAR SIR,—I am glad to learn by your favor of 15th inst. that Mrs. Brooke's health is improving, and sincerely hope that it may soon be entirely re-established.

Your objection to an immediate organization of an Opposition, upon the principles stated by me, applies rather to the time of its commencement than the principles themselves. Undoubtedly, such an Opposition should avail itself of the errors of the new Administration; but it seems to me that it would acquire greater force by availing itself also of that fatal error in its origin, which resulted from the President-elect being the designated successor of the present incumbent. If a President may name his successor, and bring the whole machinery of the Government, including its one hundred thousand dependents, into the canvass; and if by such means he achieves a victory, such a fatal precedent as this must be rebuked and reversed, or there is an end of the freedom of election. No one doubts that this has been done. And no reflecting man can doubt that, having been once done, it will be again attempted, and unless corrected by the people, it will become, in time, the established practice of the country. Now, I think that no wisdom or benefit, in the measures of the new Administration, can compensate or atone for this vice in its origin. Still this point may be pressed or not, according to circumstances, in different States. As for Virginia, I am afraid another generation must arise before she regains her former high rank. Henceforward, at least during our lives, I apprehend, she will be only a satelite of New York.

I am obliged greatly to Mr. Pleasants for cherishing his friendly sentiments toward me, and request you to assure him that they are cordially reciprocated. Nothing of interest has occurred here since the burning of the General Post-office. I understand that the opinion is general among the inhabitants of the city that it was not accidental.

SIR WILLIAM CLAY TO MR. CLAY.

FULWELL LODGE, TWICKENHAM, January 12, 1837.

DEAR SIR,—My friend and brother-in-law, Mr. Temple Bowdoin, tells me that he has the honor of your acquaintance, and that he has mentioned to you my name. I am tempted, in consequence, to take the liberty of sending you a pamphlet I have recently published, which may not be wholly without interest to you, as it relates to a question of great interest, as well in the United States as in England; and as I have endeavored to avail myself of the ample experience which your legislative bodies have had the opportunities to acquire, I trust that, by accepting this trifling work, you will permit me to consider myself not wholly a stranger to one who has conferred such celebrity on the name I bear. It is, indeed, not wholly impossible that I may have some claim to the honor of your acquaintance beyond the mere similarity of name. My lineal ancestor was related to Penn. I am not quite clear that some one of our name did not accompany him; but it is certain that at a somewhat later period (eighty or one hundred years since), a member of our family did settle in America, although his friends never had any record of his subsequent fortunes.

MR. CLAY TO FRANCIS BROOKE.

WASHINGTON, February 10, 1837.

My DEAR SIR,—I received your favor of the 8th, as I did the preceding one to which it refers, and which I postponed answering until I had something worth communicating. There is indeed some highly interesting occurrence here almost daily, but the papers generally notice it. You will have seen the letter of the President to the Committee of Investigation. Yesterday, a still more extraordinary one was presented to the Senate by Mr. Calhoun, in which the President, in the harshest and most offensive language animadverts upon a speech made by that Senator in the Senate. The majority was reminded that they alone possessed the power to vindicate the privileges of the Senate against the Executive encroachments. But they all remained mute; not one venturing to offer any motion. Such is the degradation to which Congress is reduced!

You congratulate me on my acceptance of the new appointment recently conferred on me to the Senate. I think you ought to have condoled and sympathized with me, because, by the force of circumstances, I was constrained to remain in a body, in the humiliated condition in which the Senate now is. I shall escape from it as soon as I decently can, with the same pleasure that one would fly from a charnel-house.

Mr. Webster retires positively, Mr. Ewing is ousted, and Leigh, and Clayton, and Mangum, and Porter, are gone. What good can I do, what mischief avert, by remaining?

I should be delighted to see you, but in the month of March the Cumberland route offers advantages so superior to any other, that I must follow it to Kentucky. Would to God it were for the last time!

Can you not come to Ashland from Lewisburg, when you are attending the Court there? It is an affair of but two or three days, and we should be rejoiced to have you, and Mrs. Brooke, too, if she would accompany you, under our roof.

Do me the favor to make to her assurances of my affectionate regards, and believe me always and cordially your friend.

CHANCELLOR KENT TO MR. CLAY.

NEW YORK, February 20, 1837.

MY DEAR SIR,—I hope I shall not be deemed too obtrusive, but I can not refrain from declaring my admiration of the speech delivered by you, in the Senate, in January last, on the expunging resolution, and which is published at large in "The National Intelligencer" of the 16th inst. My sympathies, and judgment, and confidence, and patriotism, and grief, and indignation, are with you in every point, and if I was in Washington, I would go directly up to you, and give your hand the hearty shake of sympathetic feeling. You have vindicated the resolution of 1834 with irresistible force, and damned the other to everlasting fame. If you, and such men as you, who are storming despotic and servile meanness in the Senatorial Hall, have no other recompense, it may possibly give you some consolation to be assured that you are receiving the silent admiration and gratitude of thousands, and by none with more hearty pulsation than by your most respectful and obedient servant.

MR. CLAY TO FRANCIS BROOKE.

WASHINGTON, March 7, 1838.

MY DEAR SIR,—I received your favor. This day the ex-President left this city, and the President, for the first time, sent in a batch of nominations. Poinsett for the War Department; Dallas for Russia; Heywood, of North Carolina, for Belgium, etc. The three mentioned were confirmed. Smith, of Alabama, and Catron, of Tennessee, were nominated by Jackson for judges of the Supreme Court, under the new law. And what judges they will make! They are not yet confirmed. Labranche, of Louisiana, was also nominated by Jackson, for Texas, and has been confirmed as Chargé d'Affaires.

You ask if I can communicate any consolation to you for the future, as to public affairs. I lament to say not much. Hopes are entertained, and with some probability, that there will be a majority in the House of Representatives at the next session, against the Administration; and if there were more concert, and a union as to the ultimate object, among the Opposition, there would be better prospects. I think there is a tendency to union among them, but it is not yet produced. Mr. Calhoun, now, as heretofore, stands in the way.

The city has been filled with strangers. The crowd from New York has been as great as it was from Scotland, when James ascended the throne in England.

My warmest regards to Mrs. Brooke. I hope to leave here on Thursday.

MR. FOX TO MR. CLAY.

WASHINGTON, March 8, 1837.

DEAR SIR,—I have to draw upon England for some money, by the next packet, of the 16th. If you can make it convenient, consequently, to draw upon me a draft for the $1,180 which I am in your debt, at ten days date from the present, I shall be much obliged to you to allow me to settle it in that way. If agreeable to you, the draft can be sent to me for acceptance, at that date, before your departure; or you can inform me in whose hands you leave it. My servant, the bearer of this, will wait for an answer, or call for one early in the morning, as you may desire.

I wish you a very happy journey, and am extremely glad to find that we are to enjoy the pleasure of your society in Washington during another session of Congress.

HARRIET MARTINEAU TO MR. CLAY.

WESTMINSTER, May 15, 1837.

DEAR MR. CLAY,—It gives me great pleasure to acknowledge, on behalf of many authors, besides myself, your exertions on the copyright business. I thought I was sure, both of what your convictions and your efforts would be; and I rejoice that my confidence has been justified. We are exceedingly pleased with your Report, and have strong hope that our object may be attained next session. The American newspapers seem to show a more and more favorable disposition toward our claim, and some solid proofs have reached the hands of one, at least, of our authors (Professor Lyell), of the feeling which honorable American publishers entertain of the injury we suffer. Several hundreds of copies of Lyell's fifth edition of his Geology, in four volumes, have been ordered from England by booksellers in Boston, New York, and Philadelphia, and the money, in full, transmitted with the order. A highly creditable proceeding. It was transacted through Professor Silliman.

Have you seen what my New York publishers (who are English) have been doing to obviate mutilation of my book? We fear we must submit to be pirated, but the risk of mutilation is much lessened by the work being divided into parts. The book has been published here only four days. I have had little hope of pleasing any body in either country with my work. I might have done so by merely copying my journal, but I felt the occasion to be too serious a one to be trifled with, and I have, accordingly, risked every thing by making an open avowal of principles which have no chance of being popular. I am very easy now the thing is done. My conscience is discharged, and I really do not care much what becomes of me in name and fortune, while I can not live without freedom of speech. This last can never, now, be taken from me.

Your new President seems to have succeeded in making himself gloriously unpopular at the very outset. I do not believe in his power of retrieving himself. We shall see. I hope you will never have another President who will venture to declare, on entering upon office, that under no circumstances will he, on a particular point, assent to a constitutional act which may become the will of the nation. Enough of him.

We are in a critical state, and the Tories may, very likely, have another short term of office. The weakness of the sovereign, the incompleteness of the Reform Bill, and the difficulties thereby left in the way of the representation, are too much for the present ministry, even without the House of Lords, which we have *pour comble de maux.* We do not fear breach of the peace, but much political struggle. We shall have your good wishes on the liberal side, though you do find our Tory ministers so very civil to the United States.

I hope you are well, and in some good degree reconciled and content in mind. My mother and I are in the best health and spirits, and talking more, it seems to me, of my beloved American friends than of all other persons in the world.

With my kind respects to Mrs. Clay and Mr. Erwin, I am, dear sir, yours affectionately.

MR. CLAY TO HIS SON JAMES.

ASHLAND, May 26, 1837.

MY DEAR JAMES,—Just as I was making preparations for my trip to St. Louis, and had resolved to start in a few days, the proclamation of the President arrived, calling Congress on the first of September. I shall be obliged to leave home, to reach Washington in time, about the middle of August. Consequently I have only two months and a half to attend to my private affairs. If I were to go to St. Louis, and examine my lands in Missouri, as I wished, it would absorb one half of that time, and not leave me enough to attend to necessary matters here. I am compelled, therefore, to abandon my contemplated journey for the present. I assure you, my dear son, that I do it with great regret; for I wanted much to see you, and to see your place and the improvements you have made upon it.

As I can not go to see you, you must come and see me. You will yourself judge of the most convenient time for you to leave home, and come here. By the first of July, I suppose your crop will be laid by, and the season of your Jack will be over; and if you can not come before then, you will be able to leave home at that time.

I wish you to say to Major Graham, how much I regret not being able to see him at his residence, as I expected and intended. I am sorry for it also on account of his suit, in which I wished to have rendered him any service in my power. But it is probable that, if his suit shall be heard at the time he expected, he may be able to engage the services of Mr. Webster, who left here on yesterday on his way to Louisville, and thence to St. Louis, which place he will reach, I suppose, about the 6th of June. His wife and his daughter accompany him, and when they get there I wish you to call and see them.

We have had a very dry spring, insomuch that I have never seen the grass so low. But two days ago the rain began, and we have had the most copious showers. Should the remainder of the season prove good, we shall be able, I trust, to make good crops.

Henry's two mares from England have arrived, and both had colts, but he had the misfortune to lose one of them. He had also imported six cows; two died on the passage, the other four arrived with four calves. I have given him nine hundred dollars for one of the cows and her calf.

Should you want money to bring you home, you must inform me, or if there be not time to inform me, draw upon me.

The family are all well, and join with me in love to you.

MR. CLAY TO A COMMITTEE OF GENTLEMEN IN NEW YORK.

ASHLAND, August 6, 1837.

GENTLEMEN,—I duly received the letter which you did me the honor to address to me on the 20th ultimo, transmitting a copy of the proceedings adopted at preliminary meetings of a number of my friends in the city of New York, in relation to the next Presidential election.

On the question of the propriety of agitating the public at this time by a discussion of that subject, I entirely concur in the opinion expressed by you, that it would be altogether premature. Six months have not yet elapsed since the termination of the last election, and more than three years and a half remain of the term which was then filled. The country is, moreover, suffering under a great calamity. Its currency and its business lie prostrate. All minds are absorbed by considerations relative to measures of immediate relief. At such a moment to disturb or distract the public attention, by introducing another exciting but remote topic, seems to me to be unwise. In expressing this sentiment, it is far from my purpose to convey any reproach or censure toward those who have taken a different view of the matter. It is quite likely they have supposed, and may be right in supposing, that the only adequate remedy which can be found for the evils with which the country is now afflicted, will be a change of those rulers by whose agency they have been produced or continued. But the necessity of some earlier relief is so great, and the expediency of bringing to the consideration of it a spirit of moderation, forbearance, and conciliation, is so obvious, that I think we should first direct our exertions exclusively to this single object. We shall soon ascertain how far the Administration will co-operate with the country in the restoration of a sound state of things.

To guard against misconception, I ought to add that too much delay as well as too much precipitation should be alike avoided, in arrangements connected with the next election of a Chief Magistrate of the Union. Precipitation would expose the disinterestedness of our patriotism to unjust animadversion; protracted delay, to the danger of division and defeat.

I also agree with you, gentlemen, entirely in thinking, in regard to a candidate for the Presidency, that some mode should be adopted of collecting the general sense of those who believe it important to the preservation of our liberties involved, the correction of abuses, and a thorough reform in the Executive Administration, that there should be a change in the Chief Magistracy. And none better appears to me to have been suggested than that of a Northern Convention. This will not supersede the previous employment of all proper means to produce union, harmony and concentration. A resort to such means is recommended by their tendency to prevent those unpleasant collisions, in the choice of delegates to the Convention, which might leave, among the friends of the respective candidates, a state of feeling, unfavorable to that hearty co-operation in the final struggle which is so essential to success.

Having said this much upon the general subject, allow me now to add a few words in relation to myself personally. You are pleased to honor me with your attachment and confidence, to appreciate highly my public services, and to desire to place me in the highest station of the Government. I am profoundly grateful to you, and to all those friends who cherish toward me similar sentiments. I think, however, that the question of the particular individual who should be selected to accomplish those patriotic purposes which we have in view, although not unimportant, is of subordinate consequence. It should not be allowed to become the paramount object, nor to divide more, than is absolutely unavoidable, those who agree in the general principle.

I have not, for several years, looked to the event of my being placed in the chair of Chief Magistrate, as one that was probable. My feelings and intentions have taken a different direction. While I am not insensible to the exalted honor of filling the highest office within the gift of this great people, I have desired retirement from the cares of public life; and although I have not been able fully to gratify this wish, I am in the enjoyment of comparative repose, and looking anxiously forward to more. I should be extremely unwilling, without very strong reasons, to be thrown into the turmoil of a Presidential canvass. Above all, I am most desirous not to seem, as I in truth am not, importunate for any public office whatever. If I were persuaded that a majority of my fellow-citizens desired to place me in their highest executive office, that sense of duty by which I have been ever guided would exact obedience to their will. Candor obliges me, however, to say that I have not seen sufficient evidence that they entertain such a desire.

Entertaining these feelings and sentiments, I think it best for the present to adhere to the passive position which I have prescribed to myself. Should a National Convention of our friends nominate any other person, he shall have my hearty wishes for success and my cordial support. And, before the assembling of such a Convention, if one should be agreed upon, there may be such indications of the public will as will enable us all clearly to trace the line of our duty toward our common country.

Requesting, gentlemen, you and all who attended the meetings, the proceedings of which you have had the goodness to forward to me, to accept my grateful acknowledgments, I am your friend and obedient servant.

MR. CLAY TO G. D. PRENTICE.

Ashland, August 14, 1837.

Dear Sir,—From numerous communications and circumstances, I think it probable that, whatever may be my own inclination or disposition, I shall be again forced into the Presidential arena. It is right that I should put you in possession of some of the information which has reached me.

In the city of New York, notwithstanding, and subsequent to the movement there for Mr. Webster, my friends spontaneously resolved to organize. From all the Wards a committee of one hundred was formed, subdivided into other Committees of Correspondence, Finance, etc., and they tell me that they have ascertained that a decided majority of the Whigs prefer me in that city. The Committee has addressed me, and I have replied. Perhaps my reply may be published. I take the ground of entire passiveness; that I do not wish my name used, unless there is reason to believe it is wanted by a majority of the country, etc.

I send you inclosed some communications which I have received, which you will be pleased to return by Mr. Erwin; and if you do not wish to retain this letter (as I have kept no copy of it), be pleased to return that also.

I still think of and hope that arrangements may be made to make it your interest to go to Washington.

MR. CLAY TO HIS WIFE.

White Sulphur Springs, August 27, 1837.

My dear Wife,—We arrived here yesterday, having parted from Mr. Erwin at Guyandotte, he proceeding up the Ohio river, and we taking the land route by this place. I was concerned to learn from him that James became worse the day on which I left home, and it was necessary to call in a physician. He assured me, however, that although threatened with a severe fever, no danger was apprehended. I sincerely hope that this may prove to be the case, but as I shall feel very uneasy until I hear again from home, I wish he would write me to Washington as soon as you get this letter.

I wrote you from Maysville, and in that letter I mentioned most of the things to which I desired James' attention in my absence. I forgot to mention that I wished the red cow with a white face (an old Hereford that was put up last winter to be killed) fattened for beef for the family, and any other of the old cows that he may think it well enough to kill. There is a little two year old at Mansfield (I believe she is an estray heifer with a black nose) that might as well be slaughtered for early beef.

We shall leave here on Wednesday morning at furthest for Washington. By that time I hope to recover from the fatigues of the journey. John looks very serious, but has conducted himself very well.

MR. CLAY TO HIS SON JAMES.

WHEELING, October 19, 1837.

MY DEAR JAMES,—I have reached this place on my return home from Congress, a good deal jaded and not very well. Prior to my departure from Washington, I received your letter communicating the death of poor Russell, which gave me sincere concern. I have been quite uneasy about you, but hope that you have escaped sickness. You ought to be very careful with yourself, for your Missouri fevers are very dangerous.

I am sorry to hear of the great loss you have sustained in sheep; and I am now convinced more than ever that it is unwise for you to keep them, unless you have a number sufficiently large to pay the expense of a shepherd to keep constantly with them. Under these circumstances, I think you had better fatten what remain and sell them for mutton.

I expect to remain at home until late in November, and then proceed again to Washington, although I am very tired of so frequently crossing the mountains. I wish you to write me often and let me know all that concerns you. I send this by the boat that carries me to Maysville.

MR. CLAY TO HIS SON JAMES.

ASHLAND, October 24, 1837.

MY DEAR JAMES,—I reached home on the 22d instant, and received your letter of the 17th. I found all well here, but it is said to be very sickly at Louisville and at Frankfort, and we have been uneasy about you. I hope that you will escape being sick. I wrote you by the journey from Wheeling, and sent my letter by the steamboat. I advised you in that letter to sell your sheep, seeing that they are not safe from the dogs and wolves. Unless you had a number sufficiently large to justify keeping a herdsman, it is useless to keep sheep.

You tell me that land is still rising in Missouri. I wish you could sell, at a fair price, my small tract in Lincoln, and also the Alton tract, if you could get a good price for it. What could you sell your land for? But I suppose that nothing could induce you to sell it and return ro Kentucky. Mr. Smith tells me that Chaumiere, the residence of the late Colonel Meade, is in market at $40 per acre, which is very low as land has sold here. It is very good land, having, I understand, about four hundred acres in the tract. That would not be large enough without the purchase of some addition to it, which probably might be made. But if you are contented with your situation and prospects, you had better not think of purchasing it.

We will try and have your cattle, etc., sent to you, as you desire. I am afraid that the river may be too low, although it is now raining. Thomas seems quite happy since his marriage.

MR. CLAY TO HIS SON JAMES.

ASHLAND, November 10, 1837.

MY DEAR JAMES,—I was glad to find by your letter of the 29th ultimo, just received, that you were in good health and spirits, and your business prosperous. I started Orphan Boy, your cow, dog, and gun, on the 7th instant, for St. Louis viâ. Louisville and steamboat, under the care of William Nelson White, a young man raised in this county, and recommended to me. He lost two days in the start by accident, as he says, and I sent Aaron to look after him and the cattle. Aaron has returned this evening and reports that he saw the man with the cattle safely across the bridge at Frankfort and going on well. So that I hope no further mishap will occur. I send you a copy of the receipt which Mr. White gave me, from which you will perceive that I advanced him $20, was to pay all expenses of himself and the cattle, and to allow him half a dollar per day as a compensation. The two days that he lost ought to be deducted from his account Although he started with the dog, he could not carry but left him.

I have written to Mr. Wm. Prather to advance the money for his freight, etc. He had charge of another calf which he was to leave between here and Louisville.

I will make arrangements in a few days to advance you the $100 which you desire.

I wrote you, on my way home, and again after my return, and advised the sale of the sheep.

I have been engaged all this week in getting in my corn. My hogs are sufficiently fat to kill when it is cold enough. Yesterday my new overseer, Mr. Florea, came and entered on business to-day.

Your mother had made up her mind to go with me to Washington, but has finally declined it.

We are all well, and she and the children send their love to you. Mr. Erwin has not yet returned.

MR. CLAY TO HIS SON JAMES.

WASHINGTON, December 18, 1837.

MY DEAR JAMES,—I received, to-day, your favor of the 6th instant, but have not received your previous letter, to which you refer, in which you made an offer of the Alton land to Mr. Tegert. I had, however, before I left home, submitted the matter of the sale of that land to you, and I shall be content with whatever you may do, being sure that your intentions will be to do the best for us all.

With respect, too, to your project of having wood cut from it for the supply of the consumption of St. Louis, I leave that affair to your judgment. If it be well attended to, I have no doubt that it may be rendered profitable; but recollect that it will depend altogether upon the degree of attention paid to it. It will have the effect of repressing trespasses upon the land.

I am sorry to hear of the loss of your heifers, but we must expect occasional losses, and increase our diligence to repair them.

Your resolution to study, and to begin with history, is a good one, and I hope you will persevere in it.

Gillie's Greece, with Plutarch's Lives; Gibbon's Rise and Fall of the Roman Empire; Tacitus; Hume, with the continuation; Russell's Modern Europe; Hallams' Middle Ages; Robertson's

Charles V., Indies, etc.; Marshall's Life of Washington; Botta's History of the American Revolution.

These books, and others, may be read with advantage; and you should adopt some systematic course as to time, that is, to read so many hours out of the twenty-four.

Give my respects to Major Graham.

MR. CLAY TO FRANCIS BROOKE.

WASHINGTON, December 19, 1837.

MY DEAR SIR,—I received your favor of the 17th. Mr. Madison's Journal is not yet ordered to be printed, and, without any such object in the delay, it may lead to the benefit of Mrs. Madison, by allowing the sale and diffusion of the European edition of the work. When printed by Congress, I will recollect your wish to obtain a copy.

Ritchie has discovered a mare's nest in the fact that the Whigs are making arrangements to establish a new paper here. They do not propose to establish it by resorting to the public crib, from which his and other papers are maintained, but by voluntary contributions, raised among an abused and betrayed people. There is no occasion to conceal the object. The Whigs mean to beat the Administration party, and the public press will be one of their instruments. The design is to establish a new paper to espouse and advance the cause generally, without reference, at present, to any particular candidate.

The committee charged with the business have under consideration the selection of suitable editors, etc. I mentioned, several days ago, to one of the committee, Mr. Blackford as one whose qualifications deserved attention. They will be, doubtless, duly weighed; but it will be best not to excite expectations, or to stimulate any direct application from him. I think very highly of his principles, and his ability. I have no doubt, however, that whatever decision may be finally made will be the result of the best intentions.

My best respects to Mrs. Brooke, and my hearty congratulations on your recent acquisition of a daughter.

MR. CLAY TO HIS SON JAMES.

WASHINGTON, January 7, 1838.

MY DEAR SON,—I received your letter of the 23d ultimo. You complain of not hearing from me. I have written to you several times since I have been here, and would have written oftener, if I had had any thing to communicate. But my correspondence is very oppressive, and I find it impossible to keep up with it. You must not suppose that I feel any want of affection toward you. Far otherwise. You are constantly in my thoughts, and in my hopes. I feel that you must be very lonesome, and regret to hear that you are not happy. You know, my dear son, that I feared you would not be, separated as you are from all who love you, and that I reluctantly consented to your going to Missouri. I hope that you will endeavor to cultivate feelings of contentment, and I shall be most happy, on my return home, if we can make any arrangement by which you can come back to Kentucky, and live in the midst of your friends.

The account you give me of your affairs is encouraging, and the account of you which I receive from others also gives me high satisfaction. What I would especially guard you against, is, every species of dissipation; and I own to you that I have feared your solitary condition might tempt you into it. But I sincerely hope that may not prove to be the case.

I suppose your offer of the Alton land was declined. It is very important to protect it against trespasses, and I trust you will take care of that. In a former letter, I gave my assent to your having wood cut for the St. Louis market.

MR. CLAY TO FRANCIS BROOKE.

WASHINGTON, January 13, 1838.

MY DEAR SIR,—The arrear which I am under in our correspondence, has proceeded from my really having nothing of interest to communicate, and I need not tell you that my correspondence and public engagements are so oppressive, that I am constrained to avoid writing whenever I can. Even now I should not address you, but from my apprehension that you would misconstrue my silence.

We have been engaged in the Senate, during the last eight or ten days, in the most unprofitable discussion that ever engrossed the attention of a deliberate body. It was upon five or six as abstract resolutions as a metaphysical mind can well devise. They are at last disposed of. Their professed object is slavery; their real aim to advance the political interest of the mover, and to affect mine. I am greatly deceived if in both respects he has not signally failed. He was caught in his own trap. You will see the series of counter-resolutions which I offered. The two most important, after undergoing some modifications, with my assent, were adopted as substitutes for his. His Texas resolution was laid on the table yesterday, by a vote of thirty-five to nine. I think that when that subject comes up, I will turn the tables upon Mr. Calhoun, as much as I did on the affair of slavery.

There is not, I think, the slightest ground of approaching war with Great Britain, on account of Canada. When the President's Message was received, respecting the capture and destruction of the Caroline, I thought it due to the occasion to reprehend in the strongest terms, the violation of our jurisdiction. My remarks are correctly published in "The National Intelligencer," and there only. "The Globe" habitually misreports me.

Resolutions have been introduced in the Kentucky Legislature, recommending me as the next President. Although I presumed that something would be done at Frankfort, I anticipated nothing in this form, and I think it displays more zeal than discretion.

MR. CLAY TO HIS SON JAMES.

WASHINGTON, January 22, 1838.

MY DEAR JAMES,—I received your letter of the 1st inst., this day, and the perusal of it gave me much concern. I had previously received from you a letter complaining of your solitary condition, and stating that you were not happy. I answered it, but as you do not acknowledge the receipt of my answer, I suppose it had not reached you.

I desire most ardently, my dear son, your happiness, and that of every child I have. You know that I was not anxious for you to go to Missouri. The very circumstances which now exist, I anticipated. But you were confident, and I yielded. I have wished to see you happily married, under the hope that with a wife whom you loved, and the prospects of a family, you might be contented and happy. You tell me that you have not the means to go into society, but you have not informed me what means you allude to. I have been very desirous that you should go much more into society than you have done, and why have you not? Do you want clothes? The slightest intimation of your wishes to me, on that subject, would have commanded them. I have refused you nothing that you have asked me. I have been, I own, exceedingly anxious that you should avoid all dissipation, but with that restriction, I have not cared how much society you enjoyed, or, rather, I have wished that you should see much of it.

In my former letter, I expressed a wish that you would attend diligently to your business, make yourself as happy as you can, and upon my return home, I would see if we could not make some arrangement by which you should return to Kentucky.

Of one thing you may be certain, that you will be happy no where, without constant employment. That is the great secret of human happiness.

I should be very glad to have you near us. Have you another overseer? You have never informed me. If you have, I do not see why you might not, at any time leave home for some weeks, go to Ashland, or make a visit to see our military lands, or to your uncle Porter.

Of one thing you may be assured, my dear son, that I not only feel the deepest interest in your welfare and happiness, but that I am always willing to do any thing to promote it. I am the more concerned about you, because John has lately given me great pain, and I almost despair of him. When you reflect how much anxiety I have suffered on account of my sons, I am sure that you will be stimulated to persevere in a course of regularity and propriety.

I have written to you frequently, but the mails are irregular. I received two or three days ago, your letter of November, transmitting a copy of that which you had addressed to your uncle Porter.

MR. CLAY TO HIS SON JAMES.

SENATE CHAMBER, March 23, 1838.

MY DEAR SON,—I received your favor of the 1st inst. I have been a little unwell, and have been so much oppressed with business, correspondence, and company, that I have been obliged to engage a young friend to act for me as amanuensis, and he wrote the letter to which you refer upon my dictation.

I return the inclosed certificate with my signature. I am perfectly satisfied with the disposition you have made of your cattle with Mr. Dorrey. I am sorry that the imported cow does not breed, and I must give you another after awhile. We will talk about the house which you wish to build, when I see you. But I still should be happy to have you back in Kentucky, if we can make some arrangement, as I hope we can, to that end. I have not yet procured the patent, but I hope to get it for your land to be issued in the name of Doctor Rogers. I have been looking out for a wife for you, but I suppose you will have to select for yourself.

I hope, my dear son, that you will continue to cultivate a cheerful disposition, and go into society as often as you can.

MR. CLAY TO FRANCIS BROOKE.

WASHINGTON, April 14, 1838.

MY DEAR SIR,—I should have written you more frequently but that I had nothing material to communicate, of which the papers would not inform you. I must add, too, that my labors, especially that of private correspondence, have greatly increased this session, from obvious causes.

In regard to the Presidential question, every thing is going on as well as my most zealous friends could desire. Public opinion every where, even in Indiana and Ohio, is rapidly concentrating as you could wish. The movement at Harrisburg for a separate nomination of General Harrison, is rebuked and discountenanced.

The Whig members of Congress have had several consultations, as to the time and place of a National Convention. Their inclination, I understand, is to Harrisburg, and to a period between January and June of the next year. They will probably definitely settle the matter the next week.

When do you return to St. Julien? I am very much jaded and fatigued, and have some thoughts of running somewhere for a few days. Possibly I may go to you, if I can be sure that I should meet only your family.

Present my respects to Mrs. Brooke.

MR. CLAY TO FRANCIS BROOKE.

SENATE CHAMBER, June 5, 1838.

MY DEAR SIR,—I am extremely sorry to hear of the loss of your servant. It is a serious misfortune, and not easily repaired, independent of the distress which such an event must necessarily occasion to every feeling heart.

I can not understand from any inquiry which I have made here the exact value of your Military Land Warrant. Mr. Allen, the Senator, from Ohio, thinks it worth seventy-five cents per acre; but recommends an application to William Creighton, Jr. (who is a man of honor and a particular friend of mine), of Chillicothe, who resides in the heart of the county set apart for the army.

If the bill making further appropriations for land scrip, now pending in the House of Representatives should pass, your warrant will be worth much more, perhaps $1 20 cents per acre. Although I can not vote for the bill, I think it very probable it will pass at this or another session, and you would probably do well not to part with it.

I should be most happy to see you here, and why can't you come? A few hours would put you in the Pennsylvania Avenue. If you visit us, come directly to Mrs. Hill's boarding-house, where I stay, and where you can be accommodated. It is nigh Gadsby's.

Every thing has passed off admirably at the Ohio Convention.

GEORGE W. LAFAYETTE TO MR. CLAY.

PARIS, le 6 Août, 1838.

MONSIEUR,—Celui qui au nom des deux Chambres Américaines réunies, fût, il y a treize ans, le brillant interprète des sentimens de la nation, pour l'heureux vétéran auquel elle prodiguoit tant de bontés, recevra j'en suis sur avec satisfaction, et bienveillance, des mains de la famille du Général Lafayette, la collection de ses manuscrits.

Qu'il me soit donc permis, monsieur, de vous offrir ce souvenir d'un ami qui n'est plus, et de vous prier en même tems, d'agréer l'hommage de ma reconnoissance, pour vos anciennes bontés pour moi. En mémoire du père que j'ai perdu, j'ose en réclamer encore aujourdhui la continuation.

J'ai l'honneur d'être, avec la plus haute considération, monsieur, votre très-obéissant et dévoué serviteur.

MR. CLAY TO FRANCIS BROOKE.

ASHLAND, August 28, 1838.

MY DEAR SIR,—I received your favor from the White Sulphur Springs, and was gratified to learn that the President had been so attentive to you. He is always courteous and civil in his manners.

Mr. Rives' determination not to be a candidate for the Senate is wise. Should he adhere to it, some embarrassment will be avoided at your next Legislature.

The elections of Kentucky and Indiana have eventuated successfully to the Whigs, without any diminution of their strength. I believe we have carried the election in Illinois, but it is not yet certainly ascertained. The Locofocos have carried that in Missouri, but by a greatly diminished majority.

I have remained at home since the adjournment of Congress, as quiet as I could be, which is not very 'quiet, for company is constantly with me. This is a very bustling week in consequence of the session at Lexington of the Board of Directors of the Charleston and Cincinnati Railroad Company. They will get more soft words than hard money in Kentucky.

Mrs. Clay unites with me in respectful compliments to Mrs. Brooke.

MR. CLAY TO FRANCIS BROOKE.

ASHLAND, October 9, 1838.

MY DEAR SIR,—I received your favor of the 27th ultimo, but I can hardly say that I had very great pleasure from its perusal; for, upon my word, if you will excuse me for saying so, the paper and the writing are so bad that I do not know that I have guessed its contents.

As to the movement in the State of Massachusetts you will have seen that it is alleged to have been without authority, and is retracted. If we succeed in the elections of Pennsylvania and New York, I attach no importance to that, or any similar movement, whether with or without authority. My impression is that the editor of "The Atlas" expressed sentiments which he supposed would be acceptable to Mr. Webster.

Your suggestion as to a Bank of the United States would do well, if it would conciliate support from those who are opposed to such an institution; but my impression is that it is to the thing, in any form, more than to a particular modification, that opposition exists. At present, however, it is useless to try to establish any Bank of the United States with any modification whatever. It should not be attempted until the people clearly call for it. This I think they will do; but if they do not, if they are opposed to it, I, for one, cheerfully acquiesce in the decision.

We have been, and yet are, terribly afflicted with drought. It has injuriously affected our crops, but I presume not as much as yours have been.

Mrs. Clay (whose health is now very good) joins me in respectful compliments to Mrs. Brooke.

MR. CLAY TO FRANCIS BROOKE.

ASHLAND, November 3, 1838.

MY DEAR SIR,—I received your favor of the 18th ultimo, and, as it informed me of your intention to go to Richmond, I address this letter to that city. You think I have too good an opinion of mankind. I confess that I have, throughout life, striven to think well of them, but the last thirteen years have shaken my faith very much. I yet, however, believe the mass to be honest, although very liable to deception.

You are certainly right as to one of the two gentlemen mentioned, perhaps as to both, being unwilling to see me elected Chief Magistrate. I was greatly surprised at the course of "The Atlas;" and although Mr. Webster disavows its authority to speak for him, in that particular, there are intelligent persons near him who believe that "The Atlas" presumed upon his concurrence. The issue of the elections, this fall, so far, have been very unfavorable to the Whig cause. From September of last year to September of this, the current ran deep and strong in our favor, and swept over every State, changing majorities against us, or, at least, diminishing them. All at once, and without any apparent cause, the current reverses its direction. What has produced it? To give you a proof that I am not too confiding, I can not forbear expressing my suspicion that a profuse and corrupt use has been made of the public money. It is almost impossible otherwise to account satisfactorily for what we have witnessed. Amos Kendall was at Columbus the week before the election. How easy was it for him to give orders throughout the State, from that central point of Ohio, to carry the election at any cost. And how can he be brought to account, if he has given such orders?

Other circumstances will enable us to account for some of the results of these elections. In Ohio, the Abolitionists are alleged to have gone against us, almost to a man. Senator Morris, you know, is one of them, and that, put together with the unfortunate case of the Methodist preacher, delivered up by Governor Vance upon the demand of the Governor of Kentucky, turned them against us. Perhaps they were previously inclined toward Mr. Van Buren.

If New York goes against us, as is to be apprehended after what has occurred, our cause will look bad. You will know the event by the time this letter reaches you. It is to be apprehended, because, whether changes have been produced in other States by voluntary impulse of the people, or by corrupt means, the same cause, whatever it may be, is likely to exert itself in New York.

The introduction of this new element of Abolition into our elections can not fail to excite, with all reflecting men, the deepest solicitude. It is, I believe, the first time it has been done. Although their numbers are not very great, they are sufficiently numerous, in several States, to turn the scale. I have now before me a letter from the Secretary of the American Anti-Slavery Society, in New York, in which he says: "I should consider (as in all candor I acknowledge I would) the election of any slaveholder to the Presidency a great calamity to the country."

The danger is that the contagion may spread until it reaches all the free States; and if it ever comes to be acted on as a rule among them, to proscribe slaveholders, they have the numbers to enforce it. Union and concert with them will throw the whole Government into their hands, and when they have once possession, the principle by which they have acquired it will urge them on to other and further encroachments. They will begin by prohibiting the slave trade, as it is called, among the slave States, and by abolishing it in the District of Columbia, and the end will be——

My own position, touching slavery, at the present time, is singular enough. The Abolitionists are denouncing me as a slaveholder, and slaveholders as an Abolitionist, while they both unite on Mr. Van Buren.

I should be extremely happy to visit Richmond and see you and the many other friends I have there, but I can not do it while I remain a *quasi* candidate for the Presidency. A candidate in fact I can not say, and have not said to any human being I would be. I am strongly inclined to promulgate that I will not be, under any circumstances. How would it do? The principal objection which I perceive, is, that they would say that I saw the grapes were sour. But then, what need I care for any thing they may say?

Pray remember me affectionately to Leigh. I rejoice to be able to infer, from a recent letter of his, addressed to another person and sent for my perusal, that his health was fully re-established. Mrs. Clay unites with me in regards to Mrs. B.

WILLIS HALL TO MR. CLAY.

NEW YORK, December 14, 1838.

DEAR SIR,—I rejoice to learn from the papers that you have arrived safe and in good health and cheerful spirits, in Washington. The accident you met with on your journey gave us much concern. You might have said, perhaps, on the occasion as Cæsar said to the boatman, "*Quid times ? Cæsarem invehis !*" I believe most implicitly in your fortunes—indeed, the great source at once of my anxiety for your health and of my confidence in your preservation is the confirmed belief that our Union and the future happy destinies of our country are bound up in your life. Yet the most devout believers do not disdain a little worldly prudence. Cromwell charged his soldiers to "Trust in Providence, but keep their powder dry!" In the same spirit I would urge you to take care of yourself. Your country never stood in so great need of you.

MR. CLAY TO FRANCIS BROOKE.

WASHINGTON, December 20, 1838.

MY DEAR SIR,—I presume that this letter will find you quiet at St. Julien. I should have written you before had I any thing interesting to communicate. To-day, on a call for information as to the relation between the Bank of the United States and the Treasury Department, Mr. Rives came out in a speech of remarkable vigor and decision, which showed conclusively that he had cut loose forever from the Administration. Of that I previously entertained no doubt, and now I think the public can entertain none. On the subject of his re-election to the Senate, it would be highly improper for me to interfere, and I do not mean to interfere; but I may to you say that those with whom I have conversed out of Virginia, think that it would be attended with very good effect.

In consequence of the Anti-Masonic and other movements, since the last session of Congress, at the commencement of this my friends were a little discouraged. They are recovering from it, think that things look much better, and entertain confidence that public opinion, in regard to the next Presidency, will remain unchanged, as it was at the last session.

My own opinion is that, with a view to arrest the unfortunate divisions which exist among us, to check the progress of intrigues, and to secure concentration, action at Richmond, by the Whig portion of the Legislature (including, if possible, the Conservatives) is highly expedient. Such a movement would probably be followed and seconded at Albany; and in that case, I think the question would be settled, and our future difficulties would afterward constantly decrease. In this opinion the most intelligent of our party, with whom I have conversed, fully concur.

It is highly important, if any thing is done, that the Conservatives should unite at Richmond, or if they can not be prevailed upon to do so, that there should be as little division as possible among the Whigs. The Northern Conservatives, including Mr. Talmadge, remain firm and decided. And my information from New York generally is full of encouragement. The mock nomination of the Anti-Masons has fallen still-born, and has produced no material effect even in the Anti-Masonic portion of the State. It appears that in the pretended Convention, there was not a delegate elected by a primary meeting whatever of the Anti-Masons; that except the Delegates from Pennsylvania (who were nominated at some previous Convention), not a member held his seat in virtue of any election whatever; and that some member from New York assumed the power to cast the whole vote of that State!

Be pleased to present my best respects to Mrs. Brooke.

HARRISON GRAY OTIS TO MR. CLAY.

BOSTON, December 24, 1838.

MY DEAR SIR,—I duly received your last favor with its inclosure, which is indeed a curiosity, which I will keep on file subject to your order. I ventured to give the substance of it to a Senator of this State, the late Lieutenant-Governor Armstrong, a very worthy and orthodox gentleman who believes that original depravity comprehends political as well as what is more strictly moral, and accounts this as a mere variety among innumerable instances. Of late "The Atlas" has been silent on a certain topic, but whether this be preliminary to a new outbreak, a few days will determine. I can not yet find that the parties concerned in the project comprehend any persons hereabout, beyond a *petit comité* who are supposed to command the back stairs of that press. But I suspect there must be others, and that there is some overt communion with "The American," etc., in New York. We shall see. Mr. Webster does not leave Boston, as I hear, until the meeting of the Legislature or about that time, January 1st. Whether he has any object in the delay, beyond his own convenience, I can not say. A rumor has prevailed of his intention to decline a re-election, but of this I have no convincing evidence. I think there is a disposition among the Whigs here to speak plainly, and as you would approve, on a certain subject. But until he unequivocally withdraws from the canvass you can easily see that they must feel under restraint. The most to be hoped prior to that event, is a declaration by the Legislature adhering to him as their first choice, and announcing yourself as the second. Some pains will be taken to affect this, and I must at present think with success. But neither my information nor influence are of the value that was attached to them, in "the days when I was young." I have also been housed for three weeks with the "unpleasant pains which infest the toe," but I hope to be on my legs to-morrow, otherwise I can do nothing, unless, like poor Judge B., I drive into the public offices. You are aware of the disturbing causes which are every where at work to pollute the political current, and of the address with which antagonist causes are too often made to co-operate in the same result. Anti-Masonry I consider as effete in itself. There is no longer zeal among its votaries. The mission from this State was an absolute burlesque. Still it will furnish pretenses for paragraphs and cabals. I have more fear in regard of abolition. The danger is that the Whigs will identify themselves, at least in appearance, with the Abolitionists, and thus souse themselves into their toils. This will be folly and madness without excuse. So deeply impressed am I with an opinion of the extreme infatuation of this officiousness that I am reconciled to Atherton's resolutions, at the avowal of which some of my friends appear to be horrified; but they forgive me as an old gentleman whose vagaries do no harm. By the by, I have been told that one of the "representatives" alluded to in H——n's letter is Mr. C——g, of this State, now in Congress.

I began this merely as an acknowledgment of yours and have rambled on. When any thing occurs that I think may be gratifying to know I will take leave to apprize you of it, and though at seventy-three I have little reason to calculate upon seeing you at the head of the nation, the hope of it is not among the least of my septuagenarian comforts.

I am very faithfully and respectfully, dear sir, yours, etc.

MR. CLAY TO FRANCIS BROOKE.

WASHINGTON, December 26, 1838.

MY DEAR SIR,—I received your two favors of the 24th. What I may say on the subject of Mr. Rives' re-election must be regarded as expressed at your instance, and as presenting opinions which prevail exterior to Virginia, without any intention on my part to interfere in a local election in a State in which I am no resident.

Those out of your State are struck by the fact that a co-operation between the Whigs and Conservatives will secure a majority against the Administration ; and that without it the majority may be the other way.

The object, therefore, to be accomplished, if it be practicable, is to secure that majority co-operation ; and to those at a distance Mr. Rives' re-election appears to be a probable means. If it be not ; if a hearty co-operation can not be produced by it ; if nothing is to be gained but Mr. Rives himself, quite a different view of the question would be entertained. Mr. Rives has himself no claim upon the Whigs but those which arise from his recent course ; and confining the question to him alone, his expunging vote and former course would more than neutralize his recent claims. But a more extended view should be taken of the matter. If he can be used as an instrument to acquire an accession of strength that would array Virginia against the Administration, the inquiry then would be, whether sound policy does not demand that we should sacrifice all feelings excited by a highly exceptionable vote, in consideration of a great object to be gained for the good of our country. I appreciate and feel sensibly all the difficulties in making such a sacrifice, but I think that I could submit to it, if I had a reasonable certainty of that object being secured.

It is manifest that, if we repel the advances of all the former members of the Jackson party to unite with us, under whatever name they may adopt, we must remain in a perpetual and hopeless minority.

Should we not extend to the repentant in politics the same forgiveness which the Christian religion promises to the contrite, even in the eleventh hour ? The difference between Mr. Rives and some others now incorporated in our party, is, that their watches did not run together.

Already has some mischief been done in Ohio, and in other places, by a refusal of all conciliation of the Conservatives. It was obvious that their position was temporary, and could not be maintained for any length of time. It was at a half-way house. They must therefore fall back into the ranks of their old associates, or be absorbed by us. And it seems to be a prevailing opinion here to be expedient to avail the country of the services of as many of them as we can get, either as allies or as a part of our consolidated force. I should add that it is feared, if he be not re-elected, the event will operate badly out of, as well as in Virginia.

This is the view which is taken by those out of Virginia. Its basis is the bringing about a co-operation in that State between the Whigs and Conservatives by his re-election. If that can not be effected (and of that those on the spot are the best judges), why, then, there will be another state of the question.

I transmit this hasty letter for your own eye only. I know how justly sensitive to all foreign intervention the people of Virginia are, and I should not have touched on this delicate topic but upon your invitation.

MR. CLAY TO FRANCIS BROOKE.

WASHINGTON, January 7, 1839.

MY DEAR SIR,—I received your favors of 29th ultimo and 5th instant. I regret extremely the existence of so much division of opinion in Virginia, respecting the election of a Senator, and sincerely hope that our friends may all become reconciled, and that what they may finally do may conduce to the success of our cause and the interest of our country. I have no individual wishes separate from the common good. What is best to be done at Richmond those alone can determine who there have a view of all circumstances. It is not, however, to be disguised, that what may be done will exercise an influence beyond the confines of the State.

I have been struggling to-day, and some previous days, on the land subject. My friends are highly gratified with my exertions, and I hope and believe they have had some effect. Whether it will be practicable much longer to save that great interest depends upon the future course of the old States. I can not much longer defeat the combined action of the Administration and the new States.

Mr. Calhoun, of our State, being on a visit of business at Richmond, I have given him a letter of introduction to you. He is intelligent, shrewd, and trustworthy. You may give him all confidence.

HARRISON GRAY OTIS TO MR. CLAY.

Boston, January 11, 1839.

My dear Sir,—Your friend Constans seems, for the present at least, to have blown his blast. I hope you may have continued to think well of the last letters, as I confess that I jump in judgment with the writer. It is evident, I think, however, that he writes under restraint, and plays with an oblique stroke, but he should drive the two balls ("ebony and topaz") into the same pocket.

I have conversed with a very respectable and intelligent member of the Massachusetts Senate, who, having taken some pains to sound opinions, reports to me that he can not find an individual who approves of the freak of "The Atlas." I know, also, that the editor of "The Courier," and I believe, that the editors of all the Whig papers here, are equally opposed to the doctrines of that journal. Still there is an under-current somewhere. Mr. W. has again disclaimed his privity to or approbation of "The Atlas" heresy, and said he thought it unlucky.

But I am satisfied he does not wish that the Legislature should move on the line of operation pointed out by Constans—repeating their quondam opinions. I can't say that he would advise to any action on the subject. Probably he thinks best to do nothing. I also apprehend that he thinks you did him ill offices by favoring H., at his expense, in 1836, and that you would still promote his (H.'s) interest next to your own. You will judge whether it is worth while to attempt, through friends, to have any *éclaircissement* on that point. I am also certain that he has no idea at present of saying *nolo episcopari*, though it seems unimaginable that he expects any important support. My opinions are not gathered from a personal interview with him, otherwise I would not feel at liberty to express them. I have met him but once since his return in summer. Nor do I violate any confidence in giving you these opinions; but they are well founded. You can easily see that individuals, knowing this to be his way of thinking, may feel embarrassed in taking a step which, though not intended to be adverse to him, might be so construed; and that the consequence may be a suppression of further action by the Legislature. As yet, however, it is impossible to judge; but that any effort will be made to nominate H. I do not believe, though it has been probably intended by the *petit comité*.

Wednesday is assigned for choice of Senator. Mr. W. will be nominated at his own request, and will, doubtless, be chosen. Rumors were afloat of his intention to abdicate, and the Government was preparing to cut in. I am " confoundedly" afraid he will be cut out next year, and that this State will be lost. The disturbing causes are inauspicious. The last Legislature passed an absurd act prohibitory of selling spirits in quantities less than fifteen gallons. Now petitions are presented for a repeal. I have been dragged into heading one, which is followed up with five thousand names ; though I have fought shy for many long years of all efforts to bring me out as an actor in the political scene, yet this strikes me as a monstrous abomination, and I yielded to urgent solicitations to become bell-wether. I still doubt the law will not be repealed ; and if not, it will be a fulcrum by which the Whig party will be capsized. The " rogues in spirit" will combine with the " rogues in grain."

Then, again, there will be abolition. Our people, I fear, will not be silent. It is clear that the efforts of the Administration are directed to the identifying Whiggism and Abolitionism, and the Whig party has not sense enough to keep free from the coils of the black snake. Your old Ghent colleague, though a person of extraordinary talents, and, as I believe, of great merit as a private citizen, is, I think, a variety *per se* in the human family. But as my old friend (and General Washington's old friend), Mrs. Powel, of Philadelphia, used to say, when puzzled by any oddity or anomaly of character : " Why, my dear, you know God Almighty makes all sorts of men, women, and children."

I have not shown H.'s letter since your last, nor shall I but with great discretion—perhaps not at all, but only state the substance of the extract to two or three friends.

I send you " The Atlas" of to-day ; it is triple brass. Think of the extract of his letter to you in a parallel column—" Think of that Master Brooke." I doubt I could print them in a handbill, and clear one of Nick's bank shares. But I suppose you are right in your forbearance, though my mouth waters for such a *bon bon*.

I express no sentiments to you that I should hesitate to avow any where, time and place fitting, yet do not wish to be " talked about ;" and I know you will govern yourself accordingly.

MR. CLAY TO FRANCIS BROOKE.

SENATE CHAMBER, January 18, 1839.

MY DEAR SIR,—I received your two favors of the 16th and 17th inst. I am highly gratified with the prospects which exists at Richmond, of general concurrence among the Opposition, as to the Presidential election, whatever divisions may unhappily exist on another question. It is of very great importance that there should be some expression of the preference which is entertained in Virginia, and its influence elsewhere would be great, if not decisive.

I lament exceedingly, the unfortunate divisions which prevail, in respect to the Senatorial elections. Is it possible that there is any danger of the election of a friend of the Administration? Is it possible that any Whig can prefer such a friend to a Conservative?

By the by, Mr. Rives, in conversation with me, expressed surprise at your opposition to his re-election. He derived different impressions from his intercourse with you at the White Sulphur Springs. His surprise was not accompanied with any complaint, but on the contrary, with declarations of high regard, and personal esteem for you.

MR. CLAY TO FRANCIS BROOKE.

SENATE CHAMBER, January 28, 1839.

MY DEAR SIR,—I have received your several favors respecting the state of things at Richmond, in reference to your Senatorial election, and thank you for them. I did not acknowledge them severally as they arrived, because they did not seem to call for any particular observation from me. The divisions and dissensions in the Legislature at Richmond, are deeply to be deplored, and I fervently hope that means may be found to heal and harmonize. At Annapolis, they have just elected, or re-elected, Mr. Merrick, and concord, it is thought, will be again restored.

The spirits of my friends are again revived, and they think that they see, in various quarters, indications of the final result which their partiality prompts them to desire. I believe myself, that the current in my favor, which for the moment appeared to be impeded, will again burst forward, with accumulated strength.

The movement which you suppose will take place at Richmond, if made, would give great impulse to that current.

Poor Mrs. Wickham, I see, is gone. Those who are falling around us, should remind us that we, ere long, must follow them, and their departure diminishes the motives of our remaining here.

MR. CLAY TO FRANCIS BROOKE.

ASHLAND, April 2, 1839.

MY DEAR SIR,—I duly received your favor of the 13th ult., and felt highly gratified with the favorable account of the state of public affairs in Virginia, which it communicates. I must, however, retort upon you a charge that is often made against me, that I fear you are too sanguine. There seems to be making a prodigious effort on the side of the Administration, and I see no evidence of corresponding or counteracting exertions on the other side. Their late Convention will strengthen them, because it is an organization of their party, and the members will return to their respective homes, animated by the confidence and hopes inspired by their interchange of opinion and feeling. Where parties are nearly balanced, that which is disciplined, and in a state of complete organization, is almost sure to prevail over its adversary in the contest. I never was more perfectly convinced than I was in 1832, of the immense importance of a Convention, followed by a county and state organization. In the autumn of that year, just before the Presidential election, the young men held a Convention in Lexington. It was well attended—filled with the *élite* of the State. They made many stirring and eloquent speeches, published an address to the State, put it into complete organization, by the appointment in all the counties of large Committees of Vigilance and Correspondence, and returned home full of enthusiasm. The result was, Jackson was beaten by upward of seven thousand votes. If you could get a similar convention of young men at Charlottesville, or Staunton, just before the election, I believe that it would be attended with a similar result.

By the by, is it possible that two of the judges of the Court of Appeals, attended and took part in the proceedings of the recent Convention, and that Judge Tucker presided? If it be true, I regard the fact as a strong mark of the degeneracy of the times.

I have not enjoyed good health since my return home, from severe colds, but I am getting better, and we have the prospect of an early and fine spring. I found Mrs. Clay in her usual good health.

Is it possible that there will be no arrangement between Messrs. Harvie and Botts; and that they will both persevere, with the certainty of both being defeated? In such a state of things, the merit is with the declining party, whatever it may be.

In Kentucky, every thing looks fair. We may carry every Congressional district, and we may be defeated in three. I think not more. From Tennessee, too, from Mississippi and Louisiana, I receive the most favorable accounts.

Do me the favor to present the warm regards of Mrs. Clay and myself to Mrs. Brooke.

MR. CLAY TO GENERAL COMBS.

MAYSVILLE, July 4, 1839.

MY DEAR GENERAL,—Having heard here that H. E. Baron de Marechal, the Austrian Minister, has gone to Lexington, I have inclosed to him a letter of introduction to you, one to Major Tilford, and one to Mrs. Clay. I wish you would all contrive to make him feel agreeable and happy. He is plain, unaffected, and intelligent.

Take him out to see Mrs. Clay, giving her some notice of his coming. And tell her to make up a little afternoon party for him, and give him some ice-creams, etc.

MR. CLAY TO GENERAL COMBS.

WASHINGTON, December 1, 1839.

MY DEAR SIR,—I transmit you inclosed a letter. I received that which you did me the favor to address to me from New York, and noted its contents.

All eyes are now turned toward your proceedings at Harrisburg, which I hope may be such as to produce union, harmony, and success.

MR. CLAY TO GENERAL COMBS.

WASHINGTON, December 3, 1839.

MY DEAR SIR,—I have received and thank you for your several letters addressed to me from New York and Philadelphia.

You have found a most extraordinary state of things in respect to the Convention at Harrisburg and General Scott.

I understand it to be conceded, by the Delegates and Members of Congress from New York, a majority of whom have waited on the General, that eight or nine tenths of the Whigs of that State prefer me. Nevertheless they prefer to make a nomination in conformity to the wishes of the one or two tenths.

Now the question is, and it may be worked by the rule of three, whether it is easier to bring over eight or nine tenths to one or two tenths, or one or two tenths to eight or nine? whether the majority (and such a majority!) can be easier drawn to the minority, or the minority, small as it is, to the majority?

What security is there that if a nomination is made, contrary to the wishes of a large majority, there is not danger of a loss, out of that majority, greater in extent than the one or two tenths who are only to be conciliated?

But I will not pursue this matter. The considerations must all be obvious to you.

CHAPTER XI.

CORRESPONDENCE OF 1840, '41, '42, AND '43.

C. HAMMOND TO MR. CLAY.

CINCINNATI, January 21, 1840.

DEAR CLAY,—Ever since the determination of the Harrisburg Convention was known, I have been watching for a little abatement of decrepitude, that I might address you a letter of congratulation, in my own hand. I have now attempted it.

I do think that you have great reason to be thankful that the burden of being a candidate for the Presidency was not put upon you. In my view the canvass was always full of degradation, and I think that now-a-days its humiliation is greatly increased. Since the categories of Sherrod Williams set the precedent, every one claims to question the candidate of his life, opinions, and general conduct. An indecent impudence marks the movements of his friends; the foulest and often most painful imputations characterize the assaults of opponents. A man has to give up his own self-respect, or every hour give offense to some pedagogue that stands over him with uplifted rod. From such a condition I would ask that all high-minded men may be delivered, and I would earnestly condole with every friend made subject to it by the imperious call of the country. And, after all, what is the station when attained? Just that in which no upright, independent man can feel himself at ease, or hold his own assurance that he makes his own opinions the basis of his public acts. I pray you take no exception to an instance I shall cite.

J. Q. Adams, in November last, wrote a strong letter on the Amistad case. How widely does it vary, in its positions of public law, from those urged upon the British Government by the Department of State, respecting slaves escaping to Canada, when

Mr. Adams was President of the United States! Thus must the man be lost in the office. At best, it requires a good scribe and an easily controlled docility.

The place you now hold has ever appeared of the highest honor to me, when held as you hold it, in ample confidence with your constituents. A Senator is the adviser and the trier of the President; a Senator, thoroughly informed of public affairs, endowed with high powers of elocution, braced with nerve for every exigency, possessed of a competent estate, and deep in the confidence of his State, is just the man I could once have so far envied as to wish that what he had in enjoyment could be some day within my reach.

I congratulate you and the country that you are a Senator, and I hope you will not lightly give up the place. Every thing we see or hear, or attempt to understand, points to approaching exigences, in which the country must call you to the rescue.

MR. CLAY TO A COMMITTEE.

WASHINGTON, March 26, 1840.

GENTLEMEN,—I have received your letter inviting me to deliver an address at a celebration of the raising of the seige of Fort Meiggs, proposed the 11th of June, 1840. Considering the highly respectable source whence the proposal of this celebration originated, the motive of it, and the friendly terms in which you have conveyed the invitation, it would afford me much satisfaction to be able to accept it; but, if my public duties do not, at that time, require my attendance here, I shall have just reached my home, after an absence of six months. I can not, therefore, contract the engagement which you invite me to make, and must leave to some other person the gratification of addressing our fellow-citizens on the occasion in contemplation.

MR. FOX (BRITISH MINISTER) TO MR. CLAY.

WASHINGTON, July 11, 1840.

DEAR SIR,—I believe it will be more correct that I should wait to see what Congress will do, before I give away any of the copies sent to me of the British Commissioner's Report. I shall then, I hope, be able to send it to you, either by Mr. Crittenden, or some other of your friends in Congress who may be returning at the close of the session to your State, and whom I can request to take charge of it.

I inclose the draft accepted at thirty days, which I will provide duly for the settlement of at the office of the United States Bank here. With high respect, yours very faithfully.

JUDGE (HENRY) BALDWIN TO MR. CLAY.

—— 1840.

MY DEAR SIR,—I have this moment come from Bamford's through the rain. The first thing I read was a paper containing your remarks on Gallatin's pamphlet. It is, in the language of Scripture, health to my soul, and marrow to my bones. It is, as we say in Pennsylvania of apple-toddy—meat, drink, washing, and lodging. Here is a token from one who always respected you as his old speaker, and schoolmaster in politics, elections, and candidates—*non obstanti*—and who in times of the highest excitement, never said of you as a statesman, a harsher thing than is in the pamphlet he put into your hands.

(Any thing connected with the pending election, to the contrary notwithstanding, which has nothing to do with the personal accounts of H. B. and H. C.)

Here is a drop of the honest stuff—genuine Pennsylvania, the true extract, the essence of the American system, the produce of the same soil which gave us birth, and whence we derive our bread. It will suit an American palate, and raise no conscientious, constitutional scruples in an American stomach. Take a drop of it to my health in memory of Auld Lang Syne.

This Florida case is a tough one. I shall have three or four evenings of leisure. When you, Creighton, Vance, and Ewing are disposed to bury old grudges, let me know it. Mrs. Bamford has a small moiety of the self same, and you will all be as welcome as the flowers of May.

This is for your eye and those named, but for no others.

GENERAL HARRISON TO MR. CLAY.

NORTH BEND, November 15, 1840.

MY DEAR SIR,—I shall set out for Louisville, in the mail boat, to-morrow. I have written to Mr. C. Wickliffe (with whom I have the business which takes me to Kentucky), to meet me in Frankfort (having understood that he has removed to Bardstown).

Since my letter to you, I have thought that our personal meeting might give rise to speculations, and even jealousies, which it might be well to avoid; for, although I have made up my mind to disregard things of that sort when they are unavoidable, yet, as all the objects to be answered by our seeing each other might be accomplished through a mutual friend or friends, I submit to you whether it would not be better to adopt this mode of communication. If you think so, I request you to name to me the friend, as heretofore, to whom I may communicate my views upon a certain important action of mine, and receive yours in return. Upon the subject to which I allude, I assure you I have had no sort of communication with any one, unless it be important suggestions by unknown individuals (with but one exception. I refer to two letters written by a man whom I know, suggesting a general principle). I inclose this to Mr. Crittenden. I shall stay but one day in Louisville, if I can get away.

MR. CLAY TO FRANCIS BROOKE.

WASHINGTON, December 8, 1840.

MY DEAR SIR,—I arrived here safely the day before yesterday. Prior to my departure from home, I received your favor addressed to me there, as I now have that of the 6th, addressed to me here. I deeply regretted the loss of the Virginia vote, but presumed it was the result of fraud, and other causes. We are looking with great interest to the course of your Legislature. The want of a quorum in the Senate has prevented the reception of the President's Message. We shall get it to-day or to-morrow.

I left General Harrison at Lexington, and I have seen and conversed a good deal with him. He is much broken, but his mind retains all its strength and vigor. He appears to be animated by the best dispositions, and if he acts in conformity to them, our hopes will be all realized. I communicated to him that, during the short time I expected to remain in public life, I had no desire to change my position in the Senate. He professed, and I have no doubt now entertains, sentiments of warm regard and attachment to me. I do not believe that he had then made up his mind as to the members of his Cabinet. I think it probable, although he did not say so, that he will invite Crittenden and Ewing to take places in it. Beyond that I will not venture even a conjecture. I thought it right to explain frankly to him my feelings and relations toward Mr. Webster, and I stated to him that, although my confidence in that gentleman had been somewhat shaken, during the last eight years, I did not see how any Whig President could overlook him; that if I had been elected, I should have felt myself constrained to offer him some distinguished station; and that if he chose to appoint him to office, it would not diminish the interest I felt in the success of his Administration, nor my zeal in its support, if it were conducted in the principles I hoped it would be. I added an expression of my opinion that he was not suited to the office of Secretary of the Treasury, which I had understood some of his friends wished him to fill.

The General is to be here in a few weeks, to go to Virginia, and to return about the 4th of March.

MR. CLAY TO FRANCIS BROOKE.

WASHINGTON, January 7, 1841.

MY DEAR SIR,—I received your favor of the 5th. I should have written to you before but I really had nothing to write. I am sorry that mere rumors about the composition of the Cabinet should fill any Virginia Whig with apprehension of the Spring elections. I venture to say that Gen. Harrison will have a better Cabinet, and less of federalism in it than even Jackson or Van Buren had. What more is wanted? Are not some of our friends too nervous? Mr. Webster, I suppose, will be a member of it; but among all the rest talked of I know of no Federalist. "The Enquirer" calls Mr. Crittenden most untruly a Federalist.

So it does me. But I hope that Virginia will no longer be affected by the slang of "The Enquirer."

The exact time is not known when General Harrison will be here. It is conjectured that it will be from the 15th to the 25th instant.

PETER B. PORTER TO MR. CLAY.

SARATOGA SPRINGS, January 28, 1841.

DEAR SIR,—I was met, on my arrival here, by a confidential communication, through my nephew, the Speaker, from Mr. Weed, who expressed some delicacy about broaching the subject of it to me personally, but hoped and intended to have a conference with me (as he had) before I left Albany. The subject was the contemplated appointment of Mr. Curtis as Collector of the Customs in New York, and the following was the purport of the communication.

That the Governor and his friends are extremely anxious for the appointment of Mr. Curtis, who, although not personally popular, is represented as possessing an extraordinary share of tact or stratagem; and as being able, by his skill in planning and combining, and his untiring industry in executing, to produce the most astonishing political results. That, with the office of Collector (which he considers as second only in influence to that of Postmaster-General) he could, on all important occasions, command the vote of the city of New York, and, *par conséquence*, of the State. That he is the intimate friend of Mr. Webster, and possesses such influence over him as to be able to direct all his important political movements, an instance of which was shown in his withdrawing Mr. Webster's name from the list of Presidential candidates without his knowledge or consultation with him, because he was fully satisfied that Mr. Webster could not then, as he now is, that he never can be elected to that office; and (although it might be disheartening and injurious to tell him so at this time) that he must not and will not be a candidate for the next term. That he (Mr. Curtis) has great respect for your political character, and opposed your nomination only because he was convinced that if you had been nominated you could not have been elected; that, your position being altered, you are now the only prominent candidate of the Whig party for the next term, and can not fail of success, unless some most unexpected event should interpose to prevent it. That he (Curtis) is so strongly fortified in his application for the Collectorship, that he thinks nothing can defeat it. Although he would feel much gratification in having your good wishes, and finally, that they (Mr. Weed and the Governor) had offered these suggestions to me under the belief that I enjoyed your confidence; and with the hope that your views in regard to Mr. Curtis may accord with those above expressed.

My reply to Mr. Weed was, in substance, that I knew but little of what was passing at the seat of Government, and was ignorant of your views, and more so of those of General Harrison, on the subject of the principal official appointments; that I knew, as indeed your recent movements had proved, that you were extremely anxious to retire from the turmoil of politics, and have as little to do with the operations of the Government as would be consistent with your duties as a citizen; but that, at the same time, it was characteristic of you not to withhold your opinions, if they should be asked, on subjects involving the interests of the country. I told him too, that I thought it would be presuming too much to expect you to interfere in behalf of Mr. Curtis, with a full knowledge, which you must be presumed to possess, of the industry and zeal he had displayed in defeating your nomination, and that too in a total disregard of the known wishes of a large majority of the Whigs of this State. Still, however, that it was proper you should know what were the opinions of the Governor and his friends, in relation to Mr. Curtis, and that I would mention the subject in my next letter to you.

Now I do not doubt that Mr. Curtis is a man of rare address and management; nor that he wields the power over Mr. Webster's volitions that is claimed for him; nor that he will exert that power, and probably with success, in preventing his (Mr. Webster's) being a candidate at the next election; nor that it is his present wish and intention (especially if you should favor his views) to support you. And I have as little doubt that if he succeeds in obtaining the office, its patronage will be disposed in favors to his particular political friends.

On the preceding facts, which I thought it my duty to communicate to you, I shall express no opinion, for surely no one is better able than yourself to weigh and decide on the various considerations which grow out of them.

As I believe I have given you quite matter enough for one dispatch, I will stop here at the end of my sheet, and probably write you again, some few days hence, from Albany.

I am, as always, with great respect and regard, your obedient servant.

PETER B. PORTER TO MR. CLAY.

Niagara Falls, February 20, 1841.

Dear Sir,—I have received your favor of the 7th instant, and am not surprised at the feeling it manifests in regard to the conduct of the gentleman in New York, who has ventured to put forth such bold views and opinions in relation to his friend, Mr. Webster, nor at the wish you express that this conduct should be made known to the latter gentleman.

But I feel that I can not, and ought not, to consent to have such communication made by or through me, for various reasons, one of which, and that decisive, is, that the matters mentioned in my letter were imparted to me in strict confidence, and under such injunctions of secrecy as would forbid their going abroad, most especially in that particular direction. Another reason is, that, although I had a conversation with Mr. Weed, predicated entirely on the facts communicated by him through my nephew, I can not now be positive whether the whole of these facts were distinctly stated by both, or by one, and which of them, only.

As you may not have correctly understood that part of my nephew's communication, I will now state it a little more at large.

Mr. Curtis was made to say that Mr. Webster was a great and ambitious man; that his affections had been long set upon the Presidency; that he had recently been quite unfortunate in his private pecuniary speculations, and repeated disappointments in these had already given a dyspeptic or hypochondriacal hue to his mind and feelings; and that his friends were afraid that he might fall into the indulgence of habits which such a state of despondency is too liable to produce, and would prove ruinous to him; that it was, therefore, incumbent on them to treat him with great delicacy, and rather to encourage than to thwart him in his ambitious aspirations; and that it was under such views of Mr. Webster's situation that Mr. Curtis thought it inexpedient to disclose to him, at present, his real opinion in regard to Mr. Webster's future prospects for the Presidency.

MR. CLAY TO FRANCIS BROOKE.

WASHINGTON, February 5, 1841.

MY DEAR SIR,—I received your two last favors. During the twelve last years I have recommended no person for any place whatever, to the appointing power of the Federal Government. All that I could do, therefore, to promote your wishes as to Dr. Berkly, was to urge Mr. Roane to exert himself, which I believe he has done most faithfully; but I am sorry to be obliged to inform you that it has been unavailingly. He this moment informed me that the appointment has been given to a Mr. Brooks.

I have been constrained, after a full consideration, and on a deliberate survey of the whole ground, to adopt the principle of non-interference with the new Administration, as to official appointments. Without it, if the day had a duration of forty-eight hours instead of twenty-four, I should be unable to attend to the applications I receive.

We have nothing new here which the papers do not communicate. There has been a little, not much, diversity of opinion as to an extra session; but opinions are settling down as to its necessity.

General Harrison probably will get to Baltimore to-night.

MR. CLAY TO FRANCIS BROOKE.

WASHINGTON, March 12, 1841.

MY DEAR SIR,—You complain of my arrearage in our mutual correspondence, and with, at least, apparent cause; but I have never passed a winter of so much pressure as the one which has just terminated, if indeed it can be said to have terminated. The painful alternative was presented to me of a neglect of my private correspondence, or of my public duties. I could not hesitate which branch of it to adopt. I have not been able to transmit an answer to one out of every hundred letters that I have received.

Moreover, I have had but little of interest to communicate of which the papers did not inform you.

The new Senate has opened with a decided, practical, and available majority of twenty-nine to twenty-two, there being one vacancy from Tennessee. That majority, I think, may be relied on in almost all of the measures of the new Administration.

The Senate will adjourn on Monday. The appointments made are, almost exclusively, to fill existing vacancies. General Payton has received that of Post-master at Richmond.

I pray you to present my affectionate regards to Mrs. Brooke.

P. B. PORTER TO MR. CLAY.

NIAGARA FALLS, February 20, 1841.

DEAR SIR,—I wrote you from Albany, a few days since, on the subject of a National Bank, to be owned by the several States in their corporate capacities; the capital to be raised on a pledge by each State of its interest, or the proceeds of it, in the national domain, guaranteed by the credit of the general Government, which would at once insure the realization of any desired amount; the power of organizing and directing the operations of the institution to be divided between and exercised by the general Government and the several States, upon the great principle of separate and yet combined and harmonious powers now exercised in relation to other great interests.

MR. CLAY TO GENERAL HARRISON.

WASHINGTON, March 15, 1841.

MY DEAR SIR,—Your incessant engagements preclude the probability of my having any opportunity of a private conversation with you, prior to my departure from this city. I therefore adopt this mode of saying a few words before I go.

I was mortified by the suggestion you made to me on Saturday, that I had been represented as dictating to you, or to the new Administration—mortified, because it is unfounded in fact, and because there is danger of the fears, that I intimated to you at Frankfort, of my enemies poisoning your mind toward me.

In what, in truth, can they allege a dictation, or even interference, on my part? In the formation of your Cabinet? You can contradict them. In the administration of the public patronage? The whole Cabinet as well as yourself can say that. I have recommended nobody for any office. I have sought none for myself, or my friends. I desire none. A thousand times have my feelings been wounded, by communicating to those who have applied to me, that I am obliged to abstain inflexibly from all interference in official appointments.

I learned to-day, with infinite surprise, that I had been represented as saying that Mr. Curtis *should not* be appointed Collector of New York. It is utterly unfounded. I never uttered such expressions in relation to that or any other office, of the humblest grade, within your gift. I have never gone beyond expressing the opinion that he is faithless and perfidious, and, in my judgment, unworthy of the place. It is one of the artifices by which he expects to succeed.

If to express freely my opinion, as a citizen and as a Senator, in regard to public matters, be dictation, then I have dictated, and not otherwise. There is but one alternative which I could embrace, to prevent the exercise of this common right of freedom of opinion, and that is retirement to private life. That I am most desirous of, and if I do not promptly indulge the feeling, it is because I entertain the hope—perhaps vain hope—that by remaining a little longer in the Senate, I may possibly render some service to a country to whose interests my life has been dedicated.

I do not wish to trouble you with answering this note. I could not reconcile it to my feelings to abstain from writing it. Your heart, in which I have the greatest confidence, will justly appreciate the motives of, whatever others may say or insinuate, your true and faithful friend.

MR. CLAY TO FRANCIS BROOKE.

ASHLAND, May 14, 1841.

MY DEAR SIR,—I have received your favor of the 6th instant. My health, or perhaps I should rather say, my strength is not fully re-established, nor do I expect it until warm weather, if that should ever again come.

I leave home for Washington on the 20th instant. I expect to go by Wheeling, and without Mrs. Clay.

I repair to my post in the Senate with strong hopes, not, however, unmixed with fears. If the Executive will cordially cooperate in carrying out the Whig measures, all will be well. Otherwise every thing is at hazard. The Western elections, as far as I have yet heard, have terminated favorably.

Mrs. Clay joins me in warm regards to Mrs. Brooke.

MR. CLAY TO FRANCIS BROOKE.

WASHINGTON, July 4, 1841.

MY DEAR SIR,—I thank you for your kind suggestions as to the best mode of preserving my health. The attack last March in Baltimore was more severe than I was aware of at the time; but, thank God, my health now, notwithstanding all my labors, is better than it was when I came here. This I attribute to the exercise which I take every morning, and to the perfectly regular life which I lead.

It is very uncertain when Congress will adjourn. I begin now to fear that it will not be until September. I shall probably return by the route of the White Sulphur, but of that there is no certainty.

Mr. Tyler's opinions about a Bank are giving us great trouble. Indeed, they not only threaten a defeat on that measure, but endanger the permanency, and the ascendency of the Whig cause. Is it not deplorable that such a cause should be put in jeopardy in such a way? He conciliates nobody by his particular notions. The Locos are more opposed to the scheme than to an old fashioned Bank, and ninety-nine out of a hundred of the Whigs are decidedly adverse to it.

COL. W. HAMPTON TO MR. CLAY.

MILLWOOD, August 20, 1841.

MY DEAR SIR,—Your favor of the 11th instant did not reach me until last evening; inclosed you will receive my acceptance of the bill of exchange you sent me, which I have stipulated to pay, at Messrs. Goodhue & Co., my agents in New York.

You will, I hope, decide upon taking Sovereign. He will, I

think, suit your countrymen, better than Monarch, being much more showy, and is also a horse, in a very high form.

We are anxiously expecting to hear the fate of the Bank bill. Should the President return it with his veto, I for one, shall despair for the Republic; if our friends betray us, what can we expect from our opponents?

MR. CLAY TO FRANCIS BROOKE.

ASHLAND, October 28, 1841.

MY DEAR SIR,—I received your favor of the 21st, to-day, from which I infer your good health, as I think I recognize in its tone, your buoyant spirits. Without ever having been laid up, I have not been always well since my return from Washington. I have worked too hard, and want rest. This feeling has given rise to a serious question which I have now under consideration, and that is, whether I shall not resign my seat in the Senate. If I should return, it will be with the hope of getting away before the close of the session; and with a resolution to take a less active part in the public business.

You inquire what will be done with the Government Land Warrants. I believe I have expressed my opinion to you heretofore, fully about them; but, without being able to specify the time when they shall be passed on by Congress, I should not be surprised if they are ultimately provided for.

So Mr. G. says we are to have no fiscal agent! That is what I have expected. Having rejected a National Bank, the State Banks, and the Sub-Treasury, I could not conceive what other project of an agent even Mr. Tyler's ingenuity could present.

The issue of the elections this fall, however much to be regretted, perhaps ought not to surprise us. An army which believes itself betrayed by its commander-in-chief, will never fight well under him, or while he remains in authority. Our defeats have not been produced by any accession of strength to our adversaries, but simply because our friends would not go to the polls. I think they were wrong, but their conduct was natural.

MR. CLAY TO FRANCIS BROOKE.

WASHINGTON, January 27, 1842.

MY DEAR SIR,—I have my old apology for not writing to you, which I have to submit to your kindness, to which I must add that I have not been very well, and really nothing of interest to write.

I was glad to learn that you had it in your power to accept the office of President of the Court of Appeals, and that you were right to decline it. As we advance in years, our labors ought to lighten. With the view to lessen mine, and in contemplation of the unhappy and disturbed state of our public councils, arising out of the course of Mr. Tyler, I mean to resign my seat in the Senate, during this session. I want rest, and my private affairs want attention. Nevertheless, I would make any personal sacrifice, if, by remaining here, I could do any good, but my belief is I can effect nothing, and perhaps my absence may remove an obstacle to something being done by others. I shall therefore go home in the spring.

The papers will inform you of the afflicting scenes passing in the House of Representatives. They will fill every patriot bosom with deep distress.

RICHARD RUSH TO MR. CLAY.

SYDENHAM, near PHILADELPHIA, February 14, 1842.

MY DEAR SIR,—I am living here on a few acres that I like so much better than the town, that although near enough to hear its bells, when the wind sets right, I never go there when I can help it, and have nothing to do with its business, which is mentioned merely to account for my being behind the world in important matters and movements that are going on. As well as I can catch some of these at present, it would seem that you are about to withdraw from the Senate, and if so, I am unable any longer to stand out against an impulse that puts the pen into my hand, making me say, how, amid all the mutations of the last ten years, I have, under all circumstances, done justice to your patriotism, in alliance with all the other qualities, to mark you out as the true head of the party, whose principles you have so pre-eminently espoused. Such a testimony can be of no value to you, but it gratifies me to give it utterance from my seclusion and leisure out here, founded as it is on convictions derived while associated with you in the public service, and although not able to side with that party in public measures, I continue to think that it will do great injustice to itself, if it does not regard you as its natural candidate for the highest honor it can bestow. At a 4th of July celebration in the neighborhood of Boston, in 1840, I expressed this sentiment as strongly as I could, General Harrison then being its candidate, which may have been too unimportant to have fallen under your notice, as published in the papers of the day, and which is only alluded to now, as the recorded and steady feelings prompting these lines to you.

I am too much out of the world to be informed if Mrs. Clay is at Washington. If she is, Mrs. Rush, who often recalls her agreable intercourse with her family, requests me to convey her affectionate remembrances to her, and her compliments to you. I am glad to say she is quite well, and beginning to think of her honeysuckles and roses as the spring approaches, if indeed we have not had it all the winter. With some grown-up daughters now around her, we are about as well content and happy as we can expect, and both of us much inclined to the old Frenchman's maxim, that "every thing is for the best, in this best of worlds."

In the sentiments I have thus thrown upon you, when supposing that you are about to retire from your present position, and in those of invariable personal esteem, I beg you to believe me, my dear sir, very faithfully yours.

RICHARD RUSH TO MR. CLAY.

SYDENHAM, near PHILADELPHIA, February 15, 1842.

MY DEAR SIR,—I follow my letter of yesterday, with this of to-day. In 1833, when I first came to live here, I threw out a volume founded on my mission to England, in the course of which (chapter 17, closing part), if so humble a production ever came under your eye, you will have seen that I alluded to your early exertions in behalf of Spanish American emancipation.

I am contemplating some continuation of the work, and may have occasion to speak somewhat more fully perhaps on that topic, as connected with the claim the English make for Mr. Canning, that it was he who first called that part of our continent into independent existence. This is not true, though he had great merit in that question—more, I think, than any statesman of England or Europe, of that day. You may perhaps remember that I had some very confidential intercourse and correspondence with Mr. Canning, on this whole matter, which, in fact, laid the foundation of Mr. Monroe's famous Message in 1823.

Now, my dear sir, will you do me so great a favor as to drop me a few lines at your convenience, giving me the date of your first movement in the House of Representatives on this subject; I mean the one which distinctly looked to our recognition of the new States? I could trace it through back newspapers and other sources, for I well remember your early speeches on the subject, but a few lines from yourself would be more satisfactory to me, and the opportunity for this correspondence seems more favorable to me now, than after you get to Lexington, should you go there soon.

I pray you to excuse the trouble it may give you, and in the renewed feelings of yesterday, I remain yours very faithfully.

MARTIN VAN BUREN TO MR. CLAY.

HILLS OF SANTEE, March 26, 1842.

MY DEAR SIR,—I have had the pleasure to receive your friendly letter at this place, and thank you very kindly for the invitation it contains. It is not quite certain that I will be able to stay long enough in Kentucky to pay Mrs. Clay and yourself a visit; but if it should be so, you may rest assured that I shall not deny myself that gratification. My movements, after leaving Tennessee, are not definitively settled, and will have to be governed by circumstances, of which I am not now fully advised. It will not, however, in any event, be in my power to be with you before the beginning of May.

CARTER BEVERLY TO MR. CLAY.

FREDERICKSBURG, VA., April 2, 1842.

DEAR SIR,—On my arrival here yesterday I received your reply to my letter of February last from Middlesex, and feel glad to find that the communication I then made to you was well received, and kindly acknowledged.

It is assuredly a matter of high satisfaction to me to believe that I discharged the obligation, which feeling and duty dictated, in doing the justice I designed of effacing the indignity cast upon you by the unfortunate, and to me unhappy Fayetteville letter that was, and has been so much the subject of injury to you in the public mind. It is now, I trust, put entirely to rest in the minds of all honorable and candid men, of whatever political persuasion; for surely none can, or will henceforward presume to countenance the miserable slander that went forth in that communication to the public against you. The entire revocation of it given by me ought to overwhelm the author of it with utter shame and mortification; and if I had any right to say, were I in his situation, it would be my province, as it should be an incumbent duty on me, to make every atonement possible for such an unfounded, unprovoked attack upon your integrity and public fame.

Believing that your letter to me, and this my reply, are calculated to benefit you in the public mind, I have sent both to "The Richmond Whig" and "Independent" for publication.

I reiterate expressions of health and happiness to you, and remain yours, etc.

MR. CLAY TO REV. GILBERT H. SAYRES.

WASHINGTON, April 12, 1842.

MY DEAR SIR,—I received, and perused with great interest and attention, the letter which you did me the favor to address to me. I cordially thank you for the sentiments of esteem and confidence, an expression of which you have so kindly communicated. And I request your acceptance of my grateful acknowledgments for the lively interest you are pleased to take in my spiritual welfare. I hope that I shall profit by it. My mind has been often seriously impressed by grave considerations of preparation for a future state; but, like the crowd in the active bustle of life and its varied occupations, I have, perhaps, too much neglected so weighty a matter. My retirement will afford me leisure for a more serious, and, I hope, more practical contemplation of it.

Do me the favor to accept a copy of a little farewell speech I recently made in the Senate, accompanying this letter under another envelop, the interest of which, if it have any is to be found in attending circumstances.

LORD ASHBURTON TO MR. CLAY.

WASHINGTON, April 11, 1842.

MY DEAR SIR,—I am truly obliged to you for your very agreeable proposal. I should have taken the liberty myself of expressing a hope of being permitted to have a little conversation with you, and to renew our acquaintance, before you execute your purpose, which I, in common with your countrymen, so much regret, of retiring from this seat of Government. At a time of life which calls me more imperatively to give up all thoughts of public business, I have been tempted to make my appearance among you, to see if we can not contrive to live on more friendly terms, and to end bickerings between two countries which have, in truth, a sincere respect and affection for each other. Your good wishes for the success of this attempt are most acceptable to me. I only wish we had to treat together on what would soon cease to be material difficulties.

I should take the earliest time you propose for the pleasure of seeing you, if it were not that I have an appointment, this morning, at your Foreign Department, and do not know exactly how long it may last. To-morrow I am at your service, as soon as you please after ten o'clock; or I would call upon you, if it were more convenient to you.

WILLIAM C. PRESTON TO MR. CLAY.

WASHINGTON, June 39, 1842.

MY DEAR SIR,—I have dispatched your letter to General Thompson in the Mexican bag, and am glad to have even so small a commission to perform for you.

The British negotiation, I believe, goes on smoothly in regard to every point except the Maine boundary, which is complicated and embarrassed by the multitude of diplomatists congregated upon it. They have been here ten days, and have not yet got to a proposition for discussion. Our hope is that Abbott Lawrence and Governor Kent will get the ascendency, and carry on the matter. The other points—all of them, I think—are in a train of very favorable adjustment. In the mean time, our internal condition is worse and worse, our separation from the Executive wider and wider, and the general confusion worse confounded. The election of Mangum has brought on a war *ad intercessionem*, and it is now generally believed (on good ground, perhaps) that there is a negotiation on foot to bring in the Locofocos to the Cabinet. Marcy and Stevenson, it is said, are the only two that lend a favorable ear, and they would have a rough navigation through the Senate.

Mr. Rives' speech, yesterday, seemed to be a new latitude and departure. He abused your distribution policy, from beginning to end, in good set terms, and with much reason, I must say. He barely stopped short of denouncing it as unconstitutional *ab initio*, and has thus retraced his own steps.

My letter was broken off by the intelligence of poor Southard's death. His funeral took place yesterday. To-day Tyler sends in his veto of the tariff. This is downright madness. God preserve us, for our condition is most sad.

A LADY TO MR. CLAY.

NEW YORK, July 13, 1842.

TO THE HON. HENRY CLAY,—The life of a political man, especially if he be pre-eminent among his cotemporaries, must, almost unavoidably, in an age of party strife, be one of great admixture of light and shade—of exulting joy and vexatious incidents—of injured feelings and of gratified pride. You, honored sir, have doubtless realized, more or less, the truth of these remarks in your own political career; a career too brilliant to escape envy —too patriotic to escape detraction—too fearless to escape opposition—too upright and honest to escape the contumely and bitter hate of those who love power more than justice, falsehood more than truth, and who would sacrifice to the Shibboleth of party the best interests of their common country. This may pass as a shade, but is it not more than balanced by the halo of light which arises from the approbation of the wisest statesmen, the honest praise of all true patriots, and the admiration of all Americans, in every condition of life, who respect honesty of purpose and integrity of principle; who approve not ruinous experiments and insulting vetoes; and who regard the welfare of their country as paramount to all other considerations? Then comes the self-approving conscience. Yes, sir; yes, bright and satisfactory must be to you the reminiscences of your public life.

"All honor to the star of the West!" I trust it will not long be permitted to revolve in its distant orbit; I trust it will not soon be permitted to set; but may He who rules over all yet cause it to rise to our political zenith, and dispel the cloud of darkness which hangs over our once prosperous and happy, but now debased and injured country; and by its genial influence and mighty power restore it to its former glorious and proud condition.

Ladies, excluded by law from a voice in the counsels of the nation, have consequently no political influence. It is right that it should be so. Their duties lie in a different direction, and their happiness is drawn from a different source. But ladies are not excluded from feeling a deep interest in the welfare of their country, and no law, and no physical incapacity, imaginary or real, prevents them from rendering it service by calling upon Him who overrules its destinies, to look down upon it in this its hour of darkness with pity and compassion, and to deliver it from its evil state. This is a canvassing which surely can be disapproved by none, and which compromises neither sex nor station. On this great source, then, of power and mercy, do I rely; and daily do I offer up my supplications that God will open the eyes of this great nation of freemen to their true interests, and in good time cause them to place the Government in the hands of one to whom all anxious eyes and honest hearts are now turned —one who will not "follow in the steps of his illustrious predecessors;" but who shall rule in wisdom and in judgment, thereby restoring a distracted, prostrated country to sanity and health. Nor do my fervent petitions end here. After a long life of honor, fame, and usefulness shall have ended, may he—leaving his testimony in favor of the laws of God—be prepared by his grace to receive a crown of glory in the kingdom above!

You will doubtless be surprised, sir, that the trouble is given you of reading so long a letter, written by a lady, without any apparent motive; and really, having none of weight to offer, I feel that an apology is due. Trifles, in the hours of relaxation, sometimes afford a momentary satisfaction even to the great; and I have thought it might possibly tinge a passing moment with a ray of pleasure, to be assured that although your countrywomen can not serve you at the ballot-box, they can, and do, remember you at the altar.

Not having the honor of your acquaintance, instead of my own unimportant name, I beg leave to subscribe, with the greatest respect, that of A TRUE NORTHERN FRIEND.

MR. CLAY TO JACOB GIBSON.

ASHLAND, July 25, 1842.

DEAR SIR,—I received your letter by my neighbor and friend Mr. Henry, and the good account he gives me of you induces me to transmit this answer.

My opinion on the subjects of slavery and Abolition was fully expressed in the Senate of the United States in February, 1839, and I have seen no reason since to change it. The speech which I delivered on that occasion may be found in a cheap, although imperfect collection of my speeches, recently published in Cincinnati, and to that I respectfully refer you. I regret that I have no copy of it by me, detached from the book, or I would send it to you.

I regard the existence of slavery as an evil. I regret it, and wish that there was not one slave in the United States.

But it is an evil which, while it affects the States only, or principally, where it abounds, each State within which it is situated is the exclusive judge of what is best to be done with it, and no other State has a right to interfere in it. Kentucky has no right to interfere with the slavery of Virginia, and Ohio has no right to interfere with it in either.

The jurisdiction of each State, where slavery exists, is among the reserved rights of the States. Congress possesses no power or authority to abolish it. Congress is invested with no power relating to it, except that which assumes its legitimate and continued existence. As to slavery, with the exception of the conservative, representative, and taxing powers of Congress, the States are as much beyond the control of Congress as if they were independent nations, unconnected by any confederative constitution.

Although I believe slavery to be an evil, I regard it as a far less evil than would arise out of an immediate emancipation of the slaves of the United States, and their remaining here mixed up in our communities. In such a contingency, I believe that a bloody civil war would ensue, which would terminate only by the extinction of the black race.

It results, from these opinions which I entertain, that I consider the movements of the Abolitionists as altogether unauthorized and most unfortunate. I believe them productive of no good whatever, but attended with positive mischief to both the white and the black races. Of all the modes of separating the free blacks from the rest of the population of the United States, in my opinion, that of colonizing them in Africa is best. They are there in the abode of their ancestors, in a climate congenial to their constitutions, and with boundless territorial scope before them. For these and other reasons I think Africa far preferable to Oregon. An emigrant can be sent to Africa much cheaper than he can be to Oregon. He would then be not only in the home of his forefathers, but he might render great service to the natives of Africa, by introducing among them the arts of civilization and the religion of Christ. He would, moreover, be secure forever against the progress of the white man, which he would be far from being in Oregon.

I have regretted extremely the agitation of abolition in the free States. It has done no good, but harm. It will do no good. The great body of Abolitionists, like the great mass of every party, I have no doubt, is honest, sincere, and humane. Their leaders deceive them, and will endeavor to profit by them. They will seek to ride into public office, and to snatch public honor, upon the delusions which they propagate.

Abolition is a delusion which can not last. It is impossible it should endure. What is it? In pursuit of a principle—a great principle, if you please, it undertakes to tread down and trample in the dust all opposing principles, however sacred. It sets up the right of the people of one State to dictate to the people of other States. It arrays State against State. To make the black man free, it would virtually enslave the white man. With a single idea some of its partisans rush on blindly, regardless of all consequences. They have dared even to threaten our glorious Union with dissolution. And suppose that unhallowed object achieved, would it emancipate the slaves? What is their next step? Is it to light up a war between the dissevered parts of the Union, and through blood, devastation, and conflagration, to march forward to emancipation? Are they at all sure that through such diabolical means they would be able finally to arrive at their object? No, my friend, let each State, and the people of each State, take care of their own interests, leaving other States, and the people of other States, to take care of theirs. We have enough to do in our respective and legitimate spheres of action— enough for the exercise of all the charities and sympathies of our nature.

But what is ultimately to become of slavery? asks the impatient Abolitionist. I can not tell him with any certainty. I have no doubt that the merciful Providence, which permitted its introduction into our country against the wishes of our ancestors, will, according to His own good pleasure and time, provide for its mitigation or termination.

In the mean time, we have had much to encourage us. Our Revolution led to the cessation of the African slave trade with the United States. It altogether ceased in 1808. Many States emancipated their slaves, not by the perilous process of an immediate liberation, but by the gradual and cautious proceeding of a slow and regulated emancipation, liberating the offspring at mature age, and leaving the parents in slavery; thus making preparation for the proper use of the liberty which their children were to enjoy. Every where a spirit of humanity was, more and more, infusing itself into the laws for the regulation of the treatment of slaves, until it was checked, in some places, by the agitation of Abolition. Some States, where the proportion of slaves was not very great in comparison with the whites, were beginning seriously to think about the practicability of a gradual emancipation within their limits, but they, too, have been checked by the intemperate zeal of Abolitionists. The feasibility of African colonization has been demonstrated, and the Society, with its limited means, has been quietly prosecuting its noble object.

By some of the means indicated, and others hidden from our view, by an all-wise Providence, we may cherish the hope that, if violent Abolitionists will cease stirring up strife and agitating the passions, we may ultimately alleviate the evils, if not eradicate the existence of slavery in our land.

The generation that established our independence achieved a great and glorious work. Succeeding generations have accomplished much in advancing the growth, the power, and the greatness of this nation. We must leave some things to posterity, and among others the task of making adequate provision for the institution of Slavery.

In spite of slavery, our arms triumphed in the revolutionary struggle. And it is not too much to assert that, if Abolition had developed itself then, as it since has done, we should have failed. We should have been unable to form the Confederation, or subsequently to have adopted the present Constitution. In spite of slavery, we were successful in the second war with Great Britain. And in neither war, it is a gratifying historical fact, was the enemy able, by all his arts of seduction, to withdraw many slaves from their fidelity. In spite of slavery, we have moved onward in our march to power and greatness, augmenting our population, in a period only co-extensive with that of my own life, from two and a half to seventeen millions.

If our country is now writhing under the agony of extreme pecuniary distress and embarrassment, it has not been produced by slavery, at least not by black slavery. It has been brought about, I think, by the exercise of arbitrary power, but not that which the master exerts over his black slave.

Let us cease to agitate a topic which divides, distracts, and inflames the community; which tends to array man against man, State against State, and section against section, and which threatens the greatest of all possible calamities which could befall this people, the dissolution of the union of these States. Let us, in place of discord and dissension, cultivate peace, harmony, and good will among the people and the States of this Confederacy. And let us recollect that we have other duties—far higher duties —to perform toward our country, toward posterity, and toward the world, than even the extirpation of African slavery, however much its original introduction among us is to be deplored.

I have thus, in answer to your inquiries, given you a full, candid, and unreserved exposition of my opinions and feelings, on the several subjects to which they relate. I hope they will be received and examined in the same friendly and frank spirit in which they are communicated.

JUDGE STORY TO MR. CLAY.

CAMBRIDGE, August 3, 1842.

MY DEAR SIR,—I return you my sincere thanks for the copy of your Lexington dinner speech, which you have been so kind as to send me. I have read it with deep interest. It abounds with passages of great eloquence and statesmanlike views, and lofty principles. I am a Whig, and although I do not pretend to mingle in the common politics of the day, there are great measures upon which I have a decided opinion, and which I would not disguise, if 1 could. I am for a National Bank, a protective Tariff, a distribution law of the public lands, and a permanent Bankrupt law. All these measures are, in my judgment, indispensable to the public prosperity and peace of our country. In promoting these measures, I know no man who has labored more perseveringly, or with more zeal, ability, and honorable devotion, than yourself, at all times. I, as one, feel grateful to you for these labors; and I trust that my country will, for many years to come, possess the services of one whose eminent talents have so justly obtained the approval of the most enlightened minds in our public councils.

With my best personal wishes for the entire restoration of your health, and for many years of life, happy as well as useful, I beg you to believe me, with the highest respect, truly your most obliged friend and servant.

MR. CLAY TO JOHN S. LITTELL.

ASHLAND, August 17, 1842.

MY DEAR SIR,—I received your obliging letter with its inclosure. The arrangement, by which Mr. Epes Sargent has undertaken to compose a biography of me, was made by the young men of New York, prior to my learning, through Mr. Toland, your friendly wishes. It would have been, otherwise, very agreeable to me to have acceded to them.

Mr. Sargent's work, I presume, from what I have heard of its progress, is now nearly ready for the press. I wish he had a better subject for his pen; and I fear that it may be with him, as it has been with many of the artists, who have taken my portrait, that, owing to the defects of the original, nothing very striking or interesting will be produced. I am sure that it will be no more his than it was their fault. I have perused your song with lively interest, and I cordially thank you for it. If my judgment is not biased by the flattering expressions and sentiments toward me, which it contains, I think it will be found to be extremely well adapted to the popular use for which it was intended.

Accept, my dear sir, my grateful acknowledgments for your friendly views and intentions toward me; and assurances of my esteem and regard.

AMOS P. GRANGER AND OTHERS TO MR. CLAY.

SYRACUSE, ONONDAGA COUNTY, NEW YORK,
September 10, 1842.

DEAR SIR,—It having recently become known among your friends in this town, that one of our citizens had received a request from you, to purchase and forward to you a quantity of Onondaga salt for use upon your farm at Ashland, a large meeting was immediately assembled at which it was resolved to ask your acceptance free of charge of a small invoice containing specimens of the various kinds of salt manufactured from our saline waters.

The undersigned were appointed a Committee to advise you of the shipment and to express to you in behalf of the meeting, the high estimation in which your character and public services are held.

We now take great pleasure in advising you of the shipment of twenty-three barrels to the care of January & Son, Maysville, Kentucky, with instructions to deliver to you free of charge. You will find specimens of common and solar salt, ground and refined dairy salt, which we venture to say will prove equal to the best quality of the imported article.

A very large number of your friends, as will be seen by the inclosed list of names, accompanying the invoice, have shared in the gratification of exhibiting this small, but sincere manifestation of the grateful sense which they entertain of your unwavering devotion to the great interests of American industry in all its branches.

Indeed, sir, those whose sentiments we are instructed to communicate, feel that your public services have laid them under a mightier debt of gratitude than they can express by this imperfect mark of their respect and esteem.

Connected as they are immediately or remotely with this important branch of domestic industry, they know that their own prosperity and happiness vitally depend upon the maintenance of the principles which have guided your public life—they gratefully remember that in the councils of the nation you have ever been the consistent friend and the eloquent advocate of American Labor. While others have sought the prostration of this and other great interests, now grown into national importance, you have always been found in opposition to the attempt. Your voice has ever been on the side of protection to the industry of your own country, against the blighting competition of foreign labor, controlled by foreign capital.

The Saline waters of Onondaga are believed to be inexhaustible, and sufficient capital has already been invested in the manufacture of salt from them to furnish half the quantity consumed in the United States. Under a system of just protection that capital was profitably employed, and thousands of laborers in this and other dependent branches of industry, received a comfortable subsistence. But under the late existing laws this important interest has just reached the lowest point of depression. Capital is without its return, and labor without its reward.

For the future, we hope much from the recent legislation of Congress in establishing a Tariff of duties upon foreign products, affording, as is believed, a fair measure of protection to domestic industry. But we can not forget that the war-cry of repeal has already been sounded.

At such a crisis, when that great system, of which the honor of being the founder, belongs to you, and which it was your glorious ambition to establish upon a sound and permanent basis, had been suddenly prostrated, and when dangers are again thickening around it, your eminent services in the public councils in behalf of that beneficent system can not but be justly appreciated. The eyes of the nation again turn to you.

In conclusion, sir, we beg leave to express the hope that your life may be long spared to your country.

We are your friends and obedient servants.

A. M. JANUARY TO MR. CLAY.

MAYSVILLE, September 22, 1842.

DEAR SIR,—We received for you this morning from Syracuse, New York, twenty-three barrels salt, and one small box, eighteen barrels of which, and the box, we have forwarded to-day in Jno. Nudegate's wagon, to be delivered at Ashland free of any charge. The carriage we pay here on return of the wagoner with a receipt of the delivery, the remaining five barrels we will forward by the first opportunity in same way.

Very respectfully your friends, etc.

MR. CLAY TO NICHOLAS O. BRITTON.

ASHLAND, September 23, 1842.

MY DEAR SIR,—I received your obliging letter, and candidly thank you for the sentiments of regard and friendship toward me which it communicates; and I am extremely happy to receive from you such strong expressions of confidence in the Whig character of your State. The apathy which you nevertheless describe as the cause of the loss of your Legislature is greatly to be deplored. Besides depriving the country of the services of an able and upright Senator, it inspires our adversaries with fresh hopes, and will stimulate them to make invigorated exertions. It is to be regretted that the force of the truth, that the price of liberty is eternal vigilance, is not more generally felt.

With respect to my becoming a candidate for the high office to which you refer, I can add nothing to what I said in a public speech delivered at a Barbecue near this place, in June last. I have no wish to be forced upon the people; no desire that my name shall be used, unless I am fully persuaded that it is wanted by a majority of my countrymen. The prevalence of the apathy noticed by you makes it difficult to comprehend their real wishes; and there is certainly some danger that the road to victory may be lost by the Whigs from the defeats which they suffer. There is, however, ample time yet to form some satisfactory opinion as to the probable views of the majority of the people of the United States. If we have our troubles, our adversaries are not free from theirs.

The course of Mr. Tyler has been such as to produce disgust and dissatisfaction. But if he has been faithless, our friends in Congress have been true and faithful. Should they be abandoned because of his perfidy? Why, when their defeat is precisely what he desires? For there can be no longer a doubt that he is wielding all the power and influence of his office for the benefit of those who opposed his election, against those whose exertions and suffrages secured it.

I wish I could see any near prospect of the restoration of a sound currency. If Mr. Tyler adheres to the opinions on which he has acted, there is none. As to his Exchequer, it would make such a fearful addition to the already enormous power of the Executive, that I have never for a moment thought it ought to be adopted.

I suppose that the only alternative left to the country is to hobble on as well as it can with the State Banks, incompetent as I am obliged to regard them to supply a general currency of uniform value.

I am unable to say when I shall have the gratification of visiting your State (Virginia). I shall seize with eagerness the first occasion I can to enjoy it.

With great regard I am your friend and obedient servant.

LORD MORPETH TO HENRY CLAY.

NEW ORLEANS, October 16, 1842.

MY DEAR MR. CLAY,—I propose at present to ascend the Mississippi by the "Henry Clay," which will probably deposit me at Louisville by the end of this month. I am not aware whether you will have reached your own shades by that period, or whether you would wish the retirement to which you have consigned yourself to be so soon broken in upon; but if it suited you to give me shelter for a day, I could not resist the temptation of diverging to Lexington, and in that case perhaps you will be good enough to address a line to me at Post-office, Louisville.

Whether it is my good fortune to meet you again or not, allow me to send you every good wish. Indeed, if I may say so without any inconvenient responsibility, I should be quite ready already to tender you my vote, if I only had one, for the next Presidential election.

Believe me, my dear sir, very faithfully yours, etc.

AMBROSE SPENCER TO MR. CLAY.

Lyons, N. Y., October 28, 1842.

My dear Sir,—I have read with deep mortification a letter addressed by my son, John C. Spencer, to certain persons in Rochester. Among the first ideas suggested by this letter, was this: Whether you would not naturally infer a coincidence on my part in the general sentiments of the letter? I feel impelled by self-respect, and the sincere regard I have for you personally, as well by my admiration of your brilliant and patriotic career through your lifetime, to remove from your mind any erroneous opinions on points affecting my own consistency and honor. I then assure you that my son has not spoken my opinions, in several, and, indeed, in the main points of his letter. I have held no counsel with him, nor even attempted to control him, but have left him free to act without any advice of mine. I heartily concur with my Whig brethren throughout the nation, that Mr. Tyler has acted most perfidiously toward those who have elevated him to power, and I feel for him that contempt which his duplicity and perfidy ought to inspire in honorable bosoms. Although I can not think my son would knowingly mistate facts, yet the advice he imputes to Mr. Tyler's first Cabinet is so extraordinary that it seems to me improbable, if not impossible.

When I last saw you in Washington, it was my wish to have a full conversation with you, but it was a period which forbade that gratification.

I have now disburdened my mind from what would have weighed upon it, and although I should object to any publicity being given to this letter through the press, I have no objection to your communicating its contents to discreet friends.

What will be the issue of our election, is impossible, in this great State, to be foretold with any certainty. Every thing depends on a full poll. If it be a full one, I think we shall succeed. I do not believe that Webster's speech, or Cushing's, or the letter, will have any material effect.

MR. CLAY TO JOHN S. LITTELL.

ASHLAND, November 11, 1842.

MY DEAR SIR,—I received your favor of the 28th ultimo, with the small volume accompanying it, containing your Biographical Notice of me. Amid preparations for my departure for Louisiana, where I propose passing at New Orleans a portion of the ensuing winter, I have not yet given it the deliberate perusal to which, I have no doubt, its merits entitle it, although I have looked a little into it with much satisfaction. But I can not delay conveying an expression of my grateful thanks for the interest which you take in me, and of which I have received many strong proofs. I appreciate these, the higher, because I am quite sure that they have been rendered from disinterested and patriotic motives. I pray you to accept my cordial acknowledgments for them all.

I am now in the hands of a Philadelphia artist, Mr. Neagle, who has advanced so far in his portrait of me, and with so much success, that I feel authorized to say that I think he will make a faithful and spirited likeness of me.

Do me the favor to present my warm regards to our friend Mr. Toland.

MR. CLAY TO FRANCIS BROOKE.

NEW ORLEANS, December 30, 1842.

MY DEAR SIR,—I received your favor by Mr. Porter, as I had received your previous letter, to which it refers. I should have before written to you, but that I really possessed nothing to communicate, and I wish now only to assure you of the receipt of your favors, and of my constant regard.

My voyage has been distinguished by enthusiastic demonstrations, wherever I have been. My effort has been rather to repress than to excite them. So far I have succeeded in avoiding my tour being given a political aspect. I expect to remain at the South until some time in February, I feel already benefited by the climate, although my health was not bad when I left home.

Your sources of political information are so much better than mine that I can add nothing to the stock which you possess. Every where I find great confidence prevailing among the Whigs of their success in 1844. All the elections of the past fall which have been lost by them, have been lost not by the increased strength of their opponents, but by voters remaining absent from feelings of mortification and disgust, created by the acting President. Such is the view which I find every where taken. The problem to be solved is, whether the Whigs can be rallied in 1844. I hope and believe they will be.

I have seen a Mr. Carter and his lady here, near relations of Mrs. Brooke, and promised them to say so. They were well, and I believe doing well.

Present my best regards to Mrs. Brooke and your daughter.

MR. CLAY TO DANIEL ULLMAN.

ASHLAND, April 13, 1843.

MY DEAR SIR—I received your favor, transmitting a letter from Mr. Gamage, which satisfactorily explains his motives in accepting a foreign appointment.

I saw that you had been pronouncing a discourse upon my poor life and poor services. I wish that you had had a better subject, but I have no doubt that you made the most of that which you selected. I presume I shall see the discourse, when published.

I lately addressed the people at home, and declared the principles which, in my opinion, ought to regulate the administration of the patronage of the general Government. I invite your attention to them, as published.

MR. BODISCO TO MR. CLAY.

GEORGETOWN, June 27, 1843.

MY DEAR MR. CLAY,—You were among the first who treated me with great kindness at my arrival at Washington. Since that time, our social intercourse has been a source of great gratification to me, and I would not pardon myself, if I were to leave this country without expressing to you all my friendly feelings. Mrs. Clay must not be so jealous, if I add how much Mrs. Bodisco is fond of you, and how well we agree in our attachment to you. Our departure for Europe has been delayed by the nomination of a first secretary coming from Persia, and whom I am to present to the Secretary of State, as Chargé d'Affaires, during my temporary absence. I expect Count Zabello by the next steamer, and intend to start immediately after his arrival, leaving here, as a pledge of our return, two fine boys, and two nephews, under the care of Mrs. B.'s parents. We hope that all will turn out well, and in accordance with our wishes.

The diplomatic corps has been rather amused by all the great discoveries lately made about Tariff treaties, and by the attempt to make out of Mr. Rumford a very smart man. The best treaty he ever negotiated, was his marriage with one of Astor's daughters. Bremen is one of the two great outlets of your important and growing trade with the German league. To disturb that trade for the sake of the few ships she employs, would be a hazardous experiment. If your Government could succeed by reciprocity stipulations, to have your grain and provisions admitted in England, we in Europe would soon enough outbid you in cheapness, and furnish all that would be required, corn not excepted, at forty-eight hours' notice. I have read with great attention, Mr. Clayton's able article in " The Philadelphia Inquirer." It put me in mind of the opinion on this subject, by one of the great men of my country. He used to say that the best commercial treaty is not worth a system of permanent and moderate protective duties at home, and full liberty for the trading community to provide herself with the cheapest markets.

Flattering myself to leave here some good friends, and having a real interest in the prosperity of the young Giant, I'll follow with undiminished solicitude, the coming events, with the hope that the contest will be settled according to our wishes.

Pray remember me to all my Kentucky friends, with Crittenden at their head, and be persuaded of Mrs. Bodisco's and my best wishes, for you and Mrs. Clay's happiness.

MR. CLAY TO HENRY T. LLOYD.

ASHLAND, August 29, 1843.

DEAR SIR,—I have duly received your friendly letter, and the box to which it refers, containing half a dozen bottles of American Cologne water, all in good order, and I tender you my warm thanks for the acceptable present, and the friendly sentiments toward me, which induced you to offer it. Mrs. Clay, who is a better judge of its quality than I am, pronounces it equal to the best German or French Cologne Water, and my opinion coincides with her's.

It was long ago remarked that any man who made a blade of grass grow, where one did not before, was a public benefactor. That citizen is an equal benefactor, by whose skill and industry an article of consumption is produced at home, and the necessity of sending abroad the money to purchase it, is avoided. To ensure the prosperity of our country, and to escape those afflicting revulsions, which are so ruinous, we must learn and practice the invaluable truth, to sell as much, and buy as little as possible, abroad. Every prudent planter and farmer acts on that principle, and what is wise in individuals, is wise in nations. I congratulate you on the perfection to which you have brought the manufacture of a very agreeable article, in extensive use, and tender you cordial wishes for your success, prosperity, and happiness.

MR. CLAY TO CALVIN COLTON.

ASHLAND, September 2, 1843.

MY DEAR SIR,—Allow me to suggest a subject for one of your Tracts which, treated in your popular and condensed way, I think would be attended with great and good effect, I mean Abolition.

It is manifest that the ultras of that party are extremely mischievous, and are hurrying on the country to fearful consequences. They are not to be conciliated by the Whigs. Engrossed with a single idea, they care for nothing else. They would see the administration of the Government precipitate the nation into absolute ruin before they would lend a helping hand to arrest its career. They treat worse and denounce most those who treat them best, who so far agree with them as to admit slavery to be an evil. Witness their conduct toward Mr. Briggs and Mr. Adams, in Massachusetts, and toward me.

I will give you an outline of the manner in which I would handle it. Show the origin of slavery. Trace its introduction to the British Government. Show how it is disposed of by the Federal Constitution. That it is left exclusively to the States, except in regard to fugitives, direct taxes and representation. Show that the agitation of the question in the free States, will first destroy all harmony, and finally lead to disunion. That the consequences of disunion—perpetual war—the extinction of the African race—ultimate military despotism.

But the great aim and object of your Tract should be to arouse the laboring classes in the free States against Abolition. Depict the consequences to them of immediate abolition. The slaves being free, would be dispersed throughout the Union; they would enter into competition with the free laborer; with the American, the Irish, the German; reduce his wages; be confounded with him, and affect his moral and social standing. And as the ultras go for both abolition and amalgamation, show that their object is to unite, in marriage, the laboring white man, and the laboring black man, and to reduce the white laboring man to the despised and degraded condition of the black man.

I would show their opposition to colonization. Show its humane, religious and patriotic aim. That they are to separate those whom God has separated. Why do the Abolitionists oppose colonization? To keep and amalgamate together the two races, in violation of God's will, and to keep the blacks here, that they may interfere with, degrade, and debase the laboring whites. Show that the British nation is co-operating with the Abolitionists, for the purpose of dissolving the Union, the World's Convention, etc.

You can make a powerful article that will be felt in every extremity of the Union.

I am perfectly satisfied it will do great good.

Let me hear from you on this subject.

GENERAL BERTRAND TO MR. CLAY.

A LEXINGTON, le 6 Octobre, au soir, 1843.

MON CHER MONSIEUR,—Etant venu à Lexington dans le but spécial de vous rendre mes devoirs, j'accepte avec empressement l'invitation que vous m'avez fait l'honneur de m'addresser pour demain, vous priant d'agréer mes remercìmens et les sentiments de ma haute considération.

PETER B. PORTER TO MR. CLAY.

NEW YORK, October 11, 1843.

MY DEAR SIR,—I received, yesterday, your favor of the 3d instant, and find it to be precisely what I knew it ought to be, and was sure it would be.

The following facts, which have been confidentially communicated to me by his confidential friend, may be relied on, viz:

That Mr. Webster, on leaving here two days ago, assured this friend, that he should return to Massachusetts with a determination to re-unite himself to the Whig party, and give it his best support. That, although there were some things in your course which he did not entirely approve, yet that he had a high respect for you, and should give you his vote and support for the Presidency. That, some few weeks since (probably when on his way to Rochester), he wrote a long letter to President Tyler, expostulating with him in the freest and most severe terms, upon the wickedness and folly of his late official course, and advising him to stop at once his wild career, or he would d——n himself and ruin his country; asking no reply to his letter, but requesting that it might be carefully put on file, as a subject of future reference and reflection. That, in his recent visit to Washington, he dined twice with the President—once alone and in private when their whole political creed was canvassed and reviewed—and once in company with the whole Cabinet, when not a word was said on politics—and that Webster had a confidential interview with Mr. Upshur, Secretary of State, in which their political views in regard both to the present and the future, were found on comparison to be perfectly harmonious, and moreover, that they were thoroughly Whig.   *   *   *   *

On the whole our political prospects are uncommonly bright and promising. The cheering and unexpected result of the elections in Maryland and Georgia, seems to have inspired our friends with new ardor and energy; and we anticipate with a confidence, that we have never before felt, on your triumphant election a year from this time.

PETER B. PORTER TO MR. CLAY.

NEW YORK, October 13, 1843.

DEAR SIR,—As it seems to have been generally known among Mr. Webster's friends here, that I had, at the pressing solicitation of one of them, although under the declared conviction that it could produce no useful result, written to you on the subject of a reconciliation, and future concert of action with the Webster party, they were extremely anxious to know what would be your reply; and, having thus committed myself by writing at all, it became necessary that I should advise them of your answer, which I have accordingly done, by reading to two or three of them, as also to Messrs. Lawrence, Webb, and one or two other Whig friends, confidentially, the following paragraphs from your letter, as comprising the whole it contained on that subject:

"I approve in the main of the answer you gave to Mr. Webster's friend. I have done him (Mr. W.) no wrong, and have therefore no reconciliation to seek. His course since Mr. Tyler's accession, but especially since the extra session, has deeply surprised me. I told him the last day of that session, 'If you mean to remain in Mr. Tyler's Cabinet, to finish some business not yet completed (alluding to the M'Leod affair), the public will justify you; but if you mean to remain there permanently, it will condemn you.'

"I defended him when his nomination for Secretary of State was before the Senate, and was very nigh getting into a personal affair with Mr. Cuthbert about it.

"Should I be a candidate for the Presidency, I shall be glad to receive his support, or that of any other American citizen; but I can enter into no arrangements, make no promises, offer no pledges to obtain it. It is impossible that I can be a party to any arrangement by which Mr. Webster, or any body else, is to be run as the candidate for Vice-President with me. I have declined all interference in behalf of Davis, Sergeant, or Clayton, or any body else, and must continue to do so. My duty is to remain perfectly passive until the nomination is made, and after that, to give to the nomination, of whoever may be proposed, such support as I can consistently with honor, delicacy, and propriety."

Our friends were delighted with this reply, and even the Webster men were obliged to acknowledge that it was perfectly correct and proper.

JOHN DAVIS TO MR. CLAY.

WORCESTER, MASS., October 14, 1843.

MY DEAR SIR,—I congratulate you upon the reviving sense and spirit of the country. How deeply must Mr. Calhoun feel the results of the late elections in Tennessee, North Carolina, and Georgia? How much astonished must he be to see the doctrines of a protective Tariff and distribution of the proceeds of the public lands prevail against his theory of politics and his scheme of nullification?

The public mind has evidently been gaining strength and courage for some months, and the fact that it has settled down upon its candidate for the Presidency has aided in this desirable event. There seems here, in the real Whig party, to be but one sentiment on that head, and it looks to your name as the rallying word. We have difficulties and embarrassments to contend with. The Abolitionists, who appear to be disinclined to all connection with the Whigs, have strength enough, which they take from us, to put us in some peril. We can, however, do nothing with them, except to let them alone, which is the wisest course. You are, however, the object at which they aim most of their shafts, and whom the leading members of the party are most desirous of defeating. We take pains to circulate your life and speeches, published by Greeley, as the best method of placing your character fairly before the public, and of refuting the calumnies to which the press gives birth. Many Abolitionists, though by no means all, are conscientious men, who view slavery as a sin, and reason to the consequences which follow. With them it constitutes the Alpha and Omega of politics and morals, and it is in vain to discuss the topic with such. * * * *

Corruption and Tyler, and Tyler and corruption, will stick together as long as Catiline and treason. The name of Tyler will stink in the nostrils of the people; for the history of our Government affords no such palpable example of the prostitution of executive patronage to the wicked purposes of bribery. The Locos of this State are equally criminal, and it will be hard for them to wipe off the stain.

Colonel Johnson has been here, and called to see me. What he hopes for, or what he anticipates, is difficult to say, though he seems in good spirits. He wears his red jacket, and the papers say, and the people think, cares nothing about dress.

Without detaining you with a long, unprofitable letter, I can not close without saying that the Whigs here have a strong feeling that you will succeed in 1844. This of itself will do much to accomplish so desirable a result. I should be much gratified to hear from you. I send without paying postage, as I see you use your frank.

J. Q. ADAMS TO MR. CLAY.

QUINCY, MASSACHUSETTS, October 17, 1843.

MY DEAR SIR,—I have received your very kind and friendly invitation, for which and for the concurring invitation of your lady to Mrs. Adams and to me, in her name and my own, I can not tender to you our sense of obligation in words adequate to the feelings by which they are inspired. Nothing could give us more pleasure than to accept your offered hospitality and to visit you at your residence at Ashland.

But the state of Mrs. Adam's health will not admit of her accompanying me on this expedition; and my own age and infirmities have admonished me that the engagement which I have contracted, is at least, as much as I can expect to perform with impunity. I have found it necessary, therefore, to limit the bounds of my journey within the State of Ohio, and to restrain all my wishes and temptations to extend my journey further. The visit to Kentucky, and particularly to yourself, will remain as a hope that I may indulge hereafter, while the kindness of your invitation will remain upon my memory with the most fervent good wishes for your health and happiness.

MR. CLAY TO CALVIN COLTON.

ASHLAND, November 9, 1843.

MY DEAR SIR,—Do not imagine that I am forgetful of you, or insensible to your exertions for the public, and for me. I have been absent from home, my correspondence is excessively oppressive, and not until this afternoon have I been able to read your life of me.* In the main, its facts are correct. It is a good outline, well-adapted to its purpose. There are a few in-

* One of the Junius Tracts.

accuracies, and too much commendation and panegyric. I do not know that it is worth while to point out the errors. I would do it if I could write on the margin.

You are unjust toward the Compromise Act. It saved our manufactures, gave them stability, and they did well, until the disorders in the currency, and consequent revulsions, affected them, and every thing, and every body else. Up to 1840, it worked well, and afforded a sufficient measure of protection. It was the duty of a Van Buren Congress to provide for the period beyond that, but it would not perform its duty.

MR. CLAY TO JOHN S. LITTELL.

ASHLAND, November 13, 1843.

MY DEAR SIR,—I have received your favor with its several inclosures, and thank you for the address, etc., of the Clay Club of Germantown. It is a fair and very able exposition of Whig principles; and I tender you cordial congratulations on the encouraging prospect of their establishment. And I beg you to accept my cordial thanks for the songs, which appear to be well calculated to excite and stimulate that spirit, which is all that is needed to insure a great and glorious triumph. To the principles announced in the declaration and resolutions, every Whig can subscribe.

I congratulate you on the auspicious prospects of our good cause.

CHAPTER XII.

CORRESPONDENCE OF 1844, '45, '46 AND '47.

MR. CLAY TO HIS SON JAMES.

NEW ORLEANS, January 22, 1844.

MY DEAR SON,—I received your two letters of the 4th and 9th inst., but I have received none from Thomas. Henry will write you about his horse. I should be glad if you could make some equitable arrangement with Bradley, to take the Woodpecker filly.

I send you inclosed a power of attorney from Henry, to sign one, and indorse another note for $5,000, which I left with you to be discounted at the Northern Bank, along with two others that I also left. I wish you to attend to that business particularly; I think the 20th February is the time. I also inclose the first number of a draft, for the sum of $——, to pay the discount on the four notes. The second I will send viâ Washington city.

It will be time, on my return home, to decide on your proposal about water rotting hemp. In the mean time, I expect Mr. Florea to put in hemp all the hemp ground I have, including the new ground and piece at Mansfield.

Tell Thomas that I think he had better make a contract with Mr. —— (I forget his name), of Clarke, for his crops of hemp offered us, at the market price between the time of delivery and the 1st of September, paying interest upon every ten tons, from time to time, as delivered. I think the probability is that hemp will fall below rather than rise above the price of $4, at which you state it now to be.

My health has been generally good, but I am suffering just now with cold and its effects. I shall leave here about the 20th of next month. Any letters for me after the 10th, had better be addressed to me at Augusta, Georgia, viâ Washington, until the 10th March; after that to Charleston, until the 25th March; after that to Raleigh, until the 10th April; and after that to Washington.

Poor Judge Porter is dead, and I regret that uncertainty should exist about his successor. A rumor has got into circulation, I believe without foundation, that he has left me a legacy.

My love to your mamma, Susan, John, and Henry.

MR. CLAY TO HENRY WHITE.

MACON, March 17, 1844.

MY DEAR SIR,—I received, at this place, your obliging letter of the 24th ultimo, and the one inclosed from the National Clay Club, to which I now transmit herein an answer. I am greatly mortified that an answer was not received from me to the communication from Mr. Gibbons, during last autumn. I am under a strong impression that I did transmit a reply to it. I hope he and the Club will be perfectly assured that I intended neither any disrespect or neglect.

I know, my dear sir, full well, the disinterested motives which prompt you and your associates in the great contest now in progress. The country ought to be grateful for your services, and it is with unfeigned pleasure that I express my personal gratitude. Allow me to suggest, that while I have no objection that the inclosed letter should be read at the Club, I do not perceive any necessity for its publication.

MR. CLAY TO HENRY WHITE AND OTHERS.

MACON, March 17, 1844.

GENTLEMEN,—I have received, at this place, the letter which you addressed to me upon the 24th ultimo, and I perused it attentively, with some feelings of concern and regret.

I received the letter which was addressed to me last autumn by the National Clay Club, and I have a strong conviction, although I would not assert positively, that I replied to it, prior to my departure from home. I know it was my intention to answer it, and to answer every communication which I received. If I did not do so, it was an unintentional omission. I must, nevertheless, say, that I have need of all the indulgence of my friends and correspondents. My correspondence is very extensive, and is becoming more and more so. It occupies, when I am at home, my time constantly. Many of the Clubs which have done me the honor to assume my name, have put themselves in correspondence with me, and some of them have even complimented me by making me an honorary member of their associations. You can judge from this how numerous the letters must be that I have to transmit.

I hope your failure to receive my reply to your letter, last autumn, was unattended with any disadvantage. On the subject of the Tariff, of which your communication treated, I have so frequently, so fully, and so clearly expressed myself, that I am sure I could not add another new word or new idea.

I assure you that I entertain a very high opinion of the motives, objects, and services of the National Clay Club. Many of the members are my personal, and all of them my political friends. It would be impossible for me to regard them with any other feelings than those of gratitude. It is quite possible that I may have received information that some of the operations of the Club were not as useful and beneficial as could be wished, although I have no distinct recollection of the tenor of such information. If I ever did receive any such, it made no unfavorable impression, and created no prejudice on my mind against the Club. I know, in the zeal and ardor of friends, that they sometimes erroneously estimate the value and importance of their respective services, and I am always ready to make allowances accordingly. But I deeply regret the existence of the jealousies and misconceptions among those between whom nothing but harmony and cordial co-operation should prevail. And if, as is to be inferred from your letter, there are any differences among my Philadelphia friends, I conjure you all to hasten to accommodate them, and to unite, in a spirit of mutual concession and conciliation, as a band of brothers in the great struggle which is before us. Most happily, concord, harmony, and union, characterize the votaries of our cause, generally, throughout the Union, and I should be greatly disappointed and mortified if Philadelphia formed an exception.

I am happy to inform you that the information which I have

received, during the progress of my journey, is of the most cheering and satisfactory kind, every where. Even in Alabama, of which I had entertained no hopes when I left home, our friends will make a great effort, and they confidently anticipate a victory.

MR. CLAY TO HIS SON JAMES.

RALEIGH, April 14, 1844.

DEAR JAMES,—I arrived here on the 12th, very much fatigued, but my general health is pretty good.

I have a note in the Branch Bank for fifteen hundred dollars, due about the 1st of next month. Inclosed I send you a check for eighteen hundred dollars, fifteen hundred of which I wish applied to the payment of that note, and the balance to the payment of my interest due to the University.

I expect to reach Washington toward the last of this month, and to remain there until the 4th or 5th of May, and shall be glad to hear from you at that place.

Tell Thomas that there is a fair prospect of selling the bagging and rope at Savannah and Charleston, and that I adhere to the opinion that it is best to send them there after I get home.

Give my love to your mamma, and tell her I will write her before I leave this place. Remember me also to Susan.

J. SLOANE TO MR. CLAY.

COLUMBUS, May 9, 1844.

DEAR SIR,—Permit me to congratulate you on the happy termination of the meeting at Baltimore, as well as the wholesome condition of our affairs in all parts of the Union. I have for some time been looking for our opponents to fall back on the slander of bargain and sale, etc. Foiled, as they are, in every thing in the way of principles and measures, it was natural that they should place their reliance on that which required nothing but assertion.

Stale and discredited as that story is, I had rather hoped that our friends would have let them have the entire field to themselves, and in no case agree to assume the defensive. But the course of some of the Whigs in Congress has, perhaps, made it necessary to meet the enemy again on the same old field.

In Ohio, I think this will be their only reliance, but I can see nothing indicating the least success from its use.

Were I referred to, by some one else, I could give information in the case perhaps more direct than any other person. It is this: About the time mentioned by Buchanan, or, perhaps, some earlier, I met with General Houston at Mr. Fletcher's boarding-house, and was accosted by him on the subject of the vote of Ohio. I told him there had been no general consultation among the members. He then observed, "What a most splendid Administration it would make, with 'Old Hickory' for President, and Mr. Clay Secretary of State." To this I assented. He then went on to address himself more earnestly to me, and said: "I feel a strong hope you will all vote for Hickory, and in that event, you know your man can get any thing he may want." To all this I replied, in substance, that the vote of the Ohio delegation, when given, I had no doubt would be satisfactory to the citizens of the State.

This conversation was in my full recollection at the time I made my statement, which was appended to your address, and an allusion of a general nature was made to it. Why I did not specify the facts as they took place, was, my knowledge of the relation which existed between Jackson and Houston, and the great probability that the latter would not dare to do other than deny the whole. This, in the then temper of the public mind, I thought might do more harm than good. What I may ultimately do in that behalf, will depend on after developments.

THEODORE FRELINGHUYSEN TO MR. CLAY.

NEW YORK, May 11, 1844.

MY DEAR SIR,—I have been rather impatiently waiting for my lame arm to write a few lines to my honored friend, that I might express to you the heartfelt gratification that I feel at the recent association of my humble name with yours, a distinction as honorable as it has been to me surprising. And should the results of the fall elections confirm the nomination, of which there now seems very strong indications, it will, I assure you, be among my richest political privileges to contribute any mite of influence in my power to render prosperous and lasting in benefits the Administration of a patriot, whose elevation I have long desired. Our names have been brought together, here, by the voice of our fellow men. My prayer for you and my own soul shall be fervent, that, through the rich grace of our Saviour, they may be found written in the Book of Life of the Lamb that was slain for our sins.

My good wife, who has never ceased to cherish the hope of your eventual elevation to the Chief Magistracy, unites with me in kindest respects to Mrs. Clay and yourself.

P. S.—My hand is still lame, and I can write only in irregular characters.

J. SLOANE TO MR. CLAY.

WOOSTER, June 20, 1844.

MY DEAR SIR,—Your favor of the 14th instant, directed to me at Columbus, reached me at this place yesterday. Your first on the same subject was also duly received here. On the first Monday of next month it is my purpose to be at Cincinnati; and I had thought of delaying my statement until then, but since the receipt of your last, I have determined to make it to-morrow. I see by the newspapers from various parts that the subject is being agitated; and, in Ohio, the Locofoco candidate for Governor is hurling it from the stump. Why Governor Letcher should feel any delicacy about making a statement, out of any amity between him and Buchanan, I am at a loss to imagine. Mr. Buchanan, by his equivocation and want of directness in his answer to Jackson's appeal, put himself beyond all claim upon the forbearance of any one. The manner in which he dragged Mr. Markley into the affair, and the cautious manner in which he spoke of Jackson, left it beyond dispute that it was his object that his statement should not be so understood as to do justice between the parties.

When my statement reaches you, and you have that of Governor Letcher, you can determine how you will dispose of them. I always intended to make the facts known to you, if for no other purpose than that it might go into the history of the case after we have gone hence.

My opinion of the necessity of the publication I will transmit to you from Cincinnati.

MR. SLOANE'S STATEMENT.

WOOSTER, June 20, 1844.

In December, 1824, about the time that the choice of President by the House of Representatives was beginning to attract attention at Washington, I happened in company with General Houston, then a member of Congress from Tennessee, when the subject of that election was introduced by him. Although the subject of the Presidential election, from the time of the commencement of the canvass before the people, had been fully discussed between us, this was the first time, after the people had failed to elect, that we had conversed in relation to it. General Houston commenced by suggesting that he supposed the Ohio delegation were all going to vote for General Jackson. To this I answered that I could not undertake to speak for them; for, so far as I knew, no meeting or consultation had taken place among them. The manner of General Houston was anxious, and evinced much solicitude; and at this point of the conversation he exclaimed, "What a splendid Administration it would make, with Old Hickory President, and Mr. Clay Secretary of State." Having often before expressed to General Houston my opinion of the several candidates, I did not, at that time, think proper to repeat it: contenting myself with an implied acquiescence in the correctness of his declaration.

The conversation was continued for a considerable time, and for the most part had relation to Western interests as connected with the Presidency, and was concluded by General Houston observing, "Well, I hope you from Ohio will aid us in electing General Jackson, and then your man (meaning Mr. Clay) can have any thing he pleases."

These expressions of General Houston made a strong impression on my mind at the time, and from the relations known to subsist between him and General Jackson, I had not then, nor at any time since, a doubt but that they embodied the feelings of that personage; and that it was the object of both that Mr. Clay and his friends should so understand it. And I have ever thought that the slanderous charge of "bargain, corruption, and intrigue," subsequently preferred by General Jackson against Mr. Clay and his friends, had its origin in the utter neglect with which every advance made to them by the friends of General Jackson was treated.

In a letter written by me, dated at Wooster, May 9th, 1827, and appended to Mr. Clay's address to the public of that year, I referred to "the importunity of some of General Jackson's friends," as indicative of a disposition to enter into a bargain. In that remark I had in my mind, among other things, those observations of General Houston. Should it now be asked why I did not then divulge the whole, my answer is, that although I held myself at all times ready to do so, if called upon, I did not then consider it necessary. The only question, then, before the public, was the charge that Mr. Clay's friends had made propositions to Jackson for a bargain. It was to repel that charge that my letter above-mentioned was written; and I chose to confine my statements to the nature of the issue. In attempting to sustain that issue, General Jackson most signally failed, being flatly contradicted by his only witness.

MR. CLAY TO STEPHEN H. MILLER.

ASHLAND, July 1, 1844.

MY DEAR SIR,—I received and thank you for your friendly letter, and the copy of "The Monitor." You have justly conceived my meaning, when I referred, in my Texas letter, to a considerable and respectable portion of the Confederacy. And you might have strengthened your construction of the paragraph by reference to the fact that, at the date of my letter, the States of Ohio, Vermont and Massachusetts had, almost unanimously, declared against annexation; the Legislature of Georgia had declined to recommend it, and other States were believed to be adverse to the measure. As to the idea of my courting the Abolitionists it is perfectly absurd. No man in the United States has been half so much abused by them as I have been.

I consider the Union a great political partnership; and that new members ought not to be admitted into the concern at the imminent hazard of its dissolution. Personally I could have no objection to the annexation of Texas; but I certainly would be unwilling to see the existing Union dissolved or seriously jeoparded for the sake of acquiring Texas. If any one desires to know the leading and paramount object of my public lite, the preservation of this Union will furnish him the key.

From developments now being made in South Carolina, it is perfectly manifest that a party exists in that State seeking a dissolution of the Union, and for that purpose employing the pretext of the rejection of Mr. Tyler's abominable treaty. South Carolina being surrounded by slave States, would, in the event of a dissolution of the Union, suffer only comparative evils, but it is otherwise with Kentucky; she has the boundary of the Ohio extending four hundred miles on three free States. What would her condition be in the event of the greatest calamity that could befall this nation?

In Kentucky the Texas question will do the Whig cause no prejudice. I am glad to perceive, in the proceedings of the Clay Club at Tuscaloosa, a similar belief expressed as to Alabama. It was a bubble blown up by Mr. Tyler in the most exceptionable manner, for sinister purposes, and its bursting has injured no body but Mr. Van Buren.

Retaining an agreeable recollection of the pleasure which I derived from forming your acquaintance last Spring, I remain your friend and obedient servant.

R. P. LETCHER TO MR. CLAY.

FRANKFORT, July 6, 1844.

MY DEAR SIR,—I send you, inclosed, a short love-letter, which I received a day or two ago from my old friend Buck. He writes like a man, as you will see, who feels the force of his subject. You can retain it until I see you.

The more I have thought about your making a publication in regard to that miserable old calumny, the less inclined I am to think favorably of it. Every thing appears to be progressing so smoothly for the Whig cause, "better let it be."

MR. BUCHANAN TO R. P. LETCHER.

LANCASTER, June 27, 1844.

MY DEAR SIR,—I have this moment received your very kind letter and hasten to give it an answer. I can not perceive what good purpose it would subserve Mr. Clay to publish the private and unreserved conversation to which you refer. I was then his ardent friend and admirer; and much of this ancient feeling still survives, notwithstanding our political differences since. I did him ample justice, but no more than justice, both in my speech on Chilton's resolutions and in my letter in answer to General Jackson.

I have not myself any very distinct recollection of what transpired in your room nearly twenty years ago; but doubtless I expressed a strong wish to himself, as I had done a hundred times to others, that he might vote for General Jackson; and if he desired it, become his Secretary of State. Had he voted for the General, in case of his election, I should most certainly have exercised any influence I might have possessed to accomplish this result; and this I should have done from the most disinterested, friendly and patriotic motives.

This conversation of mine, whatever it may have been, can never be brought home to General Jackson. I never had but one conversation with him on the subject of the then pending election, and that upon the street, and the whole of it, *verbatim et literatim*, when comparatively fresh upon my memory, was given to the public in my letter of August, 1827. The publication, then, of this private conversation could serve no other purpose than to embarrass me and force me prominently into the pending contest—which I desire to avoid.

You are certainly correct in your recollection. "You told me explicitly that you did not feel at liberty to give the conversation alluded to, and would not do so, under any circumstances without my express permission." In this you acted, as you have ever done, like a man of honor and principle.

J. C. WRIGHT TO MR. CLAY.

CINCINNATI, September 5, 1844.

MY DEAR SIR,—On the other leaf you will find the statement of my conversation with Louis M'Lane, which I promised you. My apology for not preparing it sooner is that my engagements scarcely leave me a moment of leisure.

I have your letter on the subject of the Blue Lick lie, and you will have seen in "The Gazette" the use made of it. I should certainly with you have felt no little mortification, had I thought it necessary to call upon you to refute so improbable a calumny. But the charge was reiterated upon the face of my denial, and the proof in writing said to exist under these circumstances, I thought it proper that you see the charge and have an opportunity to say if any circumstance had taken place out of which to fabricate the story. I know well, sir, that even the father of lies himself could hardly keep pace with the supporters of Polk, in inventing and giving circulation to lies, and I do not often heed them.

Upon the whole our prospects are as favorable as when I had the pleasure of meeting you. Our opponents are very active and unscrupulous in the use of the means they employ. The small majority in Kentucky has been rung in all its changes and has passed away. Your late letter on the Texas question has given the rascals a new impulse. Liberty-men, Locofocos, and timid Whigs, use the letter as a bug-a-boo to the anti-annexation. We defend it, as in accordance with what you before said, and I think it will leave little injurious impression upon the minds of our friends. But the public mind is excited—men are confederated together in appeals to the very worst passions of our nature, and the public mind is feverish, and unstable. This will not be more than a nine day's topic of vituperation. With the old issues we are safe, depend upon it. All we want is to bring the voters out.

J. C. WRIGHT TO MR. CLAY.

CINCINNATI, September 5, 1844.

DEAR SIR,—According to my promise, I give below a statement of the conversation between Mr. Louis McLane and myself, relative to the election of Mr. Adams by the House of Representatives in 1825. We were both members of the House, and of the committee to report rules for the government of the House in conducting the election. He was known to be in favor of Mr. Crawford, and I was in favor of Mr. Adams. On the morning of the election, he and I walked together from the Committee room to the House, and were conversing about the prospects of the candidates. At the door we stopped, and he asked if we could elect Mr. Adams? I answered that we could elect him, as

I thought, on the first ballot. I trust in God you will succeed, said he, and on the first ballot, and save the country from the curse of Jacksonism. You know I must vote for Crawford on the first ballot, as my State voted for him, but we all know he can not be elected, and I sincerely hope you will elect Mr. Adams. We separated, and took our seats. In a short time the vote was taken, and Mr. Adams got the votes of thirteen States, and was declared duly elected.

This is the substance of the conversation, if not the very words. Mr. McLane spoke openly, with energy, and I thought, sincerely.

MR. CLAY TO HENRY WHITE.

ASHLAND, September 19, 1844.

MY DEAR SIR,—Many thanks for your obliging letter of the 11th inst., and for its interesting contents. It demonstrates very great and patriotic activity on the part of the Commercial Committee, and I hope that the success of its labors may correspond with its good intentions. We feel the greatest anxiety about the issue of your Governor's election, and our intelligence concerning it is somewhat conflicting.

You are aware that there is a Whig Committee at Washington, consisting of the Hon. Messrs. Garrett Davis and Willis Green, the object of which is to distribute documents, of which a great many have been sent to Pennsylvania. I understand the funds of the Committee are getting low, and if you should have any surplus in your exchequer, they will be very glad to receive some assistance.

I should be very happy should it be in my power to serve your house with the sugar planters of Louisiana, and I authorize you at any time to refer them to my name.

MR. CLAY TO CALVIN COLTON.

ASHLAND, October 26, 1844.

MY DEAR SIR,—I duly received your favor of the 18th instant, communicating your desire to prepare and compose a work, to be entitled, "The Life and Times of Henry Clay," and you invite an expression of my opinion of such an undertaking, and the contribution of any materials toward it in my possession. Such a work, truly and faithfully written, might be made very interesting. But every thing will depend upon its execution. I believe you possess sufficient ability to perform the task, if you have sufficient time and sufficient materials. However, this is a moment of too great interest and excitement either to decide definitely upon the propriety of such a work, or for me to make now any contributions toward its composition. I hope we shall both live some years yet, and have many opportunities of seeing and conferring with each other upon the subject, after which we can come to a satisfactory conclusion.

A few weeks more will decide the arduous contest in which we have been engaged, and if I am to credit the confident assurances which I receive from all quarters, there is no doubt of a triumphant result.

My health is excellent, although I write by the hand of an amanuensis.

THEODORE FRELINGHUYSEN TO MR. CLAY.

NEW YORK, November 9, 1844.

MY DEAR SIR,—I address you this morning with very different feelings from my expectations a few weeks ago. The alliance of the foreign vote, and that most impracticable of all organizations, the Abolitionists, have defeated the strongest national vote ever given to a Presidential candidate. The Whigs in this city and State have struggled most nobly. All classes of American citizens have ardently, cordially, and with the freest sacrifices, contended for your just claims to patriotic confidence, and could you this morning behold the depression of spirits and sinking of hearts that pervade the community, I am sure that you would feel, " Well, in very truth, my defeat has been the occasion of a more precious tribute and vindication than even the majority of numbers."

The Abolitionists were inimicably obstinate, and seemed resolved to distinguish their importance, right or wrong. The combination of adverse circumstances has often struck me in the progress of the canvass. At the South, I was denounced as an Abolitionist, rank and uncompromising. Here, the Abolitionists have been rancorous in their hostility. A short time since,

William Jay (of illustrious name) assailed me in his Anti-Slavery prints, by a harsh, unchristian, and intolerant article, in the form of a letter addressed to me, but sent to the winds. Its object was, no doubt, to drive the party together, and it had, I suppose, some influence that way, although it was too bitter and irrational to accomplish much. And then the foreign vote was tremendous. More than three thousand, it is confidently said, have been naturalized in this city, alone, since the first of October. It is an alarming fact, that this foreign vote has decided the great questions of American policy, and counteracted a nation's gratitude.

But, my dear sir, leaving this painful subject, let us look away to brighter and better prospects, and surer hopes, in the promises and consolations of the Gospel of our Saviour. As sinners who have rebelled against our Maker, we need a Saviour or we must perish, and this Redeemer has been provided for us. Prophecy declared him from the earliest period of our fall, in Paradise, and the Gospel makes known the faithful fulfillment. "Come unto me," cries this exalted Saviour, "come unto me, all ye that are weary and heavy laden, and I will give you rest." Let us, then, repair to Him. He will never fail us in the hour of peril and trial. Vain is the help of man, and frail and fatal all trust in the arm of flesh ; but he that trusteth in the Lord shall be as Mount Zion itself, that can never be removed. I pray, my honored friend, that your heart may seek this blessed refuge, stable as the everlasting hills, and let this be the occasion to prompt an earnest, prayerful, and the Lord grant it may be a joyful, search after truth as it is in Jesus Christ.

With affectionate regards to Mrs. Clay, in which my good wife, sorely tried, heartily unites, I remain with sincere esteem and best wishes, your friend.*

* It is thought proper to introduce a few of the very large file of letters to Mr Clay on the disappointment at his defeat as candidate for the Presidency in 1844, of which the above from Mr. Frelinghuysen, the candidate for the Vice-Presidency, on the ticket with Mr. Clay, is one.

THOMAS H. BAIRD TO MR. CLAY.

PITTSBURG, November 30, 1844.

MY DEAR SIR,—The result of the late elections, although disastrous to the country, yet, when properly examined, furnishes a proud vindication of your principles and fame. No man ever before received so glorious a testimonial. I believe, in fact, you had a majority of the legal votes throughout the Union. One thing, however, is certain. You had nine tenths of the virtue, intelligence, and respectability of the nation on your side. We failed in obtaining your election through the fraud and falsehood of our opponents, who will soon feel the effects of their folly and crime. The defeat is nothing to you; it is the people who are to be the sufferers, until delusion is dispelled, and they rise in their strength to cast off the oppressors.

I have no doubt that the principles which you have so long and so ably struggled to maintain, will at last be triumphant. They are identified with your person and character, and must be vindicated.

MILLARD FILLMORE TO MR. CLAY.

BUFFALO, November 11, 1844.

MY DEAR SIR,—I have thought for three or four days that I would write you, but really I am unmanned. I have no courage or resolution. All is gone. The last hope, which hung first upon the city of New York and then upon Virginia, is finally dissipated, and I see nothing but despair depicted on every countenance.

For myself I have no regrets. I was nominated much against my will, and though not insensible to the pride of success, yet I feel a kind of relief at being defeated. But not so for you or for the nation. Every consideration of justice, every feeling of gratitude conspired in the minds of honest men to insure your election; and though always doubtful of my own success I could never doubt yours, till the painful conviction was forced upon me.

The Abolitionists and foreign Catholics have defeated us in this State. I will not trust myself to speak of the vile hypocrisy of the leading Abolitionists now. Doubtless many acted honestly but ignorantly in what they did. But it is clear that Birney and his associates sold themselves to Locofocoism, and they will doubtless receive their reward.

Our opponents, by pointing to the Native Americans and to Mr. Frelinghuysen, drove the foreign Catholics from us and defeated us in this State.

But it is vain to look at the causes by which this infamous result has been produced. It is enough to say that all is gone, and I must confess that nothing has happened to shake my confidence in our ability to sustain a free Government so much as this. If with such issues and such candidates as the national contest presented, we can be beaten, what may we not expect? A cloud of gloom hangs over the future. May God save the country; for it is evident the people will not.

J. J. CRITTENDEN TO MR. CLAY.

FRANKFORT, November 13, 1844.

MY DEAR SIR,—The intelligence brought to us this morning has terminated all our hopes, our suspense, and our anxieties, in respect to the Presidential election. We now know the worst. Polk is elected, and your friends have sustained the heaviest blow that could have befallen them. You will feel, I trust, no other concern about it than that which naturally arises from your sympathy with those friends. You are, perhaps, the only man in the nation that can lose nothing by the result. Success could have added nothing to your name, and nothing, I believe, to your happiness. You occupy now, but too truly, the position described as presenting the noblest of human spectacles—

> "A great man struggling with the storms of fate,
> And nobly falling with a falling state."

C. L. L. LEARY TO MR. CLAY.

BALTIMORE, November 14, 1844.

DEAR SIR,—The inexpressible agony which the result of the recent contest has caused me, has left me no other source of relief than the one which I have here chosen. I beg you, sir, to accept this as a sufficient apology for this intrusion. I am too well acquainted with your character to suppose that this result will affect you as it has affected your friends. That consciousness of purity of motive and of unbending rectitude, which has sustained you on former occasions, when the honor and prosperity of your country were the objects which alone you aimed at, and when your designs were purposely misconstrued by the envy and vindictive malice of your enemies, will still support you in this trying crisis ; and in the patriotic efforts and ardent personal devotion of your friends, you will, I feel assured, realize enjoyments which all the honors of public station would fail to bestow. Whatever may have been the impelling considerations in the breasts of others, I am free to confess that "Justice to Henry Clay," rather than the behests of public duty, was the ruling motive which prompted me to the humble part I acted in the late conflict. Amid the gloom and chagrin of defeat, I devoutly thank God that the family with which I am connected, including a father and four sons, native-born American citizens, and competent voters, have not been reckless of the duty they owed to you and to their country, and that our beloved and venerated old Maryland, with a devotion that has never faltered when the true issue has been presented to her sons, has proclaimed trumpet-tongued to the world her confidence in your integrity, and her stern adherence to constitutional principles. I console myself, too, (and to you it must be a source of unfailing gratulation), that I find myself arrayed in this contest on the same side with the enlightened intelligence, virtue, and patriotism of the Union, with the line of discrimination so broadly and vividly drawn, that " the wayfaring man," though a fool in other matters, "need not err therein." Whatever partial triumphs we have won, have been achieved by honest American hearts, and with unstained American hands ; no levies have been made upon the prisons and lazar-houses of Europe ; no Canadian mercenaries or Hessian auxiliaries have been either pressed or purchased into our service ; you are the only choice of the great American party, standing upon a broad American platform, supported and dependent upon an American Constitution, as framed, understood, and construed by the Patriot Fathers of the Republic. We are told in Holy Writ that " The wicked walk on every side, when the vilest men are exalted ;" and in this humiliating posture we now find American affairs. The very fountain of our political system, from whence all authority and power flow, is revoltingly corrupt. The ballot-box is poisoned by gross ignorance and wanton perjury. The ermine of justice is spotted, and the judicial bench disgraced by undisguised partisan conduct, that in the better days of the Republic would have condemned the actors to merited infamy. To what source, then, are we to look for deliverance? Alas, sir, I only speak as hundreds of American Whigs this moment feel, when I say that I shudder for the fate of my country. I know that numbers of your fellow-citizens, of the class to which I belong, have opposed your elevation, and it is because I keenly feel the reproach which this fact awakens, that I have thus ventured to address you. But be assured, sir, that wherever you have a friend you will find friendship worth possessing, flowing from warm hearts, whose every affection is yours, and wholly yours. You may never again permit yourself to be called upon the stage of public life; but whatever course your sense of duty may urge you to take, I fervently trust that the Common Father of us all may lavish his choicest blessings upon your declining years, and that, amid the contentment which retirement from political turmoil brings, you will recognize Maryland, Kentucky, and their sister Whig States, as having heartily accorded to you that tribute of justice and gratitude which an ungrateful country has failed to bestow.

P. S. GALPIN AND OTHERS TO MR. CLAY.

NEW HAVEN, CONN., November 16, 1844.

SIR,—It is with much pleasure that we execute the duty assigned to us by the Whigs of this city, of transmitting to you the inclosed proceedings of a meeting held by them, on the evening of the 14th inst.; but this pleasure is mingled with the deepest regret, that we can not hail you, as we had fondly hoped, as President of these United States. The deplorable result of the late election, has here, as every where, filled the hearts of your Whig friends with pain and mortification, and this feeling has not been confined to the voters only, but has extended itself through all ages, sexes, and conditions, from "lisping infancy to hoary age."

We were not aware, until we saw our anticipations of your

success blighted, how strong a hold you had upon our affections, and we now feel that you are President in the hearts of a vast majority of the intelligent and patriotic citizens of the country, where you can never be defeated, and where the poisonous shafts of calumny can never reach you. Had you been called to assume the reponsibilities of the office of Chief Magistrate of the Union, we feel sure that the most eminent success in the discharge of its duties could not have increased your fame, or led us to cherish any warmer feelings than we now entertain for your character and public services.

We are proud, sir, of our city, for the vote she gave you, which was larger than ever given before to any candidate in a contested election, and we are proud of our State; that amid all the deceptions and slanders which have marked the course of our opponents throughout the late contest, she has given you a majority worthy of her character, and of the intelligence of her citizens.

May your valuable life, dear sir, be spared through many years to bless the country you have so greatly honored, and whose interest in times of danger you have so often and so nobly upheld.

AMBROSE SPENCER TO MR. CLAY.

ALBANY, November 21, 1844.

MY DEAR FRIEND,—I can no longer resist the inclination which impels me to commune with you on the disastrous results of the efforts of the Whig party to do justice to you for your long and signal services to your country, by placing you at the head of the nation.

It is pretty well ascertained that had New York given you her vote, you would have been elected. This consideration is very mortifying to us; and yet, I venture to affirm, that in no State of the Union had you warmer, or more vigilant and vigorous supporters. Every thing that could be effected by human means was done. I know many, very many men, who laid aside all other business, and devoted themselves night and day in the good cause. The result of our canvass shows what mighty efforts have been made. You received 232,411 votes; Polk received 237,432; Birney, 15,875. What a monstrous poll. You received 6,594 more votes than Harrison did in 1840, when his majority exceeded 13,000. You will perceive that the Abolition vote lost you the election, as three fourths of them were firm Whigs, converted into Abolitionists. The foreign vote also destroyed your election, and there was yet another distinct cause: the utter mendacity, frauds, and villainies of Locofocoism. This untoward event has produced universal gloom, and has shaken public confidence to an unexpected extent. Even many of those who voted for Polk, now that he is elected, deeply regret the result. God only knows to what we are destined. One sentiment seems to prevail universally, that the naturalization laws must be altered; that they must be repealed, and the door forever shut on the admission of foreigners to citizenship, or that they undergo a long probation. I am for the former.

The Germans and the Irish are in the same category; the one who know not our language, and are as ignorant as the lazaroni of Italy, can never understandingly exercise the franchise; and the other, besides their ignorance, are naturally inclined to go with the loafers of our own population.

I offer you not any condolence at this sad event; the country, not you, are the sufferers. Undoubtedly, your election would have been deeply gratifying to your feelings, as the award of your countrymen on your long, unwearied, and splendid public services. You have been spared the toils of four years hard service, which could not have raised you higher in the affections and confidence of your friends and admirers. Your Administration would have put at rest all contention on the duty and necessity of protecting American industry; on the distribution of the proceeds of the public lands, and on many other vexed questions, which are now set afloat and put in jeopardy. In yielding my hearty support to the Whig cause, you are aware that I had no earthly motive but the public good. I confess that in doing all I could to promote your election, there was an additional motive: the deep respect and affection I felt for you individually, founded on your public services, and on those personal qualities which, on our first acquaintance, took a lodgment in my heart, never to be effaced.

That you may live long to enjoy, in any situation Providence may place you, the continued love and confidence of your countrymen, and all the blessings of this life, is my fervent prayer.

WILLIAM C. PRESTON* TO MR. CLAY.

COLUMBIA, November 23, 1844.

DEAR SIR,—My sense of the public calamity has, for some days, absorbed all emotions and affections of a private or personal character. I have been astonished with the result of the elections. The ways of nations, like those of Providence, are sometimes mysterious and inscrutable; and what our country has just done is of this sort. With the deepest interest in whatever concerns you personally, I have been solely occupied with these gloomy and portentous occurrences. What do they forebode to the country? As for you, they affect you in nowise but as depriving you of the means of further patriotic usefulness. You have long since passed that point when office could confer additional celebrity, or add an inch to the noble pre-eminence which history will assign to you. Though your name will not appear in the dull chronology of official succession, the times will be known as those in which the wisdom, courage and eloquence of Clay were displayed for the glory of his country. The time will come when all will be ashamed of these transactions. May God protect us from occasion to mourn over them in sorrow and bitterness of repentance. It would be vain and painful to speculate on the causes which have led to this result. The consequences of it will soon occupy the utmost anxieties of the country. For the present the Whig party of the South is dispersed; and we can not know our position until the heat and smoke of the conflict have passed away. In the mean time I content myself with the thought that I have (in however subordinate a station) fought the battle of the country under your standard, and am entitled to subscribe myself, etc.

CHRISTOPHER HUGHES TO MR. CLAY.

LONDON, November 27, 1844.

MY DEAR MR. CLAY; my chief, my old master, my venerated and beloved friend!

In an hour I shall be in the steamer for Rotterdam and the

* After the brilliant career of the Hon. Wm. C. Preston, as Senator of the United States, and at the Bar, he retired to the honorable and dignified Chair of President of Columbia College, South Carolina.

Hague. I am literally packing my trunk, and in great confusion! But I shall be too late to write from Holland by the steamer of the 4th December, and I will not lose a moment in conveying to you the heartfelt emotion, amazement, and grief with which I have received the news, just arrived, of the result of the Presidential election. Great God! is it possible! Have our people given this astonishing, this alarming proof of the madness to which party frenzy can carry them! England is astounded; on all hands I hear amazement, sorrow, uneasiness expressed; for in you and on your election depends, in the minds of this people and Government, the maintenance of harmony and peaceful relations between the two nations. The hopes of the wise and of the worthy of the New and of the Old World, rested (and seem to rest—no, now no more, for it is over) upon you. But I can not, if I would, dwell upon this matter. My heart is sad; and my time is up for embarking.

Let me, my beloved old friend, approach you in your defeat, with my ancient, my true, my invariable love, confidence, devotion and esteem; ay! let me add—and my admiration and honor. Since our first acquaintance in 1814, when we left our country to send home peace to our people, I have never—no, never—deserted you, in thought, in heart, or in deed! Never have I disguised my preference, my respect, my love and admiration for you; and I have prized, as the greatest success and honor of my life, your friendship for me, and the cheerful, amiable, playful, affectionate familiarity that you have always permitted and tolerated in me, your pupil and your friend. I know you have always loved me and trusted me. My eyes now run over—before God they do!—with the recollection of your affection and fondness for me, my great and good friend! I am weeping—as we both did, when comparatively young men—on the 2d December, 1814, the day we signed the peace of Ghent —when you threw your arms around my neck in bidding me adieu, seeing how sad I was; and exclaimed—"Hughes! my friend, what is the matter with you? I see that you are unhappy." I said that I was mortified at finding, that in the last "dispatches" to the Government at home (which I myself had copied, and was to bear home with the treaty), there was no mention of my name by my ministers, whom I had served with so much zeal, fidelity, and honor—that this mortified and pained me. You told me there had been such a sentence at the close of the last dispatch, that it had been erased as not properly belonging to a public document, and was repeated in all your private letters to the Secretary of State, and to Mr. Madison, that admirable and incomparable man, whom I knew and loved. This did not appease me, and I said, Good God! are not the character and conduct of public servants, when they are honorable, proper in the public and published archives of the country? But I loved you, my excellent and kind-hearted friend, for the kindness and tenderness of your conduct. You embraced me— you wept like a child—your heart was full of the pride and pleasure and comfort of having achieved peace for your country, and you did more at that Congress than any other of its members, by your tact, your discretion, your moderation, your angelic self-command, and your incomparable manner; you did more—and I say it, and will bear this witness before the world —than any other, to bestow this most blessed of boons, this God-like gift, Peace among men; for, like the harmony of heaven, it passeth all understanding! You wept like a child on taking leave of me; you thought of your country, of your family, of your excellent wife, of your then—alas! no longer so— numerous family of young children; of me, who was leaving you in Europe, and about to embark in the dead of winter, and in a schooner (I was sixty days on the voyage), for our awful and dangerous coast! Your heart—and a kinder and a more affectionate one never filled the bosom of mortal man—your heart was full, and you wept like a child, as I do now, my dear Mr. Clay, in recalling this scene! We were alone, in the corridor of old Madame Van Canegheu's house (for you had followed me out of the room, seeing how sad I was), where we had dined after signing the Treaty at the British Minister's—you, my chief, had signed your last dispatch, at Mme. Van C.'s, which I was to bear; and the good old lady thought it was "the Treaty," and the pen you used is in a glass case in her house, sacredly preserved to this day; for Mme. Van C. continued to believe that the peace had been made under her roof, and boasted of it till her death, twenty-five years after! and showed me proudly "the precious pen!" But I must stop. May God forever bless you! May he preserve you long for your country! No man now—I say, no man knows you as well as I do! No, not one! and I ever have loved and esteemed you, and it is my pride to feel—so have you me. Why, I could see comfort in your heart and manner whenever I have been with you. You seemed to feel as if there was a safety, an ease, a pleasing security, when I was with you. Again and again, may God bless and preserve you. I write incoherently: you would not believe my emotion. My head is confused.

I send this letter open to my beloved Joseph Ingersoll. I can not write to him. You know how I love and esteem him. You know how I have written of him to you. He will read and send you this letter. I know not, and never have known, a better man than J. R. Ingersoll. I have not written to you twice in two years! I shall do so now. I will never desert you. I will love you; honor you away, and cheer you when at home, as I suppose I shall be soon. I have been in Ireland, to see my good brother-in-law, Colonel Moore. His health is better. He returns to the United States next May. He was heart and soul for you in the election. My silence proceeded from low spirits; I have shaken them off, and my health and my heart are sound and stout.

I passed an hour with Mr. Goulburne (Chancellor of Exchequer) day before the fatal news. He asked for you, and sends respects to you. He received me most affectionately. I never was treated with more kindness than now in England. No time to read this. While I live I am yours.

P. H. SYLVESTER AND OTHERS TO MR. CLAY.

COXSACKIE, November 27, 1844.

DEAR SIR,—I write to you in behalf of the Coxsackie Clay Club. The man who said "that he stood firm and erect, unbent, unbroken, unsubdued, unawed, and ready to denounce the mischevious measures of General Jackson's Administration," needs no sympathy from us.

It is from the gushing out and fullness of our hearts that we say to you that you have been our political idol, and that we esteem you as highly, and love you as dearly as we ever have done—in defeat, more than in victory—we can not say more, how can we say less?

When we were convinced that we were defeated, we felt as if we had no country, and that all that we considered as most sacred and most cherished by us in it, was wrested from us by the insult that was offered to our own great and honest "Harry of the West."

There is one consolation to us, however, and that is, that your name will live. Yes, it must, it shall live forever, in undying, honorable fame. The measure of your glory was full to overflowing, and if success had crowned our exertions, would it have woven another wreath in the garland of fame that encircles your brow? Not one.

Your nomination was but the spontaneous and unanimous outbreaking of the feelings of a great majority of the intelligent and patriotic freemen of the land. By them you have been supported with the whole heart and soul and strength, with an intensity of feeling and exertion almost unparalleled, and every Whig heart is stricken down, and mourns that the Republic has exhibited such an instance of ingratitude.

We do not wish to burden you with our correspondence, but permit us to say in conclusion, that Henry Clay is more than ever beloved by his countrymen, and that posterity will do him justice. Our discomfiture only increases our respect and admiration for your character, and gratitude for your services. We point with unutterable pride to the fact that we cast our votes for the man "who would rather be right, than be President."

In behalf of each member of the Association, I tender you sentiments of affection, respect, and undiminished confidence and esteem.

Let me say for myself individually, may Almighty God bless you, may he lift upon you the light of his reconciled countenance, and prepare you for an abundant entrance into the abodes of more than mortal freedom.

PHILIP HONE TO MR. CLAY.

NEW YORK, November 28, 1844.

MY DEAR SIR,—I hesitate and doubt whether I ought to add to the annoyance which I know you experience at this time, but I can not deny myself the privilege of writing to you, not to condole with you on your recent defeat, I know you feel little regret on your own account, but to give vent to my own sorrow, to deplore the infatuation of my countrymen, and to mingle my prayers with yours, that the evils we anticipate from the unexpected result of the late election may be averted, and the people made happy against their own wayward wills.

You, and the holy cause of which you were the honored representative, have been sacrificed to fraud, corruption and misrepresentation, and the instruments used to effect the object were foreign voters made to order, and mischievous sectarians, who prefer to trust the success of their theory to the uncertain measures of an untried Administration than to one pledged to support the glorious Constitution and to maintain its guarantees.

The result of this election has satisfied me that no such man as Henry Clay can ever be President of the United States. The party leaders, the men who make Presidents, will never consent to elevate one greatly their superior; they suffer too much by the contrast, their aspirations are checked, their power is circumscribed, the clay can not be moulded into an idol suited to their worship. Moreover, a statesman, prominent as you have been for so long a time, must have been identified with all the leading measures affecting the interests of the people, and those interests are frequently different in the several parts of our widely extended country. What is meat in one section is poison in another. Give me, therefore, a candidate of an inferior grade, one whose talents, patriotism and public services have never been so conspicuous as to force him into the first ranks. He will get all the votes which the best and wisest man could secure, and some, which for the reasons I have stated, he could not.

But the especial object of my writing is to remove any unfavorable impressions (if such there be) from your mind as to the miserable result here. The loss of New York was fatal to the cause of the Whigs, but I pray you, dear sir, to attribute no part of this misfortune to a want of exertion on the part of your friends in the city of New York. Never before did they work so faithfully, and never, I fear, will they again; the man and the cause were equally dear to the noble Whigs, and every honorable exertion was made, every personal sacrifice submitted to, every liberal oblation poured upon the altar of patriotic devotion; nine-tenths of our respectable citizens voted for Clay and Frelinghuysen, the merchants, the professional men, the mechanics and working men, all such as live by their skill and the labor of their honest hands, who have wives whom they cherish and children whom they strive to educate and make good citizens, men who go to church on Sundays, respect the laws and love their country, such men to the number of twenty-six thousand three hundred and eighty-five redeemed their pledge to God and the country; but alas! the numerical strength lies not in those classes. Foreigners who have "no lot or inheritance" in the matter, have robbed us of our birth-right, the " scepter has departed from Israel." Ireland has re-conquered the country which England lost, but never suffer yourself to believe that a single trace of the name of Henry Clay is obliterated from the swelling hearts of the Whigs of New York.

MR. CLAY TO REV. J. M. PENDLETON.

ASHLAND, November 29, 1844.

MY DEAR SIR,—My feelings prompt me to offer you my cordial acknowledgments for your friendly letter of the 21st instant. I entertain sentiments of the liveliest gratitude for the kind interest you have taken and continue to cherish in me. And I am greatly obliged by the desire you manifest that I should seek, in the resources of religion, consolation for all the vexations and disappointments of life. I hope you will continue your prayers for me, since I trust I am not altogether unworthy of them. I have long been convinced of the paramount importance of the Christian religion. I have, for many years, fervently sought its blessings. I shall persevere in seeking them, and I hope, ultimately, to attain a firm faith and confidence in its promises. There is nothing for which I feel so anxious. May God, in his infinite mercy, grant what I so ardently desire.

Should you pass this way, at any time, I shall be most happy to see you. Meanwhile, accept my thanks and my wishes for your happiness, here and hereafter.

JOHN H. WESTWOOD TO MR. CLAY.

BALTIMORE, November 28, 1844.

RESPECTED SIR,—Now that the Presidential contest is over, and the disastrous result is known, I can address you without the fear of selfishness, or a desire of ingratiating myself to your notice for personal motives.

I was one of your early and fast friends, and have stood by you in all the phases of political strife. I imbibed those predilections from a knowledge of your history, which is identified with the glory, prosperity, and happiness of our country. My venerated father who was a Whig of the Revolution, and who recently died at the advanced age of ninety-four, was likewise your constant and fast friend—perhaps it is owing to his admiration of you that mine has been engendered. I well recollect in the family circle while a boy, sitting around the domestic hearth, hearing my father recount your patriotic deeds. One sentence from a speech of yours, "The colors that float from the mast head should be the credentials of our seamen," was indelibly fixed on my mind. Then judge my deep mortification and disappointment to find the sailors' friend, the master-spirit of the late war, "the noblest Roman of them all," rejected by the American people, and such a man as James K. Polk placed in the Presidential chair. Did I say American people? I recall that expression, for two-thirds of the native freemen of the United States are your fast friends. Yes, sir, we love you now better than ever; and when the name of Jackson and others of your vile traducers shall be forgotten, yours shall be remembered and live in the affections of all lovers of liberty.

It was foreign influence aided by the Irish and Dutch vote that caused our defeat. As a proof, in my native city alone, in the short space of two months there were over one thousand naturalized. Out of this number nine-tenths voted the Locofoco ticket. Thus men who could not speak our language were made citizens and became politicians too, who at the polls were the noisy revilers of your fair fame—thus you have been well rewarded for the interest you ever took for the oppressed of other nations. Notwithstanding the ingratitude of the Irish and German voters, if the Abolitionists of New York had done their duty, all would have been well.

WILLIAM D. LEWIS TO MR. CLAY.

PHILADELPHIA, November 30, 1844.

MY DEAR FRIEND,—After the dreadful battle is over, and, as I believe, most foully won by our opponents, I feel as if it would be some relief to my mind to express to you the deep grief with which the result has penetrated my heart. I do not class myself, in this respect, in the general list of your "hosts of friends" throughout the country, for I am sure that, earnestly and truly as I know you to be admired and beloved by the best portion of your fellow-citizens, there are but a very small number who can realize as much sorrow on the present occasion as myself. Not that I expected, or had obtruded myself, while success seemed certain, into a position to expect, that I should have sought any personal benefit from that victory which I hoped and believed was about to reward your long and faithful services to your country; but that the kindnesses I had received from you in early life had indelibly stamped your image on my heart, and that your views of public policy so entirely accorded with the dictates of my matured judgment, that I looked to your elevation to the Presidency as a great personal delight to myself, and the harbinger of long-continued prosperity to the nation.

This glorious and beneficial result has been prevented through wicked and unprincipled men, by frauds upon the elective franchise, as monstrous as they are unprecedented ; by fanaticism both religious and political, without a parallel in our history; and by a stolidity on the part of large masses of our population, which must go far to convince the most skeptical that there may be truth in the apothegm of monarchists, that the people are incapable of self-government.

All is now past. Regrets are unavailing. You will meet the untoward event as you have met all the dark hours which have preceded it in your eventful life—with manly fortitude and resignation. And viewing it in a philosophic light, you have, in fact, lost nothing. The honor attained would have brought with it an accumulation of cares, difficulties, and responsibilities ; the unreasonable expectations of many of your supporters must have been disappointed, and perhaps some of your friendships have been thereby embittered. Your reputation as a statesman and a patriot remains untouched, or is rendered by the attrition of your slanderers even more brilliant, still commanding, as it has long commanded, the admiration of the world. Whatever patriotic achievements you might have accomplished in the four years to come could have added comparatively little to those of the forty years which are gone by.

A. B. ROMAN TO MR. CLAY.

PARISH OF ST. JAMES, December 2, 1844.

DEAR SIR,—At the very moment that I learned the disastrous result of the Presidential contest, I determined to write to you; but I soon perceived that I felt too strongly to express myself with any thing like calmness, and on that account I have delayed till now to condole with you on our unexpected misfortune.

To you, personally, I have no consolation to offer. I know that you need none, for in your defeat you have lost nothing—nothing more than I and every other American citizen has lost. You have, by your want of success, obtained this advantage, that your fellow-citizens may say openly what they think of you, without being suspected of interested motives. You have done enough for fame; the station of President could have added nothing to yours. The country alone was to have been benefited by your election. When posterity shall wonder that you did not obtain the first office in the gift of your countrymen, the only answer that can be given must raise you higher than the office could ever have done; it is because "he had rather be right than President."

But what must posterity say of the people of the Union? What are we henceforward to expect from a people, when a constitutional majority has been found to reject the Whig doctrines, of which you have always been the representative and able interpreter, and to decide in favor of the principles—or, rather, the want of principles—with which we have been cursed for more than fifteen years? That the majority should sometimes be deceived in the effects and results of abstract theories, is nothing more than can be expected from the frailty of human nature; but that they should not form a correct opinion of facts, that the distressful experience of fifteen years of demagogueism and barefaced corruption should not open their eyes, is truly degrading to our national character. Are the hopes which the framers of our Government have given to the friends of liberty throughout the world to end but in a splendid proof of the incapacity of men for self-government? I begin to fear that it must be so, unless we can succeed in the almost hopeless task of retracing some of the destructive steps we have taken; unless we find the means of restoring the lost sanctity of the ballot-box.

DR. MERCER TO MR. CLAY.

NEW ORLEANS, December 7, 1844.

MY DEAR FRIEND,—I received your letter a few days ago, and soon after our arrival in town. It was a melancholy pleasure to hear from you.

The late election has mortified and distressed me more than I will attempt to express. Your friends are almost without hope, while you have consolations in abundance that are denied them. No one can deny, that without office or power, you are the first man in our country. It was Lord Ormonde, I think, who said he preferred his dead Ossary to the living son of any man in Europe.

I have never before witnessed such disappointment, distress, and disgust. The feeling seemed to pervade all classes. I have heard men of the opposite faction express their regret at the success of their party. A gray-headed man assured me that he could not restrain his tears. My own child wept bitterly. If, as I believe, you prefer reputation to power, and the approbation of the victorious and intelligent to the dignity of office, you have rather gained than lost by the defeat of your party. I can readily understand that you feel more for your country and your friends than for yourself.

Come then among them, my dear friend, you will find none elsewhere truer or warmer than those of Mississippi or of this place. Among the rest, it will afford me the greatest pleasure to see you here, for in this respect I will yield to none of them. Your old apartment is ready for you, and every one of the family would feel mortified if you were less at home with us than at your own Ashland.

I have nothing to do, and can foresee no engagement that will prevent my accompanying you, wheresoever you may wish to go—even to Cuba.

My daughter charges me to present her duty and her love to you. The ladies send their most affectionate remembrances. May I ask you to present my best respects to Mrs. Clay.

MR. CLAY TO JAMES F. BABCOCK AND OTHERS.

ASHLAND, December 17, 1844.

GENTLEMEN,—I duly received your friendly letter transmitting the proceedings of a public meeting held in the city of New Haven, in respect to the late Presidential election. The patriotic spirit, manifest in the whole of them, is worthy of Connecticut, worthy of its renowned seat of learning, and worthy of the Whig cause. For the sentiments of attachment, confidence and friendship toward myself, which they exhibit, and which you so kindly reiterate in your letter, I offer the warm acknowledgments of a grateful heart. My obligations to Connecticut and my friendly intercourse with many of her eminent sons, during a long period of time, will be faithfully remembered while I continue to live.

I share with you, gentlemen, in regrets on account of the unexpected issue of the recent election. My own personal concern in it is entitled to very little consideration, although I affect no indifference in that respect. The great importance of the event arises out of the respective principles in contest between the two parties, the consequences to which it may lead and the alleged means by which it was brought about, of which, however, I do not allow myself particularly to speak.

The policy of the country in regard to the protection of American industry, a few months ago, seemed to be rapidly acquiring a permanent and fixed character. The Southern and Southwestern portions of the Union had been reproached at the North for want of sufficient interest and sympathy in its welfare. Yielding to the joint influence of their own reflections and experience, the Slave States were fast subscribing to the justice and expediency of a Tariff for revenue, with discriminations for protection. At such an auspicious moment, instead of cordially meeting the Slave States and placing the principle of protection upon impregnable and desirable ground, a sufficient number of the free States, to be decisive of the contest, abandoned what was believed to be their own cherished policy and have aided, if not in its total subversion, in exposing it to imminent hazard and uncertainty. Discouragement has taken the place of confidence in the business of the country, enterprise is checked, and no one knows to what employment he can now safely direct his exertions. Instead of a constantly augmenting home market, we are in danger of experiencing its decline at a time when the foreign market is absolutely glutted with American productions, cotton especially, which is now selling at a lower price than was ever before known. It is probably destined to fall still lower. The final and not distant result will be, especially if large importations shall be stimulated by low duties, a drain of the specie of the country, with all its train of terrible consequences, on which I have neither inclination nor time to dwell.

If the cause of the Whigs had triumphed, the distribution of the proceeds of the sales of the public lands would have been secured, and that great national inheritance would have been preserved for the benefit of the present and future generations. I shall be most agreeably disappointed if it be not wasted in a few years by graduation and other projects of alienation, leaving no traces of permanent benefit behind.

I could not touch upon other great measures of public policy, which it was the purpose of the Whigs to endeavor to establish, without giving to this letter an unsuitable length. They may be briefly stated to have aimed at the purity of the Government, the greater prosperity of the people, and additional security to their liberties and to the Union, and, with all, the preservation of the peace, the honor and the good faith of the nation. The Whigs were most anxious to avoid a foreign war, for the sake of acquiring a foreign territory, which, under the circumstances of the acquisition, could not fail to produce domestic discord, and expose the character of the country, in the eyes of an impartial world, to severe animadversions.

But our opponents have prevailed in the late contest, and the Whigs are, for the present, denied the satisfaction of carrying out their measures of national policy. Believing that they are indispensable to the welfare of the country, I am unwilling to relinquish the fond hope that they may be finally established, whether I live to witness that event or not. In the mean time, those to whose hands the administration of public affairs is confided ought to have a fair trial. Let us ever indulge an anxious desire that the evils we have apprehended may not be realized, that the peace of our country may be undisturbed, its honor remain unsullied, and its prosperity continue unimpeded.

To guard, however, against adverse results, the resolution of the Whigs of the city of New Haven steadfastly to adhere to the Whig cause and principles, is wise and patriotic.

I should be most happy to visit once more New England, and

especially New Haven, which has done me so much honor by giving me, at the late election, the largest majority ever given by that city in a contested election. I shall embrace, with great pleasure, any opportunity, should any ever offer, to accept your obliging invitation.

I tender to you, gentlemen, my cordial thanks for your friendly wishes and kind regards for me and mine, and I hope that one and all of you may long live in health, happiness, and prosperity.

BENJAMIN J. LEEDOM TO MR. CLAY.

NEW YORK, December 20, 1844.

ESTEEMED FRIEND,—Although a member of a peaceable Society, who do not profess to take much interest in the political contests of the day, yet as a man endowed with the common feelings of humanity, and a strong desire for the promotion of the best interests of my fellow-man, do I mourn over the dark cloud which has overshadowed the political horizon of our beloved country; the prostration of those high and glorious principles, of which thou hast so long been the great and unwearied champion—that prostration brought about by fraud and calumny, is our country's loss, for I am fully aware that had the victory been ours, it could not have added one leaf to the wreath which encircles thy brow,

> "For thou art freedom's now, and fame's;
> One of the few, the immortal names
> That are not born to die."

It is for my country that I mourn, that in thy retirement, one of the strongest advocates for those high and glorious principles is removed, and I had fondly hoped that, like Cincinnatus, thou too, wouldst have left the scenes of domestic life, and once more have been heard in our legislative halls. The feeling may be a selfish one in me, for well I know that it is unreasonable to wish to draw thee from thy peaceful abode, into the turbid waters of public life again, after so many years of laborious toil.

Happy is he who carries with him into retirement the prayers of the patriotic and intelligent of his country—these thou hast.

My venerated grandsire left the peaceful society of which I

am a member, to stand by the Father of his country, in the dark hour which tried the souls of men. The same feelings, and the same love of country which nerved him to the contest in '76, prompted his descendant in '44 to deposit his vote for Henry Clay. That vote shall be handed down as an heirloom to my children; although defeated, yet that name will be the point around which freemen shall rally, until victory crowns our efforts.

With a sincere prayer that thy days may be long in the land, and that peace and happiness may be thine, I remain, etc.

ADAM BEATTY TO MR. CLAY.

PROSPECT HILL, December 24, 1844.

MY DEAR SIR,—The result of the late Presidential election has produced on my mind the deepest regret and the most profound sorrow. You may well imagine that your failure of success has had no small share in exciting these emotions. But it is the deep wound inflicted on the honor and best interests of the country, by which I have been most sorely afflicted. Your failure has relieved you from a heavy responsibility, and, I doubt not, in your retirement at Ashland, you will enjoy more real satisfaction than all the honors of the Presidential office could afford. It will be the means of carrying down to posterity your name with greater luster than if you had been elected to the Presidency, and I humbly hope that in the wise dispensation of Providence your defeat may redound to your temporal and eternal good.

But oh! what a wound has been inflicted upon the honor and interests of our country? The election has been carried in favor of Mr. Polk, by the most shameful and abominable frauds practiced to an extent which, to every reflecting mind, must create the most awful apprehensions as to the future destinies of our free institutions, and the perpetuity of the Union.

But this is not all. The foulest and most unprincipled means have been resorted to, and with great success, to excite the bitter hatred of our recently naturalized citizens, Roman Catholics and Abolitionists, against Whig principles, by the grossest and foulest misrepresentations, thus setting in hostile array against the great conservative principles of the Whig party an embittered faction, whose want of intelligence has been played upon to excite to the highest degree the ungovernable passions of a considerable portion of our population.

Reflection upon these circumstances has brought strongly to my mind the remark of an eminent modern historian, "That the great body of mankind are incapable of judging correctly on public affairs." "That the opinion of most men on the great questions which divide society, rest on prejudices, personal animosities, and private interests." He consoles his readers by the reflection that "truth is in the end triumphant, but it becomes predominant only upon the decay of interests, the experience of suffering, or the extinction of passions."

I greatly fear our country is destined to go through this ordeal, great suffering she will have to endure, but I pray God that truth may in the end prevail, and that our Republican institutions may yet be saved.

I have scarcely been able to summon resolution enough to say a word to any of my friends, in relation to the arduous contest through which the country has recently passed, but I have thought a word of consolation, if I were able to afford it, due to our long standing friendship. It affords me some satisfaction at least, under the adverse state of things which exists, to assure you of my abiding and cordial esteem and friendship. Permit me to add a request that you will present my kindest regards to Mrs. Clay.

E. PETTIGREW TO MR. CLAY.

MAGNOLIA, Tyrrell County, NORTH CAROLINA,
January 1, 1845.

MY DEAR SIR,—The storm is over, and we the people of the United States are shipwrecked, and I fear too much damaged ever to be repaired.

The result of the Presidential election was to me perfectly astounding, yet for weeks before it, I began to fear, as it is natural for me to look on the dark side of every subject, and I mentioned confidentially to some of my friends that I had apprehensions; consequently endeavored to prepare my mind for the evil day; that day which in my opinion is the beginning of the end of the peace, prosperity, and happiness of this rising country, if it did not begin in the year 1829, with the reign of Hickory the First.

My dear sir, on you rested my only hope, to stay the downward tendency of this Government, and at the Court House of my county, in a few remarks I made to the people on the day of election, I entreated them to do their utmost, to stay that decline, for four years, and it might be that affairs would be put in such a train, that misrule would not get the ascendency in four years more, and though I felt every thing for the generations to come, yet I wished of all things to be gathered to my fathers before war, pestilence, and famine should overwhelm the land. We did well in the county in which I live, and I feel proud to know that the State of North Carolina is numbered among the Law and Order party, though differing with so many of its neighboring States.

The malcontents of these United States have given the greatest blow to elective Government that ever was given. It has shown to the best friends of republican Governments that demagogues, who without principle and without honesty, to answer party and selfish purposes will rake the pit for voters, as in this case, and thereby drive from office those who could save the country and put in their stead a third-rate man. Yea, a no-rate man. Such men from want of capacity to manage the affairs of Government must submit to the dictation of artful, designing, dishonest, and irresponsible men, and every department of the Government must necessarily run into anarchy and confusion.

But on this subject I need say no more. It is all plain to you, and my remarks are only to show how much I deplore the failure of our forefathers, the patriots of the Revolution. But one word on the subject of naturalization. My opinion has been for forty years that there should be no citizens of the United States except those born within its limits. Let every foreigner be satisfied to enjoy all the other privileges that the State in which they chose to live thought proper to grant. Had that been the law, we should not now be like men in a thunder squall waiting with trembling anxiety for the next clap.

My dear sir, I must say that I feel very much for your disappointment in being prevented, by corruption, after more than forty years of devotion to your country's good, from doing to it the greatest service that could fall to the lot of any man. We all need deplore the circumstance as a national calamity; but from you, there is removed a great weight of responsibility, and you now rest under a perfect knowledge that you retire into private life with the highest honors that can fall to any man now living, the confidence, esteem, and love of hundreds of thousands of those of your fellow-citizens who know you best.

N. B. I omitted to mention, that in 1829, I was unreserved in saying that I gave this United States Government thirty years to continue; which has been my unwavering opinion and declaration up to this time, and I fear my time will be found too long, and I further fear that God has given us up as unworthy of his care and protection, and to a hard heart and reprobate mind, at all events politically.

JOHN QUINCY ADAMS TO MR. CLAY.

WASHINGTON, January 4, 1845.

DEAR SIR,—Commodore Jesse D. Elliot has committed to my charge to be transmitted to you a bronze medal which he has caused to be struck in honor of Mr. J. Fenimore Cooper, as a tribute of gratitude for Mr. Cooper's defense and vindication of the Commodore's character with reference to certain charges which have been brought before the Republic against him. Commodore Elliot proposes to distribute a limited number of these medals to certain distinguished persons and to some of his personal friends, and then to have the die broken. I take pleasure in executing his commission, by forwarding herewith the medal to you.

I have yet to acknowledge the receipt of a very kind and friendly letter from you, written shortly before the unexpected and inauspicious issue of the recent Presidential election. It has been on many accounts painful to me; but on none more or so much as on the dark shade which it has cast upon our prospects of futurity. I had hoped that under your guidance the country would have recovered from the downward tendency into which it has been sinking. But the glaring frauds by which the election was consummated afford a sad presentiment of what must be expected hereafter.

We must hope that a merciful Providence will yet preside over the destinies of our country, and avert the calamities with which she is threatened.

That your personal comforts may be multiplied in proportion to the weight of cares which a different issue would have brought upon you is the fervent wish of, dear sir, your friend and faithful servant.

MR. CLAY TO JOHN CARR.

ASHLAND, January 11, 1845.

DEAR SIR,—I received your friendly letter, and thank you for the kind feelings toward me which it expresses. Your suggestion that I would prepare a journal of my public life, embracing a narrative of all the slanders which have been so profusely propagated against me, is received in the same friendly spirit in which it was made. As to the calumnies circulated against me, many of them, I dare say, never reached me, and I wish to forget them and their vile authors as soon as I can. I hope God will forgive them. I do not desire to soil myself by any contact with them. The best demonstration of their falsehood is the testimony in my favor, borne by my neighbors, and by the people of Kentucky, uniformly, during a period of upward of forty years.

Wishing you health, happiness, and prosperity, I am, etc.

MR. CLAY TO CALVIN COLTON.

ASHLAND, February 3, 1845.

MY DEAR SIR,—I am sorry that after having remained in Lexington, I hope agreeably, for two months, you should be about to leave us in not as good health as you have enjoyed during your sojourn.

With respect to the composition of the work which you have so much at heart, and which brought you to this city, I think now, as I stated to you at first, that every thing depends upon the execution, that most important word in language. You have shown me most, if not all you have written, and, as I formed the subject of it, perhaps I am not a competent, as I certainly am not an impartial, judge. But, unless I am already biased, I do think that, so far, you have made good progress, and may ask leave to sit again. What you have written may require an attentive revisal, and some new arrangement of its parts, before it is finally sent to the press, that bourne from which a traveler does not always safely return.

I need not say that by far the most important, the historical, part of your work remains to be entered upon. I hope you will get successfully through it, to accomplish which, I hardly need say, will require great patience, much research and study, and a large measure of candor and impartiality.

I can not part from you without the expression of fervent wishes for your success and fame, and for your health and prosperity.

B. JOHNSON BARBOUR TO MR. CLAY.

BARBOURSVILLE, February, 16 1845.

MY DEAR SIR,—It has long been my wish to address you a letter, but I have been deterred until now by the fear that you were already too much wearied by an extensive correspondence. Nor had I the heart to dwell upon the subject which lay uppermost in my thoughts. I could not sit down calmly to speak of an event trifling to yourself, but portentous to the nation.

Permit me, Mr. Clay, to say that my affection for you, based upon a love of all that is bright and noble in human nature, is not the growth of a day. I claim the privilege of speaking as an original Whig, as one baptized in the faith at the fountain, as one who was taught to love the Whig cause when he knew no better, and who never knows nothing better than to love it. My love for its great representative was coeval. In my earliest youth I was taught by him who was your constant friend to honor the pure statesman and patriot pursued by calumny, but still laboring with undiminished ardor for an ungrateful country. I felt then that, when the vile passions and prejudices of the day had passed away, you would have your merited reward from an approving posterity; that your memory would be cherished when the demagogues who traduced you were

"Forgotten as fools, or remembered as worse;"

that you would be hailed as the wondrous architect that had strengthened and adorned the noble edifice whose foundation was won by the valor of Washington, and whose corner-stone was laid by the wisdom of Madison.

A brighter day seemed at length to have dawned upon the Republic. The nation seemed at length to have awakened to its true interests, and in the Presidential contest of 1844 I fondly looked forward to the confusion of your enemies, your complete justification, and the firm re-establishment of our great conservative cause. In this we have been sadly mistaken. Double-dealing, defamation and slanders are still omnipotent. A motley party, without principle or principles, with fraud for the means and the election of a demagogue for the end, have triumphed. Domestic corruption and foreign putrescence coalesced to overwhelm the virtue and honesty of the country. Plaquemine and Tammany have stifled the voice of the American people, and the late contest has only established the melancholy facts that frauds upon the ballot box have perfect impunity, that mediocrity is merit, and that every excess may be committed in the name of a spurious Democracy.

This is a mournful spectacle for the patriot, and it is perhaps better for your fame that you were not called upon to wage an ineffectual and unavailing contest with the corruption which pervades every part of the body politic. But little pleasure could be felt by the President of a nation where Dorr found mourners, disunion advocates; where a lust of territory overrides every principle of law, all fear of consequence, and all sense of justice; where rebellion puts the power of a State at defiance, and repudiation grows, prospers, and exults. Such are the terrible symptoms by which we are surrounded, telling of the decay of virtue and honor, the only safeguard of a Republic.

These are sad and gloomy thoughts, you will say, for one so young. God grant I may be mistaken, that better things may be in store for us, that the time may return when patriotism will be no crime, nor long service a subject of reproach.

As an humble member of the Whig party I shall never cease to lift my voice against the foes of my country, that I may have something at least of that proud consolation which is yours, the consciousness that every nerve was strained and nothing left undone to avert the final catastrophe.

My mother desires to be most kindly remembered to yourself and Mrs. Clay.

MR. CLAY TO CALVIN COLTON.

ASHLAND, March 5, 1845.

MY DEAR SIR,—I received your favors from Washington and from Philadelphia, the latter making inquiries concerning my paternal ancestors. I am sorry that I am unable to communicate to you any minute information about them. All that I know, in the general, is that they came from England to the colony of Virginia, some time after its establishment, and settled, I believe, on the south side of James River. The descendants of the original stock are very numerous, and much dispersed, many of them residing in Virginia and Kentucky. A branch, or branches of the family remained in England, and among their descendants was Mr. J. Clay, recently quite a distinguished member of the British House of Commons.

My maternal ancestors also came from England, and settled in Hanover county, Virginia, about the beginning of the last century. George Hudson, my maternal grandfather, died about the year 1770, in that county.

This is about as much as I can inform you in regard to my ancestors, and from this statement, you will, I hope, be able to incorporate all that is material in your narrative.

My family is well, and unite with me in assurances of our warm regard.

NOTE WITHOUT DATE.

I received to-day your favor from Philadelphia. I am sorry that you should have any trouble about my English namesakes. I am not sure that two of them have been members of the House of Commons. One, I know, has been, because I have read a speech of his, and have corresponded with him, although I can not now lay my hands upon any letter of his. He distinguished himself some years ago, on the Bank question. Most probably it was William. When I wrote you last, I thought his name was J. Clay, being uncertain whether it was John or Joseph. It was probably William.

It is not a matter of much consequence, and perhaps you had better confine what you say to the one of whom you know something.

MR. CLAY TO DR. W. A. BOOTH.

ASHLAND, April 7 1845.

DEAR SIR,—Our mutual friend, Mr. Mitchell, of Frankfort, delivered to me the day before yesterday your letter, with several publications under your name, in respect to the unfortunate controversy which has arisen in the Methodist Episcopal Church of the United States, all of which I have attentively perused. You desire an expression of my opinion on certain inquiries communicated in your letter.

I have long entertained for that Church sentiments of profound esteem and regard, and I have the happiness of numbering among its members some of the best friends I have in the world. I will add, with great truth, that I have witnessed, with much satisfaction, the flourishing condition of the Church, and the good sense and wisdom which have generally characterized the administration of its affairs, as far as I have observed it.

It was, therefore, with the deepest regret that I heard, in the course of the past year, of the danger of a division of the Church, in consequence of a difference of opinion existing on the delicate and unhappy subject of slavery. A division, for such a cause, would be an event greatly to be deplored, both on account of the Church itself and its political tendency. Indeed scarcely any public occurrence has happened for a long time that gave me so much real concern and pain as the menaced separation of the Church, by a line throwing all the Free States on one side, and all the Slave States on the other.

I will not say that such a separation would necessarily produce a dissolution of the political union of these States; but the example would be fraught with imminent danger, and, in co-operation with other causes unfortunately existing, its tendency on the stability of the Confederacy would be perilous and alarming.

Entertaining these views, it would afford me the highest satisfaction to hear of an adjustment of the controversy, a reconciliation between the opposing parties in the Church, and the preservation of its unity.

I limit myself to the political aspect of the subject, without expressing any opinion on either of the plans of compromise and settlement which have been published, which I could not do without exposing myself to improper imputations.

With fervent hopes and wishes that some arrangement of the difficulty may be devised and agreed upon, which shall preserve the Church in union and harmony, I am respectfully your obedient servant.

JOHN R. THOMPSON TO MR. CLAY.

UNIVERSITY OF VIRGINIA, April 8, 1845.

MY DEAR SIR,—Allow me to say that in venturing to offer the expression of my condolence, where condolence is doubtless inapposite, as the result of the late Presidential election, I do so as an original Whig, as a native of that " Gibraltar of Whig principles," the city of Richmond, which has always stood up nobly for you through good and evil report, and where, forty-five years ago, in the office of Chancellor Wythe, you laid the imperishable foundations of that greatness, which has since overshadowed the world. Your own generous Kentucky has not been more faithful to your fortunes. I trust, therefore, that you will recognize my right, as a citizen of Richmond, and as one who gave with honest pride his first vote for you, to lament the disaster that has befallen us.

I had fondly looked forward to November, 1844, as the day when the people of our beloved country would assert their long-violated rights, when the malevolence of a vile herd of defamatory enemies would be silenced forever, when a Republic, ceasing to be ungrateful, would reward, with the highest office in its gift, the man who of all others had deserved it. I can not tell you, sir, the sense of desolation and crushed hopes with which the painful intelligence of your defeat was received. Frauds, the most infamous in the annals of the elective franchise, stifled the voice of the people, and national disgrace was effected by a motley party of Dorrites and Agrarians, Mormons and Repudiators, the voters of Plaquemine and the outlaws of the Empire Club. Since their ill-omened success, this party have already commenced the work of destruction, and we have, but a few weeks since, seen the plainest provisions of our blessed Constitution set at naught, in the passage of the Texas bill. There is, indeed, a dark pall over the prospect before us when that sacred instrument can be trampled upon by peculation and cupidity.

For yourself, personally, the present age may not accord you justice. But I feel assured that a time will come, and I trust in God I may live to see it, when the passions and prejudices of the present state have passed away, and your stainless and splendid name will be revered by an admiring posterity.

The patriotic exertions of the women of Virginia to erect a statue in commemoration of your virtues, can not have escaped your attention. I take pleasure in stating to you that I was yesterday informed by Mrs. Lucy Barbour, the venerable and distinguished lady, who gave to the work its first impulse, that success is certain, and that next summer the corner-stone will be laid. We will erect it upon our Capitol Square, in Richmond, and it shall bear some such inscription as was once applied to Charles James Fox, a character, in many respects, kindred with your own:

"A patriot's even course he steered,
'Mid faction's wildest storms unmoved,
By all who marked his course, *revered*,
By all who knew his heart, *beloved.*"

Inclosed you will find a copy of some poor verses that I wrote for Mr. Pleasants on the occasion of Christmas, in which is atattempted a satire on the follies of the age. I hope you will not deem it impertinent if I ask that you will do me the honor to read them.

DOCTOR MERCER TO MR. CLAY.

NEW ORLEANS, April 22, 1845.

MY VERY DEAR FRIEND,—I have received here your kind letter from Natchez, whence it was forwarded. We have been detained by Miss Young's indisposition, now of several months duration, and by her desire to enjoy the benefit of Lugenburg's advice. But as she is now much relieved, I indulge the hope of returning home next week.

In regard to your affairs, or rather to a late movement on the part of your friends, however reluctant I might be on ordinary occasions to hazard one, conscious of its little authority, yet I have not the slightest hesitation to express my opinion as the case appears a very plain one.

I learn from your letter that certain of your debts have been cancelled at Lexington by some unknown and inscrutable agency, that you suspect the interposition of your friends, and that you are somewhat doubtful whether it would not be more consistent with the independence of your previous life that you should reject the kindly office thus proffered.

Now in all ages signal public services have been rewarded by national benefactions. In our own day, Sièyes and Wellington have had grants of domains, the debts of Pitt have been paid by Parliament, Fox did not disdain the assistance of his friends. Your memory will furnish innumerable other instances. If Republics are ungrateful it is the more necessary that private individuals should perform the duty neglected by the public authorities.

You have devoted more than forty years of your life to public affairs, and have rendered the most important public services. If, in this distinguished career, you have acquired fame surpassing that of your cotemporaries, it is equally true, that the same capacity, industry and zeal, would have insured to you the most ample fortune. This, it strikes me, is the true view of the case, and is conclusive beyond question, as you would also think if you were not interested.

But there is another aspect. Would it not be ungracious to repel the friendly hand that is tendered, to mortify those who are warmly attached to you, and to consult—shall I venture on the word?—your pride, at the expense of their feelings?

My dear friend, you must submit, there is no remedy; for, if your suspicions are correct, you can not overcome the precautions which may have been adopted to guard against this very contingency.

I venture to use the language which is dictated alike by my grateful sense of your sentiments toward me, as by my high respect and warm attachment for you. Most surely it is the duty of a friend to speak plainly, without, however, disregarding the delicacy and courtesy which are equally necessary.

I hope Mrs. Clay has not forgotten me, and that she will accept my respects.

MR. CLAY TO CALVIN COLTON.

ASHLAND, April 28, 1845.

MY DEAR SIR,—I duly received your letter of the 17th instant. Compression is your forte in composition; but is there not danger of your elaborating too much the old calumny of bargain, etc.? The division you propose of the subject appears to me to be natural and suitable

When I meet Governor Letcher I will endeavor to prevail on him to give the certificate you desire. He may perhaps consent to furnish it to be used only in the contingency of his death. If living, and the statement of Mr. B.'s agency should be denied, appealed to as he is as a witness, I am sure he would be willing to testify. You will find Mr. Buchanan's speech, what you want, in Gales and Seaton's Congressional Debates, although I can not refer you to the page. Governor Letcher could refer to it.

It would be well not to publish Colonel Sloan's statement until I hear from Mr. Reilly, the Texan Chargé des Affaires. I endeavored, through him, to procure from General Houston a confirmation of Colonel Sloan's testimony, and have not yet learned what success attended the effort.

Mr. Adams' appeal to heaven was at Maysville, I think in November 1843, on the occasion of his visit to Cincinnati. He made a very strong defense of me in 1829 in answer to some address from New Jersey, which you will no doubt be able to find in Niles' Register.

A GOLD PEN TO MR. CLAY.

NEW YORK, 8 Washington Square, July 12, 1845.

HONORED AND HONORABLE SIR,—Designed by my maker for actual service, and ambitious to hold a situation where I can gain the highest honor, and confer the greatest benefit on mankind, I am emboldened, at the suggestion of a friend, to present myself before you, to solicit your patronage and favor.

Truth compels me to admit that I have but little to recommend me to your notice. Although I derive my origin from a rich and powerful family, to whom even princes pay court, and whose influence is felt throughout the world, I am myself without influence, without the attraction of peculiar beauty, am worth but little money, and wholly destitute of intellectual endowments. Yet, kind sir, if you will take me by the hand and admit me to your intimate companionship, to your treasury of thoughts, I shall soon become familiar with all that is noble in sentiment, lofty in conception, wise in judgment, beautiful in imagery, honest in purpose, and truthful in expression.

Thus guided I can not fail to impart pleasure and instruction to the world ; and to gain in return, the world's admiration and applause.

Insignificant as I may appear in comparison with such of my elegant relations as have lately been presented to you, I yet hope you will deign to listen to my application, will give me a place near your person, and allow me to remain, honored sir, ever yours to command.

MR. CLAY TO J. MUIR.

ASHLAND, August 7, 1845.

DEAR SIR,—I received your kind letter and thank you for the friendly sentiments which it conveys. I have ceased to have any, I never had many, personal regrets on account of the issue of the Presidential election. Those which I most felt were excited for my country and for my friends. They remain undiminished. And for no portion of them were my sympathies more strongly awakened than for our countrywomen. Their hearts, every where, assured them of the deep and durable interests involved in the contest, and intuitively prompted them to avert all calamity from our land, if they could. Mine gratefully owns the kind partiality which they manifested toward me. The ladies of Alexandria are entitled to a large share of the great obligation which I owe to their whole sex.

I return the blank notes which you transmitted, with my name affixed to each as you desired. I add a similar one for Mrs. Mandell.

I will thank you to make my respects and my acknowledgments to the poet mechanic, of whose versification you have sent a specimen so creditable to his talent.

MR. CLAY TO CALVIN COLTON.

BLUE SULPHUR, VIRGINIA, September 5, 1845.

MY DEAR SIR,—I received your favor, proposing to send the proofs to me of your first volume. I am now *en route* to Ashland, where I shall be glad to receive them, hoping to find in the introduction, as intimated in your previous letter, an exoneration of me from any responsibility for the composition of the work. It is the best if not only mode of correcting the error committed in the prospectus.

I saw Judge Brooke at the White Sulphur Springs. He tells me that he has packed up a large bundle of my letters, and placed them in the care of a friend, to be delivered to you. He thinks that you may derive useful matter from them. He has returned to St. Julien, his residence near Fredericksburg.

I have also received a package of some forty of my letters, addressed to the late J. S. Johnston, Senator from Louisiana, sent me by the widow of his only son. I will try to find some person to forward them by to you from Lexington.

I have not yet heard from General Houston; but Mr. Reiley, the husband of my wife's niece, still believes I shall receive a communication from him.

MR. CLAY TO DR. W. A. BOOTH.

Ashland, September 15, 1845.

Dear Sir,—A temporary absence from home has delayed my acknowledgment of the receipt of your favor of the 7th ultimo. I have not received the pamphlet to which it refers. But any expression of my opinion, as to your plan of compromise between the two divisions of the Methodist Church, would be now wholly unimportant, if at any time it would have been worth any thing, since a separation seems to be inevitable. When such is the case, in human affairs, I think the best way is to seek to avoid any mischievous consequences.

I must continue to regret the separation, because I believe it to have an evil tendency. Others think differently; and my hope is that they may, in the end, prove to be right, and I wrong.

It was not my intention, in my former letter, to impute any error to the Southern portion of the Church, on the unhappy subject of Slavery, the immediate cause of division.

My opinion is, that the existence of Slavery, or the fact of owning slaves, in States which authorize the institution of Slavery, does not rightfully fall within the jurisdiction of Ecclesiastical bodies. The law of the land is paramount, and ought not to be contravened by any spiritual tribunal.

MR. CLAY TO CALVIN COLTON.

ASHLAND, September 16, 1845.

MY DEAR SIR,—I received your favor of the 2d instant. I have really no coat of arms, and if I had, I should doubt the propriety of the use of it suggested by you. In lieu of it, would it not be better to employ some object drawn from those interests which I have sought to promote in the National Councils? A loom, shuttle, anvil, plow, or any other article connected with manufactures, agriculture, or commerce. I wrote you from the Blue Sulphur. Yours respectfully.

HENRY WHITE AND OTHERS TO MR. CLAY.

PHILADELPHIA, December 21, 1845.

DEAR SIR,—The undersigned, acting for the Whigs of Philadelphia, have the honor to ask your acceptance of the book which accompanies this letter. It contains an expression of gratitude from your Whig brethren here, for your eminent services as a statesman, and a testimonial of their regard for you, as a citizen and friend.

The undersigned have the honor to send with the book a casket of jewels, manufactured in this city for Mrs. Clay. On behalf of the ladies and gentlemen whose names are contained in the book, they present them to Mrs. Clay, as a mark of their high consideration and respect for the worth and virtues of the lady of one to whom the country owes a debt of gratitude that never can be repaid.

MR. CLAY TO HENRY WHITE AND OTHERS.

ASHLAND, December 16, 1845.

GENTLEMEN,—I received to-day at this place, the letter which on the 1st inst., you did me the honor to address to me, from the hands of Henry White, Esq., one of the subscribers to it. He at the same time delivered to me the book, beautifully printed and bound, entitled " A Testimonial of Gratitude and Affection to Henry Clay," containing the proceedings of a meeting of my friends in the city of Philadelphia, publicly held at the County Court-house, on Wednesday evening, December 19, 1844, in pursuance of a call of the National Clay Club, and containing also several thousand names of both sexes, young and old, of those who have done me the great honor of contributing a testimonial to my public services, to the principles and measures which I have endeavored to establish, and to my exertions in the common cause which we have espoused.

It is utterly impossible, gentlemen, for me to find language of sufficient force and strength, to express to you the emotions of gratitude and thankfulness excited in my breast by this precious and affecting testimonial. It will be ever warmly cherished by me throughout my life, and be preserved and transmitted to my descendants, as the most honorable legacy which I could bequeath to them. And I request you to say to one and all of the contributors, that their respective names are not more indelibly recorded in the splendid book which they have sent me, than in grateful impressions on my heart.

I am also charged by Mrs. Clay to present her cordial and respectful thanks (to which I beg leave to add my own), to the ladies and gentlemen who have had the goodness to send her a casket of rich jewels, which Mr. White kindly delivered into her own hands, for their highly valuable present. Her grateful obligations for it, she enjoins me to say, are not at all diminished by the reflection that considerations apart from any merits of her own, have prompted the generous offer of it to her acceptance.

I embrace the occasion to bear my testimony, and to tender my thanks to you, gentlemen, the trustees appointed under the authority of the public meeting in Philadelphia, before mentioned, for the delicacy, the fidelity, and the honor, with which you have executed the trust confided to you. And I have great pleasure in expressing my thanks and gratitude to Mr. White, in particular, for the great trouble and inconvenience which he has encountered, by performing a long journey, at a most inclement season, to fulfill the commission intrusted to him.

I am, gentlemen, with sentiments of the highest respect and regard, your grateful and faithful friend, and obedient servant.

MR. CLAY TO W. L. WOODWARD.

ASHLAND, January 3, 1846.

DEAR SIR,—I duly received your favor, and take pleasure in answering it. The desire to trace out your ancestry is very natural. I have often felt it in respect to mine, but I have no written, and very imperfect traditional accounts of them. I am apprehensive, however, that my parental stock is different from the family of Clays described by you, as having been established in Middletown, Connecticut. My ancestors emigrated from England, and settled in the colony of Virginia, early, I believe, in the 17th century. My father was born there, not far from Richmond, on the south side of James River. He removed to Hanover county, shortly before my birth in that county. His name was John, and he was sometimes called Sir John Clay (as I have seen in the record of judicial proceedings), but he had no legitimate right to that title. It was a soubriquet which he somehow acquired. He had but one brother, Edward Clay, who removed at an early period into North Carolina, where he lived and died, leaving a large family.

I never knew my father, who died in my infancy, nor my grandfather. Left an orphan, struggling for subsistence and education, and removing, before I reached my majority, to this State, where I plunged first into an active professional business, and then into political affairs, I have had but little leisure to prosecute inquiries concerning my ancestors. And now, I shall so soon meet them in another, and I hope a better state, that I have thought it hardly necessary to institute any. I think it is quite probable that the Clays, from whom we both descended, were originally of the same family, although it may not be practicable now to trace the exact degree of connection. When I was in England, I met with some persons bearing the name of Clay, and from conversation with them, I had reason to suppose that we all sprung from the same stock.

I am very thankful for the assurance contained in your letter, that your family have all done me the honor to entertain confidence in me, and that those of them who are entitled to the exercise of the elective franchise, have voted with the Whigs. I shall be most happy, if, during the remnant of my life, I shall continue to merit their good opinion.

I pray you to communicate my respectful regards to your venerable grandfather, and accept for yourself assurances of the respect and esteem, and the wishes for your welfare and happiness of your friend and obedient servant.

P. S. My father was a Baptist preacher. Mr. Eleazer Clay

near Richmond, Va., was also a Baptist preacher for more than sixty years, and my only surviving full brother is a preacher of the same denomination.

LORD MORPETH TO MR. CLAY.

CASTLE HOWARD, April 17, 1846.

MY DEAR MR. CLAY,—I should hardly have ventured to put the locality of my date into so graphic a form, but I thought that if your Yorkshire housekeeper should be still alive, she might like to be shown the outside of a Yorkshire house. I wish I could show her master the inside. The reason for my breaking in at all upon the repose of Ashland (a repose, however, against the cause of which I protest in common with the sound sense of mankind at large), is to satisfy the request of a friend, who begs me to inquire from you whether you happen to know any thing of a Mr. William Cavendish, whom he believes to have accompanied you upon your return to America in 1815-16 (?), and if so, what befell him, whether he is still alive, and what he is now doing. I sincerely beg pardon for inflicting so much old-dated curiosity upon you, and it is only in respect of having once discharged the office of your letter-carrier, that I can hope to be excused for bothering your post-bag with so uninteresting an inquiry. The last mail brings us the account of your adding to your estimates, but I hope that the whole matters between us wear a more pacific complexion. I must say that I think upon our side there would be a sincere aversion to any conflict between us. I am afraid I must not bespeak your sympathy for our Free-Trade movement. It rather hangs fire during its progress through the Legislature, but I am inclined to believe that the House of Lords will pass the bill. I hope your groves are flourishing round you, and I must particularly inquire after your stock of cattle. We are rather proud of our breed in this place, and sold two short-horned cows last autumn for £300, which in the present times we consider a large price, when good breeds are become so much more common. I would beg to be kindly remembered to all of your family who are good enough to retain any recollection of me. I wonder whether your servant Charles is still with you?

Mr. Denison, whom you may remember as a traveler in America some twenty years ago, is now with us here, and begs to be recalled to your recollection.

HENRY CLAY JR. TO HIS BROTHER JAMES.

LOUISVILLE, May 25, 1846.

DEAR JAMES,—Your letter was thankfully received. The Governor left here yesterday morning. The night before I offered him five companies, and a sixth reported themselves through their officers the same night. I could easily raise the ten. Indeed I have been much complimented by offers to serve with me. When I offered the Governor the companies he told me that he would not be bound by their election, after having given me reason to believe that he would issue the commissions according to their choice.

At present, having done all that a proper sense of duty requires, in having offered my services, I have determined to do nothing more. The rest remains with his Excellency.

Tell Henry Erwin if he desires to go out I would advise him to be elected, if possible, captain or lieutenant of one of the companies. My love to Susan and all our friends.

MR. CLAY TO JOHN S. LITTELL.

ASHLAND, November 17, 1846.

MY DEAR SIR,—I received your friendly letter of the 9th instant, and am greatly obliged by your kind intention to send me a copy of "Graydon's Memoirs." I should receive it with pleasure, and no doubt would peruse it with profit. I saw that you were a candidate for Congress on the Native American ticket. I did not for a moment suppose that in assuming that position you had abandoned any of your long-cherished Whig principles.

There is much in the principles of the Native American party to commend it to deliberate consideration; but as a separate and distinct party, I have not imagined that it could succeed in the United States. Its tendency is to distract and divide the Whigs, for it is not to be believed that the other party, to any considerable extent, will unite with the Native American. The other party has profited too largely by the foreign vote to authorize us to expect that, as a party, it will give any considerable support or countenance to the Native Americans. If any modification of the naturalization laws shall ever be effected, it will not be at the instance, or by the co-operation, of the Democratic party.

The political evils which flow from the foreign population are confined to localities, and do not pervade the interior of the Union. Hence I suppose that the principles of the Native American party alone can never form a basis of a party commensurate with the whole Union.

I unite with you in congratulations on the recent signal triumphs of the Whigs. They encourage us to hope for a better administration of the general Government. Such a desirable result I think inevitable, if the Whigs should be wise, and not allow themselves to be intoxicated by their present successes. I look on passing scenes with calmness, though not with indifference. I am often addressed to know if I would consent to the use of my name again as a candidate for the Presidency. Although full of gratitude to my friends for their past confidence and support, I have deemed it most befitting to remain silent on these appeals, answering neither yea nor nay. In my opinion, it is too soon now to agitate the question of the next Presidency. The public mind, I think, had better be left to the full, undisturbed, and undivided consideration of the disastrous measures of the last session of Congress. It will be time enough hereafter, from among the living and the worthy, to select a suitable person to accomplish the changes so desirable in the general administration.

For the continuance of your kind and friendly feelings and sentiments toward me, I beg you to be assured of the thanks and gratitude of your friend and obedient servant.

MR. CLAY TO HENRY WHITE.

ASHLAND, November 27, 1846.

MY DEAR SIR,—At the moment of my departure from home, which I leave to-morrow for New Orleans, I take great pleasure in the acknowledgment of the receipt of your kind favor of the 21st instant. I wish I could enjoy the satisfaction of your company on the voyage, not, however, with the discomforts which we experienced in that terrible old hickory last winter.

I congratulate you on the marriage of your daughter. Say to her that I wish her all possible happiness; and that, if she does not enjoy it, so far as her husband is concerned, I must say, "white man is very uncertain."

I congratulate you also on public affairs. I think light is once more beaming upon us, and light, too, from the Key stone, as well as elsewhere.

Your information and explanations are very friendly and satisfactory.

As to the Tariff of 1846, I think our true policy is to go for its repeal, and the restoration of the Tariff of 1842, and nothing else than the repeal of the one and the restoration of the other.

My wife, and all at Ashland, unite in affectionate regards to you and all of yours.

MR. CLAY TO HIS SON JAMES.

NEW ORLEANS, January 17, 1847.

MY DEAR SON,—I received your letter of the first instant, and was much distressed by the account you gave me of dear little Lucy's health. She is one of the few links that bind me to life, and I should be quite inconsolable if we were to lose her Tell Doctor Dudley that I hope he will exert all his skill to restore her.

Give my love to Susan, and kiss Lucy for me. My health has been generally good.

MR. CLAY TO HIS SON JAMES.

NEW ORLEANS, January 30, 1847.

MY DEAR SON,—I received to-day your letter of the 19th, informing me of your having purchased thirty tons of hemp, stating that you may purchase sixty or seventy tons more, and asking me to send an authority to join my name in security for the payment of the price. I send the authority inclosed accordingly.

I am sorry to hear that poor little Lucy continues unwell. Kiss the dear child for me, and my love to Susan.

MR. CLAY TO HIS SON JAMES.

NEW ORLEANS, February 24, 1847.

MY DEAR SON,—I have at last received a letter from Henry, but he says nothing in it about his Louisville business. He is well, but writes in bad spirits, owing to his having no prospect of actual service.

My love to Susan and dear Lucy.

MR. CLAY TO HIS WIFE.

NEW ORLEANS, March 13, 1847.

MY DEAR WIFE,—Inclosed I send two bills (the first number) to guard against any accident that may befall me. I wish them kept by you until my return. I retain in my possession the other two numbers. I have been engaged to argue a case next winter in the Supreme Court of the United States.

I shall leave here on Tuesday next for Natchez, where I shall remain a few days; and I think I shall go up in the Peytona, in which case it will be near the last of the month before I get home.

We are in anxious suspense here about news from the army. Taylor has probably had some hard fighting. Rumor says he lost two thousand men, and killed four thousand; but I do not believe that there have been such heavy losses. Henry, I suppose, was in the fight, as he was with Taylor. If I should get any certain intelligence before I leave here I will write you again.

My love to John and Henry.

WM. PRESTON AND OTHERS TO MR. CLAY.

LOUISVILLE, April 10, 1847.

DEAR SIR,—The people of Louisville, deeply moved by the circumstances attending the battle of Buena Vista, and wishing to manifest their profound esteem for the brave men who fell on that memorable day, adopted a series of resolutions expressive of their feelings at the reception of the mournful, yet glorious intelligence. A copy of those resolutions have been inclosed to you by a committee appointed for that purpose.

To the undersigned this sad yet grateful duty was allotted of making the requisite arrangements to bring back to this State the remains of the brave officers and soldiers from this city, who, on that day, died in the service of the nation.

Among those who perished on that sanguinary battle-field, you, sir, sustained the loss of a brave and gallant son—a loss as afflicting to his country as to his kindred. To the city of his adoption he was endeared in life by many virtues, and the sad story of his unyielding valor and chivalric death, will long be remembered and treasured by her sons. We will not venture to dwell upon a theme so painful, yet so full of consolation to a father's heart; our duty is simpler. It is for us to bring back his last remains from the land of the foeman and stranger, that he may peacefully repose in the bosom of his own loved Kentucky, far indeed from the field of his glory, but amid hearts that knew, that loved, that honored him.

It is to ask your permission to bring back to his native State the body of Colonel Clay, to administer the last sacred rites of sepulture, and afterward to erect a monument to commemorate his virtues and perpetuate his deeds, that we address this note.

We remain, sir, with the profoundest sympathy for your affliction, and with the highest esteem, your friends and fellow-citizens.

MR. CLAY TO DANIEL ULLMANN.

ASHLAND, May 12, 1847.

MY DEAR SIR,—I duly received your letter of the 3d instant, and thank you for the friendly expression of your regret and sympathy, on account of the great and irreparable loss which I have sustained, in the death of my beloved son, on the bloody field of Buena Vista. It has been one of the most lamentable events of my life, which has been full of domestic afflictions. Although I feel some consolation in the gallant manner of my son's death in the service of his country, and in the general sympathy which the public has so generously displayed on account of it, the deep wound which I have received can only be effectually healed by Him whose dispensations have produced it.

I approach, at this time, the other subject of your letter under feelings which would not allow me to touch it, but at the instance of such a long, tried, and faithful friend, as I have ever found you to be.

And first, as to the movement in Philadelphia to bring out General Taylor as the Whig candidate for President, which you say is represented to have been made by my advice, and with my approbation. So far from that being the fact, it took me completely by surprise; and most certainly I neither did, nor is it probable that, at any time, I could advise or approve such a movement. Now, it appears to me to be premature, impulsive, and if generally concurred in by the Whig party, must place it in a false and inconsistent position.

I have thought that any serious movement, earlier than next winter or next spring, to designate the Whig candidate, would be unwise. By that time we shall have a pretty correct view of the whole ground, and of what the Whigs may be able to accomplish in 1848.

The war with Mexico is yet in progress. We do not certainly know how it will terminate, nor how General Taylor himself may finally come out of it. In the mean time, it would be very embarrassing to him to be a recognized candidate for the Presidency in opposition to the very party, to the orders of whose Administration he is subject.

Then there is General Scott. Perhaps, while I am now writing, he is in possession of the city of Mexico. Will he create no competition with General Taylor? May we not have two Whig generals in the field of politics? And as the other party may desire the *éclat* of military deeds, may they not bring forward some third general.

As to the inconsistency to which I have referred, it seems to me that the Whig party has been long and deliberately committed against the election of a military officer to the Presidency who had never developed any capacity for civil administration. The election of General Harrison was no departure from that rule; for he was quite as much distinguished in various walks in civil life as he was in his military career. The true principle, I think, is this: that great military attainments and triumphs do not qualify of themselves nor disqualify for the Presidency.

If General Taylor, who is absolutely without any experience whatever in civil administration, shall be elected, I think we may bid adieu to the election ever again of any man to the office of Chief Magistrate who is not taken from the army. Both parties will stand committed to the choice of military men. Each in future will seek to bring him forward who will be most likely to secure the public suffrage. Military chieftain will succed military chieftain, until at last one will reach the Presidency who, more unscrupulous than his predecessors, will put an end to our liberties, and establish a throne of military despotism.

If it were highly probable or certain that we must take General Taylor, or submit to the continuance in power of the present dominant party, that would present a different state of things. The question then would be between the perpetuation and increase of corruption, leading certainly to the destruction of the Government, on the one hand, and the ultimate danger of military despotism, on the other. In such a painful dilemma, it might be expedient, as an only resort, to select the General as the Whig candidate. But this ought not to be done but upon the strongest necessity; and at this early day no such necessity is manifest. On the contrary, there is much reason to hope that the Whig party may be able to elect any fair and honorable man they may choose to nominate.

As to myself, after the disastrous termination of the contest of 1844, I determined to submit to my fate, and to remain passive, and I have accordingly so remained. I have never stated to any mortal whether I would consent or not to the use of my name again as a candidate. On that question I have formed no positive determination, one way or the other. If God were to spare my life and my mind should remain in full vigor; and if there were to be such popular demonstrations of a desire to elect me as to leave no doubt of the result, I might consent to my name being again used. But the latter condition is not likely perhaps, to occur, if the former should exist. Up to the battle of Buena Vista, I had reason to believe that there existed a fixed determination with the mass of the Whig party, throughout the United States, to bring me forward again. I believe that the greater portion of that mass still cling to that wish, and that the movements we have seen, in behalf of General Taylor, are to a considerable extent superficial and limited. Such is the fact in this quarter. And even in Philadelphia I have been informed that by far the greatest enthusiasm was displayed, at the public meeting, when some allusion was made to my name.

If General Scott is successful to the extent, which we may anticipate, in Mexico, most probably a party will spring up to bring him forward; and in the collisions which may arise, it is possible that the Whig public may deem it wise and expedient finally to put aside both Generals, and select some civilian.

I am afraid that you will find this long letter a great infliction; but you must attribute it to yourself, and to the confidence and friendship which I entertain for you.

P. S. I ought to say that I have long and intimately known General Taylor; and that I regard him as an honest straightforward man; but I know nothing of his opinions upon public affairs, except by inference from the fact of his preference of me to Mr. Polk.

MR. CLAY TO MISS TOWLER.

ASHLAND, June 7, 1847.

MY DEAR MISS TOWLER,—I called this morning at Mr. McGowans' in Lexington, to see you, but you had departed for Columbia. My object was to present to you in person, what I now communicate in writing, my cordial thanks for the beautiful lines which you cordially addressed to me, on the death of my beloved son. They are highly creditable to your heart and to your head. The advice you give to restrain my grief for that melancholy event, is very good, and certainly the generous expressions of such sympathy as you, my other friends, and the public have manifested, are calculated to alleviate our sorrows. They place me under great and grateful obligations. But He only, my young friend, can effectually heal such wounds as we have received, by whose inscrutable dispensations they have been permitted to be inflicted. You have felt in early life, the bereavement of an excellent father. May your surviving parent, and your other relatives, be long spared to you, and may you enjoy all other earthly blessings. My warm regards to your mother.

MR. CLAY TO DANIEL ULLMANN.

VIRGINIA, WHITE SULPHUR SPRINGS, August 4, 1847.

MY DEAR SIR,—I received your friendly letter prior to my departure from home ten days ago, and brought it with me to this place. I thank you for the kind tender of your friendly offices, of which, if there should be need, I shall avail myself, with the fullest confidence in your fidelity to the Whig cause, and in your personal regard to me.

I think it even now very manifest that the Locofoco party does not intend to make General Taylor its Presidential candidate; and if it should not, should but designate some other candidate, the condition of popular unanimity, on which alone he states, in one of his late letters, that he will consent to run, will not exist. I think it impossible that the General should maintain silence as to his principles. He must make some public avowal of them, in other words he must say whether he is Whig or Democrat. Such silence could not, I think, be maintained by General Washington, if he were to rise from the dead and consented to be again run for the Presidency. General Jackson was constrained to proclaim his, although he did not afterward conform to them.

But suppose him to preserve silence, and the other party to designate some other candidate, what then are the Whigs to do? Will they not only forego all their objections to a mere military man, as President, but take one haphazard, without knowing whether he holds a single principle in common with them?

I have thought for some time, and continue to think, that it is highly probable that the other party will finally settle down on General Scott, and I think I have seen some indications of this, both in its conduct and in his.

You ask me what is the best mode of conducting the campaign in your State. I should think it best to rely upon the old issues, with the exception of that of a Bank of the United States, which I believe was never pressed in Pennsylvania. There is, 1st. The principle of protection, and the fraud practiced on Pennsylvania by the Kane letter. In further support of this fraud I learned yesterday from the Honorable Reverdy Johnson, that, during the canvass of 1844, when some interrogatories were addressed from your State to Polk, requesting a more explicit avowal of his opinion in regard to the Tariff of 1842, Mr. Buchanan wrote to Tennessee that the Kane letter was working well, and begging that those interrogatories might not be answered, and Mr. Polk accordingly remained silent.

Then there is, 2d. The Mexican war, its causes, the manner of conducting it, and the great National debt which it fastens on the country. 3d. The alarming increase of the vetos and the abuses of the Executive power—the improvement of the country, etc., etc. These and other topics will readily present themselves, and will be treated by you to the greatest advantage.

It is true, as you remark, that the famished condition of Europe has concealed the effects of the Tariff of 1846; but these will be more and more manifested as bread and other food become there abundant. Already have the prospects of a good crop in Europe led to a decline in the prices of American food.

I shall remain here until Monday next, when I purpose passing through your native State to Cape May, where I desire to enjoy a sea-bath, which I never in my life before had an opportunity of doing. You must not, however, infer that my health is bad. It is on the contrary very good.

MR. CLAY TO HIS SON JAMES.

WHITE SULPHUR SPRINGS, August 6, 1847.

MY DEAR SON,—I received your letter of the 28th ultimo, with its inclosures.

The latter part of the journey fatigued me very much, but I have now recovered from it. Dr. Mercer and I go to Cape May on the 9th instant, he leaving his family here. I shall return by this route on my way home.

My love to all at home, and kisses for Lucy.

Your letter is the only one I have received from home. Letters may be addressed to me at Cape May until the 18th instant, and afterward to this place.

NICHOLAS DEAN TO MR. CLAY.

NEW YORK, August 12, 1847.

MY DEAR SIR,—Three years have elapsed since I last had the honor of addressing you; not that the abiding feelings of respect and admiration with which I regard you have in any degree diminished, but the fervent hopes entertained by me, in common with millions of your fellow-citizens, were so unexpectedly and fatally crushed by the issue of the last Presidential election, that I have never yet been able perfectly to rally from its stunning effects, or to gather confidence enough to force myself upon your attention.

A calamity of a different and infinitely more afflicting character has since fallen upon your family circle, awakening the sympathies and calling forth the commisseration of all those who have hearts to feel throughout our native country;—in these, my dear sir, I deeply and truly participate, and respectfully tender to you, and those dear to you, my heartfelt condolements.

Among the numerous tributes which the gallantry and noble bearing of your lamented son upon the fatal field of Buena Vista have called forth, I have met none more touching in its inception and character than the one herewith inclosed, the production of Frances Jane Crosby, a resident graduate of the New York Institution for the Blind. It was written immediately after the announcement of his fall in that fearful conflict. The authoress but recently recited it to me, and I hasten to place it before you.

The deep, broad current of universal sorrow has forced the barriers that encompass the blind, and awakened sympathies even in their stricken state of darkness and solitude.

I can not add to the tenderness and pathos of such an offering. Accept it, I pray you.

On the death of Lieutenant Colonel Henry Clay, Jr., who fell at the battle of Buena Vista, Mexico, February 23, 1847, by Frances Jane Crosby,* of the New York Institute for the Blind.

Lo! on the gory battle-field,
A soldier brave is lying,
Mild is the luster of his eye,
Though he, alas! is dying.

Yet still with feeble hand he grasps
The sword so faithful ever;
Now drops the weapon by his side,
And to resume it—never.

Oh! gallant CLAY, though for thy brow
Its laurels Fame is weaving;
Vain trophies! for thy bosom now
Its last faint sigh is heaving.

'Back, cowards! would ye deeper make
The wounds already given?
You, from an aged father's heart
Another tie have riven.

---

* Miss Crosby has been blind since the age of six weeks.

Intrepid warrior, thou hast left
A deathless name behind thee—
That name unsullied, still shall shine,
Though the dark grave may bind thee.

Thou, by thy General's side hast fought,
Yes, Taylor will deplore thee;
And many a heart that shared thy love
Will weep in silence o'er thee!

E. C. WINES TO MR. CLAY.

THE OAKLANDS SCHOOL, near Burlington,
New Jersey, August 16, 1847.

DEAR SIR,—In the late severe affliction, through which a mysterious but doubtless ever-wise and benignant Providence has called you to pass, I have felt the deepest sympathy with you. And if I have not given utterance to these emotions, it was only because I feared that my condolence would be rather an intrusion upon your grief than any alleviation of it. Having recently seen, however, an account in the public papers of your baptism, whereby you have become a member of the visible Church of Christ, I can not refrain from conveying to you my cordial congratulations on the auspicious issue of your sorrowful bereavement. It was the experience of one of the greatest monarchs and statesmen the world ever saw; it has been the experience of thousands in every condition of life since his day; it has now, I trust, become your happy experience also: "It is good for me that I have been afflicted." The hand of affliction is heavy, but it is because it is filled with gold; the voice of affliction is stern, but its wounds are the probings of a skillful chirurgeon; the countenance of affliction is lowering, but it is the frown of a parent, soon to be followed by the serene and radiant smile of unclouded affection.

Yours, my dear sir, has been a life of incident, of stir, of agitation, of heroic doing and suffering. You have often been placed in positions where your self-possession, your wisdom, your calm energy, and your noble heroism have awakened the admiration of all beholders. But never, on any other occasion, have you displayed so true a wisdom, or appeared invested with so sublime a dignity, as when receiving the baptismal waters, and seated at the communion-table of our common Lord.

I remember well the anguish you suffered a few years ago, under the loss of an estimable and beloved daughter. I remember also your declaration that Mrs. Clay, though deeply distressed, was yet amply sustained and solaced by her religion, and the earnest expression of your wish that you had the same source of consolation, and of your hope that you some day should possess it. From that time to the present I have felt a deep interest in your religious state and welfare, and a belief that you would at length find the treasure you desired—a part in the purchased blessings of the Gospel. And such, I hope, is now the case, and that you find in this the heaviest affliction of your life—the loss of a talented, generous, and chivalrous son—all the consolation which the Gospel is fitted to bestow, and assuredly does bestow, upon all who cordially embrace it. For what can religion be worth, if there is not more in God to comfort us than there can be in the loss of any, even the dearest and most cherished, of his creatures, to distress us?

Can you not pass a day or two with us at the Oaklands, when on your way to New York? We are quite in the country, being two miles distant from Burlington; have an elevated and airy situation, and are surrounded by venerable forest-trees, whose grateful shade defends us, even in the height of summer, from the scorching heats of the sun.

When you write to your son John, be pleased to convey to him the expression of my warm regard and friendship. Mrs. Wines desires to be respectfully presented to you.

GENERAL TAYLOR TO MR. CLAY.

HEAD QUARTERS, Army of Occupation,
Camp near Monterey, November 4, 1847.

MY DEAR SIR,—By yesterday's mail I had the gratification of receiving your very welcome letter of the 27th September. Rest assured that nothing has transpired, nothing can transpire, to impair the amicable and kindly relations which it has been my pleasure and pride for so long time to maintain with you. Hints, similar to those to which you refer, have been thrown out in letters which I have recently received; but they have had no influence whatever upon me; not one word has served, in the remotest degree, to prejudice me against yourself or your friends, in either personal or political relations.

I fully agree with you in the necessity for more deliberation in the selection of a candidate for the Presidency, and I truly regret that my name should have been used in that relation. It has been permitted with the greatest reluctance on my part, and only from a sense of duty to the country. My repugnance to being a candidate before the nation for that exalted office has been frankly and sincerely made known. Most truly is it my hope that before next November the party may select a Whig in all respects worthy of the confidence of the country. To a mutual friend of ours I have recently made this announcement, asserting my greater desire for the quiet of private occupations, as not only a more appropriate termination to my services as a soldier, and more consonant with my earnest wishes, but particularly proper in reference to my limited acquaintance with matters of civil and national polity. I stated to him specifically that I was ready to stand aside, if you or any other Whig were the choice of the party, and that I sincerely hoped such might be their decision.

The importance of harmony and good feeling among the opponents of the present dynasty, is by no one appreciated more considerately than by myself, and whatever may be the decision of the party, I shall be studiously guarded in this particular, and strive to lend my best endeavors to the preservation of unity.

Permit me to repeat, that whatever representations may be made to me, from any source, conveying any expression of disrespect toward yourself or your friends, or that either entertain unfriendly feelings toward me, be assured, my dear sir, they will be repelled and discredited, as they justly merit.

I am much rejoiced that I have this opportunity to assure you, not only of my frank and full confidence in your friendship and kindly feelings, but that I warmly appreciate your wishes for my own success, and your expressed desire to contribute to it.

With my cordial assurance that what is herein written is dictated by the same candid and friendly spirit, so evident in your own letter, I subscribe myself, most sincerely and faithfully, your friend.

MR. CLAY TO MRS. JAMES B. CLAY.

ASHLAND, November 13, 1847.

MY DEAR SUSAN,—I thank you for your letter, which I should have sooner acknowledged, but that I was a week absent from home, attending the trial of a cause in Anderson.

I send you the last letter I have received from James. I hope you have still later. His trip will, I hope and believe, benefit his health.

I am delighted to hear from you that my dear Lucy is better. May God bless and restore to health one in whose welfare I feel the greatest solicitude.

At your house every thing goes on as well as could be expected. Here we are all well. My best regards to your father and your family. Kiss dear Lucy and James for me.

WILLIAM C. PRESTON TO MR. CLAY.

COLUMBIA, November 28, 1847.

MY DEAR SIR,—Your speech* is not only equal to your reputation, but in my judgment even passes what you have heretofore done. The eloquence with which you have expressed yourself gave me delight, while the dignity, wisdom and lofty spirit of patriotism throughout it inspire me with a sort of awe, and fill me with solemn emotions. It is a very noble State paper. It gave me the more profound satisfaction as it had been preceded by rumors of a different character. I can not but believe that it will be of great value to the country, and arrest the fatal policy which is hurrying us to the most disastrous consequences.

GENERAL TAYLOR TO MR. CLAY.

BATON ROUGE, La., December 28, 1847.

MY DEAR SIR,—Your kind and acceptable letter of the 13th instant, congratulating me on my safe return to the United States, and for the complimentary and flattering terms you have been pleased to notice my services, I beg leave to tender you my sincere thanks.

* On the Mexican War, at Lexington.

The warm and hearty reception I have met with from so many of my fellow-citizens, where I have mingled among them since my return, in addition to their manifestations of their high appreciation and approval of my conduct while in Mexico, has been truly gratifying, and has ten-fold more than compensated me for the dangers and toils I have encountered in the public service, as well as for the privations in being so long separated from my family and friends; yet there are circumstances connected with my operations in that country which I can never forget, and which I must always think of with feelings of the deepest sorrow and regret.

I left Mexico after it was determined the column under my orders was to act on the defensive, and after the capital of the enemy had fallen into our hands, and their army dispersed, on a short leave of absence, to visit my family, and to attend to some important private affairs, which could not well be arranged without my being present, and which had been too long neglected. After reaching New Orleans, I informed the Secretary of War that should my presence in Mexico be deemed necessary at any time, I was ready to return, and that a communication on that or any other subject connected with my public duties would reach me if addressed to this place. I therefore feel bound to remain here, or in the vicinity, until the proper authorities at Washington determine what disposition is to be made of or with me. Under this state of things I do not expect to have it in my power to visit Kentucky, although it would afford me much real pleasure to mix once more with my numerous relatives and friends in that patriotic State, to whom I am devotedly attached; as well as again to visit, if not the place of my nativity, where I was reared from infancy to early manhood. And let me assure you I duly appreciate your kind invitation to visit you at your own hospitable home, and should any thing occur which will enable me to avail myself of it, I will embrace the opportunity with much real pleasure.

I regret to say, I found my family, or rather Mrs. Taylor, on my return, in feeble health, as well as my affairs in any other than a prosperous condition; the latter was, however, to be expected, and I must devote what time I can spare, or can be be spared from my public duties, in putting them in order as far as I can do so.

Should circumstances so turn out as will induce you to visit

Washington the present winter, I trust you will take every precaution to protect yourself while traveling from the effects of the severe cold weather you must necessarily encounter in crossing the mountains, particularly so after having passed several of the last winters in the South.

The letter which you did me the honor to address me, referred to, reached me on the eve of my leaving Monterey to return to the United States, and was at once replied to, which reply I flatter myself reached you shortly after writing your last communication; in which I stated, although I had received some letters from individuals in Kentucky calculated, or perhaps intended, to produce unkind feelings on my part toward you, even admitting such was the case, their object has not been accomplished in the slightest degree, and I hope it will never be the case.

Please present me most kindly to your excellent lady, and wishing you and yours continued health and prosperity, I remain, with respect and esteem, etc.

CHAPTER XIII.

CORRESPONDENCE OF 1848, 1849.

MR. CLAY TO HIS SON JAMES.

WASHINGTON, January 16, 1848.

MY DEAR SON,—I received this moment your favor of the 10th, and was glad to hear that all are well at home. My cause is not likely to be reached, I fear, for two or three weeks, if it be reached at all. I have not changed my purpose on the subject to which you refer. I have only suspended the execution of it in deference to some friends who fear that bad consequences to the cause and the country might ensue if I were immediately to execute it.

Mr. Jacobs is to be married to-morrow, and I shall go to his wedding.

I send a list of some plants which Mr. Prince has forwarded to me.

I am sorry that you indulge in bad spirits. You are wrong to do so, and I think you have no occasion to do so. You have much to cheer and animate you. More by far than most persons.

My love to Susan and the children.

MR. CLAY TO HIS SON JAMES.

WASHINGTON, February 1, 1848.

MY DEAR SON,—I received your letter informing me of the occurrence which has taken H. E. Erwin to New Orleans. I am deeply concerned about it; but I can not but think that Mr. Prentiss will not fight him. If he should decline doing so I hope Henry will let it drop there, without resorting to any measure of violence or denunciation.

I have some hope of getting my cause tried next week, although there is not, I regret to say, entire certainty in regard to it.

I inclose a bill of lading for a barrel of sperm oil, purchased by Mr. Coffin, which I will thank you to hand to your mother.

I adhere to my purpose communicated to you before I left home. I have suspended the execution of it for the present, in consequence of strong assurances that if I take the step now it will be ruinous to the Whig party. It places me in a state of painful embarrassment.

My love to Susan and the children.

MR. CLAY TO H. T. DUNCAN.

WASHINGTON, February 15, 1848.

MY DEAR SIR,—I received your letter of the 9th instant and I was gratified with the proceedings in Bourbon, of which it gave a full account. I presume through other channels you are advised of the state of public affairs here. I see no prospect of peace at present. Upon my arrival here the strongest appeals have been made to me to take no step withdrawing my name from among those from which a selection is to be made of a candidate for the Presidency. I have been assured that, if I did, it would lead to a prostration of the Whig party, especially in the free States. Then they say that General Taylor can not be supported in his present noncommittal position. Some doubt, if he were to assume distinct Whig ground, whether he could obtain the Whig support. I have suspended any definitive action.

Great surprise exists here as to the hot haste of our Taylor friends in Kentucky. Why is it? I am often asked, without being able to give any very satisfactory answer. What will be the issue of the two Conventions in Frankfort next week? Nobody knows here. After the long period of time during which I have had the happiness to enjoy the friendship and confidence of that State, what have I done, it is inquired, to lose it?

Those Conventions, if they would act wisely, I think, would acquiesce in the National Convention and leave their own delegates to act freely, according to all circumstances.

My suit has been argued in the Supreme Court, and I shall leave this place next week for Philadelphia, where some business takes me.

MR. CLAY TO GENERAL COMBS.

WASHINGTON, February 18, 1848.

MY DEAR GENERAL,—I received your favor this morning. I have written this winter no letters to Kentucky on public affairs but in answer to letters which I received, and of this description only three. That which you thought ought to have been addressed to you was of that character.

I remain in my passive position in regard to the Presidency. To this course I have been strongly urged. It is generally approved. Whether and when I may change it depends on circumstances. There is no occasion for precipitate action. Mine at least shall be deliberate; having due regard to country, party, friends. If I were to credit all I hear and see, there would be no doubt of my election, if nominated by the National Convention, with my consent; but experience has brought diffidence, and I do not lend too ready an ear to even agreeable things.

I learn from New York that there is not a particle of doubt that, if I were a candidate, the vote of that State would be given me by an immense majority. The Legislature (I mean the Whigs) have had a caucus, in which they passed a resolution, with I believe unanimity, designating me, although not naming me, and excluding our friend General Taylor, though not naming him. Our Kentucky and other friends ought to know what an up-hill business that is of supporting the General in the free States; and yet I lose no suitable occasion to impress on all union, harmony and concord.

I am fully convinced that no preference will be expressed next week in Virginia, at Richmond, for General Taylor; most probably none will be expressed for any one.

I expect to be in Philadelphia the two or three last days of this month and the first week of the next. If I can give any impulse to your business there, I shall not fail to do it.

MR. CLAY TO HIS SON JAMES.

WASHINGTON, February 21, 1848.

MY DEAR SON,—Mr. Adams was striken to-day in his seat in the House of Representatives with paralysis, and, if not now dead, it is believed that he can not live until night. Both houses immediately adjourned.

The court has not yet decided my cause, but as it has a press of business before it, I do not draw any unfavorable conclusion from the delay. I can not lose it.

I shall leave this city the day after to-morrow for Philadelphia on Mr. Shelby's business, and shall be detained there about a week.

Mr. Trist has certainly concluded a treaty with the Mexican Commissioners, which is now in this city. I understand that it cedes the boundary of the Rio Bravo, all New Mexico, and Upper California; and that we are to pay fifteen millions of dollars, besides assuming the payment of the debt due from Mexico to our citizens. I am told that the treaty will be submitted to the Senate for its advice, etc.

I wrote to your mother that I had received the check which you sent me from New Orleans.

My love to Susan, Lucy, and your other children.

JOHN M'LEAN TO MR. CLAY.

CINCINNATI, March 1, 1848.

MY DEAR SIR,—Your favor from Baltimore was lately received at this place, it having been forwarded to me by Mr. Botts.

The manifestations of confidence and affection by your fellow-citizens in your late tour must be gratifying to you, as they certainly have been to your friends. No higher honors could be bestowed than those which you have received.

No one can so fully understand and appreciate the importance of your position, as connected with the future, as yourself; and this knowledge best qualifies you to determine your course of action. Standing in the advance of all your compeers in age and in renown, you owe much to yourself. But your fame is not exclusively your own. It belongs also to the nation. No one friendly to his country could desire a step to be taken or omitted by you, which might not result, as it would be designed, for the general good.

You can not be insensible to the claims of duty, but your friends have no right to expect from you personal sacrifices. I can only repeat what I said to you in Washington, that if, on a full view of the whole ground, your friends believe, and your own judgment shall concur with theirs, that there exists the highest probability of success, you ought not to withhold your name. But, in all frankness, I will say that you ought not to enter into a doubtful contest. Your fame is of too much value to yourself and to your country to compromise it, in any degree, on a hazardous result.

Political success is no longer a test of merit or qualification. Had this been otherwise, you would long since have been at the head of the Government. If your name shall be brought before the country, with your assent, I shall feel the utmost solicitude for your success.

GENERAL TAYLOR TO MR. CLAY.

BATON ROUGE, La., April 30, 1848.

MY DEAR SIR,—Your highly esteemed letter of the 4th inst. was duly received, for which you have my best thanks. It was highly gratifying to me to hear from you, and to learn you had returned to Ashland, after so long a travel during the most inclement season of the year, in good health, which, I flatter myself, you will long continue to enjoy. Your views, as regards our respective chances to succeed to the Presidency at the coming election, are entitled to the greatest respect and consideration, as your opportunities of knowing the opinion of the people generally throughout the country, as regards that matter, are much better than mine can possibly be, having recently made a visit to the seat of the General Government, to three or four of our largest cities, and passed through, into, and along the borders of several of the strongest States in the Union; while I have, since my return from Mexico, for the most part remained stationary at an out-of-the-way place, where I see or hear but little of political movements or matters, save through the newspapers and letters, for the most part written and published by politicians, the editors and writers of the same are sometimes mistaken in their views on the subject of President-making, as other people.

I conceive I am, owing to circumstances which I could not well avoid, placed in rather a peculiar situation, as regards my being a candidate for the Presidency. It is well known to those who had my confidence, that I was very much opposed, when the matter was first agitated in several of the public journals, which was soon after the battles of Palo Alto and Resaca de la Palma, to my name being used as a candidate for that office, which I resisted as far as I could well do so, stating to those around me that I had no aspirations for civil office of any kind; that my greatest ambition was to bring the war we were engaged in to a speedy and honorable termination; that by being considered a candidate for that situation, would have the effect to make the President hostile to me even without his being aware of it, and in such a way as to impair my usefulness in the field, if not to destroy it, as regarded the object I had nearest my heart, which has been realized to the full extent of my expectation; for ever since the battle of Monterey, until I left Mexico, the hand of the Executive was laid heavily on me.

My name continued to be constantly referred to through some of the newspapers, from the time previously mentioned, as a candidate for the Presidency, until the battle of Buena Vista, soon after which I began to receive many letters from some of the first political men of the nation, and from several States, in which they stated that it was in contemplation to bring my name before the country as the Whig candidate for the Presidency, in November, 1848. In reply, I frankly stated my objections to their doing so; among others, that I was no politician, and that it might be considered presumption in me to aspire to that high station, when there were such statesmen who might be elevated to it as yourself, Mr. Crittenden, Judge McLean, and John M. Clayton, and hundreds of others unknown to me, who were, I conceived, much better qualified to preside over the destinies of the country than I was; that you were my first choice, nor did I wish to be in the way of any prominent Whig who might be brought out for that office. To which they replied—some of whom were your warm political and personal friends—that you would not again permit your name to be brought before the country as a candidate, and that they did not believe any other Whig, owing to events which had taken place, was so likely to be elected, in opposition to the party in power, as myself; and that I owed it to the country to permit my name to be used for said object; that I "could not avoid being a candidate if I would, and ought not if I could." Under this state of things I reluctantly yielded to their wishes. About the same time, I informed a distinguished member of Congress, that the arrangements for the next Presidential campaign were to be made during the approaching session of that body, which would shortly meet; and if, after consulting the members of both branches of the same, it was thought advisable to take up some other individual of the party who was more available, he was authorized to withdraw my name from the contest, and if it was you who was fixed on, so much the better. After writing said letter, I received the proceedings of the people called together in primary assemblies in several of the States, nominating me as a candidate for the Presidency at the next election, and in several instances stating it was understood that, in the event of any distinguished Whig being brought out as a candidate, I would at once withdraw my name; but urging me not to do so, but to continue as a candidate under all circumstances, on the grounds I had taken, which was not to be the exclusive candidate of any party, etc.; and on reaching New Orleans many friends called on me to let it be publicly announced that my name as a candidate for the office in question would not be withdrawn, let who would be in the field, which I consented to, and advised my friends in Washington of my change in that respect, without delay. I therefore now consider myself in the hands of the people, a portion of whom have placed my name before the country, for the highest office in their gift, without any agency of mine in the matter, and if they should think proper to drop me and take another, which they ought to do, provided they can fix on a more available candidate, and one better qualified to serve them, and cast their votes for him at the proper time, and should succeed in electing him, it will neither be a source of mortification or disappointment to me. On the contrary, if he is honest, truthful, and patriotic, I will rejoice at the result. And I can say, in all sincerity, that should you receive the nomination of the Whig National Convention, which is to meet in Philadelphia in June, and should be elected in November, but few of your friends will be more gratified than myself. And should you be unsuccessful, and should it be thought your being a candidate had the effect of preventing my election, it will not produce the slightest feeling of unkindness toward you, but I will continue to cherish those kind feelings which I have entertained for you for many years, which I hope are reciprocal.

MR. CLAY TO SAMUEL HAIGHT.

ASHLAND, April 15, 1848.

MY DEAR SIR,—I received to-day your favor of the 10th instant. Prior to this you will have received my note addressed to the public announcing my assent to the submission of my name to the consideration of the National Convention. It so fully explained my views and feelings that I have nothing to add to it. I do not see how it is possible for any exception to be taken to it.

I concur with you in regretting the course of the "National Intelligencer" in regard to the French Revolution; but I think it ought not to operate, and I hope it will not to the prejudice of the Whig party. The editors expressly disclaim being the organ of that party, and the resolutions of congratulation to the French people have been passed, in both houses of Congress, by almost unanimous votes. My own opinion is, that our sympathies and congratulations were due to the French people for the Revolution which they had effected. In expressing these sentiments, we should not have been committed to the sanction of any future excesses which may be perpetrated in the progress of the revolution, if any such should unfortunately occur. My hope is that the foreign powers, profiting by the folly of their former interference with France, will abstain from all exterior pressure upon her, and that she, profiting by the errors which were committed in the former Revolution, will peacefully establish, without the spilling of blood, a free Government upon the basis of popular representation.

No one can doubt my feelings and sympathies who has any recollection of the course which I took in regard to the Spanish American Republics, and to Greece. While France has my cordial and hearty wishes for the triumphant establishment of liberty, I shall be ready to express the deepest regrets, if the Revolution should take an unfortunate turn.

I request you to present my respectful compliments to Mrs. Haight.

MR. CLAY TO HENRY WHITE.

ASHLAND, May 23, 1848.

MY DEAR SIR,—I received your kind letter of the 19th instant, and I feel greatly obliged by the confidence in me which it evinces. You desire, in the event of there not being a majority of the Whig Convention disposed to nominate me, to know who among the distinguished names before the Convention would be my first, second and third choice. I have hitherto maintained a position of entire impartiality between my competitors for the nomination. It was dictated by considerations of delicacy toward them. I do not think that I ought to deviate from it. To you, as soon as to any friend I have, I would make the desired communication, if I were not restrained by the motives suggested.

I hope that your apprehensions of a stormy Convention will not be realized; but that it will be found animated by a spirit of concord and patriotism, and seeking to do the best it can for our common country.

CHARLES F. ADAMS TO MR. CLAY.

QUINCY, May 24, 1848.

MY DEAR SIR,—On behalf of my mother and the few surviving relatives of my late father, as well as for myself, permit me to express the sense which I entertain of the kindness expressed in your letter of the 15th instant. Much as the sympathy has been which the painful event to which you are pleased to allude has called out from almost all quarters, from none could it have come more gratefully than from yourself. A kind providence had by a preceding warning in a measure prepared me to expect the blow, but I confess I was wholly unprepared for so deep and general a manifestation of the public regard. Besides the soothing influence of this result to the feelings of those immediately connected with him, I trust, it may have a wider bearing to prove to all that class of statesmen of which you as well as he are a prominent example, that the most vehement opposition of rivals and cotemporaries, though attended with temporary success, avails little to cloud the deliberate judgment of a later time.

Suffer me, sir, most respectfully to reciprocate the good will which you are pleased to express toward myself. I have always looked back with pleasure to the days in which as a very young man I had some extraordinary opportunities of acquaintance with the most distinguished men of the country. I have never been anxious to alloy the impressions obtained in Washington at that period with new ones to be found in the later society of that capital. Had the statesmen of that day continued to guide the destinies of the country, its prospects at this time would have been somewhat different from what they are. But the die is cast.

DAVID GRAHAM TO MR. CLAY.

NEW YORK, June 9, 1848.

MY DEAR SIR,—The mis-representatives of the Whig party have at length consummated the greatest act of national injustice it was in their power to perform, in the nomination of a man as their candidate for the Presidency who has rejected the principles and spurned the organization and discipline of the Whigs. The intelligence has fallen upon the honest and true-hearted Whigs of this city, and I doubt not of the country at large, like a clap of thunder; and the execrations of the mass of the party here, at the treachery by which they have again been overtaken, are both loud and deep. For yourself, my dear sir, it will be gratifying to know that this last act of ingratitude has only served to bind you more closely to the hearts of your friends; and I do but justice to their feelings and my own when I say that a signal, and I trust, withering rebuke will be promptly administered to the stock-jobbing politicians for whose selfish purposes this outrage upon us has been perpetrated. To you no station can bring higher honor than that which you now enjoy; and, so far as you are individually concerned, it is not too much to say that an honorable retirement, accompanied with the heartfelt affection of the whole nation, must be more grateful than the turmoil and anxieties attendant upon office, however exalted. But it can not and will not be forgotten, that in your person the integrity and the hopes of the Whig party have been stricken down, and their existence as a party blasted and destroyed. And I trust the day is far distant when a forgiveness will be extended to the base combination between the heartless rivals whom you have outstripped, both in unexampled devotion to your country and in the favor of your countrymen, and the truckling harpies, who, like the followers of a camp, are bent upon plunder alone.

I know, my dear sir, that you will indulge in no personal regrets at the issue. But at the same time, allow me, as one of your truest friends, as one who from the moment when I was invested with the right to express an opinion upon public affairs, have been a Whig, and a Clay Whig, to beg of you, as an act of justice to your faithful friends, to withhold any expression of approval of the action of this Convention. Your magnanimity will be appealed to by those who have stabbed you and outraged us, as it was when we were betrayed in 1839; but I trust that the appeal will meet with a different response.

In addressing you in this earnest and emphatic manner, I feel that I am taking a great, perhaps an unwarrantable liberty, with you. I plead, as my apology, my integrity as a Whig and my unalterable veneration for yourself. I speak, moreover, the sentiments of your hosts of friends in New York, who only find relief from the despondency which weighs them down, in the proud reflection that they have battled to the last under your glorious and honored name.

WILLIS HALL TO MR. CLAY.

NEW YORK, June, 1848.

MY DEAR MR. CLAY,—I write to you in the fullness of my heart, not to condole with you, for though I feel all the personal regard toward you which one man can feel for another, personal considerations are absorbed in those of a public nature.

The Presidency could have added nothing to your fame, and would have detracted much from your comfort.

This Government has had a national existence but little more than sixty years, during nearly forty of which it has been guided by your counsels. Glorious period! You may justly regard it with exultation! During this period you have demonstrated the great problem of the feasibility and permanency of popular government, and almost every nation in Europe, incited by the example, is now convulsed with the effort to imitate it. During this period you have impressed upon the country that high and honorable spirit in our intercourse with foreign nations, that spirit of conciliation and union among the States which have preserved us at home and made us respected abroad.

The uninterrupted and unprecedented prosperity of our national career has not been the work of accident. Three times, at least, the car of state would have taken the wrong road, if not the road to destruction, but for your guiding hand: once in 1810-12, once in 1819-20, once in 1830-31. Will no emergency of the kind ever occur again? When the next storm howls around us, this people, guilty and appalled, will shrink back covered with fear and dismay at the mischief they have done. You may say without arrogance, "Weep not for me, but rather weep for yourselves!" As the scroll of our history unrolls itself, your times will stand out in bold and bolder relief until it becomes the golden age of some future people, perhaps as unlike the present as the miserable herd that now defile the streets of Rome are unlike the associates of the elder Brutus. Convulsions and sterility immediately and abruptly following a tract of rich and elevated fertility, make the period of your counsels a stand mark to all future time.

We are on the eve of great events. Slavery will now become an immediate and bitter subject of dispute, and will not be relinquished until it is extinguished or the Union dissolved. I feel little disposition to commiserate the sufferings of the slave region. They have brought it upon themselves; they have thrust slavery upon us in the most offensive way; the policy of slavery governs all their actions; their conduct in the Convention will not be forgotten; the means they have taken to render themselves as they fancied more secure on this subject, has precipitated the discussion accompanied with an acrimony which will not tend to a friendly adjustment. The Whigs in this quarter every where are joining the Barnburners, ready to make the slave question the great issue in future. The next Presidential election (four years hence) will turn upon that point. A Barnburner will be elected.

The Whig party, as such, is dead. The very name will be abandoned, should Taylor be elected, for "the Taylor party." The last Whig Convention committed the double crime of suicide and parricide. I loved that party, and whenever and wherever I shall hereafter discover any portion of my fellow-citizens guided by its principles, I shall attach myself to them; meantime I consider myself absolved from all political connection.

It was resolved to have a ratification meeting here as usual. The General Committee met on Monday evening, they were surrounded by more than three thousand people spontaneously collected, and the Committee was compelled to postpone the meeting indefinitely, in hopes that General Taylor's letter of acceptance will place himself more distinctly upon Whig ground. They will wait in vain. The Taylorites begin to think Taylor's election is not quite as certain as they supposed.

I hasten to the sole object of this long letter, which is to assure you of my undiminished and unalterable regard. Mrs. Hall begs me to join her in the expression of these sentiments and the respectful assurances of our highest esteem.

MR. CLAY TO JAMES HARLAN.

ASHLAND, June 22, 1848.

MY DEAR SIR,—I wished much to see you, and hope soon to meet you. I got your letter from Choles' on your way home, and I have received to-day your favor of the 20th with the newspaper you sent me. Judge Robertson has returned, and has given me much information; but there are some points which you can best elucidate.

I shall take no active or partisan part in the canvass, but remain quiet, submitting to what has been done so far as relates to myself. I think this is the course prompted by self-respect and personal dignity. I shall attend no ratification meetings. How can I sanction and approve what the seven delegates from Kentucky did in the Convention, without virtually condemning what the five delegates did? How can I publicly and warmly support a candidate who declared that, in a reversal of conditions, he would not have supported, but opposed me? I am not misled by the humbuggery of the Louisiana delegates. What credentials, what instructions had they? They showed none, and had none.

In November, if I am spared, I shall, with all the lights then before me, go to the polls and vote for that candidate whose election I believe will be least prejudicial to the country. Of course I can never vote for Cass.

It is too soon to form any satisfactory opinion as to the issue of the contest. Neither candidate seems to be entirely acceptable to the party which supports him. And I suppose that party will probably succeed between whose members there will be ultimately the least division and the greatest intermediate reconciliation.

P. S. The Governor very handsomely tendered me the Executive appointment to the Senate, which I this day declined accepting.

MR. CLAY TO A COMMITTEE OF LOUISVILLE.

ASHLAND, June 28, 1848.

GENTLEMEN,—I received your favor adverting to certain reports in circulation in respect to me, with regard to the approaching Presidential election, and requesting information in relation to them.

Recognizing you as among my staunchest, truest, and most faithful friends, I shall ever feel under the greatest obligations to you, and shall be always happy when I can command your approbation, or do any thing agreeable to you. But I should not be entitled to your esteem if I did not continue to act, as I have ever endeavored to be governed, according to my own conscientious convictions of duty.

As far as I was personally concerned, I submitted to the decision of the late National Convention at Philadelphia. It has relieved me from much painful suspense and anxiety, if I had been nominated; and from great vexation, care, and responsibility, if I had been subsequently elected. I shall do nothing in opposition to it. I shall give no countenance or encouragement to any third party movements, if any should be attempted against it. I desire to remain henceforward in undisturbed tranquillity and perfect repose. I have been much importuned from various quarters to endorse General Taylor as a good Whig, who will, if elected, act on Whig principles and carry out Whig measures. But how can I do that? Can I say that in his hands Whig measures will be safe and secure, when he refuses to pledge himself to their support? when some of his most active friends say they are obsolete? when he is presented as a no-party candidate? when the Whig Convention at Philadelphia refuse to recognize or proclaim its attachment to any principles or measures, and actually laid on the table resolutions having that object in view?

Ought I to come out as a warm and partisan supporter of a candidate who, in a reversal of our conditions, announced his purpose to remain as a candidate, and consequently to oppose me, so far as it depended upon himself? Tell me what reciprocity is in this? Magnanimity is a noble virtue, and I have always endeavored to practice it; but it has its limits, and the line of demarcation between it and meanness is not always clearly discernible. I have been reminded of the course I pursued in the case of the nomination of General Harrison in 1839. But General Harrison was not merely a Whig in name. He was committed and pledged to the support of the measures of the Whigs. He did not declare that he would stand as a candidate in opposition to the nomination of the Convention. He was, moreover, a civilian of varied and extensive experience.

I lost the nomination, as I firmly believe, by the conduct of the majorities in the delegations from Kentucky in Congress and in the Convention, and I am called upon to ratify what they did, in contravention, as I also believe, of the wishes of a large majority of the people of Kentucky! I am asked to sanction and approve the course of the seven delegates from Kentucky, who, in violation of the desire of their constituents, voted against me, and virtually to censure and condemn the five who voted for me!

It seems to me, gentlemen, that self-respect, the consistency of my character, and my true fame, require that I should take no action or partisan agency in the existing contest. If it was between Locofoco principles and Whig principles, I would engage in it with all the ardor of which I am capable; but alas! I fear that the Whig party is dissolved, and that no longer are there Whig principles to excite zeal and to stimulate exertion. I am compelled, most painfully, to believe that the Whig party has been overthrown by a mere personal party, just as much having that character as the Jackson party possessed it twenty years ago.

In such a contest I can feel no enthusiasm; and I am not hypocrite enough to affect what I do not feel. There is undoubtedly a choice, but I regard it as a choice of evils, which I will make for myself in due time, under the influence of the great principles for which I have so long contended. I think my friends ought to leave me quiet and undisturbed in my retirement. I have served the country faithfully and to the utmost of my poor ability. If I have not done more, it has not been for want of heart or inclination. My race is run. During the short time which remains to me in this world, I desire to preserve untarnished that character which so many have done me the honor to respect and esteem. They may rest assured that I will intentionally do nothing to forfeit or weaken their good opinion of me. Abstaining henceforward from all active part in public affairs, and occupying myself with my private and more solemn duties, I shall, if spared, go to the polls at the proper season, like any other private citizen, and cast my vote as I may deem best and safest for the principles I have sustained and for my country. Seeking to influence nobody, I hope to be permitted to pursue for myself the dictates of my own conscience.

Such is the view which I have of the present posture of the Presidential question, and my relations to it. More light may be hereafter thrown upon it, which I shall be most happy to receive, and if it should point to a different course of duty, I shall not hesitate to follow it.

I address this letter to you in consequence of yours, and from the friendly regard I entertain for you. I should have preferred that you had not thought it necessary to appeal to me. It is manifest from the tenor of my reply that it is not intended for publication. I am, etc.

MR. CLAY TO G. W. CURTIS.

Ashland, July 4, 1848.

Dear Sir,—I comply so far with the request contained in your note of the 23d ultimo, as to acknowledge its receipt, and to say that, submitting to the decision of the Philadelphia Convention, so far as I was personally affected by it, I can not give my countenance or encouragement to the use of my name in connection with the Presidency. Abstaining from the expression of any opinion in regard to the nomination which was actually made, I will only observe that Ohio, Indiana, and Massachusetts, and other Northern States, had it in their power to prevent it, if they had chosen to unite upon one whose attachment to the Whig cause was never doubted; but they did not think proper to do so. Ought they then to complain of what was done, upon the ground that General Taylor is not pledged to the support of Whig measures and principles?

I tender my thanks to you for the friendly sentiments toward me which you were kind enough to express, and I am, etc.

MR. CLAY TO MISS SUSAN ALLIBONE.

ASHLAND, July 19, 1848.

If I have not before written to you, my dear Miss Susan, I pray you to believe that my silence has not proceeded from any want of regard to you or from any insensibility to the kindness which you have displayed toward me, in your obliging letter of the 4th March last, and in presenting me with the valuable writings of Archbishop Leighton.

With perfect truth and candor I say that I have rarely ever made a visit to any individual in my life that afforded me higher satisfaction than that which I derived from seeing you. Your physical misfortunes, your resignation to the will of our Maker, your gentle and intelligent countenance, and your interesting conversation, all combined to give to the short interview I had with you a thrilling interest. I have oftentimes thought of it, and have frequently described the touching scene to my friends.

I have looked enough into the volume which you kindly sent me to be convinced that it merits your high commendation of it; and I intend to give the whole of it an attentive perusal.

I am very thankful, dear Miss Susan, for the friendly manner in which you allude to the domestic afflictions with which it has pleased Providence to visit me. I have had a large share of them. Since my return home another has been added to the former number in the death of a most promising grandson, at New Orleans, under circumstances which greatly aggravated our grief. I am happy, however, to tell you, on the other hand, that the sweet little granddaughter, whose case of spinal affection I mentioned to you, is much better, runs about with the free use of her limbs, and we hope will have her strength and health fully re-established. In behalf of her I thank you for the little book which you had the goodness to send her. She is yet too young to read it herself, but I trust that she will be spared to be able hereafter to peruse it. In the mean time her excellent mother will make her familiar with its contents.

Relieved as I am now from the cares, the troubles and the responsibilities of public life, I hope to profit by retirement in making those preparations for another and better world which are enjoined upon us by our highest and eternal interests. In these, your example of perfect submission and complete obedience will be constantly remembered by me, with great benefit and advantage. Instead of condoling with me, as some of my friends have, on account of my failure to obtain the nomination at the late Philadelphia Convention, their congratulations on the event would have been more seasonable and appropriate.

I request you to present my respectful regards to your brothers and their families; and accept for yourself my prayers that He who has enabled you so calmly and cheerfully to bear up under the heavy privations which you suffer, may continue His watchful care over you to the end, and that we may both hereafter meet in the regions of eternal bliss.

GENERAL SCOTT TO MR. CLAY.

ELIZABETHTOWN, N. J., July 19, 1848.

MY DEAR MR. CLAY,—I have been most unfortunate in respect to your very kind note to me of May 30, addressed to this place. It followed me to Frederick, Md., then to Washington, a second time to Frederick, thence to Leonardstown (our friend John Lee's post-office), and after lying there long after I had left his hospitable mansion, it has finally just overtaken me here, via Washington.

It is now sixty days since I landed on the Jersey shore, with a Mexican disease upon me, and although obliged to travel and to engage in the most vexatious and disgusting work, I have not had the strength to walk three hundred yards at once in the whole time. I am still very feeble, and go to-morrow to the sea shore to gain vigor to meet the same court (nearly) in my own case, at the beginning of the next month.

I left Mexico in the comfortable belief that the choice of a Whig candidate for the Presidency had been narrowed down to two names, yours and that of General Taylor, and that you would be the nominee. The day after I landed a distinguished public man from a wing of the Capitol, a friend of yours, passing by got out of the train to see me. I stated my impressions and wishes to him, and was astonished to hear him say that your friends in Congress, with four exceptions—Berrien and Botts, but no Kentuckians, were two of them—had given you up on some calculation of a want of availability! I promptly said, if I could be flattered into the belief that my name on the same ticket (below yours) would add the vote of a single State, I might be considered as at the service of the party, and authorized him to say so on his return to Washington, notwithstanding my reluctance to change my army commission, etc. In a day or two I went to Washington, visited Frederick and returned, but I was confined to a sick bed, and, although I saw many political men, I was not in a condition to converse or to exercise the slightest influence. I believe the impression was quite general that I was not likely to recover. At the end of a week, however, I got back, with difficulty, to Frederick, and there the nomination of General Taylor reached me.

If he shall frankly accept the nomination as a Whig, with a pledge to administer the Government on the principles of the party, I shall fervently pray for his success. If not, I shall at least be indifferent.

MR. CLAY TO JAMES HARLAN.

ASHLAND, August 5, 1848.

MY DEAR SIR,—I received, at the Estell Springs (from which I returned yesterday), your favor transmitting a sketch of Mr. Mr. ———'s speech at Versailles, for which I thank you.

How derogatory is it for politicians to attempt to ridicule and degrade themselves in the presence of General Taylor! And how inconsistent is it to denounce party in the same breath in which the Whig party is called on to support the General as a Whig, that is, a party man! It is mortifying to behold that once great party descending from its lofty position of principle, known, avowed and proclaimed principle, and lending itself to the creation of a mere personal party, with a virtual abandonment of its old principles.

I have a letter from General Scott in which he states that he authorized, on his landing from Mexico, a distinguished gentleman from Washington, to say that he was willing to run as a candidate for the Vice Presidency on the ticket with me.

MR. CLAY TO NICHOLAS DEAN.

ASHLAND, August 24, 1848.

MY DEAR SIR,—I duly received, and perused with lively interest and gratitude, your friendly letter of the 27th ultimo.

The Whig party presents an anomalous condition. Without any candidate who recognizes his obligation to conform to their principles, the members of it are called upon as a party to support the no-party candidate; and I have been urgently and repeatedly appealed to, to indorse as a Whig General Taylor, who, while he adopts the name in a modified form, repudiates the principles of the party! I need not say, that I have done, and shall do, no such thing. Self-respect, consistency with deliberate opinions long ago formed, and my sense of public duty, will restrain me from taking any prominent or active part in the canvass. Whatever I may do, I will not expose myself to any reproaches from those—if there be any such—who might be misled by my opinion. I have submitted quietly to the decision of the Convention, and beyond that I feel under no obligations.

I consider my public career as forever terminated, and I am most anxious to preserve untarnished that character, around which so many warm-hearted friends have done me the honor to rally. I should, I think, justly incur their censure if, after all that I have thought and said (confirmed as my convictions are by observation) against the elevation of mere military men to the Presidency, could I come out in the active support of the most exclusively military candidate ever presented to the American people; one, too, who has forced himself upon the Convention, or been forced upon it. One who declared that he would stand as an independent candidate against me, or any other Whig that might be nominated—a declaration made under his own hand, and which remains uncontradicted by any thing under his own hand, which the public has been permitted to see.

I do not mean to intimate what may be my final vote, given

quietly at the polls, if I vote at all; that will depend upon a view of all existing circumstances at the time; but neither now nor then do I desire to influence any body else.

There is nothing in the contest to arouse my patriotism, or to animate my zeal. I regard the attempt to elect General Taylor as one to create a mere personal party. How such a party may work, I can not foresee; possibly better than that of either of his competitors; but this possibility is not sufficient to excite any warmth or enthusiasm with me. General Taylor has, I think, exhibited much instability and vascillation. He will inevitably fall into the hands of others, who will control his Administration. I know not who they will be, but judging from my experience of poor, weak human nature, they will be most likely those who will have favored and flattered the most.

Standing proud and erect in the consciousness of having faithfully fulfilled all my public duties, and supported and cheered by numberless intelligent and warm-hearted friends in all parts of the country, I acquiesce in the retirement in which I expect to pass the remnant of my life. Some of those friends may censure me for the inaction which I have prescribed to myself during the present canvass; but if they do, I appeal to their "sober second thoughts," or to the impartial tribunal of posterity. I am, etc.

MR. CLAY TO HENRY WHITE.

ASHLAND, September 10, 1848.

MY DEAR SIR,—I received your friendly letter, and beg you to be perfectly assured of my undiminished regard and esteem.

Although I believe that the Philadelphia Convention has placed the Whig party in a humiliating condition—one which, I fear, will impair its usefulness, if not destroy its existence—I acquiesced in its decision in not nominating me, and have submitted quietly to it. I have done nothing to oppose its nomination. I have given no countenance to any movements having for their object any further use of my name, in connection with the office of President. Beyond this I can not go. Self-respect and consistency with deliberate opinions long since formed and repeatedly avowed, against the elevation to that office of a mere military man, must restrain me from taking any active part in the canvass. I wish to leave every body freely to act for themselves, without influence from me, if I could exert any. If I were to recommend the support of General Taylor, and if he should be elected on it afterward, and in his Administration disappoint the Whigs, I should feel myself liable to reproaches.

I regret, therefore, that I can not comply with your request to make a public declaration of my intention to support General Taylor. Without compromising any one, I shall go to the polls when the day arrives, and give such a vote as I think may be most likely to be least injurious to the country.

With my warm regards to Mrs. White and your family, I am your friend.

MR. CLAY TO DANIEL ULLMAN.

ASHLAND, September 16, 1848.

MY DEAR SIR,—I received your favor of the 9th instant, informing me of the movement of some of my friends in New York to bring out my name as a candidate for the Presidency.

I feel under the greatest obligations and the warmest gratitude to them, for the sentiments of attachment, confidence, and friendship which they do me the honor to entertain. And to you, in particular, I owe an expression of my cordial thanks for your long, ardent, and ever faithful attachment to me.

But, my dear sir, after the decision of the Philadelphia Convention against my nomination, I have felt bound quietly to submit. I could not, therefore, accept a nomination, if it were tendered to me, nor do I wish any further use of my name in connection with the office of President.

I never would have consented to the submission of my name to that Convention, but under a conviction that I should have been elected if nominated. I firmly believe now that such would have been the result.

The Convention chose to nominate another, and I have ever since avoided giving the slightest countenance or encouragement to any further efforts on my behalf.

To bring me into the canvass now, would, I think, only have the effect of adding to existing embarrassments, and perhaps of throwing the election into the House of Representatives, at a time when parties are most exasperated against each other. Such an issue of the contest is to be deprecated.

I am glad to hear that you have finally established yourself in your profession in New York. I request you to accept my cordial wishes for your success, happiness, and prosperity.

MR. CLAY TO JAMES LYNCH AND OTHERS.

ASHLAND, September 20, 1848.

GENTLEMEN,—I have received your official letter as members of the (Whig) Democratic General Committee of the city and county of New York, and I take pleasure in answering it.

Never from the period of decision of the Philadelphia Convention against my nomination as a candidate for the Presidency, have I been willing, nor am I now, to have my name associated with that office. I would not accept a nomination if it were tendered to me, and it is my unaffected desire that no further use be made of my name in connection with that office. I have seen, therefore, with regret, movements in various quarters having for their object to present me as their candidate to the American people ; these movements have been made without any approbation from me. In the present complicated state of the Presidential election they can not, in my opinion, be attended with any public good, and may lead to the increase of embarrassments, and to the exasperation of parties.

While I say this much without reserve, I must nevertheless add that I feel profound gratitude to such of my warm-hearted and faithful friends as continue to indulge the vain hope of placing me in the office of Chief Magistrate of the United States. And that I neither think it just or politic to stigmatize them as factionists or by any other opprobrious epithets. Among them I recognize names which have been long distinguished for ability, for devotion to the Whig cause, and for ardent patriotism.

You advert with entire truth to the zeal and fidelity with which the delegation from New York sought in the Philadelphia Convention to promote my nomination as a candidate for the Presidency. I am most thankful to them and shall ever recollect their exertions with profound gratitude.

And here, gentlemen, I would stop but for your resquest that I would communicate my views ; this I shall do briefly and frankly, but with reluctance and regret.

Concurring entirely with you, that the peace, prosperity and happiness of the United States depend materially on the preservation of Whig principles, I should be most happy if I saw more clearly than I do that they are likely to prevail.

But I can not help thinking that the Philadelphia Convention humiliated itself, and as far as it could, placed the Whig party in a degraded condition. General Taylor refused to be its candidate. He professed indeed to be a Whig, but he so enveloped himself in the drapery of qualifications and conditions that it is extremely difficult to discover his real politics. He was and yet is willing to receive any and every nomination no matter from what quarter it might proceed. In his letter to the "Richmond Republican" of the 20th April last, he declared his purpose to remain a candidate, no matter what nomination might be made by the Whig Convention. I know what was said and done by the Louisiana delegation in the Convention, but there is a vail about that matter which I have not penetrated. The letter from him which it was stated one of that delegation possessed, has never been published, and a letter on the same subject addressed to the independent party of Maryland, has at his instance been withheld from the public. It was quite natural that after receiving the nomination he should approve the means by which he obtained it. What I should be glad to see is some revocation of the declaration in the "Richmond Republican" letter before the nomination was made.

On the great leading national measures which have so long divided parties, if he has any fixed opinions, they are not publicly known. Exclusively a military man, without the least experience in civil affairs, bred up and always living in the camp with his sword by his side, and his epaulets on his shoulders, it is proposed to transfer him from his actual position of second in command of the army, to the Chief Magistrate of this great model Republic.

If I can not come out in active support of such a candidate, I hope those who know any thing of my opinions, deliberately formed and repeatedly avowed, will excuse me; to those opinions I shall adhere with increased instead of diminished confidence. I shall think that my friends ought to be reconciled to the silence I have imposed on myself from deference to them as well as from strong objections which I entertain to the competitor of General Taylor. I wish to lead or mislead no one, but to leave all to the unbiased dictates of their own judgment.

I know and feel all that can be urged in the actual position of the present contest.

I entertain with you the strongest apprehension from the election of General Cass, but I do not see enough of hope and confidence in that of General Taylor to stimulate my exertions and animate my zeal. I deeply fear that his success may lead to the formation of a mere personal party. There is a chance indeed that he may give the country a better administration of the Executive Government than his competitor would, but it is not such a chance as can arouse my enthusiasm or induce me to assume the responsibility of recommending any course or offering any advice to others.

I have great pleasure in bearing my humble testimony in favor of Mr. Fillmore. I believe him to be able, indefatigable, industrious and patriotic. He served in the extra session of 1841 as Chairman of the committees of the two houses of Congress, and I had many opportunities of witnessing his rare merits.

I do not desire the publication of this letter, but if you deem it necessary, you may publish the four first and the last paragraphs.

SUSAN ALLIBONE TO MR. CLAY.

HAMILTON, near PHILADELPHIA, November 6, 1848.

I denied myself the gratification of giving an immediate reply to your kind and most welcome letter, respected sir, because I was aware that the communications of your numerous friends present an almost incessant demand upon your attention; but I did not design to be so very considerate as to have allowed more than three months to pass away unaccompanied by an assurance of my warm affection.

The debility which often renders me unable to use a mechanical medium for the conveyance of thought, does not deprive me of the consolation of expressing my regard for those I love by imploring for them "the blessing of the Lord," which "maketh rich and addeth no sorrow with it;" and for you, dear sir, very frequent and earnest prayers have come into my heart. I do hope God will grant you a double portion of His spirit. I should not feel satisfied if any ordinary measure of contrition, faith, love, and holy obedience were yours. We are commanded to "covet the best gifts;" and it is not presumptuous to expect much from God, if the merits of our Redeemer be our only plea. Nor would I forget to thank Him for the spiritual illumination He has granted you, nor for the desire you express to consecrate the retirement you are at last permitted to enjoy, to the interests of "another and a better world." It is indeed a better world, dear Mr. Clay. How delightful will it be to be released forever from "every day's support of wrong and outrage, with which earth is filled!" What blessedness to worship God without the intrusion of one emotion opposed to the holiness of His law, or a single wandering thought, and to satisfy the longings of the spirit after knowledge, excellence and love, by the eternal contemplation of Him who is the concentration of them all. To receive all this happiness as the free gift of a Saviour's love, and to attune a harp of thanksgiving with heaven-taught melody, ever swelling louder and clearer notes of adoration as the past and present become more fully understood, and the future hastens on with brightening glory. Oh! this will be to us a better world.

It has often occurred to me that while the believer rejoices that "to die is gain," he ought also to remember that "to live is Christ." I wish to understand the full meaning of this expression. Experience has taught me something of its import, but I hope to learn new lessons every day. One of our homilies tells us "faith is the hand that puts on Christ," and St. Paul assures us "of Him are ye in Christ Jesus, who of God, is made unto us wisdom, and righteousness, and sanctification, and redemption."

How can I, who am so sinful and so suffering, be sufficiently thankful that this glorious Redeemer is the portion of my soul? Mine has been a situation of extraordinary necessity, and the fullness of Jesus has been its supply. When my earthly friends sit down and weep because their unwearied attentions can not remove the firm pressure of disease, my Saviour draws me still more closely into the sanctuary of His presence, and my wearied spirit reposes there in peace. But there is an amputation of the heart, caused by the removal of the most cherished objects of affection, which requires the still more tender offices of Him who "came to give the oil of joy for mourning, and the garment of praise for the spirit of heaviness;" and in this sorrow also I have been greatly comforted. If I had never known bereavement I could not so fully sympathize with the deep afflictions to which your letter alludes. I am well assured that your susceptibilities of suffering are unusually acute, and I pray that the consolations of the Holy Spirit, and the sanctified uses of adversity may be given you in proportionate measure. It may be, also, that the dispensations which have caused so painful a void in your family circle may be the avenues through which many heavenly blessings may be conveyed to its surviving members. It may be your delightful privilege to teach them to consecrate the energy they have inherited from their earthly parent to the glory of their Father in Heaven; and while I condole with my country because she will be deprived of your official services at a time when they seem so greatly needed, I do indeed most heartily congratulate your children and grandchildren that they are permitted to surround you in the evening of your days.

Permit me to say that I do not think you suit the times, dear sir. Expediency has become the watchword of our nation, and your political vestments have never assumed a chameleon hue, nor has the cloak of concealment been wrapped around them. Oh! that we had many Daniel's to confess that "we, and our father's have sinned and done wickedly," and to implore that national judgments may be averted.

The beautiful petition of the Lord's Prayer, "Thy kingdom come, Thy will be done, on earth as it is in Heaven," is most appropriate at this time of danger, and how effectually will its fulfillment hush into silence the stormy elements around us! Is it not an unspeakable privilege to be the subject of a kingdom which can not be moved?

I am truly gratified to learn that the health of your little granddaughter has so greatly improved, for I feel a deep interest in all to whom you are allied. I shall not soon forget the terms of affection with which you made me acquainted with the character of Mrs. Clay, to whom you will please present my respectful regards.

I think I will be so selfish as to tell you how delighted I should be to receive another letter from Ashland.

My sister, Mrs. Allibone, is my copyist to-day, as I am still unable to attempt a greater effort than the pencilship of a letter. From her, with my brother, and other sisters, you will accept a message of warm affection, accompanied with my earnest prayers that you may ever be enabled to appropriate the assurance. "The eternal God is thy refuge, and underneath are the everlasting arms." Believe me, my beloved Mr. Clay, most sincerely and respectfully yours.

GENERAL TAYLOR TO MR. CLAY.

Baton Rouge, La., November 17, 1848.

My dear Sir,—On my return here a day or two since, after a short absence, I found your highly esteemed letter of the 23d ultimo, for which accept my most cordial thanks. The one referred to, written by you in May last, reached me by due course of mail, and I owe you an apology for not replying to it, which I deferred doing from day to day, under the expectation that certain events would occur which I wished to refer to in my reply, but which were so long in taking place as to induce me to give up doing so altogether. Said letter was entirely satisfactory, as regarded the matter alluded to (and to put an end to the misrepresentations growing out of the same, going the rounds through various newspapers, I at once caused a short article to that effect to be published in "The Picayune" of New Orleans, which may have met your eye), and relieved me from great anxiety, as I believed the course then pursuing by certain individuals touching our correspondence, was calculated, if not intended, to bring about a state of distrust, if not unkind feelings, between you and myself, as well as some of our friends; which, had they succeeded in doing, would, so far as I am concerned, been a source of much pain and mortification to me.

There certainly could be no objection or impropriety in your permitting your friends to read any of the letters I wrote you, who ought not to have made any use of them, for any purpose, without your authority, as there was an implied confidence at least, which ought not to have been violated. It is true, I allowed a few and very confidential friends to read yours to me, nor am I aware that any use was made of them, directly or indirectly, for any purpose whatever; nor was any copy taken of any one of them, and furnished to a member of Congress, or any one else, although I have no doubt you have been informed I had done so.

The hostile course pursued by the Hon. Mr. Botts toward me, since I was brought prominently before the country, as a candidate for the highest office known to our laws, has been doubtless the cause of some mortification on the part of a portion of his friends, you perhaps among the number, as I feel confident that you did not approve it. Had Mr. B., or any one else, opposed my election to the Presidency on the ground of want of qualifications to discharge the important duties connected with said office, in a becoming manner and proper spirit, it would have been all right and proper, and would not have given me one moment's concern; nor does it, at any rate; but the moment misrepresentation and scurrility were resorted to, whether it effected the object of defeating me or not, it must ultimately degrade those whoever may be concerned in it.

I trust I have many devoted personal friends, who, from various causes, were opposed to my reaching the office in question, and took every honorable and proper means in their power, and no other, to prevent my success, and I certainly would never think of censuring them, much less to permit it on my part to interrupt our friendly relations, because they have done what they thought right in opposing my election to an office which they thought another was better qualified to fill.

I beg leave to return you many thanks for your kind invitation to visit Ashland, should I go to Kentucky before you leave for the South; which it would have afforded me much pleasure to have done, and passed a few days under your hospitable roof; but I must forego this pleasure, as it will be out of my power to leave Louisiana or Mississippi for several months, at any rate during the present year; but should you carry out your intentions of visiting the South, as contemplated, and should pass the month of January in New Orleans, I will try and take you by the hand at that time, or during the same month.

Wishing you many years of health, happiness, and prosperity, I remain, etc.

J. T. HART TO MR. CLAY.

LEXINGTON, December 4, 1848.

DEAR SIR,—I hope you will accept this head I send you, which I have finished entirely with my own hands; and also another, which I will finish in a day or two, as a small token of the gratitude and obligation I feel toward yourself and family, who have extended to me so much kindness.

I will call out to see you this evening or to-morrow. With my earnest wishes for your recovery, I am, etc.

MR. CLAY TO HIS SON JAMES.

WASHINGTON, January 2, 1849.

MY DEAR SON,—I received your letter of the 27th November, and I was happy to hear of the continued health of Susan and your children, and especially that she had so easy an accouchement. That was the result of her previous exercise and the climate of Lisbon.

I am sorry to hear of the bad prospect of your getting our claims satisfied. I wrote you a few days ago, giving a long account of an interview which I had with the Portuguese minister, etc., about the case of the General Armstrong. In the course of it, he told me that he thought some of our claims were just, and so did the Minister of Foreign Affairs, and that they would be paid. If we are to come to any appeal to force, perhaps it will be as well that they should reject them all, those which are clearly just as well as those which are contestable. But, as it would be a feather in your cap, I should like that you would get them all owned, or as many as you can.

The minister told me that the owners of the General Armstrong demanded $250,000. That sum strikes me to be erroneous. If they agree to admit the claim, you might stipulate to have the amount fixed by some commission; or, which would be better, if the owners have an agent at Lisbon, you might get him to fix the very lowest sum which they would be willing to receive, which might not exceed one fifth of the sum demanded.

I mentioned confidentially to Sir H. Bulwer, the British minister, my apprehensions of a difficulty with Portugal, and he said he would write to Lord Palmerston, and suggest to him to interpose his good offices, etc. He told me that a brother of Lord Morpeth was the British Chargé at Portugal. If he resembles his brother, you will find him a clever fellow.

No certain developments are yet made of what Congress may do on the subject of slavery. I think there is a considerable majority in the House, and probably one in the Senate, in favor of the Wilmot proviso. I have been thinking much of proposing some comprehensive scheme of settling amicably the whole question, in all its bearings; but I have not yet positively determined to do so. Meantime some of the Hotspurs of the South are openly declaring themselves for a dissolution of the

Union, if the Wilmot proviso be adopted. This sentiment of disunion is more extensive than I had hoped, but I do not regard it as yet alarming. It does not reach many of the Slave States.

You complain of not hearing from Kentucky. I have the same complaint. I have not received a letter from John for a long time. My last was from Thomas, of the 18th ult. They were then all well.

I am glad to hear that Henry is placed at school, but am sorry that his defects continue to display themselves. We must hope that he will correct them as he grows older, and in the mean time console ourselves that his faults are not worse than they are.

My love to Susan, the boys, and your children.

MR. CLAY TO JAMES HARLAN.

NEW ORLEANS, January 26, 1849.

MY DEAR SIR,—I met with an accidental but violent fall a week ago, in carelessly descending a flight of stairs, to receive a gentleman who bore me a letter of introduction, and I got terribly bruised. I broke no bones, but it disabled me, for the present, from walking without assistance, and almost from writing

I received yesterday your favor of the 12th, and to-day that of the 14th. I regret extremely that the use of my name, in connection with the office of Senator, should have created any division among the Whigs, or excited any dissatisfaction with any one. God knows that I have no personal desire to return to that body, nor any private or ambitious purposes to promote by resuming a seat in it. I expressed to you and to other friends, at the period of my departure from home, the exact state of my feelings, when I declared that I could not reconcile it to my feelings to become a formal or an avowed candidate; and that if the General Assembly had any other person in view, I did not wish to interfere with him. I added that, if, nevertheless, the Legislature thought proper to require my services in the Senate, deference to their will, a sense of public duty, and the hope of doing some good, would prompt me to accept the office.

These views are unchanged. According to them, it follows

that I have no desire to have my name pressed upon the General Assembly, and I hope that it will not be presented, unless it is manifestly the free and voluntary wish of a majority of that body. It would be a great mortification to me to be thought to be solicitous for that office, and to be supposed to be seeking it from the reluctant grant of the Legislature. I hope that my friends will act in consonance with the state of my feelings, and not suffer my name to be used but on the conditions which I have stated.

MR. CLAY TO THOMAS B. STEVENSON.

NEW ORLEANS, January 31, 1849.

MY DEAR SIR,—The breaking out of the cholera here prevented my meeting General Taylor in this city, as had been expected. I met him at Baton Rouge, but only long enough to exchange friendly salutations, without any opportunity to converse on public affairs.

About a fortnight ago I met with a terrible accidental fall, which, although fortunately I broke no bones, has for the present confined me to my lodgings, disabled me from walking, and almost from writing. To that cause is owing my not having earlier acknowledged the receipt of your friendly letter of the 25th ultimo.

I suppose that I shall be elected to the Senate by the General Assembly of Kentucky, in which case I shall hardly feel myself at liberty to decline, conferred as the office will be without any solicitation from me, without my being a candidate, and with the knowledge of a strong disinclination on my part to return to that body. Deference to the will of the General Assembly, a sense of duty, and the possibility of my being able to do some good, overcome my repugnance. If I go to Washington, it will be with an anxious desire that I shall be able to support the measures of the new Administration, in consequence of their conformity with Whig policy.

There seems to be yet some slight prospect of a settlement at Washington of the Free Soil question; but we shall see.

The cholera has nearly entirely disappeared from this city.

MR. CLAY TO HIS SON JAMES.

NEW ORLEANS, March 3, 1849.

MY DEAR SON,—I was glad to hear by your letter of the 18th ultimo that you had returned from Missouri. Your journey must have been a dreadful one, but you will find some compensation for it in the profits which you expect to realize.

My health is better, and I can again walk. I hope to reach home toward the last of this month. The weather is now fine here, and I am desirous not to return until the winter breaks.

I have heard that Colonel Allen has discontinued his school, but I have not heard whether Henry is admitted at West Point. I declined going to Washington at the Call Session.

As you were absent, I sent to Richard Pendell a letter on the Emancipation question. As I regret to hear that it is not popular, I suppose that my letter will bring on me some odium. I nevertheless wish it published. I owe that to the cause, and to myself, and to posterity.

I am delighted to hear that dear little Lucy is better. You are perfectly right to take her to the sea-bath, if it be recommended ; but ought you not to think of the Arkansas Springs?

My love to Susan and your children.

MR. CLAY TO GENERAL COMBS.

NEW ORLEANS, March 7, 1849.

MY DEAR SIR,—I received your last letter, transmitting one which is returned. Many thanks are due to you for various communications received during the past winter, and which afforded me much valuable information. I should have before acknowledged them, but for the consequences of my fall, which for a time disabled me from both walking and writing.

The project of assuming the debt of Texas on the consideration of her relinquishment of her territorial claim beyond the Nucces, is worthy of serious examination. The difficulty in the way will be the Free Soil question.

I am most anxious that you should obtain some good appointment under the present Administration. You, I think, eminently deserve it. Whether I can aid you or not, I can not at present say. My relations to the President, on my part, and, as far as I know, on his, are amicable; but I have had no proof of any desire to confer or consult with me on any subject. Some of his warm and confidential friends, I have reason to know, view me with jealousy, if not enmity. While self-respect will restrain me from volunteering any opinion or advice, unless I know it will be acceptable, public duty will equally restrain me from offering any opposition to the course of his Administration, if, as I hope and anticipate, it should be conducted on principles which we have so long cherished and adhered to.

I hope to reach home, and to see you in all this month, when there will be time enough to talk over all these and other matters.

I did not go to the Call Session, because, supposing that it would be short and formal, and without any serious division, I disliked encountering, in my lame condition, a journey so long in the winter. I am, etc.

MR. CLAY TO JAMES HARLAN.

NEW ORLEANS, March 13, 1849.

MY DEAR SIR,—I received your favor of the 3d instant. I concluded not to attend the Call Session, which I could not have done without much personal discomfort.

The Cabinet of General Taylor was not, it seems, exactly as you supposed. Some of the appointments excited surprise. I think that he might have made one of greater strength. I am truly concerned that Letcher was overlooked. I had strong hopes that he would have been appointed, and I thought I had reason for them.

I think it quite likely that you may be right in supposing that neither I nor my friends will find much favor at Court. As to myself, having given no just cause for its frowns, I can bear them without difficulty; but the President will be unwise if he neglects or proscribes my friends. Without them, he never could have been elected.

While I have no desire to go into the Convention, I shall make no decision until my return. I leave this city on the 17th instant, and stopping on the river at one or two places, I hope to reach home about the last of the month.

MR. CLAY TO RODNEY DENNIS.

ASHLAND, April 15, 1849.

DEAR SIR,—Your favor of the 27th ultimo, addressed to me at New Orleans, followed and found me here.

I am very grateful and thankful for the friendly sentiments toward me which your partiality has prompted you to express. You do me too much honor in instituting any comparison between me and the renowned men of antiquity. I am in one respect better off than Moses. He died in sight of, without reaching, the promised land. I occupy as good a farm as any that he would have found, if he had reached it; and it has been acquired, not by hereditary descent, but by my own labor.

As to public honors and public offices, I have perhaps had more than my share of them. At all events I am contented, and now seek for better, if not higher offices and honors, in a better world. That we may both meet there, if we never do here, is the sincere prayer of your friend and obedient servant.

MR. CLAY TO NICHOLAS DEAN.

ASHLAND, June 21, 1849.

MY DEAR SIR,—I received your favors of the 1st and 4th instant. I regret extremely that many of the appointments of the Executive are so unsatisfactory to the public; and still more that there should be just occasion for it. I fear that the President confides that matter too much to the Secretaries, and that they have selfish and ulterior views in the selections which they make. It is undeniable that the public patronage has been too exclusively confined to the original supporters of General Taylor, without sufficient regard to the merits and just claims of the great body of the Whig party. This is both wrong and impolitic.

You tell me that it will be difficult to repress an expression of the Whig dissatisfaction, prior to the meeting of Congress. I should be very sorry if this was done so early, if it should become necessary (I hope it may not) to do it at all. I think there ought not to be any denunciation of the Administration, unless it is rendered proper for its plans of public policy. If before these are developed, the Administration should be arraigned, it would be ascribed to disappointment as to the distribution of the patronage of Government. It will be different, if, contrary to what we have a right to hope and expect, the Administration should fail to support and recommend the great measures of the Whig party.

As to myself, I need not say to you, that I shall go to Washington, if I am spared, with a firm determination to oppose or support measures according to my deliberate sense of their effects upon the interests of our country.

MR. CLAY TO HIS SON JAMES.

Ashland, October 2, 1849.

My dear James,—I returned home this day fortnight, in improved health, which, with the exception of my cough, continues good. Levi again left me at Buffalo, and has again returned to Louisville, on his way home, having reported himself there to Mr. Smith.

I received your letter dated at sea, after you had been two days out, and I was sorry to learn that there was so much seasickness in your party. I calculated that you arrived at Liverpool about the time I got home. I found all well here.

Colonel Brand died with cholera about four weeks ago. Johnson, the saddler, has purchased at private sale the whole of Mr. Hunt's land, of upward of eleven hundred acres, at sixty dollars per acre. I think it would have commanded more at public auction, land being on the rise.

You will have seen that Secretary Clayton has got into a difficulty with the French minister. I am sorry for it, and I think that with judgment and discretion it might have been avoided. But your course should be to defend the act of the Executive, if you can conscientiously; and if not to remain silent. The papers will also inform you that the Secretary has also a difficulty with the British Chargé about the Mosquito Coast. I hope it is not so serious as to threaten war.

My crops of hemp and corn are uncommonly fine, and the influx of gold from California, and the general prosperity of the country are giving an upward tendency to prices. Hemp, I fear, will, however, be an exception next year, owing to its abundance.

I suppose you will hear from Louisville. I have heard nothing to the contrary, and therefore presume all are well there.

I inclose a ticket which I received for you inclosed in a circular, similar to one addressed to me, from the American Institute.

Our love to Susan, and kiss dear Lucy and the other children for me.

MR. CLAY TO JAMES HARLAN.

ASHLAND, October 4, 1849.

MY DEAR SIR,—I saw in "The Commonwealth" with sorrow and regret, the death announced of your son, my namesake. I tender to you, on the melancholy occasion, an expression of my sincere sympathy and condolence. I knew enough of him, from frequent interviews and conversations with him, to appreciate the great distress which the lamented event must have brought upon you and Mrs. Harlan and your other children. I have been, in my time, a great sufferer from the loss of beloved children, and I can fully estimate the grief which you now feel.

Time, and a patient resignation and submission to the will of Him who, having given us our children, has the right to take them from us when He pleases, can only heal the wounds inflicted, and mitigate the sorrows which the bereavement necessarily excites.

I hope that you and Mrs. Harlan will bear with fortitude, and in a true spirit of Christianity, this sad and heavy dispensation.

MR. CLAY TO HIS SON JAMES.

ASHLAND, October 15, 1849.

MY DEAR SON,—I received your letter dated at Liverpool the 27th ultimo, and was very glad that you had all safely arrived, with so little inconvenience from sea-sickness. I hope that your excursion to Paris proved agreeable, and that you were not tempted by its many attractions to run into any extravagant expenditures.

The elections in Ohio and Pennsylvania have gone against the Administration, and, judging from present prospects, I do not see how it is to be sustained. If, therefore, you do not come home sooner, you may prepare to return on the expiration of its term. I understand indirectly that it is counting much on my exertions at the approaching session of Congress; but I fear that it is counting without any sufficient ground. I intend to leave home the first of November, but not to go to Washington until about the opening of Congress. I expect to pass two or three weeks in Philadelphia.

I suppose that you and Susan hear regularly from Louisville, from which I have heard nothing of any interest. Here we are all in health, and things move on in their ordinary channels. Yesterday (Sunday) Thomas and Mary dined with us as usual. He goes down in a few weeks to his famous saw mill, from which he calculates to make a great deal.

We expect H. Hart and his family here to-morrow or next day to make their farewell visit, preparatory to their going to St. Louis, for which he has made most of his arrangements.

Give our love to Susan and your children and to Henry Clay, and kiss dear Lucy for your affectionate father.

MR. CLAY TO HIS SON JAMES.

WASHINGTON, December 4, 1849.

MY DEAR SON,—I left home the first of last month, which throughout was a most delightful one, and, after passing two or three weeks in Philadelphia, New York, and Baltimore, arrived here last Saturday, the 1st instant. My presence in those cities excited the usual enthusiasm among my friends, and the customary fatigue, etc., to myself; but I rejoice that my health is good, with the exception of a bad cold, which I hope is passing off. I have not yet seen the President, although I called yesterday and left my card. I have seen Mr. Ewing, and other members of the Cabinet have left their cards. Up to this time there is no organization of the House, which is in a very curious state. Neither party has a majority, and divisions exist in each; so that no one can foresee the final issue. The elections this year have gone very unfavorably to the Whigs, and without some favorable turn in public affairs in their favor, they must lose the ascendency.

I received Susan's letter of the 19th October and yours of the

5th November, and the perusal of them afforded me satisfaction. I observe what you say about Mr. Hopkins' kind treatment of you. He has gone home, but if I should ever see him, I will manifest to him my sense of his friendly disposition toward you. I am acquainted with him as a former member of the House of Representatives. I shall seize some suitable occasion to examine your dispatches at the Department of State, and I am glad that you entertain confidence in your competency to discharge the duties of your official position. That is a very proper feeling, within legitimate bounds; but it should not lead to any relaxation of exertions to obtain all information within your reach, and to qualify yourself by all means in your power to fulfill all your official obligations. How do you get along without a knowledge of the French language? Are you acquiring it?

I have heard from home frequently since I left it. John had taken a short hunt in the mountains, but returned without much success. Thomas had gone down the Ohio to see about the saw mill, and is still there. All were well. Dr. Jacobs is now here from Louisville. His brother with his wife have gone to Missouri, where he has purchased another farm. You have said nothing, nor did Susan, about Henry Clay or Thomas Jacobs.

Give my love to Susan and all your children, and to the boys. I will write to her as soon as I am a little relieved from company, etc.

I hope you will adhere to your good resolution of living within your salary. From what you state about your large establishment, I am afraid that you will exceed that prudent limit. How did your predecessor in that particular? I believe he was not a man of any wealth.

MR. CLAY TO MRS. JAMES B. CLAY.

WASHINGTON, December 15, 1849.

MY DEAR SUSAN,—I received and read with great pleasure your letter of the 19th of October. All its details of information were agreeable to me, and I hope you will continue to write to me and to communicate every thing, the minutest circumstance concerning yourself or your dear family. I have taken apartments at the National Hotel (a parlor and bed-room adjoining), for the winter. I have an excellent valet, a freeman, and I am as comfortable as I can be. No advance has been yet made in Congress, in the public business, owing to the House, from its divided condition, being yet unable to elect a Speaker. When that will be done is uncertain; but I suppose from the absolute necessity of the case there will be, before long, one chosen.

I have been treated with much consideration by the President and most of his Cabinet; but I have had yet no very confidential intercourse with the President. I dined with him this week, and I have been invited to dine with two members of the Cabinet, but declined on account of a very bad cold. Mr. Clayton sent me James' diplomatic note to the Portuguese minister on the case of the General Armstrong, with the inclosed note from himself. James' note has been well spoken of by the Attorney-General to me, and I think it creditable. There are some clerical inaccuracies in it, which ought to be avoided in future copies of his official notes. James might have added, in respect to the practice of impressment, that "the Portuguese Secretary, in volunteering a sanction of it, has extended the British claim, now become obsolete, beyond any limit to which it was ever asserted by Great Britain herself, she never having pretended that she could exercise the practice within the Territorial jurisdiction of a third or neutral power, or any where but on the high seas or in her own ports."

I understood from Clayton that it was intended by the President to submit to Congress the conduct of the Portuguese Government, without recommending, at present, any measure of coercion. It is desirable to get the answer to James' note, as soon as practicable, if one be returned.

I have heard from Ashland as late as the 10th instant. All the whites were well; but there had been a number of cases of small-pox in Lexington, and one of our black men had caught it, but he was getting well. Think of your present enjoyment of a delightful climate and tropical fruits, when there fell at Lexington on the 10th instant, a snow six or eight inches deep!

Your brother, the Doctor, has returned to Louisville. You said nothing in your letter to me about Thomas, Henry Clay, or my dear Lucy, and your other children. Is Henry going to school and where?

I believe I did not mention in my former letters to James that Lucretia Erwin has determined to take the black vail.

I send herewith a letter from Mary Ann's husband. My love to James and to all the family.

MR. CLAY TO LESLIE COMBS.

WASHINGTON, December 22, 1849.

MY DEAR SIR,—I received your favor of the 17th instant, and thank you for its details. It seems that I have lost my negro man by the small-pox. I hope the measures taken will arrest its progress.

My object in writing you now is one of great importance, and I wish you to lead off in it. It will do the country good, and do you good.

The feeling for disunion among some intemperate Southern politicians, is stronger than I hoped or supposed it could be. The masses generally, even at the South, are, I believe, yet sound; but they may become influenced and perverted. The best counter-action of that feeling is to be derived from popular expressions of public meetings of the people. Now, what I should be glad to see, is such meetings held throughout Kentucky; for, you must know, that the disunionists count upon the co-operation of our patriotic State. Can't you get up a large powerful meeting of both parties, if possible, at Lexington, at Louisville, etc., to express, in strong language, their determination to stand by the Union? I hope the Legislature, and the Convention also, if it has not adjourned, may do the same. If you remain silent and passive, there is danger that the bad feeling may yet reach you. Now is the time for salutary action, and you are the man to act. I inclose some resolutions, which, or some similar to them, I should be happy to see adopted.

Prudence and propriety will suggest to you, that too free a use of my name should not be made in getting up this movement. You well know the persons to consult with; and I wish you would keep me advised of what you do.

[This advice was acted on and carried out.]

MR. CLAY TO HIS SON THOMAS.

WASHINGTON, December 25, 1849.

My DEAR THOMAS,—I received a letter from you while you were with Henry Wilkins, at your saw-mill, but none since. I expected to have heard of your return home, and to have gotten a letter from you, ere now; but I suppose that you have been detained below longer than you expected. I shall be glad to hear from you, the prospects of your mill, etc.

I am afraid that your mother and John have had much trouble and anxiety at Ashland. The loss of my man by the small-pox, and the fear of its spreading must have given them much uneasiness. It has become necessary to purchase or hire two additional hands for the farm. I should prefer the latter, and I have so written to John. I wish you would give him all the assistance you can in procuring them. His mill, too, has got out of order; but I hope that he has been able to get a millwright to repair.

Give my love and the compliments of the season to Mary and the children.

MR. CLAY TO HIS WIFE.

WASHINGTON, December 28, 1849.

MY DEAR WIFE,—There is a bundle of papers in my office up stairs, inclosed in a pasteboard paper, and tied up with tape, containing the letters from General Taylor to me. Among them is one from him to me, dated at Monterey, in Mexico, I think, in September, 1847. He and I differ about the contents of that letter; and I wish you would find it, and get Thomas to make and send me a neat copy of it, and put up the original back again where you find it.

I am still staying at the National Hotel, where I have a good parlor and bed-room, for which and my board I pay thirty dollars per week. The British Minister occupies rooms near mine, and I yesterday dined with him. He has his wife with him, a niece of the Duke of Wellington, a plain, but sensible person.

I have dined with the President, but declined to dine with Clayton and Reverdy Johnson, on account of a bad cold. These people are all civil with me, but nothing more. From every body, of both parties, I receive friendly attentions and kind consideration.

My love to John.

MR. CLAY TO HIS SON JAMES.

WASHINGTON, December 29, 1849.

MY DEAR JAMES,—I received your letter, communicating an account of Susan's confinement, and I was delighted to hear that she had given birth to a son, with so little of pain and suffering. I hope that she has continued to do well, and that the new comer has also been hearty. In the fine climate where you are, I trust that all your family enjoy good health.

I hear from home, but not as often as I could wish.

After three weeks, Mr. Cobb, of Georgia, a Democrat, was elected Speaker, and it was so much more important that the House should be organized than that whether Whig or Democrat should be chosen, that I was glad an election was made. Nothing of importance has yet been done in Congress.

The Portuguese Minister called on me to-day, and I had a long, long interview with him, both on matters personally relating to you, and on public affairs, the latter, of course, confidentially.

He tells me that you have a fine house and a delightful situation on the Tagus, with a beautiful prospect, etc., but that they made you pay too much rent for it.

I endeavored to impress him very seriously about our claims on Portugal, and that their rejection might lead to very grave consequences. I authorized him to communicate what I said to him to the Minister of Foreign Affairs. He read to me a very ingenious and plausible argument in the case of the General Armstrong, but I told him that I thought it only ingenious and plausible, and that I thought the American claim was well founded. One of his points was that the General Armstrong began the conflict. To which I replied that the British boats approached the Armstrong in hostile array; and that, when hailed, refusing to avow whether their purposes were amicable or hostile, the Armstrong was not bound to wait until they struck the first blow, but, being authorized to conclude that their purpose was to board and capture her, she had a right to defend herself, and anticipate the fall of the blow. Exactly as, when an assault is made on a man, not yet followed by a battery, he is not bound to await the battery, but may defend himself forthwith.

As to the weakness of Portugal, since the treaty of Methuen, she has been an ally, and somewhat dependent on Great Britain. Her feelings and sympathies were with the British, and against the Armstrong. She not only did not protect the Armstrong, which as a neutral power she ought to have done, but she did nothing to repel the British violation of her jurisdiction. She did worse; when the crew of the Armstrong was brought on shore, she (Portugal) suffered and connived at their being mustered by, or in presence of, British officers, that they might select from the array those whom they chose to consider British seamen! Never was such an indignity before offered! Never before or since did Great Britain ever attempt to exercise her pretended right of impressment within the jurisdictional limits of a neutral or third power, or any where but in her own ports, or on the high seas.

The Portuguese Minister cited certain provisions of our treaty with Great Britain of 1794, and other treaties, making provision for the case of captures within the waters of the respective parties by a belligerent of either of them, etc. To all which I replied, that those treaties took the case from without the operation of the general public law, but did not affect the condition of powers (of which Portugal was one) having no such treaties with us; that as to these powers, the national law furnished the rule; and that, in cases like the Armstrong, that rule required either protection or indemnity. Protection had not been afforded, and indemnity was therefore justly due.

My manner was intentionally very earnest; and I sought to impress the Minister with the belief I entertain, that if satisfaction of our claims be withheld, it will be sought for by coercion. And I told him that I should be grieved if we had any war with Portugal, especially when my son was the accredited representative of the United States at Lisbon. I told him that I hoped he would impress his Government with the gravity of existing circumstances. He was hurt at the reference in the President's Message to this affair; but I informed him that I had reason to believe that, at one time, it was contemplated to refer to it much more seriously, and I supposed this had not been done in consequence of a hope entertained that your dispatches might soon bring the welcome intelligence that our claims had been admitted and provided for.

He spoke of a proposition before the Portuguese Cortes to elevate the grade of the mission to this country. I told him that the adjustment of our claims would be an agreeable, if not indispensable preliminary to a similar elevation of the rank of our Minister to Portugal, etc.

I presume that they will send you, from the Department of State, the President's Message, and all other public documents.

My love to Susan, to dear little Lucy, and all your children, and to H. Clay, and Thomas.

CHAPTER XIV.

CORRESPONDENCE OF 1850, 1851, 1852.

MR. CLAY TO HIS SON THOMAS.

WASHINGTON, January 8, 1850.

MY DEAR THOMAS,—I received your favor of the 2d instant, and I was glad to learn from it that you had placed your pecuniary affairs on a satisfactory footing; but I hope that you had not agreed to pay to Mr. Hart exorbitant interest. You tell me that, not wanting the check I sent you for $450, you handed it to R. Pindell to deposit the amount to my credit with the B. Bank. I wish you would see that it is done, and let me know the fact.

I am greatly concerned about your poor mother. I am afraid that she has too much suffering and trouble for one person to bear. John promised me to do all in his power to promote her comfort and happiness. I wish you and Mary would do all in your power to lighten her burdens as much as possible. I do not think that I will leave her again another winter.

I wrote yesterday to John to send our mules to Greensboro', in Georgia, where I have a prospect of a good sale of them. Indeed, I consider them all already engaged at fair prices. I wish you would assist him in getting them off. It would be well to have them washed. And I desire the person in whose charge they may be placed should inform me, from time to time, as he makes progress on the journey.

I am very sorry that John has so much trouble in hiring slaves. You will, of course, continue to assist him; and I hardly know what advice to give from this place. He and you must be the best judges, being on the spot. If there be no better alternative, I suppose that I shall be obliged to purchase one or two young men, if good ones can be bought.

Give my love to Mary and your children.

MR. CLAY TO HIS SON THOMAS.

WASHINGTON, January 12, 1850.

MY DEAR THOMAS,—I received a letter from you, inclosing a copy of a letter from General Taylor to me, dated at Monterey, in November, 1847. It was the copy I wanted. I was only mistaken as to its date.

I also received the letter for Henry Clay, jun., and I have forwarded it to him.

We have a Mayday to-day.

MR. CLAY TO GENERAL COMBS.

WASHINGTON, January 22, 1850.

MY DEAR SIR,—I received your favor of the 15th, and I previously received other favors. I do not write often, because really I have nothing positive to communicate, and I have neither time nor inclination to write merely speculative letters.

Every thing here is uncertain—the Slavery question in all its bearings, California, New Mexico, Texas, etc. Of course, provision for your debt, and all other debts of Texas, is among the uncertain things.

My relation with the President and his Cabinet is amicable, but not remarkably confidential with them all. I have neither sought nor declined confidential intercourse. I do not go out at night, and in the day time both they and I are too much engaged to see much of each other.

Are you not pushing subscriptions to railroads too far? We want one to the Ohio river; two would be better, and three better yet. But we ought not to go too fast.

I am awaiting with anxiety for popular expressions in Kentucky in favor of the Union, let what come that may. Is there not danger from delay that the contagion of disunion may seize you?

MR. CLAY TO JAMES HARLAN.

WASHINGTON, January 24, 1850.

MY DEAR SIR,—If I have not written to you often, it is because of my perpetual involuntary engagements, and because I have really nothing to write about of a practical nature, and I don't like indulging in speculation. Slavery here is the all-engrossing theme; and my hopes and my fears alternately prevail as to any satisfactory settlement of the vexed question. I have been anxiously considering whether any comprehensive plan of adjustment can be devised and proposed to adjust satisfactorily the distracting question. I shall not, however, offer any scheme unless it meets my entire concurrence.

I do not know whether any thing will be done about the Marshall in Kentucky. All our Whig delegation concurred in the propriety of a change; but when we came to designate the man, there was unfortunately much division. The Executive may not, under these circumstances, deem it expedient to remove the present incumbent.

My relations to the President are civil and amicable, but they do not extend to any confidential consultations in regard to public measures. I am, etc.

MR. CLAY TO DANIEL ULLMANN.

WASHINGTON, February 2, 1850.

MY DEAR SIR,—I received your favor, and I am very glad to find that my movement to compromise the Slavery question is approved. The timid from the North hesitate, and the violent from the South may oppose it, but I entertain hopes of its success. From another quarter (the Administration) there may be a gentle breeze of approbation.

I shall need, therefore, popular support. Large public meetings (one at New York especially), indorsing my plan substantially, would do much good. Perhaps the last of next week or the week after may be early enough.

MR. CLAY TO DANIEL ULLMAN.

WASHINGTON, February 15, 1850.

MY DEAR SIR,—I received your favor of the 12th inst. I am glad to hear of the contemplated popular movement in the city of New York, on the subject of the questions concerning slavery which are producing so much unhappy division and distraction. It will do much good, if it be large, imposing, and be attended without distinction of party. But I must think that its beneficial effects will depend much upon its being conducted and regarded as a local and spontaneous assemblage, without any ground for the imputation of its being prompted from any exterior source. And I therefore think it would be best that there should not be any distant intervention from Congress or from any remote quarter. It would indeed be very difficult, putting that consideration aside, to prevail upon members of Congress, at the moment of so much interest and excitement, to quit Congress and repair to New York to address the meeting. At all events, motives of delicacy and propriety would restrain me from addressing any member of Congress to leave his official position with such purpose. I should hope that it was not necessary, and that gentlemen from New York, the fresher from the masses the better, could be induced, from patriotic considerations, to attend and address the meeting.

My accounts of the reception of my scheme of adjustment and accommodation of the slavery questions are encouraging. There is some holding back in each quarter, from a purpose of not committing itself, until the views of the other are known. But, in spite of this reserve, there are outbreaks of approbation and sanction of the scheme. And although I can not positively say so, I entertain strong hopes that it will furnish the basis of concord and a satisfactory accommodation.

MR. CLAY TO HIS SON JAMES.

WASHINGTON, March 6, 1850.

MY DEAR SON,—I have been so excessively occupied that I have written less to you than I wished. Henry Clay came safely to me, and I have placed him, for the present, at the Georgetown College, where he seems contented.

Nothing has occurred since I last wrote to you on your Portuguese affairs. And I presume that no communication will be made to Congress in respect to them, until we settle, if we ever do settle, the Slavery subject. On this subject I made a speech, and offered a plan of compromise, of which I send you a copy. The speech has produced a powerful and salutary effect in the country and in Congress. Whether the plan will be adopted or not remains to be seen. I think if any is finally adopted it will be substantially mine.

The Kentucky Legislature has passed moderate resolutions, given me no instructions, and refused to be represented in the Nashville Convention. All this is well.

My relations to the Executive are civil but not very cordial or confidential. There has been much talk all the session about changes in the Cabinet, and the retirement of Mr. Clayton especially. I am inclined to think that there is some foundation for the rumors.

All are well at home.

My love to Susan, Lucy and the rest of the children.

D. KEYES AND OTHERS TO MR. CLAY.

CLINTON, MICH., March 8, 1850.

DEAR SIR,—We are humble individuals firmly attached to the Democratic faith and the Democratic party, consequently can not indorse many things in your political creed.

But, sir, with us the preservation and harmony of our beloved Union are far above all party considerations, and we rejoice at your present position in the United States Senate, feeling that your eminent abilities and patriotic devotion to the Union are not only the property of Kentucky, but of the whole Union.

Please accept our heartfelt thanks for your conciliatory resolutions, and for the masterly manner in which you have supported and maintained them.

MR. CLAY TO HIS SON JAMES.

WASHINGTON, March 13, 1850.

MY DEAR JAMES,—I have just received your favor of the 8th ultimo. I suppose that the bad state of things here has prevented Clayton from writing to you, and probably prevented the Executive from calling the particular attention of Congress to Portuguese affairs.

You will do well, if any arrangement can be effected of any of our claims, to obtain the written concurrence of the agents of the claimants, if they have any agents near you. And if none, and a real doubt and difficulty occur, not covered by your instructions, you had better take the matter *ad referendum* to your own Government.

We are still in the woods here, on the Slavery question, and I don't know when we shall get out of them. Bad feelings have diminished, without our seeing, however, land. All other business is superseded or suspended. I do not absolutely despair of a settlement on the basis of my resolutions.

My information from home is good. All are well there. Thomas continues to be encouraged by the prospects of his saw-mill, and other prospects.

Tell Susan that I read her letter with great interest, and I have sent it to her mother. Her interview with the Queen, with all its attending circumstances, was quite imposing. As her health is so good at Lisbon, I do not think that you should be in a hurry to return home, although whenever you do come we shall be most happy to see you. Henry Clay, jr., remains at the Georgetown College.

I have seen a good deal of Sir Henry Bulwer and his lady, both of whom are intelligent and agreeable. He promised me, as I believe I informed you, to write to Lord Palmerston on our affairs with Portugal.

Give my love to Susan, to Lucy and all the children. Tell Susan that I will write to her when I can.

MR. CLAY TO JAMES HARLAN.

WASHINGTON, March 16, 1850.

MY DEAR SIR,—I have been very thankful to you for the information you have, from time to time, communicated to me during the session of Congress. While on the other hand you have found me an inattentive correspondent. My apparent neglect proceeded merely from the cause that I had nothing certain or definite to communicate.

The all-engrossing subject of slavery continues to agitate us, and to paralyze almost all legislation. My hopes are strong that the question will ultimately be amicably adjusted, although when or how can not be clearly seen.

My relations to the Executive are civil but cold. We have very little intercourse of any kind. Instead of any disposition to oblige me, I feel that a contrary disposition has been sometimes manifested. In the case of a Marshal for our State, four of the Whig members, of which I was one, united from the first in recommending Mr. Mitchell. Two others of them (making six) informed the Secretary of the Interior that they would be satisfied with Mr. Mitchell; yet Speed was nominated, and his nomination is now before the Senate. It was the act of the President, against the advice of Ewing.

I have never before seen such an Administration. There is very little co-operation or concord between the two ends of the avenue. There is not, I believe, a prominent Whig in either House that has any confidential intercourse with the Executive. Mr. Seward, it is said, had; but his late Abolition speech has, I presume, cut him off from any such intercourse, as it has eradicated the respect of almost all men for him.

I shall continue to act according to my convictions of duty, co-operating where I can with the President, and opposing where I must.

I congratulate you on your appointment as one of the Revisers.

MR. CLAY TO HIS SON JAMES.

WASHINGTON, March 17, 1850.

MY DEAR SON,—I was at the Department of State yesterday, and some of your last dispatches were shown me, and important instructions to you were also read to me. These instructions are to be sent to you in duplicate, one copy by the mail, and the other copy through Commodore Morgan, who is to proceed to Lisbon in one of the ships of the line, and to deliver to you the copy which he bears. He is then to await your orders. It is not understood that you are to act finally on these instructions until the arrival of the Commodore, but that you should, in the mean time, go on with the negotiation for our claims, and conclude, if you can, a convention for their payment.

This course of proceeding will impose on you a heavy responsibility, and you should act with great care, caution, and discretion. If you could prevail on the Portuguese Government to pay a sum in block, or in gross, for the amount and in full satisfaction of all our claims on that Government, it might save its honor in contesting the Armstrong case. It might stipulate to pay a specified sum, and leave the distribution of it, among the claimants, to our Government. I do not know whether you have a knowledge of all the claims and the means of fixing on their just amount. I was surprised to hear at the Department that it was much greater than I had supposed. I would not insist upon extravagant or extreme allowances. I should think that if the owners of the Armstrong got $50,000 they might be satisfied.

If, after the arrival of Commodore Morgan, and after you have ascertained that no arrangement of our claims can previously be made, the Portuguese Government should persist in refusing to do us justice, as I understood the instructions, you are to notify that Government of your purpose to leave Lisbon, demand your passports, and come away. The Commodore is not to employ force, which would be an act of war which the President has no power to authorize.

I suppose that this measure of sending a public vessel into the port of Lisbon has been adopted upon your advice, at least in part. I hope it may succeed; but if the Portuguese Government has the promise of British succor, it is not so likely to be successful. In the present distracted state of this country, and the weak condition of the Administration in Congress, it is much to be feared that your departure from Lisbon without the settlement of our claims, after the contemplated display of naval force, will not be followed up by the employment of the coercion which the serious steps you are authorized to take would seem to require. Hence the great importance of an amicable settlement if one can be made. And hence also I think our claims should be brought down to their minimum amount.

If your negotiation should finally fail, I suppose that we may see you back in the United States before the close of this year.

My last accounts from home represented all well. Give my love to Susan and the children.

MR. CLAY TO JAMES HARLAN.

WASHINGTON, March 22, 1850.

MY DEAR SIR,—I received your favor of the 15th instant. What you have stated, in answer to those who have inquired of you, whether under any contingency I would consent to be a candidate for the Presidency in 1852, is pretty much what I should have said myself, if I said any thing; but I have great repugnance to saying any thing about it. It would be great folly in me, at my age, with the uncertainty of life, and with a recollection of all the past, to say now that I would, under any contingences, be a candidate. I can scarcely conceive any, there are none in the range of probability, that would reconcile me to the use of my name. I have already publicly declared that I entertained no wish or expectation of being a candidate; and I would solemnly proclaim that I never would be, under any circumstances whatever, if I did not think that no citizen has a right thus absolutely to commit himself.

We can not yet see clearly how or when our slavery difficulties are to be settled.

MR. CLAY TO HIS SON JAMES.

WASHINGTON, March 25, 1850.

MY DEAR SON,—I received together, to-day, your two favors of the 15th and 28th ultimo. I am obliged to you for the articles you have shipped for your mother and me. I shall give directions about the pigs, but I am afraid there will be great difficulty in getting them home. You can not ship home any Port wine, without paying duties here. It must come back with you, and as a part of your luggage it will not be liable to duty. I should be glad to get six or eight dozen.

I have no doubt that you may return at the end of the year, if you wish it. Whether you do so or not ought to depend on your estimate of what will most conduce to the health and happiness of your family and yourself. I should be sorry if you allowed your expenses to exceed your salary. Public functionaries are too apt to think themselves more bound than they really are to dispense hospitality. He acts wisest who limits himself to his salary.

My last letter and the dispatches from Government will have apprized you that a display of naval force is to be tried as an experiment in aid of your negotiations. If it fail to induce the Portuguese Government to pay our claims, you may have to return even sooner than you wish. I suppose it will not reach the port of Lisbon before May.

The Senate confirmed your nomination to-day as soon as it was taken up, and without any opposition. At no time was there danger of any.

I wish you were honorably and safely through your negotiations. The employment of a naval force imposes on you a delicate and heavy responsibility, of the success of which I am more anxious because I understand you advised it. You may be officially interrogated as to the object of the presence of such a force. In that case, you will pursue your instructions, and I suppose have to say that the ship is intended to take you away, if our claims are not adjusted. Commodore Morgan is a particular friend of mine and a very clever fellow. You may tell him all about Yorkshire, his pet, etc.

I have got through the winter better than I expected, but I find the colds of this month very bad.

I am glad to hear that you are on good terms with the Foreign Minister. Certainly it would be a good arrangement to get them to recognize the justice of the Armstrong claim and leave the amount to arbitration; but that they won't agree to.

Give my love to Susan, dear Lucy, and your other children. All well at home when I last heard.

I believe I mentioned the death of your uncle Porter in Arkansas, in February.

MR. CLAY TO S. A. ALLIBONE.

WASHINGTON, May 10, 1850.

MY DEAR SIR,—Accept my cordial although tardy thanks for your friendly note of the 16th ultimo, with its inclosure of precious old newspapers. My public engagements will explain and excuse me, I hope, for not having earlier made this acknowledgment.

I pray you to present my warm regards to your family and to your sister, and to assure her that I often think of her amid all my occupations.

JAMES B. CLAY TO HIS FATHER.

LISBON, May 26, 1850.

MY DEAR FATHER,—You can not imagine in what a state of uncertainty, uneasiness, and expectation, we have been during this entire month. I had been informed by Mr. Clayton that it was the opinion of the Secretary of the Navy that the ship from the Mediterranean, with my final instructions, would reach here by the 1st of this month, and it is now nearly the last, and it has not arrived. I have seen by the English papers that the storeship Erie, which, I presume, took Commodore Morgan his orders, was lying, with the commodore, in the harbor of Naples, on the 27th last month, in fifteen days after he ought to have been here; why he is not, God only knows. I have been constantly uneasy for fear that his non-arrival might prejudice the settlement of our affairs; and if this Government had a grain of common sense, it would have done so very much. Their true policy, having determined not to pay, was most certainly to offer an arbitration of all the claims, and I have been every instant fearing that such an offer would be made; a rejection of it, which I would have to make, would, of course, have put us in a worse position before the world.

The English Chargé, Mr. Howard, the brother of the Earl of Carlisle, told me the other day, that Mr. Bulwer had written to Lord Palmerston, as he promised you, to advise these people to pay all the claims which were just, and to offer to arbitrate the others; and I presume he did so, for Mr. Howard told me, at the same time, that Count Fayal had informed him that he had offered to arbitrate all. This impression he has been for some time trying to create, through the papers and otherwise. You may have seen an article in "The London Times" speaking of my rejection of the offer, etc.; this, I know, was denied from Fayal, who shows every thing to the correspondent of that paper. Lord Palmerston has very little influence here. He has been always opposed to the Cabral Ministry, and there is no goodwill between them. I took occasion to inform Mr. Howard, that it was wholly untrue that Count Fayal had offered to arbitrate all our claims, and said that I had no objection to his so informing his Government.

I can not predict what will be the effect produced by the coming of the ship, if ever she does arrive, or of my demand for my passport, if they don't pay. Our action has, throughout the affair, been so dilatory, that I am sure it can not have so great influence as promptness would have done. It has always been my opinion that I ought to have been sent here in a ship of war, with the same instructions given at last. Our position at the time of my arrival was by all odds better than it is now.

Should we be suffered to go away, I am undetermined whether we shall go to Naples and to Paris, through Italy and Switzerland, or go at once to Paris. I shall be determined by Commodore Morgan's course. If he offers to take us to Naples, as it will not be out of his way, I shall accept. If we go that way, we will still reach America in November.

As the season has arrived for Southerners to be in Kentucky, perhaps my house could now be sold. I should like it to be; as on our return home, if you won't sell me Ashland, I am determined to try and buy Crutchfield's place on the Ohio. Can you write to Trotter or Pindell about the house?

28th.—Commodore Morgan has not arrived, and I am in hourly expectation of receiving, what I feared I should receive, a proposition to arbitrate all the claims. I dined last night with the Duke of Leuchtenberg, the son-in-law of the Emperor of Russia, at the Russian Legation, when the Minister asked if I had received such a proposition, as Count Fayal had told him he intended to make it. He seemed surprised when I told him I had not. I shall regret to receive it, because I think my instructions will oblige me to reject it, and I know it will place us in a worse position before the world. Either Commodore Morgan has had orders of which I was not informed, or he has not been as active as he might, and ought to have been.

Nine o'clock at night.—I have just received a note from the Minister, stating the willingness of his Government to arbitrate all the claims, but as he rejects the last of them in the same note, and as his language is not a distinct proposition to arbitrate, I shall not so consider it.

We are all well, and Susan joins me in affectionate love to you.

MR. CLAY TO HIS SON JAMES.

WASHINGTON, May 27, 1850.

MY DEAR SON,—I have written to you less of late than I wished, owing to my perpetual public occupations. We are yet in the midst of our slavery discussions, with no certainty of the final result. I have hopes of the final success of the compromise reported by me of the Committee of Thirteen, but with less confidence than I desire.

By this time, I presume that your public duties at Lisbon are brought to an unsuccessful close. I fear that the display of force in the port of Lisbon has not been attended with the benefit anticipated from it.

I have got Henry Clay admitted as a cadet in West Point, and he has gone home to see his relations, and to return to me next week to enter the Academy.

You will see in the papers that I have spoken a great deal (much more than I wished) in the Senate. In my last speech I had to attack the plan of the Administration, for compromising our slavery difficulties; its course left me no other alternative. My friends speak in terms of extravagant praise of my speeches, and especially of the last.

Since I began this letter, I received your letter of the 28th April, with Susan's long and interesting letter to her mother, which I have read and forwarded this moment.

I do not entertain much hope of the effect of the display of naval force in getting our claims allowed, and consequently I expect you will leave Lisbon soon after you receive this letter. Should they be allowed, and should Portugal raise the rank of her representatives, I suppose the measure would be reciprocated by our Executive.

I am delighted to hear that you are all so happy, and that dear Lucy has some good prospect of recovery.

I send a letter from Mary to Susan, and I am to blame for some delay in its transmission. My love to her, and to all your dear children.

MR. CLAY TO MRS. THOMAS H. CLAY.

WASHINGTON, July 13, 1850.

MY DEAR MARY,—I received your letter with its inclosure. I wish you would tell your mother not to pay the Abion's account, or any other account against me, without my direction. I will arrange these matters myself.

My health is reasonably good. Mrs. Brand, of Lexington, and her party are now here, and will to-day witness the funeral ceremonies of General Taylor, about which the whole city is now in commotion.

Tell Thomas that I think the event which has happened will favor the passage of the Compromise bill.

I can not tell you, my dear Mary, how anxious I am to be at home with your dear mother, my wife, and all of you.

MR. CLAY TO HIS SON THOMAS.

PHILADELPHIA, August 6, 1850.

MY DEAR THOMAS,—I am here on my way to Newport, for which place I proceed to-morrow, and hope to reach it during the night.

I received your letter of the 28th ultimo, and I was gratified to learn that your prospects from the saw-mill were so good.

My relations with Mr. Fillmore are perfectly friendly and confidential. In the appointment of Mr. Crittenden I acquiesced. Mr. F. asked me how we stood? I told him that the same degree of intimacy between us which once existed, no longer prevailed; but that we were on terms of civility. I added that, if he thought of introducing him into his Cabinet, I hoped that no considerations of my present relations to him would form any obstacle.

I shall be very glad if any thing can be done for Carroll, and and I will see on my return to Washington.

As to the post-office in Lexington, my wishes will, I anticipate, finally prevail.

I am very much worn down, but I hope that Newport will replace my health and strength.

My love to Mary and the children.

MR. CLAY TO HIS SON THOMAS.

NEWPORT, August 15, 1850.

MY DEAR THOMAS,—I received your two last letters, the last inclosing one from Mary to Susan, which I have forwarded. James will return in October or November; he has closed his negotiation, and although he has concluded no convention with Portugal, he has succeeded in placing our claims with that Government on a much better footing than they ever stood before. He has sent old Aaron home, and he is now in Washington

I have been benefited by my visit to this place, and shall remain here about a week longer. It is so cool here as to require the use of fires.

They are passing through the Senate, in separate bills, all the measures of our Compromise, and if they should pass the House also, I hope they will lead to all the good effects which would have resulted from the adoption of the Compromise.

I have seen Henry Piudle's wife here, and I was very glad to hear from her that your mother is in good health, and that she has been enjoying more of society than she has been accustomed to do.

Give my love to Mary and the children.

MR. CLAY TO HIS SON THOMAS.

WASHINGTON, September 6, 1850.

MY DEAR THOMAS,—I have received your letter of the 31st ult. I congratulate Louisa and her family upon her marriage, which I hope and believe may prove a happy one.

We can see no end yet of this fatiguing session. So far, nothing is definitely decided on the slavery question. Perhaps there may be to-day or to-morrow. In the mean time I am again getting very much exhausted. I wish that I had remained longer at Newport, where I was much benefited. I shall as soon as possible return home, where I desire to be more than I ever did in my life.

My love to Mary and the children.

MR. CLAY TO MRS. JAMES B. CLAY.

ASHLAND, November 21, 1850.

I was rejoiced, my dear Susan, to have seen by the newspapers, that you and your children had arrived safely at New York, and by the telegraphic dispatch, which you sent me from Pittsburg, that you had reached that city. Not knowing whether you will first come here or go to Louisville, I address this letter to you at the latter. I expect to leave home on the first or second of next month. Will you come here before I go? If not, I must try to go by Louisville to see you and the children.

I have sold James' house for nine thousand dollars, one third to be paid at New Orleans the first of January next, one third in October next, and the other third the October following, all well secured. Harvey Miller was the purchaser. Considering James' anxiety to sell, and the low price of town property, the sale is considered a good one. But if he had been at home, and could have made an arrangement with me for the purchase of Ashland, I would have allowed him ten thousand dollars for his house. Mr. Miller had left the house, and I could get no good tenant. So you see you are without house and home; but I hope you will pass as much of your time as you can at Ashland. John expects to go to New Orleans in two or three weeks. We are all well here and at Mansfield.

Write me immediately about your movements. My love to Lucy and the other children.

MR. CLAY TO HIS SON JAMES.

WASHINGTON, December 23, 1850.

MY DEAR JAMES,—Prior to the receipt of your letter, dated at Ashland the 17th instant, I had addressed a letter to you containing some things not necessary to be repeated here. I have not yet had a good opportunity of conversing with either the President or Mr. Webster about you or your late mission; but the other night at Jenny Lind's concert, sitting by Mr. Webster, he broke forth in extravagant praises of you. I do not think that you ought to put an unfriendly interpretation upon any thing which occurred about your return to Lisbon. Your letter from Geneva of September did not contain an unconditional offer to return. You submitted some point of honor to Mr. Webster. I think he might have sent earlier instructions to you; but I suppose his absence from Washington and his indisposition formed his excuse. In his letter of the 5th November (which I hastily read) he seems to have been undecided whether you wished to return or not, but left it to you to determine. After you returned to the United States I do not think that you ought to have gone back to Lisbon for the temporary purpose of concluding the Convention. And, upon the whole, I have no regrets about it, considering how well and how strongly the President speaks of you, in his annual Message, and in what favorable terms, officially and privately, Mr. Webster speaks of you, and that the public ascribes to you the success of the negotiation. I wrote you that I think you are entitled to your salary up to the 20th November and a quarter beyond, and to indemnity for any loss in furniture, etc., in consequence of your sudden departure from Lisbon. I believe it is usual also to charge for stationery, postage, etc. If you will send me your account I will endeavor to have it settled.

I was in hopes that you would stay with your mother until my return, and that we would then talk about your future. As to your purchase of Ashland, I never desired that you should make it, unless prompted by your own interests and feelings. When I go hence it must be sold, and I have never feared that it would not command a fair and full price.

I should regret deeply to see you set down doing nothing. You must engage in some occupation or you will be miserable. The law, farming, or the public service, are the only pursuits which I suppose present themselves to you. You don't like the first, which is moreover nowhere in Kentucky profitable; and your decision must be between the two others. I had inferred that you were tired of diplomacy, unless you could get a higher grade than that which you lately held. At present there is none that I know of; but perhaps some vacancy may occur. As to elevating the mission to Lisbon, I have heard here of no proposal to that effect. It does not depend, you know, exclusively on the Executive; Congress must sanction it. Possibly after the conclusion of the Convention, if Portugal should desire to elevate the rank of her minister, it may be proposed to reciprocate it by the President; but I do not apprehend that a higher rank would be thought of than that of minister resident.

You did not say whether you were satisfied or not with my sale of your house and lot. I would not have sold it but for your great anxiety to sell. It was a good house, but I never liked its external appearance. The situation was one of the finest in Lexington.

You will direct what I shall do with the draft for $3000 when I receive it from New Orleans.

My love to Susan, Lucy, and the other children.

MR. CLAY TO HIS WIFE.

WASHINGTON, March 8, 1851.

MY DEAR WIFE,—I have finally concluded to return by Cuba and New Orleans. The great difficulty I have felt in coming to the conclusion has been my long absence from you, and my desire to be with you. But my cough continues; although I do not lay up, my health is bad, and the weather has been the worst of March weather. The road, too, by Cumberland, I am told, is almost impassable. I hope that I may be benefited by the softer climate of Cuba. I expect to go on the 11th from New York in the steamer Georgia. And I think my absence from home will not be prolonged beyond a month, that is the middle of April. On settling my bank accounts, I will either from here or New York make a remittance to you.

I send herewith a check on York for $400 which I have endorsed to you, and of which you will make any use you may think proper.

I have written to John and telegraphed him, to put him at ease about Yorkshire, and I hope all will go well at home until my return.

God bless and preserve you, my dear wife.

MR. CLAY TO ADAM BEATTY.

ASHLAND, April 28, 1851.

MY DEAR SIR,—I received your favor transmitting two letters, one addressed to yourself and the other in reply to it, and I thank you for the opportunity afforded me of perusing them.

If the course of ——— affords cause of regret, I am grateful for the firmness and fidelity with which you remained attached to me in 1848, as upon all former occasions.

The nomination made of General Taylor, in Philadelphia, has now no other than an historical interest. It has long ceased to affect me. I fear, indeed, that it has had a pernicious influence upon the Whig cause, but of that we shall hereafter be able better to judge. I concur entirely in the views presented in your reply to ———. Had I been nominated I am perfectly confident that I should have obtained every electoral vote which he received, and, besides them, the vote of Ohio certainly, and that of Indiana probably. My majority in Pennsylvania would have been greater than that which was given to him. But the thing is passed, and no one has more quietly submitted to the event than I have.

I was very sorry that circumstances were such as not to admit of my calling to see you on my return home; but I hope we may yet live to meet each other. I returned by the route of Cuba and New Orleans, and was highly gratified with my visit to that delightful island.

MR. CLAY TO HIS SON JAMES.

ASHLAND, May 9, 1851.

MY DEAR SON,—I received your letter of the 28th ultimo. From Susan I had learned your plans for the future. Although they involve a separation of you and your family from me, I can not complain of them and think them judicious. I am afraid that we did not explain ourselves mutually fully to each other. It was my anxious wish that you should have succeeded me in the possession of Ashland, if it had suited your inclination and interest, and if you had been at home I think we could have made some arrangement by which you could have come into the immediate possession of it, and I could have taken your house. But you were not here; and before you went to Europe, and in your letters from Lisbon, you displayed so much anxiety to sell the house that I concluded to take the offer of Mr. Miller. Mr. Trotter too was about to give it up, and as I was on the eve of my departure for Washington, and knew of no tenant that I could get, I did not well know what to do with it. I think it ought to have brought ten thousand dollars, which is what I should have been willing to have allowed for it, but I obtained the best price I could get, and the sale of it was far better than that to Mr. Goodhue which you appeared willing to make.

My health is not good, a troublesome and inconvenient cough has hung by me for six months past; it has reduced and enfeebled me very much. Dr. Dudley thinks that my lungs are unaffected, and that it proceeds from some derangement in the functions of the stomach. Be that as it may, I must get rid of the cough or it will dispose of me. My hopes rest upon the effects of warm weather.

Susan and the children are well, and appear to be contented and satisfied. They are a source of great happiness to me, and I look forward to their leaving us with painful anticipations. Your mother and John are both quite well, and so are Thomas and his family. John is constantly occupied with our numerous horses and those which are sent to Ashland. He is in good spirits and appears much encouraged with prospects, and I think has reason to be so. My overseer is doing admirably well, and your mother is better pleased with him than she ever was with any of his predecessors. I have a great many things to say to you and to talk to you about, but among the inconveniences of my present indisposition, one is, that it is less agreeable to me than formerly to write or even to dictate, as I am now doing. I must therefore reserve for the occasion of your return to us to say whatever I now omit. Susan gets your weekly letters regularly and I hope you will continue to write, as in that way I can learn your projects and prospects.

MR. CLAY TO DANIEL ULLMAN.

ASHLAND, June 14, 1851.

MY DEAR SIR,—I duly received your favor of the 29th ultimo, stating that some of my friends in New York have it under discussion, to make a movement to bring forward my name for the Presidency; and inquiring, in entire confidence, what my own views and wishes are, upon the subject. I have delayed transmitting an answer to your letter, from a desire to give to its important contents the fullest and most deliberate consideration. That I have now done, and I will communicate the result to you.

You will recollect that the last time but one that I was in the city of New York, I had the pleasure of dining with you and a number of other friends at the house of our friend M——; that we then had a frank, full, and confidential conversation on the connection of my name with the next Presidency; and that I then declared that I did not wish ever again to be brought forward as a candidate. From that declaration, I have never since deviated in thought, word, or deed. I have said or done nothing inconsistent with it; nothing which implied any desire on my part to have my name presented as a Presidential candidate. On a review and reconsideration of the whole matter, I adhere to that declaration.

Considering my age, the delicate state of my health, the frequency and the unsuccessful presentation of my name on former occasions, I feel an unconquerable repugnance to such a use of it again. I can not, therefore, consent to it. I have been sometimes tempted publicly to announce that, under no circumstances, would I yield my consent to be brought forward as a candidate. But I have been restrained from taking that step by two considerations. The first was, that I did not see any such general allusion to me, as a suitable person for the office, as to make it proper that I should break silence and speak out; and the second was that I have always thought that no citizen has a right to ostracise himself, and to refuse public service under all possible contingencies.

I might here stop, but I will add some observations on the general subject of the next election. I think it quite clear that a Democrat will be elected, unless that result shall be prevented by divisions in the Democratic party. On these divisions the Whigs might advantageously count, if it were not for those which exist in their own party. It is, perhaps, safest to conclude that the divisions existing in the two parties will counterbalance each other.

Party ties have no doubt been greatly weakened generally, and, in particular localities, have been almost entirely destroyed. But it would be unwise to suppose that, when the two parties shall have brought out their respective candidates, each will not rally around its own standard. There may be exceptions; but those, on the one side, will probably be counterpoised by those on the other. I believe that no one in the Whig party could obtain a greater amount of support from the Democratic party than I could; but in this I may be deceived by the illusions of egotism. At all events it would be unsafe and unwise for a candidate of one party to calculate upon any suffrages of the other. While I do not think that the hopes of success on the part of the Whigs at the next Presidential election are very flattering or encouraging, I would not discourage their putting forth their most energetic exertions. There are always the chances of the war. The other party may commit great blunders, as they did recently in your State, in the course of their Senators, who opposed the enlargement of the Erie Canal; and as they are disposed to do in respect to the lake, river, and harbor improvements.

No candidate, I hope and believe, can be elected who is not in favor of the Union, and in favor of the Compromise of the last Congress (including the Fugitive Slave bill), as necessary means to sustain it. Of the candidates spoken of on the Democratic side, I confess that I should prefer General Cass. He is, I think, more to be relied on than any of his competitors. During the trials of the long session of the last Congress, he bore himself firmly, consistently, and patriotically. He has quite as much ability, quite as much firmness, and, I think, much more honesty and sincerity than Mr. Buchanan.

If I were to offer any advice to my friends, it would be not to commit themselves prematurely to either of the two Whig candidates who have been prominently put forward. Strong objections, although of a very different kind, exist against them both. They had better wait. It will be time enough next winter to decide; and I am inclined to believe that both of those gentlemen will find, in the sequel, that they have taken, or their friends have put them in, the field, too early.

Besides pre-existing questions, a new one will probably arise at the next session of Congress, involving the right of any one of the States of the Union, upon its own separate will and pleasure, to secede from the residue, and become a distinct and independent power. The decision of that momentous question can not but exert some influence, more or less, upon the next Presidential election. For my own part, I utterly deny the existence of any such right, and I think an attempt to exercise it ought to be resisted to the last extremity; for it is, in part, a question of union or no union.

You inquire if I will visit Newport this summer, with the view of ascertaining whether it might not be convenient there, or at some other Eastern place, to present me a gold medal which I understand my good friends are preparing for me. I have been absent from home fifteen out of the last nineteen months, and I feel great reluctance to leaving it, during the present summer. If I were to go to the Eastward, I should have to return early in the autumn, and soon after to go back to Washington, unless I resign my seat in the Senate of the United States. Under these circumstances, my present inclination is to remain at home and to attend to my private affairs, which need my care.

Should my friends persevere in their purpose of presenting me the proposed medal, some suitable time and place can be hereafter designated for that purpose. Surely no man was ever blessed with more ardent and devoted friends than I am, and, among them, none are more or perhaps so enthusiastic as those in the city of New York. God bless them. I wish it was in my power to testify my gratitude to them in full accordance with the fervent impulses of my heart.

MR. CLAY TO S. A. ALLIBONE.

ASHLAND, June 30, 1851.

MY DEAR SIR,—I received your friendly letter of the 23d instant. I have been so much from home during the last eighteen months that it is not my purpose at present to leave it this summer.

I have no doubt, with you, that many of the quiet and well-disposed citizens of South Carolina are opposed to the measures of violence which are threatened by others. But the danger is, as history shows too often happens, that the bold, the daring, and the violent will get the control, and push their measures to a fatal extreme. Should the State resolve to secede, it will present a new form of trial to our system; but I entertain undoubting confidence that it will come out of it with the most triumphant success.

I thank you for your friendly tender of your services. Should any occasion for the use of them arise, I will avail myself of them, with great pleasure.

Do me the favor to present my warm regards to your good sister; and I reciprocate your kind wishes and prayers, with all my heart.

MR. CLAY TO DANIEL ULLMANN.

ASHLAND, September 26, 1851.

MY DEAR SIR,—I received your favor of the 19th instant, with the memorial inclosed. On the subject of the next Presidency, my opinions and views have undergone no change since I last wrote to you. Should I be able, as I now hope to be, from my slowly improving health, to attend the next session of the Senate, we will confer more freely on that subject. In the mean time, I am glad that my friends in New York have foreborne to present my name as a candidate.

I have looked at the list of events and subjects which are proposed to be inscribed on the medal. I have made out and sent herewith a more comprehensive list, embracing most of the important matters, as to which I had any agency, during my service in the National councils. As to the Cumberland Road, no year can be properly fixed. Appropriations for it were made from year to year, for a series of years, which were violently opposed, and the support of which chiefly devolved on me. So in regard to Spanish America, the first movement was made by me in 1818, and my exertions were continued from year to year, until the measure of recognition was finally completed in 1822.

The list now sent may be too large for inscription on the medal. Of course it is my wish that it should be dealt with, by abridgment, or omission as may be thought proper. The two reports, made by me in the Senate, which gave me much credit and reputation were, 1st. That which proposed an equal distribution among the States of the proceeds of the public domain; and 2d. That which averted General Jackson's meditated war against France, on account of her failure to pay the indemnity. I carried both measures against the whole weight of Jackson; but he pocketed the Land Distribution bill, which was not finally passed until 1841. He could not, however, make war against France, without the concurrence of Congress, and my report preserved the peace of the two countries.

My Panama instructions were the most elaborate (and if I may be allowed to speak of them), the ablest State paper that I composed while I was in the Department of State. They contain an exposition of liberal principles, regulating Maritime War, Neutral Rights, etc., which will command the approbation of enlightened men and of posterity.

I was glad to see that you were nominated for Attorney-General at Syracuse, and I heartily wish for your election.

The address to me from New York, although published in the papers, has not been received officially by me. What is intended? I have had some correspondence about it with Mr. James D. P. Ogden, who sent me a copy informally. I can not venture to encounter the scenes of excitement which would attend me, if I were to go to New York; but in anticipation of the reception of the address I have prepared a pretty long answer, in which I treat of Secession, the state of the country, in regard to the Slavery question, etc. If this answer be capable of doing any good, the sooner it is published the better.

[The medal alluded to in the foregoing letter, was presented to Mr. Clay the 9th of February, 1852, and is described as follows:]

It is of pure California gold, massive and weighty, and is inclosed in a silver case, which opens with a hinge in the manner of a hunting-watch. On the face of the medal is a fine head of Mr. Clay, most felicitous in the likeness, and conveying the characteristic impression of his features in a higher degree than any of the busts or medallions usually seen. The relief is very high, and must have required a pressure of immense power to give it its fullness, sharpness, and delicacy of outline. The reverse exhibits the following inscription:

SENATE,
1806.
SPEAKER, 1811.
WAR OF 1812 WITH GREAT BRITAIN.
GHENT, 1814.
SPANISH AMERICA, 1822.
MISSOURI COMPROMISE, 1821.
AMERICAN SYSTEM, 1824.
GREECE, 1824.
SECRETARY OF STATE, 1825.
PANAMA INSTRUCTIONS, 1826.
TARIFF COMPROMISE,
1833.
PUBLIC DOMAIN, 1833—1841.
PEACE WITH FRANCE PRESERVED, 1835.
COMPROMISE, 1850.

The lines are supported on either hand by tasteful wreaths, in which the six chief American staples—wheat, corn, cotton, tobacco, rice, and hemp—are very happily intertwined.

On the silver case is represented on one side a view of the Capitol (with its contemplated additional wings fully displayed); and on the other in two distinct compartments above, an elevation of the great commemorative monument on the Cumberland road; below, a view of Ashland and its mansion.

MR. CLAY TO HIS DAUGHTER-IN-LAW, MRS. THOS. H. CLAY.

WASHINGTON, December 25, 1851.

MY DEAR MARY,—I received to-day your letter of the 19th instant, and I was very glad to get the details contained in it about yourself, your family, and affairs at Ashland. And I am under very great obligations to you and to Thomas for the kind offer which you have made, to come either one or both of you to Washington, to attend me during my present illness. If there were the least occasion for it, I should with pleasure accept the offer; but there is not. Every want, every wish, every attention which I need, is supplied. The hotel at which I stay has a bill of fare of some thirty or forty articles every day, from which I can select any for which I have a relish, and if I want any thing which is not on the bill of fare, it is promptly procured for me. The state of my case may be told in a few words. If I can get rid of this distressing cough, or can materially reduce it, I may yet be restored to a comfortable condition. That is the present aim of my physicians, and I have some hope that it has abated a little within the last few days. But if the cough can not be stopped or considerably reduced, it will go on until it accomplishes its work. When that may be, it is impossible to say, with any sort of certainty. I may linger for some months, long enough possibly to reach home once more. At all events, there is no prospect at present of immediate dissolution. Under these circumstances, I have no desire to bring any member of my family from home, when there is not the least necessity for it. With regard to the rumors which reach you from time to time, and afflict you, you must bear with them, and rest assured of what I have already communicated to your mother, that if my case should take a fatal turn, the telegraph shall communicate the fact. I occupy two excellent rooms, the temperature of which is kept up during the day at about 70°. The greatest inconvenience I feel is from the bad weather, which has confined me nearly a fortnight to my room, and I can take no exercise until the weather changes. My love to Thomas and all your children, to your mother, and to all others at Ashland.

FATHER MATTHEW TO MR. CLAY.

Cork, December 29, 1851.

My dearest Sir,—From the south of that green island which you have often, in your own eloquent and all but inspired language, made the subject of your warmest eulogy, the most grateful of your admirers presumes to intrude on your well-filled time, by presenting to you his heartfelt wishes, at the commencement of the New Year, humbly praying that the Great Bestower of every good may bless you with length of days, to promote the prosperity of that great country whose pride and glory you are, filling both it and Europe with your well-merited fame. Blessed be the remainder of your brilliant and useful life, and may the prospect of future glory gild it with felicity. Uniting your most respected lady in my humble prayer and sincere wishes, and the other amiable and beloved members of your dear family, to whom I had the honor of an introduction, with enduring remembrance of your exceeding kindness in the day of my distress, I have the honor to be, most respected sir, etc.

MR. CLAY TO HIS SON THOMAS.

Washington, January 10, 1852.

My dear Thomas,—I received two or three letters from you since I came here, and should have answered them with pleasure if my strength and health would have admitted of it. You observe now I am obliged to employ the pen of a friend. I was very thankful for the kind offer of yourself and Mary to come here and nurse me. I should have promptly accepted, if it had been necessary, but it was not. Every want and wish that I have are kindly attended to. I am surrounded by good friends, who are ready and willing to serve me; and you and Mary yourselves could not have been more assiduous in your attentions than are my friends the Calverts.

The state of my health has not very materially altered. Within the last eight or ten days there has been some improvement; not so great as my friends persuade themselves, but still some improvement. The solution of the problem of my recovery depends upon the distressing cough which I have, and I think that it is a little diminished. I am embargoed here by the severity of the winter, which has confined me to the house for the last three weeks. I hope to derive some benefit when I shall be again able to drive out in the open air. You must continue to write me without regard to my ability to reply. It is a source of great comfort to me to hear, and to hear fully, from Ashland and Mansfield. John has been very kind in writing very frequently to me. Give my love to Mary and all the children.

MR. CLAY TO SAMUEL A. ALLIBONE.

WASHINGTON, January 11, 1852.

MY DEAR SIR,—Although too unwell myself to write you, I can not withhold the expression, through the pen of a friend, of my thanks for your kind letter of the 10th instant, and for the warm interest which you take in my restoration to health. I thank you especially for your friendly offer to come hither and assist in nursing me; but I am so extremely well attended in that respect, as not to render necessary the acceptance of your obliging offer. Present my warm regards to your sister, and tell her that as the probability is that neither of us is long for this world, I hope that when we go hence we shall meet in one far better. I am, with the greatest respect, etc.

THEODORE FRELINGHUYSEN TO MR. CLAY.

NEW BRUNSWICK, January 19, 1852.

MY DEAR SIR,—I have heard with great interest and anxiety of your continued feeble health, and that it had rather been more feeble since your decided testimony in behalf of Washington's foreign policy. I was rejoiced to hear your words of soberness and truth on the exciting question of Hungarian politics; and I trust that a divine blessing will follow your counsels.

In this time of impaired health, and sometimes trying despondency that ensues, it must be refreshing to look away to Him who is a helper near in trouble, and able and willing to sustain and comfort you. This blessed Gospel, that reveals the riches of God's grace in Jesus Christ, is a wonderful remedy : so suited to our condition and character, and so full of inexpressible consolation to us, as sinners needing mercy. His blood cleansing us from the guilt of sin, His Spirit purifying our hearts, and restoring us to God's image and favor. May you, my dear friend, largely partake of its comforts, and leaning all your hopes on the Almighty Saviour's arm, hold on your way, for life and for death, for time and eternity, in His name and strength.

WILLIAM M'LAIN TO MR. CLAY.

COLONIZATION ROOMS, WASHINGTON CITY, February 9, 1852.

DEAR SIR,—At the recent annual meeting of the American Colonization Society, the following resolution was unanimously adopted:

Resolved, That we deeply sympathize with our venerable President, the Hon. Henry Clay, in his present protracted illness, by which we are deprived of his presence and able counsels at this annual meeting of our Society, to which he has, from its foundation, devoted himself with signal ability and unwavering fidelity; and that we hold him in affectionate and grateful remembrance for the distinguished services he has rendered in the prosecution of the great scheme of African colonization.

I take great pleasure, my dear sir, in furnishing you with the foregoing resolution.

Hoping that you may be restored to health, and that this Society may continue to have the honor of your name and influence as its President, I remain, etc.

MR. CLAY TO MRS. JAMES B. CLAY.

WASHINGTON, February 12, 1852.

MY DEAR SUSAN,—I received your letter of the 27th ultimo, and I had received that of James' of the 1st. I write now so uncomfortably and so slow, that I take up my pen with great repugnance. I was very glad to receive both of your letters, and was delighted to contemplate the picture of your domestic happiness with your husband and children. As the world recedes from me, I feel my affections more than ever concentrated on my children, and theirs.

My health has improved a little within the last few weeks, but the cough still hangs on, and unless I can get rid of it, or greatly diminish it, I can not look for a radical cure. The winter has been excessively rigorous, and I have not been out of the house for eight weeks. You must not believe all you see in the newspapers, favorable or unfavorable, about my health.

I hope you and James will continue to write to me, whether you receive regular replies or not. How has the dairy got through the winter?

My love to James and all my dear grandchildren.

MR. CLAY TO HIS SON JAMES.

WASHINGTON, February 24, 1852.

MY DEAR SON,—I received your letter of the 10th. I should have written you oftener, but I am so feeble, and write with so little comfort, that I take up the pen reluctantly. I hope that you and Susan, notwithstanding my apparent delinquency, will write me frequently, giving me full details of all your plans, improvements, and business. There is nothing now that interests me so much as to receive full accounts from the members of my family frequently. Although you have got more in debt than I could have wished, you ought to be very happy. In dear Susan you have an excellent wife, and you have a fine parcel of promising children, and you have ample means of support.

I gave my deposition in your case with Miller week before the last, and it was sent to Lexington. It proved all that was expected of me.

My health continues very delicate. I have not been out of the house for upward of two months. I can not recognize any encouraging change. My cough still hangs on, although I sometimes hope that it is a little abated. If I can not get rid of it, or at least greatly diminish it, I think it must prove fatal. But I may linger for months to come. I should be glad to get home once more.

My love to Susan, and kisses for all the children. I would be glad to write more, but you can not conceive how this little letter has exhausted me.

MR. CLAY TO DANIEL ULLMAN.

WASHINGTON, March 6, 1852.

MY DEAR SIR,—I received your favor transmitting an engrossed copy of the address which you did me the honor to make to me on the occasion of presenting the medal which my New York friends had offered me. I thank you for this corrected copy of the address which is very beautifully engrossed.

The medal has been in the possession of the goldsmiths of this place, who desired the custody of it to gratify public curiosity. You wish it returned that a more accurate impression may be made by striking another. I examined it to see if I could discern the defect in the letters to which you refer, and I confess I could not. If to strike it again will occasion any trouble or expense to my friends, I think it might well be avoided, but if you persist in your desire to have it done, I will have it sent to you by Adams' Express next week.

You rightly understood me in expressing a preference for Mr. Fillmore as the Whig candidate for the Presidency. This I did before I left home, and have frequently here in private intercourse, since my arrival at Washington. I care not how generally the fact may be known, but I should not deem it right to publish any formal avowal of that preference under my own signature in the newspapers. Such a course would subject me to the imputation of supposing that my opinions possessed more weight with the public than I apprehend they do. The foundation of my preference is, that Mr. Fillmore has administered the Executive Government with signal success and ability. He has been tried and found true, faithful, honest, and conscientious. I wish to say nothing in derogation from his eminent competitors, they have both rendered great services to their country; the one in the field, the other in the Cabinet. They might possibly administer the Government as well as Mr. Fillmore has done. But then neither of them has been tried; he has been tried in the elevated position he now holds, and I think that prudence and wisdom had better restrain us from making any change without a necessity for it, the existence of which I do not perceive.

MR. CLAY TO HIS SON JAMES.

WASHINGTON, March 14, 1852.

MY DEAR SON,—I received your letter of the 1st instant, and at the same time one from Susan. They both interested me, as I like to hear all the details of your business and operations. You find, as every body finds, building and improvement more expensive than you had expected.

My health continues nearly stationary, not getting better nor worse, except in one particular, and that is sleep. Although I take an opiate every night, and lie in bed fourteen hours, I can get no sound, refreshing sleep. A man whose flesh, strength, appetite and sleep have been greatly reduced, must be in a bad way, but that is my condition. I have taken immense quantities of drugs; but with little if any effect on my cough, the disease which threatens me. I may linger on some months, but if there be no speedy improvement, I must finally sink under it.

Give my love to dear Susan and all your children. I hope that she will continue to write to me.

MR. CLAY TO DANIEL ULLMAN.

WASHINGTON, March 18, 1852.

MY DEAR SIR,—I received your kind letter informing me of the loss of the medal. I am truly sorry for the occurrence, and the more so because I ought to have followed your directions to send it by Adams' Express. But Miss Lynch being in my room the evening before she started for the city of New York, and being informed that I was about to send the medal to you, she kindly offered to take charge of it, and I accordingly placed it under her care. I have no doubt she suffers as much as any of us by its loss, and I would not say one word by way of reproach to her. I should be very sorry if any trouble or expense were taken in replacing it. The fact of its presentation, and even the representations upon the medal have been so widely diffused as to render the presentation of it historical. You will recollect that I jocosely remarked while you were here that some Goth, when I was laid low in the grave, might be tempted to break off my nose and use the valuable metal which it contains! I did not then, however, anticipate the possibility of such an incident occuring so quickly.

MR. CLAY TO HIS SON JAMES.

WASHINGTON, March 22, 1852.

MY DEAR SON,—I received your letter of the 8th. I was glad to receive your letter and to peruse all the details in it.

My health continues without any material change. I am very weak, write with no comfort, sleep badly, and have very little appetite for my food.

You must not mind what you see in the newspapers about me, such as that I was going to the Senate to make a speech, etc. Not a word of truth in it.

My love to Susan and all the children.

MR. CLAY TO MRS. THOMAS H. CLAY.

WASHINGTON, April 7, 1852

MY DEAR MARY,—I received your letter of the 30th ultimo, and thank you for it. Your letters always give me satisfaction, as they go into details and tell me things which nobody else writes. The state of my health remains pretty much as it has been. But little sleep, appetite, or strength.

If I am spared, and have strength to make the journey, I think of going home in May or early in June, and in that case I wish to send for Thomas to accompany me.

I wish you would ask your mother to pay a small note of mine held by Ike Shelby. I have just heard to-day of the death of Mr. Jacobs. Poor Susan must be overwhelmed with grief.

We have had no good weather yet.

My love to Susan and the children.

MR. CLAY TO HIS SON JAMES.

WASHINGTON, April 10, 1852.

MY DEAR SON,—I have heard of the death of Mr. Jacobs, and I offer to you and to Susan assurances of my cordial condolence. Tell her that I hope she will bear the event with the fortitude of a Christian. My health continues very feeble, so much so that I write with no comfort or ease, as you may infer from this letter being written by the pen of a friend. What will be the issue of my illness it is impossible to predict. My own opinion of the case is less favorable than that of my physicians. If my strength continues to fail me, I think I can not last a great while. I feel perfectly composed and resigned to my fate, whatever it may be.

Give my love to Susan and all your children.

THOMAS H. CLAY TO JAMES B. CLAY.

WASHINGTON, May 8, 1852.

DEAR JAMES,—Summoned by a telegraphic dispatch of the 27th ultimo, I arrived here on Tuesday evening last, the 5th instant. For forty-eight hours after my arrival, my father appeared better than he had been for a week previous. He is very feeble, and there is no longer any hope of his reaching Kentucky alive.

Dr. Jackson thinks that there may be a termination of his case in a few hours, and it may be possible that he may live a week or ten days longer. He is greatly reduced in flesh; the same cough yet continues to harass and weaken him, and he is now unable even to walk across the room. Yesterday evening, supported by a friend on each side, he was very near fainting. He has now to be carried from his bed to his couch. He can not talk five minutes in the course of the day without great exhaustion.

He has directed me to say in answer to your letter of the 24th ultimo, that he is too weak to attend to the matter you write of with Corcoran and Riggs.

He is calm and composed, and will meet the enemy without any fears of the result. The Sacrament was administered to him yesterday, by Mr. Butler, the Episcopalian chaplain of the Senate. Give my love to your wife and children.

THOMAS H. CLAY TO HIS WIFE.

WASHINGTON, May 8, 1852.

MY DEAR MARY,—Had you seen, as I have, the evidences of attachment and interest displayed by my father's friends for him, you could not well help exclaiming, as he has frequently done,

"Was there ever man had such friends!" The first and best in the land are daily and hourly offering tokens of their love and esteem for him.

SIR WILLIAM CLAY TO MR. CLAY.

No. 17 Hertford St., Mayfair, May 8, 1852.

My dear Sir,—So many years have elapsed since the only intercourse I ever had the pleasure of holding with you—by letters and amity ceased—that I can hardly flatter myself you yet recollect its occurrence. I could not, however, let my son proceed to the United States without giving him at least the chance of becoming personally known to one who has so nobly illustrated the name he himself bears.

This letter, therefore, will be presented to you by my eldest son, William Dickinson Clay, who, with his friend Mr. Morris —a fellow of Oriel College, Oxford—is about to make the tour of the United States.

I know not whether you and I shall ever meet. I have the ardent wish to visit America, but whether my public duties may permit of my gratifying that wish, while I have health and strength to enjoy the journey, is more than doubtful.

Should that not occur, but should it so happen that either you or any one in whom you take an interest visits England, you will not, I hope, forget that you will afford me pleasure by showing that you perfectly rely on the friendly feeling with which I am, my dear sir, yours with great respect and regard.

[Thomas H. Clay, Mr. Clay's second son, having been summoned to the bedside of his father, arrived in Washington early in May. It will have been seen by the correspondence, that Mr. Clay had, till this time, refused his consent for any member of the family to come on. From the time of Mr. Thomas H. Clay's arrival till the death of his father, he wrote to some member of the family, at home, every day. It is thought sufficient to present extracts from this diary, at intervals of about five days, which will be found in the following extracts:]

WASHINGTON CITY, May 13, 1852.

My father passed the last night comfortable without much coughing. The only thing the doctors can do, is to alleviate as much as they can the pain arising from his cough and his excessive debility.

MAY 18, 1852.

My father has passed the last twenty-four hours much more comfortably than he had been for a week before. He has slept well and should he acquire strength with it, in spite of the predictions of the medical men, I shall begin to hope. It is the cough and that alone that has prostrated him; once relieved from that, I know not what we may not hope for. There is yet more vitality in him, than the reports in the newspapers would lead one to infer. I will keep you all correctly informed. Believe nothing that you see or hear, except it comes from me.

MAY 20, 1852.

My father coughed but little last night, yesterday he was a good deal harassed. Could it be possible to remove his cough, he would get well beyond a doubt. He is very feeble, but is not so much reduced in flesh as I had supposed before I came on here. It is the cough as he himself has always said, that is killing him. His lungs are not at all affected.

He insists on my writing to some of the family, either at Mansfield or Ashland, every day. I have but little to communicate in addition to informing you how he passes the days and nights.

MAY 26, 1852.

My father passed a tolerable night; you must be aware that any improvement in his condition must be gradual, as the prostration he labors under came on in the same way. I have been nowhere, and made as few acquaintances as I could; I am confined all day to his rooms, and last night was up until twelve o'clock, as James appeared anxious to go out. I am doing every thing that I can to render his situation as comfortable as possible, allowing myself but little time even for a walk.

JUNE 1, 1852.

My father listens attentively to the perusal of every letter from home.

He passed last night in more comfort than he did the night before. He had some appetite for his dinner yesterday.

ONE O'CLOCK AT NIGHT, June 4, 1852.

I wrote you this morning that my father had a bad night, and that he was then trying to get some rest; since I have been here, when he has passed a bad night, he was usually able to make up for the want of rest, during the following day. But such has not been the case to-day. He has coughed a great deal, and has had but little intermission from it. He took his opiate about two hours ago, and I hope that he will be enabled to get some sleep and rest in the next twenty-four hours. I shall keep my letter open to let you know how he is until tomorrow evening. He has suffered a good deal since this time last night.

JUNE 7, 1852.

My father was yesterday much depressed. He had held a long conversation with Mr. Crittenden and requested me to treat him kindly. Besides a cold sweat after dinner, all these things were sufficient to make him feel low spirited. He told me that he thought there would soon be a termination to it. The doctor thought on his afternoon visit that he was no worse than usual. God alone knows.

JUNE 9, 1852.

My father has become feeble within a few days, and I do not think it possible for him to hold out long.

JUNE 16, 1852.

My father is to-day decidedly worse than he has been since my arrival. I wrote to Mr. Theobald this morning that there was but little or no change in his condition; since then, I am satisfied he is worse. He has had a copious perspiration, which has greatly weakened him. The attending physician, Dr. Hall, rubbed him all over the person with brandy and alum. He told me this morning that he did not think he should last more than ten days.

I have been constant in my attendance on him. I think I can see a marked change in his countenance.

JUNE 20, 1852.

My father did not pass a good night, nor has he slept much this morning. A friend yesterday afternoon brought him three woodcocks; he ate a little of one of them this morning. He never now gets out of bed. He is moved occasionally from one bed to the other, for the purpose of ventilating and making up. He was too feeble this morning to carry a glass of water to his lips. The weather has been very hot during the week, the mercury rising at one time to 93°.

JUNE 25, 1852.

I now look for a termination in my father's case before many hours. I do not feel in any mood to write to any one but you, my wife. Judge Underwood coincides with me in opinion that he will not last many hours. The next you receive from me will probably be a telegraphic dispatch, directed to Mr. Harrison.

JUNE 29, 1852.

I had never before imagined that any one could live in the extreme state of debility under which my father is now suffering. The act of taking even a single swallow of water is painful to him, on account of his great feebleness. He has eaten nothing of any consequence (only a few mouthfuls of soup) for five or six days. I can not believe he can possibly survive through the week.

LEXINGTON, June 29, 1852.

The following message was received at this office to-day, dated Washington, 29th, 1852, twelve o'clock;

J. O. HARRISON—

My father is no more. He has passed without pain into eternity.

THOS. H. CLAY.

MR. THOMAS H. CLAY TO HIS WIFE.

CITY OF WASHINGTON, June 29, 1852.

MY DEAR MARY,—Shortly after I wrote to you this morning, I was summoned by James to my father's bedside. "Sit near me, my dear son," he said; "I do not wish you to leave me for any time to-day." In about an hour after, he said, "Give me some water." I gave him about half a glassful, which he drank, and still retained the tube in his mouth. In a few moments he released the tube, and said, "I believe, my son, I am going." Five minutes after, he told me "to button his shirt collar," which I did. He then caught my hand, and retained it in his pressure for some time. When he relinquished it, I discovered he was dying. I summoned Governor Jones, of Tennessee, who occupied the room above him, and in five or ten minutes after he had ceased to breathe.

May my mother, and all of you, be prepared for it. A nation mourns, but it is his gain. He is free from pain, and I thank God. Oh! how sickening is the splendid pageantry I have to go through from this to Lexington.

My love to all.

My father died at seventeen minutes past eleven. I telegraphed Mr. Harrison at twelve A. M.

ALPHABETICAL INDEX.

ADAIR, John, to Mr. Clay, 11.
Adams, Charles F., to Mr. Clay, 561.
Adams, J. Q., to Ministers at Ghent, 45.
" to Mr. Clay, 129, 149, 226, 229, 247, 311, 481, 520.
Allibone, Susan, to Mr. Clay, 577.
Ashburton, Lord, to Mr. Clay, 460.

BAIRD, T. H., to Mr. Clay, 497.
Baldwin, Judge, to Mr. Clay, 445.
Barbour, B. J., to Mr. Clay, 522.
Barbour, James, to Mr. Clay, 190, 328, 397.
Barbour, P. P., to Mr. Clay, 84.
Barbour, Mr. (confidential), to Mr. Clay, 172, 173.
Bard, Rev. Isaac, to Mr. Clay, 199.
Barger, Rev. John S., to Mr. Clay, 250.
Barnard, General, to Mr. Clay, 306.
Bayard, Mr. (Minister at Ghent), to Mr. Clay, 28.
Beatty, Adam, to Mr. Clay, 517.
Bertrand, General, to Mr. Clay, 477.
Bexley, Lord, to Mr. Clay, 138.
Biddle, Nicholas, to Mr. Clay, 287, 341, 351, 356, 386.
Blank to Mr. Clay, 182.
Blank to Judge Brooke, 104.
Bodisco, Mr., to Mr. Clay, 474.
Brooke, Francis, to Mr. Clay, 196, 222, 229, 335.
Brown, James, to Mr. Clay, 10, 12, 16, 126, 129, 221, 245, 343.
Brown, John, to Mr. Clay, 389.
Browning, R. S., to Mr. Clay, 334.
Buchanan, James, to R. P. Letcher, 491.
Burr, Aaron, to Mr. Clay, 13, 14.

CLAY, Mr., to Adair, John, 11.
" to Adams, J. Q., 171.
" to Allibone, S. A., 607, 620, 625.
" to Allibone, Susan, 569.
" to Babcock, James F., and others, 514.
" to Bailhache, John, 288, 399.
" to Beatty, Adam, 46, 47, 48, 55, 56, 61, 210, 234, 235, 237, 240, 266, 276, 280, 302, 305, 615.
" to Blair, Francis, P., 109, 111.
" to Booth, W. A., 525, 531.

Clay, Mr., to Britton, N. O., 470.
" to Brooke, Francis, 9, 17, 54, 70, 71, 74, 75, 78, 84, 86, 88, 89, 92, 93, 106, 107, 111, 113, 114, 119, 121, 126, 127, 134, 136, 139, 148, 152, 153, 156, 158, 159, 162, 164, 169, 178, 183, 185, 189, 222, 225, 232, 242, 256, 260, 262, 270, 278, 282, 291, 299, 302, 303, 305, 309, 314, 321, 322, 326, 329, 330, 331, 335, 337, 340, 341, 345, 347, 348, 349, 350, 351, 360, 367, 371, 375, 376, 377, 381, 382, 410, 412, 422, 423, 427, 428, 429, 432, 434, 436, 439, 440, 446, 447, 454, 455, 456, 473.
" to Carr, John, 521.
" to Clay, James B., 414, 419, 420, 421, 424, 426, 483, 486, 538, 545, 550, 553, 556, 582, 585, 588, 589, 590, 591, 595, 601, 602, 604, 606, 609, 612, 613, 616, 627, 629, 630.
" to Clay, Mrs. (Mr. Clay's wife), 45, 400, 418, 539, 594, 615.
" to Clay, Mrs. James B., 626.
" to Clay, Mrs. Thomas H., 623.
" to Clay, Thomas H., 594, 598, 599, 610, 611, 612, 624, 630.
" to Colton, Calvin, 476, 481, 494, 521, 524, 528, 530, 532.
" to Combs, Leslie, 404, 441, 442, 555, 585, 593, 599.
" to Committees, 412, 444, 566.
" to Crawford, W. H., 192.
" to Curtis, G. W., 568.
" to Dean, Nicholas, 572, 587.
" to Dennis, Rodney, 587.
" to Duncan, H. T., 554.
" to Gaines, General, 125.
" to Gibson, Jacob, 463.
" to Haight, Samuel, 560.

Clay, Mr., to Harlan, James, 565, 571, 583, 586, 589, 599, 603, 605.
" to Harrison, General, 175, 452.
" to Johnston, Hon. J. S., 94, 95, 97, 98, 100, 103, 104, 147, 148, 160, 169, 177, 184, 204, 226, 238, 240, 243, 245, 249, 251, 254, 255, 256, 264, 267, 268, 286, 288, 306, 353.
" to Littell, John S., 267, 473, 482, 536.
" to Lloyd, H. T., 475.
" to Lynch, James, and others, 575.
" to Madison, James, 53.
" to Miller, S. H., 490.
" to Muir, S., 530.
" to Niles, H., 213.
" Note, Diplomatic, by Mr. Clay, 42.
" to Pendleton, Rev. J. M., 509.
" to Pindell, R., 206.
" to Prentice, G. D., 418.
" to Prentis, Thomas M., 14.
" to Randolph, Thomas M., 174.
" to Rutgers, Colonel, 163.
" to Sayres, Rev. Gilbert H., 459.
" to Stevenson, Thomas B., 584.
" to Towler, Miss, 543.
" to Ullmann, Daniel, 474, 540, 543, 574, 600, 617, 620.
" to Welch, Rev. James F., 259.
" to White, Henry, 484, 494, 537, 561, 573.
" to White (Henry), and others, 484, 532.
" to Woodward, W. S., 523.
" to ———, 293, 392.
Carter, Beverly, to Mr. Clay, 459.
Cass, Lewis, to Mr. Clay, 123.
Chase, Bishop, to Mr. Clay, 96.
Cheves, Langdon, to Mr. Clay, 18, 66.
Clay, Henry, Jr., to his father, 160, 166, 214, 218, 233, 241, 280, 292, 303, 327, 336, 343, 352, 373, 400, (to James B. Clay), 536.
Clay, James B., to his father, 607.
Clay, Mrs., to Mr. Clay, 24.
Clay, Porter, to Mr. Clay, 159.
Clay, Sir William, to Mr. Clay, 409, 632.
Clay, Theodore Wythe, to his Father, 130.
Clay, Thomas H., to James B. Clay, 631.
Clay, Thomas H., to his wife, 631, 633, 634, 635, 636.
Clayton, John M., to Mr. Clay, 350.
Coffin, Alexander, to Mr. Clay, 383.
Colombia, Republic of, to Mr. Clay, 76, 77.
College, Washington, Students, to Mr. Clay, 390.
Combs, Leslie, to Mr. Clay, 325.
Cooke, Eleuth, to Mr. Clay, 387.
Cortes, Eugenio, to Mr. Clay, 65.
Crawford, William H., to Mr. Clay, 25, 33, 39, 40, 42, 191, 273.
Creighton, W., to Mr. Clay, 118.

Crittenden, J. J., to Mr. Clay, 117, 214, 498.

DAVIS, John, to Mr. Clay, 480.
Dean, Nicholas, to Mr. Clay, 545.
Dearborn, General, to Mr. Clay, 310.
Duralde, William, to Mr. Clay, 255.

ERWIN, Anne B., to her father, 269, 320, 323, 346.
Erwin, Mr., to Mr. Clay, 401.

FEATHERSTONHAUGH, G. W., to Mr. Clay, 265.
Fillmore, Millard, to Mr. Clay, 497.
Fox, Mr. (British Minister), to Mr. Clay, 412, 444.
Frelinghuysen, T., to Mr. Clay, 487, 495, 625.

GALPIN, P. S., and others, to Mr. Clay, 500.
Gallatin, Albert, to Mr. Clay, 30, 131, 161.
Gambier, Lord, to Mr. Clay, 53, 95, 150.
Gold Pen to Mr. Clay, 529.
Goulburn, Henry, to Mr. Clay, 51.
Graham, David, to Mr. Clay, 562.
Granger, A. P., and others, to Mr. Clay, 468.
Gual, P., to Mr. Clay, 213.

HALL, Willis, to Mr. Clay, 431, 563.
Hammond, C., to Mr. Clay, 443.
Hampton, Col. W., to Mr. Clay, 454.
Harrison, William Henry, to Mr. Clay, 20, 22, 258, 446.
Hart, H. T., to Mr. Clay, 581.
Hawley, Rev. William, to Mr. Clay, 251.
Henry, Patrick, to Mr. Clay, 67, 326.
Holley, President, to Mr. Clay, 124.
Horton, Howard, to Mr. Clay, 321.
Howard, Joseph, to Mr. Clay, 325.
Howe, Philip, to Mr. Clay, 507.
Hughes, Christopher, 46, (to Mr. Clay,) 503.

ITURBIDE to Mr. Clay, 64.

JANUARY, A. M., to Mr. Clay, 470.
Jeffrey, S. Caroline, to Mr. Clay, 395, 404.
Jesup, General, to Mr. Clay, 145.
" to James B. Clay, 146.
Johnson, R. M., to Mr. Clay, 64.
Johnson, Reverdy, to Mr. Clay, 349.
Johnston, J. S., to Mr. Clay, 99, 102, 103, 285.
J. W. P., to Mr. Clay, 363.

KENT, Chancellor, to Mr. Clay, 387, 411.
Keyes, D., and others, to Mr. Clay, 602.
Kirkland, President, to Mr. Clay, 127.
Krudener, Baron De, to Mr. Clay, 281.

LADY to Mr. Clay, 460.
Lafayette to Mr. Clay, 57, 62, 67, 83, 130, 131, 135, 137, 139, 140, 141, 152, 454, 155, 168, 180, 208, 223.

ALPHABETICAL INDEX. 639

Lafayette, George W., to Mr. Clay, 427.
Lawrence, Abbott, to Mr. Clay, 357.
Lawrence, John L., to Mr. Clay, 230.
Leary, C. L. L., to Mr. Clay, 498.
Lee, Richard Henry, to Mr. Clay, 219, 227.
Leedom, B. T., to Mr. Clay, 516.
Leigh, B. W., to Mr. Clay, 69, 73.
Letcher, R. P., to Mr. Clay, 171, 491.
Lewis, William D., to Mr. Clay, 510.
Lieber, Francis, to Mr. Clay, 385.
Litchfield, Franklin, to Mr. Clay, 167.

MACKINTOSH, Sir James, to Mr. Clay, 93.
Madison, James, to Mr. Clay, 52, 89, 160, 188, 284, 329, 358, 364, 388, 406.
Mallory, D., to Mr. Clay, 246.
Maneuil, Baron De, to Mr. Clay, 166.
Marshall, Chief Justice, to Mr. Clay, 121, 188, 212, 339, 352.
Martineau, Harriet, to Mr. Clay, 390, 406, 413.
Massachusetts, Daughter of, to Mr. Clay, 340.
Matthew, Father, to Mr. Clay, 624.
McDuffie, Governor, to Mr. Clay, 403.
McLain, William, to Mr. Clay, 626.
McLean, Judge, to Mr. Clay, 556.
Mercer, Dr., to Mr. Clay, 513, 527.
Monroe, James, to Mr. Clay, 19, 22, 24, 49, 53.
Morpeth, Lord, to Mr. Clay, 471, 535.

NITCHIE, John, to Mr. Clay, 384.

OTIS, Harrison Grey, to Mr. Clay, 328, 370, 433, 437.

PETTIGREU, E., to Mr. Clay, 518.
Pickering, Timothy, to Mr. Clay, 319.
Porter, Peter B., to Mr. Clay, 62, 65, 83, 205, 270, 284, 448, 450, 452, 478, 479.
Preston, William, and others, to Mr. Clay, 539.
Preston, William C., to Mr. Clay, 460, 503, 550.

RANDOLPH, Thomas M., to Mr. Clay, 174.
Real, José M. Del, to Mr. Clay, 63.
Rochester, W. B., to Mr. Clay, 85.
Roman, A. B., to Mr. Clay, 512.
Root, Erastus, to Mr. Clay, 375.
Rush, Richard, to Mr. Clay, 165, 186, 205, 299, 456, 457.
Russell, Mr. (Minister at Ghent), to Mr. Clay, 31, 32, 37.

SARCEY, Alexis De, to Mr. Clay, 241, 252, 253.
Scott, General, to Mr. Clay, 570.
Sibley, John, to Mr. Clay, 360.
Sloane, J., to Mr. Clay, 486, 488, 489.
Southard, Samuel L., to Mr. Clay, 168, 344.
Spencer, Ambrose, to Mr. Clay, 338, 372, 472, 501.
Sprague, Peleg, to Mr. Clay, 354.
Story, Judge, to Mr. Clay, 123, 467.
Sylvester, P. H., and others, to Mr. Clay, 506.

TAYLOR, General, to Mr. Clay, 548, 550, 557, 580.
Tazewell, Mr., to Mr. Clay, 378.
Thompson, John R., to Mr. Clay, 526.
Todd, C. S., to Mr. Clay, 77.
Tucker, George, to Mr. Clay, 405.
Tyler, John, to Mr. Clay, 119.

VAN BUREN, Martin, to Mr. Clay, 458
Vaughan, Mr. (British Minister), to Mr. Clay, 190, 248, 268.
Vaughan, Thomas, to Mr. Clay, 50.

WATKINS, Elizabeth, to her son, Mr. Clay, 177.
Webster, Daniel, to Mr. Clay, 122, 128, 143, 150, 156, 167, 170, 204, 205, 259, 274, 317, 366.
Westwood, John H., to Mr. Clay, 509.
Wines, E. C., to Mr. Clay, 547.
Wright, J. C., to Mr. Clay, 492, 493.